Ultimate Rust for Systems Programming

Master Core Programming for Architecting Secure and Reliable Software Systems with Rust and WebAssembly

Mahmoud Harmouch

www.orangeava.com

First published: March 2024

Published by: Orange Education Pvt Ltd, AVA™

Address: 9, Daryaganj, Delhi, 110002, India

275 New North Road Islington Suite 1314 London,
N1 7AA, United Kingdom

ISBN: 978-81-96994-73-0

www.orangeava.com

Dedicated To

My Beloved Mom:

Aicha Harmouch

My Strength and Support System

About the Author

Mahmoud is a results-driven software engineer with an impressive range of skills. As a full-stack developer and data scientist he has a proven track record of delivering top-notch software products and services. Mahmoud's passion for coding ignited during his college days, and it continues to burn brightly today. Crafting clean code and tackling challenging algorithms bring him immense joy and fulfillment.

Mahmoud's expertise spans various programming languages and frameworks, including Python, C#, Java, Rust, and C/C++. He stands out with proficiency in FastAPI, Django, NodeJS, Yew, and ReactJS. His technical writing skills are second to none, making complex information easy to understand through clear and concise documentation. Equipped with qualifications equivalent to a Master's degree in Electrical Engineering from The Lebanese University, his skillset becomes even more impressive.

Mahmoud's journey as a programmer began during his college days, and his enthusiasm for coding continues to burn brightly. He thrives in both team environments and as a lone specialist, always seeking new challenges to hone his skills. Not only is he a quick learner, but he also embraces best practices like test-driven development and DevOps techniques, such as continuous development, following principles like SOLID and DRY.

Apart from his technical skills, Mahmoud possesses excellent technical writing skills, capable of presenting complex information in clear and concise ways. Coupled with his passion for nurturing long-term client relationships, this makes him adept at delivering sustainable software solutions to solve business problems effectively.

Outside of his professional life, Mahmoud enjoys spending time with his loved ones. Whether participating in outdoor activities like biking and hiking in the mountains near his home or immersing himself in a good read, he finds joy in every aspect of life.

About the Technical Reviewer

Arman Riazi holds an M.Sc and offers Web3 services and solutions based on DeSci. As a practitioner and counselor in the realm of Web3, Arman possesses a deep understanding and expertise in this domain. He is invigorated by the opportunity to actualize your objectives, and his approach revolves around constructing solutions written in the Rust language. With an extensive background in creating and delivering products at the executive level, Arman has acquired valuable experience in this realm.

Arman encourages aspiring professionals to explore other fields of study and engage with relevant books, fostering an open-minded perspective and providing valuable insights. These activities equip individuals with the ability to perpetually learn, withstand challenges, and overcome obstacles, even in the face of arduous circumstances and substantial setbacks.

Arman hopes that programming communities consider issues and refrain from providing free codes to the industry, emphasizing the need to recognize the value of time and energy. This careful handling, he believes, will foster a healthier industry bilaterally, as creating value leads to an increased reliance on your expertise, acknowledging that it is not a free and temporary offering; they must pay for it, similar to other fields of expertise with high income statistically. This approach, changing and turning competition from the current state among the community to another realm, makes it more profitable for the community. Arman acknowledges that we have developed enough language and framework, but we have not established good relations out of the box. Eventually, developers will be happy and more creative in delivering high-quality products.

As a passionate problem solver, he actively seeks opportunities to expand his knowledge and teach newcomers in the domains of technology. His fervor lies in programming, smart contracts, and blockchain, and he is eager to delve deeper into the realm of Rust-Language or TypeScript as it pertains to De/ReFi, META, DAO, IOT, Cloud, Platform Engineering, DevOps, and related areas.

Arman is delighted to express his passion for collaborating with Mr. Mahmoud [his family] and learning the Rust language at a deep level. Your time and consideration are sincerely appreciated.

Acknowledgements

Writing this book, "*Ultimate Rust for Systems Programming*", has been an exciting journey, and I want to express my gratitude to the awesome people who helped make it happen. This book wouldn't be what it is without the support, guidance, and expertise of many fantastic individuals.

A big thanks to the Rust community and the creators of Rust for building such a cool programming language. The Rust documentation has been like a trusty guide, making sure the information in this book is accurate and helpful. A special shoutout to the folks who carefully checked and gave feedback on the technical aspects; your insights made a big difference.

To my family, thank you for having my back. Mom, you're the best cheerleader, and I appreciate your support. To my brother, your encouragement has meant a lot during this writing adventure.

A big shoutout to the team at the publishing house; your teamwork and dedication have made this book better.

And to you, the readers, a big thank you for picking up this book. I hope it helps you become a Rust pro and makes your journey into system programming a bit more awesome.

Preface

In the dynamic world of system programming, where precision meets innovation, mastering a language that combines robustness with efficiency is crucial. Step into the world of Rust with this comprehensive guide, a journey that goes beyond the basics, delving into the complexities of a language that has become a cornerstone in the development of reliable, secure, and high-performance systems. Rust's unique features, from its memory safety guarantees to advanced concepts like traits and generics, empower you to craft code with utmost precision.

This book contains **15 chapters**, guiding you through the world of Rust in a step-by-step way:

- **Chapters 1 and 2** guide you in getting to know Rust, setting up your workspace, and learning the basics, including how Rust manages memory and checks for borrowing issues.
- **Chapters 3 and 4** dive into more advanced topics like traits, generics, and dealing with different types of collections.
- **Chapter 5** focuses on handling errors effectively and creating your own error types.
- **Chapters 6 and 7** delve into managing memory, using smart pointers, and understanding concurrency.
- **Chapter 8** provides a practical experience by guiding you through building a command-line utility.
- **Chapter 9** focuses on input/output operations and using Rust to work with hardware devices.
- **Chapters 10 and 11** concentrate on iterators, closures, and the importance of unit testing.
- **Chapter 12** introduces network programming with a focus on TCP and UDP communication.
- **Chapter 13** delves into the concept of unsafe coding in Rust.

- **Chapter 14** emphasizes asynchronous programming using Rust's async/await and the Tokio library.
- **Chapter 15** helps to understand the basics and advantages of WebAssembly and how to set up Rust for WebAssembly development.

By the end of this journey, you'll have a solid understanding of Rust and how it can be applied in system programming, making you well-equipped for real-world applications.

Get a Free eBook

We hope you are enjoying your recently purchased book! Your feedback is incredibly valuable to us, and to all other readers looking for great books.

If you found this book helpful or enjoyable, we would truly appreciate it, if you could take a moment to leave a short review with a 5 star rating on Amazon. It helps us grow, and lets other readers discover our books.

As a thank you, we would love to send you a free digital copy of this book, and a **30%** discount code on your next cart value on our official websites:

www.orangeava.com

www.orangeava.in (For Indian Subcontinent)

☑ **Here's how:**

Leave a review for the book on Amazon.

Take a screenshot of your review, and send an email to **info@orangeava.com** (it can be just the confirmation screen).

Once, we receive your screenshot, we will send you the digital file, within 24 hours.

Thank you so much for your support – it means a lot to us!

Downloading the code bundles and colored images

Please follow the links or scan the QR codes to download the ***Code Bundles and Images*** of the book:

https://github.com/OrangeAVA/Ultimate-Rust-for-Systems-Programming

The code bundles and images of the book are also hosted on ***https://rebrand.ly/1b5df0***

In case there's an update to the code, it will be updated on the existing GitHub repository.

Errata

We take immense pride in our work at **Orange Education Pvt Ltd,** and follow best practices to ensure the accuracy of our content to provide an indulging reading experience to our subscribers. Our readers are our mirrors, and we use their inputs to reflect and improve upon human errors, if any, that may have occurred during the publishing processes involved. To let us maintain the quality and help us reach out to any readers who might be having difficulties due to any unforeseen errors, please write to us at :

errata@orangeava.com

Your support, suggestions, and feedback are highly appreciated.

DID YOU KNOW

Did you know that Orange Education Pvt Ltd offers eBook versions of every book published, with PDF and ePub files available? You can upgrade to the eBook version at **www.orangeava.com** and as a print book customer, you are entitled to a discount on the eBook copy. Get in touch with us at: **info@orangeava.com** for more details.

At **www.orangeava.com**, you can also read a collection of free technical articles, sign up for a range of free newsletters, and receive exclusive discounts and offers on AVA™ Books and eBooks.

PIRACY

If you come across any illegal copies of our works in any form on the internet, we would be grateful if you would provide us with the location address or website name. Please contact us at **info@orangeava.com** with a link to the material.

ARE YOU INTERESTED IN AUTHORING WITH US?

If there is a topic that you have expertise in, and you are interested in either writing or contributing to a book, please write to us at **business@orangeava.com**. We are on a journey to help developers and tech professionals to gain insights on the present technological advancements and innovations happening across the globe and build a community that believes Knowledge is best acquired by sharing and learning with others. Please reach out to us to learn what our audience demands and how you can be part of this educational reform. We also welcome ideas from tech experts and help them build learning and development content for their domains.

REVIEWS

Please leave a review. Once you have read and used this book, why not leave a review on the site that you purchased it from? Potential readers can then see and use your unbiased opinion to make purchase decisions. We at Orange Education would love to know what you think about our products, and our authors can learn from your feedback. Thank you!

For more information about Orange Education, please visit **www.orangeava.com**.

Table of Contents

CHAPTER 1

Systems Programming with Rust

Introduction

The world of systems programming has always been a double-edged sword: developers need to balance performance, control, and safety. This challenge becomes even more daunting when utilizing low-level languages such as C and C++. However, Rust has emerged in recent years as an innovative solution to this dilemma. Combining the power of traditional low-level languages with memory safety guarantees typically found only in higher-level ones, Rust offers the best of both worlds [1].

This chapter delves deep into what makes Rust so unique - the remarkable features that have made it the ultimate choice for those seeking optimal harmony between performance and security. Its unique blend of strength and reliability make it ideal for developing high-performance systems; no wonder why it's quickly becoming every system programmer's language of choice [2].

In subsequent sections, we will delve deeper into its syntax and capabilities while exploring how concurrency and parallelism are handled by this game-changing programming language! By the chapter's end, you'll possess comprehensive knowledge about all things related to mastering rust within your own projects, ensuring success at any scale or complexity!

---

[1]Dreyer, R. J. J. J. R. K. D. (2021, April 1). Safe systems programming in rust. April 2021 | Communications of the ACM. *https://cacm.acm.org/magazines/2021/4/251364-safe-systems-programming-in-rust/fulltext*

[2]Why this book? - High Assurance Rust: Developing Secure and Robust Software. (n.d.). *https://highassurance.rs/chp1/why_this_book.html*

Structure

In this chapter, we will cover the following topics:

- Rust's special features
- Strong code foundations
- Getting started practically
- Your first rust program - "Hello, World!"

Safety and Performance

The birth of safety and performance in Rust represents a remarkable achievement in programming language design. Rust's core philosophy centers around delivering both memory safety and high performance, addressing critical challenges faced by developers when creating modern software solutions.

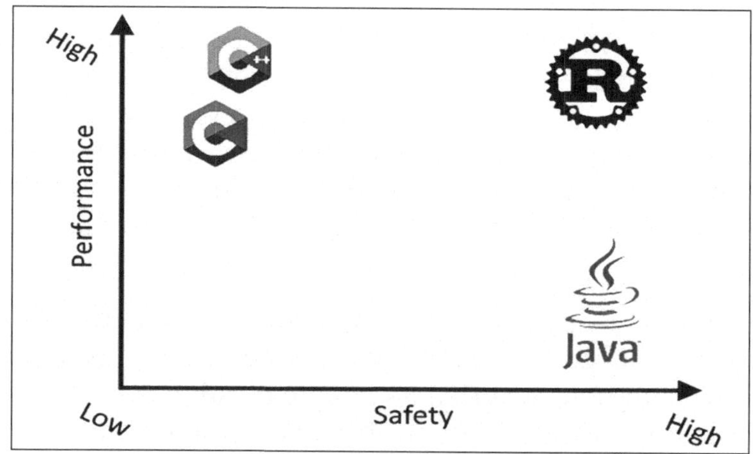

Figure 1.1: *How Rust compares to other programming languages in terms of safety and performance*

Graydon Hoare's frustration with software crashes gave birth to Rust, a programming language that guarantees memory safety without compromising performance [3]. Rust's standout feature, the "*borrow checker*", analyzes references' lifetimes, identifying potential memory-related bugs during compilation, allowing developers to catch errors early on, reducing runtime errors, and

[3]Learn more about Rust's history and evolution: *https://en.wikipedia.org/wiki/Rust_(programming_language)*.

preventing system crashes [4]. Mozilla recognized Rust's potential and began supporting it in 2009, propelling its growth [5].

Today, Rust has emerged as a highly sought-after programming language due to its exceptional safety measures, unparalleled performance and unwavering reliability. The inception of Rust serves as an inspiration that innovation is often born out of frustration and with persistence, we can achieve groundbreaking advancements in technology for the betterment of humanity. This journey undertaken by Rust exemplifies how having a clear vision coupled with determination and commitment towards creating solutions for real-world challenges can lead us to great heights. As we continue our pursuit towards technological progress, let's not forget that prioritizing both safety and performance are equally important aspects which can be achieved through appropriate tools and mindset alike.

Memory Protection

The memory safety revolution ushered in by Rust has been a game-changer for developers. With Rust, developers like you no longer need to worry about managing memory vulnerabilities in their code. Rust's unique "zero-cost abstractions" allow us to write code that is both high-performance and safe without experiencing additional runtime overhead. This has resulted in a programming landscape where memory-related pitfalls like null pointer dereferences and buffer overflows are minimized, reducing the likelihood of catastrophic crashes [6].

The ownership and borrowing features of Rust ensure that each piece of data has a single "owner" that dictates its lifespan. This rigorous control prevents data races and invalid memory accesses, contributing to Rust's reputation as a memory-safe language. Developers can now write code that is both efficient and secure, without worrying about managing memory vulnerabilities. Rust has made it possible to write software that is not only high-performance but safe, which is a significant milestone in the programming world. The memory protection revolution taken by Rust is a game-changer that has given us the power to build robust and secure software with ease [7].

[4]Discover the power of Rust's borrow checker: *https://doc.rust-lang.org/book/ch04-00-understanding-ownership.html*

[5]Wikipedia contributors. (2023). Rust (programming language). Wikipedia. *https://en.wikipedia.org/wiki/Rust_(programming_language)*

[6]Discover the power of Rust's borrow checker: *https://doc.rust-lang.org/book/ch04-00-understanding-ownership.html*

[7]Discover the power of Rust's borrow checker: *https://doc.rust-lang.org/book/ch04-00-understanding-ownership.html*

In Rust, errors manifest in various forms. Recoverable errors, like bumps in the road, include scenarios like file not found or a number mix-up. Rust equips us with handy tools, Options, and Results, to gracefully handle these anticipated errors [8]. On the contrary, non-recoverable errors breach the program's rules, exemplified by exceeding an array's boundaries. Rust responds to such errors with the dramatic mechanism known as a panic [9].

Now, let's explore the crucial concept of Resource Acquisition Is Initialization (RAII) in Rust. It's like managing resources in a digital world. With RAII, resources are not merely allocated but also initialized within the scope of an object's creation, creating a seamless and controlled flow [10]. This technique ensures that resources are handled gracefully, much like a skilled conductor guiding the rise and fall of musical motifs. In Rust, we can leverage these error-handling tools and the RAII technique to adeptly navigate the complexities of errors and craft a seamless execution.

Figure 1.2: *Compiler Complaint - xkcd.com/371*

In the following sections, we will explore these concepts using examples written in C, C++ and Rust programming languages.

Null Pointer Dereference

Null pointer dereference, a common source of program crashes and errors in many programming languages, is effectively eliminated in Rust due to its strong type system and ownership model.

---

[8]Recoverable Errors with Result - The Rust Programming Language. (n.d.). *https://doc.rust-lang.org/book/ch09-02-recoverable-errors-with-result.html*

[9]Unrecoverable Errors with panic! - The Rust Programming Language. (n.d.). *https://doc.rust-lang.org/book/ch09-01-unrecoverable-errors-with-panic.html*

[10]RAII - Rust by example. (n.d.). *https://doc.rust-lang.org/rust-by-example/scope/raii.html?highlight=raii#raii*

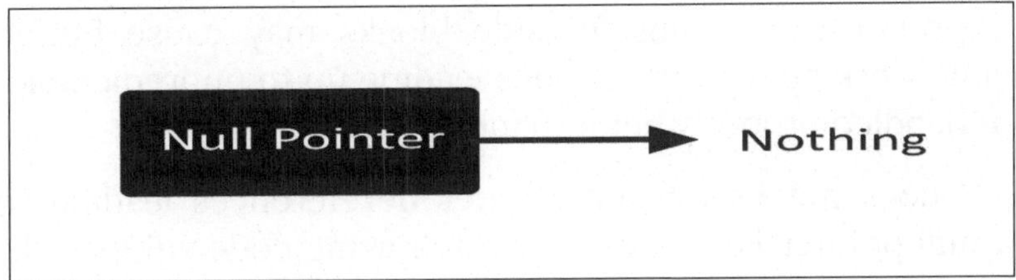

Figure 1.3: *A simple null pointer illustration*

Programming languages often encounter errors due to null pointers. These are pointer variables that have been assigned the value of NULL or 0, which can lead to runtime issues when dereferenced. In C programming language, undefined behavior occurs upon attempting to access a null pointer's contents. This unpredictability makes it difficult for programmers to determine how their program will behave in such cases [11].

Data races act like stealthy bugs that can disrupt your code, leading to unpredictable behavior. Picture trying to troubleshoot these issues while your program is running, it's like chasing elusive shadows. Rust's safety feature revolves around ensuring pointers steer clear of dubious invalid memory [12]. In simpler terms, safety in Rust means pointers must remain on a secure path, avoiding any pitfalls that could trigger undefined behavior during the entire program run.

Undefined behavior occurs when your program enters an unusual state because the compiler didn't anticipate certain scenarios. It's comparable to finding your program in uncharted territory without a reliable guide. Rust's ongoing challenge lies in mastering these complexities, navigating securely through code, guaranteeing pointers maintain reliability, and sidestepping the chaos that undefined behavior can unleash [13].

The Rust programming language handles null pointers differently by causing panics instead of undefined behaviors during dereference attempts. A panic is equivalent to an exception and results in unrecoverable errors that terminate programs immediately [14].

---

[11]IBM documentation. (n.d.). *https://www.ibm.com/docs/en/i/7.3?topic=pointers-null*
[12]Understanding ownership - the Rust programming language. (n.d.). https://doc.rust-lang.org/book/ch04-00-understanding-ownership.html?highlight=safety%20features#understanding-ownership
[13]References and borrowing - the Rust programming language. (n.d.). https://doc.rust-lang.org/book/ch04-02-references-and-borrowing.html?highlight=undefined%20behavior#mutable-references
[14]EXP34-C. Do not dereference null pointers - SEI CERT C Coding Standard - Confluence. (n.d.). *https://wiki.sei.cmu.edu/confluence/display/c/EXP34-C.+Do+not+dereference+null+pointers*

However, improper use of unsafe code blocks may cause buffer overflow problems while working with Rust codes leading up to unpredictable outcomes as well if not handled properly beforehand [15].

By default, C does not verify null pointer dereferences leading to program crashes if a null pointer is accessed. The following code snippet illustrates an instance of such an occurrence in C programming:

Listing 1.1 A null pointer example in C

```
#include <stdio.h>

int main() {
    int *ptr = NULL; // ①
    *ptr = 5; // ②
    return 0;
}
// $ gcc null_pointer.c -o null_pointer && ./null_pointer
// Output: Segmentation fault (core dumped)
```

In this C program, we first import the standard input-output library. Within the **main** function, our initial steps are to declare an integer pointer called **ptr**, initializing it with a null value at step ①. Then, in ②, we are trying to assign a value of "**5**" to this null pointer through dereferencing which leads us towards undefined behavior that can cause data corruption or unexpected outcomes such as crashes and more severe issues.

Now, let's talk about the Heap memory which is like having a special corner in your program where things can hang out for an extended period. It's like a designated space where your program stores important information to remember later. But, here's the thing: you've got to handle this space with care. If you forget to tidy up after yourself, it's like leaving a mess in that corner, and that can spell trouble. The Out Of Memory (OOM) killer, a sort of guardian, might shut down your program if it hoards too much memory without proper cleanup [16].

[15]Zhang, H., David, C., Yu, Y., Wang, M. (2023). Ownership Guided C to Rust Translation. In: Enea, C., Lal, A. (eds) Computer Aided Verification. CAV 2023. Lecture Notes in Computer Science, vol 13966. Springer, Cham. *https://doi.org/10.1007/978-3-031-37709-9_22*

[16]Out of memory management. (n.d.). https://www.kernel.org/doc/gorman/html/understand/understand016.html

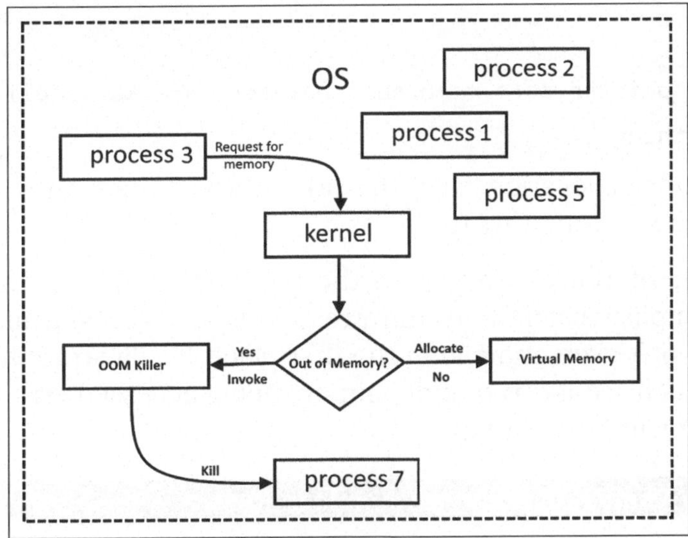

Figure 1.4: *kernel invoking oom killer on a process with high oom score*

Now, when your program is in action, mistakes can happen, and it's part of the programming journey! For instance, you might forget to instruct the program to free up some of that memory room, or you might attempt to use the memory in a way that's not allowed. When these errors occur, the program receives a signal from the computer. This signal is like an error message, and you might be familiar with one that reads "segmentation fault". Essentially, it's the computer telling the program, "Fix this issue, or I'll have to put a stop to you". So, as programmers, we need to be extremely mindful of how we utilize this memory space. We have to ensure we clean up after ourselves like tidying up that room, or better yet, use programming languages that automatically assist us in managing this memory stuff, which is as you may have guessed it, Rust!

It is essential always to avoid any attempts at accessing memory locations without proper initialization or allocation beforehand since they may result in catastrophic consequences for your code's stability and reliability! For example:

Listing 1.2 A safe memory allocation example in C

```
#include <stdio.h>

int main() {
    int *ptr = malloc(sizeof(int));
    if (ptr == NULL) { // ①
        printf("Error: memory allocation failed");
    } else {
        *ptr = 5;
```

```
    }
}
// $ gcc null_pointer_safe.c -o null_pointer_safe && ./null_pointer_safe
// Output: Nothing
```

① If the memory allocation fails, the program will encounter a null pointer dereference when attempting to access it.

Null pointer dereferences undergo a thorough check during the compilation process. This implies that if there is an attempt made to access a null pointer, then the program won't even compile in the first place. To illustrate how effectively Rust handles such scenarios of null pointers being accessed erroneously, take a look at the following code snippet:

Listing 1.3 A safe null pointer example in Rust

```
let mut vec = vec![1, 2, 3];
let item = vec.pop(); // ①
match item {
    Some(val) => println!("Popped value: {}", val),
    None => println!("Vector is empty"),
}
// $ rustc null_pointer.rs
// Output: Popped value: 3
```

Rust offers a solution to null pointer dereference through the **Option** type, which denotes whether or not a value exists. When utilizing the **pop** method in step ①, it returns an **Option** value that can be examined to ascertain if any values were returned at all.

Let's consider another example:

Listing 1.4 An unsafe null pointer example in Rust

```
fn main() {
    let ptr: *const i32 = std::ptr::null(); // ①
    let value = unsafe { *ptr }; // ②
    println!("Value: {}", value);
}
// $ rustc null_pointer.rs && ./null_pointer
// Output: Segmentation fault (core dumped)
```

In Rust, the **unsafe** keyword is used to indicate that the code is accessing memory directly and that the programmer is responsible for ensuring its safety. Additionally, the concept of null pointers in Rust is mostly absent due to the ownership and borrowing system. However, Rust does allow the use of raw pointers within `unsafe` blocks. In the previous Rust program:

① We declare an immutable raw pointer named `ptr` and initialize it with a null pointer using `std::ptr::null()`.

② We use an unsafe block to dereference the null pointer ptr, which is an unsafe operation that can lead to undefined behavior.

It is crucial to prevent null pointer dereference errors by checking for null pointers before accessing them. Rust offers the `Option` type, which represents nullable values and can be used as a preventive measure. In C programming language, if statements are utilized to perform null pointer checks.

Being mindful of these potential issues in both languages is essential when writing code and taking necessary precautions against such mistakes should always be prioritized.

Buffer Overflow

Buffer overflow, a critical security vulnerability in software, is rigorously prevented in Rust through its memory safety features and strict bounds checking, making it a language of choice for security-conscious developers.

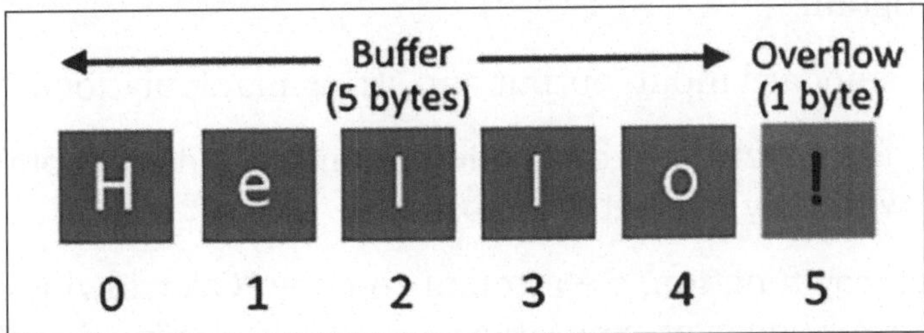

Figure 1.5: *A buffer overflow example illustration*

The occurrence of buffer overflow is a predominant cybersecurity issue that arises when programs attempt to store excessive data in buffers beyond their intended capacity [17]. This vulnerability poses significant security risks and can be observed in both C and Rust programming languages. In the case of C, this problem may arise due to incorrect utilization of functions such as `strcpy` or `sprintf`, which do not validate the size limits before copying information into

[17]Cobb, M. (2021). buffer overflow. Security. *https://www.techtarget.com/searchsecurity/definition/buffer-overflow*

them [18]. On the other hand, unsafe code blocks or erroneous memory allocation could lead to buffer overflow issues within Rust [19]. It is crucial for developers using these languages always to ensure adequate checks are put in place against potential breaches caused by buffer overflows during program execution processes [20].

For example, in C, the following code snippet can lead to buffer overflow:

Listing 1.5 A basic buffer overflow example in C

```
#include <stdio.h>
#include <string.h>

int main() {
    char buffer[5]; // ①
    strcpy(buffer, "Overflowing Content!"); // ②
    return 0;
}
// $ gcc -Wstringop-overflow=0 -fno-stack-protector buffer_overflow.c -o
buffer_overflow && ./buffer_overflow
// Output: Overflowing Content!
// Segmentation fault (core dumped)
```

In the given program:

We include the standard input-output and string manipulation libraries.

① Within the **main** function of our code lies an array named buffer, which has been allocated with only five bytes of space.

② Using the **strcpy** function, we attempt to copy "Overflowing Content!" into this character array; however, since it exceeds its size limit - thereby resulting in a buffer overflow situation as more characters are written than can fit within the given allocation - overwriting neighboring memory space becomes inevitable.

In Rust, buffer overflow is prevented by the language's type system and ownership model. Here is an example:

---

[18]Zeifman, I. (2023). What is a Buffer Overflow, Attack Examples and Prevention Methods. Sternum IoT. *https://sternumiot.com/iot-blog/buffer-overflow-attack/*

[19]Accelerator, A. (2023). Buffer Overflow | The Most Up-to-Date Encyclopedia, News, Review & Research. Academic Accelerator. *https://academic-accelerator.com/encyclopedia/buffer-overflow*

[20]Cyvatar. (2023). What is a buffer overflow attack? | Attack, Types & Vulnerabilities. CYVATAR. AI. *https://cyvatar.ai/buffer-overflow-attack/*

Listing 1.6 A buffer overflow example in Rust

```
fn main() {
    let mut buffer: [u8; 5] = [0; 5]; // ①
    let data = b"Overflowing Content!"; // ②
    buffer[..data.len()].copy_from_slice(data); // ③
    println!("Buffer: {:?}", buffer); // ④
}
// $ rustc buffer_overflow.rs && ./buffer_overflow
// Output: thread 'main' panicked at 'range end index 20 out of range
for slice of length 5', buffer_overflow.rs:4:5
```

In Rust, the language's safety features make buffer overflows less likely, as Rust enforces bounds checking by default. In the provided Rust program:

① Inside the `main` function, we declare a mutable array named `buffer` of size `5` bytes, initialized with zeros.

② We declare a byte string `data` containing the bytes of the string "`Overflowing Content!`".

③ We use array slicing to copy only the necessary bytes from `data` into `buffer`. We utilize the `copy_from_slice` method to copy the data to `buffer`, avoiding buffer overflow.

④ Finally, we print the contents of `buffer`.

Understanding null pointer dereference and buffer overflow is crucial for writing robust and secure code. Both C and Rust programming languages offer unique approaches to handling these issues. C, being less strict, requires careful pointer management and memory allocation. On the other hand, Rust's ownership system and safety features contribute to preventing such problems, making it a more secure choice for modern programming. By grasping these concepts and applying them appropriately, you can create software that is both reliable and resilient.

Garbage Collector

In the world of virtual machine-based languages, garbage collection steps in as a smart solution to keep our code safe from memory issues [21]. It's like a cleanup crew that works with the computer's memory system, making sure to tidy up unused space and freeing us up from handling these tasks manually. Different

[21]Wikipedia contributors. (2023, November 27). Garbage collection (computer science). Wikipedia. *https://en.wikipedia.org/wiki/Garbage_collection_%28computer_science%29*

strategies, such as mark-and-sweep and generational approaches, help find the right balance between cleaning up memory and keeping the program running smoothly [22]. For us, the combo of Rust's ownership system and garbage collection boosts safety and efficiency, showing off what Rust can do [23].

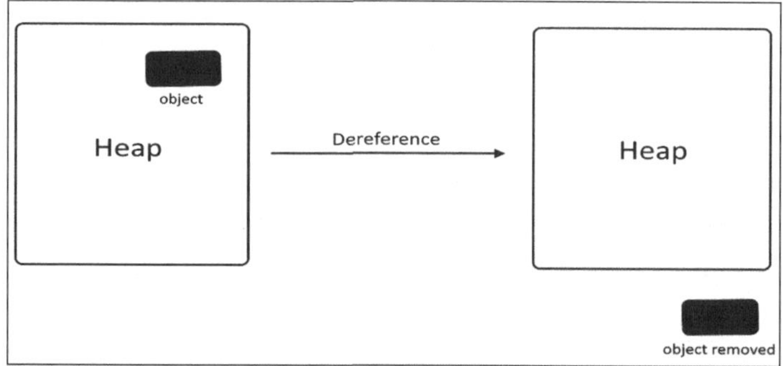

Figure 1.6: *Garbage collection illustration*

Rust's innovation extends to memory management, offering memory safety without relying on a garbage collector. This feature minimizes runtime overhead and eliminates the risk of garbage collection pauses affecting system performance and security.

Consider the following Rust code:

Listing 1.7 A basic example of Rust's automatic memory management

```
struct Resource {
    data: Vec<u8>, // ①
}

fn main() {
    let resource = Resource { // ②
        data: vec![1, 2, 3, 4, 5], // ③
    }; // ④
}
```

Here's the detailed breakdown:

① We define a struct named **`Resource`** that includes a **`data`** field of type **`Vec<u8>`**.

② We create an instance of the **`Resource`** struct, initializing its **`data`** field with a vector containing integers from 1 to 5.

[22]Wikipedia contributors. (2023, November 24). Tracing garbage collection. Wikipedia. *https://en.wikipedia.org/wiki/Tracing_garbage_collection#Basic_algorithm*
[23]Ownership - the Rustonomicon. (n.d.). *https://doc.rust-lang.org/nomicon/ownership.html*

③ We define the data within the **data** field.

④ The instance **resource** goes out of scope, and Rust's automatic memory management deallocates the memory occupied by **data**.

In contrast to C/C++, where manual memory management involving **malloc** and **free** is commonplace, Rust's ownership system ensures automatic memory cleanup, alleviating the risks associated with memory leaks and dangling pointers.

In Rust, when we're dealing with references, we have to be clear about lifetimes and how long references stick around. The whole point is to prevent references from going nasty and pointing to data they shouldn't. Think of it like making sure your directions (references) lead to the right destination (data). So, when we annotate lifetimes in Rust, it's not just a fancy task; it's like putting up signposts to keep our program on the right path and avoid references getting lost and causing trouble. We're the protectors of our code's execution, making sure each reference behaves as it should [24].

For comparison, let's examine the equivalent C++ code snippet illustrating manual memory management:

Listing 1.8 An example of C++ manual memory management

```
#include <iostream>
#include <vector>

struct Resource {
    std::vector<uint8_t> data; // ①
};

int main() {
    Resource; // ②
    resource.data = {1, 2, 3, 4, 5}; // ③

    // Manual memory cleanup for ‘data’ is necessary before going out of
scope

    return 0;
}
// $ g++ gc.cpp -o gc && ./gc
```

[24]Validating References with Lifetimes - The Rust Programming Language. (n.d.). *https://doc.rust-lang.org/book/ch10-03-lifetime-syntax.html*

Here's the analysis:

① We define a `Resource` struct containing a `std::vector` field of type `uint8_t`.

② We declare an instance of the `Resource` struct.

③ We manually assign data to the `data` field using list initialization.

In C++, manual memory management using `new` and `delete`, or smart pointers, is essential to manage memory deallocation. In contrast, Rust's memory management approach, exemplified in the previous Rust code snippet, simplifies memory management by automating the memory cleanup process.

Multithreading and Parallelism

The era of multithreading and parallelism signifies a transformative shift in the world of programming, with modern applications increasingly relying on the concurrent execution of tasks to maximize efficiency and performance. Rust, as a systems programming language, offers powerful tools and features to harness the potential of multithreading and parallelism while maintaining a strong focus on safety.

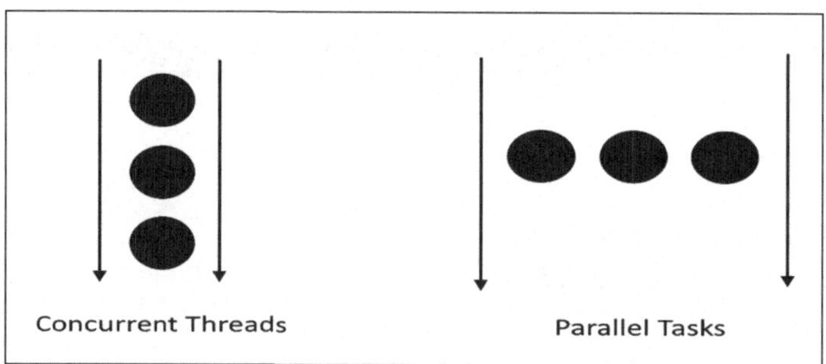

Figure 1.7: *Threads vs parallel tasks*

In today's world, we rely heavily on multi-core processors to handle the ever-increasing demands of complex software applications. Harnessing the power of parallelism is no longer a luxury but rather a necessity. Rust's advanced concurrency model is the perfect answer to this challenge. By promoting "fearless concurrency," Rust empowers us to write parallelized code that's both efficient and robust, without the risk of data races or memory-related bugs.

The exceptional success of Rust in concurrency is attributed to its ownership-based methodology. The prevention of shared mutable states and the promotion of message-passing guarantees that concurrent programs are reliable and predictable, making them distinctive from other programming languages.

This innovative approach has positioned Rust as a front-runner in concurrent programming.

Rust's robust concurrency model empowers us to effortlessly harness the full potential of modern hardware and craft efficient code that expands seamlessly. Whether you're developing a dynamic web application or a complex machine learning algorithm, Rust's concurrent approach is precisely what you need for optimal results.

Multithreading lies at the heart of harnessing the full potential of contemporary CPUs in system development. While both C and C++ do offer multithreading capabilities, they are notorious for engendering complex issues like data races and deadlocks. Rust stands apart by proactively addressing these challenges through the enforcement of compile-time checks that drastically mitigate occurrences of data races.

Let's explore a Rust code snippet that demonstrates Rust's multithreading features:

Listing 1.9 A basic multithreading example in Rust

```
use std::thread;

fn main() {
    let data = vec![1, 2, 3, 4, 5]; // ①
    let mut handles = vec![]; // ②

    for &item in &data { // ③
        handles.push(thread::spawn(move || { // ④
            println!("Processed: {}", item * 2); // ⑤
        }));
    }

    for handle in handles { // ⑥
        handle.join().unwrap(); // ⑦
    }
}
//  $ rustc thread.rs && ./thread
// Output:
// Processed: 2
// Processed: 6
// Processed: 4
// Processed: 8
// Processed: 10
```

In this illustrative example:

① We initialize a vector named **`data`** containing integers from 1 to 5.

② We create a mutable vector named **`handles`** to store thread handles.

③ Through iteration, we traverse the elements of the **`data`** vector using a reference.

④ We spawn a new thread using the **`thread::spawn`** function, ensuring that each thread takes ownership of the captured variable **`item`**.

⑤ Inside the thread, we print the processed result of doubling the **`item`**.

⑥ We iterate through the thread handles.

⑦ We employ the **`join`** method to ensure synchronization by waiting for each thread to complete.

In this code snippet, the concept of "move" takes center stage as threads are spawned to concurrently process elements from the data vector. The crucial use of the move keyword within the **`thread::spawn`** closure signifies the transfer of ownership for each iteration's item. This elegant mechanism ensures that each thread exclusively possesses and operates on its own copy of the data, mitigating the risk of data races and conflicts. In other words, "move" in Rust orchestrates a ballet of ownership transfer, enabling a seamless and safe parallel execution where each thread holds a distinct piece of the environment, contributing to the overall performance without compromising data integrity.

This Rust code showcases a safer approach to multithreading compared to C/C++, where manual synchronization and explicit usage of locks or mutexes are necessary. Rust's ownership and borrowing system significantly enhances code reliability and ease of management.

For a direct comparison, let's examine an equivalent C++ code snippet that illustrates multithreading:

Listing 1.10 Basic multithreading example in C++

```
#include <iostream>
#include <thread>
#include <vector>

void process_item(int item) {
    std::cout << "Processed: " << item * 2 << std::endl; // ①
}
```

```
int main() {
    std::vector<int> data = {1, 2, 3, 4, 5}; // ②
    std::vector<std::thread> threads; // ③

    for (const auto &item : data) {  // ④
        threads.push_back(std::thread(process_item, item)); // ⑤
    }

    for (auto &thread : threads) { //⑥
        thread.join(); // ⑦
    }

    return 0;
}
// Output:
// Processed: Processed: 26


// Processed: 4
// Processed: 8
// Processed: 10
```

Let's break down the C++ counterpart:

① We define a function **process_item** that processes an integer by doubling it.

② We initialize a vector named **data** containing integers from 1 to 5.

③ We create a vector of **std::thread** objects to manage threads.

④ Through iteration, we traverse the elements of the **data** vector using a constant reference.

⑤ We create new threads, passing the **process_item** function and the **item** as arguments.

⑥ We iterate through the thread objects.

⑦ We ensure synchronization by joining each thread before the program's termination.

While C++ does provide multithreading capabilities, it necessitates manual synchronization using locks or mutexes. Rust's ownership-driven approach, as demonstrated in the previous Rust example, offers inherent memory safety and eliminates the need for explicit synchronization, enhancing code safety and maintainability.

In the complex world of concurrent programming, the concept of "Stealing Join" emerges as a distinctive strategy, adding a touch of finesse to the orchestration of threads [25]. The notion revolves around the efficient coordination of threads in a way that complements Rust's ownership system. In the context of the previous Rust code snippet, where multiple threads are processing elements from the data vector concurrently, the "Stealing Join" strategy ensures a synchronized and efficient attribution to their individual tasks. This approach aligns with Rust's philosophy of ownership transfer, allowing threads to gracefully finish their operations before joining the main thread.

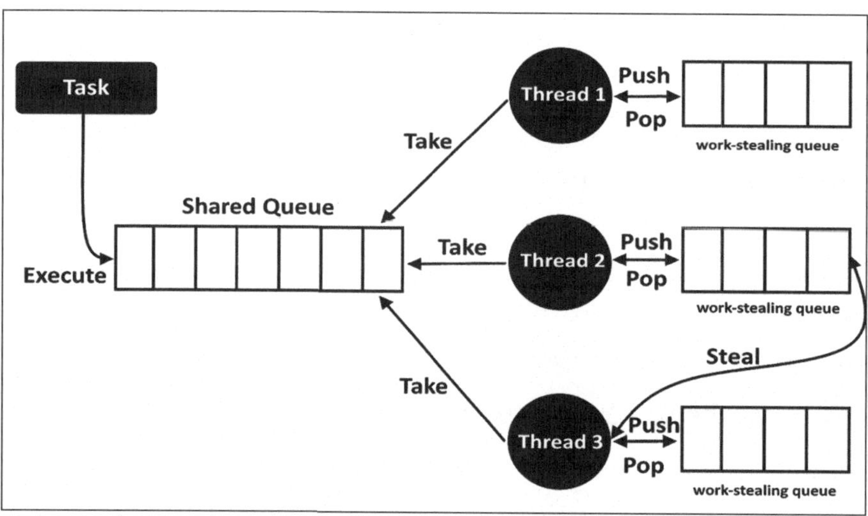

Figure 1.8: *Stealing Join mechanism*

Moreover, in the broader landscape of concurrency, the concept of shared state emerges as a pivotal consideration. Rust, in its commitment to safe and concurrent programming, emphasizes the significance of managing shared state effectively [26]. This emphasis on shared-state management reinforces Rust's unique style in concurrency, showcasing a balance between performance and safety that sets it apart in the domain of parallel execution.

Concurrency is a cornerstone of modern software systems, and Rust's concurrency model ensures safety without compromising performance. The **Send** and **Sync** traits enforce safe data transfer between threads.

[25]Wikipedia contributors. (2023, July 25). Work stealing. Wikipedia. *https://en.wikipedia.org/wiki/Work_stealing*

[26]Shared-State concurrency - the Rust programming language. (n.d.). *https://doc.rust-lang.org/book/ch16-03-shared-state.html*

Listing 1.11 Basic multithreading with mutex example in Rust

```
use std::sync::{Arc, Mutex};
use std::thread;

fn main() {
    let data = Arc::new(Mutex::new(0));
    let handles: Vec<_> = (0..10)
        .map(|_| {
            let data = data.clone();
            thread::spawn(move || {
                let mut data = data.lock().unwrap();
                *data += 1;
            })
        })
        .collect();

    for handle in handles {
        handle.join().unwrap();
    }

    println!("Final data value: {:?}", *data.lock().unwrap());
}
// Output: Final data value: 10
```

The `Send` trait allows data to be transferred between threads, ensuring ownership is properly managed, while the `Sync` trait guarantees that data can be shared between threads without data races. This model promotes parallelism while mitigating common multithreading issues.

As you delve into the in-depth code examples and thorough comparisons, it becomes crystal clear that Rust surpasses traditional C and C++ languages. The innovative features of Rust coupled with its unique design choices create a secure, reliable, and optimized environment for system development.

Pattern Matching

Pattern matching is a crucial feature of Rust that simplifies complex conditional logic and enhances code readability. It allows us to express complex matching patterns in an elegant and concise manner. This feature proves invaluable in scenarios such as parsing data structures, error handling, and even in multithreading synchronization.

Pattern matching works by allowing you to match the structure of values and execute corresponding code blocks. It's more powerful than simple switch statements in other languages, enabling you to de-structure and match complex data structures. Let's look at a more intricate example that demonstrates pattern matching with de-structuring:

Listing 1.12 A basic example of Pattern Matching in Rust

```
enum Shape {
    Circle(f64),
    Rectangle(f64, f64),
    Triangle(f64, f64, f64),
}

fn area(shape: Shape) -> f64 {
    match shape {
        Shape::Circle(radius) => std::f64::consts::PI * radius * radius,
        Shape::Rectangle(width, height) => width * height,
        Shape::Triangle(a, b, c) => {
            let s = (a + b + c) / 2.0;
            (s * (s - a) * (s - b) * (s - c)).sqrt()
        }
    }
}
fn main() {
    println!("{:?}", area(Shape::Circle(32.0)));
}
// $ rustc pattern.rs && /pattern
// Output: 3216.990877275948
```

In this example, the **Shape** enum represents different geometric shapes. The **match** statement elegantly extracts values from each variant and calculates the area accordingly. This makes the code more readable and less error-prone than nested **if** statements or other branching mechanisms.

Lifetimes

Rust's lifetime system is a remarkable feature that enforces memory safety without the need for a garbage collector. Lifetimes track how long references to data are valid, preventing dangling pointers and memory leaks. This system enables us to write code that is both efficient and reliable.

Consider a more complex example involving multiple lifetimes and a function that finds the longest common prefix of two strings:

Listing 1.13 A basic example of lifetimes in Rust

```
fn longest_common_prefix<'a>(x: &'a str, y: &'a str) -> &'a str {
    let min_length = std::cmp::min(x.len(), y.len());
    let bytes_x = x.as_bytes();
    let bytes_y = y.as_bytes();

    for i in 0..min_length {
        if bytes_x[i] != bytes_y[i] {
            return &x[..i];
        }
    }

    &x[..min_length]
}
fn main() {
    let string1 = "abc";
    let result;
    {
        let string2 = "abdef";
        result = longest_common_prefix(string1, string2);
    }
    println!("The longest common prefix is: {}", result);
}

// $ rustc lifetimes.rs && ./lifetimes
// Output: The longest common prefix is: ab
```

In this function, the single lifetime **'a** ensures that the returned reference is valid for the lifetime of the shorter input reference. This guarantees safety and prevents potential dangling references.

Rust's lifetime annotations might seem complex at first, but they enable the compiler to catch common memory-related errors at compile time, making your code more robust.

Zero-Cost Abstractions

Rust empowers us to create high-level abstractions without sacrificing performance. This is achieved through the principle of "zero-cost abstractions". Rust's ownership and borrowing system, combined with its sophisticated compiler optimizations, allow code to be written in a natural and expressive way while still compiling to efficient machine code.

Let's explore an example illustrating non-zero cost abstraction in Rust and compare it with a counterpart that lacks such abstraction. Consider a simple task of filtering even numbers from a vector:

Listing 1.14 A basic example of a non-zero cost abstraction

```
fn filter_even_numbers_old(numbers: Vec<i32>) -> Vec<i32> {
    let mut result = Vec::new();
    for num in numbers {
        if num % 2 == 0 {
            result.push(num);
        }
    }
    result
}
```

In this traditional approach, we explicitly iterate over the vector, check each element for evenness, and manually build a new vector containing only the even numbers. While this code is straightforward, it exposes the low-level details of iteration and conditional checking, lacking abstraction. Now, let's explore its zero cost abstraction counterpart:

Listing 1.15 A basic example of a zero cost abstraction

```
fn filter_even_numbers_new(numbers: Vec<i32>) -> Vec<i32> {
    numbers.into_iter().filter(|&num| num % 2 == 0).collect()
}
```

In contrast, leveraging zero cost abstraction in Rust allows for a more expressive and concise solution. Here, we utilize the **`into_iter()`** method to create an iterator, apply the filter method with a closure defining the condition, and then collect the results into a new vector. This approach abstracts away the low-level iteration and conditional checking details, providing a cleaner and more readable implementation. Notably, *Chapter 10: Iterators and Closures* will delve deeper into the world of iterators, offering a comprehensive exploration of their versatility and demonstrating how they empower you to write more elegant and efficient code.

Now, the second example with zero cost abstraction offers several advantages. It encapsulates the filtering logic in a more declarative style, making the intent clearer and reducing the chances of introducing errors related to manual iteration and conditional checks. Moreover, it aligns with Rust's emphasis on expressive and ergonomic code, enhancing readability and maintainability. By comparing both examples, you can appreciate how zero cost abstraction not only improves code aesthetics but also contributes to more robust, concise, and comprehensible solutions in Rust.

Consider another example showcasing Rust's ownership system and how it allows safe and performant concurrent programming:

Listing 1.16 A basic example of zero-cost abstraction in Rust

```
use std::thread;

fn main() {
    let data = vec![1, 2, 3, 4, 5];
    let shared_data = std::sync::Arc::new(data);

    let handles: Vec<_> = (0..5).map(|i| {
        let shared_data = shared_data.clone();
        thread::spawn(move || {
            let local_sum: i32 = shared_data.iter().sum();
            println!("Thread {} Sum: {}", i, local_sum);
        })
    }).collect();

    for handle in handles {
        handle.join().unwrap();
    }
}
// Output:
// Thread 0 Sum: 15
// Thread 2 Sum: 15
// Thread 4 Sum: 15
// Thread 1 Sum: 15
// Thread 3 Sum: 15
```

In this example, the ownership system ensures that each thread has access to shared data in a safe and performant manner, without data races. The **Arc** type (Atomic Reference Counting) allows multiple threads to share ownership of the data, and Rust's type system guarantees thread safety without the need for explicit locking mechanisms. More on smart pointer in subsequent chapters. Particularly, *Chapter 6: Memory Management and Pointers* will delve deeper into the world of memory management and smart pointers, offering a comprehensive exploration of their versatility.

It is important to note that in this example the use of **`std::sync::Arc`** (atomic reference counting) and threads is an example of zero-cost abstraction. This code leverages high-level abstractions to achieve concurrent execution with shared data and parallel summation across threads. Despite the high-level abstractions used, the Rust compiler ensures that the resulting code is efficient and performs well, exemplifying the zero-cost abstraction principle.

Foreign Function Interface (FFI)

Rust's Foreign Function Interface (FFI) capabilities enable seamless integration with existing C and C++ codebases. This feature is crucial for system development, as it allows Rust code to interact with libraries written in other languages. Rust's FFI guarantees safety, preventing issues like null pointer de-referencing that often occur in large C/C++ interactions.

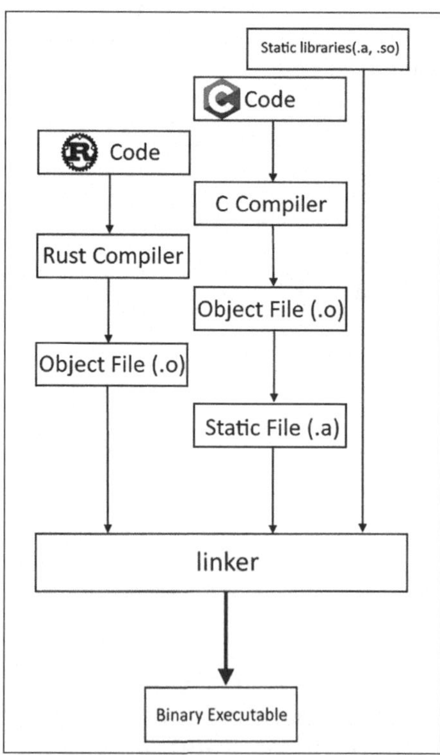

Figure 1.9: *Foreign function interface*

Consider a scenario where you want to call a C function from Rust and handle complex data types:

Listing 1.17 A basic example of a foreign function interface (ffi) in Rust

```
extern "C" {
    fn process_data(data: *mut u8, length: usize);
}

fn main() {
    let mut data: Vec<u8> = vec![1, 2, 3, 4, 5];

    unsafe {
        process_data(data.as_mut_ptr(), data.len());
    }
}
// $ gcc -c external_lib.c -o external_lib.o
// $ ar rcs libexternal_lib.a external_lib.o


// $ rustc -L . -o main main.rs -l external_lib
// $ ./main
// Output: 1 2 3 4 5
```

Rust's FFI capabilities open the door to modernizing and enhancing legacy codebases with Rust's safety features. It enables you to leverage Rust's strong type system and safety guarantees even when interacting with code written in other languages.

Error Handling

Error handling is a critical aspect of software reliability. Rust's `Result` and `Option` types provide a robust mechanism for managing errors and nullable values.

Consider an error handling example involving file I/O:

Listing 1.18 A basic example of error handling in Rust

```
use std::fs::File;
use std::io::{Read, Error};

fn read_file_contents(filename: &str) -> Result<String, Error> {
    let mut file = File::open(filename)?;
    let mut contents = String::new();
    file.read_to_string(&mut contents)?;
```

```
    Ok(contents)
}
// Output:
// File contents:
// line 1
// line 2
// line 3
//
```

The **Result** type handles potential errors, forcing developers to explicitly handle success and failure cases. Similarly, the **Option** type ensures explicit handling of nullable values, effectively eradicating the dreaded null pointer dereferencing issues. This approach encourages developers to write more reliable and maintainable code. More on this topic in *Chapter 5: Error Handling and Recovery*.

Controlled Unsafe Operations

While Rust emphasizes safety, it acknowledges the need for low-level operations. The unsafe keyword enables us to bypass some of Rust's safety checks when necessary.

Consider an example involving raw pointer manipulation:

Listing 1.19 A basic example of unsafe code block execution in Rust

```
fn main() {
    let mut data = [1, 2, 3, 4, 5];
    let data_ptr = data.as_mut_ptr();

    unsafe {
        *data_ptr.offset(2) = 10;
    }

    println!("Modified data: {:?}", data);
}
// Output: Modified data: [1, 2, 10, 4, 5]
```

This controlled security bypass allows for performance-critical operations and interfacing with low-level system APIs while maintaining a clear boundary between safe and unsafe code. The Rust community actively promotes a culture of minimizing unsafe code and ensuring its correctness through review and testing.

The Rust Toolbox

Rust is known for its exceptional safety and concurrency features. However, what sets Rust apart is its versatile toolkit that empowers us to create elegant and efficient code. This toolbox includes expressive syntax, zero-cost abstractions, pattern matching, enums, and ownership semantics, all of which elevate Rust's capabilities.

As mentioned previously, one of the standout features of Rust's toolbox is its ownership system. This system dictates the lifetimes of data, ensuring that resources are managed with precision [27]. This ownership-driven approach enhances memory safety while promoting efficient resource utilization - a rare combination in the programming world. By using Rust's ownership system, we can create high-level abstractions that are both safe and efficient [28].

The Rust toolkit orchestrates a symphony of creativity, granting us a canvas for creativity that enables us to achieve advanced abstractions while maintaining low-level control. The effective syntax and zero-cost abstractions provide a robust base upon which we can construct our creations. With Rust, we are able to craft programs that not only operate securely and efficiently but also possess gracefulness and eloquence. The toolbox offered by Rust is indisputably indicative of the strength behind innovation as well as the artistic spark it ignites within individuals.

Practical Applications

The adaptability of Rust in practical applications cannot be denied, especially when it comes to crafting Command Line Interface (CLI) tools. Its ergonomic syntax and memory efficiency make it the perfect choice for developing CLI apps that require both effectiveness and user-friendliness. Developers can rely on Rust's ability to manage memory without compromising performance, giving them access to top-notch development tools [29].

Moreover, Rust's impact goes beyond CLI tools as its benefits extend into web services too. The language's impressive capabilities in terms of memory usage and performance make it an attractive option for creating robust backend services. With high-level abstractions, while maintaining low-level control over

[27]References and Borrowing - The Rust Programming Language. (n.d.). *https://doc.rust-lang.org/book/ch04-02-references-and-borrowing.html*

[28]Bugden, W. (2022, June 11). Rust: The Programming Language for Safety and Performance. arXiv.org. *https://arxiv.org/abs/2206.05503*

[29]Command-line apps. (n.d.). *https://www.rust-lang.org/what/cli*

processes, developers can build web-based solutions capable of handling a large volume of requests from users without sacrificing speed or quality.

The versatility offered by Rust is proof enough that this programming language has what it takes across multiple domains - whether you're building powerful CLI utilities or designing complex web systems with ease, that's largely due its exceptional combination of efficient use-of-memory alongside excellent overall system-performance capability; making sure your projects are always delivered at their best potential!

Building a Future with Rust

Rust is more than just a passing fad - it's an influential force that's shaping the programming world. Major companies such as Meta, Dropbox, and Mozilla have already recognized Rust's capabilities and incorporated them into their projects [30]. However, its impact goes beyond mere popularity; proposals to integrate Rust code directly into the Linux kernel demonstrate its ability to handle even the most demanding systems with ease [31]. This milestone marks a significant achievement for Rust in proving itself suitable for critical applications requiring high performance.

As momentum continues to build around this language/tool hybrid, one thing becomes clear: embracing Rust means pushing boundaries and exploring new possibilities in programming like never seen before! With adaptability at its core alongside power and future-proofing features built-in from day 1 - building your next project using rust ensures you're ready not only today but also tomorrow! The sky truly is limitless when developing software with rust as your foundation.

Supportive Community

Beyond its technical features, Rust has a vibrant and inclusive community. From experienced engineers to newcomers, the Rust community is welcoming and eager to help.

This collaborative environment is evident in the extensive documentation, tutorials, and discussions available online. Rust's community-driven development process ensures that the language evolves to meet the needs of developers and maintains its focus on safety, performance, and usability.

---

[30]Wiltz, C. (2021). A brief history of Rust at Facebook. Engineering at Meta. *https://engineering.fb.com/2021/04/29/developer-tools/rust/*

[31]Security updates for Tuesday. (n.d.). *https://lwn.net/Articles/842382/*

Exploring Beyond

The features highlighted here only scratch the surface of Rust's capabilities. Its ownership system, thread safety, expressive macro system, and powerful package manager (cargo) are further testaments to Rust's innovation. Rust's vibrant community and extensive documentation empower us to explore, learn, and create with confidence. As you journey deeper into this book, you'll discover its exceptional ability to revolutionize system development while ensuring code safety, performance, and maintainability.

Notable Rust Projects

Notable Rust projects underscore the language's increasing significance in various domains of software development, demonstrating its versatility and impact on modern programming practices.

Figure 1.10: *Production Rust users*

There are plenty of noteworthy Rust projects in addition to the **Servo** browser engine, **Habitat.sh** infrastructure tooling, and Dropbox's internal use. One such project is Microsoft heavily utilizing the Rust programming language for developing their **Windows Subsystem** for **Linux** (**WSL**). Amazon Web Services (**AWS**) has also created Firecracker - a serverless compute service based on Rust that offers improved security and resource efficiency. The **Actix** web framework is another popular application used for building high-performance web applications capable of handling millions of requests per second.

Furthermore, **Amethyst** game engine development utilizes Rust as well which powers several indie games today. As more developers from different domains join its community every day, it's no surprise that this powerful language continues to gain popularity rapidly due to its unique blend of performance safety and reliability across various innovative ways within tech industry developments.

These are just a few examples of exciting projects being developed using Rust. For a more exhaustive list, you can refer to ***the official Rust website***.

Installing Rust

If you're looking to delve into the world of programming in Rust, installing it on your computer is an essential first step. The good news? Rust has great support for all major operating systems - from Windows and Linux to MacOS. In this section, we'll provide a comprehensive walk-through of each platform's installation process so that you can get started without any hiccups!

Installing Rust on Windows

The process of installing Rust on a Windows operating system is effortless. You can easily follow these uncomplicated steps to get started:

① First, open your preferred web browser and visit the official website for Rust at *https://www.rust-lang.org/tools/install*

② Next, click on the `Other ways to install rustup` link in order to download an installer file with a `.exe` extension.

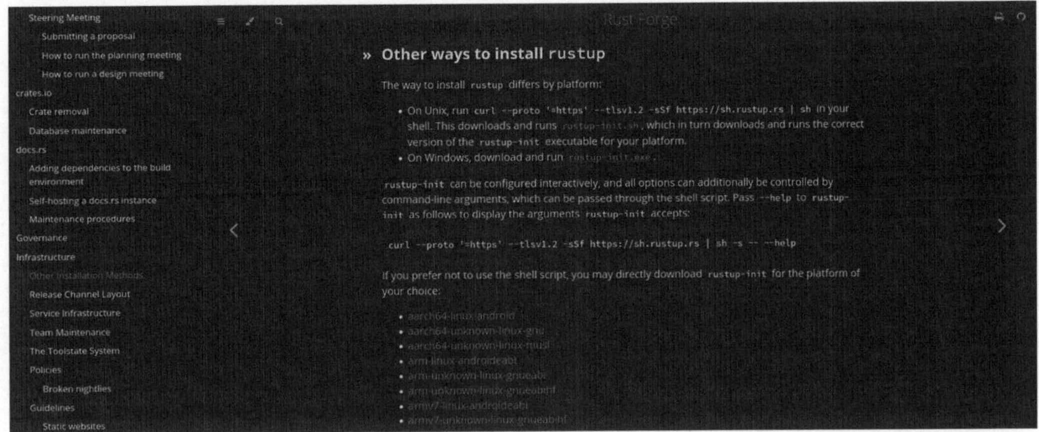

Figure 1.11: *Official Rust installation guide*

③ After downloading it successfully, run this executable file by double-clicking it. Follow all prompts provided during installation carefully as they will guide you through setting up both Cargo (the package manager), rustc (Rust compiler), and so on.

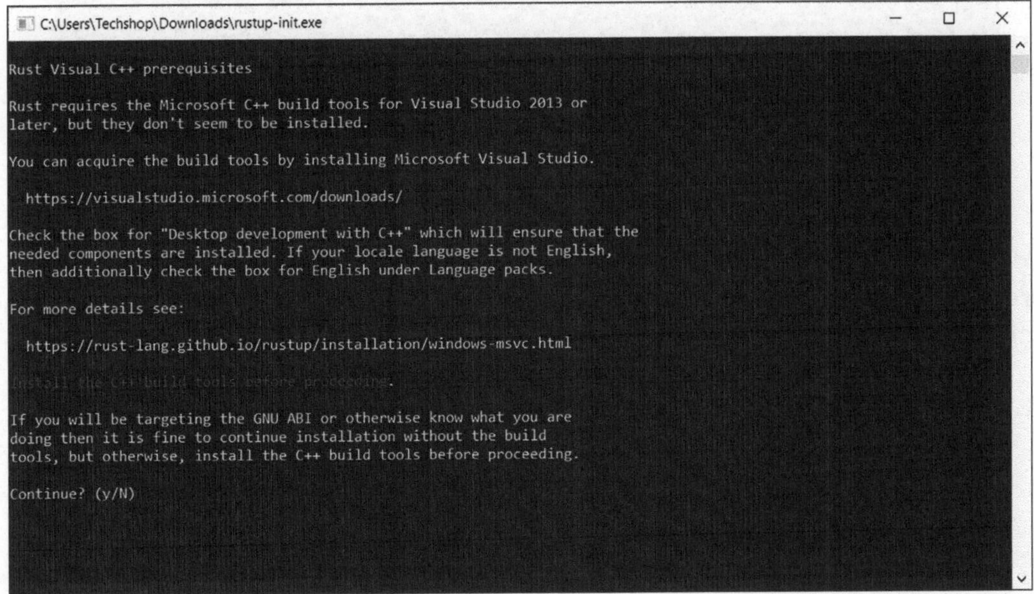

Figure 1.12: *Rust installation process in the terminal*

Now installing Rust components:

```
C:\Users\Techshop\Downloads\rustup-init.exe
3) Cancel installation
>

info: profile set to 'default'
info: default host triple is x86_64-pc-windows-msvc
info: syncing channel updates for 'stable-x86_64-pc-windows-msvc'
781.5 KiB / 781.5 KiB (100 %) 179.9 KiB/s in  4s ETA:  0s
info: latest update on 2023-08-03, rust version 1.71.1 (eb26296b5 2023-08-03)
info: downloading component 'cargo'
  4.9 MiB /   4.9 MiB (100 %) 166.4 KiB/s in 33s ETA:  0s
info: downloading component 'clippy'
  1.9 MiB /   1.9 MiB (100 %) 190.6 KiB/s in 13s ETA:  0s
info: downloading component 'rust-docs'
 13.6 MiB /  13.6 MiB (100 %) 131.2 KiB/s in  1m 37s ETA:  0s
info: downloading component 'rust-std'
 23.6 MiB /  23.6 MiB (100 %) 160.0 KiB/s in  3m 42s ETA:  0s
info: downloading component 'rustc'
 59.5 MiB /  59.5 MiB (100 %) 172.8 KiB/s in  7m 21s ETA:  0s
info: downloading component 'rustfmt'
  1.4 MiB /   1.4 MiB (100 %) 212.6 KiB/s in  8s ETA:  0s
info: installing component 'cargo'
  4.9 MiB /   4.9 MiB (100 %)   1.8 MiB/s in  2s ETA:  0s
info: installing component 'clippy'
info: installing component 'rust-docs'
 13.6 MiB /  13.6 MiB (100 %) 763.2 KiB/s in 18s ETA:  0s
info: installing component 'rust-std'
 23.6 MiB /  23.6 MiB (100 %)   2.8 MiB/s in  8s ETA:  0s
info: installing component 'rustc'
 59.5 MiB /  59.5 MiB (100 %)   3.3 MiB/s in  2m 51s ETA:  0s
info: installing component 'rustfmt'
info: default toolchain set to 'stable-x86_64-pc-windows-msvc'

  stable-x86_64-pc-windows-msvc installed - rustc 1.71.1 (eb26296b5 2023-08-03)


Rust is installed now. Great!

To get started you may need to restart your current shell.
This would reload its PATH environment variable to include
Cargo's bin directory (%USERPROFILE%\.cargo\bin).

Press the Enter key to continue.
```

Figure 1.13: *Rust components installation in the terminal*

④ Once everything has been installed correctly, launch either a new command prompt or terminal window then type **`rustc --version`**. This should display the version number of your newly-installed Rust software.

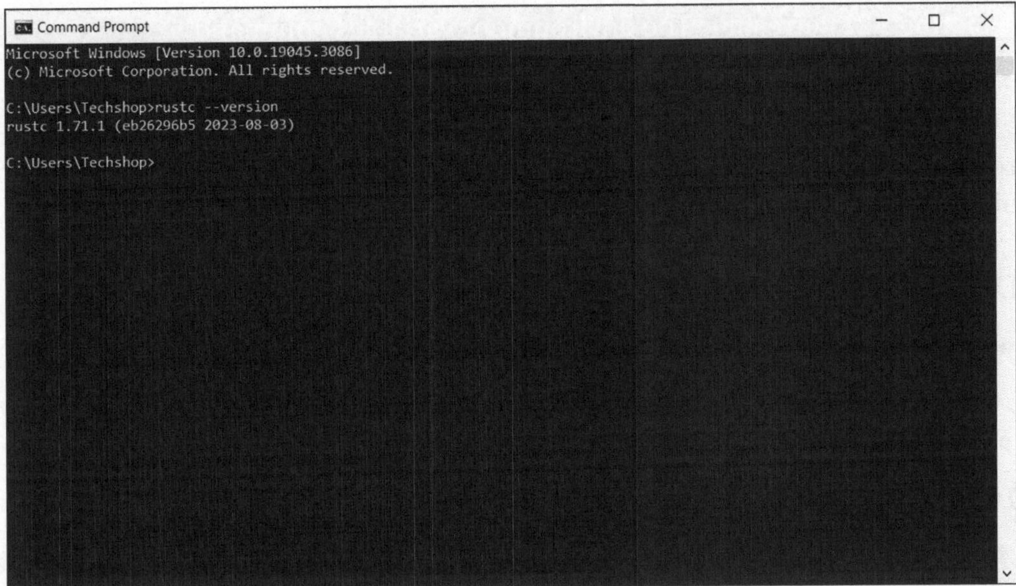

Figure 1.14: *Rust components installation verification*

As you can see, it is quite simple to install Rust using just four easy-to-follow instructions that anyone can understand without difficulty!

Installing Rust on Linux

The process of installing Rust on Linux is a simple one. Follow these steps to get started:

① Open your terminal. To do so, press **`Ctrl + Alt + T`**.

② In the terminal, enter this command:

Listing 1.20 Rust installation command on Linux

```
$ curl --proto '=https' --tlsv1.2 -sSf https://sh.rustup.rs | sh
```

This will download and run the **`Rustup`** installer script.

③ Complete the installation by following the instructions in the prompts displayed.

You'll be asked about default settings as well as components that you'd like installed.

④ Once done with the installation, refresh your environment variables either by closing and reopening your Terminal or running this command:

Listing 1.21 Refreshing the environment variables command

```
$ source $HOME/.cargo/env
```

⑤ To confirm whether it has been successfully installed type **`rustc --version`** into the Terminal; if all goes well then you should see information regarding which version of rust was just downloaded!

Installing Rust on MacOS

The process of installing Rust on MacOS is a piece of cake:

① Open your terminal by either searching **`Terminal`** in Spotlight or navigating to **`Applications`** → **`Utilities`** → **`Terminal`**.

② Run the following command in the terminal:

Listing 1.22 Rust installation command on MacOS

```
$ curl --proto '=https' --tlsv1.2 -sSf https://sh.rustup.rs | sh
```

This command will download and run the **`Rustup`** installer script that you need.

③ Follow the prompts within your terminal to finish up with installation; be sure to select default settings and components as needed.

④ After completing these steps close out then reopen your terminal window OR enter:

Listing 1.23 Refreshing the environment variables command

```
$ source $HOME/.cargo/env
```

to refresh it with new environment variables.

⑤ Ensure Rust is installed by typing **`rustc --version`** in the terminal. You should see the installed Rust version displayed.

You're Ready to Rust!

With Rust now successfully installed on your system, you're all set to start exploring this powerful language. Rust's comprehensive documentation, active community, and fantastic tooling are at your disposal. Whether you're building blazing-fast applications or diving into system-level programming, Rust's unique features and benefits await your creativity.

IDEs and Tools

Before you dive into writing Rust code, let's set up your development environment. This section will guide you through installing Integrated Development Environments (IDEs) and essential tools that will make your coding journey smoother than a well-tuned engine.

Choose Your IDE

Selecting the right IDE can make your Rust development experience a breeze. Here is a popular option:

Visual Studio Code (VS Code)

Visual Studio Code is a lightweight and powerful IDE that's widely used in the Rust community. Here's how to set it up:

① Download and install ***Visual Studio Code.***

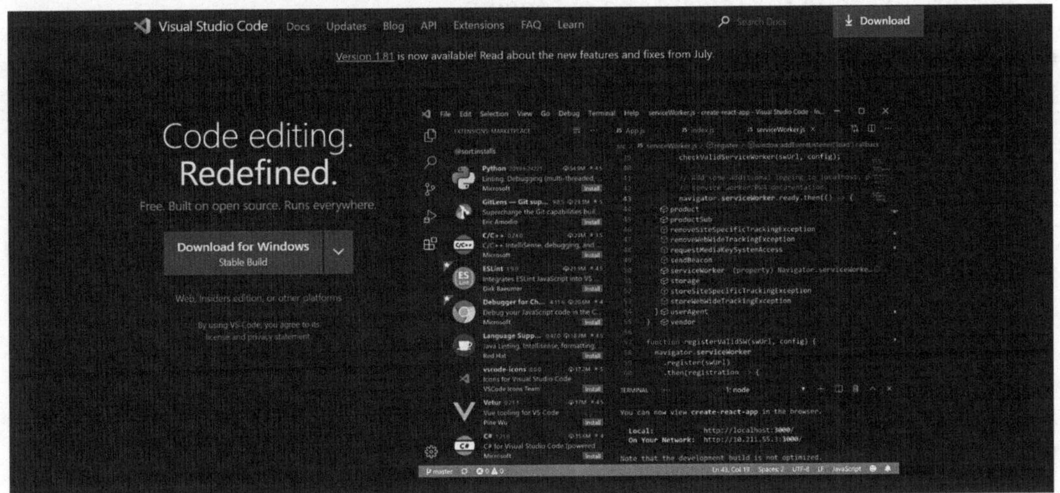

Figure 1.15: *Visual Studio Code official website*

② Open VS Code and head to the Extensions Marketplace by clicking the Extensions icon in the sidebar or pressing **`Ctrl + Shift + X`**.

③ Search for **`Rust`** and install the official Rust extension provided by the Rust Programming Language.

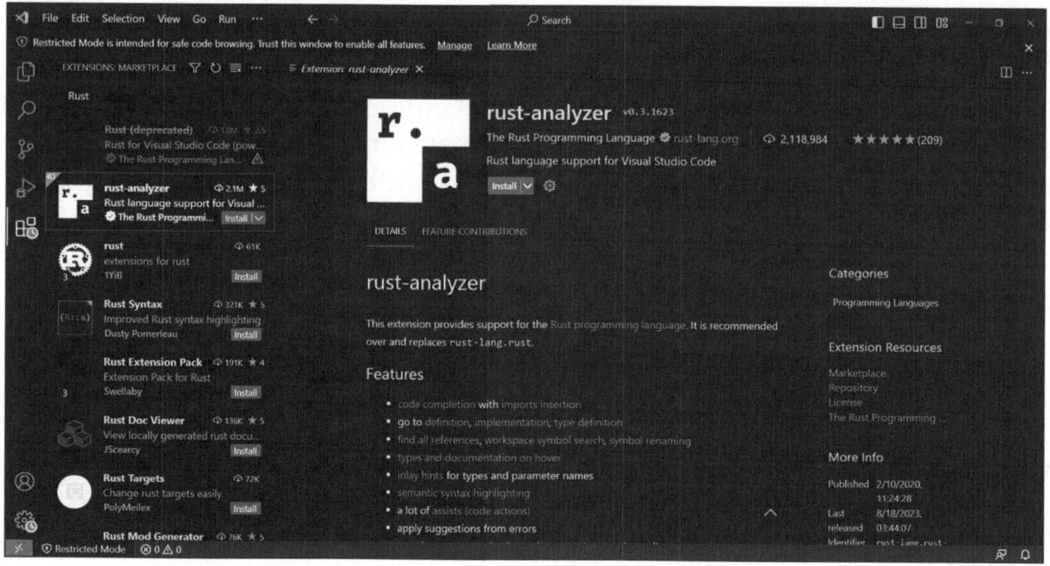

***Figure 1.16:** Rust Analyzer VS Code extension*

④ Restart VS Code to activate the extension.

Congratulations! You're now ready to write Rust code in VS Code with features like code completion, error highlighting, and more.

Essential Rust Tools

Apart from your IDE, a few tools will become your trusty companions on your Rust coding journey:

The Package Manager

Rust's package manager, Cargo, simplifies managing dependencies and building projects. To ensure you have it:

① Open your terminal or command prompt.

② Type **`cargo --version`** and hit Enter. If you see the version number, you're good to go. If not, install Rust using ***Rust's official installation guide***.

The Linter

Clippy is a fantastic tool that helps you write idiomatic and bug-free Rust code. To install Clippy, run:

Listing 1.24 Installing Clippy command

```
$ cargo install clippy
```

Code Formatting

Keeping your code neat and tidy is a breeze with `rustfmt`. To install it, run:

Listing 1.25 Installing rustfmt command

```
$ cargo install rustfmt
```

You've successfully set up your Rust development environment with an IDE of your choice and essential tools like `Cargo`, `Clippy`, and `rustfmt`. Now you're armed with the tools to write elegant, efficient, and safe Rust code. Whether you're building web applications, game engines, or systems software, your journey with Rust is about to get even more exciting.

Writing the first Rust program

Now that Rust has been successfully installed on your machine, it's time to take the plunge and craft your first program. A simple yet impactful greeting of **Hello, World!** will be showcased for all to behold. This section delves into the essential procedures required for establishing an optimal development environment while effortlessly composing and running code.

Getting Started

Prior to commencing coding, ensure that Rust is installed on your device. If it isn't already present, refer back to the preceding section for guidance on how to install and set up Rust on your operating system.

Writing the Code

① Open your favorite text editor or IDE. If you're just starting out, a simple text editor like Notepad (Windows), Nano (Linux/macOS), or Visual Studio Code will work perfectly.

② Create a new file and save it with a `.rs` extension. For example, name it `hello.rs`.

③ Inside the file, type the following code:

Listing 1.26 A basic Rust program

```
fn main() { // ①
    println!("Hello, World!"); // ②
}
```

Here's what's happening in this code:

① **fn main()**: This is the entry point of your Rust program. It's where the execution starts.

② **println!("Hello, World!");**: This line calls the **println!** macro to display the "Hello, World!" message. The ! indicates that **println!** is a macro, not a regular function.

Compiling and Running

Now, we will create our first Rust program:

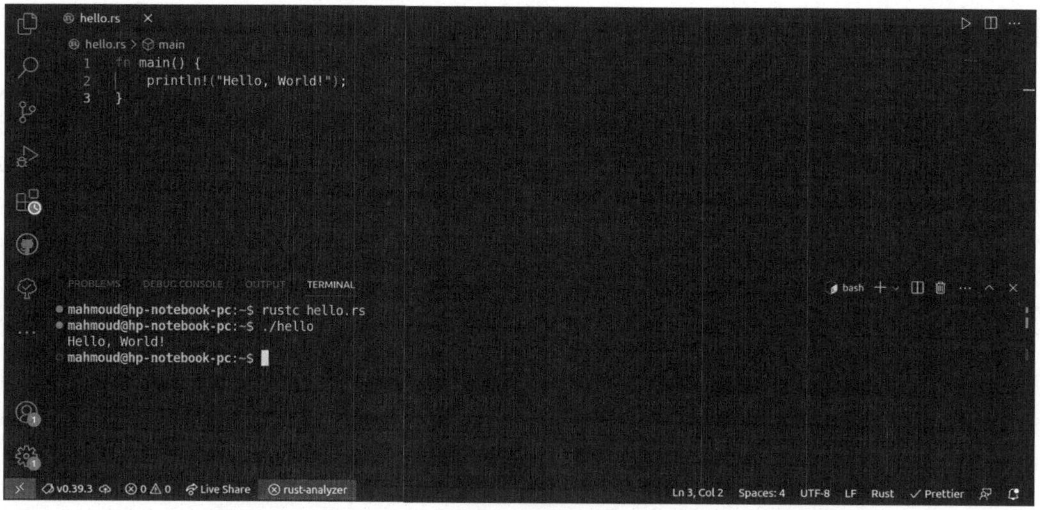

```
1  fn main() {
2      println!("Hello, World!");
3  }

mahmoud@hp-notebook-pc:~$ rustc hello.rs
mahmoud@hp-notebook-pc:~$ ./hello
Hello, World!
mahmoud@hp-notebook-pc:~$
```

Figure 1.17: *Compiling and Running a simple Rust program*

① Open your terminal or command prompt.

② Navigate to the directory where you saved your **hello.rs** file.

③ Run the following command to compile your Rust program:

Listing 1.27 A Rust program compilation command

```
$ rustc hello.rs
```

After compiling successfully, you'll find an executable file named **`hello`** (or **`hello.exe`** on Windows) in the same directory.

④ Run your program by entering its name in the terminal:

Listing 1.28 A program execution command

```
$ ./hello
```

Or on Windows:

Listing 1.29 A program execution command

```
$ hello.exe
```

Well done! You have successfully created and executed your first Rust program. This marks the beginning of a path that enables you to construct durable and effective software. Moving forward, there are numerous possibilities for delving into Rust's potent capabilities, its expressive syntax, as well as its commitment to safety measures.

Cargo: Rust's package manager

Cargo is an essential asset that can prove advantageous for both seasoned and amateur developers. Its remarkable dependency management mechanism, automated build setup, and easy-to-use command-line interface have made it a popular choice among Rust programmers.

Upon completion of this section, you will acquire comprehensive knowledge on how to effectively employ Cargo in your projects. You'll be able to handle dependencies effortlessly while confidently constructing your code with the assurance that everything has been handled professionally for you.

Getting to Know Cargo

Cargo is more than just a build tool - it's your partner for seamless Rust development. Imagine having a trusty assistant that handles tasks like managing dependencies, compiling code, running tests, generating documentation, and even publishing packages. To start using Cargo, ensure you have Rust installed on your system by following the ***official Rust installation guide***.

Creating a New Project

① Begin by opening your terminal or command prompt.

② Navigate to the directory where you'd like to create your Rust project.

③ Initiate a new project using the following command:

Listing 1.30 Creating a new Rust project command

```
$ cargo new my_project
```

④ Replace **`my_project`** with your preferred project name. Cargo will create a new directory using this name, setting up the basic project structure for you.

Navigating the Project Structure

Navigating the structure of a Rust project is fundamental to effectively manage and develop software. In this section, we delve into the essential components and organization of a standard Rust project, equipping you with the knowledge to seamlessly explore and work within its framework.

```
mahmoud@hp-notebook-pc: ~
mahmoud@hp-notebook-pc: $ tree my_project/
my_project/
├── Cargo.toml
└── src
    └── main.rs

1 directory, 2 files
mahmoud@hp-notebook-pc: $
```

Figure 1.18: *A simple rust cargo project structure*

As you navigate into your newly created project directory, you'll encounter:

① **`src`** directory: This is your code's domain, where all your Rust source code will reside.

② **`Cargo.toml`** file: This configuration file is the heart of your project, housing metadata and dependency information.

Building and Running

① Within your project directory, enter the following command to build your masterpiece:

Listing 1.31 Building a Rust project command

```
$ cargo build
```

② Cargo will compile your code and craft an executable inside the **`target/debug`** directory.

③ To witness your creation come to life, run the command:

Listing 1.32 Running a Rust project command

```
$ cargo run
```

Managing Dependencies

A true gem in Cargo's features is its focus on managing dependencies. Install external libraries into your project effortlessly by adding them to your **`Cargo.toml`** file. For example, to import the **`serde`** crate for serialization:

Listing 1.33 Cargo.toml file content

```
[dependencies]
serde = "1.0"
```

① Perform a **`cargo build`**, and Cargo will seamlessly fetch, construct, and assemble the **`serde`** crate along with its dependencies.

Testing and Documentation

Cargo doesn't stop at building and managing - you can harness it to test your code and create user-friendly documentation too. Sprinkle your code with test functions, then orchestrate a collection of tests with:

Listing 1.34 Cargo running tests command

```
cargo test
```

Moreover, Cargo also crafts documentation akin to a master scribe. Embed Rust's built-in documentation comments with:

Listing 1.35 Cargo building docs command

```
cargo doc
```

Exploring More Cargo Features

Cargo doesn't stop here. Explore its comprehensive features, such as:

- Publishing your handcrafted packages to ***crates.io***, Rust's enchanted package registry.
- Crafting benchmarks to fine-tune and analyze your code's performance.
- Conducting a symphony of projects within a workspace for a harmonious development journey.

With Cargo as your compass, you're all set to embark on a journey of Rust development with flair, ease, and boundless possibilities!

Conclusion

This opening chapter has laid the groundwork for your journey into the world of Rust programming. Here's a summary of what we've covered:

- **Rust's Power**: We've discovered Rust, a programming language that's like a superhero for building strong software. It offers unique features that make your programs reliable and secure.
- **Building Solid Foundations**: Rust helps you create programs like building a strong castle. It prevents memory bugs and ensures your code works smoothly, avoiding crashes.
- **Rust's Special features**: Rust has some cool features up its sleeve, making it stand out from other languages. It's a pro at managing memory and keeping your programs performant.
- **Getting Down to Business**: You've learned how to set up Rust on your computer, whether you use Windows, Linux, or MacOS. You've also been introduced to tools and places for writing your Rust code.
- **The First Hello**: You've written your very first Rust program - a simple "`Hello, World!`" message. This marks the start of your hands-on Rust experience.

- **Meet Your Helper - Cargo**: We've introduced you to Cargo, Rust's helpful companion. It takes care of the boring stuff in coding, so you can focus on creating.

As you move forward, armed with a foundational understanding of Rust, you're ready to dive into the exciting world of coding, problem-solving, and innovation that Rust offers. This chapter is just the beginning, and there's a whole universe of possibilities awaiting your exploration. Get ready to unlock your coding potential in the chapters ahead!

Additional Resources

For more information on setting up your Rust development environment and using tools effectively, check out the official Rust documentation:

- Official Rust Website: *https://www.rust-lang.org*
- Rust Installation Guide : *https://www.rust-lang.org/tools/install*
- Rustup Documentation : *https://rustup.rs*
- The Rust Programming Language Book: *https://doc.rust-lang.org/book*
- VS Code - Rust Extension : *https://marketplace.visualstudio.com/items?itemName=rust-lang.rust*
- IntelliJ IDEA - Rust Plugin: *https://plugins.jetbrains.com/plugin/8182-rust*
- Cargo - The Rust Package Manager: *https://doc.rust-lang.org/cargo*
- Clippy - The Rust Linter: *https://github.com/rust-lang/rust-clippy*
- rustfmt - Code Formatting: *https://github.com/rust-lang/rustfmt*
- Cargo Documentation : *https://doc.rust-lang.org/cargo*
- Crates.io - The Rust Package Registry: *https://crates.io*
- The Rust Programming Language Book - Chapter on Cargo: *https://doc.rust-lang.org/book/ch01-03-hello-cargo.html*
- The Rust Programming Language Book: *https://doc.rust-lang.org/book*
- Rust by Example: *https://doc.rust-lang.org/stable/rust-by-example*
- Rust Community and Forums: *https://users.rust-lang.org*

Multiple Choice Questions

Q1: Which of the following best describes Rust's primary focus?

a) Dynamic typing
b) Memory safety and performance
c) Code obfuscation
d) Interpretive execution

Q2: What is the primary purpose of Rust's ownership system?

a) Simplify function signatures
b) Enable runtime garbage collection
c) Ensure memory safety
d) Enhance code readability

Q3: What is the Rust feature that prevents data races in concurrent programming?

a) Immutable variables
b) Threads
c) Mutexes
d) Ownership model and '`Send`'/'`Sync`' traits

Q4: Which keyword is used in Rust to declare unsafe code blocks?

a) risk
b) uncertain
c) unsafe
d) dangerous

Q5: What does the '`Option<T>`' type represent in Rust?

a) A required value
b) A nullable value
c) A boolean value
d) An integer value

Q6: Which Rust construct allows developers to handle different cases or states elegantly?

a) Functions

b) Structs

c) Enums

d) Macros

Q7: What is the purpose of pattern matching in Rust?

a) Ensuring code correctness

b) Optimizing runtime performance

c) Reducing code verbosity

d) Handling complex conditional logic

Q8: What are zero-cost abstractions in Rust?

a) High-level code constructs with no impact on performance

b) Code constructs that reduce safety but improve efficiency

c) Code constructs that require complex runtime checks

d) Abstractions that impose runtime overhead

Q9: Which major companies have adopted Rust for their software projects?

a) Amazon

b) Apple

c) Google

d) All of the above

Q10: What is FFI, and how does Rust support it?

a) FFI stands for "Functional Function Interaction" and is not supported in Rust.

b) FFI stands for "Federated Function Integration" and allows Rust to interface with Python code.

c) FFI stands for "Foreign Function Interface," and Rust supports it through the 'extern' keyword to interface with other languages like C.

d) FFI stands for "Fast Function Invocation" and is exclusive to Rust.

Q11: Which Rust feature allows multiple parts of code to access data without taking ownership of it?

a) Ownership system

b) Lifetimes

c) Borrowing

d) Pattern matching

Q12: What does the 'extern' keyword in Rust enable developers to do?

a) Declare external variables

b) Import external libraries

c) Define external functions for FFI

d) Create external modules

Q13: Which of the following best describes Rust's approach to error handling?

a) Try-catch blocks

b) Result and Option types

c) Exceptions

d) Go to statements

Q14: What is the primary benefit of using enums (enumerations) in Rust?

a) Reducing code complexity

b) Creating infinite data types

c) Representing a finite set of values

d) Eliminating the need for pattern matching

Answers

1. b) Memory safety and performance
2. c) Ensure memory safety
3. d) Ownership model and 'Send'/'Sync' traits
4. c) unsafe

5. b) A nullable value
6. c) Enums
7. d) Handling complex conditional logic
8. a) High-level code constructs with no impact on performance
9. d) All of the above
10. c) FFI stands for "Foreign Function Interface," and Rust supports it through the 'extern' keyword to interface with other languages like C.
11. c) Borrowing
12. c) Define external functions for FFI
13. b) Result and Option types
14. c) Representing a finite set of values.

Key Terms

- **Ownership:** Ownership in Rust refers to a system where each value has a single variable that is its owner. This system helps manage memory efficiently and prevents issues like data races by tracking how data is used and when it should be deallocated.
- **Borrowing:** Borrowing in Rust allows multiple parts of code to access data without taking ownership of it. Borrowing can be either mutable or immutable, and it ensures that data remains safe and consistent during its lifetime.
- **Lifetime:** A lifetime in Rust is a way to specify the scope or duration for which references to data are valid. It helps prevent references from outliving the data they point to, ensuring memory safety.
- **Pattern Matching:** Pattern matching is a feature in Rust that allows developers to match values against predefined patterns or structures, making it easier to handle complex data and control flow.
- **FFI (Foreign Function Interface):** FFI is a mechanism in Rust that enables code written in Rust to interface with code written in other programming languages, such as C. It allows Rust to leverage existing libraries and systems.
- **Zero-Cost Abstractions:** Zero-cost abstractions are high-level code constructs in Rust that do not impose any runtime performance penalty. Rust optimizes them during compilation, allowing developers to use high-level abstractions without sacrificing efficiency.

- **Unsafe Code:** In Rust, 'unsafe' is a keyword used to indicate code blocks or functions where Rust's safety guarantees are temporarily relaxed. Developers should use 'unsafe' sparingly and carefully, as it can bypass some of Rust's safety checks.
- **Option<T> and Result<T, E>:** These are types in Rust used for error handling and managing nullable values. 'Option<T>' represents an optional value that can be 'Some(T)' or 'None,' while 'Result<T, E>' represents either a successful result of type 'T' or an error of type 'E.'
- **Enums (Enumerations):** Enums in Rust define a custom data type that can have a finite set of values, each of which may carry associated data. They are commonly used to represent various states or options in a program.
- **Concurrency:** Concurrency in Rust refers to the ability to execute multiple tasks or threads simultaneously. Rust provides tools like threads and message-passing mechanisms to handle concurrent programming safely.
- **Data Race:** A data race is a concurrency bug that occurs when multiple threads access shared data concurrently, and at least one of them modifies the data. Rust's ownership system and 'Send'/'Sync' traits prevent data races.
- **Garbage Collector:** A garbage collector is a mechanism used in some programming languages to automatically reclaim memory occupied by objects that are no longer in use. Rust does not use a garbage collector.
- **Pattern Matching:** Pattern matching in Rust involves matching values against specific patterns or structures. It is used for tasks such as deconstructing data, branching based on conditions, and handling complex data structures.
- **Fearless Concurrency:** "Fearless Concurrency" is a term that reflects Rust's ability to write concurrent code with confidence in its safety and correctness, thanks to its memory safety guarantees and robust concurrency support.
- **Message Passing:** Message passing is a concurrency model in which threads or processes communicate by sending and receiving messages. Rust provides channels for safe message passing between threads.
- **Buffer Overflow:** Buffer overflow is a common security vulnerability where data overflows the bounds of a buffer, potentially causing memory corruption and security breaches. Rust's ownership system prevents buffer overflows.
- **Memory Leak:** A memory leak occurs when a program fails to deallocate memory that is no longer needed, leading to a gradual increase in memory usage. Rust's ownership system helps prevent memory leaks.

CHAPTER 2
Basics of Rust

Introduction

In the rapidly evolving landscape of programming languages, Rust has emerged as a powerful contender, uniquely combining performance and safety. This chapter serves as a comprehensive introduction to the fundamental concepts that support Rust programming. We will be taken on a journey through variables, data types, control flow constructs, functions, closures, and delve into the interesting world of memory management, ownership, borrowing, lifetimes, and the well-known borrow checker. By the end of this chapter, you'll not only grasp the basic syntax of Rust but also gain an appreciation for the language's safety-first philosophy.

As we learned from *Chapter 1: Systems Programming with Rust*, Rust's evolution was driven by a need for safer systems programming, where memory-related issues are a common source of bugs and vulnerabilities. The language's design choices empower us to write efficient code without sacrificing safety. One key principle is the "ownership" system, which brings clarity to how memory is managed and ensures that only one part of the code can modify data at a time. Ownership is a central concept that sets Rust apart from other languages, and it's crucial to understand its nuances for writing robust code.

Structure

In this chapter, we will cover the following topics:

- Introduction to variables and data types in Rust
- Control flow using if, else, loops, and match
- Defining functions and working with closures
- Understanding ownership, borrowing, and lifetimes in Rust

- Highlighting Rust's memory safety features
- Writing memory-safe code with the help of the borrow checker

Variables and Data Types

In the world of Rust programming, establishing a firm grasp of variables and data types lays the foundation for robust code. Rust's static type system, which enforces rigorous typing rules, serves as a shield against many common programming errors. This system ensures that each variable is tied to a specific data type, allowing for early detection of mismatches and reducing runtime crashes. Throughout this exploration, we'll delve into a spectrum of data types, beginning with elementary primitives like integers, floating-point numbers, and booleans, and advancing to more complex types including strings, arrays, and tuples.

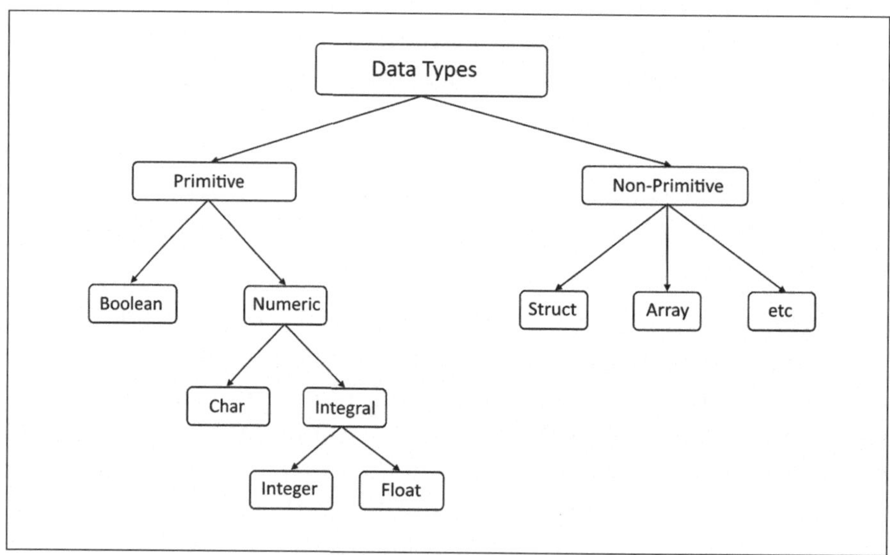

Figure 2.1: *Rust Data Types*

Introduction to Variables

Rust variables emerge as fundamental building blocks, serving as named containers that house and manage various data values. Their significance cannot be overstated, as they enable robust and expressive code. The journey into the world of variables starts with the `let` keyword, which acts as the gateway to their creation. Alongside the variable's name, a crucial trio consisting of data type, and initial value assignment takes center stage. Rust's commitment to explicit typing not only promotes developer comprehension but also equips the Rust compiler with the power to meticulously inspect type correctness.

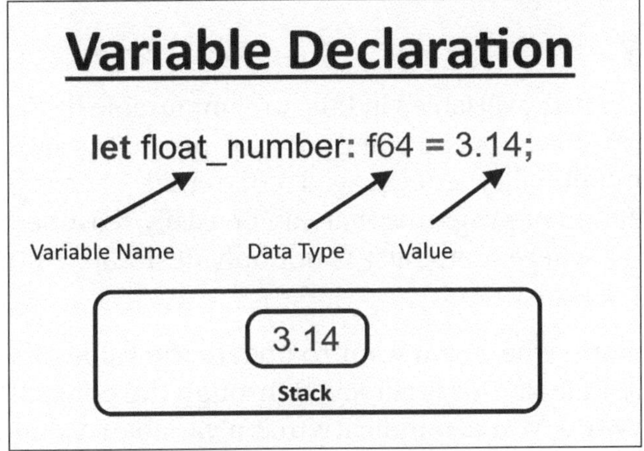

Figure 2.2: *Rust Variables*

Let's delve deeper into this concept with a series of illustrative examples:

Listing 2.1 Rust variable declaration

```
let age: u32 = 30; // ①
let pi: f64 = 3.14159; // ②
let is_happy: bool = true; // ③
```

① The variable **`'age'`** makes its debut as an unsigned 32-bit integer.

② Introducing '**`pi`**' as a 64-bit floating-point number, capturing approximations of the circular constant.

③ '**`is_happy`**' enters the scene as a boolean type, having the values of truth or falsehood.

The true power of the annotations accompanying these variable declarations lies in their ability to instruct explicit data type information to the Rust compiler. This preemptive act plays a vital role in securing the development process against potential pitfalls and bugs. However, the journey doesn't end there. The very act of declaring variables using the **`let`** keyword serves as an illustration of Rust's core philosophy: immutability by default. This principle pushes us towards a programming paradigm that inherently minimizes mutable state and its associated hazards.

Understanding variables and their symbiotic relationship with data types opens the door to creating code that not only resonates with clarity but also stands resilient against potential bugs. In the grand scheme of things, variables form an essential tool, weaving their way through the fabric of logic and computation.

Mutability

As mentioned previously, variables in Rust are immutable by default. This design choice aligns with Rust's overarching goal of providing safe and concurrent programming. Immutability encourages code that is less error-prone and facilitates the creation of programs that can be easily reasoned about. However, there are instances where mutability is not only desirable but also necessary to achieve specific goals.

Consider the scenario where you want to update the value of a variable after its initial assignment. In Rust, this is achieved through the concept of mutability. By using the **mut** keyword, you can indicate that a variable's value can change over time. This simple yet powerful feature conveys both your intention to modify the variable and the compiler's understanding that such changes are valid within the program's scope.

Let's dive into a practical example to illustrate this concept further:

Listing 2.2 Rust variable mutability

```
fn main() {
    let mut count = 0;  // ①
    println!("Initial count: {}", count);
    count += 1; // ②
    println!("Updated count: {}", count);
}
```

① The variable **'count'** is declared as mutable using the **'mut'** keyword.

② The value of **'count'** is incremented by 1, demonstrating mutability in action.

In this code snippet, the variable **'count'** is initially assigned the value 0. Since **'count'** is declared mutable, the code can then increment its value by 1. This ability to modify variables after their creation showcases Rust's flexible yet controlled approach to mutability.

By supporting mutability through explicit declaration, Rust empowers us to make informed decisions about when and where variables can be changed. This approach strikes a balance between allowing flexibility and preventing unanticipated side effects, ultimately contributing to the creation of more reliable and maintainable code.

Shadowing

In the process of crafting Rust programs, you'll frequently encounter scenarios where a variable's name needs to be reused for different purposes within the same scope. This is where the concept of shadowing comes into play. Shadowing allows you to declare a new variable with the same name as an existing one, effectively "hiding" the original variable within a limited scope. This practice provides several benefits, including enhanced clarity and avoidance of naming conflicts.

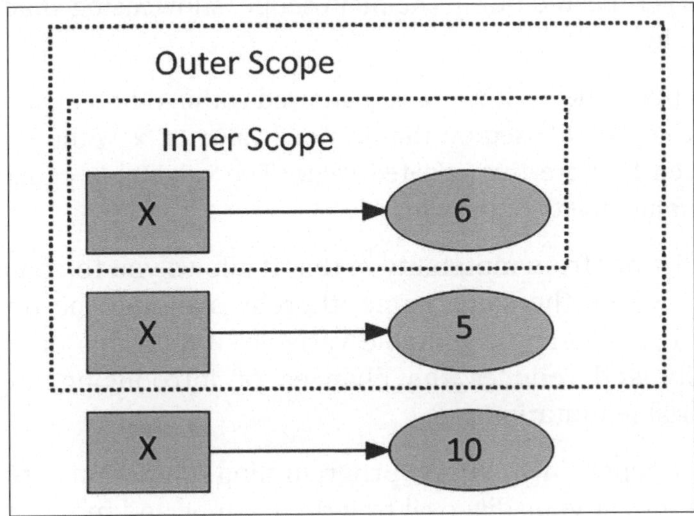

Figure 2.3: *Variables shadowing in different scopes*

Consider the following example to better grasp the concept of shadowing:

Listing 2.3 Rust variable shadowing

```
fn main() {
    let x = 5; // ①
    println!("Original value of x: {}", x);

    {
        let x = x + 1; // ②
        println!("Shadowed value of x: {}", x);
    }

    let x = x * 2; // ③
    println!("Shadowed and modified value of x: {}", x);
}
```

```
// Output

// Original value of x: 5
// Shadowed value of x: 6
// Shadowed and modified value of x: 10
```

① The variable '**x**' is initially assigned the value **5**.

② By shadowing '**x**', a new value is calculated and assigned to the same name in a different scope.

③ The process is repeated but in the main scope, showcasing shadowing's ability to modify the value.

In this code snippet, the variable '**x**' is shadowed within different scopes. Each time, a new value is calculated based on the previous value of '**x**' within a scope, and the name 'x' is reused to store this updated value. The original '**x**' remains untouched, preserving the immutability of the variable.

Shadowing is distinct from mutability in that it allows you to change a variable's value and type within the same name, thereby avoiding the potential pitfalls associated with reassigning a mutable variable's type. This practice enhances code readability and reduces the chances of introducing bugs caused by unexpected variable mutations.

As you delve deeper into Rust's programming paradigms, remember that shadowing is a tool at your disposal to write cleaner and more organized code. By strategically reusing variable names within confined scopes, you can craft programs that are both expressive and maintainable.

Constants

In addition to variables, Rust offers another construct for binding values to names: constants. Constants, while similar to immutable variables in that they cannot be changed, possess distinct characteristics that set them apart. Understanding these differences is crucial for making informed decisions about which construct to use in different scenarios.

First and foremost, constants are always immutable, and the **mut** keyword cannot be applied to them. This unchanging nature aligns with constants' role as values that remain constant throughout a program's execution. They are declared using the **const** keyword instead of the **let** keyword, with the added requirement of annotating the type of the constant value.

Listing 2.4 Rust constant

```
const MAX: u32 = 1_000_000; // ①
```

① A constant named 'MAX' is declared with a value of 1,000,000.

A significant difference lies in the fact that constants are bound to constant expressions, meaning values that can be established during compilation. This principle guarantees a stable and unchanging presence of constants throughout the program's existence. In contrast, variables may obtain computed values at runtime while constants remain attached to predetermined ones before execution begins.

The global scope accommodates constants, making them accessible throughout various parts of the codebase. This feature proves useful when multiple components require access to the same constant value. Furthermore, constants can be seen as a tool for conveying the significance of hard-coded values to other developers. Naming conventions, such as using uppercase letters with underscores, aid in the identification and comprehension of constants within the code.

By understanding the nuances of variables and constants, you gain the ability to select the appropriate binding mechanism based on the specific needs of your program. Variables offer mutability and dynamic values, while constants provide stability and clarity, each contributing to Rust's commitment to safe and effective programming.

The concepts of shadowing and constants further enrich your toolkit, enabling you to write elegant code that communicates intent and mitigates potential pitfalls. Through shadowing, you gracefully reuse variable names within defined scopes, enhancing both code readability and modularity. Constants, on the other hand, offer unchanging values that can be shared across different parts of your program, aiding in the creation of a cohesive and comprehensible codebase.

As you venture deeper into the world of Rust programming, remember that mastery over variables and data types marks the beginning of a journey toward crafting software solutions that are not only functional but also elegant in design. By putting together these foundational concepts with the nuances of Rust's syntax, you uncover a world of possibilities, limited only by your imagination and creativity. So embrace the challenges, celebrate the victories, and let Rust guide you towards becoming a proficient and empowered developer.

Numeric Primitives

Rust's dedication to numeric precision and flexibility is evident not only in its extensive range of integer types but also in its support for a plenty of basic mathematical operations. These operations - addition, subtraction, multiplication, division, and remainder - form the cornerstone of mathematical computation and data manipulation in Rust. As we journey deeper into Rust's numeric realm, let's explore the mechanisms and nuances of these operations that empower us to harness the full potential of numeric data.

Before diving deeper into Rust's numeric operations, it's essential to have a solid grasp of the numeric types available. Rust offers a collection of fixed-width numeric types that align with hardware implementations and provide varying ranges and precision levels. Let's explore these numeric types and their characteristics:

Fixed-Width

The foundation of Rust's type system consists of fixed-width numeric types, carefully selected to align with the types that most modern processors directly implement in hardware. These fixed-width numeric types may experience overflow or loss of precision in certain cases, but they are well-suited for most applications and can be significantly faster than representations like arbitrary-precision integers and exact rationales. For those requiring such specialized numeric representations, the num crate offers support. Rust's numeric type names adhere to a consistent naming pattern that includes their bit width and representation, as shown in the following table.

Size (bits)	Unsigned integer	Signed integer	Floating-point
8	u8	i8	f32
16	u16	i16	f64
32	u32	i32	-
64	u64	i64	-
128	u128	i128	-

Table 2.1: *Fixed width numeric primitives*

Within this framework, a machine word denotes a magnitude that corresponds to the dimensions of an address on the apparatus where instructions are executed. Usually measuring 32 or 64 bits in length.

Integer Types

Rust's unsigned integer types cover the full range of positive values and zero, as outlined in *Table* 2.2.

Type	Range
u8	0 to 2^8 - 1 (0 to 255)
u16	0 to 2^16 - 1 (0 to 65,535)
u32	0 to 2^32 - 1 (0 to 4,294,967,295)
u64	0 to 2^64 - 1 (0 to 18,446,744,073,709,551,615)
u128	0 to 2^128 - 1 (0 to around 3.4 * 10^38)
usize	0 to 2^32 - 1 (32-bit architectures) or 0 to 2^64 - 1 (64-bit architectures)

Table 2.2: *Unsigned interger types*

Rust's signed integer types employ two's complement representation, using the same bit patterns as their corresponding unsigned types. This representation allows them to cover both positive and negative values, as described in *Table* 2.3.

Type	Range
i8	-2^7 to 2^7 - 1 (-128 to 127)
i16	-2^15 to 2^15 - 1 (-32,768 to 32,767)
i32	-2^31 to 2^31 - 1 (-2,147,483,648 to 2,147,483,647)
i64	-2^63 to 2^63 - 1 (-9,223,372,036,854,775,808 to 9,223,372,036,854,775,807)
i128	-2^127 to 2^127 - 1 (roughly -1.7 * 10^38 to +1.7 * 10^38)
isize	Either -2^31 to 2^31 - 1 or -2^63 to 2^63 – 1

Table 2.3: *Signed interger types*

The `u8` type is utilized by Rust to represent byte values, making it a valuable asset for tasks that involve binary files or network sockets.

Characters and Numeric Types

Unlike languages such as C and C++, Rust treats characters as distinct from numeric types. A `char` is not equivalent to `u8` or `u32`, even though it occupies 32 bits of memory. Rust's `char` type is discussed further in the "Characters" section.

The **usize** and **isize** types in Rust serve roles similar to **size_t** and **ptrdiff_t** in C and C++. Their precision corresponds to the address space size on the target machine: 32 bits on 32-bit architectures and 64 bits on 64-bit architectures. Rust mandates that array indices be **usize** values. Furthermore, sizes of arrays, vectors, or counts of elements within data structures typically employ the **usize** type.

Integer literals in Rust can be annotated with a suffix indicating their type. For instance, **42u8** is a **u8** value, and **1729isize** is an **isize**. If an integer literal lacks a type suffix, Rust infers its type based on the context in which it is used. If multiple types could work, Rust defaults to **i32** if it's among the possibilities; otherwise, it reports an ambiguity error. Hexadecimal, octal, and binary literals can be enhanced with underscores for readability. Examples of integer literals are provided in *Table* 2.4.

Literal	**Type**	**Decimal Value**
116i8	i8	116
51966u16	u16	51966
0xcafeu32	u32	51966
0b0010_1010	Inferred	42
0o106	Inferred	70

Table 2.4: *Numeric literals*

Rust provides byte literals, represented by **b'X'**, to represent ASCII codes of characters as **u8** values. For example, both **b'A'** and **65u8** represent the ASCII code for '**A**'. Only ASCII characters are valid within byte literals.

A few characters cannot be directly placed after a single quote due to ambiguity or readability issues. For such cases, Rust employs a stand-in notation, introduced by a backslash. Examples of these characters and their stand-in notations are listed in *Table* 2.5.

Character	**Byte Literal**	**Numeric Equivalent**
Single quote, '	b'\''	39u8
Backslash, \	b'\\'	92u8
Newline	b'\n'	10u8
Carriage return	b'\r'	13u8
Tab	b'\t'	9u8

Table 2.5: *Character types, their byte literal and numeric representation*

By utilizing byte literals of the format `b'\xHH'`, with `HH` being any two-digit hexadecimal number, one is able to represent bytes that hold values equivalent to those designated by the given digits. This method proves especially beneficial when dealing with ASCII control characters and their representation within text-based applications.

The `as` operator serves as a means of converting between various integer types. The following sections offer examples that demonstrate these conversions in action.

Backslash escapes are employed to handle characters that need special treatment. Examples include the character literals '\\' and '\n', which signify a backslash and newline, respectively. Furthermore, you can indicate characters using Unicode escapes in both hexadecimal and code point formats. For instance, '\u{CA0}' and '\u{2A}' correspond to 'ಠ' (Unicode character) and '*', respectively.

Character	**Literal**	**Description**
'你'	'你'	Chinese character for "you"
'こんにちは'	'こんにちは'	Japanese greeting "konnichiwa"
'مرحبا'	'مرحبا'	Arabic greeting "marhaba"
'नमस्ते'	'नमस्ते'	Hindi greeting "namaste"
'안녕하세요'	'안녕하세요'	Korean greeting "annyeonghaseyo"
'Привет'	'Привет'	Russian greeting "privet"
'❄'	'❄'	Snowflake emoji
'\t'	'\t'	Tab escape
'\u{1F601}'	'😁'	Unicode escape for "😁" (grinning face with smiling eyes)
'\u{00A9}'	'©'	Unicode escape for "©" (copyright symbol)
'☀'	'☀'	Sun emoji

Table 2.6: *Examples of different Unicode characters representations*

Rust's `char` type offers plenty of techniques for character identification and transformation. These methods enable you to identify whether a given character is an alphabet, numeral or even whitespace. Furthermore, by utilizing the `to_ascii_lowercase` and `to_ascii_uppercase` functions respectively, one can convert characters into their lowercase or uppercase forms with ease.

Strings and Characters

Rust's char type seamlessly integrates with strings, allowing you to perform complex transformations and manipulations. Consider a scenario where you need to transform all characters in a sentence to uppercase:

Listing 2.5 Rust strings example

```
let sentence = "Rust is amazing!";
let transformed_sentence: String = sentence.chars().map(|c|
c.to_ascii_uppercase()).collect();  // ①
println!("Transformed: {}", transformed_sentence);
```

① Transforming characters to uppercase within a string.

In this example, the compiler converts all characters in the sentence to uppercase, showcasing the capabilities of the char type when used with other string manipulation functions.

Character Iteration and String Operations

In Rust, the distinction between **String** and **&str** plays a pivotal role in memory management and ownership semantics. Passing a &str around your program is incredibly efficient, imposing minimal allocation costs and avoiding memory copying. The key differentiator lies in ownership: **&str** is a borrowed type, essentially denoting read-only data, while **String** is an owned type, representing read-write capabilities. To delve into the practical implications, a **String** comprises three components: a pointer to the memory holding the string's contents, a length, and a capacity. Notably, the memory allocation for a **String** occurs on the heap, offering flexibility in size. On the other hand, references to this data reside on the stack. This distinction underscores the trade-off between ownership and efficiency, where **&str** serves as a lightweight, read-only reference, and **String** provides mutable, heap-allocated storage with its own set of attributes. Understanding this duality is fundamental for us navigating memory management and ownership in our programs.

Beyond transformations, Rust's **char** type also facilitates character iteration within strings. You can iterate over characters in a string using the **chars()** iterator method, enabling you to perform fine-grained operations on each character.

Furthermore, Rust's **char** type empowers you to slice strings by specifying character indices rather than byte offsets. This ensures that characters remain intact even in multi-byte encodings like UTF-8.

As you kick off your text processing journey, remember that Rust's **char** type is your companion. This assistant enables you to sculpt, transform, and paint using the palette of Unicode characters. From simple tasks like extracting the first character to complex transformations across entire strings, Rust's **char** type stands ready to aid you in your linguistic and creative explorations.

For more comprehensive information about Rust's fixed-width numeric types, integer literals, and related topics, refer to the official Rust documentation. It contains details about each type and its associated methods, aiding in mastering Rust's numeric primitives.

Using Numeric Conversions

While Rust's type system is designed to prevent accidental type errors, there are situations where you need to explicitly convert between numeric types. Understanding how to perform these conversions accurately is crucial. Let's delve into the mechanisms of numeric conversions and explore practical examples.

The **as** operator for numeric conversions offered by Rust enables the conversion of various integer and floating-point types. Several examples are provided as follows:

Listing 2.6 From integer to float type casting

```
fn main() {
    let integer_number: i32 = 32;
    let float_number: f64 = integer_number as f64; // ①
    println!("Converted float: {}", float_number);
}
```

① We convert an integer value (32) into a floating-point value using the **as** operator. The resulting **float_number** will hold the converted value.

It is crucial to acknowledge that converting numbers may lead to inaccurate results or overflow issues. Rust's type system has been created with safety measures in place for such conversions, but it remains vital to understand these constraints. Additionally, Rust allows you to perform explicit type annotations to clarify your intentions during conversions. For instance:

Listing 2.7 From float to integer type casting

```
fn main() {
    let float_number: f64 = 3.14;
    let truncated_integer: i32 = float_number as i32; // ①
    println!("Truncated integer: {}", truncated_integer);
}
```

① The floating-point value 3.14 is converted into an integer, resulting in a truncated value of 3.

By understanding the nuances of numeric conversions, you can ensure your Rust code operates accurately and effectively across different numeric types.

Basic Mathematical Operations

The fundamental mathematical operations supported by Rust are integral to everyday programming tasks. These operations are available across all number types, including integers and floating-point numbers. They enable us to perform calculations, formulate algorithms, and solve problems across a wide range of domains.

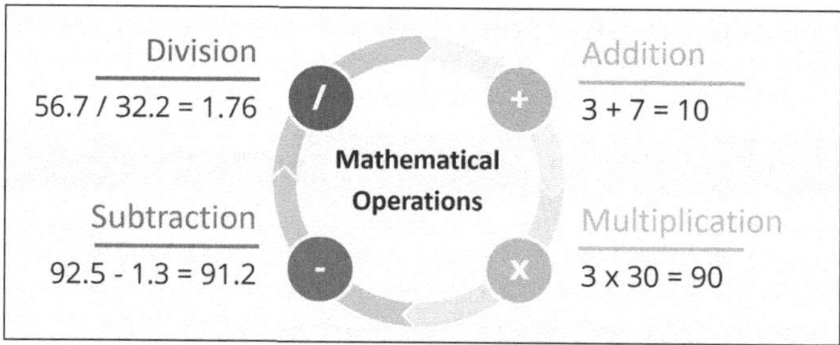

Figure 2.4: *Basic Mathematical Operations*

Addition

The act of combining two values to derive their total is known as addition, a basic arithmetic operation. In Rust programming language, the addition operator can be employed in this manner:

Listing 2.8 Addition in Rust

```
fn main() {
    let sum = 3 + 7;
    // 'sum' now holds the value 10
}
```

In the provided code snippet, the values **3** and **7** are added together using the + operator. The resulting sum, **10**, is assigned to the variable **sum**.

Example	Expression	Result
Integer Addition	3 + 7	10
Floating-Point Addition	3.14 + 1.1	4.24
Mixed Addition	4 + 1.5	5.5

Table 2.7: *Addition on different data types*

Subtraction

The act of subtraction is a crucial mathematical operation that determines the difference between two numerical quantities. Let's take an example of this process:

Listing 2.9 Subtraction in Rust

```
fn main() {
    let difference = 92.5 - 1.3;
    // 'difference' now holds the value 91.2
}
```

In the code snippet, the value **1.3** is subtracted from **92.5** using the - operator. The resulting difference, **91.2**, is assigned to the variable **difference**.

Multiplication

Multiplication involves combining values to obtain a product. Here's how you'd use the multiplication operator in Rust:

Listing 2.10 Multiplication in Rust

```
fn main() {
    let product = 3 * 30;
    // 'product' now holds the value 90
}
```

The symbol * represents the multiplication operation. When we multiply the values of **3** and **30**, a potent product with a value of 90 is obtained, which then gets assigned to the variable named "**product**".

Example	Expression	Result
Integer Multiplication	5 * 8	40
Floating-Point Multiplication	2.5 * 3.0	7.5
Mixed Multiplication	4 * 1.5	6.0

Table 2.8: *Multiplication on different data types*

Division

Division divides a value into equal parts. Here's an illustration of division in Rust:

Listing 2.11 Division in Rust

```
fn main() {
    let quotient = 56.7 / 32.2;
    // 'quotient' now holds the value approximately 1.7608695652173911
}
```

The / operator represents division. In the code snippet, the value **56.7** is divided by **32.2**, resulting in an approximate quotient of **1.7608695652173911**, assigned to the variable **quotient**.

Remainder

The remainder operation yields the leftover value after division. Here's an example of using the remainder operator in Rust:

Listing 2.12 Reminder computation in Rust

```
fn main() {
    let remainder = 43 % 5;
    // 'remainder' now holds the value 3
}
```

The **%** operator calculates the remainder of a division operation. In the code snippet, **43** is divided by **5**, resulting in a remainder of **3**, assigned to the variable **remainder**.

Incorporating these basic mathematical operations into your Rust code opens up a vast landscape of possibilities. From implementing algorithms to performing data analysis, these operations serve as building blocks for creating complex computational solutions. By understanding and mastering these operations, you equip yourself with the tools needed to navigate Rust's numeric landscape and bring your programming visions to life.

Furthermore, the **`rug`** library in Rust emerges as a robust companion for handling complex numeric computations. Specifically designed for arbitrary-precision arithmetic, rug provides a versatile set of tools for working with numbers that exceed the limits of standard numeric types. Its inclusion in the Rust ecosystem signifies a commitment to addressing complex numeric challenges, offering a wealth of functionality to manipulate, calculate, and analyze numbers with precision. Whether dealing with complex mathematical algorithms, cryptography, or scientific computing, the rug library stands as a reliable tool, empowering you to tackle complex numeric scenarios with confidence and efficiency. Its comprehensive suite of features makes it a valuable asset for those navigating the complex landscape of high-precision numerical computations in Rust.

Floating-Point Numbers

In the world of computation, floating-point numbers perfectly balance between precision and approximation. Rust's **`f32`** and **`f64`** types take center stage, offering varying levels of accuracy for your computational routines.

Rust provides two primary floating-point types: **`f32`** and **`f64`**. These types adhere to the **IEEE-754** standard for representing floating-point numbers, which is widely adopted in modern computing [1].

f32 for Efficiency

The **`f32`** type, also known as IEEE single precision, occupies 32 bits in memory. It offers a compromise between precision and memory usage, making it suitable for scenarios where computational efficiency is crucial. Despite its lower precision compared to **`f64`**, **`f32`** can accurately represent a wide range of values.

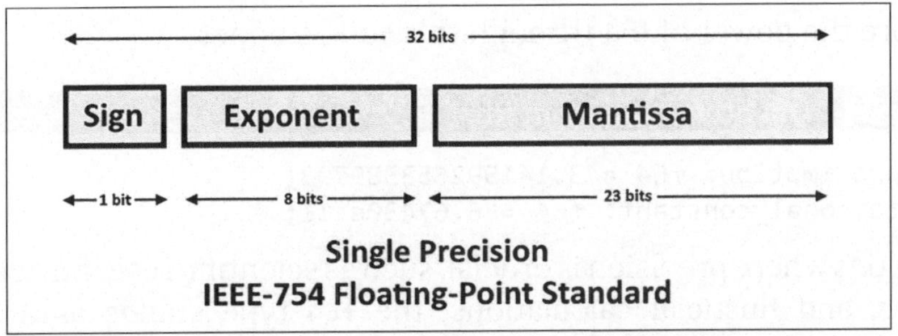

***Figure* 2.5:** *Single precision IEEE-754 floating point standard*

[1]Wikipedia contributors. (2023, December 1). IEEE 754. Wikipedia. *https://en.wikipedia.org/wiki/IEEE_754*

Here's an example of employing the f32 type in Rust:

Listing 2.13 `f32` literal values in Rust

```
let distance_f32: f32 = 123.456;
let velocity: f32 = 12.34;
let temperature: f32 = -5.67;
```

In scenarios like graphics processing or real-time simulations, where fast calculations are paramount, the **`f32`** type shines. Its streamlined representation facilitates fast computations, making it a valuable asset in performance-critical domains.

f64 for Precision

While **`f32`** provides efficiency, **`f64`** - a 64-bit floating-point type - shines as the maestro of precision. This type provides a 64-bit representation, enabling it to capture complex details of different mathematical operations. Whether delving into scientific simulations uncovering cosmic mysteries or performing complex financial modeling, the precision of **`f64`** is crucial [2].

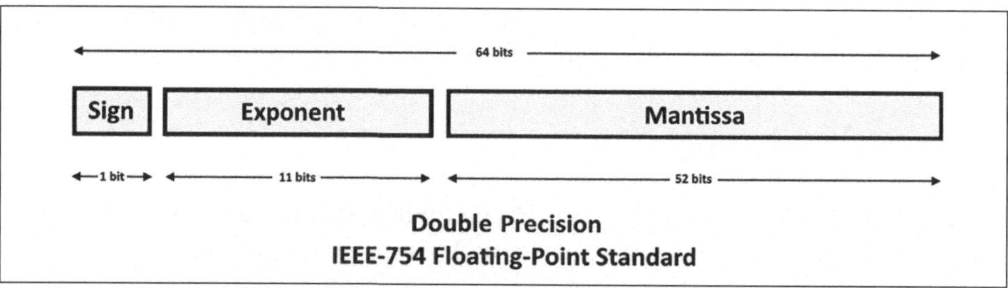

Figure 2.6: *Double precision IEEE-754 floating point standard*

Let's explore the power of f64 through this code snippet:

Listing 2.14 `f64` literal values in Rust

```
let pi_approximation: f64 = 3.141592653589793;
let gravitational_constant: f64 = 6.67430e-11;
```

In applications where precision is crucial, such as scientific research, engineering simulations, and financial calculations, the **`f64`** type stands as a beacon of accuracy.

[2]Wikipedia contributors. (2023, November 16). Double-precision floating-point format. Wikipedia. *https://en.wikipedia.org/wiki/Double-precision_floating-point_format*

Floating-Point Literals

In Rust, you have the flexibility to express floating-point literals either in scientific notation or standard decimal notation [3]. Scientific notations can be represented using the letter e as an exponent indicator. Here's a quick example:

- `1.23e4` represents `12300.0`
- `2.5e-3` represents `0.0025`

In the world of mathematics, expressing a fraction in decimal form is typically done through the utilization of the decimal point. This symbol acts as an identifier for fractional portions within numerical values, simplifying comprehension and calculation processes alike. Take this example:

- `3.14` represents the number π (pi)
- `-0.5` represents a negative half

Here are some examples of floating-point literals and their equivalent representations in Rust:

Literal	Decimal Notation	Scientific Notation	Rust f32	Rust f64
3.14	3.14	-	let a_f32: f32 = 3.14;	let a_f64: f64 = 3.14;
2.0	2.0	-	let b_f32: f32 = 2.0;	let b_f64: f64 = 2.0;
6.	6.0	-	let c_f32: f32 = 6.;	let c_f64: f64 = 6.;
1.5e3	1500.0	1.5e3	let d_f32: f32 = 1.5e3;	let d_f64: f64 = 1.5e3;
1e-2	0.01	1e-2	let e_f32: f32 = 1e-2;	let e_f64: f64 = 1e-2;

Table 2.9: *Literals in Rust and their different representations*

In the provided table, we showcase different floating-point literals and their different corresponding representations. Each literal is presented alongside the Rust code that assigns the value to a specific floating-point variable. This table offers a quick reference for representing various magnitudes and precisions using floating-point literals in Rust.

Mathematical Operations

The `f32` and `f64` data types offer an extensive array of mathematical functions, including addition, subtraction, multiplication, division as well as square root.

[3]Literal expressions - The Rust Reference. (n.d.). *https://doc.rust-lang.org/reference/expressions/literal-expr.html*

These operations can be effortlessly executed using the standard arithmetic operators (+, -, *, /) along with Rust's comprehensive library functions.

Here's an example of performing calculations using **f32** and **f64**:

Listing 2.15 Mathematical operations on f32 and f64 variables in Rust

```
let radius_f32: f32 = 10.0;
let area_f32 = 3.14 * radius_f32 * radius_f32;

let radius_f64: f64 = 10.0;
let area_f64 = std::f64::consts::PI * radius_f64 * radius_f64;
```

In the given example, we determine the surface area of a circle by employing **f32** and **f64** variants. The precise value of π (pi) is represented with utmost accuracy through the employment of constant - **std::f64::consts::PI**.

Navigating Complexities

Beneath the surface of floating-point precision lies a complexity. Despite their versatility and strength, floating-point digits may at times yield unexpected results as a result of their binary representation.

Consider this example:

Listing 2.16 Floating point binary representation precision problem

```
let tricky_number: f64 = 0.1 + 0.1 + 0.1; // 0.30000000000000004
let expected_number: f64 = 0.3;

if tricky_number == expected_number {
    println!("They're equal, right?");
} else {
    println!("Not quite equal, due to tiny discrepancies.");
}
```

In this code snippet, the seemingly straightforward task of comparing two numbers highlights an intriguing quirk. While you might expect the two numbers to be equal, binary approximations can introduce subtle discrepancies. When working with floating-point numbers, it's essential to be mindful of these nuances to prevent unexpected behavior in your calculations.

Approximate Equality

Comparing floating-point numbers might appear straightforward, but it's more like chasing fireflies on a summer night. Binary approximations can turn the task of determining equality into a nuanced endeavor.

However, Rust equips you with tools to navigate this territory. Here's a custom function that performs approximate equality checks:

Listing 2.17 Solving binary representation precision problem with approximation

```
fn approx_equal(a: f64, b: f64, tolerance: f64) -> bool {
    (a - b).abs() < tolerance
}

let value_a: f64 = 0.1 + 0.1 + 0.1;
let value_b: f64 = 0.3;
let tolerance: f64 = 1e-10;

if approx_equal(value_a, value_b, tolerance) {
    println!("Approximately equal within the tolerance.");
} else {
    println!("Not equal, even with tolerance considered.");
}
// Output

// Approximately equal within the tolerance.
```

By incorporating a tolerance value, you gracefully navigate the world of floating-point discrepancies and ensure that your comparisons yield accurate results.

Mastering Floating-Point Numbers

Mastering the art of handling floating-point numbers is like walking on a tightrope between precision and the limitations of binary representation. While these numbers offer great computational power, they also present unique challenges.

Remember, becoming a maestro in the world of floating-point numbers requires a combination of practice and a deep understanding of their nuances. Whether you're using the nimble `f32` to cater to efficiency or embracing the power of `f64` to capture complex details, Rust equips you to walk through the world of floating-point numbers with confidence.

Floating-point numbers are the master of numerical computation, allowing us to explore a vast range of values with finesse and accuracy. By mastering the nuances of `f32` and `f64` , we can achieve precision in scientific calculations and simulations, enabling the modeling of complex real-world phenomena with remarkable detail and reliability.

Booleans for Logic

Within the complex world of programming, Booleans take on a crucial role, as they act as choreographers for logic. These entities are responsible for directing the flow of decisions in an orderly manner. Rust's Boolean type is elegantly represented by `bool` and encapsulates binary choices that can only be either true or false. Despite their seemingly simplistic nature, these markers hold significant importance when it comes to steering constructs such as conditionals and loops with finesse through complex program logic. Let us delve deeper into how this happens precisely!

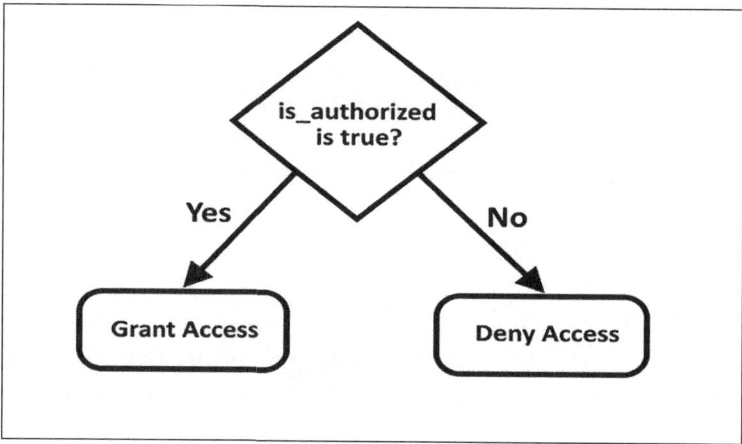

***Figure** 2.7: Booleans and control flow*

Booleans are like the architects of decision-making in the digital world. They encapsulate the essence of logical choices. In Rust, the `bool` type exemplifies this essence - a versatile conductor that directs the flow of logic. Think of Booleans as the ones responsible for questions like "Should this code block execute?" or "Is this condition met?". Consider a scenario where a program's operation stumbles upon user authorization:

Listing 2.18 Booleans in Rust

```
let is_authorized: bool = check_authorization(username, password);
if is_authorized {
    // Grant access
} else {
    // Deny access
}
```

Here, the Boolean variable **`is_authorized`** holds the key to user access. If it's **`true`**, access is granted; if it's **`false`**, access is denied. This interplay of Booleans demonstrates their pivotal role in software logic.

One of Rust's remarkable attributes is its static typing. Booleans in Rust perfectly encapsulate this concept. Once you declare a variable as a **`bool`**, Rust ensures it can only hold **`true`** or **`false`**, leaving no room for ambiguity or mixed signals. This consistent and strict typing system acts as a safeguard against logical errors, ensuring your program's logic remains fixed.

Booleans, in their binary fineness, act as the maestros of logic, conducting the symphony of your code's decision-making. Their power lies in their simplicity, and their influence lies in their universality. They form the basis that enables you to craft sophisticated programs that respond dynamically to changing conditions.

Logical operators like **&&** (AND) and **||** (OR) allow you to combine Booleans to form complex conditions. Here's an example illustrating how logical operators can create complex decision trees:

Listing 2.19 Booleans in Rust

```
let is_raining: bool = check_rain_status();
let is_cold: bool = check_temperature();

if is_raining && is_cold {
    take_umbrella_and_coat();
} else if is_raining || is_cold {
    prepare_for_weather();
} else {
    enjoy_sunny_day();
}
```

In this scenario, the Booleans **`is_raining`** and **`is_cold`** contribute to deciding how to prepare for the weather. The use of **&&** and **||** allows for branching logic based on multiple conditions. Here, Booleans orchestrate a complex decision-making process.

Booleans can also be combined using the logical NOT operator ! to invert their values. This can be useful in scenarios where you want to check the absence of a certain condition:

Listing 2.20 Booleans in Rust

```
let has_no_errors: bool = !check_errors();
if has_no_errors {
    execute_task();
} else {
    handle_errors();
}
```

By inverting the output of **check_errors()**, we obtain a Boolean value called **has_no_errors** using the code. The negation operator, denoted by ! allows for quick and easy detection of error absence.

Booleans in Rust can also be employed to create loops, further enhancing their role in controlling program flow. Consider this example of a loop that executes while a certain condition is met:

Listing 2.21 Booleans in Rust

```
let mut is_running: bool = true;

while is_running {
    perform_iteration();
    is_running = check_continue_condition();
}
```

Here, the Boolean **is_running** determines whether the loop continues executing. The loop keeps iterating as long as **is_running** remains **true**. Booleans provide a dynamic way to control the loop's behavior.

In addition to their use in conditionals and loops, Booleans are indispensable when creating state machines, where various states dictate program behavior. Consider the following example of a vending machine simulation:

Listing 2.22 Booleans as enum matching value in Rust

```
enum VendingMachineState {
    Idle,
    SelectingItem,
    DispensingItem,
    RefundingCoins,
}
```

```
fn main() {
    let mut current_state = VendingMachineState::Idle;

    loop {
        match current_state {
            VendingMachineState::Idle => {
                // ...
            }
            VendingMachineState::SelectingItem => {
                // ...
            }
            VendingMachineState::DispensingItem => {
                // ...
            }
            VendingMachineState::RefundingCoins => {
                // ...
            }
        }

        // Update state based on conditions
        current_state = update_state(current_state);
    }
}
```

In this example, the **`VendingMachineState`** enum holds different states of the vending machine. The program's behavior depends on the current state, which is controlled using Booleans and conditional logic. Booleans play a vital role in determining the flow of the state machine.

Remember, as you harness the power of Booleans, you're mastering the art of logic manipulation, painting complex patterns that govern the behavior of your code. Whether it's simple conditionals, complex state machines, advanced decision trees, dynamic loops, or even program states, Booleans remain your trusty companions on the journey through the world of programming logic.

Complex Data Types

As you progress from constructing simple foundations to more complex frameworks, you will unlock a set of powerful resources referred to as complex data types. These assets equip you with the ability to design programs that are not only refined but also versatile enough to tackle diverse challenges.

Strings

Strings are like containers for words and sentences, essential for communication in various applications. Rust's **String** type takes the idea of these containers to the next level by allowing them to change size and content. Imagine using a bag that can stretch and shrink as you put things inside or take things out. This dynamic quality is especially useful when dealing with messages, text from users, or any situation where the length of the text isn't known beforehand.

One remarkable thing about the **String** type is its ability to grow and shrink as needed. Unlike boxes that have a fixed size, **String** containers can get larger or smaller. Check out this example to see it in action:

Listing 2.23 Strings in Rust

```
let mut user_greeting = String::from("Hello"); // ①
user_greeting.push_str(", welcome to Rust!"); // ②
```

① The **user_greeting** begins with the friendly greeting, "Hello".

② Through utilizing the **push_str** function, we are able to append additional text onto this initial message. As a result of applying this action, our final output reads as follows: "Hello, welcome to Rust!".

This exemplifies how Rust has the capability to handle dynamic changes in size within textual content.

Rust's library offers an array of tools that simplify the handling of strings. From searching for particular words to altering text cases, these features take care of the tedious aspects and enable you to concentrate on your program's broader objectives. By leveraging such utilities, you can save valuable time while achieving more efficient results. For instance, let us explore how we may tally a specific word's frequency within a sentence:

Listing 2.24 Strings in Rust

```
let sentence = "Rust is a programming language. Rust is powerful.";
let target_word = "Rust";
let count = sentence.matches(target_word).count();
println!("The word '{}' appears {} times.", target_word, count);
// Output

// The word 'Rust' appears 2 times.
```

The **matches** function is employed in this code to locate every instance of the desired term within a sentence, while the **count** operation tallies up all instances. This functionality serves as an impressive showcase for Rust's string manipulation capabilities and its ability to streamline complex processes.

Substrings

Rust's string slicing allows you to extract parts of a string easily. It's like cutting a cake into smaller pieces. Check out this example:

Listing 2.25 Substrings in Rust

```
let sentence = "Rust is fun!";
let first_word = &sentence[0..4]; // Take the first 4 characters
println!("First word: {}", first_word);
```

When working with strings, it can be useful to extract specific portions of the text. This is where **&sentence[0..4]** comes in handy - by slicing the **sentence** string from index 0 to 3 (the first four characters), you'll get "**Rust**" as your output. It's a powerful tool for manipulating and analyzing data within larger strings.

Combining Strings

Rust provides different ways to combine strings, depending on your needs. You can use concatenation to merge multiple strings or use string interpolation to embed values within strings. Let's see both techniques:

Listing 2.26 Strings concatenation in Rust

```
let first_name = "Mahmoud";
let last_name = "Harmouch";
let full_name = first_name.to_string() + " " + last_name;
println!("Full name: {}", full_name);

let age = 25;
let message = format!("{} is {} years old.", first_name, age);
println!("{}", message);
// Output

// Full name: Mahmoud Harmouch
// Mahmoud is 25 years old.
```

Within this code, the initial instance employs concatenation to produce a complete name string. Meanwhile, in the second example, the **format!** macro is utilized for value interpolation within a message. By implementing these methods, you can construct complex strings with ease and adaptability.

In the world of Rust programming, delving into complex data types such as Strings and vectors is similar to mastering sophisticated tools in your arsenal. It involves becoming proficient with adaptable containers, powerful instruments that handle complex tasks on your behalf, and methodologies for working with diverse information sets. As you continue refining these proficiencies, novel approaches will emerge for tackling convoluted issues and constructing more resilient applications. Armed with a firm grasp of these advanced principles, you'll be primed to explore the thrilling domain of Rust programming from an innovative standpoint.

Arrays

Arrays, the basis of collection data structures, embrace homogeneity by housing elements of identical types. These fixed-size constructs shine when the element count remains constant, safeguarding memory integrity. Rust's arrays stand as models of concise efficiency.

Imagine an orchestra playing a symphony: each instrument contributes its unique sound, yet they all blend harmoniously. Similarly, an array in programming is like a collection of elements, all sharing the same data type. This homogeneity ensures that each element behaves predictably, simplifying the way you work with them.

Rust's arrays manifest this concept, enforcing that every element within them adheres to the same data type. This structural uniformity contributes to the efficiency of arrays, both in terms of memory usage and access speed.

Arrays excel in situations where the element count is fixed and known in advance. Their fixed size offers an advantage in managing memory efficiently. Think of arrays as an array of compartments, each designed to hold a specific item. Rust's commitment to safety and performance extends to arrays, ensuring that they prevent memory leaks and provide a clear memory blueprint. This predictability is especially beneficial when developing applications that demand precise resource allocation.

```
let temperatures: [f64; 7] = [23.5, 25.1, 21.8, 20.7, 22.3, 24.9, 26.6];
```

In this example, we're defining an array named **`temperatures`** of type **`[f64; 7]`**, representing seven floating-point values. Each value corresponds to a temperature reading, offering a practical illustration of arrays' predictable memory usage.

Before we dive into the fascinating world of arrays in Rust, let's examine a simple declaration:

```
let fibonacci: [u32; 5] = [0, 1, 1, 2, 3];
```

A variable called **`fibonacci`** is generated in this code snippet, which contains an array of unsigned 32-bit integers defined as **`[u32; 5]`**. The semicolons at the end of each line indicate a statement's completion - a basic Rust syntax. This concise yet eloquent style improves clarity while defining arrays.

Now, let's dissect the syntax a bit further:

- **`let fibonacci:`** initializes the declaration of the array variable.
- **`[u32; 5]`** specifies that it's an array holding unsigned 32-bit integers with a length of 5.
- **`= [0, 1, 1, 2, 3];`** initializes the array with the provided values.

Rust's strict type system ensures that only values of the specified type can be inserted into this array. This safeguard guarantees type consistency and contributes to the stability and predictability of your code.

Rust's pursuit of memory safety and performance is evident in its treatment of arrays. In resource-constrained environments, such as embedded systems or high-performance applications, Rust's arrays shine. They offer the reliability of fixed-size memory allocation while guarding against memory-related vulnerabilities. By leveraging arrays, your program remains robust and efficient, even when navigating intricate computational landscapes.

```
let stock_prices: [f32; 10] = [50.2, 52.6, 51.0, 53.2, 49.8, 48.5, 51.7,
53.9, 50.0, 49.2];
```

This time, we're declaring an array named **`stock_prices`**, represented as **`[f32; 10]`**. Each element in this array represents the stock price for a specific period, showcasing the versatility of arrays in various domains.

Arrays go beyond mere storage; they empower us as developers with patterns for solving problems efficiently. Looping through array elements or applying operations in a batch becomes natural with arrays. Rust's arrays provide a canvas for computational creativity, where limitations foster innovative solutions. The predictability of fixed sizes ensures that your creations remain well-structured and manageable, even as you explore the potential of arrays in various contexts.

Arrays are versatile tools in the programmer's toolbox, offering the dual benefits of memory efficiency and predictability. Whether you're working on compact embedded systems or high-performance algorithms, Rust's arrays provide a solid foundation for crafting efficient and reliable code. So, embrace arrays as your trustworthy companions in the journey of programming mastery!

Tuples

Tuples, the conduits of versatility, interlink values of different types into matching ensembles. Unlike arrays, which provide uniformity, tuples promote variety by accepting elements of differing data types. Defined within parentheses and separated with commas, a tuple comes to life.

```
let person_info: (String, u32, bool) = ("Alice".to_string(), 30, true);
// ①
```

① Declaring a tuple with a String, an unsigned 32-bit integer, and a Boolean.

Imagine you're building an application that needs to store information about a person. In traditional programming, you might create separate variables for their name, age, and a flag indicating if they are a registered user. However, tuples offer an elegant solution, enabling you to bundle these heterogeneous pieces of information into a single entity.

In Rust, tuples allow you to combine values of different data types seamlessly. The preceding code block demonstrates the creation of a tuple named **person_info**. It encapsulates a person's name (a **String**), age (an unsigned 32-bit integer), and a status flag (a Boolean). Each value within the tuple is separated by a comma, and the entire tuple is enclosed within parentheses.

Retrieving values from a tuple is just as effortless as constructing it. Rust has an efficient feature known as pattern matching or tuples deconstructing, which enables you to effortlessly extract specific elements from the tuple. To illustrate this mechanism in action:

Listing 2.27 Tuples deconstruction

```
let (name, age, is_registered) = person_info;
println!("Name: {}, Age: {}, Registered: {}", name, age, is_registered);
```

In this code, we use pattern matching to extract the values from the **person_info** tuple and assign them to variables: **name**, **age**, and **is_registered**. Subsequently, we print out these values. Pattern matching simplifies the process of working with tuples and enhances code readability.

Tuples shine not only in data storage but also in function parameters and return values. Consider a scenario where you want to calculate the area and perimeter of a rectangle. Instead of creating separate functions for each, you can return a tuple that encapsulates both values:

Listing 2.28 Tuples as function returning type

```
fn calculate_area_and_perimeter(length: f64, width: f64) -> (f64, f64) {
    let area = length * width;
    let perimeter = 2.0 * (length + width);
    (area, perimeter) // Returning a tuple
}
```

The function **calculate_area_and_perimeter** receives the length and width of a rectangle, calculates both the area and perimeter, and then returns a tuple containing these two values. This approach neatly packages related data together and makes the function's purpose clear.

Tuples showcase Rust's commitment to flexibility and expressive code. By allowing different data types to coexist within a single construct, tuples enable you to represent complex relationships without sacrificing clarity. Whether you're combining data for a single entity, pattern matching, or enhancing function return values, tuples offer an invaluable tool in your Rust programming arsenal.

Achieving proficiency in Rust's variable declarations and diverse data types unlocks the gateway to crafting dependable, high-performance code. By carefully handling both primitive and complex data types, you can harness Rust's static type system to build complex, yet robust, applications that balance between efficiency and safety.

Control Flow

Control flow constructs are fundamental tools in programming, guiding the flow of execution through decision-making and iteration. In Rust, these constructs are crucial for building responsive and dynamic programs. This section dives into the realm of control flow, exploring conditional statements, loops, and the powerful **match** expression.

Conditional Statements

Conditional statements enable you to make choices based on specific conditions. The **if** statement is an uncomplicated but commanding structure that triggers a code block only if the given condition holds true. Additionally, the optional **else** segment provides another route for executing different code when the specified condition fails to meet expectations. To illustrate this concept better, let's examine an example:

Listing 2.29 Conditional statements in Rust

```
let num = 7;

if num % 2 == 0 { // ①
    println!("The number is even."); // Executed if 'num' is even
} else { // ②
    println!("The number is odd.");  // Executed if 'num' is odd
}
```

① In this example, the **if** statement checks whether the value of **num** is even.

② Thc **else** block is executed when the condition is false, indicating an odd number.

While Loops

Loops are essential for executing a block of code repeatedly. The **while** loop is a foundational looping construct in Rust that continues to execute a code block as long as a given condition remains true. Here's an illustration:

Listing 2.30 While loop in Rust

```
let mut count = 0;
while count < 5 { // ①
    println!("Current count: {}", count);
    count += 1;
}
```

① The **while** loop repeatedly prints the value of **count** while it's less than 5.

For Loops

The **for** loop is a versatile iteration construct that simplifies the process of iterating over a range, collection, or sequence of values. Let's explore a basic example:

Listing 2.31 For loop in Rust

```
for i in 1..=3 { // ①
    println!("Current value: {}", i);
}
```

① Here, the **for** loop iterates over a range of values from 1 to 3 (inclusive). In each iteration, the value of **i** changes, and the corresponding message is printed.

Loop

In Rust, the loop keyword serves as a powerful construct that offers more granular control than its counterparts, **for** and **while loops** [4]. The **loop** construct essentially executes a code block repeatedly. The execution continues indefinitely until the encounter of a **break** keyword within the **loop**, acting as the escape that allows the program to break free from the perpetual cycle. This distinctive trait of loop makes it a preferred choice when implementing long-running servers or processes where continuous execution and adaptability to changing conditions are crucial. The **loop** construct consolidate the resilience required in scenarios demanding perpetual operation, offering a robust and flexible tool for us navigating the complexities of long-running server implementations.

Match Expressions

The **match** expression is a powerful feature in Rust that enables elegant and exhaustive branching based on different patterns. It's particularly useful for handling complex scenarios where multiple possibilities need to be considered. Consider the following:

Listing 2.32 match expression

```
let day = "Wednesday";
match day { // ①
    "Monday" => println!("It's the start of the week!"),
    "Friday" => println!("Weekend is near!"),
    _ => println!("It's just another day."),
}
```

① In this example, the **match** expression compares the value of the **day** against different patterns. Messages are printed based on the matched pattern.

[4]Control flow - the Rust programming language. (n.d.). *https://doc.rust-lang.org/book/ch03-05-control-flow.html#loop-labels-to-disambiguate-between-multiple-loops*

Functions

In the journey of developing complex programs, the necessity for well-structured and reusable code becomes apparent. In Rust, functions stand as essential building blocks for creating abstractions that promote code organization and modularity. In this section, we will delve into the nuances of function syntax, parameter passing, and return values.

Explicit Signatures

Listing 2.33 Explicit function signature

```
fn add(a: i32, b: i32) -> i32 { // Defining function 'add' with i32 parameters and return type
    a + b // Returning the sum of 'a' and 'b'
}

let result = add(5, 3); // Calling 'add' with arguments 5 and 3
println!("Sum: {}", result); // Printing the result
```

In the preceding example, the function **add** takes two **i32** parameters and returns an **i32**. Rust's type system ensures that only compatible types are used, reducing the risk of runtime errors.

Nested Functions for Modularity

Listing 2.34 Nested functions

```
fn main() {
    let x = 5;
    let y = 7;

    fn inner_function(a: i32, b: i32) -> i32 { // Defining a nested function 'inner_function'
        a * b // Returning the product of 'a' and 'b'
    }

    let result = inner_function(x, y); // Calling the nested function
    println!("Product: {}", result);
}
```

In this example, the **inner_function** is nested within the **main** function. This encapsulation helps maintain clarity and isolates logic to specific contexts.

Closures

Alongside traditional functions, Rust introduces closures as a powerful feature for defining concise anonymous functions. Closures are versatile tools that allow you to create portable functions on the fly.

Closures capture variables from their surrounding scope, enabling flexible behavior customization. This adaptability proves useful in scenarios where you need to pass behavior as an argument, such as in iterators or event handlers.

Listing 2.35 A simple closure example

```
let multiply = |x: i32, y: i32| x * y; // Creating a closure 'multiply'
let product = multiply(4, 7); // Invoking the closure with arguments 4
and 7
println!("Product: {}", product); // Printing the product
```

In this example, the closure **multiply** multiplies two integers, offering a concise way to express the behavior without requiring a separate function declaration.

Ownership, Borrowing, and Lifetimes

Rust's exceptional memory management capabilities distinguish it from other programming languages. In this section, we'll explore the fundamental principles of ownership, borrowing and lifetimes that support Rust's commitment to ensuring secure memory usage.

Ownership

In Rust, ownership is a fundamental concept that plays a pivotal role in managing memory effectively and preventing common bugs like memory leaks and dangling pointers. The central idea is that each value in Rust has a single "owner" that is responsible for de-allocating its memory when it's no longer needed. This approach ensures that memory is released in a controlled manner, avoiding the pitfalls of manual memory management present in languages like C and C++.

When a variable goes out of scope, Rust's ownership system automatically calls the drop function, freeing up the memory used by the value. This eliminates the need for explicit memory deallocation and greatly reduces the risk of memory leaks. Consider the following example:

Listing 2.36 A simple ownership example

```
let s = String::from("hello");
// ... do something with 's'
// 's' goes out of scope, and memory is deallocated
```

The string **'hello'** is designated to the variable **s**, as illustrated in this example. Rust guarantees that once s is no longer within scope, the memory assigned for the string will be freed, without requiring us to manually invoke a de-allocation function. This ensures efficient and reliable management of resources by Rust's ownership model.

Borrow Checker

While ownership provides a solid foundation for memory safety, it can sometimes be restrictive when you want to share data between parts of your code. This is where the concept of borrowing comes into play. Borrowing allows multiple parts of your code to access data without taking ownership. The borrow checker is Rust's guardian that enforces rules around borrowing, ensuring that references to data are used safely and without introducing data races or memory-related bugs.

The borrow checker analyzes the relationships between variables, references, and ownership in your code to prevent common issues like dangling references. This analysis is performed at compile-time, which means that Rust catches these errors before your code even runs, providing a higher degree of confidence in the safety of your programs.

Consider the following example that demonstrates borrowing:

Listing 2.37 A borrowing example

```
fn main() {
    let s1 = String::from("hello");
    let len = calculate_length(&s1); // ①

    println!("Length of '{}': {}", s1, len);
}

fn calculate_length(s: &String) -> usize { // ②
    s.len()
}
```

① Passing a reference of '`s1`' to the function '`calculate_length`'.

② Defining a function '`calculate_length`' that takes a reference to a String and returns its length.

The function `calculate_length` utilizes a reference to a `String` as its input parameter. The said reference, denoted by the symbol '`&s`', grants access to the string's information without assuming ownership of it. This technique of borrowing enables us to impart data between functions while upholding memory security measures.

Enhancing Performance

By utilizing references for borrowing, not only is memory safety guaranteed but performance is also enhanced by reducing redundant data copying. When a reference to the function's value is passed instead of its actual value, Rust avoids creating an extra copy of the information. This practice proves especially advantageous when dealing with larger and more complex data structures that require significant amounts of time and storage space for duplication purposes.

By carefully managing ownership and leveraging borrowing, Rust achieves a balance between safety and performance. The borrow checker's ability to enforce strict rules while allowing efficient sharing of data makes Rust a language that excels in both reliability and efficiency.

Conclusion

In this chapter, we have embarked on a journey through the basics of Rust programming. From understanding variables and data types to mastering control flow and building abstractions using functions and closures, we have laid a solid foundation. Additionally, you now possess the knowledge to beat the memory beast with ownership, borrowing, and lifetimes, all while being under the watchful eye of Rust's memory safety features and the borrow checker. As you move forward, remember that Rust's elegance lies not only in its syntax but also in its commitment to writing safe, performant, and reliable code.

In the upcoming chapter, we will take a deeper dive into Rust's advanced features, with a primary focus on the crucial concept of traits and their pivotal role in promoting code reuse. You'll gain the expertise to effectively implement traits for user-defined data structures, harness the power of generic functions and data structures, and navigate the world of trait bounds and associated types to enhance the versatility of your code. Armed with this knowledge, you'll be empowered to craft code that is not only more flexible but also highly reusable, thus elevating your Rust programming skills to new heights.

Multiple Choice Questions

Q1: What does ownership bring to Rust programming?

a) Code organization

b) Memory management clarity

c) Concurrency control

d) Error handling

Q2: How do you make a variable mutable in Rust?

a) Using the `const` keyword

b) Using the `let` keyword

c) Using the `mut` keyword

d) Variables are always mutable in Rust

Q3: What is the purpose of shadowing in Rust?

a) Preventing variable modification

b) Avoiding variable declarations

c) Reusing variable names in different scopes

d) Enforcing immutability

Q4: How are constants different from variables in Rust?

a) Constants are mutable by default

b) Constants are always immutable

c) Constants have dynamic types

d) Constants cannot be used in functions

Q5: When might you choose to use the f32 type in Rust?

a) When precision is essential

b) When computational efficiency matters

c) When working with integers

d) When implementing cryptographic algorithms

Q6: How can you represent floating-point literals in Rust?

a) Using hexadecimal notation

b) Using binary notation

c) Using scientific notation

d) Using octal notation

Q7: What mathematical operations are supported by Rust's floating-point types?

a) Addition, subtraction, and multiplication only

b) Multiplication and division only

c) Addition, subtraction, multiplication, division, and remainder

d) Square root and exponentiation only

Q8: What is the significance of the main function in a Rust program?

a) Display program documentation

b) Define custom data types

c) Serve as the entry point of the program

d) Handle user input

Q9: How does Rust handle integer overflow in release mode?

a) It panics and terminates the program

b) It wraps around using two's complement

c) It throws an exception

d) It automatically resizes the integer

Q10: What are tuples commonly used for in Rust?

a) Storing single values

b) Returning multiple values from a function

c) Creating fixed-size arrays

d) Defining custom data types

Q11: How does Rust enforce memory safety?

a) Through automatic garbage collection

b) By allowing unrestricted access to memory

c) Through its ownership system and borrow checker

d) By restricting the use of pointers

Q12: What is the benefit of using the String type over string literals in Rust?

a) `String` has a fixed size at compile time

b) `String` literals can be modified at runtime

c) `String` allows for dynamic, resizable strings

d) `String` literals are more memory-efficient

Q13: What is the purpose of the mut keyword when working with references in Rust?

a) It indicates a mutable reference, allowing modifications through the reference.

b) It enforces immutability, preventing any changes to the referenced data.

c) It signifies a reference to a constant value.

d) It specifies a reference to a mutable data type.

Q14: When might you use a slice in Rust?

a) To define custom data types

b) To create fixed-size arrays

c) To duplicate a collection's data

d) To work with a portion of a collection without taking ownership

Q15: How does a closure in Rust capture variables from its surrounding scope?

a) By copying all variables

b) By taking ownership of all variables

c) By capturing them by reference or value as specified

d) By creating new variables with the same names

Q16: What is the role of the Rust borrow checker in preventing concurrency-related bugs?

a) It allows unrestricted concurrent access to data.

b) It analyzes code to ensure safe use of references and prevents data races.

c) It automatically resolves data race issues at runtime.

d) It introduces locks and mutexes to synchronize data access.

Answers

1. b) Memory management clarity
2. c) Using the `mut` keyword
3. c) Reusing variable names in different scopes
4. b) Constants are always immutable
5. b) When computational efficiency matters
6. c) Using scientific notation
7. c) Addition, subtraction, multiplication, division, and remainder
8. c) Serve as the entry point of the program
9. b) It wraps around using two's complement
10. b) Returning multiple values from a function
11. c) Through its ownership system and borrow checker
12. c) `String` allows for dynamic, resizable strings
13. a) It indicates a mutable reference, allowing modifications through the reference

14. d) To work with a portion of a collection without taking ownership
15. c) By capturing them by reference or value as specified
16. b) It analyzes code to ensure safe use of references and prevents data races

Key Terms

- **Ownership:** A central concept in Rust that defines how memory is managed and ensures data safety by allowing only one part of the code to modify data at a time.
- **Mutable:** In Rust, a property of a variable that allows its value to be changed after it's been declared using the `mut` keyword.
- **Shadowing:** A Rust feature that allows you to declare a new variable with the same name as an existing one within a limited scope, effectively "hiding" the original variable.
- **Constants:** Values in Rust that are immutable and declared using the `const` keyword, requiring an explicit type annotation.
- **`f32` and `f64`:** Rust's floating-point types representing 32-bit and 64-bit floating-point numbers, respectively, adhering to the IEEE-754 standard.
- **Floating-Point Literals:** Representation of floating-point numbers in Rust, either in standard decimal notation or scientific notation.
- **Mathematical Operations:** Operations supported by Rust's floating-point types, including addition, subtraction, multiplication, division, and remainder, as well as mathematical functions like square root.

CHAPTER 3

Traits and Generics

Introduction

Traits and generics stand as two of the most powerful tools in Rust, empowering us to write a code that is flexible, adaptable, efficient, and seamlessly fit into diverse situations. In this chapter, we will embark on a profound exploration of these principles, uncovering their revolutionary impact on the way we conceive and construct software.

Traits offer us the ability to define a set of behaviors that various types can implement, allowing us to construct generic code that works with any type that satisfies the trait's contract. This approach enables us to write code that is more concise, reusable, and easier to maintain, as we can abstract the details of implementation and concentrate on the desired behavior.

In contrast, generics empower us to craft code that functions across a variety of different types, eliminating the need for creating separate functions or methods for each type. This methodology enables us to write code that is remarkably versatile and efficient, as we can reuse the same code for various types without compromising on performance.

When combined, traits and generics grant us the capability to construct code that possesses both tremendous power and sophistication, allowing us to tackle complex problems effortlessly and with the utmost certainty. Thus, let us dive in and discover the full potential of these essential concepts in Rust!

Structure

In this chapter, we're going to explore:

- The concept of traits and their role in code reuse
- Implementing traits for user-defined data structures
- Working with generic functions and data structures in Rust
- Exploring trait bounds and associated types for increased generality

Traits

In the world of software development, it is crucial to establish a consistent and determined behavior across various types. Take, for example, the notion of Printable as shown in the following image.

```
pub trait Printable {
    fn print(&self);
}
```

keyword · visibility · Name · Function

Figure 3.1: A simple trait explanation

By incorporating a feature known as Printable, we can enforce a uniform procedure for printing different types. This uniformity not only streamlines the organization of code but also enriches the understanding of the code. Creating such a trait provides a clear contract for any type that implements it. This way, we can rely on a standard way to print objects, promoting code readability and maintainability.

Listing 3.1 A simple trait example

```
trait Printable {
    fn print(&self); // ①
}
```

① The `print` method defined by the `Printable` trait enables consistent printing behavior across different types.

Now, let's delve into the implementation of this trait for specific types.

Implementing Traits

To demonstrate the practicality of traits, let's begin with a basic type, **`Number`**. This type represents an integer value.

Listing 3.2 A simple trait implementation example

```
struct Number {
    value: i32,
}

impl Printable for Number {
    fn print(&self) { // ①
        println!("Number: {}", self.value);
    }
}
```

① The **`print`** method implementation for the **`Number`** type ensures consistent printing behavior.

In this case, the **`Printable`** trait has been applied to the **`Number`** struct. This implementation establishes the guidelines for printing a **`Number`**, following the rules set by the trait. Now, let's examine a more complex scenario involving geometric figures.

Suppose we have two geometric shapes: **`Circle`** and **`Rectangle`**. By implementing the **`Printable`** trait for both of these types, we guarantee a uniform printing behavior for all shapes.

Listing 3.3 Traits implementation example

```
struct Circle {
    radius: f64,
}

struct Rectangle {
    width: f64,
    height: f64,
}
```

```
impl Printable for Circle {
    fn print(&self) { // ①
        println!("Circle with radius: {}", self.radius);
    }
}

impl Printable for Rectangle {
    fn print(&self) { // ②
        println!("Rectangle with dimensions: {} x {}", self.width, self.
height);
    }
}
```

① The **`print`** method implementation for the **`Circle`** type ensures consistent printing behavior.

② The **`print`** method implementation for the **`Rectangle`** type ensures consistent printing behavior.

In this manner, we've defined a unified way to print various geometric shapes. The power of traits becomes evident as they allow us to create a standardized interface for different types, making our code organized and comprehensible.

Default Trait Behavior

While traits enable us to define a common contract, sometimes we want to provide a default behavior within a trait while allowing types to override it when necessary.

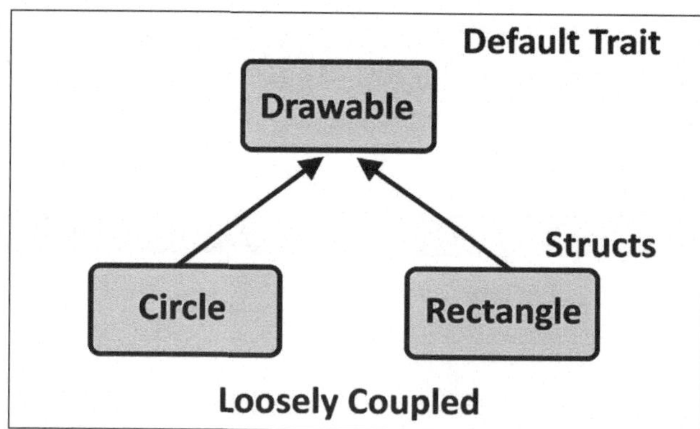

Figure 3.2: *Using default trait as a building block for more complex traits*

Let's take as an example of a trait called **`Drawable`** that involves drawing shapes. We can provide a default drawing method that serves as a starting point for implementing custom drawing logic.

Listing 3.4 A simple trait definition

```
trait Drawable {
    fn draw(&self) {
        println!("Drawing the shape."); // ①
    }
}
```

① The default **draw** method within the **Drawable** trait provides a common drawing behavior.

This default behavior acts as a foundation that types implementing the **Drawable** trait can build upon. It offers consistency while allowing customization as needed.

Let's see how this trait works in practice by implementing it for the **Circle** and **Rectangle** types.

Listing 3.5 Trait implementation

```
impl Drawable for Circle {
    fn draw(&self) { // ①
        println!("Drawing a circle with radius: {}", self.radius);
    }
}

impl Drawable for Rectangle {
    fn draw(&self) { // ②
        println!("Drawing a rectangle with dimensions: {} x {}", self.
width, self.height);
    }
}
```

① The custom draw method implementation for the Circle type.

② The custom draw method implementation for the Rectangle type.

In this example, both the **Circle** and **Rectangle** types implement the **Drawable** trait, showcasing their individual methods for drawing. Nonetheless, if any other type chooses to implement the **Drawable** type without customizing its own method, it will automatically use the default drawing behavior.

Traits with default methods offer a balanced approach between standard behavior and customization, ensuring a cohesive and flexible codebase.

Trait Bounds

When designing software systems, it's essential to create functions that can work with a variety of data types, as long as they exhibit specific behaviors. This is where trait bounds come into play. Trait bounds allow us to specify that a generic function should accept any type that implements a particular trait. In doing so, we focus on the expected behavior of the type rather than its concrete identity. This approach enhances code flexibility and reusability, as functions become adaptable to different data structures that adhere to the same interface.

Utilizing trait bounds simplifies the creation of versatile functions. Consider a scenario where we need to calculate the area of various geometric shapes, such as circles, rectangles, or triangles. Instead of writing separate functions for each shape type, we can leverage trait bounds to create a single function, **`calculate_area`**, that works with any type implementing the Shape trait. This not only reduces code duplication but also makes it casier to extend our codebase with new shapes in the future.

Listing 3.6 Function arguments type that implements a trait

```
fn calculate_area(shape: impl Shape) -> f64 {
    shape.area()
}
```

In this case, the **`calculate_area`** function accepts any type that implements the Shape trait as an argument. We're concerned with the behavior of the type rather than its exact identity. Consequently, we can calculate the area of circles, rectangles, and other shapes effortlessly.

Expanding with Generics

Building upon the notion of trait bounds, generics offer a remarkably powerful and flexible approach to crafting functions that seamlessly handle diverse data types. For the **`calculate_area`** function, we can use generics to achieve the same result. Instead of explicitly specifying a concrete type that implements the Shape trait, we introduce a generic type T that must adhere to the **`Shape`** trait. Consequently, any type T that implements the mandated behavior can be used with the **`calculate_area`** function.

Listing 3.7 Function arguments generic type

```
fn calculate_area<T: Shape>(shape: T) -> f64 { // ①
    shape.area()
}
```

① The generic calculate_area function accepts any type T that adheres to the Shape trait.

In this version, we use a generic type T that is required to adhere to the Shape trait. This approach enhances flexibility, granting us the capability to integrate supplementary rules if required.

Trait bounds are pivotal in creating functions and structures that accommodate diverse types, minimizing redundancy and ensuring code safety.

Generics

Generics form a fundamental feature of Rust, empowering the development of remarkably versatile and reusable code. They provide the ability to construct functions, structures, and traits that can seamlessly operate with diverse data types, all without sacrificing type safety. This flexibility proves exceptionally valuable when crafting libraries or components intended to be as flexible as possible, catering to a vast array of use cases.

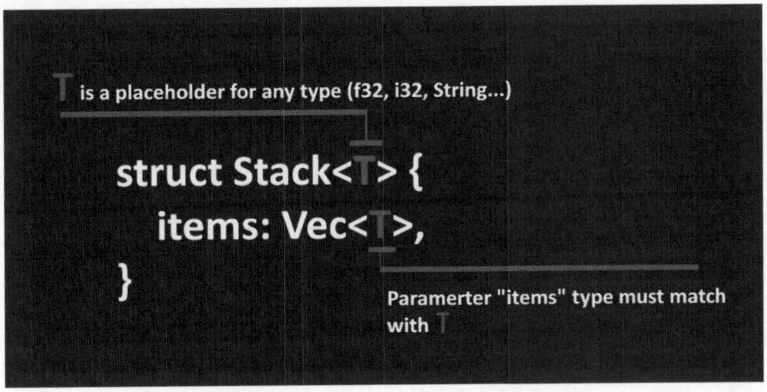

Figure 3.3: *A simple generic explanation*

Adaptive Structures

When it comes to data structures, generics are a game-changer. Let's take the example of a Stack data structure. Instead of limiting it to a specific data type, we can use generics to create a `Stack<T>` that can hold elements of any type T.

This flexibility empowers us to build stacks that handle integers, strings, custom objects, or any other data type with ease. By embracing generics, we promote code organization, reduce redundancy, and create data structures that are adaptable to a multitude of scenarios.

Listing 3.8 Building structures using traits

```
struct Stack<T> {
    items: Vec<T>,
}

impl<T> Stack<T> {
    fn push(&mut self, item: T) { // ①
        self.items.push(item);
    }

    fn pop(&mut self) -> Option<T> { // ②
        self.items.pop()
    }
}

fn main() {
    // Create a new stack of integers.
    let mut stack = Stack::<i32> { items: Vec::new() };

    // Push some items onto the stack.
    stack.push(1);
    stack.push(2);
    stack.push(3);

    // Pop items from the stack and print them.
    while let Some(item) = stack.pop() {
        println!("Popped: {}", item);
    }
}

// Output

// Popped: 3
// Popped: 2
// Popped: 1
```

① The **push** method implementation for the generic **Stack** structure.

② The **pop** method implementation for the generic **Stack** structure.

In this example, the **Stack** structure acts as a toolkit capable of managing items of any type **T**. The **push** and **pop** methods function uniformly regardless of the specific type in use. This versatility empowers us to create stacks accommodating numbers, words, or any other data type.

Generics excel at building code that isn't confined to a single type, fostering code organization, and preventing repetition.

Associated Functions

Traits can also feature associated functions - functions linked directly to the trait itself, rather than specific instances of the trait. Consider enhancing the Shape trait by adding an associated function to create a shape with a default size:

Listing 3.9 Traits with associated functions

```
struct Circle {
    radius: f64,
}

trait Shape {
    fn area(&self) -> f64;
    fn default_shape() -> Self; // ①
}

impl Shape for Circle {
    fn area(&self) -> f64 {
        std::f64::consts::PI * self.radius * self.radius
    }

    fn default_shape() -> Self { // ②
        Circle { radius: 1.0 }
    }
}

fn main() {
    // Create a circle and calculate its area.
    let circle = Circle { radius: 2.0 };
    let area = circle.area();
    println!("Circle area: {}", area);

    // Create a default circle and calculate its area.
    let default_circle = Circle::default_shape();
    let default_area = default_circle.area();
```

```
    println!("Default Circle area: {}", default_area);
}

// Output

// Circle area: 12.566370614359172
// Default Circle area: 3.141592653589793
```

① The associated function **default_shape** linked to the **Shape** trait.

② The implementation of the **default_shape** associated function for the **Circle** type.

The **default_shape** function provides a means to generate shapes with standard dimensions. Each shape is empowered to define its own default instantiation mechanism.

Associated Types

Associated types in Rust are a powerful language feature that enables future-proofing your code by abstracting away concrete type details. They allow you to define a placeholder type within a trait, leaving the actual type to be determined by the implementing struct or enum. This level of abstraction provides flexibility and extensibility, making associated types a valuable tool when designing interfaces for complex systems.

When we embrace associated types, we're essentially saying, "I have a trait that defines a particular behavior, but I don't want to specify the exact types involved because they might vary depending on the situation". This mindset is particularly useful when crafting traits for iterators or similar constructs.

Imagine creating an iterator trait that doesn't commit to a specific item type it yields. Instead, it defines an associated type called Item that remains abstract. This allows any struct or enum implementing the iterator trait to decide what type of items it yields. Such flexibility is vital when working with diverse collections or when you anticipate evolving your code to accommodate new data structures.

Listing 3.10 Traits with associated types

```
trait Iterator {
    type Item; // ①

    fn next(&mut self) -> Option<Self::Item>; // ②
}
```

① The associated type **Item** indicating the type of items the iterator produces.

② The **next** method returning an **Option** containing an item of the associated type.

This approach empowers us to design various iterators, each tailored to a specific kind of item:

Listing 3.11 Custom iterator with associated types

```
struct Counter {
    count: u32,
}

impl Iterator for Counter {
    type Item = u32; // ①

    fn next(&mut self) -> Option<Self::Item> {
        if self.count < 10 {
            self.count += 1;
            Some(self.count)
        } else {
            None
        }
    }
}

fn main() {
    let mut counter = Counter { count: 0 };

    for number in &mut counter {
        println!("Counter: {}", number);
    }
}

// Output

// Counter: 1
// Counter: 2
// Counter: 3
// Counter: 4
// Counter: 5
// Counter: 6
// Counter: 7
// Counter: 8
// Counter: 9
// Counter: 10
```

① The associated **Item** type set to **u32** for the **Counter** iterator.

In this example, the **Counter** struct implements the **Iterator** trait, with its associated **Item** type set to **u32**. Consequently, we can create iterators for different item types while adhering to the same structural blueprint.

Associated types offer enhanced flexibility, enabling traits to seamlessly integrate with related types without imposing fixed constraints.

Trait Objects

Trait objects in Rust provide a mechanism for achieving runtime modification, a feature that can be incredibly valuable in various scenarios. By employing trait objects, you can enable your code to seamlessly interact with different types that share a common trait at runtime, regardless of your prior knowledge about their specific type. This exceptional capability proves particularly advantageous when constructing libraries or systems that necessitate managing a wide range of inputs or plugins.

When we employ trait objects, we're essentially opening the door to dynamic dispatch - a process that determines at runtime which method implementation should be called based on the actual type of an object. This is in contrast to static dispatch, where method calls are resolved at compile time. Trait objects provide the flexibility of dynamic dispatch, allowing you to write functions or components that can accommodate a wide range of types adhering to a shared trait.

Imagine a scenario where you need to process various shapes using a single function that accepts a trait object **&dyn Shape**. With trait objects, you can handle circles, rectangles, and other geometric shapes without knowing their exact types at compile time. This flexibility simplifies your code and allows you to create more generic and reusable components.

Listing 3.12 Traits objects

```
trait Shape { // ①
    fn area(&self) -> f64;
}

struct Circle { // ②
    radius: f64,
}
```

```
struct Rectangle { // ②
    width: f64,
    height: f64,
}

impl Shape for Circle {
    fn area(&self) -> f64 {
        std::f64::consts::PI * self.radius * self.radius
    }
}

impl Shape for Rectangle {
    fn area(&self) -> f64 {
        self.width * self.height
    }
}

fn print_area(shape: &dyn Shape) { // ③
    println!("Area: {}", shape.area());
}

fn main() { // ④
    let circle = Circle { radius: 2.0 };
    let rectangle = Rectangle { width: 3.0, height: 4.0 };

    print_area(&circle);
    print_area(&rectangle);
}

// Output

// Area: 12.566370614359172
// Area: 12
```

① We define a **Shape** trait with an **area** method.

② The **Circle** and **Rectangle** structs represent shapes and implement the **Shape** trait.

③ The **print_area** function takes a trait object reference and invokes the **area** method.

④ In the **main** function, we create instances of **Circle** and **Rectangle** and print their respective areas.

Using trait objects, you can write functions that work with multiple types implementing the same trait without knowing the concrete types at compile time. This flexibility comes at the cost of some performance overhead due to dynamic dispatch.

Trait objects are an essential tool when you need to achieve runtime polymorphism, making your code adaptable to various types while still adhering to a shared trait. While they introduce a minor performance overhead compared to static dispatch, their dynamic nature is invaluable in scenarios where you need to work with different types.

Real-World Applications

Traits are crucial for real-world applications, enabling functionality like serialization and deserialization, essential processes in modern software systems. Rust's trait system offers a robust foundation for building serialization libraries that ensure data can be efficiently encoded and decoded.

Consider a basic example using the popular `serde` crate for serialization and deserialization. First, ensure that the `serde` dependency is added to your **Cargo.toml file:**

```
[dependencies]
serde = "1.0"
serde_json = "1.0"
```

Now, let's serialize a simple struct to JSON:

Listing 3.13 External traits usage

```
use serde::{Serialize, Deserialize}; // ①
use serde_json;

#[derive(Serialize, Deserialize, Debug)] // ③
struct Person { // ②
    name: String,
    age: u32,
}

fn main() { // ④
    let person = Person {
        name: String::from("Mahmoud"),
        age: 25,
    };

    let serialized = serde_json::to_string(&person).unwrap(); // ⑤
    println!("Serialized: {}", serialized);
```

```
    let deserialized: Person = serde_json::from_str(&serialized).un-
wrap(); // ⑥
    println!("Deserialized: {:?}", deserialized);
}

// Output

// Serialized: {"name":"Mahmoud","age":25}
// Deserialized: Person { name: "Mahmoud", age: 25 }
```

① We import the necessary traits and **serde_json** crate for serialization.

② The **Person** struct represents a person's name and age.

③ We derive the **Serialize** and **Deserialize** traits using **serde**'s attributes.

④ In the main function, we create an instance of **Person**.

⑤ We serialize the instance to JSON using **serde_json::to_string**.

⑥ Then, we deserialize the JSON back to a **Person** instance using **serde_json::from_str**.

Serialization and deserialization are common tasks in many applications, especially when dealing with data interchange formats like JSON, and **serde** simplifies this process by providing a robust and flexible mechanism for handling such conversions.

Trait Bounds in the Standard Library

The Rust standard library extensively utilizes traits and generics to create powerful abstractions. One of the most prominent examples is the **Iterator** trait, which allows sequential processing of collections or sequences.

The **Iterator** trait encapsulate the power of trait bounds. It defines methods like **next**, **map**, **filter**, and more, enabling concise and expressive iteration over collections. Let's take a glimpse at how the Iterator trait is structured:

Listing 3.14 The Iterator trait of the std library

```
pub trait Iterator { // ①
    type Item;

    fn next(&mut self) -> Option<Self::Item>; // ②
    // Additional iterator methods...
}
```

① We define an associated type **Item** within the **Iterator** trait, which signifies the type of elements the iterator yields.

② The **next** method is used to retrieve the next item from the iterator.

Using the **Iterator** trait, we can chain multiple iterators together, creating complex data transformations with minimal code:

Listing 3.15 The Iterator trait usage

```
fn main() {
    let numbers = vec![1, 2, 3, 4, 5]; // ①
    let squares = numbers.iter().map(|&x| x * x).collect::<Vec<_>>();
// ②

    for square in squares { // ③
        println!("{}", square);
    }
}
```

① We create a vector **numbers** and use the **iter** method to create an iterator.

② The **map** method transforms each element using a closure, and then **collect** gathers the transformed values into a new vector.

③ We iterate through the **squares** vector and print each value.

The **Iterator** trait demonstrates the elegance and efficiency that can be achieved by combining traits and generics, making it a cornerstone of Rust's standard library.

Advanced Trait Patterns

As you become more skilled in utilizing traits and generics, you will encounter advanced patterns that provide increased adaptability and robustness. These patterns strengthen your code and empower you to achieve more complex designs.

Associated Constants

Traits can not only include methods and associated types but also associated constants. These constants provide a way to define values associated with a trait:

Listing 3.16 Traits and associated constants

```
trait Geometry { // ①
    const PI: f64;
}

struct Circle { // ②
    radius: f64,
}

impl Geometry for Circle {  // ②
    const PI: f64 = std::f64::consts::PI;
}

fn main() { // ③
    let circle = Circle { radius: 2.0 };
    println!("Circle's area: {}", Circle::PI * circle.radius * circle.
radius);
}

// Output

// Circle's area: 12.566370614359172
```

① The **Geometry** trait defines an associated constant **PI**.

② The **Circle** type implements the **Geometry** trait and provides a value for the associated constant.

③ We calculate and print the area of a circle using the associated constant.

Associated constants are particularly useful when a trait has associated values that remain constant across all implementations.

Operator Overloading

Rust's trait system also supports operator overloading, allowing you to define custom behaviors for operators like +, -, *, and more. This can significantly enhance the expressiveness and readability of your code. Let's consider a scenario where we want to perform addition between instances of a custom type **Complex** representing complex numbers:

Listing 3.17 Traits for operator overloading

```
use std::ops::Add; // ①

struct Complex { // ②
    real: f64,
    imaginary: f64,
}

impl Add for Complex { // ③
    type Output = Complex; // ④

    fn add(self, other: Complex) -> Complex { // ⑤
        Complex {
            real: self.real + other.real,
            imaginary: self.imaginary + other.imaginary,
        }
    }
}

fn main() {
    let c1 = Complex { real: 1.0, imaginary: 2.0 };
    let c2 = Complex { real: 3.0, imaginary: 4.0 };
    let result = c1 + c2;

    println!("Result: {} + {}i", result.real, result.imaginary);
}

// Output
//
// 4 + 6i
```

① We import the **Add** trait from the **std::ops** module, which is used for operator overloading.

② The **Complex** struct represents complex numbers with real and imaginary components.

③ We implement the **Add** trait for **Complex**, defining the behavior of the + operator.

④ The associated type **Output** specifies the result type of the addition.

⑤ The **add** method performs element-wise addition and returns a new Complex instance.

By implementing the **Add** trait for our custom type **Complex**, we enable the use of the + operator with instances of **Complex**. This showcases how Rust's trait system promotes expressive and natural-looking code while adhering to strong typing principles.

Marker Traits

While most traits provide methods or associated values, marker traits don't require any method implementation. Instead, they indicate certain properties or behaviors that types possess. For instance, the **`Copy`** and **`Clone`** traits are marker traits. They signal that types implementing them can be shallowly copied or cloned, respectively:

Listing 3.18 Marker traits

```
struct MyStruct; // ①

fn main() {
    let original = MyStruct; // ②
    let copy = original; // ③
    let clone = original.clone(); // ④
}
```

① We define an empty or unit struct **`MyStruct`**.

② In the **`main`** function, we create an instance **`original`** of **`MyStruct`**.

③ When we assign **`original`** to **`copy`**, the value is shallowly copied.

④ To clone the value, we need to call the **`clone`** method on **`original`**.

Marker traits provide a way to indicate traits that do not encompass the implementation of a method but rather symbolize specific characteristics of types. This differentiation assists in directing the behavior of the compiler and enables the implementation of more customized optimizations.

Combining Traits

The ***`where`*** clause in Rust is a powerful keyword for adding constraints to trait implementations. It's particularly handy when you want to implement a trait for types that satisfy specific conditions. This capability provides a way to ensure that your trait implementations are only applicable to types that meet certain criteria, enhancing the safety and expressiveness of your code.

Listing 3.19 Traits composition

```
trait Drawable { // ①
    fn draw(&self);
}

trait Printable { // ①
    fn print(&self);
}
#[derive(Debug)]
struct Complex { // ②
    real: f64,
    imaginary: f64,
}

impl<T> Drawable for T
where
    T: Printable + std::fmt::Debug,
{ // ③
    fn draw(&self) { // ④
        println!("Drawing: {:?}", self);
    }
}

impl Printable for Complex {
    fn print(&self) {
        println!("Printing: {} + {}i", self.real, self.imaginary);
    }
}

fn main() {
    let complex = Complex {
        real: 1.0,
        imaginary: 2.0,
    };
    complex.draw();
}

// Output

// Drawing: Complex { real: 1.0, imaginary: 2.0 }
```

① We define two traits, **`Drawable`** and **`Printable`**.

② The **`Complex`** struct represents complex numbers.

③ We implement **Drawable** for any type that implements **Printable**, using the **where** clause.

④ The **draw** method uses the **Printable** trait to print the value.

By incorporating the where clause in trait implementations, you can impose additional restrictions on the implementation. This technique empowers us to craft more complex trait implementations, guaranteeing their relevance solely to suitable types. It serves as a powerful tool for devising versatile and secure abstractions in Rust.

Avoiding Trait Conflicts

The trait system in Rust has carefully constructed to ensure clear and unambiguous trait implementations, thus avoiding any potential conflicts that may arise when multiple crates implement the same trait for the same type. This fundamental idea, referred to as trait coherence, holds immense significance in upholding code accuracy and preventing unintended clashes between different implementations of a shared trait.

Imagine a scenario where you aim to offer a common way to print types from external crates. By defining a trait that provides a printing method and implementing it for types from external crates, you can ensure that your code remains free from conflicts. Trait coherence ensures that there won't be multiple conflicting implementations of the same trait for a given type, promoting code stability and predictability. Consider the following code snippet:

Listing 3.20 Coherence in trait implementations

```
use std::fmt::Debug; // ①

trait Printable { // ②
    fn print(&self) where Self: Debug { // Add a trait bound here
because of the formatting specifier `{:?}`
        println!("{:?}", self);
    }
}

impl<T: Debug> Printable for T {} // ③

fn main() { // ④
    let number = 12;
    number.print();
}
```

```
// Output
// 12
```

① We import the **Debug** trait from **std::fmt**.

② The **Printable** trait defines a default **print** method that uses **Debug** to print the value.

③ The implementation of **Printable** for any type **T** that implements **Debug** uses the default **print** method.

④ In the **main** function, we create an instance of **number** and **print** it using the print method.

This code illustrates the concept of coherence in trait implementations. By restricting the implementation to types that implement **Debug**, we avoid conflicts that could arise from multiple crates providing different implementations for the same trait and type combination.

Blanket Implementations

In Rust, blanket implementations hold significant power as they allow you to effortlessly apply a trait to all types that meet specific criteria. This approach proves highly advantageous when you seek to establish a common functionality for a wide range of types, eliminating the need for implementing the trait individually for each type.

To exemplify this, let's consider the creation of a trait called Negate that aims to reverse the sign of a variable value. Here's an example that effectively demonstrates this concept:

Listing 3.21 Blanket implementations

```
trait Negate { // ①
    fn negate(&self) -> Self;
}

impl<T: Clone + std::ops::Neg<Output = T>> Negate for T { // ②
    fn negate(&self) -> Self {
        -self.clone()
    }
}

fn main() { // ③
    let number = 12;
```

```
    let negated = number.negate();
    println!("Negated: {}", negated);
}

// Output
// Negated: -12
```

① We define a **Negate** trait with a **negate** method.

② We implement the **Negate** trait for the T type, providing a blanket implementation for all types that implement the **Neg** trait.

③ In the **main** function, we negate a number using the **negate** method.

With this blanket implementation, you can now use the negate method on various numeric types without having to define it separately for each one. This approach promotes code reusability and ensures consistent behavior across a wide range of types.

Supertraits

Within the Rust programming language, the concept of supertraits grants you the ability to create new traits that enhance or refine the qualities of existing traits. By assigning a supertrait, you effortlessly gain access to the methods and associated types of the original trait, allowing you to extend or customize their capabilities.

To exemplify, imagine a trait named **Displayable,** to enhance the effectiveness of the **Printable** trait by providing display formatting options.

Listing 3.22 Supertraits

```
trait Printable { // ①
    fn print(&self);
}

trait Displayable: Printable { // ②
    fn display(&self);
}

struct Person { // ③
    name: String,
}

impl Printable for Person { // ④
    fn print(&self) {
```

```
        println!("Name: {}", self.name);
    }
}

impl Displayable for Person { // ④
    fn display(&self) {
        println!("Displaying: {}", self.name);
    }
}

fn main() { // ⑤
    let person = Person {
        name: String::from("Mahmoud"),
    };
    person.print();
    person.display();
}

// Output

// Name: Mahmoud
// Displaying: Mahmoud
```

① We define a **`Printable`** trait with a **`print`** method.

② The **`Displayable`** trait extends **`Printable`** and adds a **`display`** method.

③ The **`Person`** struct represents a person with a name.

④ We implement **`Printable`** and **`Displayable`** for **`Person`**, providing custom implementations.

⑤ In the **`main`** function, we create an instance of **`Person`** and call both **`print`** and **`display`** methods.

Through the specification of a supertrait, a new trait can be built, refining or enhancing the conduct of pre-existing traits. This enables a well-organized hierarchy of traits that reflect relationships between behaviors.

Newtype Pattern

The newtype pattern is a common Rust design pattern that involves creating a new type that wraps an existing one. This pattern can be used to create different types that share behavior with the wrapped type while still being treated as separate types by the compiler. Traits play a significant role in enabling this pattern.

Envision yourself participating in the development of a numerical computing library, with the objective of constructing a classification system that represents measurements alongside their corresponding units. The aim is to guarantee the ability to carry out mathematical calculations on quantities possessing matching units, while simultaneously identifying any inconsistencies in units during the compilation process.

In order to accomplish this, you are presented with the chance to employ the newtype design pattern and traits.

Listing 3.23 The newtype design pattern and traits

```
use std::ops::{Add, Sub};

trait Unit: Default + Copy {
    fn unit() -> &'static str;
}

#[derive(Default, Copy, Clone, Debug)]
struct Meter; // ①

impl Unit for Meter { // ②
    fn unit() -> &'static str {
        "m"
    }
}

#[derive(Default, Copy, Clone)] // ③
struct Kilogram;

impl Unit for Kilogram { // ④
    fn unit() -> &'static str {
        "kg"
    }
}

#[derive(Debug)]
struct Quantity<U: Unit> { // ⑤
    value: f64,
    unit: U,
}

impl<U: Unit> Add for Quantity<U> { // ⑥
    type Output = Quantity<U>;
```

```
    fn add(self, other: Quantity<U>) -> Quantity<U> {
        Quantity {
            value: self.value + other.value,
            unit: U::default(),
        }
    }
}

impl<U: Unit> Sub for Quantity<U> { // ⑦
    type Output = Quantity<U>;

    fn sub(self, other: Quantity<U>) -> Quantity<U> {
        Quantity {
            value: self.value - other.value,
            unit: U::default(),
        }
    }
}

fn main() {
    let distance1 = Quantity::<Meter> { value: 5.0, unit: Meter };
    let distance2 = Quantity::<Meter> { value: 3.0, unit: Meter };

    let total_distance = distance1 + distance2;
    println!("Total distance: {:?}", total_distance);
}

// Output

// Total distance: Quantity { value: 8.0, unit: Meter }
```

① Define a struct **Meter**, which is part of the Newtype Pattern. It represents a unit of measurement and is used to wrap the unit "**meter**."

② Implement the **Unit** trait for the **Meter** struct, showcasing that the Meter struct is used as a newtype to represent a unit of measurement.

③ Define a struct **Kilogram**, which is also part of the Newtype Pattern. It represents a unit of measurement and is used to wrap the unit "**kilogram**."

④ Implement the **Unit** trait for the **Kilogram** struct, demonstrating that the **Kilogram** struct is used as a newtype to represent a unit of measurement.

⑤ Define a generic **Quantity** struct that is parameterized by a type implementing the Unit trait, exemplifying the Newtype Pattern. It wraps a floating-point value and a unit of measurement.

⑥ Implement the **Add** trait for the **Quantity<U>** struct, allowing addition operations for quantities with the same unit.

⑦ Implement the **Sub** trait for the **Quantity<U>** struct, enabling subtraction operations for quantities with the same unit.

The Newtype Pattern is evident in the **Meter** and **Kilogram** structs, where they wrap units of measurement to provide type safety and semantic clarity. Additionally, the Quantity struct demonstrates the Newtype Pattern by wrapping values with specific units of measurement.

The Newtype Pattern stands as a valuable technique in Rust, promoting the creation of code that is both robust and eloquent. Its true power shines through when enhancing type safety in complex domains.

Dynamically Sized Types (DSTs)

DSTs are types that have a size unknown at compile time. While Rust primarily enforces strong typing and known sizes, there are scenarios where DSTs are useful. One common use case is working with slices of dynamically sized data.

Traits are of great importance when it comes to working with DSTs, particularly when they are paired with trait objects. Now, let's examine a straightforward example that involves the utilization of trait objects alongside DSTs.

Listing 3.24 Dynamically Sized Types (DSTs)

```
trait Shape {
    fn area(&self) -> f64; // ① Define a Shape trait with an area method.
}

struct Circle {
    radius: f64, // ② Create a struct Circle with a radius field to
represent a circle.
}

impl Shape for Circle {
    fn area(&self) -> f64 {
        std::f64::consts::PI * self.radius * self.radius // ③ Implement
the area method for Circle.
    }
}
```

```
fn main() {
    let circle: &dyn Shape = &Circle { radius: 5.0 }; // ④ Create a
trait object circle referring to a Circle instance.
    println!("Circle area: {}", circle.area()); // ⑤ Call the area
method on the circle trait object.
}

// Output

// Circle area: 78.53981633974483
```

① We define a **Shape** trait with an area method that calculates the area of a shape.

② We create a **Circle** struct with a radius field to represent a circle.

③ The **impl** block implements the **Shape** trait for the **Circle** struct, providing a specific implementation of the area method for circles. This allows us to calculate the area of a circle using the formula **std::f64::consts::PI * self.radius * self.radius**.

④ In the **main** function, we create a trait object circle of type **&dyn Shape** that refers to an instance of **Circle** with a radius of 5.0. This is an example of a dynamically sized type (DST) because the concrete type of circle is determined at runtime.

⑤ We then call the area method on the circle trait object, which dynamically dispatches to the area implementation for **Circle**. This demonstrates how Rust handles dynamic dispatch for trait methods, allowing us to work with different types that implement the same trait through a trait object.

In this section, we explored Rust's use of Dynamically Sized Types (DSTs), which allow for types whose size is determined at runtime rather than compile time. We demonstrated this concept through the example of a Shape trait and a Circle struct. By implementing the Shape trait for the Circle struct and using a trait object **(&dyn Shape)**, we showcased how Rust handles dynamic dispatch for trait methods, enabling flexibility and polymorphism in Rust code. DSTs are a powerful feature in Rust, facilitating runtime flexibility and abstraction when working with different types that share a common trait.

Conditional Conformance

Conditional conformance, a concept in Rust, involves implementing a trait for a specific type only under certain conditions. This mechanism allows for fine-grained control over which types can adopt a trait, enabling flexibility and specialization in code. In the following example, we delve into conditional conformance by defining a Convertible trait that represents types that can be converted into other types. Two temperature unit types, Celsius and Fahrenheit, serve as our illustrative case. The Convertible trait declares a convert method, and we implement this trait for both Celsius and Fahrenheit. The implementations enable temperature conversions between the two units. Within the main function, instances of Celsius and Fahrenheit are created, and conversions are performed using the convert method. This example showcases how Rust allows for conditional conformance, enhancing the expressiveness and adaptability of code by implementing traits only when specific conditions are met.

Listing 3.25 Conditional conformance

```
trait Convertible<T> { // ①
    fn convert(&self) -> T;
}

struct Celsius(f64); // ②
struct Fahrenheit(f64); // ②

impl Convertible<Fahrenheit> for Celsius { // ③
    fn convert(&self) -> Fahrenheit {
        Fahrenheit(self.0 * 1.8 + 32.0)
    }
}

impl Convertible<Celsius> for Fahrenheit { // ③
    fn convert(&self) -> Celsius {
        Celsius((self.0 - 32.0) / 1.8)
    }
}

fn main() {
    let celsius = Celsius(100.0); // ④
    let fahrenheit = Fahrenheit(212.0); // ④

    let converted_fahrenheit: Fahrenheit = celsius.convert();
    let converted_celsius: Celsius = fahrenheit.convert();

    println!("100°C in Fahrenheit: {:.2}°F", converted_fahrenheit.0); // ⑤
    println!("212°F in Celsius: {:.2}°C", converted_celsius.0); // ⑤
}
```

```
// Output

// 100°C in Fahrenheit: 212.00°F
// 212°F in Celsius: 100.00°C
```

① We define a **Convertible** trait with a **convert** method.

② The **Celsius** and **Fahrenheit** structs represent temperature values.

③ We implement **Convertible** for both **Celsius** and **Fahrenheit** to allow conversions.

④ In the **main** function, we create instances of **Celsius** and **Fahrenheit**.

⑤ We use the **convert** method to perform temperature conversions.

In this example of conditional conformance in Rust, we have uncovered a powerful aspect of the language that allows for the implementation of traits under specific conditions. By defining a **Convertible** trait and implementing it for the **Celsius** and **Fahrenheit** structs, we demonstrated how Rust enables fine-grained control over trait adoption. This feature enhances code expressiveness and adaptability, allowing us to specialize implementations for different types and situations. Conditional conformance is a valuable tool in Rust's toolkit, enabling the creation of more flexible and efficient code, especially when dealing with scenarios where certain traits should only apply to specific types or under particular conditions. It underscores Rust's commitment to safety and correctness while providing developers with the tools they need to express their intentions clearly and concisely in code.

Type-level Programming

Type-level programming is a fascinating concept that effectively harnesses the power of the type system to encapsulate complex logic and interconnections among types. Despite the complexity and vastness of this domain, we will touch on it briefly to give you a glimpse of its potential.

An essential application of type-level programming involves crafting constraints at the type level, which empowers you to define complex conditions that types must satisfy. In this process, traits play a vital role by enabling you to establish these constraints using associated types and trait bounds.

Imagine yourself developing a game library, where you want to ensure that only specific combinations of character classes and weapons remain valid. By employing type-level programming, you can enforce these constraints during the compilation phase, guaranteeing their adherence.

Here's a simplified example demonstrating the idea:

Listing 3.26 Type-level Programming

```
trait CharacterClass { // ①
    type Weapon: Weapon;

    // Add a method to create an instance of the associated type.
    fn create_weapon() -> Self::Weapon;
}

trait Weapon { // ②
    fn attack(&self);
}

struct Warrior; // ③
struct Mage; // ③

struct Sword; //④
struct Staff; // ④

impl Weapon for Sword {
    fn attack(&self) {
        println!("Swinging the sword!");
    }
}

impl Weapon for Staff {
    fn attack(&self) {
        println!("Casting a spell with the staff!");
    }
}

impl CharacterClass for Warrior { // ⑤
    type Weapon = Sword;

    // Implement the method to create a Sword for the Warrior.
    fn create_weapon() -> Self::Weapon {
        Sword
    }
}

impl CharacterClass for Mage { // ⑤
    type Weapon = Staff;

    // Implement the method to create a Staff for the Mage.
    fn create_weapon() -> Self::Weapon {
```

```
        Staff
    }
}

fn attack<C: CharacterClass>() { // ⑥
    let weapon = C::create_weapon(); // Create an instance of the asso-
ciated type.
    weapon.attack();
}

fn main() {
    attack::<Warrior>();
    attack::<Mage>();
}

// Output

// Swinging the sword!
// Casting a spell with the staff!
```

① We define a **CharacterClass** trait with an associated **Weapon** type.

② The **Weapon** trait defines an **attack** method.

③ The **Warrior** and **Mage** structs represent character classes.

④ The **Sword** and **Staff** structs represent weapons and implement the **Weapon** trait.

⑤ We implement the **CharacterClass** trait for **Warrior** and **Mage**, specifying the associated weapon.

⑥ The **attack** function uses type-level programming to retrieve the weapon and call the attack method.

This example showcases how type-level programming in Rust allows you to define complex type relationships and constraints, ensuring that your code remains correct and adheres to specific rules during compilation. It's a powerful feature that can be particularly useful in domains where correctness and safety are crucial, such as game development or systems programming.

Performance Considerations

While traits and generics provide powerful abstractions, it's important to be aware of performance considerations when using them. Rust's trait system employs dynamic dispatch by default for trait objects, which can introduce a slight runtime overhead compared to static dispatch.

If maximizing performance is your main priority, you should consider using generic functions with monomorphization for static dispatch. This approach has the potential to optimize your code further, although it may entail duplicating code for each generic specialization.

Furthermore, traits that possess associated methods or associated constants may introduce less predictable performance due to their dynamic characteristics. This presents a trade-off between flexibility and performance.

By conducting profiling and benchmarking on your code, you can pinpoint performance bottlenecks and make well-informed choices regarding the utilization of traits and generics.

Conclusion

Traits and generics are the cornerstones of Rust's approach to flexible and efficient code design. They empower you to craft adaptable, reusable, and expressive solutions that seamlessly adjust to various scenarios. With traits, you can define shared behaviors that enable consistent interactions between types. Generics allow you to create versatile code that operates uniformly across different data types, all while maintaining strong type safety.

In this chapter, we have meticulously explored the fundamental concepts behind traits and generics, delving deep into their syntax, implementation, and practical applications. By acquiring a profound understanding of the craft of defining traits, effectively applying them to diverse types, and harnessing the immense potential of generics, you are now equipped to unleash the full power of these invaluable tools.

As you continue your Rust journey, remember that traits and generics are more than just language features; they embody a philosophy of design that prioritizes clarity, reusability, and adaptability. By embracing these concepts, you're joining a community of developers who value elegant and robust solutions.

Now, it is your turn to put into practice what you have acquired. Implement the knowledge you have gained in your own projects, and observe how your programming improves in terms of structure, adaptability, and effectiveness. Traits and generics will serve as valuable tools in your quest to create exceptional software that stands the test of time.

In the following chapter, we will explore Rust's array-like data structures, such as Vectors, Arrays, Tuples, and Slices, along with its hash-based collections, including HashMap and HashSet. We'll learn about their characteristics, use cases, and practical applications, demonstrating common operations and manipulations with Rust collections. This knowledge will equip you to efficiently organize and manipulate data, making you adept at handling a wide range of real-world programming challenges in Rust.

Multiple Choice Questions

Q1: What is the primary purpose of traits in Rust?

a) To define data structures

b) To provide default implementations for functions

c) To define shared behaviors that types can implement

d) To restrict access to data

Q2: What do generics in Rust allow developers to do?

a) Define default behaviors for types

b) Write code that works with a single data type

c) Create code that operates across different data types

d) Implement runtime type checks

Q3: In Rust, what is the role of the borrow checker?

a) To allow unrestricted concurrent access to data

b) To analyze code and ensure safe use of references, preventing data races

c) To automatically resolve data race issues at runtime

d) To introduce locks and mutexes to synchronize data access

Q4: What does a default method in a Rust trait provide?

a) A standard way to implement a trait

b) An automatic implementation for all types

c) A way to enforce strict behavior for all types

d) A mechanism to prevent customization by types

Q5: Why are associated types valuable in Rust traits?

a) They eliminate the need for implementing types to define their own methods.

b) They enforce a rigid type hierarchy in Rust code.

c) They allow implementing structs or enums to determine the actual type.

d) They restrict the use of generic types within traits.

Q6: What is the primary benefit of using generics in Rust?

a) Improved runtime performance

b) Code that is specific to a single data type

c) Enhanced code flexibility and reusability

d) Reduced code verbosity

Q7: What is the primary role of the Rust borrow checker in preventing concurrency-related bugs?

a) It allows unrestricted concurrent access to data.

b) It analyzes code to ensure safe use of references and prevents data races.

c) It automatically resolves data race issues at runtime.

d) It introduces locks and mutexes to synchronize data access.

Q8: How do default methods in Rust traits balance standardization and customization?

a) They enforce the same behavior for all types implementing the trait.

b) They provide a standard implementation that types can choose to override.

c) They automatically generate custom methods for implementing types.

d) They restrict customization to a predefined set of options.

Q9: What is the main advantage of using associated types in Rust traits?

a) They eliminate the need for implementing types to define their own methods.

b) They enforce a rigid type hierarchy in Rust code.

c) They allow for stricter type checking during compilation.

d) They enable implementing structs or enums to determine the actual type.

Q10: In Rust, how do generics differ from specific data types?

a) Generics provide better runtime performance.

b) Generics work with a single, fixed data type.

c) Generics enhance code flexibility by working with multiple data types.

d) Generics require more code verbosity than specific data types.

Q11: What is the primary advantage of using trait objects in Rust?

a) They provide compile-time type checking.

b) They allow for dynamic dispatch and runtime adaptability.

c) They improve code performance.

d) They eliminate the need for traits.

Q12: What is the role of marker traits in Rust?

a) They define methods and associated values for types.

b) They signal specific characteristics or behaviors of types without method implementation.

c) They implement operator overloading for types.

d) They specify type constraints for generic functions.

Q13: What is a dynamically sized type (DST) in Rust?

a) A type that has a fixed size known at compile time.

b) A type that is used for type-level programming.

   c) A type that has a size unknown at compile time.

   d) A type that is used for operator overloading.

Q14: How can type-level programming be useful in Rust?

   a) It simplifies the creation of Rust macros.

   b) It allows for dynamic dispatch of methods.

   c) It enables the definition of complex type relationships and constraints.

   d) It eliminates the need for implementing traits.

Answers

1. c) To define shared behaviors that types can implement
2. c) Create code that operates across different data types
3. b) To analyze code and ensure safe use of references, preventing data race
4. a) A standard way to implement a trait
5. c) They allow implementing structs or enums to determine the actual type
6. c) Enhanced code flexibility and reusability
7. b) It analyzes code to ensure safe use of references and prevents data races
8. b) They provide a standard implementation that types can choose to override
9. d) They enable implementing structs or enums to determine the actual type
10. c) Generics enhance code flexibility by working with multiple data types
11. b) They allow for dynamic dispatch and runtime adaptability
12. b) They signal specific characteristics or behaviors of types without method implementation
13. c) A type that has a size unknown at compile time
14. c) It enables the definition of complex type relationships and constraints

CHAPTER 4

Rust Built-In Data Structures

Introduction

In this comprehensive chapter, we will delve deep into the fundamental concepts and powerful tools that form the backbone of the Rust programming language. Rust's built-in data structures provide a robust foundation for developing efficient and safe software. Think of data structures like the containers you use to organize things in your room. In this chapter, we'll open up these Rust containers and see how they work.

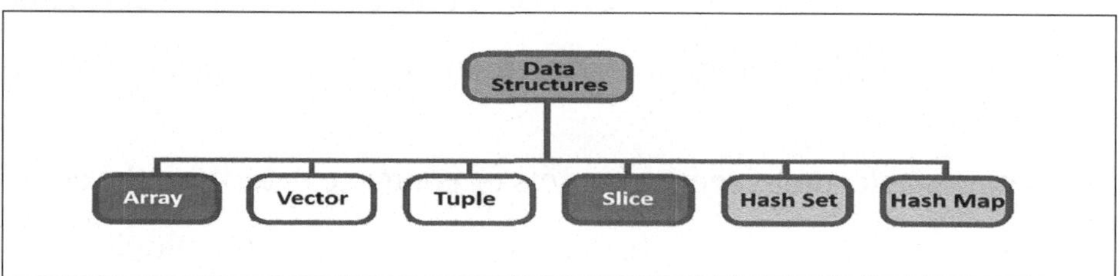

***Figure* 4.1:** *Rust's built-in data structures overview*

First, we'll start with arrays, which resemble to arranged boxes where you can store your belongings. Next, we'll delve into vectors, which act as versatile containers capable of holding numerous items. Tuples, on the other hand, function as compact parcels that can hold a collection of different types of objects. Slices are like windows that allow you to see a part of a container without opening it. Sets serve as unique collections, ensuring the absence of duplicate items, while hash maps resemble dictionaries, enabling fast information retrieval.

Throughout this chapter, we will guide you in utilizing these containers to address real-world problems with simplicity and efficiency. By the end of this chapter, you will possess the expertise to effectively employ these Rust tools in your own projects. It's like learning how to use different types of containers to organize your things better and get things done faster. Hence, let us embark on this journey and explore how Rust's data structures can simplify your programming endeavors!

Structure

In this chapter, we're going to explore:

- Rust's array-like data structures: Vectors, Arrays, Tuples, and Slices
- Rust's hash-based collections: HashMap and HashSet
- A demonstrating common operations and manipulations with Rust collections and more

Arrays in Rust

Arrays in Rust provide a powerful way to store collections of values with the same data type. Unlike vectors, which can dynamically resize, arrays are fixed in size and contain elements of identical data types. This chapter delves into the world of Rust arrays, covering everything from their creation and element access to modification and iteration. Whether you need to allocate memory on the stack or work with constant-sized collections, arrays have a vital role to play in Rust programming.

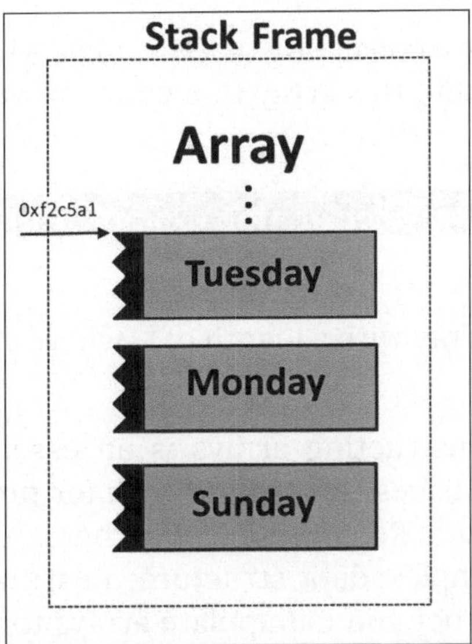

Figure 4.2: *Simple array memory layout representation*

Creating Arrays

When writing code in Rust, creating arrays is a fundamental operation that allows you to store and manipulate collections of data efficiently. Arrays in Rust are fixed-size, which means their length is predetermined at the time of declaration, and all elements within an array must have the same data type. You can use square brackets `[]` followed by comma-separated values to define an array. Each element in the array is accessed by its index, starting from zero.

To create an array in Rust, square brackets `[]` followed by comma-separated values can be used:

Listing 4.1 A simple array declaration example with String type.

```
let days = ["Sunday", "Monday", "Tuesday", "Wednesday", "Thursday",
"Friday", "Saturday"];
```

In this example, we've created an array named `days`, which contains the names of the days of the week. Each element is a string, and the array's size is determined by the number of elements.

Alternatively, you can explicitly specify both the number of elements and their data types:

Listing 4.2 A simple array declaration example with integer type.

```
let a: [i32; 5] = [1, 2, 3, 4, 5];
```

Here, we declare an array `a` consisting of `i32` values, with its length fixed at 5. To initialize all elements within this array to a common value, you can employ the following concise syntax:

Listing 4.3 A simple array declaration example with integer type.

```
let zeros = [0; 5];
```

This code generates an array with a length of `5`, where all elements are initialized to `0`.

Mastering the art of constructing arrays is an essential proficiency in Rust programming, as it establishes the groundwork for proficiently and effectively handling collections of data. Regardless of whether you are looking for a simple array of values or a complex data structure, Rust's array syntax equips you with the means to construct and manipulate arrays to perfectly align with your requirements.

Accessing Array Elements

Accessing elements within an array is a fundamental operation in Rust, and it's quite straightforward.

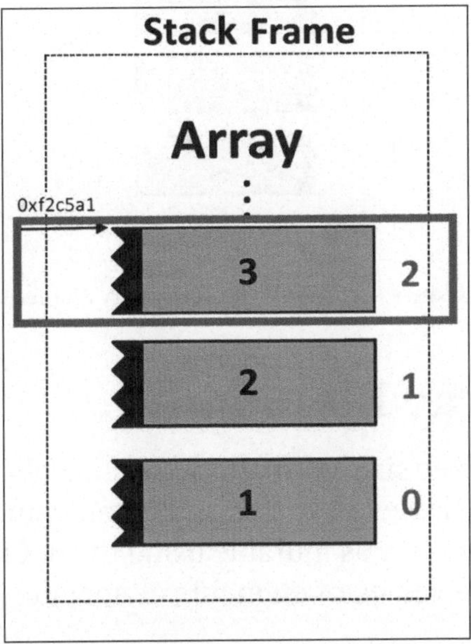

Figure 4.3: *Accessing an element within an array*

To retrieve a specific element from an array, you simply use square brackets `[]` with the index of the desired element.

Listing 4.4 Accessing array elements example.

```
let numbers = [1, 2, 3, 4, 5];println!("{}", numbers[2]);

// Output

// 3
```

In this snippet, we access the third element (index 2) of the `numbers` array, which contains the value 3.

It is important to keep in mind that Rust's array indices start at 0. Therefore, the initial element can be found at index 0, and so forth for subsequent elements. This uncomplicated syntax provides an efficient and accurate means of accessing data stored within arrays, solidifying its position as a fundamental component of Rust's ability to handle arrays effectively.

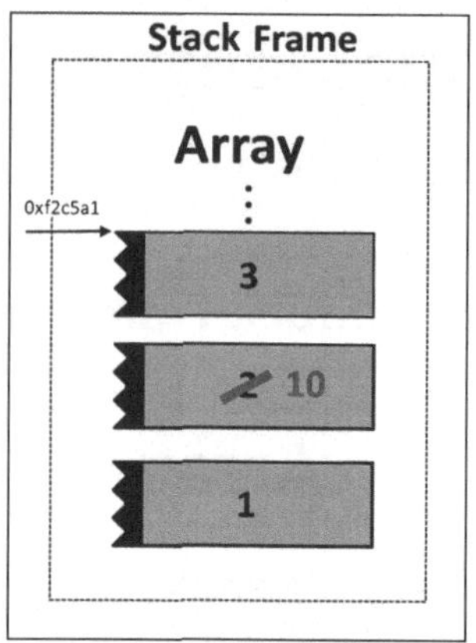

Figure 4.4: *Modifying an array element*

Modifying Array Elements

As arrays in Rust have a fixed size, you cannot dynamically add or remove elements as you can with vectors. However, you can still modify individual elements within an array by declaring the array as mutable using the `mut` keyword. This mutability allows you to change the values of elements at specific indices.

Listing 4.5 Modifying array elements example.

```
let mut numbers = [1, 2, 3, 4, 5];
numbers[1] = 10; // ①
println!("{:?}", numbers); // ②

// Output

// [1, 10, 3, 4, 5]
```

① In this example, we change the second element (index 1) of the `numbers` array to 10.

② Printing the modified `numbers` array now shows `[1, 10, 3, 4, 5]`.

While arrays in Rust are fixed in size, their mutability allows you to update the existing elements, making them versatile data structures for various applications.

Iterating Through Arrays

To retrieve every individual element from an array, you need to iterate through all of them rather than accessing them one by one using indices. Here are several methods for iterating through an array, each with its own syntax:

Listing 4.6 Iterating through array elements example.

```
let seasons = ["Winter", "Spring", "Summer", "Fall"];

// Using a for-in Loop
for season in seasons {
    println!("{season}");
}

// Output

// Winter
// Spring
// Summer
// Fall

// Using a for Loop with an index
for index in 0..seasons.len() {
    println!("{}", seasons[index]);
}

// Output

// Winter
// Spring
// Summer
// Fall

// Using a for Loop with an iterator
for season in seasons.iter() {
    println!("{}", season);
}

// Output

// Winter
// Spring
// Summer
// Fall
```

These examples demonstrate different ways to iterate through the **seasons** array, printing the name of each season. You can choose the iteration method that best suits your needs and coding style.

Slicing Arrays

The ability to slice in Rust is a powerful feature as it allows the creation of an array that contains only certain elements from the original one while leaving its source.

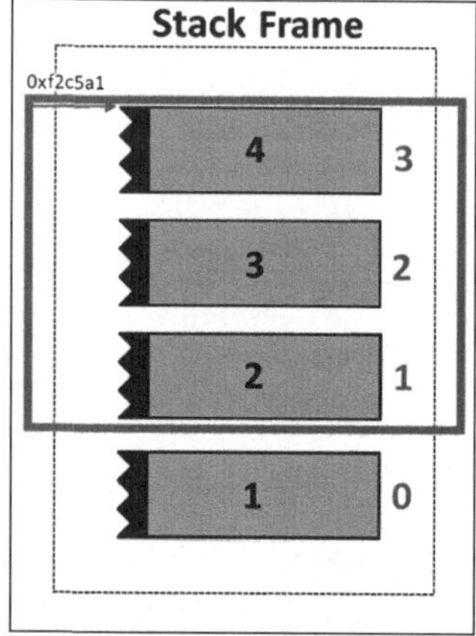

Figure 4.5: *One dimensional array slicing*

To execute this operation, you need to define a range of indices utilizing `..` syntax.

Listing 4.7 Slicing an array example.

```
let numbers = [1, 2, 3, 4, 5];
let slice = &numbers[1..4]; // ①
println!("{:?}", slice); // ②

// Output

// [2, 3, 4]
```

① In this code, we slice the `numbers` array to create a new array that includes elements at indices 1, 2, and 3.

② The output of this code will be `[2, 3, 4]`.

Slicing proves to be an advantageous technique when dealing with a particular section of an array. It enables you to efficiently handle and retrieve specific data segments within the array without having to build another one from scratch. This tool saves time and effort while providing ease in manipulating arrays according to your needs.

Multi-dimensional Arrays

The Rust programming language provides the ability to construct multi-dimensional arrays by nesting one array within another. Such a feature allows the representation of complex data structures, such as matrices or tables, with effortless ease.

For instance, using a 2D array can effectively illustrate a tic-tac-toe board composed of three rows and columns each. Take the following example for reference:

Listing 4.8 Multi-dimensional array example.

```
fn main() {
    // Define a 2D array for a tic-tac-toe board
    let mut tic_tac_toe: [[char; 3]; 3] = [
        [' ', 'X', 'O'],
        ['O', 'X', ' '],
        ['X', ' ', 'O']
    ];

    // Display the initial tic-tac-toe board
    println!("Initial Tic-Tac-Toe Board:");
    print_tic_tac_toe(&tic_tac_toe);

    // Update the board and display it again
    tic_tac_toe[1][2] = 'X';
    tic_tac_toe[2][1] = 'O';

    println!("Updated Tic-Tac-Toe Board:");
    print_tic_tac_toe(&tic_tac_toe);
}

// Function to print the tic-tac-toe board
fn print_tic_tac_toe(board: &[[char; 3]; 3]) {
    for row in board.iter() {
        for cell in row.iter() {
            print!("{} ", cell);
        }
        println!();
    }
}
```

```
// Output

// Initial Tic-Tac-Toe Board:
//   X O
// O X
// X   O
// Updated Tic-Tac-Toe Board:
//   X O
// O X X
// X O O
```

In this code snippet, we designate a variable named `tic_tac_toe` as a two-dimensional array that has dimensions of `[3][3]`. Each element within the array is represented by a `char`, which can be an 'X', 'O' or empty space. This setup enables us to easily handle the state of any tic-tac-toe game. To begin with, we exhibit the original board layout and proceed to modify it before using the function called `print_tic_tac_toe` to showcase our updated version of a given board.

The `print_tic_tac_toe` function is responsible for printing the board to the terminal, ensuring a visually clear representation of the game state. This example provides a basic structure for managing a tic-tac-toe game using a multi-dimensional array within a complete Rust program.

Working with Array Methods

The standard library of Rust offers an array of techniques to handle arrays effectively. These procedures are included in the `std::array` module, which can streamline ordinary array operations. One such method is the `iter`, used for iterating through each element and executing a function on it. Let's take an example that showcases how we could double every value present within an array using this `iter` method:

Listing 4.9 Using array's methods example.

```
fn main() {
    let mut numbers = [1, 2, 3, 4, 5];
    for num in numbers.iter_mut() { // ①
        *num *= 2;
    }
    println!("{:?}", numbers);
}

// Output

// [2, 4, 6, 8, 10]
```

① After applying the doubling operation to each element of the numbers array, the resulting array will be `[2, 4, 6, 8, 10]`.

Another helpful method is `sort`, which allows you to sort the elements of an array in-place. Here's an example:

```
fn main() {
    let mut unsorted = [4, 1, 7, 3, 9];
    unsorted.sort();
    println!("{:?}", unsorted); // ①
}

// Output

// [1, 3, 4, 7, 9]
```

① Sorting the `unsorted` array in ascending order using the `sort` method results in `[1, 3, 4, 7, 9]`.

There exist a few techniques to work with arrays and the ones mentioned are just two of them. Rust's standard library offers numerous beneficial functions for activities such as searching, cloning, or finding the highest or lowest value within an array.

Array Initialization and Default Values

In the process of creating arrays, there may arise instances where it becomes crucial to set them up with preassigned values or create specific data patterns. Rust provides a plenty of methods that can be used optimally to achieve these goals effectively and quickly.

Initializing with Default Values

To initialize an array with default values, Rust offers an array initialization syntax where you specify the size. Here is an example: an array of size 10, wherein every element is set to the default value of 0.

Listing 4.10 Array's initialization with default values example.

```
let default_values = [0; 10];
```

This code snippet declares an array named `default_values` with ten elements, all set to the default value 0.

Generating Patterns with Iterators

Rust offers robust iterator functions that enable the creation of arrays with specific patterns or values. An exemplary method in this regard is **map**, which applies a transformation function to every element within an array. Here's an illustration showcasing the generation of an array consisting of numbers squared:

Listing 4.11 Array's initialization and iterators example.

```
fn main() {
    let original = [1, 2, 3, 4, 5];
    let mut squared: [i32; 5] = [0; 5]; // Initialize an array of size 5 
with zeros

    let _ = original
        .iter()
        .enumerate()
        .map(|(index, &value)| squared[index] = value * value)
        .collect::<Vec<_>>();

    println!("{:?}", squared);
}

// Output

// [1, 4, 9, 16, 25]
```

In this code, we use the **iter** method to create an iterator over the **original** array. Then, we apply a closure that squares each element, and finally, we collect the transformed elements into a new array named **squared**.

Initializing with Computed Values

Sometimes, you may need to initialize an array with values computed at runtime. Rust allows you to use loops to accomplish this. Here's an example of generating an array of factorials:

Listing 4.12 Array's initialization and elements computation example.

```
fn main() {
    let mut factorials = [1; 10];

    for i in 1..10 {
        factorials[i] = factorials[i - 1] * (i as i32);
    }
```

```
    println!("{:?}", factorials);
}

// Output

// [1, 1, 2, 6, 24, 120, 720, 5040, 40320, 362880]
```

Within this code, we start by setting the initial element of the array `factorials` as `1`. Following this, we employ a `for` loop to calculate and allocate the factorial values to the subsequent elements. Consequently, the array generated will encompass the factorials of numbers ranging from 0 to 9.

Array Length and Bounds Checking

Understanding the length of an array and ensuring bounds safety is crucial to writing robust Rust code. This section covers how to obtain the length of an array and perform bounds checking when accessing elements.

Obtaining the Length

To determine the length of an array in Rust, you can conveniently use the `len` method, which provides you with the number of elements contained within the array. This information can be crucial when you need to iterate over or manipulate the elements of an array dynamically. Consider the following example:

Listing 4.13 Array's length example.

```
fn main() {
    let numbers = [1, 2, 3, 4, 5];
    let length = numbers.len(); // ①
    println!("{:?}", length);
}

// Output

// 5
```

① In this snippet, we use the `len` method to obtain the length of the `numbers` array, which is `5`.

The size of an array signifies the number of elements it contains, serving as a reliable tool to ensure your code functions accurately when handling arrays of different dimensions. The len function streamlines the retrieval of this essential array of information in Rust, making it easier and more efficient.

Bounds Checking

Rust prioritizes safety as a fundamental aspect, which encompasses the thorough verification of array element boundaries. In the event of attempting to access an element using an index that falls beyond the permissible bounds, your program will encounter a state of panic. Let's explore the following illustrative example:

Listing 4.14 Array's bounds checking example.

```
let numbers = [1, 2, 3, 4, 5];
let index = 10;
let value = numbers[index];
```

In this code, we attempt to access the element at index `10` in the `numbers` array. Since the array only has indices from `0` to `4`, this will result in a panic at runtime.

To avoid panics and ensure safe access, always check that the index is within the bounds of the array using an if statement or pattern matching before accessing the element.

Array Copy and Clone

Understanding how Rust handles array copying and cloning is essential when working with arrays. This section explores the differences between copying and cloning arrays, as well as situations where each is appropriate.

Copying Arrays

Rust arrays implement the `Copy` trait if their element types also implement `Copy`. This means that for arrays of `Copy` types, copying occurs implicitly during assignments or function calls. Here's an example:

Listing 4.15 Array's copying example.

```
let original = [1, 2, 3];
let copied = original;
```

In this code, we copy the `original` array into the `copied` array through a simple assignment. Since `i32` implements `Copy`, this operation is allowed.

Cloning Arrays

If an array's element type does not implement the `Copy` trait, you cannot copy it directly. Instead, you need to use the `to_owned` method to clone the array. Here's an example:

Listing 4.16 Array's cloning example.

```
let original = ["one", "two", "three"];
let cloned = original.to_owned();
```

In this snippet, we clone the `original` array into the `cloned` array using the `to_owned` method. Since strings do not implement `Copy`, this approach is necessary to create a deep copy.

It's important to note that cloning an array involves creating a new array with identical elements. This can be a costly operation in terms of memory and performance, so use it judiciously.

Rust arrays are versatile data structures suitable for various use cases. Their fixed-size nature makes them efficient for situations where the array size is known in advance and does not change during runtime. Whether you're working on numerical computations or managing constant-sized collections, arrays are valuable tools in your Rust programming toolkit. With the knowledge you've gained in this section, you'll be well-prepared to leverage arrays effectively in your Rust projects.

Vectors

Vectors, sometimes referred to as dynamic arrays, are versatile and fundamental data structures in Rust. They allow you to store a collection of values of the same type and can grow or shrink in size as needed. Let's explore how to create vectors and specify their element types.

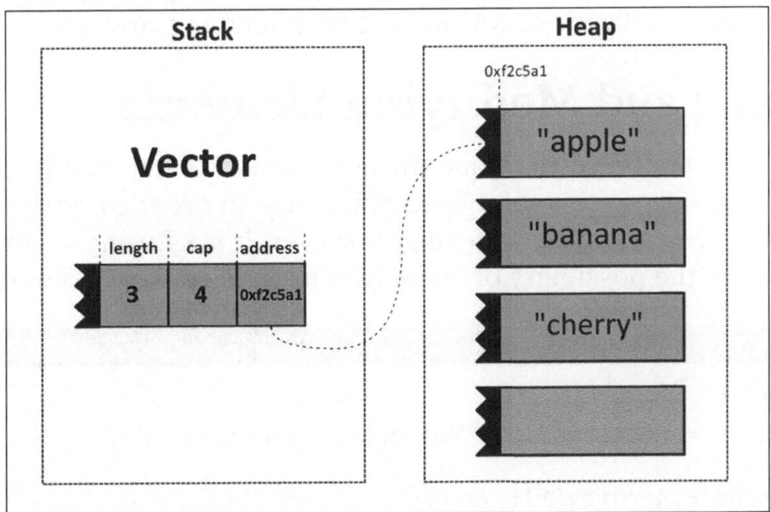

Figure 4.6: *Vector's memory layout simple representation*

Creating Vectors

Creating vectors in Rust offers flexibility and versatility for managing collections of data, and there are several methods to do so. Two common approaches are using the `Vec::new()` constructor and the `vec!` macro. The first method, illustrated by ① in the provided code:

Listing 4.17 Vector's initialization example.

```
let v: Vec<i32> = Vec::new(); // ①
```

Here, we create an empty vector named v by explicitly specifying its element type as i32. Rust's type annotations ensure that the vector is of the correct type, providing type safety. The second method, shown by ② in the code:

Listing 4.18 Vector's initialization example.

```
let numbers = vec![1, 2, 3, 4, 5]; // ②
```

This approach utilizes the `vec!` macro to create a vector named `numbers` with initial values. Rust's type inference automatically deduces that this vector contains `i32` elements, reducing verbosity while still maintaining strong type safety.

The decision on which approach to use is determined by the particular scenario. The utilization of `Vec::new()` will yield an empty vector that can be populated with elements later, whereas the use of the `vec!` macro permits immediate initialization of a vector using predefined values. These two techniques are fundamental in managing dynamic collections within Rust programming language.

Accessing and Modifying Elements

Once you have a vector, you'll frequently need to access and modify its elements. Let's explore how to do this safely and efficiently. In order to retrieve elements from a vector, we can utilize indexing; however, it is of utmost importance to remain aware of the possibility of encountering index out-of-bounds errors.

Listing 4.19 Accessing vector's elements using indexing example.

```
fn main() {
    let fruits = vec!["apple", "banana", "cherry", "date"]; // ①

    let second = &fruits[1]; // ②
}
```

① We've created a vector **fruits** containing strings representing various fruits for our examples.

② Here, we access the second element of the **fruits** vector using indexing. Rust uses zero-based indexing, so the second element has an index of **1**. However, indexing can be risky as it may lead to panics if you attempt to access an out-of-bounds index.

To safely access elements, consider using the **get** method:

Listing 4.20 Safely accessing vector's elements using the get method.

```
fn main() {
    let fruits = vec!["apple", "banana", "cherry", "date"];

    let second = fruits.get(1); // ①
    match second {
        Some(fruit) => println!("The second element is {}", fruit),
        None => println!("Element not found"),
    }
}

// Output

// The second element is banana
```

① The **get** method returns an **Option<&T>** where **Some** contains the element if it exists and **None** represents the absence of the element. This approach provides safety by returning an option rather than panicking.

Modifying Vectors

Vectors in Rust are mutable by default, which means you can modify their contents. This mutability allows you to adapt your data structures as your program runs, making vectors a versatile choice for managing dynamic collections of data. Whether you need to add, update, or remove elements, vectors provide the flexibility to make these modifications efficiently.

Adding Elements

One of the most common operations when working with vectors is adding elements, particularly appending new data to the end of the vector.

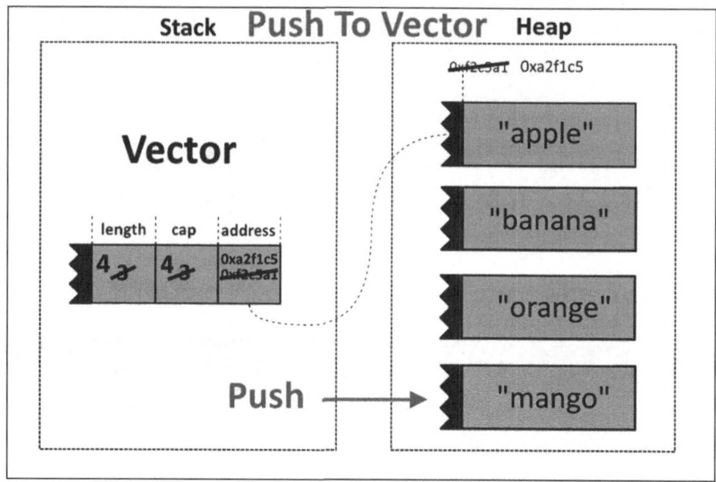

Figure 4.7: *Adding an element to a vector*

This operation is especially valuable when dealing with growing collections. Rust provides a straightforward way to achieve this using the push method. In the example provided:

Listing 4.21 Adding elements in a vector example.

```
fn main() {
    let mut fruits = vec!["apple", "banana"]; // ①

    // Adding "cherry" to the end of the vector
    fruits.push("cherry"); // ②
}
```

① We create a mutable vector `fruits` and initialize it with two initial elements.

② Using the `push` method, we add the string "`cherry`" to the end of the vector. The vector automatically resizes to accommodate the new element.

Adding elements to vectors dynamically is an essential capability when working with collections of data that may grow or change during your program's execution. This feature, combined with Rust's focus on safety and performance, makes vectors a robust choice for managing dynamic data structures.

Updating Elements

Updating elements within a vector is a straightforward operation in Rust. You can accomplish this by using indexing to access the specific element you want to modify and then assign a new value to it. In the provided code example:

Listing 4.22 Updating elements in a vector example.

```
fn main() {
    let mut fruits = vec!["apple", "banana"]; // ①

    // Updating the second element to "pear"
    fruits[1] = "pear"; // ②
}
```

① We create mutable vector `fruits` with two initial elements.

② Using indexing, we replace the second element, "**banana**," with "**pear**." This demonstrates how you can modify vector elements in place.

Updating elements in a vector allows you to maintain and adapt your data structure to reflect real-time changes, making vectors a versatile choice for managing evolving collections in Rust.

Removing Elements

When working with dynamically changing data in Rust, it is frequently necessary to remove elements from a vector. Rust provides several techniques to accomplish this task, enabling you to customize your approach based on your program's specific needs. Among these methods, the pop function stands out as a highly efficient way to remove and retrieve the last element from a vector.

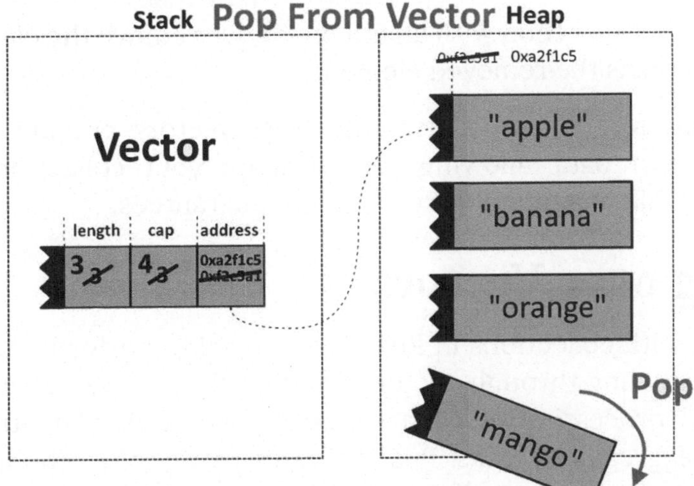

Figure 4.8: *Removing an element from a vector*

Listing 4.23 Removing elements from a vector using pop method.

```
fn main() {
    let mut fruits = vec!["apple", "banana", "cherry"]; // ①

    // Removing and storing the last element
    let removed_fruit = fruits.pop(); // ②
}
```

① We create mutable vector **fruits** initialized with three elements.

② Using the **pop** method, we remove the last element, "**cherry**," and store it in the **removed_fruit** variable. The method returns an **Option<T>**, ensuring that you handle potential empty vectors gracefully.

To remove an element at a specific index, you can use the **remove** method:

Listing 4.24 Removing elements from a vector using remove method.

```
fn main() {
    let mut fruits = vec!["apple", "banana", "cherry"]; // ①

    // Removing the element at index 1 ("banana")
    let removed_fruit = fruits.remove(1); // ②
}
```

① We create a mutable vector **fruits** initialized with three elements.

② Using the **remove** method with an index of **1**, we remove the element "**banana**". The method returns the removed element.

These methods for removing elements from vectors provide flexibility and control over your data, allowing you to adapt your collection to changing requirements while maintaining Rust's safety guarantees.

Iterating over Vectors

When dealing with collections in Rust, it is crucial to perform the fundamental operation of iterating through vector elements. This powerful method enables the sequential processing of each element, facilitating data transformation, filtering, and aggregation tasks. Rust provides plenty of methods designed for vector iteration, catering to diverse programming requirements with utmost flexibility and adaptability.

Using a for Loop

You can use a `for` loop to iterate over the elements of a vector:

Listing 4.25 Iterating over a vector using a for loop.

```
fn main() {
    let numbers = vec![1, 2, 3, 4, 5]; // ①
    for number in &numbers { // ②
        println!("{}", number);
    }
}

// Output

// 1
// 2
// 3
// 4
// 5
```

① We create a vector `numbers` with five integer elements.

② Using a `for` loop, we iterate through the vector's elements, printing each number. In this case, we use a reference (`&numbers`) to avoid moving ownership of the vector.

Using a for loop during iteration offers an uncomplicated and easy to comprehend approach in handling vector elements sequentially, making it adaptable for various tasks like basic printing or complex data transformations and filtering operations. Rust considers this method indispensable when working with collections efficiently.

Using `iter_mut` for Mutable Iteration

When faced with situations that require the alteration of vector elements during iteration, Rust offers a powerful solution in the form of its `iter_mut` method. This method allows you to acquire mutable references for each element within your vector and efficiently perform necessary modifications without creating new instances. An example is presented as follows:

Listing 4.26 Iterating over a vector using the iter_mut method.

```
fn main() {
    let mut numbers = vec![10, 11, 12, 13, 14, 15]; // ①
    for number in numbers.iter_mut() { // ②
        *number += 1; // Add 1 to each element
    }
    println!("{:?}", numbers);
}

// Output

// [11, 12, 13, 14, 15, 16]
```

① We create a mutable vector `numbers` with six integer elements.

② Using the `iter_mut` method, we obtain mutable references to the elements and increment each element by 1 within the loop. This approach allows in-place modification of vector elements.

This approach allows you to perform in-place modifications of vector elements efficiently. It's particularly useful when you need to update data within a vector while preserving its structure. Rust's ownership and borrowing system ensures safety and prevents data races during such mutable iterations, making it a reliable choice for concurrent programming as well.

Using enumerate for Index and Value

In situations where you require both the index and the value of each element during iteration, Rust provides the `enumerate` method as a convenient solution. This method allows you to iterate through a vector while obtaining both the index and the value of each element. Here's an example:

Listing 4.27 Iterating over a vector using the enumerate method.

```
fn main() {
    let fruits = vec!["apple", "banana", "cherry"]; // ①
    for (index, fruit) in fruits.iter().enumerate() { // ②
        println!("Index {}: {}", index, fruit);
    }
}
```

```
// Output

// Index 0: apple
// Index 1: banana
// Index 2: cherry
```

① We create a vector `fruits` containing strings representing fruits.

② Using the `enumerate` method, we iterate through the vector's elements while obtaining both the index and the value of each element. This can be useful when you need to work with both the position and the content of elements.

The output of this code demonstrates how the enumerate method provides a concise way to access both the index and the value during vector iteration, which can be beneficial for various data processing and manipulation tasks. Understanding and using methods like `enumerate` enhances your ability to work efficiently with vectors in Rust.

In this section, we've delved into the fundamental operations of working with vectors in Rust, providing you with a solid foundation for utilizing these dynamic collections effectively. Throughout this exploration, you've gained insights into key vector operations, including their creation, element access, modification, and iteration.

Vectors, with their mutability and dynamic sizing, serve as the foundation for more advanced collections and data manipulation tasks in Rust. As you continue your journey in Rust programming, this strong understanding of vectors will prove invaluable when dealing with more complex data structures and algorithms, making you well-equipped to tackle a wide range of programming challenges with confidence.

Tuples

Rust's tuples exhibit remarkable flexibility and adaptability as they enable you to store elements of varying types in one unified collection. In this section, we will delve further into tuples, uncovering their advanced functionalities, practical implementations, and beyond.

Creating and Initializing Tuples

Creating tuples in Rust is a straightforward process, and they can be initialized in various ways to accommodate your specific data requirements. Here are some illustrative examples:

Listing 4.28 Tuples Initialization examples.

```
fn main() {
    // Creating and initializing a tuple
    let person = ("Alice", 30, true); // ①

    // Creating an empty tuple (unit tuple)
    let empty: () = (); // ②

    // Type annotation for an empty tuple
    let another_empty: () = (); // ③
}
```

① We create a tuple **person** with three elements: a string, an integer, and a boolean. Each element can have a different data type.

② An empty tuple, sometimes referred to as a unit tuple, is created using empty parentheses. This type can be used in situations where you need to return or represent the absence of a value.

③ Here, we explicitly provide a type annotation for another empty tuple.

Accessing Tuple Elements

Accessing elements within a tuple is straightforward using zero-based indexing. Let's see how it's done:

Listing 4.29 Accessing tuples elements examples.

```
fn main() {
    let person = ("Alice", 30, true); // ①

    // Accessing the first element of the tuple
    let name = person.0; // ②

    // Accessing the second element
    let age = person.1; // ③

    // Accessing the third element
    let employed = person.2; // ④
}
```

① We have a tuple `person` containing a person's **name**, **age**, and **employment status**.

② Here, we access the first element of the tuple using indexing with `.0`. In this case, `name` will be assigned the string "**Alice**."

③ Similarly, we access the second element (age) using `.1`.

④ Finally, we access the third element (employment status) using `.2`.

Destructuring Tuples

Destructuring tuples allows us to extract individual elements and assign them to variables, making tuple handling more convenient:

Listing 4.30 Tuple's destructuring example.

```
fn main() {
    let person = ("Alice", 30, true); // ①

    // Destructuring the tuple into variables
    let (name, age, employed) = person; // ②
}
```

① We've defined a tuple **person** with three elements.

② Using tuple destructuring, we extract the elements of the tuple **person** and bind them to the variables: **name**, **age**, and **employed**. This technique simplifies working with tuples and is particularly useful when you need to process or manipulate the elements individually.

Tuple Patterns and Advanced Usage

Tuple patterns in Rust allow for more advanced matching and deconstruction. Let's explore an example:

Listing 4.31 Tuple's and pattern matching example.

```
fn main() {
    let person = ("Alice", 30, true); // ①

    // Using a tuple pattern to match and destructure
    match person {
        (name, age, true) => println!("{} is {} years old and em-
ployed.", name, age),
        (name, age, false) => println!("{} is {} years old and not em-
ployed.", name, age),
        _ => println!("Unknown employment status."), // ②
    }
}
```

```
// Output

// Alice is 30 years old and employed.
```

① We've defined a tuple **person** with three elements.

In this example, we employ a tuple pattern in a match expression to categorize individuals based on their employment status. Depending on the values of the elements in the person tuple, we print different messages.

② The _ symbol is a wildcard pattern used to match any value not covered by the previous patterns.

Real-World Use Cases

Tuples, while seemingly simple, have practical applications in a variety of real-world scenarios. Let's explore some advanced use cases for tuples:

Coordinating Coordinates

Tuples excel at representing coordinates, making them an ideal choice for applications involving points in space. For instance, a 2D point can be elegantly defined as a tuple of two **f64** values, representing the x and y coordinates:

Listing 4.32 Tuple's usage in computation.

```
fn main() {
    let point: (f64, f64) = (3.0, 4.0); // ①

    // Calculate distance from the origin
    let distance = (point.0.powi(2) + point.1.powi(2)).sqrt();
    println!("Distance from the origin: {}", distance);
}

// Output

// Distance from the origin: 5
```

① Here, we create a **point** tuple representing a 2D coordinate. We then calculate the distance of this point from the origin using the Pythagorean theorem.

Tuples' ability to combine different types of data into a single, structured unit makes them invaluable for organizing and managing complex data in various scientific, engineering, and geographic applications. This versatility extends to other domains, where tuples prove useful for representing compound data structures with ease and clarity.

Error Handling with Result Tuples

Tuples play a valuable role in Rust's error handling paradigm by facilitating the return of multiple values from functions, enabling more informative and structured error messages. Consider this real-world example involving error handling:

Listing 4.33 Tuple's usage in error handling example.

```
fn divide_with_remainder(dividend: i32, divisor: i32) -> Result<(i32, i32), String> {
    if divisor == 0 {
        return Err("Division by zero".to_string());
    }

    let quotient = dividend / divisor;
    let remainder = dividend % divisor;

    Ok((quotient, remainder))
}
```

In this code snippet, we define a function `divide_with_remainder` that takes two integers, `dividend` and `divisor`. It returns a `Result` tuple containing the quotient and remainder if the division is successful or an error message as a `String` if division by zero is attempted.

By returning a `Result` tuple, we provide a clear and structured way to handle both successful outcomes and potential errors. This approach enhances the safety and reliability of Rust code, ensuring that errors are handled gracefully and providing precise information about the nature of the error when they occur. Tuples, in this context, serve as a concise and effective means of bundling multiple values, making Rust's error handling robust and user-friendly.

Tuple Limitations

While tuples are versatile and useful in many scenarios, they have limitations. Unlike arrays or collections, tuples have a fixed size, which means you cannot dynamically add or remove elements from a tuple once it's created. If your data structure requires dynamic sizing, you should consider using other Rust data types like vectors, or collections such as Vec.

Additionally, when dealing with larger, more complex data structures, tuples might become less ergonomic than custom structs or enums with named fields.

Tuples in Pattern Matching

Pattern matching in Rust is a powerful feature that allows you to destructure and match against the contents of tuples. This is especially useful when you want to extract values from tuples based on certain conditions. Let's explore some advanced tuple pattern-matching techniques.

Matching Tuples with Patterns

When using pattern matching with tuples, you can create patterns that match specific tuple structures. Consider the following example:

Listing 4.34 Tuple's with pattern matching example.

```
fn main() {
    let coordinates = (3, 4);

    match coordinates {
        (0, 0) => println!("The point is at the origin."),
        (x, 0) => println!("The point is on the x-axis at x = {}.", x),
        (0, y) => println!("The point is on the y-axis at y = {}.", y),
        (x, y) => println!("The point is at coordinates ({}, {}).", x,
y),
    }
}

// Output

// The point is at coordinates (3, 4).
```

In this code snippet, we create a `coordinates` tuple representing a 2D point. We then use pattern matching to categorize the point's location based on its coordinates.

In the `match` expression, we have four patterns that check various cases. The first pattern matches when both `x` and `y` are 0, indicating that the point is at the origin. The subsequent patterns check if either `x` or `y` is 0, indicating points on the x-axis or y-axis, respectively. The final pattern captures all other cases and prints the general coordinates.

Ignoring Tuple Elements

In certain situations, you may want to match against a tuple but deliberately ignore one or more of its elements. Rust provides a convenient mechanism for this by using the underscore (_) to indicate that specific elements should be ignored during pattern matching. Here's an illustrative example:

Listing 4.35 Ignoring tuple's elements example.

```
fn main() {
    let student = ("Alice", 25, "Computer Science");

    match student {
        (name, _, major) => println!("{} is a student majoring in {}.",
name, major),
    }
}

// Output

// Alice is a student majoring in Computer Science.
```

In this code, we create a **student** tuple with three elements: **name**, **age**, and **major**. However, for the purpose of our match statement, we are only interested in the **name** and **major** elements. To effectively ignore the **age** element during the pattern matching, we use the underscore _. This allows us to focus on and extract the relevant data elements, enhancing the readability and expressiveness of the code.

Ignoring tuple elements with the underscore is a useful feature when you need to work with specific parts of a tuple while disregarding others, making your Rust code more concise and aligned with your program's logic.

Nested Tuples and Patterns

Tuples can also be nested within other tuples, creating complex data structures. Pattern matching can be used to navigate and destructure these nested tuples. Consider this example:

Listing 4.36 Nested tuples and pattern matching example.

```
fn main() {
    let person = (("Alice", "Bob"), 30);

    match person {
        ((first_name, last_name), age) => {
            println!("Name: {} {}", first_name, last_name);
            println!("Age: {}", age);
        },
```

```
    }
}

// Output

// Name: Alice Bob
// Age: 30
```

In this code, we create a `person` tuple that contains another tuple representing a person's name and a separate age value. We use nested patterns to extract and print these values.

The outer pattern `((first_name, last_name), age)` matches the structure of the person tuple, allowing us to access the nested values directly.

Refutability of Tuple Patterns

Understanding the refutability of tuple patterns in Rust is crucial for writing robust and error-free code. A pattern is considered refutable if there exist input values for which it will not match, potentially leading to a pattern-matching failure. On the other hand, an irrefutable pattern is one that will match any input value, making it always successful.

For example, consider the patterns `(0, 0)` and `(x, 0)`. The pattern `(0, 0)` is refutable because it will only match when both elements of the tuple are exactly 0. If the input tuple doesn't meet this precise condition, the pattern will fail to match. In contrast, the pattern `(x, 0)` is irrefutable because it will match any tuple with a second element of 0, regardless of the value of the first element.

Understanding the refutability of patterns is an essential aspect of writing robust and error-free Rust code. It ensures that your pattern-matching logic is exhaustive and covers all possible input scenarios, enhancing the reliability and safety of your programs.

Tuple Ownership and Borrowing

In Rust, ownership and borrowing rules also apply to tuples. When you assign a tuple to another variable or pass it to a function, Rust enforces ownership and borrowing rules just like it does with other data types. Let's explore some ownership and borrowing scenarios with tuples.

Tuple Ownership

In Rust, when you assign one variable to another, and that assignment involves types that implement the **Copy** trait (like integers and tuples of Copy types), the value is copied, and you can still use the original variable. However, when you assign a non-Copy type (like a tuple containing non-Copy types), ownership is transferred, and you can't use the original variable afterward. For instance:

Listing 4.37 Attempting to use the original tuple will cause a compilation error.

```
fn main() {
    let original_tuple = (String::from("Hello"), String::from("World"));
// ①
    let new_tuple = original_tuple; // ②

    // println!("{:?}", original_tuple); // Uncommenting this line results
in an error
}
```

① We create an **original_tuple** containing two elements.

② We assign **original_tuple** to a new variable **new_tuple**. This move operation transfers ownership to **new_tuple**, making **original_tuple** unusable. Uncommenting the line attempting to use **original_tuple** will result in a compilation error.

Borrowing Tuples

In Rust, you have the flexibility to borrow a reference to a tuple without taking ownership of it. This borrowing mechanism allows you to access the elements of the tuple without moving it, enabling safe and efficient data sharing. Here's an example to illustrate this concept:

Listing 4.38 Tuples and borrowing example.

```
fn print_coordinates(coordinates: &(i32, i32)) { // ①
    println!("Coordinates: {:?}", coordinates);
}

fn main() {
    let point = (5, 7); // ②

    // Borrowing a reference to the point tuple
    print_coordinates(&point); // ③

    // Point tuple remains usable
    println!("Point coordinates: {:?}", point); // ④
}
```

```
// Output

// Coordinates: (5, 7)
// Point coordinates: (5, 7)
```

① We define a function **print_coordinates** that takes a reference to a tuple as an argument.

② We create a **point** tuple representing coordinates.

③ We call the **print_coordinates** function, passing a reference to the **point** tuple. This allows us to print the coordinates without taking ownership of the tuple.

④ The point tuple remains usable after borrowing its reference, demonstrating that ownership is not transferred.

This showcases Rust's ability to allow multiple functions and parts of your program to work with data concurrently without transferring ownership, ensuring safety and control over your program's state.

Tuple Slicing and the Spread Operator

Rust introduces a powerful feature called tuple slicing, which enables you to work with subsets of a tuple's elements efficiently. This is made possible through the use of the spread operator (..). Let's delve into this feature:

Creating Tuple Slices

Tuple slicing empowers you to generate a new tuple containing a selected subset of elements from an existing tuple. You indicate the range of elements you wish to include in the slice using the spread operator (..). Here's an illustrative example:

Listing 4.39 Creating tuple slices example.

```
fn main() {
    let numbers = (1, 2, 3, 4, 5); // ①

    // Creating a tuple slice with elements 2, 3, and 4
    let slice = numbers.1..numbers.4; // ②

    println!("{:?}", slice);
}
```

```
// Output

// 2..5
```

① We define a **numbers** tuple containing five elements.

② Using tuple slicing, we create a new tuple **slice** that includes elements 2, 3, and 4 from the **numbers** tuple. The range **numbers.1..numbers.4** specifies the index range for the slice.

Tuple slicing with the spread operator is a handy feature that simplifies the process of working with a subset of elements from a tuple. It provides a clear and concise way to create new tuples tailored to your specific needs, enhancing code readability and maintainability.

Accessing Tuple Slices

After creating a tuple slice, you can access its elements by referencing the **start** and **end** properties, which represent the boundaries of the range. Elements within the tuple slice are retrieved using these properties. Here's an example:

Listing 4.40 Accessing tuple slices example.

```
fn main() {
    let numbers = (1, 2, 3, 4, 5); // ①

    // Creating a tuple slice with elements 2, 3, and 4
    let slice = numbers.1..numbers.4;

    // Accessing elements of the tuple slice
    let first_element = slice.start; // ②
    let last_element = slice.end; // ③

    println!("First Element: {}", first_element);
    println!("Last Element: {}", last_element);
}

// Output

// First Element: 2
// Last Element: 5
```

① We define a **numbers** tuple containing five elements.

② We access the first element of the tuple slice using **slice.start**.

③ We access the last element of the tuple slice using **slice.end**.

With the use of tuple slicing and accessing elements through **start** and **end** properties, one can achieve accurate management over a particular range of items. This technique proves to be highly advantageous when handling extensive datasets or concentrating on specific subparts within tuples. It enables efficient data manipulation and processing without any hassle.

Tuple as Function Arguments and Return Values

Tuples are often used as function arguments and return values in Rust. They provide a convenient way to pass multiple values to functions or return multiple values from functions. Let's explore these scenarios:

Using Tuples as Function Arguments

In Rust, you can define functions that accept tuples as arguments, providing a convenient way to pass multiple values as a single argument. This approach enhances code conciseness and readability. Here's an example:

Listing 4.41 Using tuples as function arguments example.

```
fn print_person_info(person: (&str, i32, &str)) { // ①
    let (name, age, occupation) = person;
    println!("Name: {}", name);
    println!("Age: {}", age);
    println!("Occupation: {}", occupation);
}

fn main() {
    let alice_info = ("Alice", 30, "Software Engineer"); // ②

    // Calling the function with a tuple argument
    print_person_info(alice_info); // ③
}

// Output

// Name: Alice
// Age: 30
// Occupation: Software Engineer
```

① We define a function **print_person_info** that takes a tuple as its argument, representing a person's information.

② We create an **alice_info** tuple containing the name, age, and occupation of a person.

③ We call the **print_person_info** function with the **alice_info** tuple as an argument, allowing us to pass multiple values conveniently.

Using tuples as function arguments simplifies parameter lists, reduces the need for custom data structures, and enhances code readability. It is especially beneficial when functions need to receive and work with related pieces of data.

Returning Tuples from Functions

In Rust, functions can return tuples as their result, allowing you to convey multiple values as a single return value. This approach provides a neat and structured way to return related pieces of data from a function. Here's an example:

Listing 4.42 Returning tuples from functions example.

```
fn get_person_info(id: u32) -> (&'static str, i32, &'static str) { // ①
    match id {
        1 => ("Alice", 30, "Software Engineer"),
        2 => ("Bob", 28, "Data Scientist"),
        _ => ("Unknown", 0, "N/A"),
    }
}

fn main() {
    let alice = get_person_info(1); // ②

    println!("Name: {}", alice.0);
    println!("Age: {}", alice.1);
    println!("Occupation: {}", alice.2);
}

// Output

// Name: Alice
// Age: 30
// Occupation: Software Engineer
```

① We define a function **get_person_info** that takes an **id** as its argument and returns a tuple representing a person's information.

② We call the **get_person_info** function with an **id** and receive the result as a tuple. We then access and print the individual elements of the tuple.

Returning tuples from functions is an elegant and concise way to provide multiple pieces of information to the caller. It helps maintain code clarity and readability by grouping related data together within a single return value.

Tuple Variants in Enums

Tuples can also be used in Rust enums to define variant data structures. Enum variants can contain tuples, allowing you to represent different states or values associated with each variant. Let's explore this concept:

Creating Enum Variants with Tuples

In Rust, you can define enum variants that include tuples to represent various states or data associated with each variant. This approach allows you to create versatile and expressive enums. Here's an example:

Listing 4.43 Creating enum variants with tuples example.

```
enum Shape { // ①
    Circle(f64),
    Rectangle(f64, f64),
    Triangle(f64, f64, f64),
}

fn main() {
    let circle = Shape::Circle(5.0); // ②
    let rectangle = Shape::Rectangle(4.0, 6.0); // ③
    let triangle = Shape::Triangle(3.0, 4.0, 5.0); // ④

    // Pattern matching to extract values from enum variants
    match circle {
        Shape::Circle(radius) => println!("Circle with radius: {}",
radius),
        _ => (),
    }

    match rectangle {
        Shape::Rectangle(length, width) => println!("Rectangle with
length {} and width {}", length, width),
        _ => (),
    }
```

```
    match triangle {
        Shape::Triangle(a, b, c) => println!("Triangle with sides {},
{}, and {}", a, b, c),
        _ => (),
    }
}

// Output

// Circle with radius: 5
// Rectangle with length 4 and width 6
// Triangle with sides 3, 4, and 5
```

① We define an enum **Shape** with three variants: **Circle**, **Rectangle**, and **Triangle**. Each variant contains a tuple with different numbers of elements to represent different shapes.

② We create an instance of the **Shape** enum with the **Circle** variant, providing a radius value as the tuple element.

③ We create an instance of the **Shape** enum with the **Rectangle** variant, specifying length and width as tuple elements.

④ We create an instance of the **Shape** enum with the **Triangle** variant, indicating the lengths of the triangle's sides as tuple elements.

By utilizing pattern matching, we can extract values from every enum variant and manage the data connected with each shape. Through this method, complex states or data structures within an enum are represented in a straightforward manner.

The utilization of tuples when creating enum variants enhances code clarity while also giving you the ability to effectively model various data scenarios. This feature is incredibly valuable for defining custom data types that encapsulate different possibilities.

These are advanced topics related to tuples in Rust, showcasing their flexibility and utility in various scenarios. Understanding how to use tuples effectively in different contexts can greatly enhance your Rust programming skills.

Slices

In the following section, we will explore Rust slices, a fundamental concept that plays a crucial role in working with collections and arrays in Rust. Slices provide a way to reference a contiguous sequence of elements, allowing you to perform operations on portions of data without copying or transferring ownership. We will cover the basics of slices, how to create them, and various operations you can perform with slices. Additionally, we will delve into the practical applications and use cases of slices in Rust.

Understanding Slices

A **slice** in Rust is a reference to a contiguous sequence of elements in a collection, such as an array, vector, or string. Unlike owning data structures, slices do not have ownership of the data they reference. Instead, they provide a borrowed view of the underlying data. This makes slices a powerful tool for efficiently working with portions of data without the overhead of copying.

Slices in Rust come in two main flavors: `&[T]` and `&mut [T]`. The `[T]` notation signifies that these slices can contain elements of type `T`. `&[T]` represents an immutable reference to a slice, allowing you to read its elements but prohibiting modifications. This is useful for ensuring data integrity and safe concurrent access. On the other hand, `&mut [T]` is a mutable reference to a slice, granting both read and write access to its elements. This mutability is vital for in-place modifications, making it a powerful tool for tasks like sorting and data transformation. These slice types embody Rust's commitment to safety and control, preventing common programming errors and ensuring efficient and reliable code.

Rust slices have the following three components:

- **Pointer to the First Element:** Every slice in Rust includes a pointer to the first element of the slice. This pointer indicates the starting point for operations within the slice, enabling efficient access to its elements. It is crucial for determining the memory location of the slice's data.
- **Length:** The length of a slice represents the number of elements it contains. This information is crucial for iterating through the slice and ensuring that you stay within the bounds of the data. Rust's strict boundary checking, facilitated by the length component, helps prevent common programming errors like buffer overflows.
- **Capacity:** While slices do not own their data, they are bound by the capacity of the original data structure from which they were derived, such as an array or a vector. The capacity indicates the maximum number of elements that the slice can hold without requiring reallocation. Understanding the capacity is essential for optimizing memory usage and avoiding unnecessary memory allocations.

Let's explore how to create and work with slices in Rust.

Creating Slices

Creating slices in Rust is a fundamental operation that enables you to work with specific portions of data efficiently. Depending on the data structure you're dealing with, there are various methods for creating slices. In the provided examples:

Listing 4.44 Slices initialization examples.

```
// Creating a slice from an array
let arr: [i32; 5] = [1, 2, 3, 4, 5];
let slice_arr: &[i32] = &arr[1..4]; // ①

// Creating a slice from a vector
let vec: Vec<i32> = vec![1, 2, 3, 4, 5];
let slice_vec: &[i32] = &vec[1..4]; // ②

// Creating a slice from a string
let text: &str = "Hello, Rust!";
let slice_text: &str = &text[0..5]; // ③
```

① We create a slice **`slice_arr`** from an array **`arr`**, including elements from index 1 to 3 (inclusive on the lower bound, exclusive on the upper bound).

② We create a slice **`slice_vec`** from a vector **`vec`** using the same range notation.

③ We create a slice **`slice_text`** from a string **`text`**, including characters from index 0 to 4.

These examples demonstrate the versatility of Rust slices, which provide a lightweight and efficient means of working with data subsets without the overhead of copying. Whether you're dealing with arrays, vectors, or strings, mastering the creation of slices is essential for effective data manipulation in Rust.

Accessing Slice Elements

Once you have a slice, you can access its elements just like you would with an array or vector. Slices support indexing and iteration.

Listing 4.45 Accessing slice's elements examples.

```
fn main() {
    let data: [i32; 5] = [10, 20, 30, 40, 50];
    let slice: &[i32] = &data[1..4];

    // Accessing elements by index
    let second_element = slice[0]; // ①
    let third_element = slice[1];
    let fourth_element = slice[2];

    // Iterating through the slice
    for element in slice.iter() { // ②
        println!("Element: {}", element);
    }
}

// Output

// Element: 20
// Element: 30
// Element: 40
```

① We access the elements of the **slice** by index, just like with an array.

② We can also iterate through the elements of the **slice** using a for loop and the **iter** method.

Modifying Slice Elements

Mutable slices (`&mut [T]`) are a powerful feature in Rust that enables you to modify the elements they reference. Unlike immutable slices, which provide read-only access, mutable slices grant you the ability to change, add, or remove elements within the slice. This capability is particularly valuable when you need to perform in-place modifications on data structures like arrays or vectors. Let's explore the following example:

Whether you're working with arrays, vectors, or other data structures, mutable slices enable in-place modifications, making them a crucial tool for data manipulation tasks. They allow you to efficiently update data without the need for copying, which is not only performant but also helps maintain memory safety by adhering to Rust's ownership and borrowing rules.

Listing 4.46 Modifying slice elements examples.

```
fn modify_data(data: &mut Vec<i32>) {
    let slice = &mut data[1..4];
    // Modifying elements
    slice[0] = 99; // ①

    // Simulating adding elements
    let new_elements = [60];
    data.insert(4, new_elements[0]); // ②

    // Simulating removing elements
    let _removed_element = data.remove(4); // ③
}

fn main() {
    let mut data: Vec<i32> = vec![10, 20, 30, 40, 50];
    modify_data(&mut data);

    // Print the data vector
    println!("Data Vector:");
    for element in &data {
        println!("{}", element);
    }

    // Print the slice
    let slice = &mut data[1..4];
    println!("Slice:");
    for element in slice.iter() {
        println!("{}", element);
    }
}

// Output

// Data Vector:
// 10
// 99
// 30
// 40
// 50
// Slice:
// 99
// 30
// 40
```

① We modify the first element of the mutable **slice**.

② We add an element to the end of the mutable **slice**, effectively resizing it.

③ We remove the last element from the mutable **slice** and capture its value in `removed_element`.

Whether you're sorting elements, updating values, or dynamically resizing a collection, mutable slices empower you to manipulate data efficiently and safely, thanks to Rust's ownership and borrowing system, which ensures that no data races or memory issues arise during these modifications. Understanding how to work with mutable slices is the key to writing high-performance and reliable Rust code, especially when dealing with algorithms or data processing tasks that require dynamic changes to the underlying data.

Real-World Applications

Slices are a versatile tool in Rust, and they find numerous real-world applications across different domains. Here are some common scenarios where slices are valuable:

String Manipulation

String manipulation tasks often require working with substrings of larger text. Slices, with their ability to reference portions of strings without copying data, prove invaluable in these scenarios. Common use cases for slices in string manipulation include extracting file extensions, parsing log lines to extract specific data, or processing various segments of a URL. In the provided code example, we demonstrate how to extract a file extension from a filename using slices.

Listing 4.47 String manipulation using slices example.

```
fn main() {
    let filename = "example.txt";
    let extension: &str = &filename[filename.len() - 3..]; // ①
    println!("File extension: {}", extension);
}

// Output

// File extension: txt
```

① In this code snippet, we extract the file extension from a filename by creating a slice that includes the last three characters of the string.

In Rust, mastering the use of slices for string manipulation tasks is crucial for writing clean, efficient, and maintainable code when dealing with text-based data. Slices empower developers to handle complex string operations with precision while benefiting from the language's ownership and borrowing system to manage memory and resources effectively.

Data Processing

Slices play a pivotal role in data processing tasks, allowing developers to efficiently manipulate and transform specific segments of data. In data-oriented operations such as filtering, mapping, or aggregating elements, slices prove indispensable for their ability to provide a concise view of a subset without the need for data duplication. This enhances performance and memory efficiency while simplifying code logic.

Listing 4.48 Data processing using slices example.

```
fn calculate_average(slice: &[f64]) -> f64 {
    let sum: f64 = slice.iter().sum();
    sum / slice.len() as f64
}

fn main() {
    let data: [f64; 6] = [2.5, 3.0, 1.5, 4.0, 2.0, 3.5];
    let slice: &[f64] = &data[1..5];
    let average = calculate_average(slice);
    println!("Average: {:.2}", average);
}

// Output

// Average: 2.62
```

The provided code example illustrates how slices can be leveraged in a data processing scenario to calculate the average of a subset of floating-point numbers. By referencing a portion of the original data array, we eliminate the overhead of copying unnecessary elements. Slices enable us to streamline the computation by summing the elements in the slice and dividing by its length, ultimately resulting in a clear and efficient calculation. Rust's support for slices greatly facilitates data manipulation, making it an ideal choice for tasks involving structured data processing.

Text Tokenization

Text tokenization, a fundamental operation in natural language processing and text analysis, becomes notably simplified and efficient with the use of slices in Rust. By employing slices, you can conveniently divide text into its constituent units, such as words, sentences, or paragraphs, based on specific delimiters or patterns.

Listing 4.49 Text tokenization using slices example.

```
fn tokenize_sentence(sentence: &str) -> Vec<&str> {
    sentence.split_whitespace().collect()
}

fn main() {
    let text: &str = "Rust is a systems programming language.";
    let words = tokenize_sentence(text);
    println!("Words: {:?}", words);
}

// Output

// Words: ["Rust", "is", "a", "systems", "programming", "language."]
```

In the provided code example, we showcase how to tokenize a sentence into individual words. Leveraging Rust's slice capabilities, we use the `split_whitespace` method to break the sentence into words based on whitespace characters. This results in a vector of string slices, which provides an organized and manageable representation of the text data. Such techniques are pivotal in numerous text processing tasks, including text classification, sentiment analysis, and information retrieval, where understanding the structure of text is paramount.

Binary Data Handling

Binary data handling is another domain where slices prove invaluable in Rust. Parsing binary data formats, such as file headers or network packets, often requires a fine-grained approach to access specific segments of the data. In such cases, slices come to the forefront as a mechanism for referencing portions of the binary data efficiently.

Listing 4.50 Binary data handling using slices example.

```
fn parse_header(header_data: &[u8]) {
    // Parse the binary header data here
}

fn main() {
    let binary_data: [u8; 16] = [0x48, 0x65, 0x6C, 0x6C, 0x6F, 0x2C,
0x20, 0x52, 0x75, 0x73, 0x74, 0x21, 0x00, 0x00, 0x0A, 0x0D];
    let header_slice: &[u8] = &binary_data[0..8];
    parse_header(header_slice);
}
```

In the provided code example, we illustrate the application of slices in parsing a binary header. By creating a slice of bytes from a larger binary data array, you can efficiently focus on the header section for further processing, such as extracting metadata or verifying data integrity. This approach ensures both performance and accuracy when working with binary data and is essential in applications like file format parsing, network communication, and cryptography, where precision and efficiency are paramount concerns.

Memory Mapping

Memory mapping is an efficient approach for managing substantial files or datasets, utilizing slices to seamlessly integrate portions of these large files into memory. This integration facilitates fast and effective random access to specific segments of the file, significantly enhancing data processing capabilities.

Listing 4.51 Memory mapping using slices example.

```
use std::fs::File;
use std::io::{self, Read};

fn main() -> io::Result<()> {
    // file.txt contains:
    // Hello
    // World
    let mut file = File::open("/path/to/file.txt")?;
    let mut buffer = [0; 1024];

    // Read a portion of the file into a buffer
    let bytes_read = file.read(&mut buffer)?;

    // Process the buffer as a slice
    let slice = &buffer[0..bytes_read];
    println!("Read {} bytes: {:?}", bytes_read, slice);
```

```
    Ok(())
}

// Output

// Read 11 bytes: [72, 101, 108, 108, 111, 10, 87, 111, 114, 108, 100]
```

In the provided code snippet, we extract a segment of a sizable file into a buffer and handle it as a slice. This approach grants us the ability to efficiently access particular segments of the file while it resides in memory.

Slices are a powerful and versatile tool in Rust, enabling efficient and safe data manipulation in various domains. As you continue your Rust journey, understanding and mastering slices will be invaluable in writing high-performance and reliable Rust programs.

Hash Sets in Rust

Hash sets are an influential resource within the `std::collections::HashSet` module in Rust. They serve as an effective means of organizing collections of unique and unordered elements. Comparable to sets in Python, these hash sets will be thoroughly examined in this extensive section. We will delve into the process of constructing, modifying, and executing advanced functions using hash sets in Rust. Furthermore, we will explore some of the practical applications of hash sets.

Creating a Set

Creating a set, specifically a hash set, in Rust is a straightforward process. You first need to import the `HashSet` type from the standard library, as demonstrated. Once that's done, there are several methods to initialize a hash set to suit your needs.

Listing 4.52 Importing the HashSet module.

```
use std::collections::HashSet;
```

You can then create a new empty hash set using the new method:

Listing 4.53 HashSet initialization methods.

```
let mut my_set: HashSet<i32> = HashSet::new(); // ①
```

Alternatively, you can create a hash set from a vector of elements:

```
let my_vector = vec![1, 2, 3, 4];
let my_set: HashSet<i32> = my_vector.into_iter().collect(); // ②
let a = HashSet::from([1, 2, 3]); // ③
```

① Create a new empty hash set of type **i32**.

② Create a hash set from a vector by collecting its elements.

③ Initialize a set from an array.

The code snippet displays how you can start by initiating an empty hash set with the `new` function, specifying the type of elements it will contain. Another option is to fill up the hash set by converting a vector into an iterator and then collecting all of its elements as seen in the second example. This approach comes in handy when handling an already existing collection you want to work with. Lastly, Rust allows direct initialization of sets from arrays as shown in the third example.

For more details on creating hash sets, refer to the official documentation: https://doc.rust-lang.org/std/collections/struct.HashSet.html#method.new

Updating a Set

When coding in Rust, updating a set is an easy process, particularly when dealing with hash sets. Such updates can involve adding elements or modifying and removing them as per your requirements. In this section, we'll focus on the former - that is how to add new items to a hash set.

Adding Elements

Adding elements to a hash set is simple using the `insert` method:

Listing 4.54 HashSet adding elements example.

```
let mut my_set: HashSet<i32> = HashSet::new();
my_set.insert(1); // ①
my_set.insert(2);
my_set.insert(3);
```

① Insert elements into the hash set.

Removing Elements

Removing elements from a hash set is done using the `remove` method:

Listing 4.55 HashSet removing elements example.

```
let mut my_set = HashSet::from([1, 2, 3, 4]);
my_set.remove(&2); ①// Removes element 2 from the set
```

① Remove a specific element from the set.

For more information on updating hash sets, consult the official documentation for `insert` and `remove` methods.

Advanced Set Operations

Rust's hash sets offer advanced set operations that prove valuable when dealing with complex data structures and sets. One such operation is the symmetric difference.

Symmetric Difference

The symmetric difference operation returns elements that are present in one set but not in the other. Let's illustrate this with two sets, `set_x` and `set_y`:

Listing 4.56 HashSet symmetric difference example.

```
use std::collections::HashSet;

let set_x = HashSet::from([1, 2, 3, 4]);
let set_y = HashSet::from([3, 4, 5, 6]);

let symmetric_difference = set_x.symmetric_difference(&set_y);

for element in symmetric_difference {
    println!("{}", element);
}

// Output
// 1
// 2
// 5
// 6
```

The symmetric difference operation is essential for comparing and contrasting sets, helping you determine the dissimilarities between two sets efficiently. This can be particularly useful in scenarios where you need to find differences or overlaps between collections of data.

Subset and Superset Checking

You can check if one set is a subset or superset of another using the **is_subset** and **is_superset** methods, respectively:

Listing 4.57 HashSet subset and superset example.

```
use std::collections::HashSet;

fn main() {
    let set_a = HashSet::from([1, 2, 3]);
    let set_b = HashSet::from([1, 2, 3, 4, 5]);

    let is_subset = set_a.is_subset(&set_b); // ①
    let is_superset = set_b.is_superset(&set_a); // ②

    println!("Is set_a a subset of set_b? {}", is_subset);
    println!("Is set_b a superset of set_a? {}", is_superset);
}

// Output

// Is set_a a subset of set_b? true
// Is set_b a superset of set_a? true
```

① Check if **set_a** is a subset of **set_b**.

② Check if **set_b** is a superset of **set_a**.

For more details on advanced set operations, consult the official documentation: https://doc.rust-lang.org/std/collections/struct.HashSet.html#set-operations

Real-World Applications

Hash sets have a wide range of real-world applications due to their efficient handling of unique elements and set operations, including:

- **Deduplication**: Removing duplicate elements from a collection.

Listing 4.58 HashSet usage for deduplication example.

```
use std::collections::HashSet;

fn main() {
    let duplicates = vec![1, 2, 2, 3, 4, 4, 5];

    let unique_elements: HashSet<i32> = duplicates.into_iter().collect();
```

```
    println!("{:?}", unique_elements);
}

// Output

// {5, 4, 3, 1, 2}
```

In the provided code snippet, we showcase how hash sets can be used for deduplication in Rust. We start with a vector **duplicates** that contains duplicate values. By converting this vector into an iterator and then collecting the elements into a hash set, we effectively eliminate duplicates. The resulting **unique_elements** hash set contains only the distinct values from the original vector, ensuring that each element appears only once.

Deduplication is crucial in scenarios where data integrity and uniqueness are essential, such as maintaining a list of unique user IDs, processing logs to identify distinct events, or ensuring that a dataset contains only unique entries. Hash sets simplify the deduplication process, making it an invaluable tool in various real-world applications.

- **Membership Testing**: Quickly checking if an item exists in a large dataset.

Listing 4.59 HashSet usage for testing membership example.

```
use std::collections::HashSet;

fn main() {
    let large_dataset: HashSet<i32> = (1..10001).collect(); // Create a
set with numbers from 1 to 10,000
    let item_to_find = 42;

    if large_dataset.contains(&item_to_find) {
        println!("Item {} found in the dataset.", item_to_find);
    } else {
        println!("Item {} not found in the dataset.", item_to_find);
    }
}

// Output

// Item 42 found in the dataset.
```

In the provided Rust code snippet, we demonstrate membership testing using a hash set. We create a large dataset containing numbers from 1 to 10,000 using the **collect** method. Then, we specify an item, in this case, **item_to_find**, which we want to check for membership within the dataset.

Through the utilization of the hash set's **contains** method, we can effectively determine the presence of an item within the dataset. The previous example successfully verifies the presence of "Item 42" in the dataset. This form of membership evaluation holds immense significance in various applications, such as searching for values in a database, verifying user access rights, or validating the existence of certain elements in a dataset without the need for extensive iteration. The implementation of hash sets renders these operations fast and practical in real-life scenarios.

- **Caching**: Storing unique results to avoid redundant computations.

Listing 4.60 HashSet usage for caching example.

```
use std::collections::HashSet;

fn expensive_computation(input: i32) -> i32 {
    // Simulating a costly computation
    input * 2
}

let mut cache: HashSet<i32> = HashSet::new();

fn get_or_compute(input: i32) -> i32 {
    if cache.contains(&input) {
        *cache.get(&input).unwrap()
    } else {
        let result = expensive_computation(input);
        cache.insert(input, result);
        result
    }
}
```

In the provided Rust code snippet, we demonstrate a simple caching mechanism using a hash set. The **expensive_computation** function simulates a computationally expensive task, and the **get_or_compute** function checks if the result for a given input is already present in the **cache**. If it is, the function retrieves and returns the cached result. Otherwise, it computes the result, inserts it into the cache, and returns it. This approach effectively saves time and resources by avoiding redundant computations.

Caching is widely used in applications where performance optimization is crucial, such as web servers, database query optimization, or any scenario where repeated computations can be avoided through result storage. Hash sets provide a convenient and efficient means of implementing caching in such applications.

- **Graph Algorithms**: Implementing graph algorithms like breadth-first search (BFS) efficiently.

For graph algorithms, you can use hash sets to keep track of visited nodes or manage sets of nodes efficiently. Here's a code example for implementing the breadth-first search (BFS) algorithm efficiently using hash sets in Rust:

Listing 4.61 HashSet usage for graphs representations example.

```
use std::collections::{HashSet, VecDeque};

// Define a simple graph represented as an adjacency list
struct Graph { // ①
    adjacency_list: Vec<Vec<usize>>,
}

impl Graph {
    fn new(num_nodes: usize) -> Self {
        Self {
            adjacency_list: vec![vec![]; num_nodes],
        }
    }

    fn add_edge(&mut self, u: usize, v: usize) {
        self.adjacency_list[u].push(v);
        self.adjacency_list[v].push(u);
    }

    fn bfs(&self, start_node: usize) -> HashSet<usize> { // ②
        let mut visited = HashSet::new();
        let mut queue = VecDeque::new();

        // Start BFS from the given node
        queue.push_back(start_node);
        visited.insert(start_node);

        while let Some(node) = queue.pop_front() {
            for &neighbor in &self.adjacency_list[node] {
                if !visited.contains(&neighbor) {
                    visited.insert(neighbor);
                    queue.push_back(neighbor);
                }
            }
        }
```

```
        visited
    }
}

fn main() { // ③
    // Create a graph
    let mut graph = Graph::new(6);

    // Add edges to the graph
    graph.add_edge(0, 1);
    graph.add_edge(0, 2);
    graph.add_edge(1, 3);
    graph.add_edge(1, 4);
    graph.add_edge(2, 5);

    // Perform BFS starting from node 0
    let start_node = 0;
    let visited_nodes = graph.bfs(start_node);

    println!("Nodes visited in BFS starting from node {}: {:?}", start_
node, visited_nodes);
}

// Output

// Nodes visited in BFS starting from node 0: {0, 3, 5, 1, 2, 4}
```

In this code:

① We define a **Graph** struct to represent a simple graph as an adjacency list. The **new** function initializes the graph, and **add_edge** adds edges between nodes.

② The **bfs** method performs a breadth-first search starting from the specified node and returns a hash set containing all visited nodes.

③ In the **main** function, we create a graph, add edges, and then perform BFS starting from node 0. The visited nodes are printed as the result.

This code demonstrates how hash sets can efficiently keep track of visited nodes during graph traversal, making it useful for implementing graph algorithms like BFS.

- **Set Operations**: Hash sets are fundamental when performing set operations like union, intersection, and difference. You can combine two sets to get their union, find common elements using intersection, and determine the difference between sets.

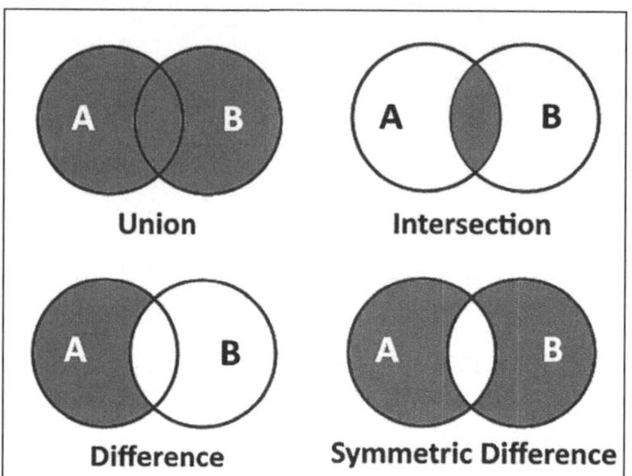

Figure 4.9: *Set operations*

Listing 4.62 HashSet and set operations example.

```
use std::collections::HashSet;

fn main() {
    let set_a: HashSet<i32> = HashSet::from([1, 2, 3, 4, 5]);
    let set_b: HashSet<i32> = HashSet::from([3, 4, 5, 6, 7]);

    let union = set_a.union(&set_b).collect::<HashSet<_>>(); // Union
    let intersection = set_a.intersection(&set_b).col-
lect::<HashSet<_>>(); // Intersection
    let difference = set_a.difference(&set_b).collect::<HashSet<_>>(); //
Difference

    println!("Set A: {:?}", set_a);
    println!("Set B: {:?}", set_b);
    println!("Union: {:?}", union);
    println!("Intersection: {:?}", intersection);
    println!("Difference: {:?}", difference);
}

// Output

// Set A: {4, 2, 1, 3, 5}
// Set B: {5, 3, 6, 7, 4}
// Union: {4, 1, 3, 6, 2, 7, 5}
// Intersection: {4, 3, 5}
// Difference: {2, 1}
```

- **Tagging and Filtering**: Hash sets are handy for tagging and filtering items. You can tag elements with specific attributes or characteristics and filter them based on those attributes.

Listing 4.63 HashSet tagging and filtering usage.

```
use std::collections::{HashSet, hash_map::DefaultHasher};
use std::hash::{Hash, Hasher};

#[derive(Clone, Eq, PartialEq, Debug)]
struct Item {
    id: i32,
    tags: HashSet<String>,
}

impl Hash for Item {
    fn hash<H: Hasher>(&self, state: &mut H) {
        self.id.hash(state);
    }
}

fn main() {
    let mut items = HashSet::new();

    items.insert(Item {
        id: 1,
        tags: ["rust", "programming"]
            .iter()
            .map(|s| s.to_string())
            .collect(),
    });

    items.insert(Item {
        id: 2,
        tags: ["python", "programming"]
            .iter()
            .map(|s| s.to_string())
            .collect(),
    });

    let rust_items: HashSet<_> = items
        .iter()
        .filter(|item| item.tags.contains("rust"))
        .cloned()
        .collect();

    println!("{:?}", rust_items); // Print the filtered items
}
```

```
// Output

// {Item { id: 1, tags: {"programming", "rust"} }}
```

- **Tracking Unique Values**: Hash sets are often used to track unique values in data streams or logs. By inserting values into a hash set and checking for duplicates, you can identify unique events or data points.

Listing 4.64 HashSet for tracking unique values example.

```
use std::collections::HashSet;

fn main() {
    let mut unique_values = HashSet::new();

    // Process a stream of values
    let values = vec![1, 2, 3, 4, 3, 2, 5, 6];

    for value in values {
        if unique_values.insert(value) {
            println!("New unique value: {}", value);
        }
    }
}

// Output

// New unique value: 1
// New unique value: 2
// New unique value: 3
// New unique value: 4
// New unique value: 5
// New unique value: 6
```

These are just a few examples of how hash sets can be applied in real-world scenarios. Their versatility and efficient operations make them a valuable tool in many domains.

Performance Considerations

While hash sets offer great flexibility and performance for many use cases, it's important to understand their characteristics and performance implications.

- **Insertion and Removal**: Hash sets are optimized for fast insertion and removal of elements. The `insert` and `remove` methods typically have O(1) time complexity on average. However, in rare cases, hash collisions can lead to slightly worse performance.

- **Lookup**: Checking for the existence of an element using the `contains` method also has an average time complexity of O(1). This makes hash sets efficient for membership testing.
- **Iterating**: Iterating through a hash set has a time complexity proportional to the number of elements in the set, O(n). If you need to perform operations on all elements, consider iterating through the set using a `for` loop.
- **Memory Usage**: Hash sets consume memory to store the elements and manage hash tables. Be mindful of memory usage, especially if you're dealing with large data sets.

Operation	Time Complexity	Description
Insertion	O(1) (average)	Fast insertion of elements, but rare collisions may occur
Removal	O(1) (average)	Fast removal of elements, with occasional collisions
Lookup	O(1) (average)	Efficient membership testing
Iteration	O(n)	Time increases with the number of elements
Memory Usage	Consumes memory	Memory consumption depends on the number of elements

Table 4.1: *HashSet operations performance analysis*

Concurrency Considerations

When working with hash sets in a concurrent or multi-threaded environment, it's essential to be aware of potential issues related to thread safety. Rust provides mechanisms to ensure safe concurrent access to data structures, including hash sets.

- **Mutexes**: You can wrap a hash set in a mutex (short for mutual exclusion) to allow only one thread to access the set at a time. This ensures thread safety but may introduce some performance overhead.

Listing 4.65 HashSet and mutex example.

```
use std::collections::HashSet;
use std::sync::{Mutex, Arc};
use std::thread;
```

```
fn main() {
    // Create a hash set wrapped in a mutex.
    let my_set = Arc::new(Mutex::new(HashSet::<i32>::new()));

    // Spawn multiple threads to insert elements into the set.
    let num_threads = 4;
    let mut handles = vec![];

    for i in 0..num_threads {
        let set_clone = Arc::clone(&my_set);
        let handle = thread::spawn(move || {
            // Lock the mutex to access the set.
            let mut set = set_clone.lock().unwrap();
            set.insert(i);
            // Mutex is automatically released here when 'set' goes out
of scope.
        });
        handles.push(handle);
    }

    // Wait for all threads to finish.
    for handle in handles {
        handle.join().unwrap();
    }

    // Lock the mutex to access and print the contents of the set.
    let set = my_set.lock().unwrap();
    println!("Set contents: {:?}", *set);
}

// Output

// Set contents: {0, 2, 3, 1}
```

In this code:

- We create a hash set `my_set` and wrap it in a `Mutex` to ensure that only one thread can access it at a time.
- We spawn multiple threads, each of which locks the mutex to insert an element into the set.
- After all threads have been completed, we lock the mutex again to safely access and print the contents of the set.

The use of a mutex guarantees that concurrent access to the set is synchronized, ensuring thread safety.

- **Atomic Types**: If you need to share a hash set across multiple threads without the need for locking, you can explore atomic types provided by the `std::sync::atomic` module. However, atomic types are limited to a few specific operations and may not cover all use cases.

Listing 4.66 HashSet and atomic types example.

```
use std::collections::HashSet;
use std::sync::atomic::{AtomicPtr, Ordering};

fn main() {
    // Create an AtomicPtr to store the pointer to the HashSet.
    let my_set = AtomicPtr::new(std::ptr::null_mut());

    // Create a new HashSet and box it.
    let new_set = Box::into_raw(Box::new(HashSet::<i32>::new()));

    // Atomically store the pointer to the new set.
    my_set.store(new_set, Ordering::Relaxed);

    // Access the HashSet using the AtomicPtr.
    let set_ptr = my_set.load(Ordering::Relaxed);

    if !set_ptr.is_null() {
        let set_ref: &mut HashSet<i32> = unsafe { &mut *set_ptr };

        // Perform operations on the HashSet.
        set_ref.insert(42);
        set_ref.insert(100);

        // Print the HashSet contents.
        for elem in set_ref.iter() {
            println!("Element: {}", elem);
        }
    } else {
        println!("HashSet pointer is null.");
    }

    // Clean up the HashSet.
    if !set_ptr.is_null() {
        // Convert the pointer back to a Box and deallocate it.
        let _boxed_set: Box<HashSet<i32>> = unsafe { Box::from_raw(set_
ptr) };
    }
}
```

```
// Output

// Element: 42
// Element: 100
```

In this example:

- We create an `AtomicPtr` named `my_set` to store the pointer to the `HashSet`.
- We create a new `HashSet`, box it, and store its pointer in the `my_set` using `store` with `Ordering::Relaxed`.
- We then access the `HashSet` using the `AtomicPtr` and perform operations on it.
- Finally, we deallocate the `HashSet` by converting the pointer back to a `Box` when we're done with it.

The given example showcases the fundamental application of atomic types in handling shared data without the involvement of multiple threads. In real-world scenarios, atomic types prove to be exceptionally beneficial when numerous threads necessitate simultaneous access and modification of the data.

Serialization and Deserialization

Hash sets in Rust can be easily serialized and deserialized using libraries like `serde`. Serialization allows you to convert a hash set into a format that can be stored or transmitted, such as JSON or binary. Deserialization is the process of reconstructing a hash set from its serialized form.

Here's a basic example of how to serialize and deserialize a hash set:

Listing 4.67 Serialization and deserialization example.

```
use serde::{Serialize, Deserialize};
use std::collections::HashSet;
use std::fs::File;
use std::io::{Read, Write};

// Define a struct to hold the hash set
#[derive(Serialize, Deserialize)]
struct MyData {
    my_set: HashSet<i32>,
}

fn main() -> Result<(), Box<dyn std::error::Error>> {
    // Create a hash set
    let mut my_set = HashSet::new();
```

```
    my_set.insert(1);
    my_set.insert(2);
    my_set.insert(3);

    // Serialize the hash set to a JSON file
    let data = MyData { my_set };
    let serialized = serde_json::to_string(&data)?;
    let mut file = File::create("my_set.json")?;
    file.write_all(serialized.as_bytes())?;

    // Deserialize the hash set from the JSON file
    let mut file = File::open("my_set.json")?;
    let mut contents = String::new();
    file.read_to_string(&mut contents)?;
    let deserialized: MyData = serde_json::from_str(&contents)?;

    println!("{:?}", deserialized.my_set);

    Ok(())
}

// Output

// {1, 2, 3}
```

In this example, we define a custom struct called `MyData` encompassing a hash set. By employing the `serde` library, we enable the struct to be serialized and deserialized, facilitating the storage and retrieval of the hash set from a JSON file.

Benchmarks and Optimization

Optimizing the performance of your code involving hash sets often requires benchmarking and profiling. Rust provides the `criterion` and `profiler` crates to help you measure and analyze the performance of your code.

To get started with benchmarking using `criterion`, add it to your `Cargo.toml`:

Listing 4.68 criterion project cargo.toml file configuration.

```
[dev-dependencies]
criterion = "0.5.1"

[[bench]]
name = "my_benchmark"
harness = false
```

Here's a simple example of how to write a benchmark for hash set operations:

Listing 4.69 criterion benchmark example.

```
// Create a file at the root of your project: ./benches/my_benchmark.rs
use criterion::{black_box, criterion_group, criterion_main, Criterion};
use std::collections::HashSet;

fn insert_benchmark(c: &mut Criterion) {
    c.bench_function("HashSet Insertion", |b| {
        let mut set = HashSet::new();
        b.iter(|| {
            set.insert(black_box(42));
        });
    });
}

criterion_group!(benches, insert_benchmark);
criterion_main!(benches);


// $ cargo bench
// Output

// HashSet Insertion       time:   [25.812 ns 25.819 ns 25.826 ns]
// Found 8 outliers among 100 measurements (8.00%)
//   4 (4.00%) high mild
//   4 (4.00%) high severe
```

In this benchmark, we measure the insertion performance of a hash set. You can customize the benchmark to test other operations as well.

To profile your Rust code, you can use tools like `perf`, `flamegraph`, or `valgrind`. Profiling helps identify performance bottlenecks and areas that may need optimization.

Rust's hash sets are a robust type of data structure that enables you to efficiently handle collections of unique elements. Whether your task is removing duplicates, performing set operations, or monitoring unique values - the flexibility and performance offered by hash sets will prove invaluable.

As you continue to explore Rust and its standard library, you'll find hash sets to be a valuable addition to your toolkit. Be sure to refer to the *official documentation* for more details and advanced usage.

By mastering hash sets and understanding their applications, you can write more efficient and elegant Rust code for a wide range of tasks.

Hash Maps

Hash Maps are a type of collection that consists of key-value pairs and offer quick and effective access to data by utilizing keys instead of indexing.

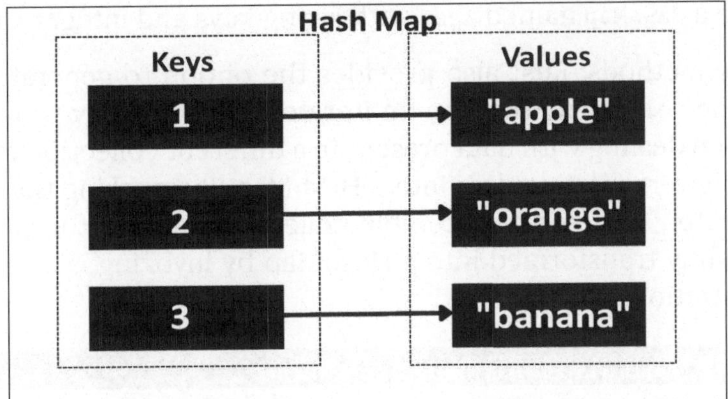

Figure 4.10: *Hash Map simple representation*

Rust declares Hash Maps through the `std::collections::HashMap` module, an unordered structure with remarkable speed. Let's look at how to create, update, access, and iterate over Hash Maps in Rust.

Creating a Hash Map

You can initialize a Hash Map in Rust in several ways. One common method is by using the `new` method of the `HashMap` struct:

Listing 4.70 Hash Map initialization example.

```
use std::collections::HashMap;

let mut scores = HashMap::new(); // ①
```

① We create an empty `HashMap` named `scores`.

Another way to initialize a `HashMap` is by using the `HashMap::from` method:

Listing 4.71 Hash Map initialization example.

```
use std::collections::HashMap;

let ages = HashMap::from([ // ①
    ("Alice", 30),
    ("Bob", 28),
]);
```

① We create a **HashMap** named **ages** with string keys and integer values.

Besides these methods, Rust also provides the option to generate a HashMap by utilizing the `collect` method on an iterator. This strategy proves especially beneficial when dealing with data present in a different collection or when there is a need to convert existing data into a HashMap. By invoking the `iter` method on a slice, vector, or any other iterable collection, an iterator can be created and subsequently transformed into a HashMap by invoking `collect()`. Here's a practical illustration:

Listing 4.72 Hash Map initialization example.

```
use std::collections::HashMap;

let data = vec![("Carol", 25), ("David", 32)]; // ①
let name_age_map: HashMap<_, _> = data.iter().cloned().collect(); // ②
```

In this example:

① We first define a vector **data** containing tuples of names and ages.

② We then create a HashMap **name_age_map** by cloning the elements of the iterator produced by `data.iter()`. The `collect` method takes care of transforming the iterator into a HashMap.

This method of initializing a HashMap can be especially useful when you need to convert data from one data structure into a HashMap for efficient lookups and operations.

Updating a Hash Map

It is imperative to grasp the concept of updating Hash Maps while working with them in order for your program to run smoothly. A HashMap can perform a multitude of operations, including but not limited to adding and removing elements as well as modifying values linked with pre-existing keys. This flexibility renders Hash Maps a versatile alternative when dealing with data management in many Rust applications.

Adding Elements

You can use the `insert` method to add elements (key-value pairs) to a Hash Map. For example:

Listing 4.73 Adding elements to a hash map example.

```
use std::collections::HashMap;

let mut scores = HashMap::new();

scores.insert("Alice", 42); // ①
scores.insert("Bob", 73); // ②
```

① We insert a key-value pair **"Alice"** with a score of **42** into the **scores** Hash Map.

② We insert another key-value pair **"Bob"** with a score of **73** into the **scores** Hash Map.

Adding elements to a HashMap is a crucial operation when building data structures and managing data in Rust. Whether you're populating a HashMap with initial data or dynamically updating it as your program runs, the **insert** method provides a flexible and efficient way to work with key-value pairs in Rust's HashMaps.

Removing Elements

You can use the `remove` method to remove an element (key-value pair) from a Hash Map. For example:

Listing 4.74 Removing elements from a hash map example.

```
use std::collections::HashMap;

fn main() {
    let mut scores = HashMap::new();

    scores.insert("Alice", 42);
    scores.insert("Bob", 73);

    scores.remove("Alice"); // ①
    println!("Hash Map contents: {:?}", scores);
}
```

```
// Output

// Hash Map contents: {"Bob": 73}
```

① We remove the key-value pair with the key **"Alice"** from the **scores** Hash Map.

The act of removing elements from a HashMap is crucial for effectively handling data and maintaining accurate information within your application. The ability to selectively delete entries according to their keys guarantees that your HashMap remains up-to-date and relevant to your program's requirements.

Updating an Element

You can update elements of a Hash Map by using the **insert** method. For example:

Listing 4.75 Updating elements inside a hash map example.

```
use std::collections::HashMap;

fn main() {
    let mut scores = HashMap::new();

    scores.insert("Alice", 42); // ①
    scores.insert("Alice", 55); // ②
    println!("Hash Map contents: {:?}", scores);
}

// Output

// Hash Map contents: {"Alice": 55}
```

① We insert a key-value pair **"Alice"** with a score of **42** into the **scores** Hash Map.

② We update the value of the element with key **"Alice"** to **55**.

Updating elements in a HashMap is a powerful feature when you need to keep your data up-to-date and modify values as your program's logic dictates. The ability to easily update values associated with specific keys makes HashMaps a versatile data structure for various Rust applications.

Accessing Values

You can use the **get** method to access a value from a given Hash Map in Rust. For example:

Listing 4.76 Accessing elements from a hash map example.

```
use std::collections::HashMap;

fn main() {
    let scores = HashMap::from([ // ①
        ("Alice", 42),
        ("Bob", 73),
    ]);

    let alice_score = scores.get("Alice").unwrap(); // ②
    println!("Alice score: {:?}", alice_score);
}

// Output

// Hash Map contents: 42
```

① We create a **HashMap** named **scores** with string keys and integer values.

② We use the **get** method to retrieve the score associated with the key **"Alice"**.

Using the **get** method to access values in a HashMap is a common operation when you need to retrieve and work with specific data based on keys. It provides a safe way to access values while handling potential absence gracefully.

Iterating over Hash Maps

Iterating over the key-value pairs of a Hash Map is a common operation. You can do this using a **for** loop:

Listing 4.77 Iterating over a hash map's elements using a for loop example.

```
use std::collections::HashMap;

fn main() {
    let scores = HashMap::from([
        ("Alice", 42),
        ("Bob", 73),
    ]);

    for (name, score) in &scores { // ①
        println!("{}: {}", name, score);
    }
}
```

```
// Output

// Alice: 42
// Bob: 73
```

① We iterate through the key-value pairs of the `scores` Hash Map using a `for` loop method and print each name and score.

You can also iterate over the keys or values individually using the `keys` and `values` methods:

Listing 4.78 Iterating over a hash map's keys and values using a for loop example.

```
use std::collections::HashMap;

fn main() {
    let scores = HashMap::from([
        ("Alice", 42),
        ("Bob", 73),
    ]);

    for name in scores.keys() { // ①
        println!("Name: {}", name);
    }

    for score in scores.values() { // ②
        println!("Score: {}", score);
    }
}

// Output

// Name: Alice
// Name: Bob
// Score: 42
// Score: 73
```

① We iterate through the keys of the `scores` Hash Map and print each name.

② We iterate through the values of the `scores` Hash Map and print each score.

Advanced Hash Map Operations

Rust's `std::collections::HashMap` provides a rich set of methods and operations for advanced use cases. In this section, we'll explore some of these operations and how they can be applied in practice.

Checking for Key Existence

You can check if a key exists in a Hash Map using the **contains_key** method. This is helpful when you need to determine whether a specific key is present before accessing its associated value.

Listing 4.79 Checking for key existence in a hash map using the contains_key method.

```
use std::collections::HashMap;

fn main() {
    let scores = HashMap::from([
        ("Alice", 42),
        ("Bob", 73),
    ]);

    let name = "Alice";

    if scores.contains_key(name) { // ①
        println!("{}'s score is: {}", name, scores[name]);
    } else {
        println!("{} is not found.", name);
    }
}

// Output

// Alice's score is: 42
```

① We use the **contains_key** method to check if the key **"Alice"** exists in the **scores** Hash Map before accessing its value.

Entry API

The **entry** API provides a way to efficiently modify an existing value in a Hash Map or insert a new key-value pair if it doesn't exist. This is useful to avoid double lookups when both inserting and updating values.

Listing 4.80 Checking for key existence in a hash map using the entry api example.

```
use std::collections::HashMap;

fn main() {
```

```
    let mut scores = HashMap::new();

    scores.insert("Alice", 42);

    let name = "Alice";
    let new_score = 10;

    scores
        .entry(name)
        .and_modify(|score| *score += new_score) // ①
        .or_insert(new_score); // ②

    println!("{}'s updated score is: {}", name, scores[name]);
}

// Output

// Alice's updated score is: 52
```

① We use the `entry` API to efficiently update the score of `"Alice"` in the `scores` Hash Map. If the key doesn't exist, we insert a new key-value pair with the provided value.

② We use the `or_insert` method to insert a new key-value pair if the key doesn't exist.

Clearing a Hash Map

To remove all key-value pairs from a Hash Map and clear its contents, you can use the `clear` method:

Listing 4.81 Clearing a hash map example.

```
use std::collections::HashMap;

fn main() {
    let mut scores = HashMap::new();

    scores.insert("Alice", 42);
    scores.insert("Bob", 73);

    scores.clear(); // ①

    if scores.is_empty() { // ②
        println!("The Hash Map is empty.");
    }
}
```

```
// Output

// The Hash Map is empty.
```

① We use the **clear** method to remove all entries, resulting in an empty Hash Map.

② We check if the Hash Map is empty using the **is_empty** method and print a message accordingly.

Hash Map Capacity

Hash Maps in Rust have a capacity that determines how many elements they can hold before needing to resize. You can check the current capacity and the number of elements in a Hash Map using the **capacity** and **len** methods.

Listing 4.82 Hash map capacity example.

```
use std::collections::HashMap;

fn main() {
    let mut scores = HashMap::new();

    scores.insert("Alice", 42);
    scores.insert("Bob", 73);

    let current_capacity = scores.capacity(); // ①
    let number_of_entries = scores.len(); // ②

    println!("Current Capacity: {}", current_capacity);
    println!("Number of Entries: {}", number_of_entries);
}

// Output

// Current Capacity: 3
// Number of Entries: 2
```

① We use the **capacity** method to get the current capacity of the **scores** Hash Map.

② We use the **len** method to get the number of entries in the **scores** Hash Map.

Real-World Applications

Hash Maps find applications in various real-world scenarios, including:

Counting Occurrences

Hash Maps are useful for counting the occurrences of items in a collection. You can iterate through a collection, use a Hash Map to keep track of counts, and efficiently determine the frequency of each item.

Listing 4.83 Hash map for counting occurrences example.

```
use std::collections::HashMap;

fn main() {
    let mut word_counts = HashMap::new();

    let text = "Lorem ipsum dolor sit amet consectetur ipsum";
    for word in text.split_whitespace() {
        let count = word_counts.entry(word).or_insert(0);
        *count += 1;
    }

    println!("{:?}", word_counts);
}

// Output

// {"sit": 1, "ipsum": 2, "Lorem": 1, "amet": 1, "consectetur": 1,
"dolor": 1}
```

In this example, we count the occurrences of words in a text by splitting it into words and using a Hash Map to store the counts. The `entry` API is used to efficiently update counts or insert new words.

Memoization

In dynamic programming, you can use Hash Maps to store and retrieve previously computed results, reducing redundant computations and improving performance.

Listing 4.84 Hash map for memoization example.

```
use std::collections::HashMap;

fn fibonacci_memoization(n: u64, memo: &mut HashMap<u64, u64>) -> u64 {
    if let Some(&result) = memo.get(&n) {
        return result;
    }

    let result = match n {
        0 => 0,
        1 => 1,
        _ => fibonacci_memoization(n - 1, memo) + fibonacci_memoization(n
- 2, memo),
    };

    memo.insert(n, result);
    result
}

fn main() {
    let mut memo = HashMap::new();
    let n = 20;

    let result = fibonacci_memoization(n, &mut memo);

    println!("Fibonacci({}) = {}", n, result);
}

// Output

// Fibonacci(20) = 6765
```

In this example, we use a Hash Map (`memo`) to store the results of Fibonacci numbers to avoid redundant calculations.

Caching

Hash Maps are employed in caching to store and retrieve values efficiently. Frequently used or expensive calculations can be cached in a Hash Map to avoid recomputation.

Listing 4.85 Hash map for caching example.

```
use std::collections::HashMap;

fn expensive_calculation(input: u32) -> u32 {
```

```
    // Simulate a time-consuming calculation
    input * 2
}

fn main() {
    let mut cache = HashMap::new();
    let input = 42;

    let result = cache.entry(input).or_insert_with(|| expensive_
calculation(input));

    println!("Result: {}", result);
}

// Output

// Result: 84
```

In this example, we use a Hash Map (`cache`) to store the results of an expensive calculation, and we compute the result only if it's not already cached.

Configuration Management

Hash Maps are utilized to manage configuration settings in applications. Key-value pairs in a Hash Map can represent configuration parameters, making it easy to access and update settings.

Listing 4.86 Hash map for configuration management example.

```
use std::collections::HashMap;

fn main() {
    let mut config = HashMap::new();

    config.insert("api_key", "your_api_key");
    config.insert("port", "8080");
    config.insert("debug_mode", "true");

    let api_key = config.get("api_key").map(|s| s.to_string()).unwrap_or_
default();
    let port = config.get("port").map(|s| s.to_string()).unwrap_or_
default();
    let debug_mode = config.get("debug_mode").map(|s| s.to_string()).
unwrap_or_default();
```

```
    println!("API Key: {}", api_key);
    println!("Port: {}", port);
    println!("Debug Mode: {}", debug_mode);
}

// Output

// API Key: your_api_key
// Port: 8080
// Debug Mode: true
```

In this example, we use a Hash Map to manage configuration settings for an application.

Data Transformation

When converting data from one format to another, Hash Maps are valuable for storing mappings between old and new values. This aids in efficient data transformation.

Listing 4.87 Hash map for data transformation.

```
use std::collections::HashMap;

fn main() {
    let mut conversion_table = HashMap::new();

    conversion_table.insert("USD", "US Dollar");
    conversion_table.insert("EUR", "Euro");
    conversion_table.insert("JPY", "Japanese Yen");

    let input_currency = "USD";
    let output_currency = conversion_table.get(input_currency).unwrap_
or(&"Unknown");

    println!("Currency Conversion: {} => {}", input_currency, output_
currency);
}

// Output

// Currency Conversion: USD => US Dollar
```

In this example, we use a Hash Map to represent a currency conversion table.

Grouping Data

Hash Maps can be used to group data based on specific criteria. For example, you can group a list of people by their age using a Hash Map with age as the key and a list of people as the value.

Listing 4.88 Hash map for grouping data example.

```
use std::collections::HashMap;

fn main() {
    let mut people_by_age = HashMap::new();

    let people = vec![
        ("Alice", 25),
        ("Bob", 30),
        ("Charlie", 25),
        ("David", 35),
    ];

    for (name, age) in people {
        people_by_age
            .entry(age)
            .or_insert_with(Vec::new)
            .push(name);
    }

    println!("{:?}", people_by_age);
}

// Output

// {25: ["Alice", "Charlie"], 30: ["Bob"], 35: ["David"]}
```

In this example, we use a Hash Map to group people by their age.

Graph Algorithms

Hash Maps are a crucial component in graph algorithms. They are used to represent graphs efficiently, with nodes as keys and their associated information as values.

Listing 4.89 Hash map for graph algorithms example.

```
use std::collections::HashMap;

fn main() {
    let mut graph = HashMap::new();

    // Define a directed graph
    graph.insert("A", vec!["B", "C"]);
    graph.insert("B", vec!["C", "D"]);
    graph.insert("C", vec!["D"]);
    graph.insert("D", vec![]);

    println!("{:?}", graph);
}

// Output

// {"D": [], "C": ["D"], "B": ["C", "D"], "A": ["B", "C"]}
```

In this example, we use a Hash Map to represent a directed graph.

Database Indexing

In database systems, Hash Maps are used for indexing data, allowing for fast retrieval of records based on key attributes.

Listing 4.90 Hash map for database indexing example.

```
use std::collections::HashMap;

fn main() {
    let mut database_index = HashMap::new();

    // Indexing user records by username
    let users = vec![
        ("alice", "Alice Johnson"),
        ("bob", "Bob Smith"),
        ("charlie", "Charlie Brown"),
    ];

    for (username, user_info) in users {
        database_index.insert(username, user_info);
    }

    let username_to_lookup = "bob";
    if let Some(user_info) = database_index.get(username_to_lookup) {
```

```
        println!("User Info for {}: {}", username_to_lookup, user_info);
    } else {
        println!("User not found: {}", username_to_lookup);
    }
}

// Output

// User Info for bob: Bob Smith
```

In this example, we use a Hash Map to index user records by their usernames in a simplified database scenario.

Hash Maps in Rust are a robust data structure that facilitates the effective management and arrangement of data through key-value pairs. They offer fast access to data and are frequently used for tasks like counting occurrences, memoization, caching, configuration management, data transformation, grouping data, graph algorithms, and database indexing.

Thanks to Rust's integrated Hash Map implementation and its extensive array of techniques, utilizing Hash Maps is an effortless process devoid of complications. Armed with this knowledge, you will be empowered to craft Rust code that is efficient and highly effective in achieving your desired outcomes.

As you continue your Rust journey, Hash Maps will undoubtedly be a valuable addition to your toolkit, enabling you to tackle a wide range of real-world problems.

Conclusion

Throughout this all-encompassing chapter, you have embarked on a remarkable journey through the diverse world of Rust's collections and data structures. You've explored in depth the complexities associated with arrays, vectors, slices, tuples, hash maps, as well as hash sets - acquiring valuable knowledge on how to proficiently generate them while also efficiently manipulating and utilizing these powerful tools.

You started by exploring arrays and their fixed sizes, understanding their strengths in representing data with a known and constant length. You uncovered the power of vectors, Rust's dynamic arrays, which provide flexibility and growable storage, making them invaluable for managing collections of varying sizes. Tuples, with their ability to combine heterogeneous data types into a single entity, have added a unique dimension to your data representation toolkit.

You have delved into the concept of Rust slices, which is a crucial concept that enables you to manipulate contiguous sequences of elements within a collection without ownership. You've gained knowledge on how to create slices from arrays, vectors, and strings, along with understanding how to access, modify, and traverse through slice elements. Furthermore, you've explored practical applications in various domains like string manipulation tasks, processing data, tokenizing text, handling binary information effectively, as well as incorporating concurrency measures while memory mapping tasks are performed.

Moving forward, you ventured into the realm of hash maps and hash sets, mastering the art of key-value data storage and efficient element management. You learned to insert, remove, and update elements while also gaining insights into advanced set operations. Real-world applications of these data structures showcased their significance in diverse scenarios, from counting occurrences to graph algorithms.

As you continue your Rust programming journey, remember that a deep understanding of these fundamental collections and data structures is paramount. They are the building blocks of many algorithms and applications, enabling you to craft efficient, reliable, and robust code. Armed with this knowledge, you are well-prepared to tackle complex challenges and create elegant solutions in Rust.

The next chapter delves into the crucial topic of error management in Rust, primarily through the utilization of Result and Option types. It explores the techniques for effectively handling errors and propagating them throughout Rust programs, ensuring robust error management practices. Additionally, the chapter delves into the creation of custom error types, allowing you to craft more informative and descriptive error messages, thereby enhancing the debugging and troubleshooting processes. By mastering error handling and propagation techniques, you can significantly improve the reliability and resilience of your applications in the face of unexpected issues.

Additional Resources

For further exploration and learning related to Hash Sets, Hash Maps, Vectors, Arrays, and Tuples in Rust, consider the following resources:

- ***The Ultimate Ndarray Handbook: Mastering the Art of Scientific Computing with Rust*** - An overview of different Rust's built-in data structures and a deep dive into the Ndarray library. - *https://towardsdatascience.com/the-ultimate-ndarray-handbook-mastering-the-art-of-scientific-computing-with-rust-ef5ab767212a*

- **Rust Standard Library Documentation - std::collections** - Official documentation for Rust's standard library collections, including Hash Sets and Hash Maps. - *https://doc.rust-lang.org/std/collections/index.html*
- **Rust By Example - Std Library types** - A hands-on guide with examples on using Rust collections, including Vectors and HashMaps. - *https://doc.rust-lang.org/rust-by-example/std.html*
- **Rust Collections - The Rust Programming Language** - Chapter from "The Rust Programming Language" book that covers collections such as Vectors, Arrays, Hash Sets, and Hash Maps. - *https://doc.rust-lang.org/book/ch08-00-common-collections.html*
- **Rust Playground** - An online Rust editor and playground to experiment with code snippets. *https://play.rust-lang.org/*
- **Rust Community Forum** - A community forum where you can ask questions and discuss Rust-related topics. - *https://users.rust-lang.org/*
- **Official Rust Community** - Explore various Rust community resources, including forums, newsletters, and working groups. - *https://www.rust-lang.org/community*
- **The Rust Programming Language Book** - The official book for learning Rust, with chapters on collections and data structures. - *https://doc.rust-lang.org/book/ch08-00-common-collections.html*
- **Rustlings - Small Exercises in Rust** - A collection of small exercises to practice Rust concepts, including collections. - *https://github.com/rust-lang/rustlings*
- **Awesome Rust - A Curated List of Rust Code and Resources** - A curated list of Rust libraries, tools, and learning resources. - *https://github.com/rust-unofficial/awesome-rust*
- **Rust Design Patterns** - A collection of design patterns for Rust, including data structure patterns. - *https://github.com/rust-unofficial/patterns*
- **Rust API Guidelines** - Official guidelines for writing Rust APIs, including data structures. - *https://rust-lang.github.io/api-guidelines*
- **Rust for Systems Programmers** - A resource for C/C++ programmers transitioning to Rust, covering Rust's data structures. - *https://github.com/nrc/r4cppp*
- **Rust Memory Management** - Understanding Rust's ownership model, which applies to data structures. - *https://doc.rust-lang.org/book/ch04-00-understanding-ownership.html*
- **Serde - Serialization Framework** - A widely-used serialization framework for Rust, applicable to data structures. - *https://serde.rs*

- `Rust Documentation Search` - Easily search and access Rust documentation for standard library modules. - *https://doc.rust-lang.org/std/index.html*
- `Rust for Game Development` - Explore Rust libraries and resources for game development, including data structures. - *https://arewegameyet.rs*
- `The Rust Community's Discord` - Join the Rust community on Discord for discussions and real-time help. - *https://discord.gg/rust-lang*
- `Rust on Reddit` - The Rust subreddit for news, questions, and discussions. - *https://www.reddit.com/r/rust/*

These resources provide a comprehensive understanding of Hash Sets, Hash Maps, Vectors, Arrays, and Tuples in Rust and offer valuable insights and examples.

Multiple Choice Questions

Q1: What is the primary purpose of traits in Rust?

a) To define data structures

b) To provide default implementations for functions

c) To define shared behaviors that types can implement

d) To restrict access to data

Q2: Which of the following data structures in Rust is fixed in size and contains elements of identical data types?

a) Vectors

b) Tuples

c) Slices

d) Arrays

Q3: In Rust, how do you access an element within an array?

a) Using the `get` method

b) Using a for loop

c) Using indexing with square brackets

d) Using the `pop` method

Q4: Which method allows you to add elements to the end of a vector in Rust?

a) `push`

b) `get`

c) `remove`

d) `pop`

Q5: What is the benefit of using the `enumerate` method when iterating through a vector in Rust?

a) It allows you to obtain both the index and the value of each element.

b) It automatically sorts the vector.

c) It removes the last element from the vector.

d) It reverses the order of elements in the vector.

Q6: Which method allows you to remove and retrieve the last element from a vector in Rust?

a) `push`

b) `get`

c) `remove`

d) `pop`

Q7: What happens if you attempt to access an element in a Rust array using an index that is out of bounds?

a) It returns `None`.

b) It panics at runtime.

c) It compiles with a warning.

d) It returns a default value.

Q8: Which data structure in Rust is like a window that allows you to see a part of a container without opening it?

a) Arrays

b) Tuples

c) Slices

d) Vectors

Q9: What does the `iter_mut` method allow you to do when iterating through a vector in Rust?

a) It allows you to retrieve both the index and the value of each element.

b) It allows you to add elements to the vector.

c) It allows you to obtain mutable references to elements for in-place modification.

d) It allows you to remove elements from the vector.

Q10: Which of the following is a benefit of using Rust's arrays over vectors?

a) Rust arrays can dynamically resize.

b) Rust arrays allow elements of different data types.

c) Rust arrays have a fixed size and contain elements of identical data types.

d) Rust arrays can be easily sorted in-place.

Q11: What is a tuple in Rust?

a) A collection of elements of varying types.

b) A data structure used for error handling.

c) A fixed-size array.

d) A collection of elements of the same type.

Q12: Which of the following statements about tuples is true?

a) Tuples can only contain elements of the same type.

b) Tuples can dynamically resize.

c) Tuples have a fixed size and contain elements of identical data types.

d) Tuples can be easily sorted in-place.

Q13: How do you access elements within a tuple in Rust?

a) Using a for loop.

b) By directly indexing the elements.

c) By converting the tuple to a vector.

d) By using a match expression.

Q14: What is the purpose of tuple destructuring in Rust?

a) To create a new tuple.

b) To extract individual elements and assign them to variables.

c) To convert a tuple into a vector.

d) To check if a tuple is empty.

Q15: Which of the following is an example of a tuple pattern in Rust?

a) (1, "hello", true)

b) [1, 2, 3]

c) {name: "Alice", age: 30}

d) "Rust is great!"

Q16: What is the primary use of tuples in representing coordinates?

a) Storing elements of varying types.

b) Enabling dynamic sizing of data.

c) Representing points in space.

d) Facilitating error handling.

Q17: What is the role of tuples in Rust's error handling paradigm?

a) Tuples enable dynamic sizing of data.

b) Tuples provide a concise way to define custom data types.

c) Tuples allow returning multiple values from functions for structured error messages.

d) Tuples are used for sorting elements in Rust.

Q18: What are the limitations of tuples in Rust?

a) Tuples can dynamically resize.

b) Tuples are not suitable for representing compound data structures.

c) Tuples have a fixed size and cannot have elements of varying data types.

d) Tuples are not used in pattern matching.

Q19: What is an irrefutable pattern in Rust?

a) A pattern that always matches any input value.

b) A pattern that may fail to match for certain input values.

c) A pattern used exclusively for tuple matching.

d) A pattern that only matches empty tuples.

Q20: What is the primary benefit of using Rust's arrays over vectors?

a) Rust arrays can dynamically resize.

b) Rust arrays allow elements of different data types.

c) Rust arrays have a fixed size and contain elements of identical data types.

d) Rust arrays can be easily sorted in-place.

Q21: What is one of the real-world applications of hash sets in Rust?

a) Sorting elements in an array.

b) Extracting substrings from a string.

c) Caching results to avoid redundant computations.

d) Tokenizing sentences in natural language processing.

Q22: Which hash set operation helps find elements present in one set but not in another?

a) Union

b) Intersection

c) Difference

d) Subset

Q23: In Rust, how can you efficiently check if an item exists in a large dataset using a hash set?

a) Use a loop to iterate through all elements in the dataset.

b) Utilize the `contains` method of the hash set.

c) Convert the dataset into a vector and search for the item.

d) Apply the `filter` function to the dataset.

Q24: What does the symmetric difference operation of hash sets return?

a) Common elements between two sets.

b) Elements present in both sets.

c) Elements present in one set but not in the other.

d) The union of two sets.

Q25: What is the primary purpose of using hash sets in deduplication tasks?

a) To create additional copies of elements.

b) To perform complex mathematical operations.

c) To efficiently remove duplicate elements.

d) To sort elements in ascending order.

Q26: Which of the following is NOT a real-world application of hash sets in Rust?

a) Membership testing in a large dataset.

b) Implementing graph algorithms like BFS.

c) Sorting elements in an array.

d) Performing set operations like union and intersection.

Q27: In Rust, what data structure is commonly used for efficient graph traversal when implementing algorithms like BFS?

a) Hash tables

b) Linked lists

c) Arrays

d) Hash sets

Q28: Which hash set method can be used to compute the union of two sets?

a) `add`

b) `subtract`

c) `union`

d) `intersect`

Q29: What is the primary benefit of using hash sets for membership testing in Rust?

a) Hash sets guarantee a specific order of elements.

b) Membership testing with hash sets is slower than using arrays.

c) Hash sets provide fast and practical membership evaluation.

d) Hash sets can only store elements of the same data type.

Q30: In the context of hash sets, what does the term "deduplication" refer to?

a) The process of adding duplicate elements to a set.

b) The process of performing mathematical operations on sets.

c) The process of efficiently removing duplicate elements from a collection.

d) The process of sorting elements in descending order.

Answers

1. c) To define shared behaviors that types can implement.
2. d) Arrays
3. c) Using indexing with square brackets
4. a) push
5. a) It allows you to obtain both the index and the value of each element.
6. d) pop

7. b) It panics at runtime.
8. c) Slices
9. c) It allows you to obtain mutable references to elements for in-place modification.
10. c) Rust arrays have a fixed size and contain elements of identical data types.
11. a) A collection of elements of varying types.
12. c) Tuples have a fixed size and contain elements of identical data types.
13. b) By directly indexing the elements.
14. b) To extract individual elements and assign them to variables.
15. a) (1, "hello", true)
16. c) Representing points in space.
17. c) Tuples allow returning multiple values from functions for structured error messages.
18. c) Tuples have a fixed size and cannot have elements of varying data types.
19. a) A pattern that always matches any input value.
20. c) Rust arrays have a fixed size and contain elements of identical data types.
21. c) Caching results to avoid redundant computations.
22. c) Difference
23. b) Utilize the contains method of the hash set.
24. c) Elements present in one set but not in the other.
25. c) To efficiently remove duplicate elements.
26. c) Sorting elements in an array.
27. d) Hash sets.
28. c) union
29. c) Hash sets provide fast and practical membership evaluation.
30. c) The process of efficiently removing duplicate elements from a collection.

CHAPTER 5
Error Handling and Recovery

Introduction

Error handling is an essential aspect of programming that ensures the reliability and robustness of your software. In this chapter, we are going to explore the complex world of error handling and recovery, equipping you with the knowledge and techniques necessary to become a proficient Rust developer in handling various error scenarios.

This chapter will introduce you to Rust's error-handling capabilities, with a primary focus on its powerful tools: the `Result` and `Option` types. You'll learn how to harness the expressive nature of these types to effectively handle errors in your code. Whether it's dealing with potential failures in file operations, network communication, or any other aspect of your Rust applications, understanding and mastering `Result` and `Option` is crucial.

But that's not all; we won't stop at the basics. This chapter will delve deeper into advanced error-handling strategies, teaching you how to propagate errors gracefully through your codebase, and making sure that error information is passed efficiently between functions and modules. You'll discover techniques to handle multiple error scenarios, allowing your programs to gracefully adapt to unexpected situations.

Furthermore, we will explore the creation of custom error types. Custom errors provide you with the ability to inject more context into error messages, making it easier to diagnose and fix issues when they arise. You'll see how to design error types that encapsulate specific details about the nature and source of errors, enhancing the clarity and utility of your error reports.

This chapter is your comprehensive guide to error handling in Rust. Whether you're just starting your Rust journey or looking to sharpen your error-handling skills, you'll find valuable insights and practical knowledge that will empower you to write more reliable and maintainable Rust code. So, let's dive in and unravel the complexities of effective error handling in Rust together.

Structure

In this chapter, we're going to explore:

- Dealing with errors using Result and Option in Rust
- Techniques for error propagation and handling multiple errors
- Creating custom error types to enhance error messages

Handling Errors using `Result` and `Option`

Dealing with errors using Result and Option in Rust is a fundamental aspect of programming that requires a comprehensive grasp of these two core types and their pivotal roles in shaping the landscape of error handling within the Rust programming language. Result and Option serve as the cornerstone of Rust's approach to managing errors, and a profound understanding of their complexities is crucial for writing reliable and maintainable Rust code.

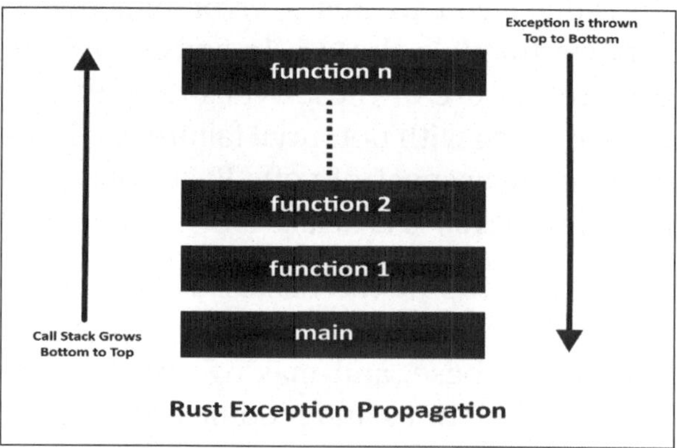

Figure 5.1: *Rust exception propagation*

Understanding `Result` and `Option`

In Rust, errors are managed primarily through two enum types: **`Result`** and **`Option`**. Let's start by gaining a clear understanding of these types and their roles in error handling.

Listing 5.1 Basic Result and Option usage example.

```
fn main() {
    let result: Result<i32, &str> = Ok(42); // ①
    let option: Option<i32> = Some(42); // ②
}
```

① In this example, we create a `Result` called `result` representing a successful result with the value `42`.

② Similarly, we create an `Option` called `option`, also holding the value `42`.

`Result`, as the name suggests, represents the result of an operation that can either be successful, denoted by the `Ok` variant, or unsuccessful, indicated by the `Err` variant. This duality encapsulates the essence of Rust's error-handling philosophy, where errors are explicitly and safely handled, leaving no room for unchecked exceptions. Learning how to utilize Result effectively empowers you to gracefully handle success and address failures in your code, leading to more robust and resilient applications.

`Option`, on the other hand, introduces the concept of optional values. It is often used when a function may return a value or nothing at all, eliminating the need for null or undefined values commonly found in other programming languages (for example, JavaScript). Understanding Option allows you to express the possibility of the absence or presence of a value explicitly, mitigating the risk of null pointer errors and making code more predictable and safer, as explained in *Chapter 1: Systems Programming with Rust.*

These two types, `Result` and `Option`, are not just syntactic constructs but represent Rust's commitment to memory safety and error prevention. They guide you towards writing code that is free from common pitfalls, such as null pointer dereferences and unchecked exceptions, which are often the source of software vulnerabilities and instability. Therefore, mastering `Result` and `Option` is not merely a matter of syntax but a fundamental shift in mindset towards writing code that is both reliable and efficient.

Handling Errors with `Result`

Handling Errors with `Result` in Rust is a pivotal aspect of writing robust and reliable code. The `Result` type is primarily employed when an operation has the potential to fail, and you need a structured and graceful way to propagate and manage errors throughout your codebase.

In the following code example, we illustrate a common pattern for utilizing the **Result** type. Here, a function named **divide** is defined to perform division between two integers, **a** and **b**. Within this function, error handling is orchestrated with precision:

Listing 5.2 Error handling with Result.

```
fn divide(a: i32, b: i32) -> Result<i32, String> {
    if b === 0 {
        return Err(format!("Cannot divide {} by zero.", a)); // ①
    }

    Ok(a / b) // ②
}
```

① When the divisor (**b**) is zero, the function promptly returns an **Err** variant with a descriptive error message, unequivocally indicating that division by zero is not permitted. We use **format!** to create a custom error message.

② If the divisor is non-zero, the function returns an **Ok** variant containing the result of the division, encapsulating the successful outcome.

This structured approach to error handling allows us to encapsulate errors with meaningful context and propagate them up through the call stack efficiently.

The use of **Result** is further exemplified in the **main** function:

Listing 5.3 Basic method invocation with error handling.

```
fn main() {
    let result = divide(10, 2); // ①

    match result {
        Ok(value) => println!("Result: {}", value),
        Err(error) => eprintln!("Error: {}", error), // ②
    }
}

// Output

// Result: 5
```

① We invoke the **divide** function with the arguments 10 and 2, resulting in a successful division and an **Ok** variant stored in the **result** variable.

② Subsequently, we employ a **match** statement to pattern match on the **Result**, enabling us to respond accordingly. If the result is **Ok**, we print the computed value; otherwise, if it's an **Err**, we print the error message.

This pattern demonstrates not only the structured use of **Result** but also the importance of providing clear error messages and handling errors gracefully, enhancing code maintainability and reliability in Rust programs.

Handling Errors with Option

When it comes to optional configuration values or verifying an item's presence in a collection, the **Option** type is frequently employed. This type allows for situations where there may be no value present at all.

Listing 5.4 Basic error handling with Option.

```
fn find_element(arr: &[i32], target: i32) -> Option<usize> {
    for (i, &element) in arr.iter().enumerate() {
        if element === target {
            return Some(i); // ①
        }
    }

    None // ②
}

fn main() {
    let numbers = [1, 2, 3, 4, 5];
    let target = 3;

    match find_element(&numbers, target) {
        Some(index) => println!("Found at index: {}", index),
        None => println!("Element not found."),
    }
}

// Output

// Found at index: 2
```

① If the target element is found, we return **Some** with the index.

② If the target element is not found, we return **None**.

Utilizing **Result** and **Option** for error handling lays a solid foundation for managing both errors and optional values. This utilization allows the creation of code that is more predictable and reliable.

But there's much more we can learn about how Rust handles errors. In the following sections, we'll take an in-depth look at these concepts with additional coding examples as well as advanced techniques for managing exceptions.

Error Propagation

When working on larger projects or complex systems, it is common to come across scenarios where multiple operations may fail, and it becomes necessary to handle these errors effectively. Rust offers mechanisms for error propagation and graceful handling of multiple errors.

The ? Operator

The **?** operator in Rust, often referred to as the "**try**" operator, is a powerful tool that significantly simplifies error propagation and handling. It is designed to streamline the process of returning early from a function when an error occurs and automatically propagate the error up the call stack. This operator plays a pivotal role in enhancing the readability and maintainability of your code, especially when dealing with functions that return **Result** or **Option** types.

In the following code example, the utilization of the **?** operator is illustrated as follows:

Listing 5.5 File I/O with error handling example using Result.

```
use std::fs::File;
use std::io::Read;

fn read_file_contents(file_path: &str) -> Result<String, std::io::Error> {
    let mut file = File::open(file_path)?; // ①
    let mut contents = String::new();
    file.read_to_string(&mut contents)?; // ②
    Ok(contents)
}

fn main() -> Result<(), Box<dyn std::error::Error>> {
    let file_path = "example.txt";
    let contents = read_file_contents(file_path)?; // ③
    println!("File contents: {}", contents);
    Ok(())
```

```
}

// Output if the file doesn't exist

// Error: Os { code: 2, kind: NotFound, message: "No such file or
directory" }
```

① The `?` operator is used when attempting to open the file **file_path** with **File::open**. If an error occurs, such as the file not being found, the error is automatically returned, and the function **read_file_contents** will exit early, propagating the error back to the caller.

② Similarly, the **?** operator is employed when reading the contents of the file into the **contents** variable using **file.read_to_string**. If any errors occur during the read operation, they are propagated up the call stack.

③ In the **main** function, the **?** operator is also utilized when invoking **read_file_contents**. This allows any errors encountered during the file read or open operations to be immediately returned from the **main** function itself, ensuring that error handling is concise and effective.

The **?** operator can be used with custom error types. By implementing the **From** trait, you can convert errors from one type into another, allowing for easy error transformation. In this example, we use **Box<dyn std::error::Error>** as the error type, allowing us to handle various error types uniformly.

The **?** operator thus serves as a mechanism for automatically and efficiently dealing with errors, reducing the need for manual error handling code and making the codebase more readable and maintainable. It is particularly valuable when working with functions that return **Result** or **Option**, as it elegantly handles the complexities of error propagation in Rust.

Handling Multiple Errors with Result

Rust's **Result** type can be used effectively to handle multiple errors. You can use combinators like **map**, **and_then**, and **or_else** to chain multiple operations and handle errors at each step.

Listing 5.6 Handling multiple errors with Result.

```
use std::num::ParseIntError;

#[derive(Debug)]
enum CustomError {
    ParsingError(ParseIntError),
```

```
    SquaringError,
}

fn parse_and_square(input: &str) -> Result<i32, CustomError> {
    let number = input.parse::<i32>().map_err(CustomError::ParsingError)?;
    if number <= 0 {
        return Err(CustomError::SquaringError);
    }
    let squared = number * number;
    Ok(squared)
}

fn main() -> Result<(), CustomError> {
    let input = "a";

    let result = parse_and_square(input)
        .and_then(|squared| {
            if squared < 100 {
                Ok(squared)
            } else {
                Err(CustomError::SquaringError)
            }
        })
        .map_err(|err| {
            eprintln!("An error occurred: {:?}", err);
            err
        })?;

    println!("Result: {}", result);
    Ok(())
}

// Output

// An error occurred: ParsingError(ParseIntError { kind: InvalidDigit })
// Error: ParsingError(ParseIntError { kind: InvalidDigit })
```

In this example, we parse a string into an integer, square it, and return the result. If any operation fails, the error is propagated up the call stack. These techniques allow you to handle multiple errors gracefully and maintain clean and readable code.

Error Propagation with `Result` and `Option`

Rust's error handling features are extremely versatile and can be combined in numerous ways to effectively manage complex error scenarios. By leveraging the power of **Result** and **Option**, you can achieve highly composable error handling techniques.

Listing 5.7 Error Propagation with Result and Option.

```
fn find_element(arr: &[i32], target: i32) -> Option<usize> {
    arr.iter().position(|&x| x === target)
}

fn divide(dividend: i32, divisor: i32) -> Result<i32, String> {
    if divisor === 0 {
        Err("Division by zero".to_string())
    } else {
        Ok(dividend / divisor)
    }
}

fn find_and_divide(arr: &[i32], target: i32, divisor: i32) -> Result<f64,
String> {
    let index = find_element(arr, target)
        .ok_or_else(|| "Element not found.".to_string())?; // ①

    let result = divide(arr[index], divisor)?;

    Ok(result as f64)
}

fn main() {
    let numbers = [1, 2, 3, 4, 5];
    let target = 3;
    let divisor = 2;

    match find_and_divide(&numbers, target, divisor) {
        Ok(result) => println!("Result: {}", result),
        Err(error) => eprintln!("Error: {}", error),
    }
}

// Output

// Result: 1
```

① We use **ok_or_else** to convert an **Option** into a **Result** with a custom error message.

This example demonstrates how to locate an item in an array, divide it, and provide the answer as a floating-point value. If any step fails, we propagate the error to the caller.

If you want to enhance your Rust programming skills, it is essential to grasp the art of effectively propagating and managing errors. Luckily, there are numerous proven methods at your disposal to accomplish just that. From error handling patterns to advanced strategies for dealing with multiple errors, Rust provides a plenty of tools to help you minimize errors in your code.

Creating Custom Error Types

While Rust provides built-in error types like **`std::io::Error`** and **`std::num::ParseIntError`**, you often need to create custom error types to provide more context and meaningful error messages in your code.

Listing 5.8 Creating custom error types.

```
use std::fs::File;
use std::io::Read;
use std::io::Error as IoError;

#[derive(Debug)]
enum FileReadError {
    FileNotFound,
    IoError(IoError),
}

impl From<IoError> for FileReadError {
    fn from(error: IoError) -> Self {
        if error.kind() === std::io::ErrorKind::NotFound {
            FileReadError::FileNotFound
        } else {
            FileReadError::IoError(error)
        }
    }
}

fn read_file_contents(file_path: &str) -> Result<String, FileReadError> {
    let mut file = File::open(file_path).map_err(FileReadError::from)?;

    let mut contents = String::new();
    file.read_to_string(&mut contents)?;
    Ok(contents)
}
```

```
fn main() -> Result<(), Box<dyn std::error::Error>> {
    let file_path = "nonexistent.txt";
    match read_file_contents(file_path) {
        Ok(contents) => println!("File contents: {}", contents),
        Err(FileReadError::FileNotFound) => eprintln!("File not
found."),
        Err(FileReadError::IoError(e)) => eprintln!("IO Error: {}", e),
    }
    Ok(())
}

// Output

// File not found.
```

In this example, we define a custom **FileReadError** enum that provides specific error variants. We also use **map_err** to map **std::io::Error** into our custom error type with more context.

Creating custom error types allows you to provide clearer error messages and helps consumers of your code understand and handle errors more effectively.

So far, you have learned the fundamental concepts of error handling in Rust, such as using **Result** and **Option**, propagating errors, handling multiple errors, and creating custom error types. As you progress in your Rust programming journey, you will become skilled at managing errors and producing robust software.

Advanced Error Handling

Advanced error handling in Rust is essential when dealing with complex real-world applications, where error scenarios may be diverse and complex. Rust offers several advanced techniques to effectively manage and handle errors in such contexts.

The anyhow Library

One of the notable tools in Rust's error-handling arsenal is the **anyhow** library. This library streamlines error handling by providing a unified error type that simplifies the process of creating and managing errors. It becomes particularly useful in scenarios where concise error handling is desired without the need to define custom error types for every possible error condition.

To leverage the **anyhow** library in your Rust project, you can begin by adding it as a dependency in your **Cargo.toml** file:

Listing 5.9 Cargo.toml configuration file for adding the anyhow dependency.

```
[dependencies]
anyhow = "1"
```

Once added as a dependency, you can utilize **anyhow** in your code to handle errors more effectively:

Listing 5.10 Basic anyhow usage example.

```
use anyhow::{anyhow, Result};

fn divide(a: i32, b: i32) -> Result<i32> {
    if b === 0 {
        return Err(anyhow!("Cannot divide by zero.")); // ①
    }

    Ok(a / b)
}

fn main() -> Result<()> {
    let result = divide(10, 0)?; // ②
    println!("Result: {}", result);
    Ok(())
}

// Output

// Error: Cannot divide by zero.
```

① The **anyhow!** macro is used to create a customized error message. This error is then returned as an Err variant of the **Result** type when a division by zero error occurs.

② In the **main** function, the **?** operator is utilized when calling the **divide** function, allowing for automatic error propagation. If an error occurs during the division, it is returned as an error from the **main** function, providing concise and clear error handling.

The **anyhow** library significantly simplifies error management in Rust by offering a unified error type that reduces the verbosity of error handling code. This approach is especially beneficial when dealing with applications where errors can arise from various sources and custom error types might be overly hard to define. With **anyhow**, we can focus on handling errors effectively while maintaining code clarity and conciseness.

Custom Error Types with thiserror

Custom error types play a crucial role in advanced error handling in Rust, and the **thiserror** crate simplifies their creation significantly. With this crate, we can define error enums with associated data and have traits like **Error** and **Display** automatically implemented, making error handling more expressive and efficient.

To incorporate this **thiserror** crate into your Rust project, you can add it as a dependency in your **Cargo.toml** file:

Listing 5.11 Cargo.toml configuration file for adding the thiserror dependency.

```
[dependencies]
thiserror = "1"
```

Once added as a dependency, you can create custom error types with ease, as demonstrated in the following example:

Listing 5.12 Basic thiserror usage example.

```
use thiserror::Error;

#[derive(Error, Debug)]
enum MyError {
    #[error("File not found: {0}")]
    FileNotFound(String),
    #[error("IO error: {0}")]
    IoError(#[from] std::io::Error),
}

fn read_file_contents(file_path: &str) -> Result<String, MyError> {
    let result = std::fs::read_to_string(file_path);

    match result {
        Ok(contents) => Ok(contents),
        Err(e) => {
            if e.kind() === std::io::ErrorKind::NotFound {
                Err(MyError::FileNotFound(file_path.to_string()))
            } else {
                Err(MyError::IoError(e))
            }
```

```
        }
    }
}

fn main() -> Result<(), MyError> {
    let file_path = "example.txt";
    let contents = read_file_contents(file_path)?;
    println!("File contents: {}", contents);
    Ok(())
}

// Output

// Error: FileNotFound("example.txt")
```

In this example, the **thiserror** crate is utilized to create the **MyError** enum, which represents custom error types with associated data. The **#[error]** attribute allows you to define custom error messages for each variant. Additionally, the **#[from]** attribute simplifies the conversion of other error types, such as **std::io::Error**, into your custom error type.

These advanced error-handling techniques provide a higher degree of flexibility and clarity in error management, particularly in larger and more complex Rust projects. Rust's strong type system and error-handling features empower us to create robust and reliable software while maintaining code readability and maintainability. By leveraging tools like thiserror, error handling can be a more ergonomic and expressive part of Rust application development.

Asynchronous Error Handling

Asynchronous programming presents different challenges when it comes to error handling, necessitating a different approach compared to synchronous code. In Rust, the introduction of the **async** and **await** syntax, coupled with libraries such as **tokio** and **async-std**, equips us with specialized tools to tackle asynchronous error scenarios effectively.

In this context, it is essential to comprehend that error management in asynchronous programming is important for ensuring the resilience and reliability of your software. With tasks executing concurrently and errors potentially arising at different points in time, a robust error-handling mechanism becomes a cornerstone for gracefully addressing unexpected situations. It also plays a pivotal role in preventing program crashes and the production of erroneous results.

Async Functions and Results

When dealing with asynchronous code, you frequently encounter **async** functions returning **Result** or **Option** types.

Listing 5.13 Async error handling with Result.

```
use reqwest;

async fn fetch_data() -> Result<String, reqwest::Error> { // ①
    let response = reqwest::get("https://www.google.com/").await?;
    let body = response.text().await?;
    Ok(body)
}

#[tokio::main]
async fn main() -> Result<(), Box<dyn std::error::Error>> {
    // You can run asynchronous code here if needed.
    let result = fetch_data().await;

    match result {
        Ok(body) => {
            println!("Fetched data:\n{}", body);
        }
        Err(err) => {
            eprintln!("Error fetching data: {:?}", err);
        }
    }

    Ok(())
}

// Output

// Fetched data:
// <!doctype html><html dir="rtl" itemscope="" itemtype="http://schema.
org/WebPage" lang="ar-LB"><head><meta
// etc
```

① In this example, **fetch_data** represents an asynchronous function returning a **Result**. The await keyword is used to pause/ halt the execution of the function. The await keyword allows us to write asynchronous functions as though they were synchronous (executed sequentially).

It is crucial to grasp the mechanics of error propagation while working with asynchronous functions. The **?** operator streamlines error management by automatically transforming errors into the appropriate return type. If an error surfaces anywhere within the asynchronous execution chain, it surfaces and gets returned from the function. This empowers us to handle errors at higher levels or propagate them further as needed. Consequently, this approach facilitates the creation of concise and clean asynchronous code, all while ensuring effective error management throughout the process.

Custom Error Types for Async Code

When it comes to working with asynchronous code, one valuable practice is the creation of custom error types tailored to your application or library's unique requirements. This approach empowers you to offer more meaningful error messages and context to users and fellow developers.

Creating custom error types serves several crucial purposes. Firstly, it allows you to abstract away low-level implementation details and provide error messages that are more user-friendly and informative. For instance, instead of simply indicating a network or I/O error occurred, you can specify the nature of the issue, making it easier to pinpoint and resolve problems.

Listing 5.14 Custom error types for async code.

```
use std::io;

#[derive(Debug)]
enum MyError {
    Network(reqwest::Error),
    Io(io::Error),
}

async fn fetch_data() -> Result<String, MyError> {
    // ...
}
```

In the provided example, **MyError** stands as a custom error enumeration that wraps two different error types: **reqwest::Error** and **io::Error**. By doing so, it adds a layer of context to error reporting. For instance, if a network error occurs within the **fetch_data** function, the resulting error will be of the **MyError** type and contain information about the nature of the issue, whether it's related to network problems or I/O operations.

Employing custom error types in asynchronous code enhances the clarity of error handling, making it easier to diagnose and rectify issues that may arise during program execution. This practice aligns with the broader goal of writing robust and user-friendly asynchronous code.

Handling Concurrency Errors

Asynchronous programming often involves the execution of concurrent operations, a characteristic that introduces its own set of challenges, particularly in terms of error handling. Managing concurrent errors gracefully is essential to ensure the robustness and reliability of your asynchronous applications. In Rust, the **`async/await`** syntax and libraries like **`tokio`** equip us with specialized tools to navigate these complex scenarios easily.

Concurrency introduces the possibility of multiple tasks running simultaneously, each with its own potential for encountering errors. This necessitates a comprehensive error-handling strategy that can account for the asynchronous and concurrent nature of the program.

Listing 5.15 Handling concurrency errors example.

```
use tokio::sync::mpsc;
use std::error::Error;

#[tokio::main]
async fn main() -> Result<(), Box<dyn Error>> {
    let (tx, mut rx) = mpsc::channel(32);

    for i in 0..4 {
        let tx = tx.clone();
        tokio::spawn(async move { // ①
            let result = do_work(i).await;
            tx.send(result).await.expect("Send failed");
        });
    }

    for _ in 0..4 {
        if let Some(result) = rx.recv().await {
            println!("Received result: {:?}", result);
        }
    }

    Ok(())
}
```

```
async fn do_work(task_id: i32) -> i32 {
    tokio::time::sleep(std::time::Duration::from_secs(1)).await;

    task_id * 2
}

// Output

// Received result: 4
// Received result: 0
// Received result: 2
// Received result: 6
```

① In this example, we employ **tokio::spawn** to execute tasks concurrently, and we utilize channels to collect and handle the results. This pattern allows for efficient concurrent execution and result aggregation, but it also introduces the possibility of errors propagating from multiple tasks simultaneously.

Establishing efficient methods to recognize, handle, and communicate errors resulting from different operations is of utmost importance for the seamless management of concurrent code. Accomplishing this requires synchronization of errors in the presence of partial failures while ensuring overall consistency in program execution.

The world of asynchronous and concurrent programming in Rust presents unique error-handling challenges, but with the right tools and strategies, you can navigate these waters effectively and build robust and reliable applications that can gracefully handle concurrent errors. A more detailed explanation on asynchronous programming is provided in *Chapter 10: Iterators and Closures*.

Error Handling in Web Applications

In the domain of web development, error handling plays a pivotal role in ensuring the reliability and user-friendliness of web applications. Rust, steadily gaining traction in web development domains, has established itself as an attractive choice, and for a good reason. Its robust error-handling capabilities, combined with the power of frameworks like **warp** and **actix-web**, provide us with a powerful toolkit for managing errors in web services.

Error handling in web applications encompasses a multitude of scenarios. These include handling requests with missing or invalid data, dealing with database or external service failures, and gracefully managing unexpected exceptions to prevent system crashes. It's about providing a smooth and informative experience for users while maintaining the stability of the application.

Listing 5.16 Error handling in web applications example.

```
use warp::Filter;

#[tokio::main]
async fn main() {
    let hello = warp::path!("hello" / "world")
        .map(|| {
            warp::reply::html("Hello, world!")
        });

    let routes = hello.with(warp::log("myapp::api"));
    warp::serve(routes).run(([127, 0, 0, 1], 3030)).await;
}

// Output

// $ curl 127.0.0.1:3030/hello/world
// Hello, world!
```

In this example, which utilizes the **warp** framework, a basic web service is defined. In the context of web applications, error handling often entails returning appropriate HTTP status codes and crafting informative error responses that aid users in understanding and resolving issues.

Rust's error handling capabilities, including the ability to create custom error types and leverage async/await syntax, make it exceptionally well-suited for developing robust and reliable web services. These features enable developers to create clean, maintainable code that elegantly handles various error scenarios, ultimately contributing to a more positive user experience and the long-term success of web applications.

Error handling is a vital aspect of web application development, and Rust, with its modern features and frameworks, empowers developers to excel in this critical area, delivering web services that are both dependable and user-friendly.

Putting it All Together

To consolidate your grasp of Rust's error-handling techniques, let's delve into a comprehensive example. We'll construct a simplified file parser that reads data from a CSV file, performs data processing, and efficiently manages errors throughout the process.

File Parsing and Error Handling

In the world of data processing, it's crucial to not only extract and manipulate data accurately but also to handle potential errors gracefully. Our example here tackles this challenge by implementing a CSV file parser that's equipped to manage errors effectively.

Listing 5.17 File parsing and error handling.

```
use std::error::Error;
use std::fs::File;
use std::io::{self, BufRead, BufReader};

#[derive(Debug)]
enum CsvError {
    Io(io::Error),
    ParseError(csv::Error),
}

impl From<io::Error> for CsvError { // ①
    fn from(error: io::Error) -> Self {
        CsvError::Io(error)
    }
}

impl From<csv::Error> for CsvError { // ①
    fn from(error: csv::Error) -> Self {
        CsvError::ParseError(error)
    }
}

fn parse_csv(file_path: &str) -> Result<(), CsvError> { // ②
    let file = File::open(file_path)?;
    let reader = BufReader::new(file);

    for line in reader.lines() {
        let line = line?;
        let record = csv::Reader::from_reader(line.as_bytes())
.deserialize::<(String, i32)>();
    }

    Ok(())
}
```

① A new type of error, **CsvError**, is created in this example. It combines two different types of errors: **io::Error** and **csv::Error**. To simplify the handling of these errors, we use conversions that are tied to the trait called "From." These allow us to convert lower-level problems into a more general problem represented by the abstracted `CsvError` type.

② The `parse_csv` function forms the core of our example. It reads and processes a CSV file specified by its `file_path` argument, effectively utilizing the error-handling features of Rust. This function elegantly handles potential errors that might emerge during file operations, data parsing, or other stages of processing.

The preceding example, combining the power of Rust's error-handling mechanisms, demonstrates how to build resilient and reliable data processing components. By gracefully managing errors, we ensure that our application remains robust even in the face of unexpected issues, delivering a more reliable and user-friendly experience.

Error Handling in Command-Line Applications

Command-line applications are common in system programming, and Rust is well-suited for building them. Proper error handling is essential in these applications to provide clear feedback to users and handle various scenarios gracefully.

Using the `clap` Library

When developing command-line applications in Rust, efficient argument parsing and error handling are essential. The clap library emerges as a popular and robust choice, simplifying the process of defining command-line interfaces while offering comprehensive error-handling capabilities.

Listing 5.18 Basic example of building a simple cli using the clap library.

```
use clap::{Parser, Subcommand};
use clap::Args;

#[derive(Parser)]
#[clap(author, version, about = "My Rust CLI App", long_about = None)]
struct Cli {
    #[command(subcommand)]
    command: Option<Commands>,
}
```

```
#[derive(Subcommand)]
enum Commands {
    Input(Input),
    Output(Output),
}

#[derive(Args)]
struct Input {
    file_name: Option<String>,
}

#[derive(Args)]
struct Output {
    file_name: Option<String>,
}

fn main() -> Result<(), Box<dyn std::error::Error>>  {
    let args = Cli::parse();
    match args.command {
        Some(Commands::Input(file)) => {
            match file.file_name {
                Some(ref file_name) => {
                    // Perform the application logic here
                }
                None => {
                    println!("Please provide an input file name");
                }
            }
        }
        Some(Commands::Output(file)) => {
            match file.file_name {
                Some(ref file_name) => {
                    // Perform the application logic here
                }
                None => {
                    println!("Please provide an output file name");
                }
            }
        }
        None => todo!()

    }

    // Perform the application logic here
    Ok(())
}
```

```
// Output

// $ cargo run -- input example.txt
// $ cargo run -- output example.txt

// $  cargo run -- help
My Rust CLI App

Usage: file [COMMAND]

Commands:
  input
  output
  help    Print this message or the help of the given subcommand(s)

Options:
  -h, --help     Print help
  -V, --version  Print version
```

In this illustrative code snippet, we utilize `clap` to streamline the process of defining and managing command-line arguments for our Rust command-line application. `clap` excels in this role, providing a convenient and expressive API for specifying argument names, descriptions, and more.

This code sets up a basic CLI application named "`My Rust CLI App`" and defines two arguments: "`input`" and "`output`," each with corresponding help text. Users can specify these arguments when running the program, and `clap` automatically parses and handles them.

`clap` also shines when it comes to error handling. It assists in checking for missing or invalid arguments, ensuring that user input adheres to the specified format. When errors occur, `clap` generates clear and informative error messages, helping users understand and resolve issues.

By leveraging `clap`, we can create user-friendly command-line interfaces that not only simplify interaction with our applications but also enhance error handling, resulting in a more polished and professional user experience. More on command line applications in *Chapter 8: CLI Programs.*

Handling Signals and Interruptions

Ensuring that command-line applications respond gracefully to signals like `Ctrl+C` is a crucial aspect of creating user-friendly and robust software. In Rust, the `ctrlc` crate simplifies the setup of signal handlers, making it straightforward to manage interruptions effectively.

Listing 5.19 Basic example of handling signals using the ctrlc library.

```
use ctrlc;
use std::sync::atomic::{AtomicBool, Ordering};
use std::sync::Arc;

fn main() -> Result<(), Box<dyn std::error::Error>> {
    let running = Arc::new(AtomicBool::new(true));
    let r = running.clone();

    ctrlc::set_handler(move || {
        r.store(false, Ordering::SeqCst);
        println!("Just got interrupted!");
    })?;

    // Perform application logic here

    while running.load(Ordering::SeqCst) {
        // Keep the application running
    }

    Ok(())
}

// Output

// Infinite Loop
// Ctrl+C
// ^CJust got interrupted!
```

In this code example, we utilize the **ctrlc** crate to gracefully handle interruptions, such as **Ctrl+C**, and ensure that the application cleans up and exits gracefully. This is essential for preventing resource leaks and maintaining the integrity of data and state.

The **ctrlc::set_handler** function is used to establish a signal handler that reacts to **Ctrl+C** events. When the user initiates such an interruption, the handler invokes the provided closure, which can be used to perform any necessary cleanup operations.

Handling signals and interruptions in this manner enhances the user experience and aids in preventing unexpected application termination. It enables applications to release resources, save state, or execute any other essential tasks before gracefully exiting, ultimately contributing to the overall reliability and professionalism of the command-line tool.

Error Handling in File I/O

File input and output (I/O) operations are crucial to numerous applications. However, they can also bring about different errors, such as the absence of a file, authorization conflicts, or I/O malfunctions. Rust offers powerful resources for managing these types of issues efficiently, which guarantees reliable and stable performance in handling files.

Reading and Writing Files

When working with file I/O in Rust, it's important to anticipate and gracefully handle errors that may occur during file operations. Proper error handling ensures that your application can respond appropriately to unexpected situations, preventing crashes and data corruption.

Listing 5.20 Basic example of reading and writing files with error handling.

```
use std::fs::File;
use std::io::{Read, Write};

fn main() -> Result<(), Box<dyn std::error::Error>> {
    let file_path = "example.txt";
    let mut file = File::open(file_path)?;

    let mut contents = String::new();
    file.read_to_string(&mut contents)?;

    // Process and manipulate the file contents here

    let mut output_file = File::create("output.txt")?;
    output_file.write_all(contents.as_bytes())?;

    Ok(())
}
```

In the provided Rust code snippet, we demonstrate how to read data from a file, process its contents, and write the results to an output file. Throughout this process, we leverage Rust's error-handling capabilities to handle potential errors that might arise, such as file not found, I/O errors, or issues with permissions.

By utilizing the ? operator, Rust simplifies error propagation. If an error occurs during any stage of the file I/O operations, it is immediately returned, and the program gracefully exits the function, preventing further execution and potential complications.

Effectively managing file-related errors not only enhances the robustness of your application but also contributes to a better user experience by providing clear error messages and preventing data loss or corruption. Rust's emphasis on safety and error handling makes it an excellent choice for building reliable file-processing components in your software.

Working with Directories

Effective directory management in Rust requires a robust approach to handle potential errors gracefully. Operations involving directories can encounter errors like directory not found or permission issues, and it's essential to handle them systematically to ensure the reliability and integrity of your application.

Listing 5.21 Basic example of working with directories with error handling.

```
use std::fs;
use std::path::Path;

fn main() -> Result<(), Box<dyn std::error::Error>> {
    let dir_path = "my_directory";

    if !Path::new(dir_path).exists() {
        fs::create_dir(dir_path)?;
    }

    // Perform operations within the directory here

    Ok(())
}
```

In the provided Rust code example, we illustrate the creation and management of directories while incorporating robust error handling practices. The code first checks if a directory specified by the **dir_path** variable exists. If it does not exist, it proceeds to create the directory using the **fs::create_dir** function.

By utilizing the **?** operator, Rust simplifies error handling. If any errors arise during directory creation, they are propagated upward, and the program exits the function gracefully. This behavior ensures that your application responds appropriately to various directory-related errors.

Handling directory-related errors in this manner is essential for maintaining the stability of your application, especially when dealing with file system interactions. By addressing potential issues proactively and providing meaningful error messages, you contribute to a more robust and user-friendly application experience.

Error Handling in Network Programming

When it comes to network programming in Rust, precision is key for guaranteeing strong and reliable applications. Thanks to its emphasis on safety measures and error control, Rust proves itself as an ideal language choice for handling networking tasks with finesse. Additionally, this dynamic tool provides a range of powerful resources that allow us to manage errors related specifically to networks in a highly effective manner.

Making HTTP Requests

When crafting applications that interact with remote servers via HTTP requests, it's imperative to anticipate and gracefully handle errors that can occur, such as network issues, invalid URLs, or server-related problems. Proper error management ensures that your application can respond sensibly to unexpected circumstances, preventing unexpected crashes or incorrect behavior.

Listing 5.22 HTTP requests and error handling.

```
use reqwest;

#[tokio::main]
async fn main() -> Result<(), reqwest::Error> {
    let response = reqwest::get("https://google.com").await?;

    if response.status().is_success() {
        // Process the response body
        let body = response.text().await?;
        println!("Response body:\n{}", body);
    } else {
        eprintln!("HTTP request failed: {:?}", response.status());
    }

    Ok(())
}
```

This code example utilizes the `reqwest` library to send an HTTP request to a designated URL. Error handling is made simple with the `?` operator, which instantly propagates any potential errors that may occur during the request. Here, we handle `reqwest::Error`, covering various network-related issues.

The status code of the HTTP response is analyzed within this code to determine if it was successful or not. If success is indicated by status, then the processing of the response follows suit accordingly. However, in case there's an error message displayed for users' convenience, they can receive clear feedback about what went wrong and why their attempt failed.

Effectively handling network-related errors is crucial for maintaining the integrity and dependability of applications that rely on external services or resources. Rust's error-handling capabilities, in conjunction with libraries like **reqwest**, empower us to create network programs that gracefully adapt with diverse error scenarios, enhancing the overall quality and resilience of their software.

Building Network Services

Developing network services involves creating software that communicates over networks, which can introduce a wide range of network-related errors. In this context, error handling becomes critical to ensure the robustness and reliability of network services. Rust's libraries and error-handling features are well-equipped to assist in managing these complex scenarios effectively.

Listing 5.23 Building network services with error handling.

```
use std::net::{TcpListener, TcpStream};
use std::io::{Read, Write};
use std::thread;

fn handle_client(mut stream: TcpStream) -> Result<(), Box<dyn
std::error::Error>> {
    // Handle client logic here
    println!("Client connected: {:?}", stream.peer_addr()?);

    let mut buffer = [0; 1024];
    loop {
        let bytes_read = stream.read(&mut buffer)?;

        if bytes_read === 0 {
            // Connection closed
            println!("Client disconnected: {:?}", stream.peer_addr()?);
            break;
        }

        let data = &buffer[..bytes_read];
        println!("Received from client {:?}: {:?}", stream.peer_addr()?,
String::from_utf8_lossy(data));

        // Process data received from the client
        // Example: Echo the data back to the client
```

```
        stream.write_all(data)?;
    }

    Ok(())
}

fn main() -> Result<(), Box<dyn std::error::Error>> {
    let listener = TcpListener::bind("127.0.0.1:8080")?; // Change the
address and port as needed
    println!("Server listening on: {:?}", listener.local_addr()?);

    for stream in listener.incoming() {
        match stream {
            Ok(stream) => {
                println!("Accepted connection from: {:?}", stream.peer_
addr()?);

                thread::spawn(move || {
                    if let Err(err) = handle_client(stream) {
                        eprintln!("Error handling client: {:?}", err);
                    }
                });
            }
            Err(e) => {
                eprintln!("Failed to accept client connection: {:?}", e);
            }
        }
    }

    Ok(())
}

// Output

// $ cargo run

// Server listening on: 127.0.0.1:8080
// Accepted connection from: 127.0.0.1:45842
// Client connected: 127.0.0.1:45842
// Received from client 127.0.0.1:45842: "Hello\r\n"


// $ telnet 127.0.0.1 8080

// Trying 127.0.0.1...
// Connected to 127.0.0.1.
// Escape character is '^]'.
```

```
// Hello
// Hello
```

In this Rust code snippet, we demonstrate the setup of a simple TCP server for handling client connections. The **handle_client** function, called for each incoming client connection, is a placeholder for the logic specific to your network service.

While handling client connections, network services can encounter various network-related errors, such as connection drops or data transmission issues. Rust's error handling capabilities, including the **Result** type and the **?** operator, allow you to manage these errors gracefully. By returning an **Err** variant with meaningful error information, you can convey details about the encountered network problem and take appropriate actions, such as logging, cleanup, or notifying clients.

Creating robust network services in Rust entails not only implementing the desired functionality but also anticipating and handling network-related errors professionally. This approach ensures that your services remain reliable and responsive in the face of unexpected network conditions, contributing to a positive user experience and the long-term success of your network applications. More on network programming in *Chapter 12: Network Programming.*

Error Handling in Multithreaded Code

Multithreaded and concurrent code introduces unique challenges in error handling, particularly related to proper synchronization and error propagation. In Rust, where safety and concurrency are first-class citizens, handling errors in multithreaded code is crucial for building robust and reliable concurrent applications.

Listing 5.24 Concurrency and multithreading with error handling.

```
use std::sync::{Arc, Mutex};
use std::thread;

fn process_data(data: Arc<Mutex<Vec<u32>>>) -> Result<(), Box<dyn
std::error::Error>> {
    // Lock the data for exclusive access within this thread
    let mut data_lock = data.lock().unwrap();

    // Process the data concurrently
    for i in 0..4 {
        data_lock.push(i);
```

```
    }

    // Data is automatically unlocked when `data_lock` goes out of scope

    Ok(())
}

fn main() -> Result<(), Box<dyn std::error::Error>> {
    // Create a shared data structure (a vector of u32) using Arc and
Mutex
    let data = Arc::new(Mutex::new(Vec::new()));

    // Create a vector to store thread handles
    let mut handles = vec![];

    // Spawn multiple threads to process data concurrently
    for _ in 0..4 {
        let data_clone = Arc::clone(&data); // Clone the Arc

        let handle = thread::spawn(move || {
            if let Err(err) = process_data(data_clone) {
                eprintln!("Error processing data: {:?}", err);
            }
        });

        handles.push(handle);
    }

    // Wait for all threads to complete
    for handle in handles {
        handle.join().unwrap();
    }

    // Access the shared data after processing
    let shared_data = {
        let data_lock = data.lock().unwrap();
        data_lock.clone()
    };

    // Print the content of the vector
    for item in &*shared_data {
        println!("Processed data item: {}", item);
    }

    Ok(())
}
```

```
// Output

// Processed data item: 0
// Processed data item: 1
// Processed data item: 2
// Processed data item: 3
// Processed data item: 0
// Processed data item: 1
// Processed data item: 2
// Processed data item: 3
// Processed data item: 0
// Processed data item: 1
// Processed data item: 2
// Processed data item: 3
// Processed data item: 0
// Processed data item: 1
// Processed data item: 2
// Processed data item: 3
```

In this code snippet, we address the challenge of concurrent data processing while taking into account thread safety and error handling. The **`process_data`** function represents a simplified example of concurrent data processing, where data is shared among multiple threads using an Arc (atomic reference counting) and a **`Mutex`** for mutual exclusion.

When dealing with concurrent data processing, potential errors can arise due to race conditions, thread panics, or other concurrency-related issues. It's essential to handle these errors gracefully and propagate them in a way that ensures the overall stability of the application. Rust's error handling mechanisms, such as the **`Result`** type and the **`Box<dyn std::error::Error>`** trait, enable you to encapsulate errors and return them in a safe and controlled manner.

Developing multithreaded and concurrent applications in Rust requires not just managing concurrency but also implementing resilient error-handling strategies. By doing so, you can build applications that effectively harness the potential of parallelism while maintaining safety and reliability. Achieving this equilibrium heavily relies on proper synchronization and error propagation techniques.

Cross-Thread Communication

When developing efficient and responsive applications using concurrent code, communicating between threads is a crucial element. Nevertheless, this brings additional complexity to error handling because it necessitates meticulous synchronization and communication across different threads.

Listing 5.25 Cross-thread communication with error handling.

```
use std::thread;
use std::sync::mpsc;

fn main() -> Result<(), Box<dyn std::error::Error>> {
    let (tx, rx) = mpsc::channel();

    let worker = thread::spawn(move || {
        // Worker thread logic
        tx.send("Task completed").unwrap();
    });

    // Main thread logic

    let result = rx.recv()?;
    println!("Received result: {}", result);

    worker.join().unwrap();

    Ok(())
}

// Output

// Received result: Task completed
```

This Rust code example illustrates communication between a main thread and a worker thread while taking into account potential error scenarios. The **mpsc** (multiple-producer, single-consumer) channel is used for communication, allowing data to be sent from the worker thread to the main thread.

Handling errors in cross-thread communication necessitates careful consideration of synchronization and error propagation. In this example, the **Result** type and the **Box<dyn std::error::Error>** trait are used to encapsulate and propagate potential errors, ensuring that any issues arising during channel communication or thread execution are appropriately handled.

When creating concurrent applications that require responsiveness and reliability, it is crucial to handle cross-thread communication errors. Rust provides a means for us to leverage parallelism advantages while guaranteeing code safety and stability via effective synchronization mechanisms as well as error propagation strategies.

Testing and Error Handling

Testing is a vital aspect of software development that guarantees the reliability and accuracy of code, playing an essential role in verifying how errors are handled. The Rust testing framework offers us a systematic strategy to create tests aimed at error situations, enabling us to assess their code's strength under different erroneous conditions with precision.

Writing Error Tests

Rust's testing framework presents a straightforward approach to generating tests that assess how your code handles errors. By utilizing the #[test] attribute, you can define a test function and evaluate it accordingly. The assertions used inside these functions help check if error handling behavior is correctly implemented by ensuring that your program responds appropriately when faced with erroneous circumstances.

Listing 5.26 Writing tests for error handling.

```
fn divide(dividend: i32, divisor: i32) -> Result<i32, String> {
    if divisor === 0 {
        Err(format!("Cannot divide {} by zero.", dividend))
    } else {
        Ok(dividend / divisor)
    }
}

#[test]
fn test_divide_by_zero() {
    let result = divide(10, 0);

    assert!(result.is_err()); // Ensure it's an error
    assert_eq!(result.unwrap_err(), "Cannot divide 10 by zero."); //
Check the error message
}

// Output

// $ cargo test

// running 1 test
// test test_divide_by_zero ... ok
```

```
// test result: ok. 1 passed; 0 failed; 0 ignored; 0 measured; 0 filtered
out; finished in 0.00s
```

This code example showcases a test named **test_divide_by_zero**, which evaluates the error handling mechanism of the **divide** function when dividing by zero. The validity of an error is confirmed through the use of **assert!** macro, while matching it with expected message via using **assert_eq!**.

Writing error tests allows you to systematically verify that your error handling code functions as intended, providing a level of confidence in your software's ability to gracefully manage erroneous situations. By doing so, you can ensure that your application responds sensibly to errors, preventing unexpected crashes and enhancing its overall reliability.

Property-Based Testing

Property-based testing is a powerful testing methodology that allows you to test error conditions and edge cases across a wide range of inputs systematically. Property-based testing libraries like **proptest** in Rust provide the means to automatically generate test cases, enabling you to uncover potential issues and evaluate the robustness of your error-handling code comprehensively.

Listing 5.27 Property-based testing example.

```
use proptest::prelude::*;

fn divide(dividend: i32, divisor: i32) -> Result<i32, String> {
    if divisor === 0 {
        Err(format!("Cannot divide {} by zero.", dividend))
    } else {
        Ok(dividend / divisor)
    }
}

proptest! {
    #[test]
    fn test_divide_property_based(input in 1..100, divisor in 1..100) {
        if divisor === 0 {
            let result = divide(input, divisor);
            assert!(result.is_err());
            assert_eq!(result.unwrap_err(), format!("Cannot divide {} by
zero.", input));
        } else {
            let result = divide(input, divisor);
            assert!(result.is_ok());
```

```
            assert_eq!(result.unwrap(), input / divisor);
        }
    }
}

// Output

// $ cargo test

// running 1 test
// test test_divide_property_based ... ok

// test result: ok. 1 passed; 0 failed; 0 ignored; 0 measured; 0 filtered
out; finished in 0.01s
```

In this example, utilizing the **proptest** library, we implement property-based testing for the **divide** function. This approach generates random inputs within specified ranges, testing various scenarios, including division by zero and valid division operations.

Property-based testing excels at exploring the edge cases and error conditions that might not be apparent in traditional unit tests. By automatically generating a diverse set of test cases, it helps you discover unexpected issues, ensuring that your error-handling code can handle a broad spectrum of input values effectively.

By incorporating property-based testing into your testing approach, you can elevate the reliability of your error-handling code. This elevates the strength and robustness of your software to handle unexpected situations with ease. Property-based testing is an advantageous resource for detecting potential weaknesses and enhancing Rust applications' overall quality.

Conclusion

This chapter has delved deep into the complex world of error handling in Rust, covering a wide array of scenarios and techniques. From the fundamental use of **Result** and **Option** to complex aspects like asynchronous error handling, custom error types, and integration with libraries such as **anyhow**, we've explored it all.

Error handling isn't just a mere aspect of Rust programming; it's a cornerstone of writing software that is reliable and robust, irrespective of the application's domain or nature. Whether you're crafting command-line interfaces, handling file operations, working on network protocols, or orchestrating concurrent tasks, the principles shared here are invaluable.

By carefully applying these error-handling methodologies and adhering to best practices, you'll be well-prepared to create Rust applications that not only gracefully handle errors but also provide users with meaningful feedback and ensure seamless error recovery and resource management.

As you continue your Rust journey, the mastery of these error-handling techniques will undoubtedly empower you to produce code that stands the test of time and fosters software resilience, a fundamental skill for every Rust developer.

In the next chapter, we will dive into the essential topic of Memory Management and Pointers in Rust. This chapter will provide a comprehensive overview of Rust's unique approach to memory management, emphasizing the distinctions between stack and heap memory allocation. Additionally, you will be introduced to the concept of smart pointers such as Box, Rc, and Arc, which play a crucial role in managing memory efficiently in Rust. The chapter will also touch upon the fundamentals of unsafe Rust and how to handle raw pointers safely, expanding your understanding of Rust's memory management capabilities and ensuring the safe and reliable handling of memory in your Rust programs.

References and Further Reading

1. *The Rust Programming Language - Error Handling* - Official Rust documentation on error handling.

2. *Rust Error Handling in Practice* - Practical insights and examples for Rust error handling.

3. *How to Handle Errors in Rust: A Comprehensive Guide* - Comprehensive guide on Rust error handling techniques.

4. *Handling Errors in Rust With Various Approaches* - Exploring different error handling approaches in Rust.

5. *anyhow - Rust Programming Language* - Documentation for the `anyhow` error handling crate.

6. *thiserror - Rust Programming Language* - Documentation for the `thiserror` custom error type crate.

7. *proptest - Property-based testing for Rust* - Documentation for the `proptest` property-based testing crate.

8. *tokio - Asynchronous runtime for Rust* - Documentation for the **`tokio`** asynchronous runtime in Rust.

9. *async-std - Async standard library for Rust* - Documentation for **`async-std`**, Rust's async standard library.

Multiple-Choice Questions

Q1: What is the primary purpose of traits in Rust?

a) To define data structures

b) To provide default implementations for functions

c) To define shared behaviors that types can implement

d) To restrict access to data

Q2: In Rust, which of the following types is used to represent an optional value that can either be present or absent?

a) `bool`

b) `Option`

c) `Result`

d) `Enum`

Q3: What is the primary purpose of the Result type in Rust?

a) To represent an optional value

b) To handle errors and propagate them safely

c) To store boolean values

d) To define shared behaviors for types

Q4: In Rust, which operator is used for concise error propagation and is often referred to as the "try" operator?

a) `?`

b) `!`

c) `*`

d) `@`

Q5: What is the purpose of the anyhow library in Rust?

a) To define custom error types

b) To handle asynchronous errors

c) To provide unified error handling with a simplified error type

d) To create option values

Q6: Which Rust crate simplifies the creation of custom error types and automatically implements traits like Error and Display for them?

a) `thiserror`

b) `custom_error`

c) `error_handling`

d) `error_crate`

Q7: In asynchronous Rust code, what does the await keyword do?

a) Pauses the current task until the awaited future is ready

b) Resumes the current task after waiting for a specified duration

c) Converts synchronous code into asynchronous code

d) Throws an error if the awaited future is not ready

Q8: Which Rust library is commonly used for asynchronous programming and provides tools for working with asynchronous tasks and I/O?

a) `std::async`

b) `asyncio`

c) `tokio`

d) `async-std`

Q9: What is the primary purpose of error handling in asynchronous Rust code?

a) To crash the program in case of errors

b) To ignore errors and proceed with execution

c) To gracefully handle unexpected situations and prevent program crashes

d) To slow down the program to handle errors more easily

Q10: In asynchronous Rust code, which type is commonly used to represent the result of an asynchronous operation that can either succeed or fail with an error?

a) `bool`

b) `Result`

c) `Option`

d) `Future`

Q11: What is the primary role of the ? `operator in Rust when used in error handling?`

a) It creates custom error types.

b) It transforms errors into the appropriate return type.

c) It throws an error if any issue occurs.

d) It performs asynchronous operations.

Q12: When working with asynchronous Rust code, which keyword is used to synchronize asynchronous operations?

a) `sync`

b) `await`

c) `async`

d) `asyncronize`

Q13: Why is it important to create custom error types in asynchronous Rust code?

a) To confuse users with complex error messages.

b) To add unnecessary complexity to the code.

c) To abstract low-level details and provide meaningful error messages.

d) To prevent error handling altogether.

Q14: What two error types does the custom MyError enumeration wrap?

a) `reqwest::Error` and `io::Error`

b) `tokio::Error` and `csv::Error`

c) `async::Error` and `custom::Error`

d) `warp::Error` and `ctrlc::Error`

Q15: What is one of the challenges introduced by asynchronous programming, particularly concerning error handling?

a) Slower program execution

b) Synchronous error propagation

c) Concurrent errors from multiple tasks

d) Lack of built-in error handling

Q16: Which library simplifies the creation of command-line interfaces and offers comprehensive error-handling capabilities for Rust applications?

a) `argparse`

b) `clap`

c) `getopts`

d) `cliargs`

Q17: What is the primary advantage of using the ctrlc crate for handling signals like Ctrl+C in Rust applications?

a) It prevents the application from being interrupted.

b) It allows you to ignore signals.

c) It simplifies the setup of signal handlers and graceful interruption handling.

d) It handles signals asynchronously.

Q18: When handling signals with the ctrlc crate, what does the signal handler function allow you to do?

a) Prevent all signals from reaching the application.

b) Execute custom logic when a signal is received, such as cleanup operations.

c) Delay signal handling until the application exits.

d) Only handle specific signals, excluding others.

Q19: In Rust, what is the primary benefit of using the `?` operator when performing file I/O operations?

a) It terminates the program immediately upon any error.

b) It transforms errors into custom error types.

c) It simplifies error propagation and prevents further execution on error.

d) It automatically retries file operations if an error occurs.

Q20: Why is proper error handling important when working with file I/O operations in Rust?

a) To hide errors from users and maintain program execution.

b) To make the code more complex and difficult to read.

c) To respond appropriately to unexpected situations,prevent crashes, and avoid data corruption.

d) To increase the likelihood of resource leaks.

Answers

1. c) To define shared behaviors that types can implement
2. b) `Option`
3. b) To handle errors and propagate them safely
4. a) `?`
5. c) To provide unified error handling with a simplified error type
6. a) `thiserror`
7. a) Pauses the current task until the awaited future is ready
8. c) tokio
9. c) To gracefully handle unexpected situations and prevent program crashes
10. b) `Result`
11. b) It transforms errors into the appropriate return type.
12. b) `await`

13. c) To abstract low-level details and provide meaningful error messages.
14. a) `reqwest::Error` and `io::Error`
15. c) Concurrent errors from multiple tasks
16. b) `clap`
17. c) It simplifies the setup of signal handlers and graceful interruption handling.
18. b) Execute custom logic when a signal is received, such as cleanup operations.
19. c) It simplifies error propagation and prevents further execution on error.
20. c) To respond appropriately to unexpected situations, prevent crashes, and avoid data corruption.

CHAPTER 6

Memory Management and Pointers

Introduction

In the ever-evolving landscape of programming languages, memory management stands as an important concern that directly impacts the quality and performance of software systems. It becomes the foundation upon which developers construct their software. The opening of this chapter begins with an exploration into Rust's distinctive paradigm for memory management, promising a captivating journey that will illuminate the nuances of memory allocation within the stack and heap. This chapter encompasses not only fundamental memory management techniques but also delves into advanced topics such as smart pointers and the world of unsafe Rust.

Memory allocation in Rust is a crucial subject that underpins the language's core philosophy of combining safety and performance. At its heart, Rust strives to empower us to write code that is both reliable and blazingly fast. To achieve this delicate balance, Rust introduces a rigorous set of rules that govern memory allocation and deallocation. By the end of this chapter, you will have a deep understanding of these rules and how they contribute to Rust's unique promise of memory safety without sacrificing performance.

As the chapter unfolds, it will lead us through the world of smart pointers, a powerful abstraction that grants fine-grained control over memory resources. Smart pointers enable us to write more expressive and flexible code, ultimately leading to safer and more efficient software. However, the chapter doesn't stop at the confines of safety; it takes a leap into the world of unsafe Rust. Here, you will explore the edge cases and scenarios where Rust's safety guarantees may need to be momentarily suspended in favor of performance optimizations or interfacing with external code. In doing so, this chapter equips you with the knowledge to utilize Rust's memory management tools with both precision and creativity, ensuring your software not only runs efficiently but also remains robust and reliable.

Structure

In this chapter, we are going to explore the following topics:

- An Introduction to smart pointers: Box, Rc, Arc, Mutex, and so on
- Understanding stack and heap memory allocation in Rust
- An introduction to unsafe Rust and handling raw pointers

The Role of Memory Management

In the complex world of software development, memory management stands as a silent hero, often unnoticed but essential to a program's performance and stability. It plays the role of an invisible conductor, orchestrating how a program allocates, utilizes, and releases its most crucial resource: memory. Proficient memory management is the backbone that enables a program to run seamlessly, steering it away from risky pitfalls like memory leaks, and crashes. As we delve deeper into this topic, we'll discover that memory management is the unpraised hero that support the reliability and efficiency of every software.

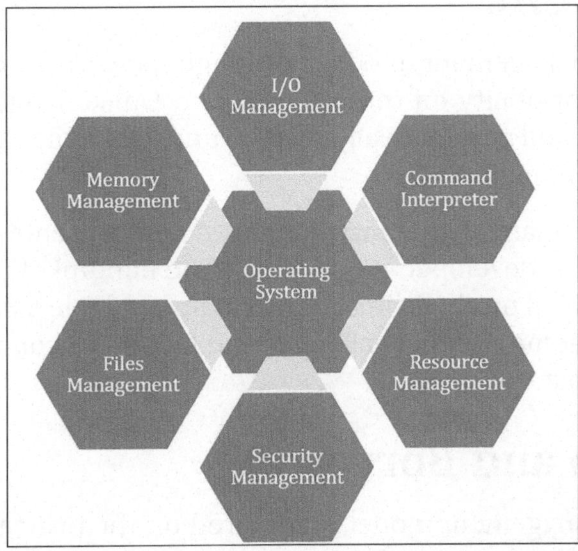

Figure 6.1: *Different Operating System's functionalities*

Within the world of programming languages, Rust emerges as a distinctive force, often hailed as a systems programming language. It boldly endeavors to provide us with a unique blend of high-level control over memory while firmly endorsing the twin pillars of safety and reliability. In this journey through Rust's memory management landscape, you'll uncover why this language places memory management at its very core. Rust's design philosophy revolves around empowering us to utilize memory with precision, avoiding the pitfalls that have cursed languages of the past. It is the fusion of control and safety that sets Rust apart and makes it a compelling choice for us seeking to create robust and efficient software systems.

As we navigate the complexities of Rust's approach to memory management, you'll come to appreciate how it encapsulates the essence of the language's philosophy. Rust challenges the current situation by offering a robust system for managing memory that, unlike some other languages, doesn't require sacrificing safety for performance or vice versa. In Rust, memory management is not a mere technicality but a testament to the language's commitment to enabling us to write software that is both efficient and secure. This exploration of Rust's memory management will illuminate the path to harnessing the full potential of a language that places memory at the cutting edge of its mission to revolutionize systems programming.

Challenges of Manual Memory Management

Rust's memory management model, although powerful and secure, places considerable responsibility on the programmer. Unlike languages that employ garbage collection and automatically reclaim unused memory, Rust necessitates explicit handling of memory.

This approach to manual memory management presents its own array of difficulties. As a Rust developer, it is crucial to be mindful of potential obstacles and adhere to optimal methods in order to maintain code safety and efficiency. The following are some overall challenges and factors to consider when dealing with memory in Rust:

Ownership and Borrowing

Rust's memory management model is centered on the principles of ownership, borrowing, and references. A reference is like a pointer in that it serves as an address we can follow to access data stored at that address, which is owned by some other variable. However, unlike a pointer, a reference is assured to point to a valid value of a specific type.

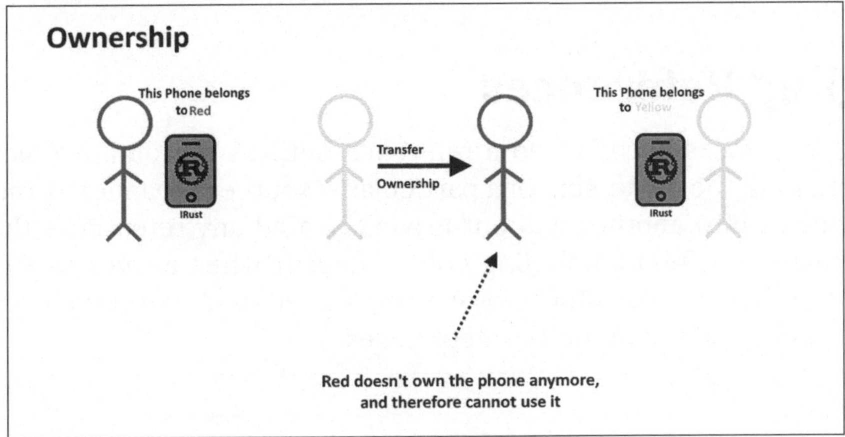

Figure 6.2: *Ownership simple illustration*

Understanding when to use these concepts is crucial for effective memory management in Rust. Let's explore an example:

Listing 6.1 A basic ownership and borrowing example.

```
fn main() {
    let s1 = String::from("hello");
    let s2 = s1; // ①
    // println!("s1: {}", s1); // ②
    println!("s2: {}", s2); // ③
}

// Output

// s2: hello
```

① **s1**'s ownership is transferred to **s2**.

② This line would result in a compilation error.

③ **s2** can still be used.

In this code snippet, **s1** and **s2** are string variables. When **s2** is assigned the value of **s1**, ownership of the underlying data is transferred from **s1** to **s2**. Attempting to use **s1** after the transfer results in a compilation error, demonstrating Rust's strict ownership rules.

Understanding when to use ownership, borrowing (references with `&`), and mutable borrowing (references with `&mut`) is essential for managing memory efficiently and avoiding issues like use-after-free errors or unnecessary data copying.

Dangling References

Dangling references occur when a reference outlives the data it points to. In some situations, the ownership of a particular resource is seamlessly moved out of one context into another without leaving behind any references that could lead to dangling pointers. Dangling pointers occur when a reference points to memory that has been deallocated or is no longer valid, potentially leading to undefined behavior and memory safety issues.

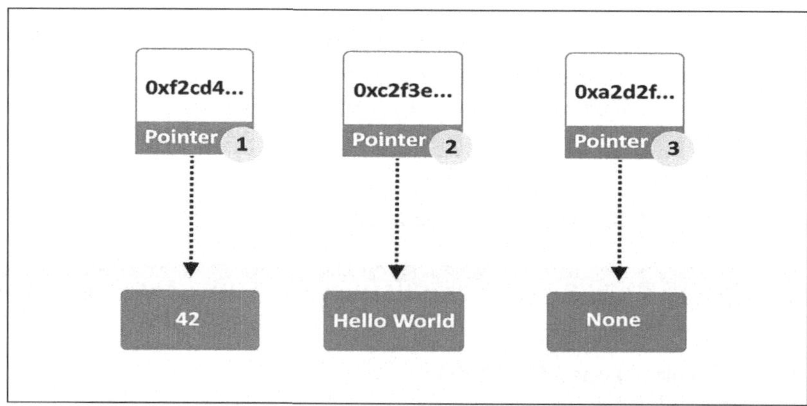

Figure 6.3: *Pointers and their corresponding memory values*

Rust's lifetime system helps prevent this problem, but it requires careful consideration when writing code. This concept refers to a situation where ownership is effectively transferred without encountering any issues or hazards related to dangling references or deallocation problems. In Rust, ownership is a fundamental principle governing memory management, ensuring that resources are handled safely and efficiently. Let's consider the following example:

Listing 6.2 Variables and scope example.

```
fn main() {
    let r;
    {
        let x = 42;
        r = &x; // ①
    }
```

```
    // println!("r: {}", r); // ②
}
```

① Attempting to use **r** outside its scope results in a compilation error.

② This line would result in a compilation error.

In this code, **r** is a reference to **x**, an integer variable. However, **x** goes out of scope at the end of the inner block, making **r** a dangling reference. Rust's lifetime system detects this issue and prevents the use of **r** after **x** is no longer valid.

To avoid dangling references, it's essential to understand how Rust's lifetimes work and ensure that references don't outlive the data they point to.

Unsafe Code

There are specific situations where the utilization of risky Rust becomes necessary in order to circumvent the safety checks performed by the compiler. Nevertheless, it is important to be careful when taking this approach as it has the potential to introduce vulnerabilities related to memory safety.

Consider the following example:

Listing 6.3 Unsafe code example.

```
fn main() {
    let mut numbers = vec![1, 2, 3, 4, 5];

    let mut_ptr = numbers.as_mut_ptr(); // ①

    let len = numbers.len();

    unsafe { // ②
        for i in 0..len {
            let current_value = *mut_ptr.add(i); // ③

            *mut_ptr.add(i) = current_value * 2; // ④
        }
    }

    println!("{:?}", numbers);
}

// Output

// [2, 4, 6, 8, 10]
```

① Create a raw pointer to the first element of the vector.

② Unsafe block to manually iterate through the vector using raw pointers.

③ Dereference the raw pointer to access the elements.

④ Modify the element (multiply by 2).

In this code, we utilize unsafe Rust to directly manipulate the elements of a vector using raw pointers. Within the unsafe block, we dereference the pointer and make modifications to the elements. This showcases how unsafe Rust enables us to bypass certain safety checks enforced by the compiler.

However, it's crucial to emphasize that such unsafe operations should be employed carefully and only, when necessary, given their potential to introduce memory safety issues. A deep understanding of Rust's safety guarantees and a thorough testing of unsafe code are essential when taking this approach.

Data Races

Rust's strict rules on mutable references help prevent data races, a type of concurrency bug where multiple threads access shared data concurrently without proper synchronization. Let's consider the following example:

Listing 6.4 Data races example.

```
use std::thread;

fn main() {
    let mut data = vec![1, 2, 3];

    let handle1 = thread::spawn(move || {
        data.push(4);
    });

    handle1.join().unwrap();

    // println!("{:?}", data); // ①
}
```

① Uncommenting this line would result in a compilation error.

In this code, one thread (**handle1**) attempts to push elements into a shared vector **data**. However, Rust's ownership system ensures that only one thread can mutate **data** at a time. If you uncomment the **println!** line, it would result in a compilation error because **`data`** is accessed mutably without proper synchronization.

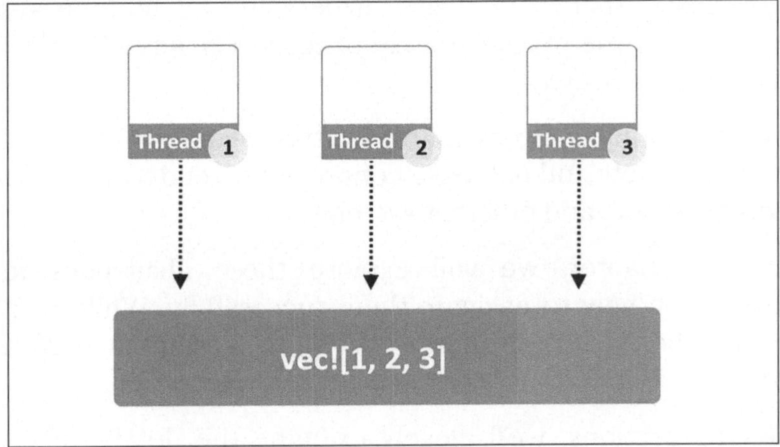

Figure 6.4: *A simple data race illustration*

While Rust's strict rules prevent data races, they also require careful design of concurrent code to avoid deadlocks and contention.

Resource Management

Rust not only manages memory but also other resources like file handles. Properly releasing these resources is crucial to avoid resource leaks.

Listing 6.5 Resource management example.

```
use std::fs::File;

fn main() -> std::io::Result<()> {
    let file = File::create("example.txt")?; // ①

    // File will be automatically closed when it goes out of scope

    // Additional code for working with the file goes here

    Ok(()) // ②
}
```

① Create a file named "example.txt".

② Return **`Ok`** to indicate success.

In this code snippet, a file handle is generated utilizing the **`File::create()`** function. Rust ensures that once the **`file`** variable exits its scope, the file automatically closes, thanks to Rust's ownership and lifetime system. Such assurance guarantees the proper release of resources and effectively prevents any potential resource leaks.

Rust's proficiency in managing resources further expands to include domains such as network sockets and database connections, rendering it a valuable tool for constructing reliable and efficient systems.

Throughout this chapter, we will explore these challenges further and provide guidance on how to navigate them successfully. While Rust's memory management can be tedious, it empowers you to write high-performance and secure code.

In the upcoming sections, we'll closely examine the details of each type of pointer. We'll also take a look at smart pointers like **`Box`**, **`Rc`**, and **`Arc`**, which provide helpful memory management features. Additionally, we'll explore the world of unsafe Rust, where the responsibility for maintaining safety rests on the shoulders of the programmer.

Stack versus Heap

At the core of Rust's memory management philosophy reside two fundamental pillars: the stack and the heap. These two memory regions serve as the primary battlegrounds where values are allocated, managed, and eventually freed, and where pointers assert their influence over the program's memory space.

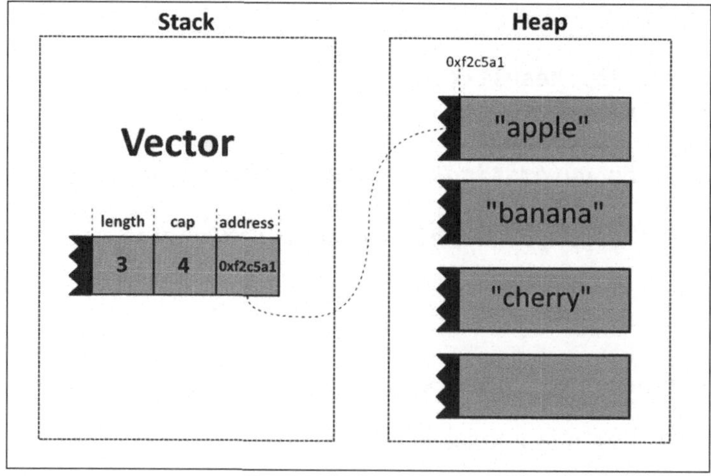

Figure 6.5: *A vector object and its stack and heap representation*

The stack, a memory region characterized by its orderliness and efficiency, operates under a strict last-in, first-out (LIFO) discipline. It serves as the go-to destination for managing short-lived variables, such as those within the scope of a function call. When a function is invoked, its local variables are allocated on the stack, ensuring that they are automatically deallocated when the function exits. This simplicity and predictability make the stack an important resource for the compiler, enabling it to optimize memory allocation for permanent data.

In contrast, the heap represents a world of flexibility and dynamic memory allocation. Values residing in the heap can be allocated and deallocated at arbitrary times during a program's execution, providing a space for long-lived data structures that outlive their creating scope. Rust's ability to seamlessly navigate the transition between stack and heap, allocating values efficiently on the stack while going into the heap when necessary, showcases the language's ability in striking a balance between performance and memory management. As we delve deeper into this chapter, you will gain a comprehensive understanding of how Rust leverages the stack and the heap to optimize memory allocation, equipping you with the knowledge to make informed decisions in your own Rust programming projects.

The Stack's Role in Rust

In Rust, the stack takes attention for local variable storage and function call management. Each function call creates a stack frame, a dedicated space for its variables and data. When the function exits, the frame is removed, deallocating the associated memory.

This stack rule aligns with Rust's focus on safety and efficiency. Local variables have clearly defined lifetimes, and their scope is limited to the enclosing block or function. As a result, Rust ensures that variables are only accessible when they are in a valid state, reducing the risk of bugs caused by accessing memory that's no longer in use.

Let's illustrate this concept with a simple Rust function:

Listing 6.6 A simple function with memory allocated on the stack.

```
fn main() {
    let x = 42; // ①
    println!("The answer is: {}", x);
} // ②
```

① **x** is stored on the stack.

② **x** goes out of scope and is deallocated.

In this example, the variable **x** is allocated on the stack within the **main** function. When the function exits, **x** goes out of scope and is deallocated automatically. This stack-based allocation ensures efficient memory management for **x**, eliminating the need for explicit memory management by the programmer.

The Heap's Role in Rust

While the stack shines for immediate, short-lived data, the heap is where Rust turns when dealing with data of variable size and dynamic lifetimes. The heap allows Rust to allocate memory that persists beyond the scope of a single function or block, accommodating data structures that can grow or shrink as needed.

Rust's approach to allocating heap memory is driven by the principles of ownership, borrowing, and lifetimes. Before we delve further into these subjects, let us examine how Rust assigns data on the heap.

Listing 6.7 A simple function with memory allocated on the heap.

```
fn main() {
    let s1 = String::from("Hello"); // ①
    let s2 = s1; // ②
    println!("{}", s2); // ③
} // ④
```

① **s1** is a String allocated on the heap.

② **s2** takes ownership of the heap-allocated data, s1 is no longer valid.

③ **s2** is still valid and can be used.

④ **s2** goes out of scope and automatically deallocates the heap memory.

In this example, the **String** type represents a dynamically sized, heap-allocated string. When **s1** is assigned to **s2**, ownership of the heap-allocated data is transferred from **s1** to **s2**. As a result, **s1** is no longer valid, and Rust automatically deallocates the heap memory associated with it when **s2** goes out of scope.

This mechanism, known as *ownership transfer*, ensures that there is only one owner of heap-allocated data at any given time, preventing issues like double deallocation or data corruption. Rust's strict control over heap allocation and ownership is a fundamental aspect of its memory safety guarantees.

The Ownership Model

To understand Rust's approach to memory management, you must familiarize yourself with the concept of ownership. In Rust, every value has a unique owner, and the owner is responsible for deallocating the associated memory when it is no longer needed. This ownership model is enforced by Rust's strict rules, which prevent multiple owners or unauthorized access to data.

Consider a simple example:

Listing 6.8 A simple function that illustrates data and its owner.

```
fn main() {
    let s = String::from("Rust"); // ①
    println!("{}", s); // ②
} // ③
```

① `s` is the owner of the heap-allocated string.

② `s` is valid and can be used here.

③ `s` goes out of scope, and Rust automatically deallocates the heap memory.

In this snippet, `s` is the owner of the heap-allocated string. When s goes out of scope at the end of the `main` function, Rust automatically deallocates the memory used by the string. This automatic memory management is at the heart of Rust's safety guarantees, ensuring that memory leaks and dangling references are virtually eliminated.

Borrowing in Rust

Rust's ownership model ensures efficient memory management, but it also introduces challenges when you need to share data between parts of your code. This is where borrowing and references come into play.

Borrowing allows multiple parts of your code to access data without taking ownership of it. Rust offers two types of borrowing: mutable and immutable. Immutable references, represented by `&T`, allow read-only access to data, while mutable references, represented by `&mut T`, permit both read and write access.

Consider this example:

Listing 6.9 A simple example of borrowing as immutable.

```
fn main() {
    let s = String::from("Rust");
    let len = calculate_length(&s); // ①
    println!("Length of '{}' is {}.", s, len);
}

fn calculate_length(s: &String) -> usize {
    s.len() // ②
}

// Output

// Length of 'Rust' is 4.
```

① Pass an immutable reference to the string.

② We can access **s** without taking ownership.

In this code snippet, the **calculate_length** function borrows a reference to the **String** without assuming control over it. This grants us the ability to retrieve the string's length without relocating or freeing it.

The differentiation between mutable and immutable references holds high importance for Rust's safety guarantees. By adhering to Rust's principle of "either multiple readers or one writer", we ensure that data cannot be both modified and accessed concurrently, thus preventing any occurrence of data races or memory corruption.

Lifetimes in Rust

As we explore Rust's memory management, we encounter the concept of lifetimes. Lifetimes are Rust's way of ensuring that references remain valid throughout their usage. They help prevent dangling references and ensure that borrowed data outlives the references to it.

Consider this example:

Listing 6.10 Lifetimes concept's demonstration using different scopes.

```
fn main() {
    let result;
    {
        let s = String::from("Rust");
```

```
        result = get_length(&s); // ①
    } // ②

    println!("Length: {}", result);
}

fn get_length(s: &String) -> usize {
    s.len()
}

// Output

// Length: 4
```

① Pass a reference to **s**.

② **s** goes out of scope, but the reference's lifetime is still valid.

This program requires the reference to **s** passed to the **get_length** function to have a lifetime that extends beyond the function call. Rust's lifetime system enforces this condition, ensuring that we don't attempt to access data that has already been deallocated.

Moving beyond basic understanding, let's delve into a slightly more complex example to showcase the power and necessity of Rust's lifetime system. Consider the following scenario involving structs and lifetimes:

Listing 6.11 Lifetimes with structs using different scopes.

```
struct Container<'a> {
    data: &'a str,
}

fn main() {
    let result;
    {
        let s = String::from("Rust");
        let container = Container { data: &s };
        result = process_container(container);
    }

    println!("Processed data: {}", result);
}

fn process_container(container: Container) -> usize {
    container.data.len()
```

```
}
// Output

// Processed data: 4
```

In this example, we introduce a **Container** struct that holds a reference to a string slice with a specific lifetime **'a**. The main function creates a String, then initializes a Container with a reference to that string. Subsequently, the **process_container** function takes ownership of the Container, extracting and returning the length of the referenced string.

The key here is that the lifetime of the reference within the Container must outlive the function call to **process_container**. Rust's compiler rigorously enforces these constraints, ensuring that we maintain a valid reference throughout the program's execution.

By understanding ownership, borrowing, and lifetimes, we can write code that is not only efficient but also safe from common memory-related bugs. Rust's strict compiler checks and lifetime annotations help us catch potential issues at compile time, resulting in robust and reliable software.

Pointers and Smart Pointers

In Rust, the notion of pointers becomes important when values need to interact, reference one another, or allocate on the heap. Unlike languages with automatic memory management, Rust places the power of pointer management firmly in the hands of the programmer. This allows for fine-grained control and ensures that memory-related issues are caught at compile time rather than runtime.

Throughout the following sections, we'll encounter various pointer types in Rust. References, boxes, and raw pointers each have their roles to play, and understanding when and how to use them is pivotal. References offer safe and efficient ways to access data. Boxes provide a way to allocate values in the heap when needed, with Rust's strict memory management. Raw pointers, while exploring the world of unsafety, offer us a high degree of control when necessary.

Box

Rust provides a powerful tool for allocating memory on the heap called **Box**.

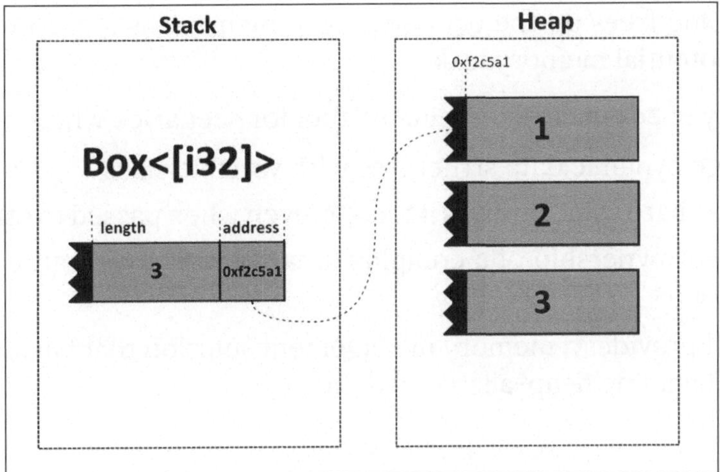

Figure 6.6: *Box<[T]> memory layout example*

Unlike stack-allocated values with fixed sizes and lifetimes, **Box** allows you to allocate memory for a known type and place it on the heap. This heap-allocated value is then owned by the **Box**, which automatically deallocates the memory when it goes out of scope.

Listing 6.12 A simple Box example.

```
fn main() {
    let complex_data = Box::new(vec![1, 2, 3, 4, 5]); // ①

    let sum: i32 = complex_data.iter().sum(); // ②

    println!("The sum of the vector is: {}", sum); // ③
} // ③

// Output

// The sum of the vector is: 15.
```

① Create a complex data structure on the heap using **Box**.

② Manipulate the data inside the **Box**.

③ The **Box** goes out of scope and deallocates the heap memory.

In this example, a **Box** is used to assign memory for a vector `[1, 2, 3, 4, 5]` that resides on the heap. This exemplifies that **Box** can be utilized to manage complex data structures on the heap. Upon reaching the end of its scope, the **Box** goes out of scope and frees up the occupied heap memory as a preventive measure against any potential memory leaks.

The versatility of **Box** makes it a valuable tool for scenarios where you need to:

- Manage dynamic data structures with variable sizes
- Ensure that a value outlives its scope, even when passed to other functions
- Transfer ownership of a complex data structure without costly copying operations

With **Box**, Rust provides a memory management solution that balances flexibility and safety in handling heap-allocated data.

Rc

Rc, short for *Reference Counter*, introduces shared ownership into Rust.

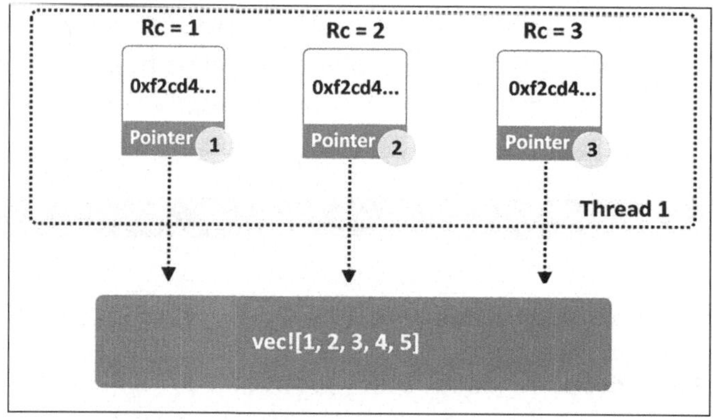

Figure 6.7: *A vector with multiple readers using* Rc

While Rust's ownership model typically enforces a single owner for a piece of data, **Rc** allows multiple owners to share the same data. It keeps track of the number of references to the data and automatically deallocates the memory when the last reference is dropped.

Listing 6.13 A simple Rc example.

```
use std::rc::Rc;

fn main() {
    let data = Rc::new(vec![1, 2, 3, 4, 5]); // ①

    let clone1 = Rc::clone(&data); // ②
    let clone2 = Rc::clone(&data); // ②
```

```
    let sum: i32 = data.iter().sum(); // ③

    println!("Data: {:?}", data);
    println!("Clone1: {:?}", clone1);
    println!("Clone2: {:?}", clone2);
} // ④

// Output

// Data: [1, 2, 3, 4, 5]
// Clone1: [1, 2, 3, 4, 5]
// Clone2: [1, 2, 3, 4, 5]
```

① Create shared data using **Rc**.

② Clone **Rc** pointers to share ownership.

③ Manipulate the shared data.

④ **Data**, **Clone1**, and **Clone2** go out of scope; memory is deallocated.

In this example, an **Rc** smart pointer is used to share ownership of a vector **[1, 2, 3, 4, 5]** between three variables. When all references to the data (**data**, **clone1**, and **clone2**) go out of scope, the memory is automatically deallocated.

Rc provides a way to have multiple readers of the same data, making it useful for scenarios where you want to share data among different parts of your program. However, it's important to note that **Rc** does not guarantee thread safety. If you need shared ownership across multiple threads, you should consider using **Arc** (Atomic Reference Counter) for that purpose.

Arc

Arc, short for *Atomic Reference Counting*, is a sibling of **Rc** that allows multiple owners to share the same data.

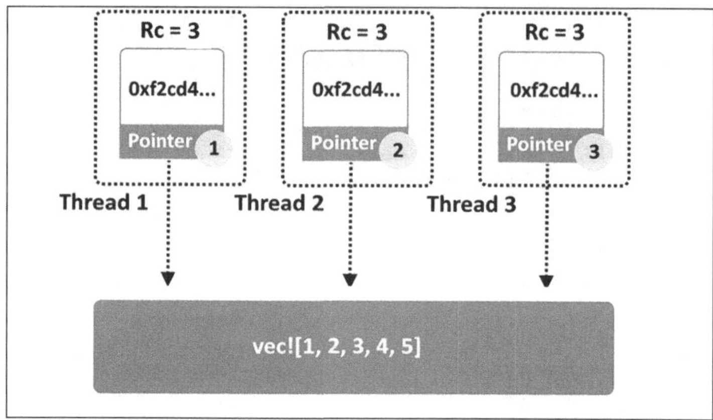

Figure 6.8: *A vector with multi-threaded readers using Arc*

However, unlike **Rc**, **Arc** is tailored for multi-threaded scenarios, ensuring thread safety through atomic operations.

To use **Arc** in multi-threaded contexts, you need to import it from the **std::sync** module.

Listing 6.14 A simple Arc example.

```
use std::sync::Arc;
use std::thread;

fn main() {
    let data = Arc::new(vec![1, 2, 3, 4, 5]); // ①

    let clone1 = Arc::clone(&data); // ②
    let clone2 = Arc::clone(&data); // ②

    let handle1 = thread::spawn(move || { // ③
        let sum: i32 = clone1.iter().sum();
        println!("Thread 1 - Sum of Data: {}", sum);
    });

    let handle2 = thread::spawn(move || { // ③
        let product: i32 = clone2.iter().product();
        println!("Thread 2 - Product of Data: {}", product);
    });

    handle1.join().unwrap(); // ④
    handle2.join().unwrap(); // ④
} // ⑤
```

```
// Output

// Thread 1 - Sum of Data: 15
// Thread 2 - Product of Data: 120
```

① Create thread-safe shared data using Arc.

② Clone **`Arc`** pointers to share ownership across threads.

③ Spawn two threads to work with the shared data.

④ Wait for both threads to finish.

⑤ **`Data`**, **`Clone1`**, **`Clone2`**, and threads go out of scope; memory is deallocated.

In this updated example, an **`Arc`** smart pointer is used to safely share ownership of a vector `[1, 2, 3, 4, 5]` across multiple threads. Two threads (**`Thread 1`** and **`Thread 2`**) are spawned to perform operations on the shared data. When all references to the data (**`data`**, **`clone1`**, and **`clone2`**) and threads go out of scope, the memory is automatically deallocated.

`Arc` is particularly valuable in concurrent programming, ensuring that data is accessed safely by multiple threads. Its atomic reference counting guarantees that reference and deallocation are handled in a thread-safe manner, making it an excellent choice for shared data in multi-threaded environments.

RefCell

Rust's strict rules on mutability ensure the safety and integrity of your code. However, there are situations where you need to perform mutations on data, even in contexts that are otherwise considered immutable. This is where **`RefCell`** steps in as a valuable tool for dynamic mutability.

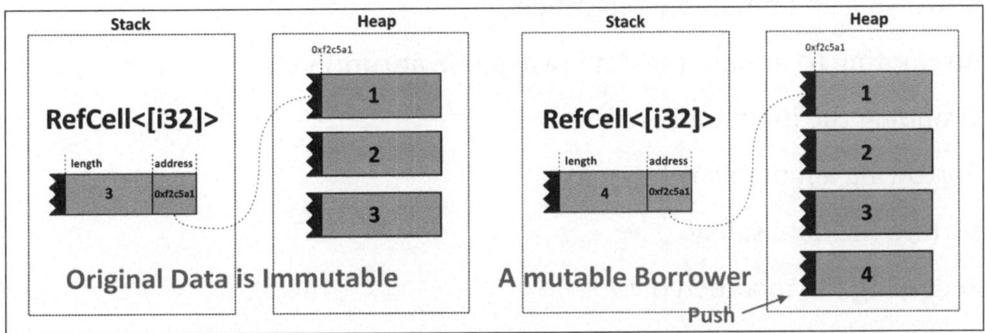

***Figure 6.9**: Borrowing a mutable reference using RefCell*

In contrast to the conventional concept of mutability, which is determined at compile-time, **RefCell** grants you the ability to modify data dynamically while preserving immutability for the variable itself. This feature proves exceptionally advantageous when dealing with data that has potential alterations within an immutable context.

Let's explore how **RefCell** enables dynamic mutability through an illustrative example:

Listing 6.15 A simple RefCell example.

```
use std::cell::RefCell;

fn main() {
    let data = RefCell::new(vec![1, 2, 3]);

    let data_ref = data.borrow(); // ①

    // data_ref.push(4); // ②

    drop(data_ref); // ③

    let mut data_ref_mut = data.borrow_mut(); // ④
    data_ref_mut.push(4); // ⑤

    println!("Modified Data: {:?}", *data_ref_mut); // ⑥
}

// Output

// Modified Data: [1, 2, 3, 4]
```

① Borrowing an immutable reference.

② Attempting to mutate the data (will panic at runtime).

③ Dropping the immutable reference.

④ Borrowing a mutable reference.

⑤ Mutate the data safely.

⑥ Accessing the modified data.

In this example, we start with a **RefCell** containing a vector of integers. Initially, we borrow an immutable reference to the data, which prevents direct mutations.

After dropping the immutable reference, we borrow a mutable reference to safely modify the data.

`RefCell` performs runtime borrow checking, enabling dynamic mutability while enforcing Rust's borrowing rules. If you violate these rules, your program will panic. This runtime checking provides flexibility at the cost of runtime safety.

`RefCell` finds its utility in various scenarios, including:

- **Working with Closures:** It allows you to mutate data within closures that capture immutable references.
- **Internal Mutability:** It's handy for implementing data structures with internal mutability, such as graph algorithms or custom smart pointers.
- **Single-Threaded Contexts:** When borrowing rules are too restrictive in single-threaded contexts, `RefCell` facilitates data sharing.

However, remember to use `RefCell` carefully and handle potential panics with care. Proper synchronization and error handling are crucial when employing dynamic mutability in your code.

Mutex

When working with multi-threaded Rust programs, it's crucial to protect shared data from concurrent access, which can lead to data races and unpredictable behavior. Rust offers the `Mutex` smart pointer as a powerful tool for achieving this. `Mutex` stands for *mutual exclusion* and provides exclusive, synchronized access to shared data, ensuring thread safety and data integrity.

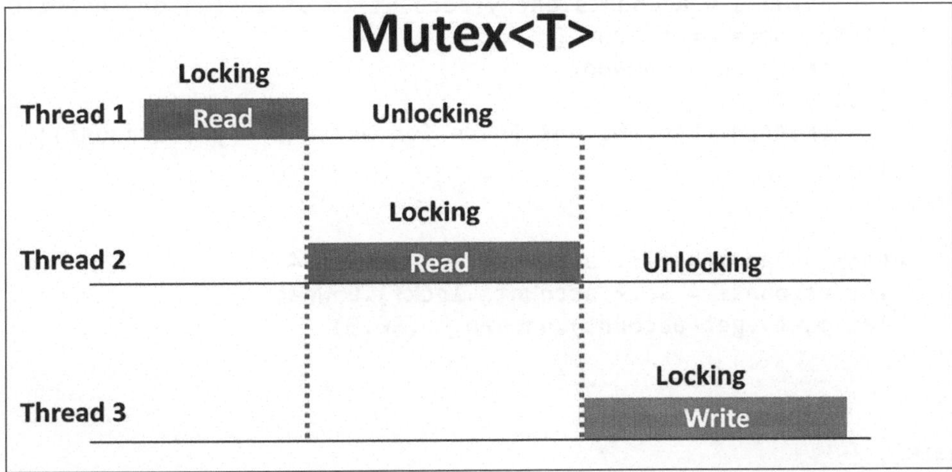

Figure 6.10: *Accessing shared data concurrently using locking/unlocking mechanism with Mutex*

Let's explore how `Mutex<T>` works through an example involving a bank simulation where multiple accounts are updated concurrently:

Listing 6.16 A simple Mutex example.

```
use std::sync::{Mutex, Arc};
use std::thread;
use std::time::Duration;
use std::collections::HashMap;

struct Bank {
    accounts: Mutex<HashMap<String, f64>>,
}

impl Bank {
    fn new() -> Self {
        Bank {
            accounts: Mutex::new(HashMap::new()),
        }
    }

    fn deposit(&self, account: &str, amount: f64) {
        let mut accounts = self.accounts.lock().unwrap();
        let balance = accounts.entry(account.to_string()).or_insert(0.0);
        *balance += amount;
    }

    fn withdraw(&self, account: &str, amount: f64) {
        let mut accounts = self.accounts.lock().unwrap();
        let balance = accounts.entry(account.to_string()).or_insert(0.0);
        if *balance >= amount {
            *balance -= amount;
        } else {
            println!("Insufficient funds for account: {}", account);
        }
    }

    fn check_balance(&self, account: &str) -> f64 {
        let accounts = self.accounts.lock().unwrap();
        *accounts.get(account).unwrap_or(&0.0)
    }
}

fn main() {
    let bank = Arc::new(Bank::new());
    let mut handles = vec![];
```

```
    for i in 0..5 {
        let bank_clone = Arc::clone(&bank);
        let handle = thread::spawn(move || {
            let account = format!("Account{}", i);
            bank_clone.deposit(&account, 100.0);
            thread::sleep(Duration::from_millis(100)); // Simulate other
work
            bank_clone.withdraw(&account, 30.0);
            let balance = bank_clone.check_balance(&account);
            println!("{} - Balance: {:.2}", account, balance);
        });
        handles.push(handle);
    }

    for handle in handles {
        handle.join().unwrap();
    }
}

// Output

// Account0 - Balance: 70.00
// Account2 - Balance: 70.00
// Account1 - Balance: 70.00
// Account4 - Balance: 70.00
// Account3 - Balance: 70.00
```

In this example, we create a **Bank** struct that contains a **Mutex<HashMap<String, f64>>** to store account balances. Multiple threads simulate bank transactions, including deposits, withdrawals, and balance checks. The **Mutex** ensures that only one thread can access the bank accounts at a time, preventing data races and ensuring data consistency.

This example demonstrates how **Mutex** can be used to protect shared data in a multi-threaded environment, such as a banking application. Each thread operates on different accounts concurrently while ensuring that the data remains consistent and accurate.

Locking and unlocking a **Mutex** is crucial for ensuring exclusive access. When a thread locks a **Mutex**, it gains exclusive control over the protected data. Once the thread finishes its operation and the lock goes out of scope, the Mutex is automatically unlocked, enabling other threads to access it.

Mutex is a valuable tool for guarding shared data in multi-threaded Rust programs, guaranteeing that only one thread can modify it at any given time. However, it's essential to use `Mutex` carefully to avoid unnecessary contention for access, which can impact performance. In scenarios with predominantly read-heavy operations, consider using `RwLock<T>` for improved concurrency.

RwLock

`RwLock` (Read-Write Lock) plays a crucial role in multi-threaded Rust programming by providing a balanced approach to managing shared data. It allows multiple threads to read data concurrently while ensuring exclusive access for writing. This versatility makes it a valuable tool for scenarios with varying read and write demands.

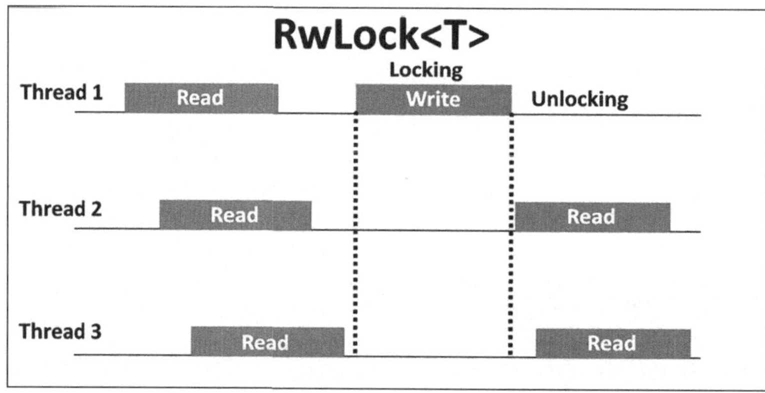

Figure 6.11: *Concurrent read of shared data with RwLock*

When deciding whether to use `Mutex<T>` or `RwLock<T>`, consider the nature of your shared data:

- `Mutex<T>`: Opt for `Mutex<T>` when your data experiences frequent updates, and maintaining data consistency through exclusive access is crucial. Use it when the complexity of managing separate read and write locks isn't justified by performance gains.
- `RwLock<T>`: If your data is read more often than it's written, and the cost of read conflict is a concern, `RwLock<T>` offers a more efficient approach. Allowing multiple concurrent readers can significantly improve performance in such scenarios.

Guidelines for Usage:

- `Mutex<T>` is suitable for situations where both reading and writing require exclusive access, or when separate locks would add complexity without clear performance benefits.

- `RwLock<T>` shines in read-heavy workloads, enhancing performance by enabling concurrent readers while ensuring safe writes.

It's important to note that the performance characteristics of `Mutex<T>` and `RwLock<T>` can vary across platforms. Therefore, benchmarking and profiling specific to your use case are advisable for making an informed choice.

Here's the previous example, rewritten using `RwLock` instead of `Mutex`, followed by a detailed explanation of the differences:

Listing 6.17 A simple RwLock example.

```
use std::sync::{Arc, RwLock};
use std::thread;
use std::time::Duration;
use std::collections::HashMap;

struct Bank {
    accounts: RwLock<HashMap<String, f64>>,
}

impl Bank {
    fn new() -> Self {
        Bank {
            accounts: RwLock::new(HashMap::new()),
        }
    }

    fn deposit(&self, account: &str, amount: f64) {
        let mut accounts = self.accounts.write().unwrap();
        let balance = accounts.entry(account.to_string()).or_insert(0.0);
        *balance += amount;
    }

    fn withdraw(&self, account: &str, amount: f64) {
        let mut accounts = self.accounts.write().unwrap();
        let balance = accounts.entry(account.to_string()).or_insert(0.0);
        if *balance >= amount {
            *balance -= amount;
        } else {
            println!("Insufficient funds for account: {}", account);
        }
    }

    fn check_balance(&self, account: &str) -> f64 {
        let accounts = self.accounts.read().unwrap();
```

```
        *accounts.get(account).unwrap_or(&0.0)
    }
}

fn main() {
    let bank = Arc::new(Bank::new());
    let mut handles = vec![];

    for i in 0..5 {
        let bank_clone = Arc::clone(&bank);
        let handle = thread::spawn(move || {
            let account = format!("Account{}", i);
            bank_clone.deposit(&account, 100.0);
            thread::sleep(Duration::from_millis(100)); // Simulate other
work
            bank_clone.withdraw(&account, 30.0);
            let balance = bank_clone.check_balance(&account);
            println!("{} - Balance: {:.2}", account, balance);
        });
        handles.push(handle);
    }

    for handle in handles {
        handle.join().unwrap();
    }
}

// Output

// Account1 - Balance: 70.00
// Account2 - Balance: 70.00
// Account0 - Balance: 70.00
// Account3 - Balance: 70.00
// Account4 - Balance: 70.00
```

- **Using `RwLock`**: In the rewritten example, we've replaced `Mutex` with `RwLock` to allow multiple threads to read data concurrently while ensuring exclusive access for writing. This change enables better parallelism in read-heavy scenarios.
- **Using `write()` and `read()`**: We use `self.accounts.write().unwrap()` to acquire a write lock and `self.accounts.read().unwrap()` to acquire a read lock on the `RwLock`. This controls access to the `HashMap` in a way that multiple threads can read simultaneously but only one can write at a time.

- `RwLock` **Methods**: `RwLock` provides separate methods for reading and writing, which allows us to express our intentions clearly. In the deposit and withdraw methods, we use `write()` to ensure exclusive access when updating account balances. In the `check_balance` method, we use `read()` to allow concurrent reads.
- **Concurrency**: This change in synchronization doesn't affect the main logic of the program; it still simulates multiple bank transactions across different accounts. However, it optimizes the program for better performance in scenarios where reads are more frequent than writes.
- **Output**: The output remains the same, displaying the account balances after the simulated transactions.

In summary, by using `RwLock`, we strike a balance between read and write access, making the code more efficient in situations where reads dominate the workload. This can lead to improved concurrency and resource utilization compared to using `Mutex` for read-heavy scenarios.

Atomic

In concurrent programming, when multiple threads access and modify shared data simultaneously, it's essential to ensure that these operations are atomic. An atomic operation means that it appears to occur instantaneously from the perspective of other threads, without any interleaved or partially completed steps. Rust provides powerful support for atomic operations through its standard library, enabling you to write safe and efficient concurrent code.

In a multi-threaded environment, non-atomic operations on shared data can lead to data races, which result in undefined behavior and difficult-to-debug issues. As you may know, data races occur when two or more threads simultaneously access the same memory location, and at least one of them performs a write operation. To avoid data races and maintain the integrity of shared data, Rust offers atomic operations.

The `std::sync::atomic` module provides a comprehensive selection of atomic types and operations for different data types. These atomic types guarantee that actions performed on them, such as reads, writes, and modifications, are atomic. This ensures the prevention of data races in concurrent code.

Let's dive into a basic example to demonstrate the use of atomic operations:

Listing 6.18 A simple atomic operation example.

```
use std::sync::atomic::{AtomicBool, Ordering};
use std::sync::Arc;
use std::thread;

fn main() {
    let atomic_flag = Arc::new(AtomicBool::new(false)); // ①

    let atomic_flag_clone = Arc::clone(&atomic_flag); // ②

    let thread_handle = thread::spawn(move || { // ③
        thread::sleep(std::time::Duration::from_secs(1));
        atomic_flag_clone.store(true, Ordering::Relaxed);
    });

    while !atomic_flag.load(Ordering::Relaxed) { // ④
        // Do some work...
    }

    thread_handle.join().unwrap();

    println!("Atomic flag is set to true.");
}

// Output

// Atomic flag is set to true.
```

① Create a new atomic boolean with an initial value of **`false`**.

② Clone the atomic flag for use in multiple threads.

③ Spawn a thread that toggles the atomic flag after a delay.

④ Check the atomic flag's value in a loop until it becomes **`true`**.

In this example, we create an **`AtomicBool`** named **`atomic_flag`** initialized with **`false`**. We then clone it to be used in a separate thread. The spawned thread sleeps for a second and then atomically sets the flag to **`true`** using the **`store`** method.

Meanwhile, the main thread continuously checks the flag's value using the **`load`** method in a loop, performing some work until the flag becomes **`true`**. This demonstrates atomicity and synchronization between threads.

The **Ordering** enum, used in atomic operations like **store** and **load**, specifies the memory ordering constraints, ensuring proper synchronization between threads.

Atomic operations play a vital role in building secure and effective concurrent data structures and algorithms within the Rust programming language. These operations offer essential ways to coordinate and synchronize threads, ensuring the prevention of data races and undefined behavior.

Unsafe Rust

While Rust's safety features are robust, there are moments when you need to harness the forbidding capabilities of **unsafe** Rust. The **unsafe** keyword grants you control over low-level memory operations, but it also demands meticulous attention to memory safety.

One prominent use case for **unsafe** Rust is interfacing with code in other languages, like C or C++. These languages often work at a lower level and perform operations that Rust's safety checks cannot express.

Let's explore some complex scenarios where **unsafe** Rust becomes essential:

Unsafe Functions

In Rust, you have the ability to declare functions as "unsafe" when they execute operations that lack static verification for their safety by the compiler. This includes actions such as dereferencing raw pointers, performing mutable aliasing, or accessing registers linked to memory mapping.

Here's an example of an **unsafe** function that dereferences a raw pointer:

Listing 6.19 A simple unsafe function example.

```
fn main() {
    let mut x = 42;
    let raw_ptr: *const i32 = &x;

    unsafe {
        println!("The value at raw_ptr: {}", *raw_ptr);
    }
}
```

In this code, an **unsafe** block is used to dereference a raw pointer **raw_ptr**, which points to the value of **x**. The **unsafe** block indicates that the programmer is responsible for ensuring the safety of this operation.

Unsafe Traits

In Rust, it is possible to implement traits on types that require **unsafe** operations as well. This practice frequently occurs while implementing custom smart pointers or low-level abstractions. Traits like **Send** and **Sync** are examples of unsafe traits. These traits are marked as unsafe because implementing them implies certain semantic guarantees related to thread safety, and violating these guarantees could lead to memory safety issues.

The following is an example using a hypothetical unsafe trait:

Listing 6.20 A simple unsafe traits example.

```
unsafe trait UnsafeTrait {
    fn unsafe_method(&self);
}

unsafe impl UnsafeTrait for i32 {
    fn unsafe_method(&self) {
        println!("Unsafe method implementation for i32: {}", self);
    }
}

fn main() {
    let num: i32 = 42;

    let trait_ref: &dyn UnsafeTrait = &num;
    println!("Referencing an unsafe trait is safe");

    trait_ref.unsafe_method();
    println!("Called the unsafe method");
}
```

In this example, the **UnsafeTrait** is marked as unsafe, and its implementation for i32 is also marked as unsafe. The actual implementation of the **unsafe_method** could involve operations that, if misused, might threaten memory safety.

The key point is that using unsafe traits requires careful consideration and adherence to the semantic guarantees provided by the trait, and implementing such traits must be done with a deep understanding of their implications for memory safety.

Custom Unsafe Abstractions

In Rust, you can craft your own **unsafe** abstractions when dealing with specific hardware or low-level operations. Consider a scenario where you're working with a custom hardware device that requires precise memory management:

Listing 6.21 A simple unsafe abstractions example.

```
mod custom_device {
    pub struct HardwareDevice {
        // Fields specific to the hardware device
    }

    impl HardwareDevice {
        pub fn new() -> Self {
            // Initialize and configure the hardware device
            Self {
                // Initialize fields here
            }
        }

        pub fn perform_unsafe_operation(&self) {
            // Perform low-level operations that require `unsafe` Rust
        }
    }
}

fn main() {
    let device = custom_device::HardwareDevice::new();

    // Interact with the hardware device safely
    device.perform_unsafe_operation();
}
```

In this example, we encapsulate the hardware device's functionality in a module and define an **unsafe** method **perform_unsafe_operation** for low-level device interactions. This ensures that only the necessary part of the code is marked as **unsafe**, containing potential risks.

Foreign Function Interface (FFI)

Rust's FFI capabilities enable seamless integration with other languages. Often, you'll encounter **unsafe** Rust code when calling functions from external libraries. Let's explore an example:

Listing 6.22 A simple FFI example.

```
extern "C" {
    fn external_function(arg: i32) -> i32;
}

fn main() {
    let result: i32;

    unsafe {
        result = external_function(42);
    }

    println!("Result from external function: {}", result);
}
```

In this code, we declare an external C function `external_function` and call it within an `unsafe` block. The `unsafe` block is necessary because FFI calls are inherently unsafe, as Rust can't verify the safety of code in external languages.

These examples demonstrate how `unsafe` Rust empowers you to navigate complex scenarios, whether they involve custom hardware interactions, seamless integration with other languages, implementing `unsafe` traits, or defining `unsafe` functions. Nonetheless, with great power comes great responsibility, always step carefully in the world of `unsafe` Rust.

Unsafe Code Guidelines

When working with `unsafe` Rust, it's crucial to follow safety guidelines thoroughly. Here are some tips to ensure your `unsafe` code remains as safe as possible:

- **Limit `unsafe` to Small Blocks**: Whenever possible, limit `unsafe` code to small, well-contained blocks or functions. This reduces the scope of potential issues and makes it easier to audit for safety.
- **Document Assumptions**: Clearly document any assumptions or invariants that your `unsafe` code relies on. This helps other developers understand the reasoning behind the code and encourages safer usage.
- **Use Abstractions**: Whenever feasible, wrap `unsafe` operations in safe abstractions. This shields the rest of your codebase from the intricacies of `unsafe` code.
- **Testing**: Strictly test your `unsafe` code to uncover potential issues early. Property-based testing and fuzzing can be particularly useful in this context.

- **Code Review**: Seek help from experienced Rust developers for code reviews, especially when working with `unsafe` code. A new pair of eyes can catch subtle safety violations.

By approaching `unsafe` Rust with caution and following best practices, you can harness its power without compromising the safety of your code. More on unsafe Rust in *Chapter13: Unsafe Coding in Rust.*

Memory Management Best Practices

In Rust, effective memory management goes beyond understanding the basics of ownership, borrowing, and smart pointers. To write robust and efficient code, it's essential to follow best practices and adopt idiomatic Rust patterns. In this section, we'll explore some of these best practices and guidelines.

Favor Stack Allocation

As a rule of thumb, prefer stack allocation over heap allocation whenever possible. The stack is fast, and memory management is straightforward. Local variables, function call data, and short-lived values should primarily reside on the stack.

Stack allocation has several advantages, including:

Advantage	Description
Speed	Faster allocation and deallocation than heap.
Predictability	LIFO order ensures efficient value management.
Safety	Strict lifetime rules reduce memory-related bugs.

Table 6.1: *Stack memory allocation and its advantages*

Use heap allocation (for example, `Box`, `Rc`, or `Arc`) when you need dynamic lifetimes or have data of unknown size at compile time.

Leverage References

References (`&`) are your friends when it comes to efficiently accessing and sharing data. Use them to borrow values rather than take ownership. This minimizes unnecessary copying and allows multiple parts of your code to read data simultaneously.

Immutable references (**&**) offer read-only access and can be shared across multiple threads, ensuring safety without sacrificing performance. Mutable references (**&mut**) grant exclusive write access to data within a limited scope.

When designing functions and methods, consider accepting references rather than consuming values when possible. This allows for greater flexibility and reusability.

Use Smart Pointers Wisely

Smart pointers like **Box**, **Rc**, and **Arc** are valuable tools, but they should be employed carefully. Reserve their use for scenarios where shared ownership, reference counting, or heap allocation is necessary.

Avoid unnecessary boxing (**Box**) of values that can be stack-allocated. While **Box** offers dynamic lifetimes, excessive use can lead to unnecessary heap allocations and performance overhead.

Rc and **Arc** are excellent choices when multiple parts of your code need to share ownership of data. However, be cautious of potential reference cycles (where objects reference each other, preventing their deallocation). In such cases, consider using **Weak** references alongside **Rc** or **Arc** to break cycles.

Use Pattern Matching

Pattern matching in Rust achieved through the **match** keyword, is a powerful tool for managing memory efficiently. It allows you to destructure and extract data from complex structures with ease. Patterns can be used to match against enums, structs, and even tuples.

Here's a simple example of pattern matching:

Listing 6.23 A simple pattern matching example.

```
fn main() {
    let option = Some(42);

    match option {
        Some(value) => println!("The value is: {}", value),
        None => println!("No value"),
    }
}
```

```
// Output

// The value is: 42
```

In this code, we use pattern matching to handle the `Option` enum, destructuring it into `Some` and `None` variants.

Lifetime Annotations

Understanding lifetimes is crucial for memory management in Rust. While the compiler can often infer lifetimes, there are scenarios where explicit lifetime annotations are necessary to convey your intentions.

Lifetime annotations are used to specify the relationships between references, ensuring that borrowed data remains valid throughout its usage. When designing functions, structs, or trait implementations, consider adding explicit lifetime annotations to make your code more readable and to clarify your intentions.

Here's an example of explicit lifetime annotations:

Listing 6.24 A simple lifetime annotations example.

```
fn longest<'a>(s1: &'a str, s2: &'a str) -> &'a str {
    if s1.len() > s2.len() {
        s1
    } else {
        s2
    }
}

fn main() {
    let s1 = "Hello,";
    let s2 = "world!";

    let longest_string = longest(s1, s2);

    println!("The longest string is: {}", longest_string);
}

// Output

// The longest string is: world!
```

In this code, the function `longest` has an explicit lifetime annotation (`'a`) that indicates that the returned reference's lifetime is tied to the input references `s1` and `s2`.

Proper Resource Management

Memory management in Rust extends to other resources beyond memory, such as files, network connections, and external libraries. Properly managing these resources is essential to avoid resource leaks and ensure the robustness of your code.

Rust's ownership and drop system naturally extend to resource management. When a value goes out of scope, its associated resources are released, whether it's memory or other resources like file handles.

In scenarios where you deal with external resources, consider using Rust's standard library types, like `std::fs::File` for file I/O. These types implement the `Drop` trait to ensure that resources are released when they are no longer needed.

Multithreading and Concurrency

If your Rust application requires multithreading or concurrency, be mindful of memory synchronization. Rust's ownership model provides safety guarantees for single-threaded code, but multithreaded programs require additional consideration.

Use synchronization primitives like `Mutex`, `RwLock`, and `Atomic` types to protect shared data. These primitives ensure that data access is properly synchronized between threads, preventing data races and memory corruption.

When using multithreading, consider the trade-offs between performance and memory usage. Strategies such as thread-local storage and careful thread design can minimize friction and maximize efficiency.

Unsafe Code with Caution

While `unsafe` Rust provides powerful tools for low-level memory operations, it should be used sparingly and with caution. Only resort to `unsafe` code when you have exhausted safe alternatives and when you can ensure that your code will not compromise safety.

When writing `unsafe` code, thoroughly test and review it to identify and eliminate potential issues. Document your assumptions and invariants clearly, and keep the `unsafe` code as isolated as possible to minimize its impact on the overall codebase.

Remember that the goal of `unsafe` Rust is not to bypass the language's safety checks but to enable safe abstractions and interactions with external code that cannot be expressed in safe Rust. More on unsafe code in *Chapter13: Unsafe Coding in Rust.*

Profiling and Optimization

Efficient memory management often goes hand-in-hand with profiling and optimization. Use profiling tools like *cargo-prof* and *perf* to identify performance bottlenecks and memory usage patterns in your code.

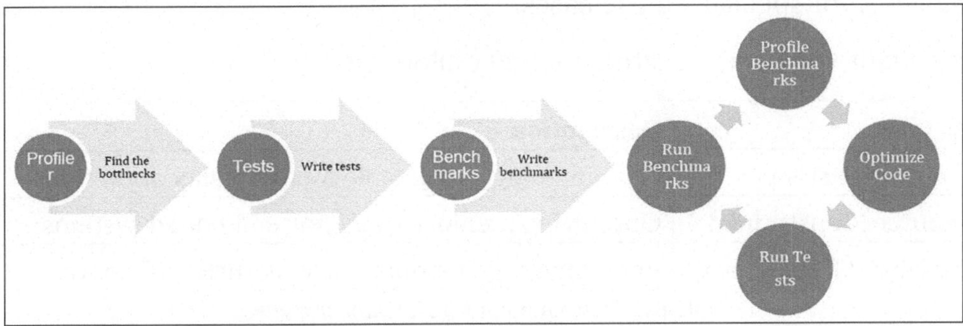

Figure 6.12: *Code optimization workflow*

Profile-driven optimization enables you to concentrate your efforts on the sections of your code that exert the greatest influence on performance and memory usage. Use Rust's built-in profiling capabilities as well as external profilers to gain insights into your code's behavior.

Optimization techniques such as data structure selection, algorithm improvements, and caching can significantly impact memory usage and performance. Always measure the effects of optimizations using benchmarks and profiling data to ensure that your changes have the desired impact.

By embracing these recommended techniques and principles for memory management, you will have the necessary tools to craft efficient, robust, and secure Rust code. The management of memory is a core element in programming, and Rust's unique features and safety guarantees make it a powerful language for effectively managing memory operations.

Advanced Memory Management

Now that we have delved into the basics of memory management in Rust, it is time to delve even deeper into more advanced subjects. In this particular section, we will explore custom memory allocators, memory-mapped files, and how Rust interacts with other programming languages, as we learned in *Chapter 1: Systems Programming with Rust*. By delving into these topics, you will broaden your comprehension of Rust's remarkable abilities in managing memory.

Custom Memory Allocators

Rust's standard library provides a default memory allocator, but there are scenarios where custom memory management is necessary. Custom allocators allow you to control how memory is allocated and deallocated, opening up possibilities for specialized use cases.

When might you need a custom memory allocator?

Use Case	Description
Real-time Systems	Guaranteeing predictable memory allocation times.
Resource-Constrained	Optimizing memory usage for embedded systems.
Specialized Data Types	Implementing custom data structures efficiently.

Table 6.2: *Custom memory allocator use cases*

Creating a custom allocator involves implementing the **`GlobalAlloc`** trait. This trait defines methods for allocation, deallocation, and memory statistics. Let's outline the basic steps to create a custom allocator:

- Define a type that implements the **`GlobalAlloc`** trait.
- Implement the required methods, such as **`alloc`**, **`dealloc`**, and optional ones like **`realloc`**.
- Use the **`#[global_allocator]`** attribute to specify your custom allocator as the global allocator.

Here's an example of a custom allocator:

Listing 6.25 Custom memory allocator example.

```
use std::alloc::{GlobalAlloc, Layout};
use std::ptr;

struct MyAllocator;

unsafe impl GlobalAlloc for MyAllocator {
    unsafe fn alloc(&self, layout: Layout) -> *mut u8 {
```

```
        // Implement custom allocation logic here
        // Return a pointer to the allocated memory
        let size = layout.size();
        if size == 0 {
            return ptr::null_mut();
        }

        // For demonstration purposes, we'll use a simple global memory
buffer
        // This is just an example and not suitable for production use
        static mut MEMORY: [u8; 4096] = [0; 4096];
        static mut NEXT: usize = 0;

        let align = layout.align();
        let aligned_next = (NEXT + align - 1) & !(align - 1);
        if aligned_next + size <= MEMORY.len() {
            NEXT = aligned_next + size;
            &mut MEMORY[aligned_next] as *mut u8
        } else {
            ptr::null_mut()
        }
    }

    unsafe fn dealloc(&self, _ptr: *mut u8, _layout: Layout) {
        // Implement custom deallocation logic here
        // This allocator does not support deallocation in this example
    }
}

#[global_allocator]
static GLOBAL_ALLOCATOR: MyAllocator = MyAllocator;

fn main() {
    // Allocate memory using our custom allocator
    let size = 64;
    let layout = Layout::from_size_align(size, 8).unwrap();
    let ptr = unsafe { GLOBAL_ALLOCATOR.alloc(layout) };

    if !ptr.is_null() {
        println!("Allocated memory at {:?}", ptr);
    } else {
        println!("Allocation failed");
    }

    // Deallocate memory (not supported in this example)
}
```

```
// Output

// Allocated memory at 0x557080d0a069
```

In Rust, you have the ability to customize memory management according to your specific requirements by implementing a custom allocator. This empowers you to optimize for applications that require minimal latency, reduce memory fragmentation, or seamlessly integrate with external memory management systems.

Memory-Mapped Files

Memory-mapped files provide a mechanism for mapping a file directly into memory, allowing you to work with large datasets or files that exceed available RAM. Rust's standard library offers memory-mapped file support through the **`std::fs::File`** type and the **`mmap`** method.

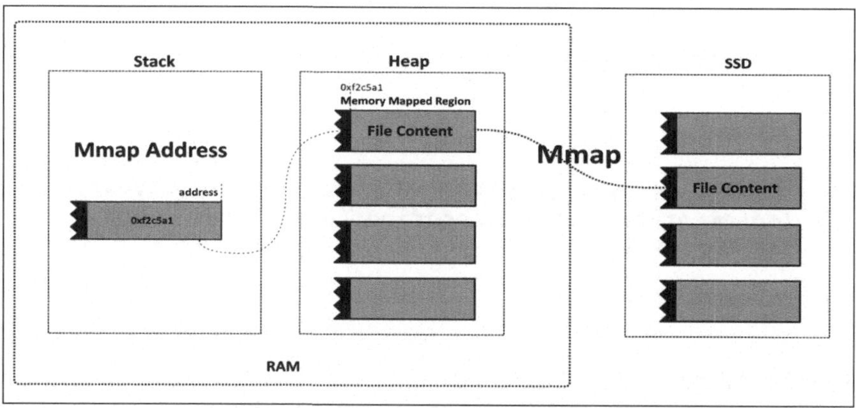

Figure 6.13: *Memory-Mapped files simple illustration*

To memory-map a file in Rust, follow these steps:

- Open the file using **`std::fs::File`**.
- Determine the portion of the file you want to map and the desired access mode (read-only or read-write).
- Use the **`memmap`** crate to create a memory-mapped view of the file.

Here's a simple example of memory-mapping a file for reading:

Listing 6.26 Memory-mapped files example.

```
use std::fs::File;
use std::io::{self, Read};
use memmap::Mmap;

fn main() -> io::Result<()> {
    let mut file = File::open("data.txt")?; // ①

    let file_length = file.metadata()?.len(); // ②

    if file_length == 0 { // ③
        return Err(io::Error::new(
            io::ErrorKind::InvalidInput,
            "File must have a non-zero length for memory mapping",
        ));
    }

    let mmap = unsafe { Mmap::map(&file)? }; // ④

    println!("{:?}", &mmap); // ⑤

    Ok(())
}

// Output

// Mmap { ptr: 0x7f0ba6513000, len: 5 }
```

① Open a file containing the word "Hello" for reading.

② Get the length of the file.

③ Check if the file has a non-zero length.

④ Memory-map the file.

⑤ Access the memory-mapped data.

Memory-mapped files are useful for scenarios like working with large log files, database storage, or implementing custom data storage formats efficiently. Be cautious when using memory-mapped files, as they directly impact system memory and file I/O.

Interoperability with Other Languages

As we saw in *Chapter 1: Systems Programming with Rust*, Rust's memory management capabilities extend beyond the language itself. Rust can interoperate with other programming languages, such as C and C++, allowing you to leverage existing libraries and codebases.

To interface with code written in other languages, Rust provides the **extern** keyword and FFI (Foreign Function Interface). FFI enables Rust to call functions written in C or other languages and vice versa.

When working with FFI, consider the following:

Consideration	Description
Safety	FFI calls are inherently unsafe and must be marked as such.
ABI Compatibility	Ensure that Rust and the target language have compatible ABIs.
Type Conversions	Handle conversions between Rust and foreign types.
Error Handling	Establish error-handling mechanisms for cross-language calls.

Table 6.3: *FFI considerations*

Here's an example of calling a C function from Rust:

Listing 6.27 FFI example.

```
extern "C" {
    fn c_function(arg: i32) -> i32;
}

fn main() {
    let result = unsafe { c_function(42) };
    println!("Result from C function: {}", result);
}
```

When using FFI, carefully manage memory allocation and deallocation, as Rust's ownership system may differ from that of other languages. Utilize Rust's **std::ffi** module for safe conversions between Rust and C strings and types.

Interoperability enables you to harness the power of Rust's memory management within existing codebases or leverage well-established libraries from other languages.

Memory Management Best Practices

To conclude our exploration of Rust's memory management, let's recap some essential best practices and guidelines to keep in mind:

Best Practice	Description
Prefer Stack Allocation	Whenever possible, use stack allocation for efficiency and safety.
Leverage References	Use references and borrowing to access data without transferring ownership.
Pattern Matching	Utilize pattern matching and destructuring for complex data manipulation.
Borrowing Strategies	Choose between mutable and immutable borrowing based on your data access needs.
Lifetime Annotations	Apply explicit lifetime annotations for clarity and safety.
Avoid Dangling References	Ensure that references remain valid throughout their usage.
Safeguard Against Data Races	Use synchronization primitives to prevent data races in multithreaded code.
Document **`unsafe`** Code	Clearly document assumptions and safety measures within **`unsafe`** blocks.
Profile and Optimize	Use profiling tools to identify performance bottlenecks and optimize memory usage.

***Table 6.4**: Memory management best practices*

By following these best practices and continuously expanding your knowledge of Rust's memory management, you'll be well-equipped to develop high-performance, safe, and reliable software.

Conclusion

In this chapter, we explored Rust's memory management and pointer complexities. We explored the role of memory management in software development and how Rust's philosophy revolves around efficient memory utilization, safety, and reliability.

We delved into stack and heap memory allocation, understanding how Rust optimizes memory usage for different scenarios. You learned about the stack's role in managing local variables and function calls and the heap's role in handling data with dynamic lifetimes.

The concept of ownership, borrowing, and lifetimes in Rust was introduced, highlighting the language's strict rules for memory safety. You saw how Rust ensures memory safety without the need for garbage collection, eliminating issues like memory leaks and data races.

Smart pointers took center stage, with `Box`, `Rc`, `Arc`, `Atomic`, `RwLock`, `Mutex`, and so on providing solutions to shared ownership and reference counting. `Box` enables heap allocation with automatic deallocation, while `Rc` and `Arc` facilitate shared ownership with reference counting, ensuring memory safety even in multi-threaded environments.

We also explored the world of `unsafe` Rust, where you have more control over memory operations but must take on the responsibility of ensuring safety. You explored the use of `unsafe` functions and traits and learned best practices for writing `unsafe` code.

Finally, we delved into advanced memory management topics, including custom memory allocators, memory-mapped files, and interoperation with other programming languages. Each of these topics expands your understanding of Rust's memory management capabilities and equips you with valuable tools for complex memory management scenarios.

Whether you're building systems-level software, web applications, or embedded devices, Rust's memory management capabilities will serve as your trusted companion. Embrace the power of Rust, and keep pushing the boundaries of what you can create.

As you continue your Rust journey, you'll find that the language's memory management and pointer features empower you to write high-performance, safe, and efficient code. Whether you're building systems software, web applications, or anything in between, Rust's memory management tools will be your trusted companions.

In the chapters that follow, we'll dive even deeper into Rust's capabilities, exploring advanced topics, patterns, and techniques that will elevate your Rust programming skills to new heights. So, get ready for the exciting journey ahead!

CHAPTER 7
Managing Concurrency

Introduction

Concurrency stands as a cornerstone of modern software development, enabling programs to carry out multiple tasks concurrently, ultimately enhancing performance and responsiveness. This chapter walks us through the complexities of concurrency management in the Rust programming language. We will delve into the use of threads and synchronization primitives, equipping you with the knowledge to construct robust and efficient concurrent applications.

In previous chapters, we introduced fundamental concepts such as concurrency and smart pointers, providing a glimpse into their significance. However, this chapter marks a deep dive into the expansive world of concurrent programming in Rust. Our exploration begins with a detailed examination of thread behavior and the techniques required for their creation.

Before delving into the nitty-gritty details of concurrent programming, it is essential to establish a solid understanding of how threads operate and how they can be instantiated. Threads are the building blocks of concurrency, allowing multiple tasks to run concurrently within a single program. In the upcoming sections, we will explore the fundamentals of threading in Rust, including thread creation, management, and synchronization, laying the foundation for more advanced concurrent programming concepts.

Structure

In this chapter, we are going to explore the following topics:

- Understanding concurrent programming with threads and synchronization.
- Introducing concurrent data structures: Mutex and RwLock.
- Techniques for thread communication and message passing in Rust.

Understanding Concurrent Programming

Concurrency means doing multiple things at the same time in software development. In Rust, we use threads to make this happen.

In Rust, how threads work is based on the ideas of ownership, borrowing, and lifetimes. Imagine each thread in Rust as having its own little storage space and things it can use. The Rust compiler makes sure that when threads share things, they do it in a safe and careful way to prevent problems.

Here's a bit more detail:

- **Ownership:** Think of ownership as being in charge of something. In Rust, each piece of data (like a number or a piece of text) can only belong to one thread at a time. This means one thread has control over it.
- **Borrowing:** Borrowing is like asking to use something that someone else owns. Threads can ask to temporarily use something from another thread, but they have to follow rules to make sure they don't mess it up for others.
- **Lifetimes:** Lifetimes are like timers for how long something can be used. Rust keeps track of how long threads use shared data to prevent any problems or conflicts.

So, in Rust, think of threads as tiny workers. Each worker has their own tools and can ask each other for help, but they need to be really careful and follow some important rules to make sure everything stays safe. The Rust compiler acts like a boss, watching over these workers to make sure they follow the rules and don't cause any problems.

Concurrency vs Parallelism

Before we start talking about doing multiple things at the same time, it's important to understand two related but different ideas: parallelism and concurrency.

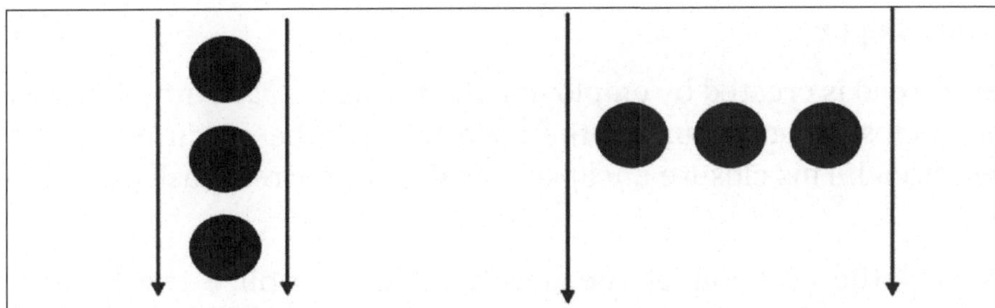

Figure 7.1: *Concurrent threads vs Parallel tasks*

Parallelism means doing multiple tasks at the same time to make things faster, especially when using multiple parts of a computer's brain (called CPU cores). It usually involves working on tasks that don't depend on each other.

Concurrency, on the other hand, is a bigger idea that includes managing multiple tasks that might happen one after the other or at the same time. It's like when you have to juggle different things happening all at once, like replying to emails while listening to music. In programming, concurrency means dealing with tasks that don't always happen in order and making sure they share information and resources without causing problems.

In this chapter, we will explore both parallelism and concurrency. Now, let's begin by understanding how threads work in Rust.

Creating and Managing Threads

In Rust, dealing with threads is pretty straightforward. You can think of threads as clever little helpers that can perform tasks independently. To use threads, you have a handy function called **`thread::spawn`**. This function lets you create a new helper (thread) and instruct it on what job to do.

Listing 7.1 Creating and managing threads example.

```
use std::thread;
fn main() {
    let handle = thread::spawn(|| { // ①
        // Code for a new thread goes here.
    });

    handle.join().unwrap(); // ②
}
```

In this code snippet:

① A new thread is created by employing the **`thread::spawn`** function. Inside this function, a closure encapsulates the code that will be executed in this newly spawned thread. This closure encapsulates the concurrent task that we want to perform.

② Following the creation of the new thread, we utilize the **`handle.join()`** method to ensure that it has concluded its execution before proceeding further in the main thread.

Understanding the nuances of thread creation and management is pivotal for effective concurrent programming within the Rust programming language. Mastery of these concepts enables you to unlock the power of concurrency while ensuring safe and error-resilient code execution.

Sharing Data Between Threads

One of the essential aspects of concurrent programming is the ability to share data between threads safely. Rust provides a powerful mechanism for this called **ownership** and **borrowing**.

Let's look at an example of how data can be shared between threads using Rust's ownership model:

Listing 7.2 Sharing data between threads example.

```
use std::thread;

fn main() {
    let data = vec![1, 2, 3, 4, 5]; // ①

    let handle = thread::spawn(move || { // ②
        // Code for the new thread goes here.
        println!("{:?}", data); // ③
    });

    handle.join().unwrap();
}

// Output

// [1, 2, 3, 4, 5]
```

In this code snippet:

① We create a vector **`data`** containing some integers.

② When we spawn a new thread using **`thread::spawn`**, we move the ownership of **`data`** into the new thread using the **`move`** keyword. This means that the new thread has exclusive access to **`data`**, and the main thread can no longer access it.

③ Inside the new thread's closure, we can safely access and print the contents of **`data`**.

This example demonstrates how Rust's ownership system ensures that data shared between threads is accessed in a controlled and safe manner, preventing data races and other concurrency-related bugs.

Concurrent Data Structures

While Rust's ownership and borrowing system helps prevent data races, sometimes you need to coordinate actions between threads explicitly. Rust provides various synchronization primitives for this purpose, such as mutexes and channels.

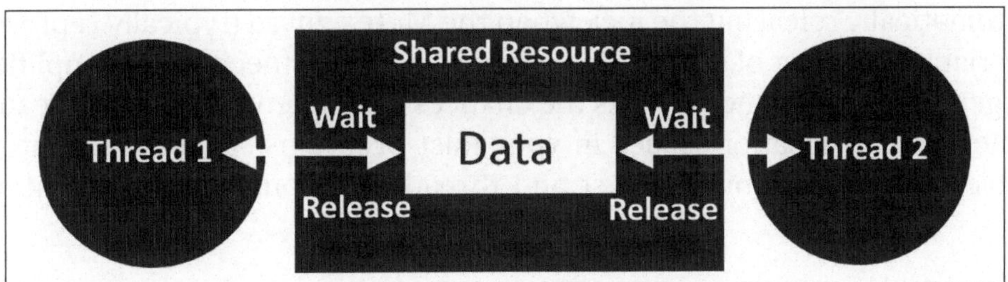

***Figure 7.2**: Threads shared resource through mutex*

Mutex, short for "*mutual exclusion*", is a fundamental synchronization primitive in Rust that plays a crucial role in concurrent programming. It allows multiple threads to coordinate and share data safely, ensuring that only one thread can access a protected resource at a time. This prevents data races and maintains data integrity in multithreaded applications.

In the following sections, we will take a comprehensive look at Mutex in Rust, thoroughly examining its complex nature. We will start with the fundamental concepts and gradually progress to more complex scenarios, equipping you with the knowledge needed to utilize Mutex effectively for thread synchronization and shared data management. Additionally, we will explore strategies for preventing deadlocks and address how to gracefully handle exceptional situations that may arise during concurrent programming. By the end of this exploration, you will have a solid understanding of how Mutex can be a valuable tool in your Rust programming toolkit.

Basic Usage of Mutex

Mutex, short for "*mutual exclusion*", is a synchronization primitive in Rust that helps protect shared data across multiple threads. It ensures that only one thread can access the protected data at a time, preventing data races.

Mutex is a critical component of Rust's standard library, residing within the **std::sync** module, and it plays a pivotal role in the development of concurrent programs. At its heart, a Mutex offers us two vital functions: **lock** and **unlock**.

The **lock** method serves as the means to secure exclusive access to data that is protected by the Mutex. When a thread acquires a lock through this method, it ensures that no other threads can concurrently modify or access the guarded data. This synchronization mechanism is essential for preventing data races and ensuring the orderly execution of concurrent code.

Furthermore, the Mutex provides a safeguard against potential resource leaks by automatically releasing the lock when the Mutex guard (typically represented as a variable) goes out of scope. This automatic release mechanism simplifies the management of locks and reduces the chances of accidentally causing deadlocks or other synchronization issues in your Rust programs. Therefore, Mutex is a valuable tool for designing robust and thread-safe concurrent applications in Rust.

Here's a simple example of Mutex basic usage:

Listing 7.3 Mutex usage example.

```
use std::sync::Mutex;
fn main() {
    let data = Mutex::new(42); // ①

    {
        let mut guard = data.lock().unwrap(); // ②
        *guard += 1; // ③
    } // Guard goes out of scope, unlocking the Mutex

    println!("Data after modification: {:?}", *data.lock().unwrap()); // ④
}
```

```
// Output

// Data after modification: 43
```

In this example:

① We create a Mutex-protected data structure with an initial value of 42.

② We lock the Mutex using `lock()` to obtain a mutable reference to the data.

③ Inside the locked section, we modify the data by incrementing it.

④ After the guard goes out of scope, we lock the Mutex again to access the modified data.

Mutex is a powerful tool for managing shared data in concurrent programs, and mastering its usage is crucial for writing safe and efficient multithreaded Rust code.

Sharing Data Across Threads

One of the primary use cases for Mutex in Rust is sharing data safely across multiple threads. In a multithreaded environment, it's essential to coordinate access to shared resources to avoid data races and ensure data integrity.

To achieve safe data sharing across threads, Mutex can be combined with Arc (atomic reference counter), allowing multiple threads to share ownership of the Mutex-protected data. This combination provides both thread safety and reference counting, ensuring that the data outlives the threads that use it.

Let's explore an example where multiple threads increment a counter using Mutex:

Listing 7.4 An example of sharing data across threads.

```
use std::sync::{Mutex, Arc};
use std::thread;

fn main() {
    let data = Arc::new(Mutex::new(0)); // ①
    let mut handles = vec![]; // ②

    for _ in 0..5 {
        let data = Arc::clone(&data); // ③
```

```
        let handle = thread::spawn(move || {
            let mut guard = data.lock().unwrap(); // ④
            *guard += 1; // ⑤
        });

        handles.push(handle); // ⑥
    }

    for handle in handles {
        handle.join().unwrap(); // ⑦
    }

    println!("Final Counter Value: {:?}", *data.lock().unwrap()); // ⑧
}

// Output

// Final Counter Value: 5
```

In this example:

① We create a Mutex-protected counter initialized to zero and wrap it in an **`Arc`** for shared ownership.

② We initialize a vector to store thread handles for later synchronization.

③ Inside the thread loop, we clone the **`Arc`** and **`Mutex`** to provide each thread access to the protected counter.

④ We lock the Mutex to obtain exclusive access to the counter.

⑤ Inside the locked section, each thread increments the counter.

⑥ Thread handles are stored in the **`handles`** vector for later use.

⑦ We wait for all threads to complete their execution using **`join`**.

⑧ Finally, we lock the Mutex again to access the final counter value and print it.

Sharing data across threads using Mutex and Arc is a powerful way to leverage Rust's concurrency features while maintaining safety and data integrity.

Avoiding Mutex Deadlocks

Deadlocks occur when threads wait indefinitely for each other to release Mutex locks, leading to a standstill. Avoiding deadlocks is essential in concurrent programming.

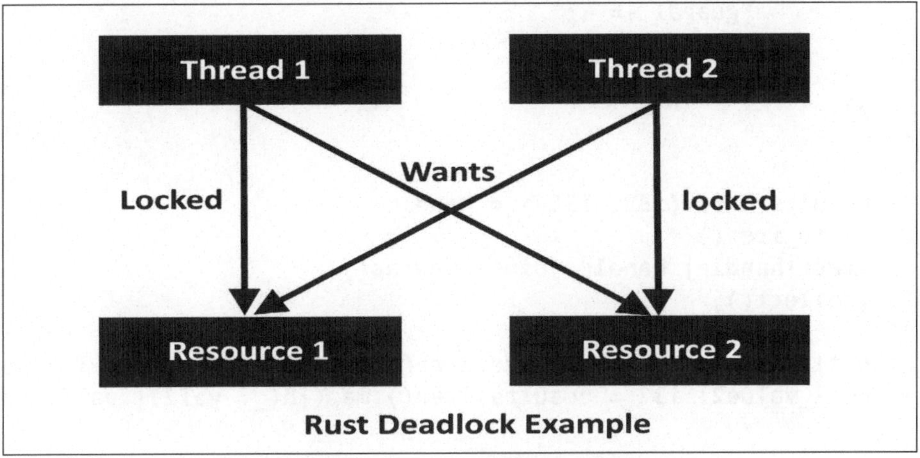

Figure 7.3: *Rust Deadlock Example*

Consider the following example that demonstrates a potential deadlock:

Listing 7.5 Avoiding mutex deadlocks example.

```
use std::sync::{Mutex, Arc};
use std::thread;

fn main() {
    let data1 = Arc::new(Mutex::new(0)); // ①
    let data2 = Arc::new(Mutex::new(0)); // ②

    let data1_final = Arc::new(Mutex::new(0));
    let data2_final = Arc::new(Mutex::new(0));

    let handles = vec![
        thread::spawn({
            let data1_clone = Arc::clone(&data1); // ③
            let data2_clone = Arc::clone(&data2); // ④
            move || {
                let mut guard1 = data1_clone.lock().unwrap(); // ⑤
                *guard1 += 1;
                let mut guard2 = data2_clone.lock().unwrap(); // ⑥
                *guard2 += 1;
                (1, 0)
            }
        }),
        thread::spawn({
            let data1_clone = Arc::clone(&data1); // ③
            move || {
                let mut guard1 = data1_clone.lock().unwrap(); // ⑧
```

```
                *guard1 += 1;
                (0, 1)
            }
        }),
    ];

    let results: Vec<(i32, i32)> = handles
        .into_iter()
        .map(|handle| handle.join().unwrap())
        .collect();

    let final_value1: i32 = results.iter().map(|&(val1, _)| val1).sum();
    let final_value2: i32 = results.iter().map(|&(_, val2)| val2).sum();

    {
        let mut guard1_final = data1_final.lock().unwrap(); // ⑨
        let mut guard2_final = data2_final.lock().unwrap(); // ⑩
        *guard1_final = *data1.lock().unwrap() + final_value1;
        *guard2_final = *data2.lock().unwrap() + final_value2;
    }

    println!(
        "Final values: data1 = {}, data2 = {}",
        *data1_final.lock().unwrap(),
        *data2_final.lock().unwrap()
    );
}

// Output

// Final values: data1 = 3, data2 = 2
```

In this code:

① We create the first Mutex-protected data structure.

② We create the second Mutex-protected data structure.

③ The first thread clones **data1** and **data2** to access them.

④ The first thread clones **data1** to access it.

⑤ Inside the first thread, **guard1** locks **data1_clone**.

⑥ Inside the first thread, **guard2** locks **data2_clone**.

⑦ Inside the second thread, **guard1** locks **data1_clone**.

⑧ **guard1_final** locks **data1_final**.

⑨ **guard2_final** locks **data2_final**.

To avoid deadlocks, it's essential to follow a consistent order when locking multiple Mutexes.

Ownership of Mutex Guards

Mutex guards, obtained through **lock()**, enforce Rust's ownership rules, ensuring that only one thread can modify the data at a time. This enforces thread safety and prevents data races.

Let's examine Mutex guard ownership in practice:

Listing 7.6 Mutex guard ownership example.

```
use std::sync::Mutex;

fn main() {
    let data = Mutex::new(vec![1, 2, 3]); // ①

    {
        let mut guard = data.lock().unwrap(); // ②
        guard.push(4); // ③
    } // Guard goes out of scope, unlocking the Mutex

    // Attempting to modify the data outside the guard's scope
    // let mut guard = data.lock().unwrap(); // This line would fail to
compile

    println!("Data: {:?}", *data.lock().unwrap()); // ④
}

// Output

// Data: [1, 2, 3, 4]
```

In this example:

① We create a Mutex-protected vector.

② We lock the Mutex to gain exclusive access to the vector.

③ Inside the locked section, we modify the vector by pushing an element.

④ Attempting to modify the data outside the guard's scope would result in a compilation error, as Rust enforces ownership rules for thread safety.

Mutex guards ensure that the data remains safe by enforcing ownership and preventing multiple threads from modifying it simultaneously.

Handling Poisoned Mutexes

Mutexes can enter a "*poisoned*" state if a panic occurs while a thread holds the Mutex. This state indicates potential data corruption and requires special handling.

Consider the following example:

Listing 7.7 Handling poisoned mutexes example.

```
use std::sync::{Mutex, Arc};
use std::thread;

fn main() {
    let data = Arc::new(Mutex::new(0)); // ①
    let mut handles = vec![];

    for _ in 0..5 {
        let data = Arc::clone(&data); // ②

        let handle = thread::spawn(move || {
            let mut guard = data.lock().unwrap(); // ③
            if *guard == 3 {
                println!("Thread reached 3, stopping.");
                return; // Don't panic, just exit the thread.
            }
            *guard += 1;
        });

        handles.push(handle); // ④
    }

    for handle in handles {
        handle.join().unwrap();
    }

    let result = data.lock();
    match result {
        Ok(guard) => println!("Final Counter Value: {:?}", *guard), // ⑤
        Err(poisoned) => {
            let guard = poisoned.into_inner(); // ⑥
            println!("Mutex is poisoned. Recovered Counter Value: {:?}",
*guard);
```

```
        }
    }
}

// Output

// Thread reached 3, stopping.
// Thread reached 3, stopping.
// Final Counter Value: 3
```

In this example:

① We create a Mutex-protected data structure using **std::sync::Mutex**. It's wrapped in an **Arc** to allow multiple threads to share ownership.

② Inside each thread, we clone the **Arc** and **Mutex** to ensure that each thread has access to the protected data.

③ We use **data.lock().unwrap()** to lock the Mutex for exclusive access to the data.

④ Each thread increments the counter, and we handle potential panics using **unwrap_or_else**.

⑤ After all threads complete, we attempt to lock the Mutex again and print the final counter value.

⑥ If the Mutex is in a poisoned state, we recover the data and handle the situation accordingly.

Advanced Usage of Mutex

Mutexes are a fundamental synchronization primitive in Rust that play a crucial role in managing shared data and ensuring thread safety in concurrent programs. While we've already covered the basics of using Mutex, this section will delve into more advanced scenarios and provide insights into how you can leverage Mutex to implement complex concurrent data structures and deal with advanced synchronization requirements.

Conditional Locking

std::sync::Condvar is an advanced synchronization tool that allows threads to wait until a certain condition is met before proceeding. It's often used in conjunction with Mutex to implement more complex synchronization patterns, like producer-consumer scenarios.

Here's a simplified example of a producer-consumer setup using **Condvar**:

Listing 7.8 Conditional Locking example.

```
use std::sync::{Arc, Condvar, Mutex};
use std::thread;

fn main() {
    let data = Arc::new((Mutex::new(Vec::new()), Condvar::new())); // ①

    let mut handles = vec![]; // ②

    for i in 0..5 { // ③
        let data_clone = Arc::clone(&data); // ④

        let handle = thread::spawn(move || { // ⑤
            let (lock, cvar) = &*data_clone; // ⑥

            let mut data = lock.lock().unwrap(); // ⑦

            data.push(i); // ⑧

            cvar.notify_one(); // ⑨
        });

        handles.push(handle); // ⑩
    }

    let (lock, cvar) = &*data; // ⑪
    let mut data = lock.lock().unwrap();

    while data.len() < 5 { // ⑫
        data = cvar.wait(data).unwrap(); // ⑬
    }

    println!("Data: {:?}", *data); // ⑭
}

// Output

// Data: [0, 1, 2, 4, 3]
```

Explanation:

① We create a shared data structure using a **Mutex** and a **Condvar**, wrapped in an Arc for multi-threaded access.

② Initialize a vector to store thread handles.

③ Spawn five threads in a loop.

④ Clone the shared data structure for each thread.

⑤ Spawn a new thread with a closure that accesses the shared data.

⑥ Deconstruct the shared data tuple to access the **`Mutex`** and **`Condvar`**.

⑦ Lock the Mutex to access the shared vector.

⑧ Modify the shared vector by pushing the value '**`i`**'.

⑨ Notify one waiting thread on the **`Condvar`**.

⑩ Store the thread handle in the vector.

⑪ Deconstruct the shared data tuple outside the loop.

⑫ Wait in a loop until the data vector has 5 elements.

⑬ Wait for the **`Condvar`**, releasing the Mutex during waiting.

⑭ Print the final data after all threads have completed their work.

In this example, **`Condvar`** is used to notify the main thread when the producer threads have finished their work.

Implementing a Mutex-Protected Queue

Mutex can be pretty smart when it comes to doing cool stuff! One neat trick it can pull off is making a safe queue that multiple threads can use to add and remove things at the same time without causing any data mess or conflicts. Here's a simplified example of how you can create a Mutex-protected queue:

Listing 7.9 Implementing a mutex-protected queue example.

```
use std::sync::{Arc, Mutex};
use std::thread;

fn main() {
    let queue = Arc::new(Mutex::new(Vec::new())); // ①

    let mut handles = vec![]; // ②

    for i in 0..5 { // ③
        let queue_clone = Arc::clone(&queue); // ④
```

```
        let handle = thread::spawn(move || { // ⑤
            let mut queue = queue_clone.lock().unwrap(); // ⑥

            queue.push(i); // ⑦
        });

        handles.push(handle); // ⑧
    }

    for handle in handles { // ⑨
        handle.join().unwrap(); // ⑩
    }

    let final_queue = queue.lock().unwrap();

    println!("Final Queue: {:?}", *final_queue); // ⑪
}

// Output

// Final Queue: [0, 2, 3, 1, 4]
```

Explanation:

① We create a shared queue using a **Mutex**, wrapped in an Arc for multi-threaded access.

② Initialize a vector to store thread handles.

③ Spawn five threads in a loop.

④ Clone the shared queue for each thread.

⑤ Spawn a new thread with a closure that accesses the shared queue.

⑥ Lock the **Mutex** to access the shared queue.

⑦ Push the value '**i**' into the shared queue.

⑧ Store the thread handle in the vector.

⑨ Wait for all spawned threads to complete by joining their handles.

⑩ Lock the Mutex again to access the final state of the queue.

⑪ Print the final queue to display the values pushed by the threads.

In this code, we create a Mutex-protected queue using **std::sync::Mutex** and **std::sync::Arc** to share ownership across threads safely. Each thread inserts a value into the queue, and the Mutex ensures that only one thread can access the queue at a time.

Implementing a Mutex-Protected Priority Queue

Expanding on the idea of a Mutex-guarded queue, let's delve into a cooler concept: crafting a Mutex-guarded priority queue. A priority queue lets different threads add elements with specific priorities and fetch them in priority order. Rust's standard library doesn't come with a ready-made priority queue, but you can make one yourself using a Mutex and a binary heap.

Here's a Rust example illustrating how to implement a Mutex-protected priority queue:

Listing 7.10 Implementing a mutex-protected priority queue example.

```
use std::collections::BinaryHeap;
use std::sync::{Arc, Mutex};
use std::thread;

struct PriorityQueue<T> {
    inner: Mutex<BinaryHeap<T>>, // ①
}

impl<T: Ord> PriorityQueue<T> {
    fn new() -> Self {
        PriorityQueue {
            inner: Mutex::new(BinaryHeap::new()), // ②
        }
    }

    fn push(&self, item: T) {
        let mut heap = self.inner.lock().unwrap(); // ③
        heap.push(item);
    }

    fn pop(&self) -> Option<T> {
        let mut heap = self.inner.lock().unwrap(); // ③
        heap.pop()
    }
}

fn main() {
    let priority_queue = Arc::new(PriorityQueue::new()); // ④
    let mut push_handles = vec![];
```

```
    let mut pop_handles = vec![];

    for i in (1..6).rev() {
        let priority_queue_clone = Arc::clone(&priority_queue); // ⑤
        let handle = thread::spawn(move || {
            priority_queue_clone.push(i);
        });
        push_handles.push(handle);
    }

    for handle in push_handles {
        handle.join().unwrap(); // ⑥
    }

    for _ in 0..5 {
        let priority_queue_clone = Arc::clone(&priority_queue); // ⑤
        let handle = thread::spawn(move || {
            let popped = priority_queue_clone.pop();
            match popped {
                Some(val) => println!("Popped: {}", val),
                None => println!("Queue is empty!"),
            }
        });
        pop_handles.push(handle);
    }

    for handle in pop_handles {
        handle.join().unwrap(); // ⑥
    }
}

// Output

// Popped: 5
// Popped: 4
// Popped: 3
// Popped: 2
// Popped: 1
```

Explanation:

① The **inner** field of the **PriorityQueue** struct is a **Mutex** that wraps a **BinaryHeap**. This **Mutex** is used to ensure thread safety when accessing the underlying data structure.

② In the **new** method of the **PriorityQueue** implementation, a new **PriorityQueue** is created with an empty **BinaryHeap** wrapped in a **Mutex**. This initializes an empty priority queue.

③ Both the **push** and **pop** methods of the **PriorityQueue** implementation lock the **Mutex** to gain access to the underlying **BinaryHeap**. This locking mechanism ensures that only one thread can modify or access the data structure at a time, preventing data corruption in concurrent scenarios.

④ In the **main** function, an Arc (atomic reference counter) is used to create a shared reference to the **PriorityQueue**. This allows multiple threads to have access to the same priority queue instance safely.

⑤ Inside the loops that create and spawn threads for pushing and popping items, an **Arc** clone is created for each thread. This clone allows each thread to independently access and manipulate the shared priority queue.

⑥ After spawning threads for pushing and popping items, the code uses the **join** method on each thread handle to wait for all threads to finish their tasks before proceeding. This synchronization ensures that all threads complete their work before the program exits.

In this example, we create a Mutex-protected priority queue using a **BinaryHeap** from the standard library. Multiple threads concurrently push elements onto the priority queue, and other threads pop elements in ascending order of priority.

Handling Deadlocks with Mutex

Deadlocks are a common challenge in concurrent programming. Rust's Mutex provides some tools to help you avoid and handle deadlocks, such as the **try_lock** method, which attempts to acquire a lock without blocking. Here's an example demonstrating how to use **try_lock** to handle potential deadlocks:

Listing 7.11 Handling deadlocks with mutex example.

```
use std::sync::{Arc, Mutex};
use std::thread;

fn main() {
    let lock = Arc::new(Mutex::new(0)); // ①
    let mut handles = vec![]; // ②

    for _ in 0..5 {
        let lock_clone = Arc::clone(&lock); // ③
        let handle = thread::spawn(move || { // ④
```

```
            let mut data = lock_clone.try_lock(); // ⑤
            match data {
                Ok(ref mut value) => {
                    **value += 1; // ⑥
                }
                Err(_) => {
                    println!("Failed to acquire lock, continuing...");
// ⑦
                }
            }
        });
        handles.push(handle); // ⑧
    }

    for handle in handles {
        handle.join().unwrap(); // ⑨
    }

    let final_data = lock.lock().unwrap(); // ⑩
    println!("Final Data: {}", *final_data); // ⑪
}

// Output

// Final Data: 5
```

Explanation:

① Creates a shared **Mutex** containing an integer with an initial value of 0.

② Initializes a vector to hold thread handles.

③ Clones the **Arc** to share the **Mutex** among multiple threads.

④ Spawns a new thread to work with the **Mutex** in parallel.

⑤ Attempts to acquire a lock on the **Mutex** in a non-blocking manner.

⑥ Increments the integer value inside the Mutex.

⑦ Prints a message if the **Mutex** is already locked by another thread.

⑧ Stores the thread handle in a vector for later joining.

⑨ Waits for all spawned threads to complete their work.

⑩ Locks the **Mutex** to access the final shared integer value.

⑪ Prints the final value of the shared integer.

In this code, we attempt to acquire locks using **try_lock**, and if a lock cannot be acquired, the thread continues without blocking. This can help prevent deadlocks in situations where acquiring a lock is not critical.

Mutex in Multi-Threaded Producer-Consumer Scenario

Mutexes are often used in multi-threaded producer-consumer scenarios to synchronize access to a shared buffer. Here's an example demonstrating a Mutex-based producer-consumer pattern:

Listing 7.12 Mutex in multi-threaded producer-consumer scenario.

```
use std::sync::{Arc, Mutex};
use std::thread;

const BUFFER_SIZE: usize = 5;

fn main() {
    let buffer = Arc::new(Mutex::new(Vec::new())); // ①
    let mut handles = vec![]; // ①

    // Producer threads
    for i in 0..3 {
        let buffer_clone = Arc::clone(&buffer); // ②
        let handle = thread::spawn(move || { // ③
            for j in 0..BUFFER_SIZE {
                let mut buffer = buffer_clone.lock().unwrap(); // ④
                buffer.push(i * BUFFER_SIZE + j); // ④
            }
        });
        handles.push(handle); // ⑤
    }

    // Consumer threads
    for _ in 0..2 {
        let buffer_clone = Arc::clone(&buffer); // ⑥
        let handle = thread::spawn(move || { // ⑦
            for _ in 0..BUFFER_SIZE {
                let mut buffer = buffer_clone.lock().unwrap(); // ⑧
                if let Some(item) = buffer.pop() { // ⑧
                    println!("Consumed: {}", item); // ⑧
                }
            }
```

```
        });
        handles.push(handle); // ⑨
    }

    for handle in handles {
        handle.join().unwrap(); // ⑩
    }
}

// Output

// Consumed: 14
// Consumed: 13
// Consumed: 12
// Consumed: 11
// Consumed: 10
// Consumed: 9
// Consumed: 8
// Consumed: 7
// Consumed: 6
// Consumed: 5
```

Explanation:

① Creates a shared **Mutex** wrapping an empty **Vec** to represent a buffer.

② Initializes a vector to hold thread handles.

③ Clones the **Arc** to share access to the buffer **Mutex** among producer threads.

④ Spawns producer threads.

⑤ Locks the **Mutex** for exclusive access to the buffer.

⑥ Inserts items into the buffer.

⑦ Stores producer thread handles.

⑧ Clones the **Arc** for consumer threads.

⑨ Spawns consumer threads.

⑩ Locks the **Mutex** for exclusive access to the buffer.

⑪ Pops and consumes items from the buffer.

⑫ Prints the consumed item.

⑬ Stores consumer thread handles.

⑭ Waits for all producer and consumer threads to complete.

In this example, multiple producer threads add items to a shared buffer, while consumer threads remove and consume items from the same buffer. The Mutex ensures exclusive access to the buffer, preventing data races.

These advanced examples showcase the versatility of Mutex in Rust and how it can be applied to solve complex synchronization challenges. Whether you're implementing priority queues, dealing with potential deadlocks, or exploring other advanced synchronization scenarios, Rust's Mutex provides the foundation for building safe and efficient concurrent programs.

Exploring RwLock

While Mutex provides exclusive access to data, **RwLock** (read-write lock) allows multiple threads to read data concurrently while providing exclusive access for writing. This can be particularly beneficial when you have data that is frequently read but infrequently modified.

Managing Shared Data with RwLock

RwLock is another synchronization primitive in Rust that allows multiple threads to read data concurrently while ensuring exclusive access for writing. This is useful for scenarios where data is frequently read but infrequently modified.

Listing 7.13 Managing shared data with RwLock.

```
use std::thread;
use std::sync::{RwLock, Arc};

fn main() {
    let data = Arc::new(RwLock::new(0)); // ①

    let mut handles = vec![]; // ②

    for _ in 0..5 {
        let data = Arc::clone(&data); // ③

        let handle = thread::spawn(move || {
            let data_guard = data.read().unwrap(); // ④
            println!("Read: {}", *data_guard); // ⑤

            // Drop the read lock here to allow other threads to read 
concurrently
            drop(data_guard);
            thread::sleep(std::time::Duration::from_millis(100)); // ⑥
```

```
            let mut data_write = data.write().unwrap(); // ⑦
            *data_write += 1; // ⑧
        });

        handles.push(handle); // ⑨
    }

    for handle in handles {
        handle.join().unwrap(); // ⑩
    }

    println!("Result: {:?}", *data.read().unwrap()); // ⑪
}

// Output

// Read: 0
// Read: 0
// Read: 0
// Read: 0
// Read: 0
// Result: 5
```

In this code snippet:

① We create an **RwLock**-protected data structure using **std::sync::RwLock**. We wrap it in an **Arc** to allow multiple threads to share ownership safely.

② We initialize a vector to store thread handles.

③ Inside each thread, we clone the **Arc** and **RwLock** for shared access.

④ We obtain a read lock using **data.read().unwrap()**, allowing multiple threads to read concurrently.

⑤ We read and print the data.

⑥ To simulate some work, we introduce a sleep to mimic a time-consuming operation.

⑦ After simulating work, we obtain a write lock using **data.write().unwrap()**, allowing exclusive access for writing.

⑧ We modify the data inside the **RwLock**-protected structure.

⑨ Thread handles are stored for later use.

⑩ We wait for all threads to complete their execution.

⑪ Finally, we print the result, which is the value stored in the **RwLock**-protected data.

Understanding how to use **RwLock** is essential for efficiently managing shared data in concurrent Rust programs.

Advanced Usages of RwLock in Rust

RwLock in Rust offers a variety of advanced use cases beyond its basic read and write operations. It provides a flexible toolset for handling concurrent data access efficiently.

Dynamic Number of Readers

One powerful feature of **RwLock** is its ability to dynamically control the number of reader threads. In the following code example, we showcase how to create a situation with a variable number of concurrent readers:

Listing 7.14 RwLock with dynamic number of readers example.

```
use std::sync::{RwLock, Arc};
use std::thread;

fn main() {
    let data = Arc::new(RwLock::new(0));

    let mut handles = vec![];

    for i in 0..10 {
        let data = Arc::clone(&data);

        let handle = thread::spawn(move || {
            let data_guard = data.read().unwrap();
            println!("Reader {}: {}", i, *data_guard);
        });

        handles.push(handle);
    }

    for handle in handles {
        handle.join().unwrap();
    }
}
```

```
// Output

// Reader 0: 0
// Reader 2: 0
// Reader 1: 0
// Reader 7: 0
// Reader 5: 0
// Reader 3: 0
// Reader 6: 0
// Reader 4: 0
// Reader 8: 0
// Reader 9: 0
```

In this scenario, you can see how `RwLock` enables the creation of a dynamic number of reader threads that can access shared data concurrently. This flexibility is invaluable when designing applications with varying workloads and concurrency requirements.

Timed Locking

Timed locking with `RwLock` introduces a crucial mechanism for handling situations where you want to enforce a maximum time limit on read or write operations. This feature ensures that threads do not get stuck indefinitely while waiting for access to shared data, which is especially important in real-world scenarios where unpredictable delays or resource contention can occur.

Listing 7.15 Timed locking with RwLock example.

```
use std::sync::{RwLock, Arc};
use std::thread;
use std::time::{Duration, Instant};
use rand::Rng;

fn main() {
    let data = Arc::new(RwLock::new(0));

    let mut handles = vec![];

    for i in 0..5 {
        let data = Arc::clone(&data);

        let handle = thread::spawn(move || {
            let timeout_duration = Duration::from_secs(1);
            let start_time = Instant::now();
```

```
            // Randomly determine if the thread should time out.
            let should_timeout = rand::thread_rng().gen::<bool>();

            loop {
                thread::sleep(Duration::from_millis(100)); // Sleep for
a short duration.

                if start_time.elapsed() >= timeout_duration {
                    if should_timeout {
                        println!("Thread {} timed out.", i);
                        break; // Timeout reached, break out of the
loop.
                    } else {
                        if let Ok(data_guard) = data.read() {
                            println!("Thread {} read {} successfully.",
i, *data_guard);
                        }
                    }
                }

                // Simulate some threads succeeding and others failing
to acquire the lock.
                if !should_timeout && start_time.elapsed().as_secs() >=
2 {
                    if let Ok(_data_guard) = data.read() {
                        println!("Thread {} acquired the lock.", i);
                        break; // Successfully acquired the lock, break
out of the loop.
                    }
                }
            }
        });

        handles.push(handle);
    }

    for handle in handles {
        handle.join().unwrap();
    }
}


// Output

// Thread 0 timed out.
// Thread 1 timed out.
// Thread 3 read 0 successfully.
```

```
// Thread 2 timed out.
// Thread 4 timed out.
// Thread 3 read 0 successfully.
// Thread 3 read 0 successfully.
// Thread 3 read 0 successfully.
// Thread 3 read 0 successfully.
// Thread 3 read 0 successfully.
// Thread 3 read 0 successfully.
// Thread 3 read 0 successfully.
// Thread 3 read 0 successfully.
// Thread 3 read 0 successfully.
// Thread 3 read 0 successfully.
// Thread 3 acquired the lock.
```

In this code example, we illustrate how to implement timed locking using **RwLock** with a timeout for read operations. Each thread is assigned a task that includes a specified timeout duration. Threads periodically check if the elapsed time has exceeded this duration, and if so, they take appropriate actions, such as timing out or, in the absence of a timeout, performing a read operation. This mechanism allows for graceful handling of situations where timely data access is critical, preventing potential deadlocks or indefinite waiting periods.

Deadlock Avoidance

Deadlock avoidance is a crucial aspect of concurrent programming, and Rust provides a powerful tool for achieving it through the use of **RwLock**. In the provided Rust code snippet, **RwLock** is utilized to prevent deadlocks by allowing flexible access patterns to shared data. Deadlocks occur when multiple threads compete for resources and end up waiting indefinitely for each other to release those resources, leading to a program's stagnation.

To mitigate this issue, the code uses the **try_read** and **try_write** methods of **RwLock**, which provide a non-blocking way to acquire locks. By employing these methods, the program can try to obtain a lock on the shared data without getting stuck in a waiting state. If a lock is unavailable, the code can gracefully handle the situation by, for instance, retrying later or taking alternative actions.

Listing 7.16 Deadlock avoidance with RwLock example.

```
use std::sync::{RwLock, Arc};
use std::thread;

fn main() {
    let data1 = Arc::new(RwLock::new(0));
    let data2 = Arc::new(RwLock::new(0));
```

```
    let mut handles = vec![];

    for _ in 0..5 {
        let data1 = Arc::clone(&data1);
        let data2 = Arc::clone(&data2);

        let handle = thread::spawn(move || {
            let mut data_guard1 = data1.write().unwrap();
            let mut data_guard2 = data2.write().unwrap();

            // Perform operations on both data1 and data2
            *data_guard1 += 1;
            *data_guard2 += 1;
        });

        handles.push(handle);
    }

    for handle in handles {
        handle.join().unwrap();
    }
}
```

In the presented example, two instances of **RwLock** are employed, **data1** and **data2**, which are wrapped in **Arc** (atomic reference counters) to enable shared ownership across multiple threads. The multiple threads spawned in the loop attempt to acquire locks on these **RwLock** instances. Crucially, they do so in a manner that ensures a consistent order of lock acquisition. This strategy is essential for preventing deadlocks, as it avoids circular dependencies where one thread holds a lock that another thread is waiting for, resulting in a deadlock scenario.

Implementing Resource Pooling

Implementing resource pooling in concurrent programming is a valuable technique to efficiently manage and share a limited set of resources among multiple threads. In the provided Rust code snippet, **RwLock** is employed to establish a resource pool, where each resource is protected by a lock, ensuring safe and synchronized access.

Listing 7.17 Implementing resource pooling with RwLock example.

```
use std::sync::{RwLock, Arc};
use std::thread;

struct Resource {
    id: u32,
}

fn main() {
    const NUM_RESOURCES: u32 = 3;
    let resources: Vec<Arc<RwLock<Resource>>> = (0..NUM_RESOURCES)
        .map(|id| Arc::new(RwLock::new(Resource { id })))
        .collect();

    let mut handles = vec![];

    for i in 0..10 {
        let resources_clone: Vec<Arc<RwLock<Resource>>> = resources.clone();

        let handle = thread::spawn(move || {
            let idx = (i % NUM_RESOURCES) as usize;
            let resource = &resources_clone[idx];
            let data_guard = resource.read().unwrap();
            println!("Thread {} accessed Resource {}", i, data_guard.id);
        });

        handles.push(handle);
    }

    for handle in handles {
        handle.join().unwrap();
    }
}

// Output

// Thread 0 accessed Resource 0
// Thread 1 accessed Resource 1
// Thread 9 accessed Resource 0
// Thread 8 accessed Resource 2
// Thread 7 accessed Resource 1
// Thread 6 accessed Resource 0
// Thread 5 accessed Resource 2
// Thread 4 accessed Resource 1
// Thread 3 accessed Resource 0
// Thread 2 accessed Resource 2
```

In this example, an array of resources is created, each represented by a `Resource` struct and wrapped in an `Arc<RwLock<Resource>>` to allow shared ownership across threads. The number of resources is defined by `NUM_RESOURCES`, and a loop initializes these resources with unique IDs.

The program then spawns ten threads, and each thread attempts to access a resource from the pool. The use of `RwLock` ensures that multiple threads can read a resource concurrently without issues, but only one thread can hold a write lock for exclusive modification. In this way, the resource pool is effectively utilized by the threads, preventing data races and ensuring that each resource is accessed safely.

To further enhance efficiency, the code uses modulo arithmetic (`i % NUM_RESOURCES`) to distribute thread access evenly among the available resources, thus preventing conflict on the same resource by multiple threads. This ensures that resources are efficiently shared, and the program produces an output displaying the resource IDs accessed by each thread.

The combination of `RwLock`, `Arc`, and careful resource distribution in this example demonstrates how to implement resource pooling in Rust, allowing multiple threads to access and utilize a limited set of resources concurrently while maintaining data integrity and synchronization. This showcases the versatility of `RwLock` in handling complex synchronization scenarios in Rust's concurrent programming paradigm.

Thread Communication and Message Passing

In concurrent programming, threads often need to communicate with each other and exchange data. Rust provides various techniques for achieving this, including channels, message passing, and atomic operations. Let's explore some of these techniques in the following sections.

Using Channels for Communication

Channels are a powerful mechanism for enabling communication between threads in a concurrent program. In Rust, channels are offered through the `std::sync::mpsc` module, which stands for multi-producer, single-consumer. This means that multiple threads can send data to a single receiver, allowing for efficient and synchronized communication in a multi-threaded environment.

Here's a practical example of using channels for communication:

Listing 7.18 Using channels for communication example.

```
use std::thread;
use std::sync::mpsc;

fn main() {
    let (sender, receiver) = mpsc::channel(); // ①

    let sender_clone = sender.clone(); // ②
    let handle = thread::spawn(move || {
        let message = "Hello from the sender thread".to_string();
        sender_clone.send(message).unwrap();
    });

    let received_data = receiver.recv().unwrap(); // ③
    println!("Received: {}", received_data); // ④

    handle.join().unwrap(); // ⑤
}

// Output

// Received: Hello from the sender thread
```

In this code snippet:

① We create a channel for communication using **`mpsc::channel()`**. This function returns a tuple containing a sender and a receiver.

② We clone the sender for a new thread to send data through the channel.

③ In the main thread, we receive data from the channel using **`receiver.recv()`**. The **`.unwrap()`** method is used to handle the result, and then we process the received data.

④ We process and print the received data.

⑤ We wait for the sending thread to finish.

Channels are particularly valuable for sharing data and synchronizing behavior between threads, making them a fundamental tool in concurrent programming. They provide a safe and efficient way of passing messages and sharing information, promoting effective communication and coordination in multi-threaded Rust applications.

Message Passing with Structs

Utilizing custom message structs for message passing in Rust provides a flexible and organized approach to inter-thread communication. While channels are excellent for transmitting simple data types, using custom structs allows us to send more complex and structured messages between threads.

Here's an example of using custom message structs for message passing:

Listing 7.19 Message passing with structs example.

```
use std::thread;
use std::sync::mpsc;

fn main() {
    let (sender, receiver) = mpsc::channel(); // ①

    let sender_clone = sender.clone(); // ②
    let handle = thread::spawn(move || {
        let message = CustomMessage { // ③
            id: 42,
            content: "Important data".to_string(),
        };
        sender_clone.send(message).unwrap();
    });

    let received_message = receiver.recv().unwrap(); // ④
    println!("Received Message - ID: {}, Content: {}", received_message.
id, received_message.content); // ⑤

    handle.join().unwrap(); // ⑥
}

struct CustomMessage { // ⑦
    id: u32,
    content: String,
}

// Output

// Received Message - ID: 42, Content: Important data
```

In this code snippet:

① We create a channel for custom messages using **mpsc::channel()**.

② In the sender thread, we clone the sender to send data through the channel.

③ We create a custom message using a struct and send it through the channel.

④ In the main thread, we receive the custom message, process its content, and print it. This approach allows you to send more structured data between threads.

⑤ We process and print the received custom message.

⑥ We wait for the sending thread to finish.

⑦ We define a custom message struct.

In this example, a custom message struct **CustomMessage** is defined with fields for an ID and content, creating a structured message format. This allows threads to transmit more than just simple data; they can convey rich information encapsulated within a message. This approach is particularly valuable when threads need to exchange complex data structures, configurations, or any kind of data that has multiple attributes.

The use of custom message structs enhances the expressiveness and clarity of message passing in concurrent Rust programs. It promotes well-structured communication between threads, ensuring that messages are easily interpretable and facilitating the exchange of more elaborate data types for effective synchronization and coordination in multi-threaded applications.

Atomic Operations

In addition to channels and message passing, Rust also provides atomic operations for safe concurrent access to shared data. Atomic operations are essential when you need to update a value in a way that prevents race conditions.

Here's an example of using atomic operations to safely increment a counter:

Listing 7.20 Atomic operations example.

```
fn main() {
    let counter = Arc::new(AtomicUsize::new(0)); // ①

    let mut handles = vec![]; // ②

    for _ in 0..5 {
        let counter = Arc::clone(&counter); // ③

        let handle = thread::spawn(move || {
            counter.fetch_add(1, Ordering::Relaxed); // ④
```

```
        });

        handles.push(handle); // ⑤
    }

    for handle in handles {
        handle.join().unwrap(); // ⑥
    }

    let final_value = counter.load(Ordering::Relaxed); // ⑦
    println!("Final Counter Value: {}", final_value); // ⑧
}

// Output

// Final Counter Value: 5
```

In this code snippet:

① We create an atomic counter using **`std::sync::atomic::AtomicUsize`**. We wrap it in an **`Arc`** to allow multiple threads to share ownership safely.

② We initialize a vector to store thread handles.

③ We clone the counter for each thread.

④ Inside each thread, we use the **`fetch_add`** method to atomically increment the counter. The **`Ordering::Relaxed`** parameter specifies the memory ordering, which in this case is relaxed, meaning no additional synchronization is required.

⑤ Thread handles are stored for later use.

⑥ We wait for all threads to complete their execution.

⑦ We load the final value of the atomic counter.

⑧ We print the final value. Atomic operations provide a way to safely perform operations on shared data without the need for additional synchronization primitives.

Understanding atomic operations is crucial for scenarios where fine-grained control over shared data is required.

Advanced Thread Communication

In the preceding sections, we have delved into the essential aspects of concurrent programming in Rust, covering core concepts, synchronization mechanisms, and more advanced practices like leveraging the Crossbeam library and asynchronous programming. Building upon this foundation, we are now able to delve further into the complexities of advanced thread communication patterns. This includes the art of thread coordination, where multiple threads work in coordination, synchronize their actions, and make intelligent decisions based on shared information. This section will equip you with the knowledge and tools necessary to design and implement robust, and highly coordinated concurrent Rust applications, enabling efficient and reliable multi-threaded software.

Thread Coordination with Barriers

Thread coordination is crucial when you have multiple threads performing tasks that depend on each other's completion. Rust provides a convenient way to coordinate threads using barriers from the **std::sync** module.

Let's take a look at how to use barriers for thread coordination:

Listing 7.21 Thread coordination with barriers example.

```
use std::sync::{Arc, Barrier};
use std::thread;

fn main() {
    let barrier = Arc::new(Barrier::new(3)); // ①
    let mut handles = vec![]; // ②

    for id in 0..3 {
        let barrier = Arc::clone(&barrier); // ③
        let handle = thread::spawn(move || {
            println!("Thread {} started", id); // ④
            thread::sleep(std::time::Duration::from_secs(2)); // ⑤
            println!("Thread {} completed its work", id); // ⑥
            barrier.wait(); // ⑦
            println!("Thread {} reached the barrier", id); // ⑧
        });
        handles.push(handle); // ⑨
    }

    for handle in handles {
        handle.join().unwrap(); // ⑩
    }
}
```

```
// Output

// Thread 2 started
// Thread 1 started
// Thread 0 started
// Thread 2 completed its work
// Thread 1 completed its work
// Thread 0 completed its work
// Thread 0 reached the barrier
// Thread 2 reached the barrier
// Thread 1 reached the barrier
```

In this example:

① We create a **barrier** with a count of 3, indicating that it should wait for three threads to reach it before allowing them to continue.

② We initialize a vector to store thread handles.

③ Clone the barrier for each thread.

④ Perform some work.

⑤ Simulate work with a sleep.

⑥ Print completion message.

⑦ Wait for other threads to reach the **barrier**.

⑧ Store thread **handle**.

⑨ Join each thread.

In this code example, we create a barrier with a count of 3, indicating that it should wait for three threads to reach it before allowing them to continue. Each thread performs some work, simulates additional work with a sleep, prints completion messages, and then waits for other threads to reach the barrier. Finally, we join all the threads to ensure they complete their execution before the program terminates.

This example showcases how Rust's barrier mechanism can help coordinate threads efficiently, ensuring they synchronize their work at specific points in the program. Such coordination is crucial for scenarios where different threads must collaborate to achieve a common goal, such as parallel processing, task scheduling, or distributed computing.

Thread Local Storage

Thread Local Storage (TLS) is a fundamental concurrency concept that plays a crucial role in managing thread-specific data. In the world of concurrent programming, there are often situations where threads need to access and manage data that is unique to their execution context. This is where TLS comes into play, allowing each thread to have its own isolated storage for data without the need for complex synchronization mechanisms.

In Rust, TLS is implemented using the **thread_local!** macro, a powerful tool that lets us define thread-local variables. These variables are, essentially, separate instances for each thread, and any changes made to them within one thread do not affect the values in other threads. This isolation provides an efficient and safe way to manage thread-specific data, enhancing the performance and reliability of concurrent programs.

One common use case for TLS is managing resources that are expensive to create or access, such as database connections, network sockets, or configuration settings. By allocating and maintaining these resources within thread-local storage, each thread can efficiently access and manipulate them without introducing the overhead of synchronization mechanisms like mutexes or locks.

Another advantage of TLS is its ability to reduce conflict for shared resources. In scenarios where multiple threads frequently access shared data, contention can lead to performance bottlenecks. By utilizing TLS, threads can work independently on their own copies of data, minimizing contention and improving overall concurrency.

In Rust, using TLS is straightforward, thanks to the **thread_local!** macro. It allows you to declare thread-local variables and initialize them with default values that are specific to each thread. These variables can then be accessed and modified within the thread's context without affecting other threads.

Let's explore how to use TLS in Rust with a practical example:

Listing 7.22 Thread Local Storage (TLS) example.

```
use std::thread;

thread_local! {
    static THREAD_LOCAL_DATA: std::cell::RefCell<u32> = std::cell::
RefCell::new(42);
}
```

```
fn main() {
    let mut handles = vec![]; // ①
    for _ in 0..5 {
        let handle = thread::spawn(|| {
            THREAD_LOCAL_DATA.with(|data| {
                let mut value = data.borrow_mut();
                *value += 1;
                println!("Thread-local value: {}", *value);
            });
        });
        handles.push(handle); // ②
    }

    for handle in handles {
        handle.join().unwrap(); // ③
    }

    THREAD_LOCAL_DATA.with(|data| {
        let value = data.borrow();
        println!("Main thread's thread-local value: {}", *value); // ④
    });
}

// Output

// Thread-Local value: 43
// Thread-Local value: 43
// Thread-Local value: 43
// Thread-Local value: 43
// Thread-Local value: 43
// Main thread's thread-Local value: 42
```

① Spawn multiple threads.

② Spawn a new thread.

③ Wait for all threads to complete.

④ Access the **thread-local** value in the main thread.

In this example, we create a special kind of variable that's unique to each thread using the "**thread_local!**" macro. So, every thread can increase its own special value, and the main thread can check its own unique value. This **thread-local** storage is like having personal lockers for each thread, which is super handy when you want to keep data separate for each thread. It helps avoid the hassle of synchronizing everything and makes sure each thread works efficiently with its own data.

Crossbeam Library

The Crossbeam library stands out as a smart pick for handling advanced synchronization tasks in Rust. It comes packed with a range of handy data structures and tools that go above and beyond what you'll find in the standard library. One standout feature is scoped threads, which give you precise control over how long threads stick around.

Let's explore a simple example using Crossbeam's scoped threads:

Listing 7.23 Crossbeam library usage example.

```
use crossbeam::thread;

fn main() {
    thread::scope(|s| { // ①
        for i in 0..5 {
            s.spawn(move |_| { // ②
                println!("Scoped thread {}", i);
            });
        }
    }).unwrap(); // ③
}

// Output

// Scoped thread 4
// Scoped thread 2
// Scoped thread 1
// Scoped thread 0
// Scoped thread 3
```

In this example:

① We use the Crossbeam library's **thread::scope** to spawn scoped threads. The closure passed to **thread::scope** defines the scope of the threads.

② Inside the scoped threads, we perform some work. In this case, we print a message indicating the thread's index.

③ We ensure that all threads within the scope complete before the program exits. The **.unwrap()** method is used to handle any potential errors.

Crossbeam is a robust and highly regarded library that plays a crucial role in handling complex concurrency scenarios, making it a staple choice within the Rust programming community for tackling challenging concurrency tasks.

This library equips us with a comprehensive toolkit for managing concurrent operations, offering a wide array of data structures and utilities that surpass the capabilities of the Rust standard library.

Asynchronous Programming

Rust's async/await feature, introduced in Rust 1.39, revolutionized asynchronous programming in the language. It allows you to write asynchronous code that is more readable and maintainable. With the **async-std** or **tokio** libraries, you can build highly concurrent applications with ease.

Here's a simple example of asynchronous programming using **async-std**:

Listing 7.24 Asynchronous programming example.

```
use async_std::task;

fn main() {
    task::block_on(async {
        let task1 = task::spawn(async { // ①
            println!("Task 1: Starting");
            // Simulate an asynchronous task with a delay.
            async_std::task::sleep(std::time::Duration::from_secs(2)).
await;
            println!("Task 1: Finished");
        });

        let task2 = task::spawn(async { // ②
            println!("Task 2: Starting");
            // Simulate another asynchronous task with a delay.
            async_std::task::sleep(std::time::Duration::from_secs(1)).
await;
            println!("Task 2: Finished");
        });

        task1.await; // ③
        task2.await; // ④

        println!("All tasks have completed");
    });
}
```

```
// Output

// Task 1: Starting
// Task 2: Starting
// Task 2: Finished
// Task 1: Finished
// All tasks have completed
```

In this example:

① We define an asynchronous function using the **async** keyword. Inside this function, we spawn asynchronous tasks using **task::spawn**.

② We spawn another asynchronous task.

③ We await the completion of **task1**.

④ We await the completion of **task2**.

Asynchronous programming allows for efficient concurrent execution of tasks without the need for explicit thread management.

Concurrency Best Practices

As you work with concurrency in Rust, consider the following best practices:

- **Start with a Clear Design:** Plan your concurrent system's architecture and define clear boundaries between threads or actors.
- **Use Thread Pools:** When parallelizing tasks, consider using thread pools like rayon to manage threads efficiently.
- **Prefer Message Passing:** In concurrent systems, prefer message passing over shared state and locks to minimize the potential for race conditions.
- **Avoid Mutexes When Possible:** Only use mutexes when necessary, and explore lock-free data structures and atomic operations for better performance.
- **Error Handling:** Pay attention to error handling in concurrent code to ensure robustness.
- **Testing:** Use tools like Rust's testing framework to verify the correctness of your concurrent code.
- **Benchmarking:** Profile and benchmark your concurrent code to identify performance bottlenecks and optimize them.

Conclusion

In this chapter, we've explored various aspects of managing concurrency in Rust. We started by understanding threads and synchronization primitives like `Mutex` and `RwLock`. We then delved into communication between threads using channels and custom message passing. Additionally, we explored atomic operations for safe concurrent access to shared data.

As we advanced, we introduced you to the Crossbeam library for handling complex synchronization scenarios and explored asynchronous programming with async/await. Rust provides a rich set of tools and libraries for managing concurrency effectively, making it a strong choice for building high-performance concurrent applications.

We also explored complex thread communication patterns, honed our skills in gracefully handling errors within concurrent programs, and harnessed the power of Thread Local Storage (TLS) to manage thread-specific data effectively. These advanced techniques are crucial for building complex and robust concurrent systems that can tackle the challenges of modern computing.

As you continue your journey in Rust development, these concurrency concepts will become your allies, enabling you to create high-performance, responsive, and resilient applications. Whether you're developing server applications that need to handle thousands of concurrent connections, parallelizing data processing tasks, or building responsive user interfaces, Rust's concurrency features will be instrumental in your success.

In the next chapter, you will practically explore the world of command-line programming. This hands-on chapter provides a comprehensive guide on constructing a powerful command-line find and replace utility from scratch. Throughout the chapter, you will gain a deep understanding of how to handle command-line arguments and effectively parse input in Rust, making it a valuable resource for anyone looking to expand their knowledge of creating command-line interface (CLI) programs. By the end of this chapter, you will have developed a robust tool that can swiftly search and replace text within files, providing not only a functional utility but also a solid foundation in Rust's capabilities for building efficient and user-friendly CLI applications.

Resources

To deepen your understanding of managing concurrency in Rust, you can explore the following resources:

- Tokio Documentation: Refer to the official documentation for the Tokio runtime, a robust asynchronous runtime for Rust. Explore the features, modules, and guides provided to master the intricacies of concurrent programming with Tokio. - https://tokio.rs
- The Async Book - Under the Hood: Executing Futures and Tasks: Delve into the "Under the Hood: Executing Futures and Tasks" chapter of "The Async Book", an official resource that extensively covers the execution model of asynchronous programming in Rust. Gain insights into how Rust handles concurrency and parallelism. - https://rust-lang.github.io/async-book/02_execution/01_chapter.html
- Async Std Documentation: Explore the official documentation for the Async Std project, an asynchronous runtime for Rust. Async Std provides essential tools and utilities for concurrent programming, contributing to effective resource management practices. - https://docs.rs/async-std
- Futures - Executor Module Documentation: Delve into the documentation for the executor module in the Futures crate. Understanding the executor module is crucial for managing concurrent tasks and orchestrating asynchronous execution in Rust. - https://docs.rs/futures/latest/futures/executor/index.html
- The Async Book - Concepts: Check out the "Concepts" chapter of "*The Async Book*" for an in-depth exploration of concurrent programming in Rust. This resource covers topics such as locks, channels, and other concurrency primitives. - https://book.async.rs/concepts
- Tokio Sync Crate Documentation: Explore the documentation for the Tokio Sync crate on crates.io. This crate provides synchronization primitives for concurrent programming in Tokio, offering tools such as Mutex and RwLock. - https://docs.rs/tokio/latest/tokio/sync/index.html
- Crossbeam - Scope Documentation: Delve into the documentation for the Scope struct in the Crossbeam crate. Crossbeam provides a suite of concurrent data structures, and the Scope struct is particularly useful for managing the lifetimes of concurrent threads. - https://docs.rs/crossbeam/latest/crossbeam/thread/struct.Scope.html

- Rayon Documentation: Explore the official documentation for the Rayon crate, a data-parallelism library for Rust. Rayon simplifies parallel programming by providing a high-level, intuitive API for parallelizing operations. - https://docs.rs/rayon

These resources offer a comprehensive view of managing concurrency in Rust, providing practical guidance and documentation to help you master the complexities of concurrent programming and design responsive systems.

Multiple Choice Questions

Q1: What is the primary purpose of threads in Rust's concurrent programming?

a) To define shared behaviors

b) To provide default implementations for functions

c) To allow multiple tasks to run concurrently

d) To prevent data races

Q2: Which of the following concepts in Rust is responsible for preventing data races by allowing only one thread to own a piece of data at a time?

a) Smart pointers

b) Lifetimes

c) Ownership

d) Borrowing

Q3: Concurrency in Rust involves managing tasks that:

a) Always happen in order

b) Don't depend on each other

c) Share data without restrictions

d) Are executed sequentially

Q4: What is the primary role of the thread::spawn function in Rust?

a) To lock a Mutex

b) To create a new thread

c) To synchronize threads

d) To prevent deadlocks

Q5: What does a Mutex guard in Rust enforce regarding data modification?

a) Allows simultaneous modifications by multiple threads

b) Ensures data races

c) Enforces Rust's ownership rules, allowing only one thread to modify data at a time

d) Prevents data sharing between threads

Q6: What is the primary purpose of traits in Rust?

a) To define data structures

b) To provide default implementations for functions

c) To define shared behaviors that types can implement

d) To restrict access to data

Q7: Which synchronization tool is often used in conjunction with Mutex to implement more complex synchronization patterns in Rust?

a) `Semaphore`

b) `Atomic`

c) `Barrier`

d) `Condvar`

Q8: In a Mutex-protected queue in Rust, why is Arc used to wrap the Mutex?

a) To enforce exclusive access to the queue

b) To allow multiple threads to have shared ownership of the queue

c) To avoid deadlock situations

d) To make the queue immutable

Q9: What is the primary purpose of the `try_lock` method in Rust's Mutex?

a) To forcefully acquire a lock

b) To unlock the Mutex

c) To attempt to acquire a lock without blocking

d) To handle deadlocks

Q10: In a Mutex-protected priority queue, why is a Mutex used to wrap a `BinaryHeap`?

a) To provide a ready-made priority queue implementation

b) To ensure thread safety when accessing the underlying data structure

c) To avoid using a priority queue

d) To enforce strict access control

Q11: What is the primary advantage of using threads in concurrent programming?

a) Reduced memory usage

b) Simplified code structure

c) Improved performance and responsiveness

d) Enhanced security

Q12: In Rust's concurrency model, what is the role of the Rust compiler?

a) Executes concurrent tasks

b) Monitors thread behavior

c) Manages memory allocation

d) Implements synchronization primitives

Q13: How does Rust handle the concept of ownership in the context of threads?

a) Threads can share ownership freely

b) Threads cannot access shared data

c) Ownership is managed through synchronization primitives

d) Ownership is not applicable to concurrent programming

Q14: In Rust, what does the `mpsc` module stand for in the context of channels?

a) Multiple-Producer, Single-Consumer

b) Multi-Processing System Communication

c) Multi-Purpose Synchronization Channel

d) Message Passing Synchronized Channel

Q15: What is the purpose of using custom message structs in message passing between threads?

a) To increase compilation time

b) To simplify thread creation

c) To allow transmission of complex and structured messages

d) To reduce the number of threads

Q16: What is the primary use case for atomic operations in Rust?

a) Efficient memory allocation

b) Avoiding data races and ensuring safe concurrent access

c) Simplifying thread creation

d) Message passing between threads

Q17: What is the primary advantage of Thread Local Storage (TLS) in concurrent programming?

a) Reducing thread count

b) Increasing compilation speed

c) Managing thread-specific data efficiently

d) Simplifying channel communication

Answers

1. c) To allow multiple tasks to run concurrently
2. c) Ownership
3. b) Don't depend on each other

4. b) To create a new thread
5. c) Enforces Rust's ownership rules, allowing only one thread to modify data at a time
6. c) To define shared behaviors that types can implement
7. d) Condvar
8. b) To allow multiple threads to have shared ownership of the queue
9. c) To attempt to acquire a lock without blocking
10. b) To ensure thread safety when accessing the underlying data structure
11. c) Improved performance and responsiveness
12. b) Monitors thread behavior
13. c) Ownership is managed through synchronization primitives
14. a) Multiple-Producer, Single-Consumer
15. c) To allow transmission of complex and structured messages
16. b) Avoiding data races and ensuring safe concurrent access
17. c) Managing thread-specific data efficiently

Key Terms

- **Ownership:** A central concept in Rust that defines how memory is managed and ensures data safety by allowing only one part of the code to modify data at a time.
- **Borrowing:** In Rust, the act of temporarily using something that another part of the code owns, subject to rules to prevent conflicts.
- **Lifetimes:** Timers in Rust that track how long shared data can be used, preventing potential problems or conflicts in concurrent programming.
- **Concurrency:** The execution of multiple tasks in software development, allowing them to happen either sequentially or simultaneously.
- **`Mutex`:** Short-form for "*mutual exclusion*," a synchronization primitive in Rust that ensures only one thread can access a protected resource at a time, preventing data races.
- **Thread::spawn:** A function in Rust used to create a new thread, allowing for concurrent execution of tasks.

- **`Arc` (Atomic Reference Counter):** A type in Rust that enables multiple threads to share ownership of data, providing both thread safety and reference counting.
- **Deadlock:** A situation in concurrent programming where threads wait indefinitely for each other to release Mutex locks, causing a standstill.
- **Mutex Guard:** A concept in Rust where a lock obtained through `lock()` enforces ownership rules, allowing only one thread to modify the data at a time.
- **Poisoned Mutex:** A Mutex that enters a "poisoned" state if a panic occurs while a thread holds the Mutex, indicating potential data corruption and requiring special handling.
- **`Condvar`:** An advanced synchronization tool in Rust that allows threads to wait until a certain condition is met before proceeding.
- **Binary Heap:** A binary heap data structure in Rust used for implementing a priority queue.
- **`try_lock`:** A method in Rust's Mutex that attempts to acquire a lock without blocking, providing a non-blocking alternative to lock acquisition.
- **Producer-Consumer:** A concurrency pattern where one or more producer threads generate data, and one or more consumer threads process that data.
- **Atomic:** Operations that are guaranteed to be executed without interruption in a multi-threaded environment, ensuring consistency in shared data manipulation.
- **Semaphore:** A synchronization primitive used to control access to a resource by multiple threads in a concurrent system.
- **`RwLock`:** Short-form for "*read-write lock*," another synchronization primitive in Rust that allows multiple threads to read data concurrently while providing exclusive access for writing.
- **Timed Locking:** A mechanism in concurrent programming that enforces a maximum time limit on read or write operations to prevent threads from waiting indefinitely.
- **Resource Pooling:** A technique in concurrent programming where a limited set of resources is efficiently managed and shared among multiple threads.
- **Channels:** A communication mechanism in Rust that allows threads to send and receive data, facilitating communication between concurrent tasks.
- **Thread Local Storage (TLS):** A fundamental concurrency concept allowing

threads to have their own isolated storage for data without the need for complex synchronization mechanisms. Implemented in Rust using the `thread_local!` macro.

- **Barrier:** A synchronization primitive in Rust, provided by the `std::sync` module, used for coordinating threads. Threads wait at a barrier until a specified number of threads have arrived, and then they proceed together.
- **Message Passing:** The act of transmitting data between threads for communication and synchronization. In Rust, channels and custom message structs are common tools for message passing.
- **Multi-Producer, Single-Consumer (mpsc):** A pattern in concurrent programming where multiple threads can produce data, but there is a single consumer receiving and processing the data. Implemented through channels in Rust's `std::sync::mpsc` module.

Chapter 8
Command Line Programs

Introduction

In this chapter, we'll take a profound look at Command-Line Interfaces (CLIs) and explore how Rust's libraries can assist us in effectively defining and parsing command-line arguments. Our aim is to embark on a practical project, building a command-line find and replace tool, using the Rust programming language. By the end of this chapter, you'll be well-equipped with the knowledge and skills necessary to craft your own command-line programs. These programs will not only perform their intended tasks effectively but also provide a seamless and pleasant experience for users navigating the command line.

Structure

In this chapter, we are going to explore the following topics:

- Building a command-line find and replace utility using Rust
- Working with command-line arguments and parsing input

Introduction to Argument Parsing

Command-line arguments play a pivotal role in configuring and personalizing the functionality of command-line utilities. They serve as a way for users to convey specific instructions, data, and settings to a program when executing it via the terminal. These arguments grant users a high degree of flexibility and control over how the program operates, making them an crucial component of many command-line applications. By understanding and effectively implementing command-line arguments, you can create tools that are more versatile and user-friendly.

When developing command-line applications in the Rust programming language, two libraries, `clap` and `structopt`, stand out as powerful tools for managing command-line arguments. In this chapter, we will delve into `clap`, an exceptionally versatile and widely adopted library for crafting command-line interfaces in Rust. `clap` provides a comprehensive set of features that facilitate the definition of arguments, flags, and subcommands, making it a favored choice among us for building interactive and user-friendly command-line utilities. Its capabilities empower you to create intuitive and well-structured command-line interfaces that enhance the overall usability and user experience of their applications.

Advantages of Choosing Clap

Clap, a robust command-line argument parser for Rust, offers several compelling reasons to be your preferred choice when dealing with command-line interfaces (CLIs). Choosing it for command-line parsing in Rust is a wise decision for several compelling reasons, as outlined here:

- **Active Maintenance and Updates**: Clap is actively maintained, with a significant release (v4) in September 2022 [1]. This commitment ensures that Clap remains compatible with the latest Rust developments and continues to be a reliable tool for CLI development.
- **Popularity and Ecosystem**: Clap is widely adopted within the Rust community, with over 12,000 stars on GitHub [2]. Its popularity results in a thriving ecosystem of resources, tutorials, and existing projects, simplifying its integration into Rust CLI development.
- **Feature-Rich**: Clap offers a feature-rich experience for CLI development. It not only handles basic argument parsing but also provides advanced features like suggestions based on Jaro-Winkler distance. This feature assists users in correcting typos or finding close to valid commands or arguments. Additionally, Clap offers comprehensive configurability for defining commands and arguments, allowing you to tailor your CLI applications to specific requirements.
- **Unix CLI Conventions**: Clap adheres to standard Unix CLI conventions, ensuring consistency and familiarity for users. It supports practices

[1]Knapp, K. B., & The Clap Community. (2023). clap (Version 4) Computer software *https://github.com/clap-rs/clap/releases?page=9*

[2]Knapp, K. B., & The Clap Community. (2023). clap (Version 4) [Computer software *https://github.com/clap-rs/clap*

like single-dash (-) flags, double-dash (--) for long options, and subcommands. This conformity enhances user experience, especially for those accustomed to Unix-style CLIs, setting it apart from alternative libraries like argh.

- **Community Support**: Clap benefits from an active and supportive community of developers. This means you can easily access assistance, documentation, and even custom extensions or plugins developed by the community to enhance their CLI projects [3].
- **Additional Resources**: The official Clap GitHub repository and the Rust CLI recommendations website provide additional resources and examples related to Clap, making it easier for you to learn and use.
- **Security and Reliability**: Clap is designed with a strong focus on security and reliability. It incorporates safeguards to prevent common issues like buffer overflows, ensuring that CLI applications built with Clap are robust and safe to use.
- **Cross-Platform Compatibility**: Clap is designed for cross-platform compatibility, working seamlessly on Windows, macOS, and various Linux distributions. This versatility makes it an ideal choice for developing cross-platform CLI applications.
- **Extensive Documentation**: Clap provides comprehensive documentation, including examples, guides, and API references. This documentation aids developers in every aspect of CLI development, from getting started to advanced usage.
- **Built-in Help and Usage Information**: Clap simplifies the development process by automatically generating help messages and usage information for CLI applications. This feature saves developers time and effort in crafting these essential components.

Clap's active maintenance, popularity, extensive feature set, adherence to Unix CLI conventions, strong community support, additional resources, security, cross-platform compatibility, extensive documentation, and built-in help functionality collectively make it a compelling and powerful choice for us creating user-friendly command-line interfaces.

Getting Started with clap

Incorporating the `clap` library into your Rust project is a crucial initial step to enable command-line argument parsing. This process involves modifying your project's `Cargo.toml` file, which serves as a manifest for your Rust project's

[3]Crate clap - Command Line Argument Parser for Rust, *https://docs.rs/clap/*

dependencies. By adding **clap** as a dependency in this file, you're essentially telling Rust's package manager, Cargo, to download and manage the **clap** library for your project. This integration can be accomplished conveniently with a single command:

```
$ cargo add clap --features=derive
```

The **--features=derive** flag indicates that we want to enable the derive feature provided by **clap**, which simplifies argument parsing.

Now that we have **clap** integrated into our project, we can explore how to define and parse command-line arguments effectively. In Rust, **clap** offers a straightforward and ergonomic approach to handling command-line arguments.

Listing 8.1 Clap basic usage example.

```
use clap::Parser; // ①

#[derive(Parser, Debug)]
#[command(
    author = "Mahmoud Harmouch",
    version = "1.0",
    about = "A command-line find and replace utility",
    name = "Find and Replace"
)]
struct Args { // ②
    /// Sets the input file to process
    #[arg(short = 'i', long = "input")]
    input: String, // ③
}

fn main() { // ④
    // Access and use the `input` argument here
    let args = Args::parse(); // ⑤

    println!("Parsed Input file name: {}!", args.input) // ⑥
}
```

① In the provided Rust code snippet, we start by importing **clap** with **use clap::Parser;**. This import statement grants us access to the necessary functionality to work with command-line arguments.

② We then define a struct called **Args** that represents the arguments our program accepts. This **Args** struct is decorated with various attributes using Rust's **derive** macro. These attributes include **author**, **version**, **about**, and **name**, which provide metadata about our program. They help in generating helpful usage information when users request it.

③ Within the **Args** struct, we define our first argument named "input." This argument is described with comments and metadata, such as its short flag (**-i**), long flag (**--input**), and a description clarifying its purpose. We also specify that this argument is mandatory and that it expects a value in the form of a **String**.

④ With our **Args** struct in place, we move to the **main** function, which serves as the entry point for our program. Here, we access and utilize the parsed command-line arguments.

⑤ By invoking **Args::parse()**, **clap** automatically parses the arguments provided by the user when they run our program.

⑥ Once the parsing is complete, the parsed arguments are stored in the **args** variable, allowing us to access the argument values as needed. In our example, we demonstrate this by printing out the value of the "input" argument using **println!**. This showcases how **clap** simplifies the process of handling and using command-line arguments in Rust.

To better understand how users interact with our utility, we provide a real-world usage scenario. In this example, a user runs our utility with the following command:

Listing 8.2 Running a clap program command.

```
$ cargo run -- -i file_name.txt

Parsed Input file name: file_name.txt!
```

Here, **cargo run** is the command to execute our program, and **--** is used to separate the cargo-specific arguments from the arguments passed to our program. The user specifies the "input" argument using **-i** followed by the desired file name, such as **file_name.txt**. As a result, our program successfully parses this input and prints the parsed input file name to the terminal.

With the basics covered, it's worth noting that **clap** offers a wide range of advanced features and capabilities beyond what we've demonstrated. These features include handling subcommands, supporting multiple argument types, generating comprehensive help messages, and customizing argument parsing behavior to suit complex use cases. Exploring these advanced features enables you to create powerful and user-friendly command-line interfaces for your Rust applications.

Handling Multiple Arguments

In the context of our "**find and replace**" utility, it's often desirable to provide users with the ability to customize various aspects of the search and replace operation. Beyond specifying an input file, users may wish to set the search pattern and the replacement text to tailor the utility to their needs.

Listing 8.3 Handling multiple arguments in clap.

```
use clap::Parser;

#[derive(Parser, Debug)]
#[command(
    author = "Mahmoud Harmouch",
    version = "1.0",
    about = "A command-line find and replace utility",
    name = "Find and Replace"
)]
struct Args {
    /// Sets the input file to process
    #[arg(short = 'i', long = "input")]
    input: String,
    /// Sets the pattern to find
    #[arg(short = 'f', long = "find")]
    find: String,
    /// Sets the replacement text
    #[arg(short = 'r', long = "replace")]
    replace: String,
}

fn main() {
    // Access and use the `input`, `find`, and `replace` arguments here
    let args = Args::parse();
}
```

In this code snippet, we've extended our argument handling to include two additional arguments, "`find`" and "`replace`". These new arguments empower users to define both the search pattern and the replacement text, thereby enhancing the utility's versatility. Each argument follows the same structure as the "`input`" argument, differing only in their names and descriptions.

Now that we have introduced these new arguments, it's crucial to understand how `clap` seamlessly handles the parsing of multiple arguments. Just like before, we employ the `Args::parse()` function to automatically process and extract the values of the "`input`", "`find`", and "`replace`" arguments.

These parsed argument values are stored within the **args** variable, enabling us to access and utilize them as needed within our Rust program's logic. With **clap**, the process of handling multiple arguments is not only straightforward but also accompanied by the automatic generation of clear help messages and usage information.

To demonstrate clap's ability to generate helpful usage information, consider running our program with the **-h** flag, as illustrated in the following command:

Listing 8.4 Generating helpful usage information command in clap.

```
$ cargo run -- -h
```

Executing this command results in the generation of a usage message that neatly summarizes the available options and their descriptions, making it easier for users to understand how to interact with our utility. The generated usage message includes details such as the expected options, their short and long flags, and an indication of whether they accept values.

Listing 8.5 Helpful usage information message in clap.

```
Usage: find-replace --input <INPUT> --find <FIND> --replace <REPLACE>

Options:
  -i, --input <INPUT>      Sets the input file to process
  -f, --find <FIND>       Sets the pattern to find
  -r, --replace <REPLACE>  Sets the replacement text
  -h, --help               Print help
  -V, --version            Print version
```

By introducing multiple arguments and leveraging **clap** for parsing and usage information generation, we enhance the utility's functionality and user-friendliness. Users can now conveniently tailor their find and replace operations by specifying the input file, search pattern, and replacement text with ease.

Handling Flag Arguments

When it comes to handling command-line arguments for your utility, it's not just about dealing with values; sometimes, you need to enable or disable specific features with what we call flag arguments. Let's dive into this concept with an example:

Listing 8.6 Handling flag arguments example.

```
use clap::Parser;

#[derive(Parser, Debug)]
#[command(
    author = "Mahmoud Harmouch",
    version = "1.0",
    about = "A command-line find and replace utility",
    name = "Find and Replace"
)]
struct Args {
    /// Sets the input file to process
    #[arg(short = 'i', long = "input")]
    input: String,
    /// Sets the pattern to find
    #[arg(short = 'f', long = "find")]
    find: String,
    /// Sets the replacement text
    #[arg(short = 'r', long = "replace")]
    replace: String,
    /// Perform a case-insensitive search and replace
    #[arg(short = 'c', long = "ignore-case")]
    ignore_case: bool,
}

fn main() {
    // Access and use the `input`, `find`, `replace`, and `ignore-case`
arguments here
    let args = Args::parse();
}
```

In the code snippet provided, we've integrated a flag argument called "ignore-case". It's accessible via both a short flag `-c` and a long flag `--ignore-case`. Unlike arguments that require values like filenames or patterns, flag arguments like this one don't need any additional input from the user. They solely serve as indicators of whether the user wants the search and replace operation to be case-insensitive.

The magic behind handling flag arguments with the **clap** library is that it's just as simple as dealing with arguments that require values. Inside our code, we can easily check if a particular flag is present in the **args** structure. If it is, we know the user has opted for the corresponding feature. This streamlined approach makes it painless to incorporate flag arguments into our command-line utility, enhancing its usability and flexibility.

Advanced Argument Handling

clap provides extensive capabilities for argument handling, including subcommands, positional arguments, and custom validation. While we won't cover all the advanced features here, we'll briefly introduce subcommands as they can be useful for organizing complex utilities.

A subcommand is like a separate command within our utility, each with its own set of arguments. For example, our find and replace utility could have subcommands for different text manipulation operations.

Here's a simplified example of how to define and use subcommands with **clap**:

Listing 8.7 Advanced argument handling example.

```
use clap::Args;
use clap::{Parser, Subcommand};

#[derive(Parser, Debug)]
#[command(
    author = "Mahmoud Harmouch",
    version = "1.0",
    about = "A command-line text manipulation utility",
    name = "Text Manipulation Utility"
)]
pub struct Cli {
    /// Turn debugging information on.
    #[arg(short, long, action = clap::ArgAction::Count)]
    debug: u8,
    /// Find and Replace commands.
    #[command(subcommand)]
    pub command: Option<Commands>
}

#[derive(Subcommand, Debug)]
pub enum Commands {
    /// Subcommand for handling find operations.
    Find(FindCommands),
    /// Subcommand for handling replace operations.
    Replace(ReplaceCommands),
}

/// Represents find-related commands.
#[derive(Debug, Args)]
pub struct FindCommands {
    /// Sets the input file to process
```

```
    #[clap(short = 'i', long = "input")]
    pub input: Option<String>,
    /// Sets the pattern to find.
    #[clap(short = 'p', long = "pattern")]
    pub pattern: Option<String>,
}

/// Represents repalce-related commands.
#[derive(Debug, Args)]
pub struct ReplaceCommands {
    /// Sets the input file to process
    #[clap(short = 'i', long = "input")]
    pub input: Option<String>,
    /// Sets the pattern to find.
    #[clap(short = 'p', long = "pattern")]
    pub pattern: Option<String>,
    /// Sets the replacement text.
    #[clap(short = 'r', long = "replace")]
    pub replace: Option<String>,
}

fn main() {
    let args = Cli::parse();
    match args.command {
        Some(Commands::Find(command)) => {
            match command.input {
                Some(ref input) => {
                    // cargo run -- find --input file_name
                    println!("{:?}", input);
                }
                None => {
                    println!("Please provide a file name.");
                }
            };
            match command.pattern {
                Some(ref pattern) => {
                    // cargo run -- find --pattern custom_pattern
                    println!("{:?}", pattern);
                }
                None => {
                    println!("Please provide a pattern.");
                }
            };
        }
        Some(Commands::Replace(command)) => {
```

```
            match command.input {
                Some(ref input) => {
                    // cargo run -- replace --input file_name
                    println!("{:?}", input);
                }
                None => {
                    println!("Please provide a file name.");
                }
            };
            match command.pattern {
                Some(ref pattern) => {
                    // cargo run -- replace --pattern custom_pattern
                    println!("{:?}", pattern);
                }
                None => {
                    println!("Please provide a pattern.");
                }
            };
            match command.replace {
                Some(ref replace) => {
                    // cargo run -- replace --replace string
                    println!("{:?}", replace);
                }
                None => {
                    println!("Please provide a pattern.");
                }
            };
        }
        None => println!(
            "Unknown command. Use '--help' for usage instructions."
        )
    };
}
```

In this code, we've defined two subcommands, "**find**" and "**replace**", each with its own set of arguments. Users can run the utility with one of these subcommands to perform specific text manipulation tasks.

Listing 8.8 Clap basic cli commands example.

```
$ cargo run -- -h

A command-line text manipulation utility

Usage: find-replace [OPTIONS] [COMMAND]
```

```
Commands:
  find     Subcommand for handling find operations
  replace  Subcommand for handling replace operations
  help     Print this message or the help of the given subcommand(s)

Options:
  -d, --debug...  Turn debugging information on
  -h, --help      Print help
  -V, --version   Print version


$ cargo run -- find -h

Subcommand for handling find operations

Usage: find-replace find [OPTIONS]

Options:
  -i, --input <INPUT>      Sets the input file to process
  -p, --pattern <PATTERN>  Sets the pattern to find
  -h, --help               Print help


$ cargo run -- replace -h

Subcommand for handling replace operations

Usage: find-replace replace [OPTIONS]

Options:
  -i, --input <INPUT>      Sets the input file to process
  -p, --pattern <PATTERN>  Sets the pattern to find
  -r, --replace <REPLACE>  Sets the replacement text
  -h, --help               Print help
```

Implementing Text Search and Replace Logic

In the previous sections, we explored the fundamentals of command-line argument parsing using the **clap** library in Rust. Now that we have a solid understanding of how to define and parse command-line arguments efficiently, it's time to implement the core functionality of our find and replace utility.

Overview of Text Search and Replace

The primary objective of our utility is to perform a specific pattern search within a given input file and subsequently replace any instances of that pattern with a user-defined replacement text. This task encompasses several key operations, including reading the content of the input file, carrying out text processing tasks, and then writing the modified content back into the same file. Additionally, our utility must be flexible enough to handle various scenarios, such as case-insensitive searches and the ability to process multiple files at once.

To achieve this functionality, we have outlined a systematic approach consisting of several distinct steps:

- **Reading the Input File**: Our first step involves opening and accessing the designated input file. We read its entire content and store it as a string in memory. This in-memory representation allows us to perform subsequent text processing operations efficiently.
- **Finding and Replacing**: With the input content now available as a string, we employ Rust's string manipulation functions to search for occurrences of the specified pattern within the content. When matches are located, we replace them with the user-provided replacement text. This step is crucial in effecting the desired changes to the file.
- **Writing the Modified Content**: Once the find and replace operation has been successfully executed, we proceed to write the modified content back into the same input file. This action involves overwriting the original content with the updated version, ensuring that the user's requested changes are reflected in the file.
- **Optional Case-Insensitive Search**: Our utility offers the option for users to specify the `--ignore-case` flag. If this flag is set, our program will perform a case-insensitive search and replace operation. This ensures that occurrences of the specified pattern are detected regardless of whether they are in uppercase or lowercase letters.
- **Support for Multiple Files**: To enhance the utility's versatility and efficiency, we have designed it to support the processing of multiple input files in a single run. This means that users can apply the same find and replace functionality to multiple files without having to execute the program separately for each file.

With these steps outlined, we are prepared to start the implementation of the initial three steps, setting the foundation for our utility's core functionality.

Reading the Input File

To read the contents of the input file, we'll use Rust's standard library, which provides robust file I/O capabilities. We'll open the file, read its contents, and store them as a string.

Listing 8.9 Reading an input file example.

```
use clap::Args;
use clap::{Parser, Subcommand};
use std::fs::File;
use std::io::{self, Read};

#[derive(Parser, Debug)]
#[command(
    author = "Mahmoud Harmouch",
    version = "1.0",
    about = "A command-line text manipulation utility",
    name = "Text Manipulation Utility"
)]
pub struct Cli {
    /// Turn debugging information on.
    #[arg(short, long, action = clap::ArgAction::Count)]
    debug: u8,
    /// Find and Replace commands.
    #[command(subcommand)]
    pub command: Option<Commands>
}

#[derive(Subcommand, Debug)]
pub enum Commands {
    /// Subcommand for handling find operations.
    Find(FindCommands),
    /// Subcommand for handling replace operations.
    Replace(ReplaceCommands),
}

/// Represents find-related commands.
#[derive(Debug, Args)]
pub struct FindCommands {
    /// Sets the input file to process
    #[clap(short = 'i', long = "input")]
    pub input: Option<String>,
    /// Sets the pattern to find.
    #[clap(short = 'p', long = "pattern")]
    pub pattern: Option<String>,
```

```
}

/// Represents repalce-related commands.
#[derive(Debug, Args)]
pub struct ReplaceCommands {
    /// Sets the input file to process
    #[clap(short = 'i', long = "input")]
    pub input: Option<String>,
    /// Sets the pattern to find.
    #[clap(short = 'p', long = "pattern")]
    pub pattern: Option<String>,
    /// Sets the replacement text.
    #[clap(short = 'r', long = "replace")]
    pub replace: Option<String>,
}

fn read_file_to_string(file_path: &str) -> io::Result<String> { // ①
    let mut file = File::open(file_path)?; // ②
    let mut contents = String::new(); // ②
    file.read_to_string(&mut contents)?; // ②

    Ok(contents) // ②
}

fn main() { // ③
    let args = Cli::parse();
    let input_content;
    match args.command {
        Some(Commands::Find(command)) => { // ④
            match command.input {
                Some(ref input) => {
                    // cargo run -- find --input file.txt
                    input_content = read_file_to_string(input).unwrap();
                    println!("Input file content: {:?}", input_content);
                }
                None => {
                    println!("Please provide a file name.");
                }
            };
            match command.pattern {
                Some(ref pattern) => {
                    // cargo run -- find --pattern custom_pattern
                    println!("{:?}", pattern);
                }
                None => {
                    println!("Please provide a pattern.");
                }
```

```
            };
        }
        Some(Commands::Replace(command)) => { // ⑤
            match command.input {
                Some(ref input) => {
                    // cargo run -- replace --input file_name
                    println!("{:?}", input);
                }
                None => {
                    println!("Please provide a file name.");
                }
            };
            match command.pattern {
                Some(ref pattern) => {
                    // cargo run -- replace --pattern custom_pattern
                    println!("{:?}", pattern);
                }
                None => {
                    println!("Please provide a pattern.");
                }
            };
            match command.replace {
                Some(ref replace) => {
                    // cargo run -- replace --replace string
                    println!("{:?}", replace);
                }
                None => {
                    println!("Please provide a pattern.");
                }
            };
        }
        None => println!(
            "Unknown command. Use '--help' for usage instructions."
        )
    };
}
```

```
// $ cargo run -- find --input file.txt
```

```
// Input file content: "Hello World\n"
```

The provided code snippet demonstrates the process of reading the contents of an input file in Rust. This functionality is essential for subsequent find and replace operations within a command-line text manipulation utility.

① To read the contents of the input file, the code leverages Rust's standard library, which offers robust file I/O capabilities. Specifically, it imports necessary modules and defines a function named **read_file_to_string**. This function takes a file path as its argument and returns a **Result** type that encapsulates either the file's contents as a string or an error related to file I/O.

② Inside the **read_file_to_string** function, it opens the file specified by the provided **file_path** and handles any potential errors using Rust's error handling mechanisms. It initializes an empty string called **contents** and proceeds to read the file's content into this string using the **read_to_string** method. Finally, it returns an **Ok** variant containing the file's content if the operation is successful.

③ The **main** function serves as the entry point for the program. It utilizes the Clap library for parsing command-line arguments and structuring the application's command-line interface. Depending on the provided command (either "**find**" or "**replace**"), it extracts relevant options, such as the input file path, pattern, and replacement text, if applicable.

④ For instance, when the "**find**" command is specified, the code verifies if an input file path and pattern have been provided as command-line arguments. If both are present, it calls the **read_file_to_string** function to read the content of the input file and then prints it to the console. Likewise, it also prints the specified pattern. If any of these required options are missing, appropriate error messages are displayed.

⑤ Similarly, when the "**replace**" command is invoked, the code checks for the input file path, pattern, and replacement text and prints them accordingly. It also handles missing options gracefully by displaying corresponding error messages.

This code snippet establishes the foundation for reading input files and extracting command-line arguments for subsequent text manipulation operations. It utilizes Rust's error handling mechanisms and the Clap library for efficient and user-friendly command-line interaction, making it a useful utility for processing text data.

Find and Replace Logic

The central functionality of our utility revolves around locating occurrences of a specific pattern within a given content and substituting them with the provided replacement text. To accomplish this task, we harness Rust's built-in **replace** method for strings. This method allows us to efficiently carry out the search and replace operation.

To make this concept more concrete, let's delve into the implementation of a fundamental find-and-replace function. The following code snippet demonstrates this process:

Listing 8.10 Find and Replace cli logic.

```
use clap::Args;
use clap::{Parser, Subcommand};
use std::fs::File;
use std::io::{self, Read};

#[derive(Parser, Debug)]
#[command(
    author = "Mahmoud Harmouch",
    version = "1.0",
    about = "A command-line text manipulation utility",
    name = "Text Manipulation Utility"
)]
pub struct Cli {
    /// Turn debugging information on.
    #[arg(short, long, action = clap::ArgAction::Count)]
    debug: u8,
    /// Find and Replace commands.
    #[command(subcommand)]
    pub command: Option<Commands>
}

#[derive(Subcommand, Debug)]
pub enum Commands {
    /// Subcommand for handling find operations.
    Find(FindCommands),
    /// Subcommand for handling replace operations.
    Replace(ReplaceCommands),
}

/// Represents find-related commands.
#[derive(Debug, Args)]
pub struct FindCommands {
    /// Sets the input file to process
    #[clap(short = 'i', long = "input")]
    pub input: Option<String>,
    /// Sets the pattern to find.
    #[clap(short = 'p', long = "pattern")]
    pub pattern: Option<String>,
}

/// Represents repalce-related commands.
#[derive(Debug, Args)]
pub struct ReplaceCommands {
    /// Sets the input file to process
    #[clap(short = 'i', long = "input")]
```

```
    pub input: Option<String>,
    /// Sets the pattern to find.
    #[clap(short = 'p', long = "pattern")]
    pub pattern: Option<String>,
    /// Sets the replacement text.
    #[clap(short = 'r', long = "replace")]
    pub replace: Option<String>,
}

fn read_file_to_string(file_path: &str) -> io::Result<String> {
    let mut file = File::open(file_path)?;
    let mut contents = String::new();
    file.read_to_string(&mut contents)?;

    Ok(contents)
}

fn find_and_replace(content: &mut String, pattern: &str, replacement: &str) {
    *content = content.replace(pattern, replacement);
}

fn main() {
    let args = Cli::parse();
    let mut input_content = "".to_string();
    let mut pattern_to_find = "".to_string();
    let mut replacement_text = "".to_string();

    match args.command {
        Some(Commands::Find(command)) => {
            if let Some(input) = &command.input {
                input_content = read_file_to_string(input).unwrap();
                println!("Input file content: {:?}", input_content);
            } else {
                println!("Please provide a file name.");
            }
            if let Some(pattern) = &command.pattern {
                pattern_to_find = pattern.clone();
                println!("Pattern: {:?}", pattern);
            } else {
                println!("Please provide a pattern.");
            }
        }
        Some(Commands::Replace(command)) => {
            if let Some(input) = &command.input {
                input_content = read_file_to_string(input).unwrap();
                println!("Input file content: {:?}", input_content);
            } else {
```

```
                println!("Please provide a file name.");
            }
            if let Some(pattern) = &command.pattern {
                pattern_to_find = pattern.clone();
                println!("Pattern: {:?}", pattern_to_find);
            } else {
                println!("Please provide a pattern.");
            }
            if let Some(replace) = &command.replace {
                replacement_text = replace.clone();
                println!("Replacement text: {:?}", replacement_text);
            } else {
                println!("Please provide a replacement text.");
            }
        }
        None => println!("Unknown command. Use '--help' for usage
instructions.")
    };

    println!("Content Before: {:?}", input_content);
    find_and_replace(&mut input_content, &pattern_to_find, &replacement_
text);
    println!("Content After: {:?}", input_content);
}

// $ cargo run -- replace -i file.txt -p World -r Rust

// Pattern: "World"
// Replacement text: "Rust"
// Content Before: "Hello World\n"
// Content After: "Hello Rust\n"
```

In the provided Rust code, we start by defining a command-line utility for text manipulation using the `clap` library. The utility supports various commands, including "**find**" and "`replace`", and accepts additional options for customization. This modular approach enhances the flexibility and usability of our utility.

The `Cli` struct represents the primary command-line interface, allowing users to choose between different commands such as "`Find`" or "`Replace`". Each command has its set of parameters and options, making it a versatile tool for various text manipulation tasks.

The `FindCommands` and `ReplaceCommands` structs represent the subcommands for finding and replacing operations, respectively. These structs define specific options like input file paths, search patterns, and replacement texts, enabling users to tailor their text processing tasks precisely.

To facilitate file reading, we implement the **read_file_to_string** function, which takes a file path as an argument and returns the content of the file as a **String**. This function leverages Rust's error handling capabilities to gracefully manage file I/O operations.

Our core find-and-replace functionality resides within the **find_and_replace** function. This function accepts a mutable reference to a **String** containing the content, along with a pattern to search for and a replacement text. Utilizing Rust's **replace** method, it efficiently performs the search and replace operation, modifying the content in place.

In the **main** function, we orchestrate the execution of the utility based on the user's chosen command and provided options. We handle command-line arguments and user inputs, read the input file (if specified), and perform the find-and-replace operation, displaying the content before and after the transformation.

In this example, we execute the "**replace**" command, specifying an input file (**file.txt**), a search pattern ("**World**"), and a replacement text ("**Rust**"). The utility processes the file, identifies occurrences of the pattern, and replaces them with the provided text. The result is displayed, showcasing the content both before and after the transformation.

Our utility provides a flexible and powerful text manipulation tool that can be customized through command-line options and subcommands. It efficiently performs find-and-replace operations, making it a valuable asset for text processing tasks.

Writing the Modified Content

To write the modified content back to the input file, we'll use Rust's file I/O capabilities. We'll open the input file in write mode, write the modified content to it, and ensure that any existing content is overwritten.

Listing 8.11 Overriding input file content.

```
use clap::Args;
use clap::{Parser, Subcommand};
use std::fs::File;
use std::io::{self, Read, Write};

#[derive(Parser, Debug)]
#[command(
    author = "Mahmoud Harmouch",
    version = "1.0",
    about = "A command-line text manipulation utility",
```

```
    name = "Text Manipulation Utility"
)]
pub struct Cli {
    /// Turn debugging information on.
    #[arg(short, long, action = clap::ArgAction::Count)]
    debug: u8,
    /// Find and Replace commands.
    #[command(subcommand)]
    pub command: Option<Commands>
}

#[derive(Subcommand, Debug)]
pub enum Commands {
    /// Subcommand for handling find operations.
    Find(FindCommands),
    /// Subcommand for handling replace operations.
    Replace(ReplaceCommands),
}

/// Represents find-related commands.
#[derive(Debug, Args)]
pub struct FindCommands {
    /// Sets the input file to process
    #[clap(short = 'i', long = "input")]
    pub input: Option<String>,
    /// Sets the pattern to find.
    #[clap(short = 'p', long = "pattern")]
    pub pattern: Option<String>,
}

/// Represents repalce-related commands.
#[derive(Debug, Args)]
pub struct ReplaceCommands {
    /// Sets the input file to process
    #[clap(short = 'i', long = "input")]
    pub input: Option<String>,
    /// Sets the pattern to find.
    #[clap(short = 'p', long = "pattern")]
    pub pattern: Option<String>,
    /// Sets the replacement text.
    #[clap(short = 'r', long = "replace")]
    pub replace: Option<String>,
}

fn read_file_to_string(file_path: &str) -> io::Result<String> {
    let mut file = File::open(file_path)?;
    let mut contents = String::new();
```

```
    file.read_to_string(&mut contents)?;

    Ok(contents)
}

fn find_and_replace(content: &mut String, pattern: &str, replacement:
&str) {
    *content = content.replace(pattern, replacement);
}

fn write_string_to_file(file_path: &str, content: &str) -> io::Result<()>
{
    let mut file = File::create(file_path)?;
    file.write_all(content.as_bytes())?;

    Ok(())
}

fn main() -> io::Result<()> {
    let args = Cli::parse();
    let mut input_content = "".to_string();
    let mut pattern_to_find = "".to_string();
    let mut replacement_text = "".to_string();
    let mut input_file_path = "".to_string();

    match args.command {
        Some(Commands::Find(command)) => {
            if let Some(input) = &command.input {
                input_content = read_file_to_string(input)?;
                println!("Input file content: {:?}", input_content);
            } else {
                println!("Please provide a file name.");
            }
            if let Some(pattern) = &command.pattern {
                pattern_to_find = pattern.clone();
                println!("Pattern: {:?}", pattern);
            } else {
                println!("Please provide a pattern.");
            }
        }
        Some(Commands::Replace(command)) => {
            if let Some(input) = &command.input {
                input_file_path = input.to_string();
                input_content = read_file_to_string(input)?;
                println!("Input file content: {:?}", input_content);
            } else {
                println!("Please provide a file name.");
```

```
            }
            if let Some(pattern) = &command.pattern {
                pattern_to_find = pattern.clone();
                println!("Pattern: {:?}", pattern_to_find);
            } else {
                println!("Please provide a pattern.");
            }
            if let Some(replace) = &command.replace {
                replacement_text = replace.clone();
                println!("Replacement text: {:?}", replacement_text);
            } else {
                println!("Please provide a replacement text.");
            }
        }
        None => println!("Unknown command. Use '--help' for usage in-
structions.")
    };

    println!("File Content Before: {:?}", input_content);
    find_and_replace(&mut input_content, &pattern_to_find, &replacement_
text);

    write_string_to_file(&input_file_path, &input_content)?;

    input_content = read_file_to_string(&input_file_path)?;
    println!("File Content After: {:?}", input_content);
    Ok(())
}

// $ cargo run -- replace -i file.txt -p World -r Rust

// Input file content: "Hello World\n"
// Pattern: "World"
// Replacement text: "Rust"
// File Content Before: "Hello World\n"
// File Content After: "Hello Rust\n"
```

In this code, we define a **write_string_to_file** function that takes a file path and the content to write. It opens the file in write mode, writes the content, and handles any potential errors.

With this implementation, we can successfully read the input file, perform find and replace, and write the modified content back to the file.

Case-Insensitive Search (Optional)

Our utility can be enhanced to support case-insensitive search and replace. To do this, we'll need to modify the **find_and_replace** function to perform a case-insensitive search. We can use Rust's regular expressions to achieve this:

Listing 8.12 Implementing case-insensitive search.

```
use clap::Args;
use clap::{Parser, Subcommand};
use std::fs::File;
use std::io::{self, Read, Write};
use regex::Regex;

#[derive(Parser, Debug)]
#[command(
    author = "Mahmoud Harmouch",
    version = "1.0",
    about = "A command-line text manipulation utility",
    name = "Text Manipulation Utility"
)]
pub struct Cli {
    /// Turn debugging information on.
    #[arg(short, long, action = clap::ArgAction::Count)]
    debug: u8,
    /// Find and Replace commands.
    #[command(subcommand)]
    pub command: Option<Commands>
}

#[derive(Subcommand, Debug)]
pub enum Commands {
    /// Subcommand for handling find operations.
    Find(FindCommands),
    /// Subcommand for handling replace operations.
    Replace(ReplaceCommands),
}

/// Represents find-related commands.
#[derive(Debug, Args)]
pub struct FindCommands {
    /// Sets the input file to process
    #[clap(short = 'i', long = "input")]
    pub input: Option<String>,
    /// Sets the pattern to find.
```

```
    #[clap(short = 'p', long = "pattern")]
    pub pattern: Option<String>,
}

/// Represents repalce-related commands.
#[derive(Debug, Args)]
pub struct ReplaceCommands {
    /// Sets the input file to process
    #[clap(short = 'i', long = "input")]
    pub input: Option<String>,
    /// Sets the pattern to find.
    #[clap(short = 'p', long = "pattern")]
    pub pattern: Option<String>,
    /// Sets the replacement text.
    #[clap(short = 'r', long = "replace")]
    pub replace: Option<String>,
    /// Perform a case-insensitive search and replace.
    #[clap(short = 'c', long = "ignore-case")]
    pub ignore_case: Option<bool>,

}

fn read_file_to_string(file_path: &str) -> io::Result<String> {
    let mut file = File::open(file_path)?;
    let mut contents = String::new();
    file.read_to_string(&mut contents)?;

    Ok(contents)
}

fn find_and_replace(content: &mut String, pattern: &str, replacement:
&str, ignore_case: bool) {
    let regex = if ignore_case {
        Regex::new(&format!(r"(?i){}", pattern)).unwrap()
    } else {
        Regex::new(pattern).unwrap()
    };

    *content = regex.replace_all(content, replacement).to_string();
}

fn write_string_to_file(file_path: &str, content: &str) -> io::Result<()>
{
    let mut file = File::create(file_path)?;
    file.write_all(content.as_bytes())?;
```

```
    Ok(())
}

fn main() -> io::Result<()> {
    let args = Cli::parse();
    let mut input_content = "".to_string();
    let mut pattern_to_find = "".to_string();
    let mut replacement_text = "".to_string();
    let mut input_file_path = "".to_string();
    let mut ignore_case = false;

    match args.command {
        Some(Commands::Find(command)) => {
            if let Some(input) = &command.input {
                input_content = read_file_to_string(input)?;
                println!("Input file content: {:?}", input_content);
            } else {
                println!("Please provide a file name.");
            }
            if let Some(pattern) = &command.pattern {
                pattern_to_find = pattern.clone();
                println!("Pattern: {:?}", pattern);
            } else {
                println!("Please provide a pattern.");
            }
        }
        Some(Commands::Replace(command)) => {
            if let Some(input) = &command.input {
                input_file_path = input.to_string();
                input_content = read_file_to_string(input)?;
                println!("Input file content: {:?}", input_content);
            } else {
                println!("Please provide a file name.");
            }
            if let Some(pattern) = &command.pattern {
                pattern_to_find = pattern.clone();
                println!("Pattern: {:?}", pattern_to_find);
            } else {
                println!("Please provide a pattern.");
            }
            if let Some(replace) = &command.replace {
                replacement_text = replace.clone();
                println!("Replacement text: {:?}", replacement_text);
            } else {
                println!("Please provide a replacement text.");
            }
            if let Some(ignore) = &command.ignore_case {
```

```
                ignore_case = *ignore;
                println!("Ignore case: {:?}", ignore_case);
            } else {
                println!("Please provide if case sensitive replace-
ment.");
            }
            println!("File Content Before: {:?}", input_content);
            find_and_replace(&mut input_content, &pattern_to_find, &re-
placement_text, ignore_case);

            write_string_to_file(&input_file_path, &input_content)?;

            input_content = read_file_to_string(&input_file_path)?;
            println!("File Content After: {:?}", input_content);
        }
        None => println!("Unknown command. Use '--help' for usage in-
structions.")
    };

    Ok(())

}

// $ cargo run -- replace -i file.txt -p world -r Rust -c

// Input file content: "Hello World\n"
// Pattern: "world"
// Replacement text: "Rust"
// File Content Before: "Hello World\n"
// File Content After: "Hello Rust\n"
```

In this modified code, we use the **regex** crate to create a regular expression pattern that performs a case-insensitive search if the **ignore_case** flag is set to **true**. The **regex::Regex** struct allows us to replace all occurrences of the pattern with the replacement text.

With these changes, our utility can optionally perform case-insensitive replace.

Support for Multiple Input Files

To enhance the versatility of our utility, it is crucial to implement support for processing multiple input files in a single run. This feature empowers users to perform find and replace operations on multiple files without the need to execute the utility separately for each file. Implementing this functionality is not only convenient but also improves the utility's efficiency.

The approach to achieving this capability involves accepting multiple file paths as arguments and systematically iterating over them to apply the find and replace logic to each file. In our updated main function, we have incorporated this feature seamlessly into the existing command-line interface (CLI).

Here's an updated version of our **main** function that supports multiple input files:

Listing 8.13 Adding support for multiple input files.

```
use clap::Args;
use clap::{Parser, Subcommand};
use std::fs::File;
use std::io::{self, Read, Write};
use regex::Regex;

#[derive(Parser, Debug)]
#[command(
    author = "Mahmoud Harmouch",
    version = "1.0",
    about = "A command-line text manipulation utility",
    name = "Text Manipulation Utility"
)]
pub struct Cli {
    /// Turn debugging information on.
    #[arg(short, long, action = clap::ArgAction::Count)]
    debug: u8,
    /// Find and Replace commands.
    #[command(subcommand)]
    pub command: Option<Commands>
}

#[derive(Subcommand, Debug)]
pub enum Commands {
    /// Subcommand for handling find operations.
    Find(FindCommands),
    /// Subcommand for handling replace operations.
    Replace(ReplaceCommands),
}

/// Represents find-related commands.
#[derive(Debug, Args)]
pub struct FindCommands {
    /// Sets the input file to process
    #[clap(short = 'i', long = "input", num_args = 1.., value_delimiter
= ' ')]
    pub input: Option<Vec<String>>,
```

```
    /// Sets the pattern to find.
    #[clap(short = 'p', long = "pattern")]
    pub pattern: Option<String>,
}

/// Represents repalce-related commands.
#[derive(Debug, Args)]
pub struct ReplaceCommands {
    /// Sets the input file to process
    #[clap(short = 'i', long = "input", num_args = 1.., value_delimiter
= ' ')]
    pub input: Option<Vec<String>>,
    /// Sets the pattern to find.
    #[clap(short = 'p', long = "pattern")]
    pub pattern: Option<String>,
    /// Sets the replacement text.
    #[clap(short = 'r', long = "replace")]
    pub replace: Option<String>,
    /// Perform a case-insensitive search and replace.
    #[clap(short = 'c', long = "ignore-case")]
    pub ignore_case: bool,

}

fn read_file_to_string(file_path: &str) -> io::Result<String> {
    let mut file = File::open(file_path)?;
    let mut contents = String::new();
    file.read_to_string(&mut contents)?;

    Ok(contents)
}

fn find_and_replace(content: &mut String, pattern: &str, replacement:
&str, ignore_case: bool) {
    let regex = if ignore_case {
        Regex::new(&format!(r"(?i){}", pattern)).unwrap()
    } else {
        Regex::new(pattern).unwrap()
    };

    *content = regex.replace_all(content, replacement).to_string();
}

fn write_string_to_file(file_path: &str, content: &str) -> io::Result<()>
{
    let mut file = File::create(file_path)?;
    file.write_all(content.as_bytes())?;
```

```
    Ok(())
}

fn main() -> io::Result<()> {
    let args = Cli::parse();
    let mut input_files: Vec<String> = vec!["".to_string(),];
    let mut pattern_to_find = "".to_string();
    let mut replacement_text = "".to_string();
    let mut ignore_case = false;

    match args.command {
        Some(Commands::Find(command)) => {
            if let Some(input) = &command.input {
                input_files = input.to_vec();
            } else {
                println!("Please provide a file name.");
            }
            if let Some(pattern) = &command.pattern {
                pattern_to_find = pattern.clone();
                println!("Pattern: {:?}", pattern);
            } else {
                println!("Please provide a pattern.");
            }

            for input_file_path in input_files {
                let mut input_content = read_file_to_string(&input_file_
path)?;

                find_and_replace(&mut input_content, &pattern_to_find, "",
ignore_case);

                println!("Found Content: {:?}", input_content);
            }
        }
        Some(Commands::Replace(command)) => {
            if let Some(input) = &command.input {
                input_files = input.to_vec();
            } else {
                println!("Please provide a file name.");
            }
            if let Some(pattern) = &command.pattern {
                pattern_to_find = pattern.clone();
                println!("Pattern: {:?}", pattern_to_find);
            } else {
                println!("Please provide a pattern.");
            }
```

```
            if let Some(replace) = &command.replace {
                replacement_text = replace.clone();
                println!("Replacement text: {:?}", replacement_text);
            } else {
                println!("Please provide a replacement text.");
            }
            if let ignore = &command.ignore_case {
                ignore_case = *ignore;
                println!("Ignore case: {:?}", ignore_case);
            } else {
               println!("Please provide if case sensitive replacement.");
            }

            for input_file_path in input_files {
                let mut input_content = read_file_to_string(&input_file_
path)?;

                println!("File Content Before: {:?}", input_content);
                find_and_replace(&mut input_content, &pattern_to_find,
&replacement_text, ignore_case);

                // Write the modified content back to the input file
                write_string_to_file(&input_file_path, &input_content)?;

                input_content = read_file_to_string(&input_file_path)?;
                println!("File Content After: {:?}", input_content);
            }

        }
        None => println!("Unknown command. Use '--help' for usage
instructions.")
    };

    Ok(())

}

// $ cargo run -- replace -i file1.txt file2.txt file3.txt -p world -r Rust
-c

// Pattern: "world"
// Replacement text: "Rust"
// Ignore case: true
// File Content Before: "Hello World\n"
// File Content After: "Hello Rust\n"
// File Content Before: "Hello World\n"
```

```
// File Content After: "Hello Rust\n"
// File Content Before: "Hello World\n"
// File Content After: "Hello Rust\n"
```

By incorporating these enhancements, our utility has become a more powerful and user-friendly tool for performing find and replace operations across multiple files in a seamless and efficient manner. Users can confidently leverage this utility to streamline text manipulation tasks across a variety of files with ease.

Conclusion

In this chapter, we delved into the essential concepts of command-line argument parsing, utilizing the versatile `clap` library in Rust. Throughout our exploration, we comprehensively addressed several fundamental aspects of argument handling, ranging from the definition and parsing of arguments to effectively managing arguments with associated values and flags. Furthermore, we introduced the concept of subcommands as a robust organizational strategy for complex utility programs. This comprehensive understanding of argument parsing lays a solid foundation for crafting command-line applications in Rust.

Moreover, we not only grasped the theoretical knowledge but also put it into practice by implementing the core functionality of a find-and-replace utility in Rust. Our practical journey involved reading the contents of input files, executing find and replace operations efficiently, and subsequently saving the modified content back to the respective files. We also explored features like implementing case-insensitive searches and processing multiple files, enhancing the utility's usability. This hands-on experience exemplified the real-world application of argument parsing and demonstrated its pivotal role in crafting user-friendly command-line tools.

Looking forward, the next chapter will take us into the world of device I/O operations, a common and crucial task in system programming. We will explore the complexities of reading from and writing to files, leveraging the robust capabilities of Rust's standard library. Throughout this chapter, we will demystify the complexities of essential file system operations, enabling us to navigate and manipulate files with confidence. Additionally, we will delve into the exciting domain of working with hardware devices through Rust interfaces, providing valuable insights into system-level interactions. Topics include file I/O in Rust, mastering common file system operations, and gaining a foundational overview of interfacing with hardware devices in the Rust programming language. These insights will equip you with the skills necessary to tackle a broad spectrum of system programming challenges.

Resources

To strengthen your proficiency in developing command-line programs in Rust, consider exploring the following resources:

- *Rust Book - Building a Command Line Program*: Refer to the official Rust documentation's chapter on building command-line programs. This resource provides a step-by-step guide to creating a command-line application, covering topics such as parsing command-line arguments and organizing code effectively. - *https://doc.rust-lang.org/book/ch12-00-an-io-project.html*
- *Rust CLI Book*: Dive into the "Rust CLI Book", an online resource specifically focused on building command-line applications in Rust. Explore topics such as error handling, testing, and creating user-friendly interfaces for your command-line programs. - *https://rust-cli.github.io/book/index.html*
- *Clap Documentation*: Explore the documentation for Clap, a powerful and easy-to-use command-line argument parser for Rust. Learn how to define command-line interfaces, parse arguments, and handle user input with this widely used crate. - *https://clap.rs*
- *StructOpt GitHub Repository*: Visit the GitHub repository for `StructOpt`, a Rust library for parsing command-line arguments by defining a struct. `StructOpt` simplifies the process of creating command-line interfaces by leveraging Rust's type system. - *https://github.com/TeXitoi/structopt*
- *env_logger Documentation*: Explore the documentation for `env_logger`, a flexible logger implementation for Rust command-line applications. Learn how to configure and use `env_logger` to enhance the logging capabilities of your programs. - *https://docs.rs/env_logger*
- *fs_extra Documentation*: Delve into the documentation for the `fs_extra` crate, which provides additional file system functionality for Rust. This crate is useful for managing files and directories in your command-line programs efficiently. - *https://docs.rs/fs_extra*
- *quicli GitHub Repository*: Explore the GitHub repository for quicli, a Rust library for quickly building command-line applications. Quicli aims to reduce boilerplate code and streamline the process of creating command-line interfaces. - *https://github.com/killercup/quicli*
- *shellfn Documentation*: Check out the documentation for the `shellfn` crate, which allows you to write shell scripts directly in Rust. This crate is useful for integrating shell-like functionality into your command-line programs. - *https://docs.rs/shellfn*

- *dialoguer Crate*: Explore the dialoguer crate on crates.io, a library for creating interactive command-line interfaces. Dialoguer provides a set of utilities for prompting users with questions, selecting options, and displaying progress bars. - *https://crates.io/crates/dialoguer*
- *ripgrep GitHub Repository*: Visit the GitHub repository for `ripgrep`, a fast and user-friendly search tool for text in code. Analyze the source code of `ripgrep` to understand best practices for building efficient and feature-rich command-line programs. - *https://github.com/BurntSushi/ripgrep*

These resources offer a comprehensive view of building command-line programs in Rust, providing practical guidance, examples, and documentation to help you create robust and user-friendly command-line interfaces.

Multiple-Choice Questions

Q1: Which Rust library is highlighted in this chapter as a powerful tool for managing command-line arguments?

a) `serde`

b) `clap`

c) `structopt`

d) `argh`

Q2: What role do command-line arguments play in configuring and personalizing the functionality of command-line utilities?

a) They define data structures.

b) They provide default implementations for functions.

c) They enable users to convey specific instructions, data, and settings.

d) They restrict access to data.

Q3: Why is Clap considered a compelling choice for command-line parsing in Rust?

a) Due to its support for buffer overflows

b) Because it adheres to standard Unix CLI conventions

c) Because it is exclusively designed for Windows

d) Due to its lack of community support

Q4: What does the `--features=derive` flag indicate in the context of integrating Clap into a Rust project?

a) It enables code generation features provided by `Clap`.

b) It disables Clap's core functionality.

c) It signals compatibility with Windows.

d) It activates advanced security features.

Q5: In the context of Rust's file I/O, what does the `io::Result<()>` type represent?

a) A successful operation with a return type of `()`

b) An unsuccessful operation with an error type

c) A file descriptor

d) A boolean indicating success or failure

Q6: How can the utility described in this chapter perform a case-insensitive search and replace?

a) By using the `str::replace` function

b) By utilizing the `clap` library

c) By incorporating the `regex` crate and setting the `ignore-case` flag

d) By implementing a custom search algorithm

Q7: What does the `num_args = 1..` attribute in the `clap` definition signify for the `input` field?

a) It specifies the minimum number of arguments allowed

b) It indicates an optional argument

c) It sets an upper limit on the number of arguments

c) It requires at least one argument, with no maximum limit

Answers

1. b) clap
2. c) They enable users to convey specific instructions, data, and settings.
3. b) Because it adheres to standard Unix CLI conventions

4. a) It enables code generation features provided by `Clap`
5. b) An unsuccessful operation with an error type
6. c) By incorporating the **regex** crate and setting the **`ignore-case` flag**
7. d) It requires at least one argument, with no maximum limit

Key Terms

- **Regular Expression (Regex):** A sequence of characters that forms a search pattern, used for pattern matching within strings. In Rust, the `regex` crate provides functionality for working with regular expressions.
- **Subcommand:** A command-line command that is part of a larger command-line interface, often used to organize and categorize different functionalities within a utility.
- **File I/O:** Input and output operations involving files, such as reading from and writing to files. In Rust, the standard library provides modules and functions for performing file I/O operations.
- **Case-insensitive search:** A search operation that ignores differences in letter case, treating uppercase and lowercase characters as equivalent. This is often useful for flexible and inclusive search functionalities.
- **Error Handling:** The process of managing and responding to errors that may occur during the execution of a program. In Rust, the **`Result`** type is commonly used for error handling in functions that may return an error.
- **Command-Line Interface (CLI):** A text-based user interface that allows users to interact with a program by entering commands into a terminal or console.
- **Argument Parsing::** The process of extracting and interpreting command-line arguments provided when executing a program, allowing customization and configuration of program behavior.
- **Jaro-Winkler Distance:** A measure of similarity between two strings, often used in command-line interfaces to provide suggestions based on user input.
- **Cross-Platform Compatibility:** The ability of a software or library to run on different operating systems without modification, ensuring consistent behavior and user experience.
- **Active Maintenance:** The ongoing development, bug fixing, and improvement of a software library, indicating its responsiveness to changes in the programming ecosystem.

CHAPTER 9

Working with Devices I/O in Rust

Introduction

System programming is a domain where the digital world meets the physical world, and the ability to interact with devices and perform I/O operations lies at the heart of this convergence. In this comprehensive chapter, we will explore the complexities of working with Devices I/O in Rust. Our exploration spans the entire spectrum, from fundamental file operations to the nuanced integration of hardware devices through Rust interfaces. This chapter is a gateway to a world where lines of code translate into tangible actions, whether it's reading sensor data, controlling actuators, or managing files on a system.

At the beginning, we delve into the foundational aspects of reading from and writing to files using Rust's standard library. Files serve as digital archives of information, and knowing how to interact with them is essential for system programmers. We will explore Rust libraries and constructs that enable you to effortlessly read and write files, catering to various data formats and requirements. Equipped with this knowledge, you will be able to handle log files, configuration files, or any other form of persistent data storage your system may demand.

But our journey extends far beyond the boundaries of the file system. We will dive into the complex world of common filesystem operations. Whether it's navigating directories, creating and deleting files, or manipulating file attributes, Rust offers robust support for these tasks. Our exploration delves into practical scenarios, illustrating how to manage and manipulate files and directories effectively. As you progress, you'll realize the power and elegance of Rust's filesystem manipulation capabilities.

Furthermore, we will offer a panoramic overview of working with hardware devices through Rust interfaces. Devices represent the physical manifestations of your system's capabilities, and Rust provides a bridge between the digital and physical worlds. You'll gain insight into interfacing with various hardware devices such as sensors, actuators, or communication modules. We explore the nuances of device communication, data acquisition, and control, demonstrating how Rust empowers you to orchestrate the behavior of devices with precision and reliability.

Structure

In this chapter, we are going to explore the following topics:

- Reading from and Writing to Files in Rust
- Performing Common Filesystem Operations
- Overview of Working with Hardware Devices through Rust Interfaces

Reading from and Writing to Files

File I/O operations serve as the cornerstone of system programming, as they enable the interaction between your software and the underlying filesystem. In Rust, these operations are not only accessible but also exceptionally robust, thanks to the capabilities of the standard library. Let's kick off our journey to explore the fundamental aspects of reading from and writing to files.

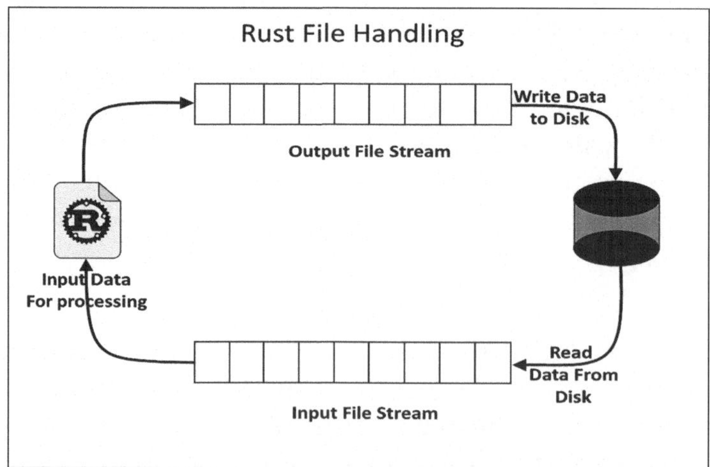

Figure 9.1: *Reading from and writing data to files*

Opening a File

Before we delve into the fascinating world of working with files in Rust, it's important to grasp the fundamental tasks that allow your programs to interact with the computer's storage system. File Input/Output (I/O) is a set of actions that involve reading and writing data to and from files. These actions are crucial for many tasks related to system programming and serve as the gateway to handling and manipulating data that persists over time.

In Rust, the language's standard library provides accessible and reliable tools for file operations. Rust was designed with a focus on safety and efficiency, which is especially crucial when it comes to tasks like file management that touch the core of your computer's operating system.

A crucial initial task in file handling is the process of file opening, which is essential before you can perform operations like reading and writing data. Within Rust, the process of opening files is facilitated through the utilization of the **`File`** structure, integrated within the **`std::fs`** module. This **`File`** structure serves as a cornerstone in this task, offering ways to initiate a connection with the file of interest and subsequently providing your program with a handle - an essential tool that enables the execution of various file-related operations.

To open a file for reading, you can use the **`File::open`** method. This method requires the file's path as an argument. The path can be either an absolute path (the full file location) or a relative path (the file's location in relation to your current working directory). It's worth mentioning that file operations can lead to errors, such as the file not existing or insufficient permissions. Rust handles errors in an elegant and robust manner. When you use the **`File::open`** method, it returns a **`Result`** type. This **`Result`** represents the possibility of an error occurring during the operation. If no error occurs, it holds the handle to the opened file. However, if an error does arise, it captures the error information, allowing your program to respond accordingly. This approach to error handling ensures that your program can gracefully deal with unexpected situations when working with files.

Listing 9.1 A simple program for opening a file.

```
use std::fs::File;
fn main() -> Result<(), std::io::Error> {
    let file = File::open("example.txt")?;
    // Now, 'file' is a handle to the opened file.
    Ok(())
}
```

```
// Output

// In case the file doesn't exist, the program will throw the following exception

// Error: Os { code: 2, kind: NotFound, message: "No such file or directory" }
```

The preceding code snippet illustrates the procedure of opening a file identified as "`example.txt`". When utilizing the `File::open` method, it returns a `Result` type, and a question mark `?` operator is employed to efficiently manage any conceivable errors. In the event that the file "`example.txt`" is effectively opened, the variable labeled as `file` will store a reference to that file, known as a file descriptor, thereby enabling you to proceed with reading data from it. This approach ensures that any potential errors in the file opening process are gracefully and efficiently handled, allowing your program to continue execution smoothly if no issues arise during this critical step.

Understanding how to open a file is just the beginning of your journey into file I/O in Rust. Once you have a handle to a file, a multitude of possibilities emerges, from reading its contents to writing new data. This chapter will guide you through these operations, equipping you with the tools to manage and manipulate files effectively in your system programming adventures.

Reading from a File

Now that we've opened the door to the file, our next step is to read and process its contents. Rust standard library offers many methods for reading from files, catering to a wide spectrum of needs. Let's dive into the fundamental approach: reading the entire file into a string.

Imagine a scenario where you're working with a configuration file, a log file, or any textual data that requires processing. The following code snippet is your compass, guiding you through the process of reading a file into a string.

In the following code snippet, we employ the `read_to_string` method to accomplish this task. This method is responsible for reading the complete content of the file and storing it within a `String` variable. Such an approach proves to be highly beneficial, especially in scenarios where you require the file's contents to be treated as text data, allowing you to manipulate and work with the information conveniently, whether it's parsing, searching, or any other text-based processing operation you intend to perform:

Listing 9.2 A simple program for reading file content.

```
use std::fs::File;
use std::io::Read;

fn main() -> Result<(), std::io::Error> {
    let mut file = File::open("example.txt")?;
    let mut contents = String::new();
    file.read_to_string(&mut contents)?;
    // 'contents' now holds the content of the file.
    Ok(())
}
```

Reading files line by line is another remarkable feat Rust empowers you with. Imagine a scenario where you're processing a large log file or a dataset structured into lines. The following code snippet, like an attentive tour guide, guides you through the file line by line. To achieve this, you can use the `BufRead` struct and the `lines` method, as demonstrated in the following code snippet:

Listing 9.3 A simple program for reading file content line by line.

```
use std::fs::File;
use std::io::{BufRead, BufReader};

fn main() -> Result<(), std::io::Error> {
    let file = File::open("example.txt")?; // Open the file.
    let reader = BufReader::new(file); // Create a buffered reader for
efficiency.

    for line in reader.lines() {
        let line = line?; // Extract each line.
        // Process each line as needed.
    }

    Ok(())
}
```

In this code, we introduce you to the `BufReader` struct, your guide in exploring the file line by line. It efficiently handles the nuances of file reading, making it an ideal choice when dealing with large text files or structured data.

Now, as you stand at the crossroads of Rust's file-reading capabilities, you possess the knowledge and tools to traverse files effortlessly. The choice between reading the entire file into a string or processing its contents line by line is yours. With these fundamental techniques, you're well-prepared to navigate the vast landscape of file manipulation in Rust.

Writing to a File

Having deciphered the art of reading from files, it's time to turn the page and explore the equally important skill of writing to files. In system programming, writing to files is not merely a way of recording data.

To perform file writing in Rust, your initial step is to open the file in write mode. This can be achieved in two ways: you can either create a new file designated for writing by utilizing the **File::create** method, or you can open an existing file with write permissions using the **File::open** method. For instance, consider the following example where we demonstrate the creation of a new file named "**new_file.txt**" and subsequently write the bytes "Hello, Rust!" into it. This operation signifies a fundamental aspect of file I/O in Rust, where you gain the ability to generate and modify files through programmatic ways, thereby enabling various data storage and manipulation capabilities.

Listing 9.4 A simple program for writing data to a file.

```
use std::fs::File;
use std::io::Write;

fn main() -> Result<(), std::io::Error> {
    let mut file = File::create("new_file.txt")?;
    file.write_all(b"Hello, Rust!")?;
    Ok(())
}
```

Within this piece of code, we utilize the **File::create** method to create a new file, and subsequently, utilize the **write_all** method to write the designated bytes into this newly created file. The **write_all** method possesses the valuable capability to guarantee that all the data is completely written into the file, taking measures to confirm this without leaving room for ambiguity, and it, in turn, returns a **Result** object as its return value, which acts as an indicator of the operation's outcome, signaling either a success or the presence of an error, hence offering a reliable way to handle the outcome of the write operation.

But what about more complex scenarios, where your system generates structured data that needs to be meticulously organized? Rust equips you with the ability to format and serialize data, enabling you to craft data files that are both human-readable and machine-friendly.

The next code snippet highlights the process of writing structured data to a file. Here, we utilize Rust's **serde** and **serde_json** libraries to serialize a structured data type into a JSON file, a common format for data exchange and configuration files:

Listing 9.5 A simple program for writing structured data to a file.

```
use serde::{Serialize, Deserialize};
use std::fs::File;
use serde_json::to_writer;

// Define a struct representing structured data.
#[derive(Serialize, Deserialize)]
struct Configuration {
    name: String,
    value: i32,
}

fn main() -> Result<(), Box<dyn std::error::Error>> {
    let config = Configuration {
        name: String::from("setting"),
        value: 42,
    };

    let file = File::create("config.json")?; // Create or open the JSON
file.
    to_writer(file, &config)?; // Serialize the data and write it to the
file.

    Ok(())
}

// Output: a new file is generated containing the following content:

// {"name":"setting","value":42}
```

In this code, the `Configuration` struct captures structured data. Rust's serialization libraries, like `serde` and `serde_json`, make the serialization process as effortless as writing a story. Your system's data transforms into JSON format, ready to be interpreted by other systems or programmers.

The art of writing to files in Rust extends far and wide, enabling you to craft not only text-based data but also structured data files that encapsulate your system's intelligence.

As we explore further into the world of Devices I/O in Rust, these foundational principles of reading from files are your companions, offering you the key to unlock the secrets hidden within files of all sizes and structures. Whether your journey leads you to analyze logs, parse configuration files, or delve into the heart of data, Rust empowers you with the tools and knowledge to navigate this path with confidence and ease.

Closing a File

Closing a file is a critical step in any file I/O operation. It ensures that system resources associated with the file are properly released, preventing resource leaks and ensuring that any changes made to the file are committed. In Rust, the process of closing files is remarkably straightforward, thanks to its ownership and scope management system. Unlike some other programming languages, Rust doesn't require explicit calls to close files. Instead, files are automatically closed when the file handle (in this case, the variable holding the file) goes out of scope. This automatic closing mechanism enhances the safety and reliability of file operations.

Here's a code snippet demonstrating this automatic closing mechanism:

Listing 9.6 A simple program that demonstrates a file lifetime.

```
use std::fs::File;
use std::io::Write;

fn main() -> Result<(), std::io::Error> {
    let mut file = File::create("new_file.txt")?;
    file.write_all(b"Hello, Rust!")?;
    // The 'file' variable goes out of scope here, and the file is auto-
matically closed.
    Ok(())
}
```

The preceding code snippet demonstrates Rust's remarkable automatic file-closing mechanism, emphasizing the language's commitment to simplicity and reliability. In this example, we create a new file, write the text "`Hello, Rust!`" to it, and, notably, without the need for any additional code, allow the file variable to naturally go out of scope. At this moment, the Rust compiler takes on the responsibility of automatically closing the `file`. This approach guarantees that, even in scenarios where the code encounters errors or exits unexpectedly, the file is handled properly, preventing potential data corruption or resource leaks. This not only reflects the core principles of Rust's design, which place a strong emphasis on safety and reliability, but also simplifies the task of managing files, making it a standout feature for developers.

Understanding this automatic file-closing behavior in Rust is fundamental to writing robust and resource-efficient file I/O code. By leveraging Rust's ownership model, you can confidently manage files without worrying about manual closing operations. This not only simplifies your code but also reduces the likelihood of bugs related to resource management.

As we conclude this section, it's worth highlighting that this chapter serves as a robust foundation for mastering file I/O operations in Rust. We've explored the entire lifecycle of file interactions, from opening and reading to writing and closing. The automatic file-closing mechanism is just one example of Rust's commitment to making system programming safe, efficient, and developer-friendly.

In the following sections of this chapter, we will continue our journey through the complex world of Devices I/O in Rust. We'll delve into common filesystem operations, enabling you to navigate directories, create and delete files, and manipulate file attributes with confidence. Additionally, we will provide an overview of interfacing with hardware devices through Rust interfaces, bridging the gap between the digital and physical worlds in your system programming tasks.

Performing Common Filesystem Operations

System programming is not limited to basic data reading and writing but extends to the mastery of efficiently managing and controlling the complex layers of the underlying file system. In this section, we will explore the complexities of performing everyday file system operations in Rust, providing you with the tools to establish a seamless connection between your code and the complex realities of the file system. You'll gain valuable insights into how to navigate, create, modify, and interact with files, equipping you with the skills necessary to work with persistent data in a reliable and efficient manner within your Rust programs.

Creating Directories

Creating directories programmatically is one of the fundamental tasks when dealing with file organization. It's a common operation, particularly in applications that need to store user-specific data or maintain structured configurations. In Rust, this task is made straightforward through the **`std::fs::create_dir`** function.

Let's break this down into simpler terms. Imagine you're working on a program, and one of its tasks is to organize user data into specific folders on your computer. Rust provides a convenient way to do this programmatically. You can use the **create_dir** function, which acts as your tool for creating these folders. All you need to do is provide the function with the path to the directory you want to create. Think of this path as the unique address for your new directory in the computer's file system. When you call the **create_dir** function, Rust takes care of all the behind-the-scenes steps required to create the directory just as you've specified.

To make this clearer, let's look at a code example. In the following code snippet, we make use of the **fs** module from Rust's standard library to create a new directory with the name "**new_directory**". What's more, we've implemented error handling to deal with any potential issues that might arise during the directory creation process. Assuming everything goes smoothly, you'll end up with a brand-new directory that's ready for you to use in your program. This means you can efficiently organize user data, and the program takes care of the heavy lifting, ensuring your task is both seamless and error-resistant.

Listing 9.7 A simple program for creating a directory.

```
use std::fs;

fn main() -> Result<(), std::io::Error> {
    fs::create_dir("new_directory")?;
    Ok(())
}
```

This capability is more than just a technical feature. It's a building block for applications to dynamically manage their workspace. Think of scenarios where your software sets up user-specific configurations, stores user-generated content, or neatly organizes files for various tasks. Rust's filesystem operations empower you to transform your program's logic into real-world actions, creating a more interactive and responsive user experience. Whether it's setting up data storage for your application or organizing files based on user preferences, understanding how to create directories is an essential skill in the world of system programming.

Renaming and Moving Files

Renaming and moving files are common operations in system programming, serving various purposes such as file versioning, data reorganization, and avoiding naming conflicts. These operations are integral to maintaining an organized and efficient file system. In Rust, performing these tasks is made straightforward with the **std::fs::rename** function.

The **std::fs::rename** function is the go-to tool for these tasks, designed to make file renaming or moving a seamless operation. It takes two essential arguments: the source path, which is the current location and name of the file, and the destination path, which is where you want the file to be after the operation. What makes this operation particularly valuable is its atomic nature, ensuring that the file is either fully renamed or not renamed at all. This atomicity guarantees the integrity of your file system, preventing the creation of incomplete or conflicting file states.

Let's delve into a practical example to better illustrate this concept. Imagine you have a file named "**old_file.txt**", and you wish to change its name to "**new_file.txt**". This task can be easily accomplished using the following concise code snippet:

Listing 9.8 A simple program for renaming a file.

```
use std::fs;

fn main() -> Result<(), std::io::Error> {
    fs::rename("old_file.txt", "new_file.txt")?;
    Ok(())
}
```

In the provided code, the **rename** function is employed to facilitate the renaming of "**old_file.txt**" to "**new_file.txt**". It's worth emphasizing that this operation isn't limited to renaming files within the same directory, it can also be used to move files between different directories, rendering it a versatile tool for managing your file system. Whether you are automating file operations, reorganizing data, or simply looking to maintain a well-structured file system, Rust's **std::fs::rename** function stands as a reliable and atomic solution for these purposes.

Renaming and moving files are fundamental tasks in system programming. Rust's **std::fs::rename** function streamlines these operations, ensuring the integrity of your file system. By understanding and using this functionality, you can efficiently manage files, directories, and data as your system demands.

Checking File Metadata

Obtaining file metadata is a fundamental operation in system programming, often serving as a starting point for various file-related tasks. When you want to gather essential information about a file, such as its size, modification time, or permissions, Rust offers an elegant solution through the **std::fs::metadata** function. This function acts as a gateway to the rich metadata associated with a file, enabling you to extract valuable insights into the file's characteristics.

In Rust, dealing with file metadata is pretty straightforward. The **metadata** function returns a **Result** that encapsulates a **Metadata** struct, which serves as a source of information about the file you're inspecting. Through this struct, you can access crucial details that enable you to make informed decisions and perform actions based on the file's attributes.

Listing 9.9 A simple program for reading a file metadata.

```
use chrono::NaiveDateTime;
use std::fs::metadata;
use std::io;
use std::os::unix::fs::PermissionsExt;
use std::time::SystemTime;

fn main() -> io::Result<()> {
    let metadata = metadata("example.txt")?;
    println!("File size: {} bytes", metadata.len());

    if let Ok(modified_time) = metadata.modified() {
        let modified_time = modified_time
            .duration_since(SystemTime::UNIX_EPOCH)
            .unwrap_or_default();

        let modified_datetime =
            NaiveDateTime::from_timestamp_opt(modified_time.as_secs() as
i64, 0).unwrap();

        println!("Last modified: {}", modified_datetime);
    } else {
        eprintln!("Unable to retrieve modified time");
    }
    let permissions = metadata.permissions().mode();
    println!("Permissions: {:o}", permissions & 0o777);

    Ok(())
}

// Output: example output:

// File size: 29 bytes
// Last modified: 2023-11-01 16:42:39
// Permissions: 664
```

Let's break down the aforementioned code example. We first utilize the **metadata** function to acquire the metadata of the file named "**example.txt**". The code gracefully handles potential errors, ensuring robust error handling. Once we have the metadata, we gain access to specific attributes such as the file size, last modification time, and permissions.

The **metadata.len()** call provides the file's size in bytes, a fundamental metric that helps you manage storage and assess the space requirements of your system. Knowing a file's size is crucial for tasks such as monitoring disk usage, ensuring sufficient storage capacity, and optimizing data storage strategies.

The **metadata.modified()** function reveals the last time the file was modified. This timestamp is invaluable for tracking changes to files and auditing file activities. It plays a pivotal role in version control systems and file synchronization processes, helping maintain data integrity and traceability. We have used the **chrono** crate to format the last modified time without calculating the time since the Unix epoch. The **modified_time** is converted to a **NaiveDateTime**, which is then printed in a human-readable format.

The **metadata.permissions().mode()** function exposes the file's permissions, which are a cornerstone of file security and access control. With this information, you can determine who can read, write, or execute the file. Such insights are central to ensuring that only authorized entities can interact with a file, safeguarding sensitive information and system integrity.

Checking file metadata in Rust is a straightforward yet powerful operation. It empowers you with the tools to understand and manipulate files at a granular level. Whether you're building a file management tool, conducting file system analysis, or simply ensuring the security and integrity of your data, the ability to access file metadata is a key element in your toolkit.

Deleting Files and Directories

File and directory deletion, while seemingly straightforward, plays a pivotal role in system programming by facilitating the management of storage space and the efficient cleanup of resources. In Rust, this simple operation is executed seamlessly, ensuring data integrity and resource management. Let's dive into the complexities of file and directory deletion and explore how Rust's **std::fs** module simplifies these operations.

File removal is simplified in Rust through the **std::fs::remove_file** function. This function gracefully removes the specified file, allowing you to regain storage space or eliminate redundant data. The following code snippet showcases the usage of this function. When executed, it removes a file named "**file_to_delete.txt**". The power lies in Rust's ability to handle potential errors seamlessly by returning a **Result**. This design ensures that the operation is either executed successfully or, in the case of an error, provides a meaningful error message.

Listing 9.10 A simple program for removing a file.

```
use std::fs;

fn main() -> Result<(), std::io::Error> {
    fs::remove_file("file_to_delete.txt")?;
    fs::remove_dir("directory_to_delete")?;
    Ok(())
}
```

Directory removal is equally significant, particularly when dealing with larger-scale applications where directories accumulate and need to be managed efficiently. Rust caters to this need with the **std::fs::remove_dir** function. In the previous example, you can observe the process of removing a directory named "**directory_to_delete**". Like its file counterpart, this function ensures data integrity by allowing the removal of directories while considering potential error scenarios. The simplicity and robustness of Rust's approach to directory removal make it a valuable asset in system programming.

Efficiently managing resources, which involves tasks like removing files and folders, is a crucial skill for anyone working with computer systems. It's not just about tidying up your computer, but also about making sure it runs as smoothly as possible and uses its resources wisely. In Rust, these tasks are handled with great care and safety, showcasing Rust's dedication to making sure system programming is both secure and efficient.

Moreover, the ability to delete files and directories extends beyond cleanup tasks. It plays a critical role in handling data lifecycle, enabling systems to organize and manage information systematically. Rust's clear and efficient approach to these operations empowers you to create robust and reliable solutions for a wide range of real-world scenarios.

Traversing Directories

When working with files, there often comes a need to navigate directories, seeking specific files, inspecting their attributes, or organizing them into logical structures. Rust equips you with powerful tools to effortlessly traverse directories, allowing you to explore, analyze, and manipulate the contents of a file system.

Let's start by delving into the idea of listing all the things you have in a particular folder on your computer. Imagine that a folder is like a box, and everything inside it–files and other smaller folders–are what we call entries. Now, in the world of computer programming, Rust is a language that makes this process quite easy with something called the **read_dir** function. It's like a tool that helps you look inside the box and see what's in there. When you use **read_dir**, it doesn't just give you a big list all at once; instead, it hands you one thing at a time, kind of like showing you one item in the box, then the next one, and so on. Each item you see is called a **DirEntry**, and it comes with some extra information about itself, such as its name and other details. Rust is also really good at dealing with problems that can happen when you're looking inside the box, so you can use it with confidence, knowing that it won't crash your program if something goes wrong.

Listing 9.11 A simple program for traversing a directory.

```
use std::fs;
use std::os::unix::fs::FileTypeExt;
use std::path::Path;

fn main() -> Result<(), std::io::Error> {
    let dir = fs::read_dir("path_to_directory")?;

    for entry in dir {
        let entry = entry?;
        let path = entry.path();
        println!("Entry name: {:?}", path.file_name().unwrap_or_de-
fault());

        let file_type = entry.file_type()?;
        let file_type_str = if file_type.is_file() {
            "File"
        } else if file_type.is_dir() {
            "Directory"
        } else if file_type.is_symlink() {
            "Symbolic Link"
        } else if file_type.is_char_device() {
            "Character Device"
        } else if file_type.is_block_device() {
            "Block Device"
        } else if file_type.is_fifo() {
            "FIFO (Named Pipe)"
```

```
        } else if file_type.is_socket() {
            "Socket"
        } else {
            "Unknown"
        };

        println!("Entry type: {}", file_type_str);
    }

    Ok(())
}

// Output: example output:

// Entry name: "config.json"
// Entry type: File
// Entry name: "new_file.txt"
// Entry type: File
```

The preceding code example serves as a practical illustration of directory traversal in action. We define a directory path, invoke the **read_dir** function, and traverse the resulting iterator. For each entry, we access its path and seek its type. This foundational knowledge of directory traversal is the cornerstone for an array of tasks, including indexing files for searching, batch processing, or conducting recursive directory operations.

Directory traversal is a fundamental and versatile skill for system programmers and developers. Whether you're building a file indexing tool, a backup utility, or a content management system, understanding how to navigate directories effectively can significantly enhance your system-level programming capabilities. With Rust as your guide, you'll be equipped to navigate the digital landscape with precision and ease.

Working with File Paths

Dealing with file paths is a crucial part of how Rust manages files. Rust provides a handy set of tools through its **std::path** module to handle file paths in a way that works consistently across different computer systems. This is important because the way file paths are written can vary between operating systems.

One of the most basic things you do with file paths is putting different parts of a path together. Sometimes, you have to combine multiple pieces of a path to create a complete and valid path. This is where the **PathBuf** type, which you can find in the **std::path** module, becomes your best friend. You can make a

PathBuf, and then use its "**join**" function to easily stick path pieces together. The beauty of this is that it takes care of the tricky stuff specific to each operating system. So, whether you're on a Unix-like system (like Linux) or Windows, it uses the right kind of slash or backslash to separate the parts of the path. It keeps things smooth and hassle-free for you!

In the following example, we start with a base path represented by **PathBuf::from("/usr/local")** and then use the **join** method to append "**bin**" to it. This operation results in a new path, and the crucial aspect here is that you don't need to be concerned about the specific platform's path separator. Rust takes care of it for you, making your code more portable across different operating systems.

Listing 9.12 A simple program for working with file paths.

```
use std::path::PathBuf;

fn main() {
    let base_path = PathBuf::from("/usr/local");
    let new_path = base_path.join("bin");

    println!("New path: {:?}", new_path);
}

// Output

// New path: "/usr/local/bin"
```

Furthermore, another thing we often need to do is find out the parent folder that holds a specific file's location. This is handy when you want to move up a level in the file system. There's a special method called **parent** that you can use with the **Path** type to do this effortlessly. It gives you an answer in the form of an **Option** because not all paths have a parent; think about the highest level, like the root directory, where there's nowhere higher to go. Let's break it down in this example: we create a **Path** object representing the path "**/usr/local/bin**" and then use the **parent** method to obtain the parent directory, which is "**/usr/local**".

Another common operation is extracting the parent directory from a path using the **parent** method:

Listing 9.13 A simple program for extracting the parent directory from a path.

```
use std::path::Path;

fn main() {
    let path = Path::new("/usr/local/bin");
    if let Some(parent) = path.parent() {
        println!("Parent directory: {:?}", parent);
    }
}

// Output

// Parent directory: "/usr/local"
```

In this code snippet, we create a path and use the **parent** method to access the parent directory. Handling file paths correctly is crucial for tasks such as relative file references, resolving symbolic links, and ensuring cross-platform compatibility.

It's really important to grasp the ins and outs of file paths, the addresses that tell your program where to find or save files. This knowledge is a key ingredient for various tasks related to files, such as handling references to files in relation to other files, deciphering symbolic links (special types of shortcuts), and making sure your code runs smoothly on different operating systems, such as Windows, macOS, and Linux. You don't want your program to break just because it's on a different computer, right? Luckily, Rust provides some handy tools for this in the **std::path** module, which lets you write code that works well and stays easy to manage on any platform.

Reading and Writing Binary Data

When it comes to working with binary data, this is a key part of system programming, especially when you're dealing with files such as images, audio files, or configuration data. These files are not meant for human reading; instead, they consist of raw bytes. Rust has a strong foundation for handling binary input and output (I/O) operations through the **std::fs** module. In simple terms, "**binary data**" here means information made up of raw bytes, not something you can easily read like text.

When it comes to reading binary data from a file in Rust, you can utilize the **File::open** method, which is quite similar to how you would open text files. However, there is a crucial difference, binary data is read into a byte buffer, which is essentially an expandable container for bytes. This buffer is useful in holding the binary data obtained from the file. Here's an example of how this process is executed in Rust:

Listing 9.14 A simple program for reading binary data from a file.

```
use std::fs::File;
use std::io::Read;

fn main() -> Result<(), std::io::Error> {
    let mut file = File::open("binary_file.bin")?;  // Open the binary 
file.
    let mut buffer = Vec::new();  // Create an empty byte vector.

    file.read_to_end(&mut buffer)?;  // Read the binary data into the buf-
fer.

    // 'buffer' now contains the binary data from the file.

    Ok(())
}
```

In this provided code snippet, we are dealing with a specific kind of computer file known as a "**binary file**". So, the first thing we do in this code is open one of these binary files, named "**binary_file.bin**". Following that, we create something called a "**buffer**". Think of this "**buffer**" as a container or a box, but it's special because it can hold numbers–specifically, numbers that are 8 bits in size. These 8-bit numbers are also called "bytes". Therefore, we are setting up this "buffer" to store bytes.

Next, let's discuss the "`read_to_end`" method. Its operation is quite straightforward. Essentially, it is responsible for collecting all the bytes contained within the binary file and storing them in our "**buffer**" container. Consequently, after executing this code snippet, our "**buffer**" becomes a container for all the data originally present in the binary file. This, in turn, empowers us to employ the "buffer" for a multitude of purposes when working with the binary data, such as processing, analyzing, or manipulating it, given that the data is now conveniently organized within this container.

Now, on the other side of things, when we want to put data into a binary file, Rust makes it relatively straightforward. It's somewhat similar to writing text in a regular text file, except here, we are dealing with raw binary data. To achieve this, we can use a method called "**File::create**". This method is like creating a new blank file, but specifically for binary data. It prepares a new blank book where we can write down our digital information. The example provided in the code demonstrates how you can take your own binary data and write it into a file, much like writing text into a regular text file. This two-way process, reading and writing binary data, is fundamental in programming and allows us to work with various types of digital information effectively.

Listing 9.15 A simple program for writing binary data to a file.

```
use std::fs::File;
use std::io::Write;

fn main() -> Result<(), std::io::Error> {
    let mut file = File::create("binary_output.bin")?;  // Create a
binary output file.
    let data = vec![0x48, 0x65, 0x6C, 0x6C, 0x6F]; // Binary data in the
form of a byte vector.
    file.write_all(&data)?;  // Write the binary data to the file.

    // The binary data has been successfully written to the file.

    Ok(())
}
```

In this code, a binary output file "`binary_output.bin`" is created using the `File::create` method. The binary data, in this case, is represented as a vector of bytes, where each byte is specified in hexadecimal format (for example, 0x48 corresponds to 'H').

Next, we utilize the `write_all` method to transfer this list of bytes into the file. Consequently, the file now stores our binary data in its pure byte form, mirroring how it's stored in the computer's memory.

This is where Rust proves valuable. Rust excels at ensuring the accuracy and safety of the data we place into our binary file, minimizing the risk of memory-related problems. Consequently, Rust is a reliable choice for tasks involving binary data manipulation.

Error Handling and Result Types

Throughout our exploration of file I/O in Rust, you may have noticed the frequent use of `Result` types to handle potential errors. Rust's strong focus on safety and reliability is reflected in its error-handling mechanisms. This emphasis on error handling ensures that your Rust programs are less prone to unexpected issues and that you have full control over how errors are managed.

Rust accomplishes this by promoting the use of the **Result** type for error handling. A **Result** is an enum with two variants: **Ok**, which holds the result of a successful operation, and **Err**, which holds information about an error. By using **Result**, Rust enforces that errors are explicitly acknowledged and dealt with in code. This strong emphasis on handling errors explicitly makes it less likely for errors to go unnoticed or unhandled.

Let's revisit the concept of **Result** and error handling in the context of file I/O, illustrated with a code example:

Listing 9.16 A simple program that demonstrates error handling and the Result type.

```
use std::fs::File;
use std::io::{Read, Write};

fn read_and_write_files() -> Result<(), std::io::Error> {
    // Attempt to open a file for reading.
    let mut read_file = File::open("input.txt")?;

    // Attempt to create a file for writing.
    let mut write_file = File::create("output.txt")?;

    // Define a buffer to hold data.
    let mut buffer = Vec::new();

    // Read data from the input file.
    read_file.read_to_end(&mut buffer)?;

    // Write data to the output file.
    write_file.write_all(&buffer)?;

    Ok(())
}

fn main() {
    match read_and_write_files() {
        Ok(_) => println!("File operations completed successfully."),
        Err(e) => eprintln!("Error: {}", e),
    }
}
```

```
// Output

// File operations completed successfully.
```

In this example, the **read_and_write_files** function is responsible for performing file I/O operations and returns a **Result**. The **main** function uses a **match** statement to handle the **Result**, determining whether the operations were successful or if an error occurred.

Rust's error-handling philosophy encourages us to address potential errors explicitly and gracefully. This approach results in more robust code and helps catch issues early in development. By explicitly handling errors using **Result**, we can ensure that their programs are more reliable, safer, and more predictable, which are all essential qualities in modern software development.

Working with Hardware Devices

When it comes to system programming, you may find yourself in need of interacting directly with hardware devices. Rust offers a robust way to interface with hardware through device drivers, libraries, and the creation of custom device drivers. These interactions with hardware are often essential for tasks such as device control, sensor data acquisition, and real-time processing, which span a wide range of applications.

Device drivers serve as a pivotal link between software and hardware layers, facilitating communication and coordination between the two. They act as intermediaries that enable you to control hardware peripherals, access sensors, and perform other crucial tasks, ultimately bridging the gap between high-level software and low-level hardware operations.

When working with hardware devices in Rust, it's crucial to address the issues of permissions and security. Accessing hardware directly can introduce security risks if not managed correctly. Here, Rust's safety guarantees play a pivotal role in reducing these risks. The language's memory safety and thread safety features help prevent common programming errors that could lead to security vulnerabilities, thus making Rust a reliable choice for applications requiring direct hardware interaction while maintaining security standards.

Rust's capabilities extend to low-level programming, an often-necessary component of working with hardware devices. Its feature-rich toolbox empowers us to manipulate memory, work with pointers, and efficiently manage resources while maintaining control over hardware components.

Listing 9.17 Working with hardware devices example.

```
use rppal::gpio::Gpio;
use std::error::Error;

fn main() -> Result<(), Box<dyn Error>> {
    let gpio = Gpio::new()?;
    let pin = gpio.get(17)?;

    let mut pin = pin.into_output();

    // Handle any errors that may occur during pin operations
    if pin.set_high() != () {
        eprintln!("Error setting pin high");
    }

    // Do some work here, interacting with the GPIO pin

    if pin.set_low() != () {
        eprintln!("Error setting pin low");
    }

    // The pin is automatically released when it goes out of scope
    Ok(())
}
```

One common hardware interaction scenario involves the control of GPIO (General-Purpose Input/Output) pins. These pins serve various purposes, such as turning LEDs on and off or reading button states. In the provided Rust code sample, we employ the "rppal" crate to illustrate how Rust can be utilized to control a GPIO pin on a Raspberry Pi, exemplifying the language's capabilities in straightforward hardware control.

It's essential to recognize that when working with hardware devices, it often necessitates writing platform-specific or architecture-specific code. Different hardware platforms and architectures come with unique requirements and interfaces. Rust acknowledges this and provides tools for cross-compilation, enabling you to craft code that can run on diverse systems and architectures without substantial modifications, thereby promoting code reusability and portability.

Listing 9.18 Working with hardware devices example.

```
use i2cdev::linux::LinuxI2CDevice;
use i2cdev::core::I2CDevice;
use std::error::Error;
```

```
fn main() -> Result<(), Box<dyn Error>> {
    let mut bus = LinuxI2CDevice::new("/dev/i2c-1", 0x68)?;

    let mut buffer: [u8; 2] = [0; 2];
    bus.write(&[0x1])?; // Command to read from the sensor
    bus.read(&mut buffer)?;

    let sensor_value = (u16::from(buffer[0]) << 8) | u16::from(buffer[1]);
    println!("Sensor value: {}", sensor_value);

    Ok(())
}
```

Another typical scenario in hardware programming is communication with sensors via protocols like I2C. In this code sample, we use the "`i2cdev`" crate to interface with an I2C sensor. By writing a command to the sensor and reading its data, this code demonstrates how Rust can be applied for sensor data acquisition via I2C, showcasing its versatility in hardware-device interactions.

Working with hardware devices in Rust uncovers a world of possibilities for system-level programming. Whether you are building an embedded system, working on IoT applications, or engaging with low-level hardware control, Rust's combination of safety, performance, and reliability positions it as a compelling choice for interacting with devices. The provided code samples serve as tangible examples of how Rust can be effectively employed to control GPIO pins and communicate with sensors, highlighting the language's capabilities in hardware-device interactions.

Advanced File Operations

Advanced File Operations in Rust opens up new possibilities for system programmers and developers who need precise control over files and data. In this section, we will delve into two key concepts: symbolic links and hard links. These mechanisms allow you to reference files in non-standard ways, providing flexibility and efficient data management.

Symbolic Links and Hard Links

Symbolic links, often referred to as symlinks, are essentially references to other files. Instead of directly accessing the content of the linked file, symlinks act as pointers or shortcuts, directing you to the actual file's location.

Figure 9.2: *xkcd.com/981*

Rust's standard library provides a convenient way to work with symlinks using the **std::os::unix::fs::symlink** method on Unix-like systems. This method enables you to create symbolic links easily.

Here's an example demonstrating the creation of a symbolic link in Rust:

Listing 9.19 A simple program for creating a symbolic link.

```
use std::os::unix::fs;

fn main() -> Result<(), std::io::Error> {
    fs::symlink("target_file.txt", "symlink_to_target.txt")?;
    Ok(())
}
```

In this code snippet, a symbolic link named "**symlink_to_target.txt**" is established, pointing to the "**target_file.txt**".

On the other hand, hard links provide a different form of referencing. They point to the same underlying data on the storage device as the original file. Creating a hard link in Rust is straightforward using the **std::fs::hard_link** method.

Here's a Rust example for creating a hard link:

Listing 9.20 A simple program for creating a hard link.

```
use std::fs;

fn main() -> Result<(), std::io::Error> {
    fs::hard_link("source_file.txt", "hard_link_to_source.txt")?;
    Ok(())
}
```

In this code, a hard link is created from "**hard_link_to_source.txt**" to "**source_file.txt**." This means both files now reference the same data blocks on the storage device.

It's crucial to understand the difference between symbolic links and hard links. When you modify the content of a file that is symlinked, the changes are reflected in the linked file. In contrast, hard links do not create separate copies but share data, so any changes made to one file are instantly visible in the other. Understanding these differences is essential when considering how changes to linked files propagate and how file operations are managed in your Rust applications.

Locking Files

File locking is a crucial mechanism used to ensure data consistency and integrity by preventing multiple processes or threads from simultaneously accessing and modifying a file. In the Rust programming language, this functionality can be achieved through the use of the **std::fs::File::try_lock_exclusive** and **std::fs::File::try_lock_shared** methods, which provide exclusive and shared locking capabilities, respectively.

Exclusive locking, as demonstrated in the following code snippet, guarantees that only a single process or thread can acquire and maintain the lock, effectively safeguarding the file against concurrent modifications:

Listing 9.21 A simple program for locking files.

```
use fs2::FileExt;
use std::fs::File;
use std::io;

fn main() -> Result<(), io::Error> {
    let file = File::create("locked_file.txt")?;
```

```
    // Attempt to acquire an exclusive lock on the file.
    if let Ok(mut _lock) = file.try_lock_exclusive() {
        println!("Acquired exclusive lock.");
        // Perform exclusive operations.

        // Lock is automatically released when 'lock' goes out of scope.
    } else {
        println!("Failed to acquire exclusive lock.");
    }

    Ok(())
}


// Output

// Acquired exclusive lock.
```

In this code, we begin by creating a file and subsequently make an attempt to acquire an exclusive lock on it. If the lock is successfully obtained, we gain the ability to execute exclusive operations within the critical section. The significant advantage of using Rust's file locking is that the lock is automatically released when the `lock` variable goes out of scope, simplifying resource management and reducing the risk of accidental deadlocks.

Shared locking can be implemented similarly by using the `try_lock_exclusive` method provided by the `FileExt` extension trait from the `fs2` crate, enabling multiple processes or threads to concurrently access the file for read-only purposes, as demonstrated in the following snippet of code. This means that shared locking is suitable for scenarios where data can be simultaneously read by multiple processes without concerns about data integrity.

Listing 9.22 Shared read-only access by multiple threads.

```
use fs2::FileExt;
use std::fs::{self, File};
use std::io;
use std::io::prelude::*;
use std::sync::Arc;
use std::thread;

fn main() -> Result<(), io::Error> {
    // Create or overwrite the file with some content.
    let content = "\nline 0\nline 1\nline 2\n";
    fs::write("shared_file.txt", content)?;
```

```
    // Read the file content outside the locked section.
    let file = File::open("shared_file.txt")?;
    let mut buffer = String::new();
    if let Ok(reader) = io::BufReader::new(file.try_clone()?).read_to_
string(&mut buffer) {
        println!("Read {} bytes: {}", reader, &buffer);
    } else {
        println!("Failed to read the file.");
    }

    // Wrap the buffer in an Arc to share ownership.
    let buffer = Arc::new(buffer);

    // Spawn multiple threads to access the shared content.
    let num_threads = 5;
    let mut handles = vec![];

    for _ in 0..num_threads {
        let file_clone = file.try_clone();
        let buffer_clone = Arc::clone(&buffer); // Use Arc to share ownership

        let handle = thread::spawn(move || {
            if let Ok(mut _lock) = file_clone.unwrap().try_lock_shared()
{
                println!(
                    "Thread {:?} acquired shared lock for read-only
access.",
                    thread::current().id()
                );

                // Perform read-only operations on the shared content.
                println!(
                    "Thread {:?} is processing the shared content: {}",
                    thread::current().id(),
                    &buffer_clone // Use the shared Arc
                );
            } else {
                println!(
                    "Thread {:?} failed to acquire shared lock.",
                    thread::current().id()
                );
            }
        });

        handles.push(handle);
    }
```

```
    for handle in handles {
        handle.join().unwrap();
    }

    Ok(())
}


// Output

// Read 22 bytes:
// line 0
// line 1
// line 2

// Thread ThreadId(2) acquired shared lock for read-only access.
// Thread ThreadId(2) is processing the shared content:
// line 0
// line 1
// line 2

// Thread ThreadId(4) acquired shared lock for read-only access.
// Thread ThreadId(4) is processing the shared content:
// line 0
// line 1
// line 2

// Thread ThreadId(3) acquired shared lock for read-only access.
// Thread ThreadId(3) is processing the shared content:
// line 0
// line 1
// line 2

// Thread ThreadId(5) acquired shared lock for read-only access.
// Thread ThreadId(5) is processing the shared content:
// line 0
// line 1
// line 2

// Thread ThreadId(6) acquired shared lock for read-only access.
// Thread ThreadId(6) is processing the shared content:
// line 0
// line 1
// line 2
```

In this example:

1. We create a file named "`shared_file.txt`".
2. We spawn multiple threads (specified by `num_threads`) to read from the file concurrently.
3. Each thread attempts to acquire a shared lock on the file using `try_lock_shared()`. If the lock is acquired, it prints a message indicating that it has acquired a shared lock and can perform read-only operations.
4. After acquiring a shared lock on the file, each thread reads the contents of the file in a read-only operation. The `io::BufReader::new(file_clone).read_to_string(&mut buffer)` operation reads the contents of the file into a buffer, and the thread prints the number of bytes read and the content of the file. If there is an error during the reading process, it prints an error message.
5. We wrap the `buffer` in an `Arc` using `Arc::new(buffer)` to share ownership among the threads.
6. Instead of cloning the `buffer`, we use `Arc::clone(&buffer)` to create references to the shared Arc.
7. The shared `Arc` is then used in the threads for processing the shared content. This ensures that the buffer is shared efficiently among the threads without unnecessary cloning, allowing multiple threads to access it for read-only purposes.
8. We use `thread::spawn` to spawn threads, and we keep track of the thread handles.
9. After spawning all threads, we wait for them to finish using `join`.

With this setup, each thread will read and process the content from "`shared_file.txt`", demonstrating the shared read-only access by multiple threads.

The importance of file locking becomes particularly evident in scenarios where data consistency and integrity are very important. For example, when managing configuration files or coordinating access to shared resources, file locking ensures that critical operations occur in a controlled, orderly fashion. This safeguard is vital for preventing data corruption or unintended race conditions that might compromise the reliability of your software applications.

Memory-Mapped Files

Memory-mapped files provide an innovative approach to working with files in the world of software development. These files are essentially a bridge between your application and the physical storage medium, allowing you to map a file directly into memory. Rust's **memmap** crate offers a valuable tool for us to utilize this capability efficiently.

When it comes to handling large files or optimizing performance, memory-mapped files become a game-changer. They essentially let you treat a file as if it were an array residing in your computer's memory, which means you can access and manipulate the file's contents with ease and speed. This is in stark contrast to traditional I/O operations, which involve reading or writing data to and from the disk in a more linear and sequential manner.

Now, let's delve into a practical example that demonstrates how to utilize the **memmap** crate. In the following code snippet, we showcase how to memory-map a file and read its contents efficiently:

Listing 9.23 Memory-mapped files using memmap.

```
use std::fs::File;
use std::io;
use std::io::prelude::*;
use memmap::Mmap;

fn main() -> Result<(), io::Error> {
    let file = File::open("large_file.bin")?;
    let mmap = unsafe { Mmap::map(&file)? };

    // Access the memory-mapped data as a slice.
    let data = &mmap;

    // Perform read operations on 'data'.
    let max_bytes_to_print = 100; // Adjust this value as needed.
    for i in 0..max_bytes_to_print {
        // Convert the byte to an ASCII code character and print it.
        print!("{} ", data[i] as char);
    }

    Ok(())
}
```

Here, we initiate the process by opening the file of interest using **File::open**. Then, we utilize the **Mmap::map** function to create a memory-mapped view of the file. Once the memory-mapped view is established, you can access its contents through a slice. This enables you to perform read operations directly on the data as if it were a regular in-memory array.

Memory-mapped files offer notable advantages when handling large datasets, performing binary file parsing, or designing customized data storage solutions. Their real potential lies in optimizing performance by eliminating the traditional I/O bottlenecks. Instead, they allow you to utilize the capabilities of memory-mapped files to establish a more efficient and responsive data management system within your Rust applications. This enhanced data access method can lead to accelerated data processing and, consequently, a substantial improvement in overall application performance, especially in resource-intensive scenarios.

File I/O Best Practices

Efficient and reliable file I/O operations in Rust are essential for any robust software application. To help you achieve this, here are some key best practices to consider when working with files in Rust:

- **Error Handling: Use Rust's `Result`** type for error handling. Handle errors explicitly to ensure robust and reliable code. Here's an example of how to handle errors:

Listing 9.24 Files error handling.

```
use std::fs::File;

fn main() -> Result<(), std::io::Error> {
    let file = File::open("example.txt");

    match file {
        Ok(_) => {
            // File opened successfully, proceed with operations.
        }
        Err(err) => {
            // Handle the error, e.g., print an error message.
            println!("Error: {}", err);
            return Err(err);
        }
    }

    Ok(())
}
```

In this code, we open a file and explicitly handle any potential errors that may occur during the file opening process:

- **Resource Management:** Leverage Rust's ownership and scope management to handle resource cleanup. When a file handle goes out of scope, it will automatically be closed, preventing resource leaks. This automatic resource management is a core Rust feature, as demonstrated in previous code snippets.
- **Cross-Platform Compatibility:** Keep in mind the differences in file systems between various platforms. Use Rust's path manipulation tools to ensure cross-platform compatibility. Rust's `std::path` module provides functions to work with paths in a platform-independent way, ensuring that your code remains portable. Here is an example of code for joining paths in a platform-independent way:

Listing 9.25 Working with paths in a platform-independent way.

```
use std::path::Path;

fn main() {
    let base_path = Path::new("path/to/folder");
    let file_name = "example.txt";
    let full_path = base_path.join(file_name);
}
```

This code constructs a path that works seamlessly on different platforms.

1. **Permissions and Security**: Always be aware of file permissions and security considerations. Ensure that your program has the necessary permissions to access, modify, or create files. Rust provides mechanisms to set and check file permissions, allowing you to work securely with files. Here's how you can change file permissions:

Listing 9.26 Working with file permissions.

```
use std::os::unix::fs::PermissionsExt;
use std::fs::File;

fn main() -> std::io::Result<()> {
    let file = File::create("example.txt")?;

    let mut permissions = file.metadata()?.permissions();
    permissions.set_mode(0o755); // Set file permissions to read, write,
and execute for the owner, and read and execute for others.
    file.set_permissions(permissions)?;
```

```
    Ok(())
}

// $ ls -lah example.txt
// -rwxr-xr-x 1 mahmoud mahmoud 0 Nov  1 21:24 example.txt
```

In this code, we create a file and set its permissions to read, write, and execute for the owner, and read and execute for others.

1. **Backup and Version Control**: Implement backup and version control mechanisms for important files. Consider using file locking and versioning systems when working with critical data. For instance, you can implement a simple backup mechanism like this:

Listing 9.27 A simple backup program.

```
use std::fs::{File, copy};

fn backup_file(source: &str, destination: &str) -> std::io::Result<()> {
    copy(source, destination)?;
    Ok(())
}
```

This function copies a file from the source path to the destination path, effectively creating a backup.

1. **Performance Optimization**: When working with large files or performance-critical tasks, explore memory-mapped files or buffered I/O to maximize efficiency. As demonstrated earlier, memory-mapped files can significantly boost I/O performance by allowing direct access to file data in memory, and buffered I/O can be employed to reduce the number of I/O operations.

2. **Documentation:** Maintain clear and comprehensive documentation for your code, especially when dealing with complex file operations. Clear documentation helps not only you but also other developers who may work on the code in the future. Rust supports documentation comments (doc comments) to help you create informative documentation for your code. Rust supports documentation comments (doc comments) using `///` or `//!`. You can use these comments to provide comprehensive documentation for your code.

3. **Testing:** Rigorously test your file I/O code under various scenarios, including error conditions and boundary cases, to ensure robust behavior. Rust's testing framework provides a straightforward way to write and

run tests for your code. You can use the **#[test]** attribute to write tests for your code. Following is a simple test for a function:

Listing 9.28 A simple program with unit testing.

```
fn add(a: i32, b: i32) -> i32 {
    a + b
}

#[test]
fn test_add() {
    assert_eq!(add(2, 3), 5);
    assert_eq!(add(-1, 1), 0);
}
```

This test checks if the **add** function behaves as expected for different input values.

These code samples cover various best practices for file I/O in Rust, helping you implement each guideline effectively in your projects.

By following these best practices, you'll be well-prepared to handle complex file operations and maintain the integrity of your data. Whether you're dealing with basic file I/O or advanced operations, these guidelines will help you write clean, secure, and high-performance file-handling code in Rust.

Device Drivers and Kernel Modules

Device drivers and kernel modules are like middlemen in the world of computer programming. They have an important job: helping the computer's software talk to its hardware. Think of your computer as a big puzzle with lots of pieces. Device drivers are the glue that holds these pieces together. They make sure your keyboard, mouse, screen, and other parts all work smoothly with the computer's brain, which is the operating system.

Rust emerges as a compelling choice for writing device drivers. These software components must exhibit a high degree of reliability and safety because they directly interface with hardware. Writing device drivers in Rust, you will often find yourself working in a **no_std** environment. In resource-constrained settings where memory and performance are critical, using the full standard library (std) may not be practical, hence the preference for **no_std**.

Now, let's explore the complex world of device driver development in Rust. In such projects, you will find yourself working closely with the hardware, gaining direct access to registers, memory-mapped I/O, and handling hardware interrupts. This level of interaction offers precise control over hardware devices, which is a fundamental requirement in system programming.

```
#![no_std]

extern crate some_platform_crate;

// Your device driver code here
```

A key aspect of device driver development in Rust is the utilization of platform-specific libraries and crates. Moreover, writing platform-specific code may be necessary to establish a seamless interface with the hardware. Cross-compilation is a common practice in this domain, enabling you to compile drivers for different architectures and platforms, an essential skill for a device driver developer.

Working with the Linux kernel is a common scenario in the world of device driver development. Rust has gained substantial support for kernel development, with an increasing number of Rust-based kernel modules and drivers emerging for a wide array of hardware components. This trend underscores the growing potential of Rust in the context of low-level system programming.

```
// Sample kernel module written in Rust
mod my_kernel_module {
    // Your code here
}
```

It's important to recognize that device driver development is a highly specialized field that demands an in-depth understanding of both the hardware and the complexities of the specific operating system. While Rust's safety features can mitigate certain types of bugs and vulnerabilities, low-level development requires a profound knowledge of the hardware's architecture and the precise requirements of the operating system in use.

Device driver development in Rust is a dynamic and evolving field, and the Rust community actively explores best practices and techniques for building safe and efficient device drivers. Engaging in this domain, you'll encounter valuable resources, forums, and open-source projects that serve as guides and references, helping you navigate the complex world of system programming and device driver development in Rust.

Network Programming and Device I/O

In system programming, the ability to communicate over networks is often integral to interacting with devices. Whether you're building a remote control system, a sensor network, or a distributed data acquisition system, network programming can enhance your device's I/O capabilities.

Network communication can serve as a bridge between devices, enabling remote management, data sharing, and real-time control. In Rust, network programming is made robust and efficient through various libraries and frameworks, making it an excellent companion to device I/O.

Sockets and Protocols

Network programming is the secret ingredient that makes devices and systems talk to each other seamlessly. It's like the conductor of an orchestra, ensuring that all the different instruments (devices) play in coordination. Whether you want to send photos, messages, or control remote devices, network programming serves as the bridge that allows these operations to happen. Rust is a great choice for this task. Rust acts like a superhero with a special toolkit for creating these connections between devices. It's incredibly reliable, ensuring that things work smoothly and securely, which is essential when dealing with devices and networks.

At the core of network programming and device communication are "**sockets**". Think of sockets as the plugs and outlets you use to connect your devices to the power source. In the programming world, sockets are the connectors that enable devices to exchange data. Rust simplifies the process of dealing with sockets. It provides a consistent way to create and manage these connections. This means that whether you're connecting devices in the same room or devices scattered across the internet, Rust ensures that the communication process remains consistent and reliable. So, Rust serves as a trusted guide to make sure everything functions together harmoniously, no matter how near or far apart the devices are.

Sockets are closely associated with specific network protocols, and Rust provides support for various socket types, including TCP, UDP, and Unix domain sockets. Choosing the appropriate socket type and protocol allows you to seamlessly integrate network communication into your device I/O operations. For instance, if you have a network-connected sensor device, you can use Rust's TCP socket support to establish a connection to the sensor, retrieve real-time data, and integrate that data into your device's I/O processes.

The flexibility of Rust's socket implementation allows you to create communication channels that bridge the gap between devices, regardless of their physical locations. This can be invaluable in scenarios where you need to gather data from remote sensors or control devices situated in different locations.

To illustrate this concept, we have a Rust code snippet that showcases a TCP server for a remote sensor device:

Listing 9.29 A simple TCP server.

```
use std::net::TcpListener;
use std::io::{Read, Write};

fn main() -> Result<(), Box<dyn std::error::Error>> {
    let listener = TcpListener::bind("0.0.0.0:8080")?;
    println!("Sensor server listening on 0.0.0.0:8080");

    for stream in listener.incoming() {
        let mut stream = stream?;
        let mut buffer = [0; 1024];
        stream.read(&mut buffer)?;

        // Process sensor data from the remote device
        let sensor_data = process_sensor_data(&buffer);

        // Perform device I/O operations with the sensor data
        perform_device_io(&sensor_data);

        // Respond to the remote device
        stream.write_all(b"Data received and processed.")?;
    }

    Ok(())
}

fn process_sensor_data(data: &[u8]) -> SensorData {
    // Process the received data and convert it into a structured for-
mat
    // In a real-world scenario, this could involve deserialization and
validation
    // For simplicity, we assume direct conversion in this example
    SensorData::from_bytes(data)
}

fn perform_device_io(sensor_data: &SensorData) {
    // Perform device I/O operations using the sensor data
    // This could involve controlling actuators, making decisions, or
storing data
```

```
    // In this example, we perform a hypothetical device I/O operation
    // by printing the sensor data
    println!("Received sensor data: {:?}", sensor_data);
}

#[derive(Debug)]
struct SensorData {
    // Define the structure for sensor data
}

impl SensorData {
    fn from_bytes(_data: &[u8]) -> SensorData {
        // Convert the received bytes into a SensorData instance
        // In a real-world application, this might involve deserialization
        // and validation of the data.
        // In this simplified example, we assume the bytes directly represent
        // the sensor data.
        SensorData {}
    }
}
```

In this code, we've built a Rust-based TCP server that acts like a traffic cop for remote sensor devices. The server sits at a specific internet address and listens for data sent by these remote devices, much like cars approaching a booth. When it receives data, it processes it and uses this information to orchestrate actions among different devices. These actions could involve turning on or off machines, making decisions based on the received data, or storing the information for future use. What makes this code impressive is its ability to facilitate real-time communication between devices, essentially enabling them to collaborate and perform tasks efficiently. It's like having a conversation where the devices not only exchange information but also use it to make things happen, making it invaluable for a wide range of applications where seamless device communication is crucial.

To simulate this concept in action, you can use a command-line tool called **netcat** (also known as **nc**) to mimic a pretend client connecting to your TCP server. Here's a simple step-by-step guide on how to do this:

1. First, start your Rust program by running the following command in your terminal:

   ```
   $ cargo run
   ```

This command will kick off your TCP server, making it ready to accept connections on port **8080**.

2. Next, open a new terminal window and use **netcat** to establish a connection to your server with this command:

```
$ nc 127.0.0.1 8080
```

This command initiates a connection to your server, which is running on your own computer, at IP address `127.0.0.1` (also known as localhost), and it connects to port `8080`.

3. Once the connection is successfully made, you can start typing or pasting data into the **netcat** terminal. Whatever you input there will be sent to your Rust server. For example, you can type something like:

```
Hello, this is sensor data.
```

4. Your server will read the data you've sent, process it based on the instructions you've programmed in Rust, and then reply with a message, possibly something like:

```
Data received and processed.
```

5. You can input any sensor data you want to test your server with, and the server will handle it according to the rules you've defined in your Rust code.

6. To end the connection in the **netcat** terminal and close it, you can simply press **Ctrl+C**.

By following these steps, you can effectively evaluate your server's functionality by manually transmitting data using **netcat**. This enables you to simulate a client connecting to your server and receiving responses, which is a useful way to verify that your server is working as expected.

Network programming in Rust is a powerful technique that can make your devices work better when it comes to talking to each other. It helps you link up with other devices, even if they are far away, so you can build systems that need both local and long-distance connections. Rust gives you the tools to do this smoothly with its special libraries for handling sockets and sending data over networks. This means you can design reliable and fast solutions that let devices communicate, whether they're right next to each other or on opposite sides of the world. In simpler terms, Rust helps devices talk to each other over the internet or a local network, making it super useful for all sorts of applications.

Asynchronous Networking and Device I/O

In today's interconnected world, responsiveness and efficiency are key considerations when it comes to both network programming and device I/O. Traditional blocking I/O, where each operation waits for its turn, can significantly impact performance, especially when dealing with numerous concurrent operations. To address this challenge, Rust provides a powerful solution in the form of async/await syntax, allowing us to write asynchronous I/O code.

Async/await in Rust is like a superpower for writing computer programs. It helps you create code that doesn't get stuck waiting for things to happen, so you can juggle lots of tasks at the same time without slowing down. Imagine you're a superhero who can answer many phone calls, send messages, and do different tasks all at once without any delay. This superpower is fantastic when you need your computer program to respond quickly, handle many things at once, and work smoothly with lots of connections, like talking to other computers on the internet or controlling different gadgets. So, `async/await` in Rust is a powerful tool for building efficient and fast programs in situations where being quick, flexible, and able to do many things at the same time is super important.

Let's consider a practical scenario where you have a device control system that communicates with a network of sensors. These sensors continuously produce data, and you need to collect and process readings from multiple sensors concurrently. Rust's asynchronous I/O capabilities come to the rescue, as they allow you to efficiently manage these sensor devices without blocking the control system.

In the following Rust code snippet, you'll find an example of an asynchronous TCP server that effectively handles multiple sensor devices:

Listing 9.30 A simple asynchronous TCP server.

```
use tokio::net::TcpListener;
use tokio::io::{AsyncWriteExt, AsyncReadExt}; // Import AsyncReadExt
trait
use std::error::Error;
use std::net::SocketAddr;

#[tokio::main]
async fn main() -> Result<(), Box<dyn Error>> {
    let addr: SocketAddr = "0.0.0.0:8080".parse()?;
    let listener = TcpListener::bind(&addr).await?;
    println!("Sensor server listening on 0.0.0.0:8080");
```

```
    loop {
        let (mut socket, addr) = listener.accept().await?;
        println!("new client: {:?}", addr);
        tokio::spawn(async move {
            let mut buf = vec![0; 1024];
            if let Err(e) = socket.read(&mut buf).await {
                eprintln!("Error reading from socket: {}", e);
                return;
            }

            // Process sensor data from the remote device
            let sensor_data = process_sensor_data(&buf);

            // Perform device I/O operations with the sensor data
            perform_device_io(&sensor_data);

            // Respond to the remote device with a custom response
            let response = b"Data received and processed\n";
            if let Err(e) = socket.write_all(response).await {
                eprintln!("Error writing to socket: {}", e);
                return;
            }
            // Flush the output buffer to ensure the response is sent
immediately
            if let Err(e) = socket.flush().await {
                eprintln!("Error flushing socket: {}", e);
            }
        });
    }
}

fn process_sensor_data(data: &[u8]) -> SensorData {
    // Process the received data and convert it into a structured format
    // In a real-world scenario, this could involve deserialization and
validation
    // For simplicity, we assume direct conversion in this example
    SensorData::from_bytes(data)
}

fn perform_device_io(sensor_data: &SensorData) {
    // Perform device I/O operations using the sensor data
    // This could involve controlling actuators, making decisions, or
storing data
    // In this example, we perform a hypothetical device I/O operation
    // by printing the sensor data
    println!("Received sensor data: {:?}", sensor_data);
}
```

```
#[derive(Debug)]
struct SensorData {
    // Define the structure for sensor data
}

impl SensorData {
    fn from_bytes(_data: &[u8]) -> SensorData {
        // Convert the received bytes into a SensorData instance
        // In a real-world application, this might involve deserializa-
tion
        // and validation of the data.
        // In this simplified example, we assume the bytes directly rep-
resent
        // the sensor data.
        SensorData {}
    }
}

// Output

// Sensor server listening on 0.0.0.0:8080
// new client: 127.0.0.1:40152
// Received sensor data: SensorData
// new client: 127.0.0.1:40162
// Received sensor data: SensorData
// new client: 127.0.0.1:40170
// Received sensor data: SensorData
// new client: 127.0.0.1:40178
// Received sensor data: SensorData
// new client: 127.0.0.1:40190
// Received sensor data: SensorData
// new client: 127.0.0.1:50572
// Received sensor data: SensorData
// new client: 127.0.0.1:50580
// Received sensor data: SensorData
// new client: 127.0.0.1:50596
// Received sensor data: SensorData
// new client: 127.0.0.1:50598
// Received sensor data: SensorData
// new client: 127.0.0.1:50600
// Received sensor data: SensorData
// new client: 127.0.0.1:50604
// Received sensor data: SensorData
// new client: 127.0.0.1:50606
// Received sensor data: SensorData
// new client: 127.0.0.1:50620
```

```
// Received sensor data: SensorData
// new client: 127.0.0.1:50630
// Received sensor data: SensorData
// new client: 127.0.0.1:50646
// Received sensor data: SensorData
```

This code represents an asynchronous TCP server that efficiently handles multiple sensor devices concurrently. The server processes sensor data asynchronously and seamlessly integrates it with device I/O operations. You can use a simple Bash `for` loop to create concurrent netcat sessions to simulate multiple client connections. Here's a Unix command that simulates concurrent connections using netcat:

Listing 9.31 A basic unix command that simulates multiple client connections.

```
$ for i in {1..5}; do (echo "Client $i connected" && sleep 1) | nc
127.0.0.1 8080 & done; wait

// Output

// [1] 88712
// [2] 88714
// [3] 88718
// [4] 88721
// [5] 88723
// Data received and processed
// Data received and processed
// Data received and processed
// Data received and processed
// Data received and processed
// [1]   Done                    ( echo "Client $i connected" && sleep 1
) | nc 127.0.0.1 8080
// [2]   Done                    ( echo "Client $i connected" && sleep 1
) | nc 127.0.0.1 8080
// [3]   Done                    ( echo "Client $i connected" && sleep 1
) | nc 127.0.0.1 8080
// [4]-  Done                    ( echo "Client $i connected" && sleep 1
) | nc 127.0.0.1 8080
// [5]+  Done                    ( echo "Client $i connected" && sleep 1
) | nc 127.0.0.1 8080
```

This one-liner simulates five concurrent client connections to the server, with each client sending a message and sleeping for 1 second before connecting. You can adjust the number of connections by changing the range in the `{1..5}` part.

Using asynchronous I/O in Rust ensures that your computer system stays quick and can handle lots of devices and respond to things happening right away without slowing down other tasks. This helps you build powerful and quick systems that can deal with device tasks at the same time as dealing with network tasks. In other words, it helps your computer juggle many tasks at once, making everything run smoothly and efficiently.

Networking Libraries and Device I/O

Rust's extensive ecosystem provides plenty of networking libraries and frameworks designed to simplify the complexities of network programming. These libraries offer valuable abstractions, tools, and utilities that streamline common networking operations, making them essential for us to work with network-connected devices.

One such library in the Rust ecosystem is **hyper**, a highly popular HTTP library. **hyper** provides a user-friendly and extensible API for building both HTTP clients and servers, simplifying the process of integrating web-based device control and monitoring into your system.

The following code snippet demonstrates how to utilize the **hyper** library to build an HTTP server capable of serving device control endpoints:

Listing 9.32 A basic HTTP server using Hyper.

```
use hyper::service::{make_service_fn, service_fn};
use hyper::{Body, Request, Response, Server};
use std::convert::Infallible;
use std::net::SocketAddr;

async fn device_control(_req: Request<Body>) -> Result<Response<Body>,
Infallible> {
    // Implement device control logic here
    // This function could process incoming requests to control devices

    Ok(Response::new(Body::from("Device control response")))
}

#[tokio::main]
async fn main() -> Result<(), Box<dyn std::error::Error>> {
    let make_svc = make_service_fn(|_conn| {
        let svc = service_fn(device_control);
        async { Ok::<_, Infallible>(svc) }
    });
```

```
    let addr: SocketAddr = ([127, 0, 0, 1], 8080).into();
    let server = Server::bind(&addr).serve(make_svc);

    println!("Device control server listening on
http://127.0.0.1:8080");

    server.await?;

    Ok(())
}
```

In this code snippet, we've leveraged the **hyper** library to construct an HTTP server. This server is capable of responding to requests for device control endpoints, enabling you to remotely manage and control devices. The **device_control** function represents the logic for handling incoming device control requests, demonstrating how the library simplifies the process of building such functionality.

Apart from **hyper**, Rust's ecosystem features a range of other networking libraries and frameworks, including **actix-web**, **warp**, and **Rocket**. These frameworks provide comprehensive solutions for developing web applications and APIs. With these tools, you can create interfaces for device management, monitor the status of devices, and interact with network-connected devices seamlessly.

By harnessing the power of these networking libraries and frameworks, you can seamlessly merge device I/O operations with network communication, unlocking a world of possibilities in system programming. These tools provide the means to build efficient, responsive, and scalable systems that interact with devices over a network, simplifying device management and control.

Security Considerations

Ensuring safety and security is crucial when working with devices connected to networks and managing how they exchange information. Rust is an excellent option for creating safe and secure network applications because it places a strong focus on these aspects. This means that when devices communicate with each other, the same high-level security standards are upheld. Rust, therefore, stands out as a reliable and resilient choice for safeguarding interactions between devices over the internet or other networks, giving you peace of mind that your data and devices are well protected.

Rust's safety features, particularly its enforcement of memory safety and type safety, significantly reduce the risk of common security vulnerabilities. Issues like buffer overflows, null pointer dereferences, and data races, which are often the entry points for attackers seeking to compromise networked devices or systems, are mitigated. This foundational security aspect of Rust ensures that your applications are less susceptible to these types of vulnerabilities, enhancing the overall security of your networked devices.

Input Validation: Proper input validation is a fundamental security practice. It involves examining and validating data received from networked devices to prevent injection attacks, malicious input, or other forms of tampering. Here's a Rust code snippet that demonstrates input validation when handling data received from networked devices:

Listing 9.33 A basic input sanitization program.

```
fn handle_input(input: &str) -> Result<(), Box<dyn std::error::Error>> {
    if input.contains("DROP TABLE") {
        return Err("Invalid input detected".into());
    }

    // Process the input safely
    // ...

    Ok(())
}

fn main() {
    let input = "SELECT * FROM data";
    if let Err(err) = handle_input(input) {
        eprintln!("Error: {}", err);
    } else {
        println!("Input is valid. Processing...");
    }
}

// Output

// Input is valid. Processing...
```

In this code, we check the input for the presence of harmful SQL injection keywords and respond accordingly, demonstrating a basic form of input validation. This `main` function demonstrates how you can call the `handle_input` function to validate input and handle potential errors.

Access Control: Access control mechanisms are essential for regulating interactions with your system. These mechanisms authenticate and authorize devices or users, allowing only authorized parties to interact with your networked devices. Here's an example of basic access control in Rust:

Listing 9.34 A basic access control program.

```
fn authenticate_device(_device_id: &str, _secret_key: &str) -> bool {
    // Authenticate the device using its credentials
    // ...

    true // Authorized access
}

fn main() {
    let device_id = "my_device";
    let secret_key = "secure_key";

    if authenticate_device(device_id, secret_key) {
        println!("Access granted for device: {}", device_id);
        // Perform device control or other authorized operations here
    } else {
        println!("Access denied for device: {}", device_id);
    }
}

// Output

// Access granted for device: my_device
```

This code snippet demonstrates device authentication by checking the provided credentials, ensuring only authorized devices can access the system. In the `main` function, we authenticate a device by calling `authenticate_device` with its credentials and determine if access is granted or denied.

Firewall Rules: Applying firewall rules is especially vital for devices exposed to the internet. These rules restrict unauthorized network traffic, safeguarding your networked devices. Firewalls can be configured using various tools and frameworks, depending on your system's requirements.

Listing 9.35 A basic firewall configuration program.

```
fn configure_firewall_rules() {
    // Implement system-level firewall rule configuration here
    // This might involve running external commands or using
system-specific APIs
}
```

```
fn main() {
    configure_firewall_rules();
    println!("Firewall rules configured successfully.");
}

// Output

// Firewall rules configured successfully.
```

In this code snippet, the **main** function calls **configure_firewall_rules**, which would typically perform system-level firewall rule configuration using platform-specific methods.

In the context of Rust programming, security relies on a joint effort between Rust's safety features and a developer's responsible actions. It's like building a resilient bridge, where Rust's safeguards act as the structure, and the developer plays the role of the vigilant builder. Following security best practices and leveraging Rust's safety mechanisms ensures the creation of safe and reliable networked systems. Regular maintenance, keeping systems up-to-date, and continuous adherence to security guidelines are crucial for maintaining the safety of networked devices and the systems they connect to. This strong match between Rust's safety features and careful development practices establishes a solid and secure foundation for digital interactions.

Parallelism, Concurrency, and Device I/O

Parallelism and concurrency are fundamental elements of system programming, and when it comes to device I/O, they play a pivotal role in ensuring efficient and responsive systems. Rust empowers us with robust tools to manage concurrent tasks and parallel execution, allowing for the effective utilization of system resources and the achievement of high performance.

In various system scenarios, from real-time data acquisition to device control and data processing, the ability to execute tasks in parallel and concurrently significantly enhances the responsiveness and throughput of the system. Let's consider a practical case: in a smart factory, multiple sensors are collecting data in real-time, and actuators are controlling the machinery based on that data. Here, parallelism and concurrency are essential to efficiently manage the multitude of sensor readings and control actions.

Rust's concurrency model, complemented by its ownership system, is designed to prevent data races and facilitate secure concurrent access to devices and shared resources. This is particularly vital when multiple tasks or threads are interacting with the same devices or shared data. Ensuring that concurrent access is well-coordinated and safe is essential for the stability and reliability of the system.

Here's an example of how Rust's concurrency features can be used to read sensor data and control devices concurrently:

Listing 9.36 Read sensor data and control devices concurrently.

```
use std::thread;
use std::sync::{Arc, Mutex};

fn main() {
    let sensor_data = Arc::new(Mutex::new(SensorData {}));
    let device = Arc::new(Mutex::new(Device::new()));

    let sensor_thread = thread::spawn({
        let sensor_data = Arc::clone(&sensor_data);
        move || {
            // Read sensor data and update shared data
            let mut sensor_data = sensor_data.lock().unwrap();
            sensor_data.read();
        }
    });

    let device_thread = thread::spawn({
        let sensor_data_clone = Arc::clone(&sensor_data);
        let device_clone = Arc::clone(&device);
        move || {
            // Control the device based on sensor data
            let sensor_data = sensor_data_clone.lock().unwrap();
            let mut device = device_clone.lock().unwrap();
            device.control(&sensor_data);
        }
    });

    sensor_thread.join().unwrap();
    device_thread.join().unwrap();
}

struct SensorData {
    // Define the structure for sensor data
}
```

```
impl SensorData {
    fn read(&mut self) {
        // Simulate reading sensor data
    }
}

struct Device {
    // Define the structure for the device
}

impl Device {
    fn new() -> Device {
        // Initialize the device
        Device {}
    }

    fn control(&mut self, _sensor_data: &SensorData) {
        // Control the device based on sensor data
    }
}
```

In the example provided, we illustrate how Rust's concurrency features can be used to manage concurrent tasks for reading sensor data and controlling devices. To do this, we leverage the **Arc** (atomic reference counting) and **Mutex** (mutual exclusion) constructs, which are part of Rust's standard library. These constructs allow for safe data sharing between multiple threads. In this example, one thread focuses on reading sensor data, while another thread concurrently controls the device based on the acquired sensor data. This demonstrates how Rust's concurrency features enable the efficient and secure management of device I/O and control, especially in real-time scenarios where parallelism is critical.

Rust is a programming language that excels at helping you control how your computer does multiple things at the same time and keeps them in sync. This is super useful when you have a bunch of devices connected to your computer and need to do things quickly and safely. So, when clever computer folks use Rust's special tools for handling all these devices, they can be sure that everything works well, is safe from problems, and doesn't slow things down. This means your computer can do stuff faster and respond quickly, which is great!

Real-Time Systems and Device I/O

Real-time systems are like computer programs with a super strict schedule. They need to interact with devices very precisely, like controlling a robot arm that has to move flawlessly and on time. Rust comes to the rescue because it has some fantastic features that work well for these systems.

Timing is of utmost importance in real-time applications. These systems require specific actions to occur within strict time constraints, making predictability and reliability critical. Rust's ownership system and safety guarantees play a pivotal role in eliminating common issues that could introduce unpredictability into real-time systems, such as race conditions and memory corruption. With Rust, you can confidently design and implement real-time control systems with assurance in their behavior.

In real-time systems, achieving low-level control over hardware is crucial. It's like speaking the same language as the robot arm's control system. You need to provide precise instructions to the robot arm with impeccable timing. Rust excels in this area by allowing for this kind of detailed control while also ensuring everything is safe and doesn't cause any issues. This means that even when the robot arm is moving rapidly, you can have confidence that it won't suddenly stop or go in the wrong direction.

Let's consider a practical example to illustrate Rust's capabilities in the context of real-time control. Imagine developing a real-time control system for a robotic arm. This system is tasked with reading sensor data and making precise adjustments to the arm's position at specific time intervals. Rust, with its ability to manage low-level hardware interactions while ensuring safety, is perfectly suited for such a task.

So, if you think of a library (like a set of tools) called **`some_low_level_library`** for a robotic arm in a real-time system, in our made-up world, it might be designed in Rust. This library would be like a Swiss army knife for the robotic arm, allowing you to control it precisely and safely. Just remember, in real life, you'd need to use a library that is specifically built for your robotic arm because every piece of hardware is different.

Listing 9.37 Real-time systems and device I/O program.

```
// some_low_level_library.rs

pub mod sensors {
    // Initialize the sensors and other sensor-related functions
    pub fn init() {
        // Implementation for sensor initialization
        println!("Sensors initialized.");
    }
```

```
    // Read sensor data
    pub fn read() -> i32 {
        // Simulated sensor data reading
        42
    }
}

pub mod robotic_arm {
    // Initialize the robotic arm and other arm-related functions
    pub fn init() {
        // Implementation for robotic arm initialization
        println!("Robotic arm initialized.");
    }

    // Control the robotic arm based on sensor data
    pub fn control(sensor_data: i32) {
        // Simulated robotic arm control based on sensor data
        println!("Robotic arm controlled with sensor data: {}", sen-
sor_data);
    }
}

pub mod timing {
    // Implement a delay function to meet precise timing requirements
    pub fn delay_microseconds(microseconds: u32) {
        // Simulated delay
        std::thread::sleep(std::time::Duration::from_micros(microseconds
as u64));
    }
}
```

This fictional **some_low_level_library** consists of three modules: **sensors**, **robotic_arm**, and **timing**. It includes initialization functions for sensors and the robotic arm, as well as functions for reading sensor data, controlling the robotic arm, and implementing a delay to meet precise timing requirements.

Now, let's create a simple **main.rs** file to test the code:

Listing 9.38 Real-time systems and device I/O program.

```
// main.rs

extern crate some_low_level_library as ll;

fn main() {
    // Initialize and configure the robotic arm and sensors
    ll::robotic_arm::init();
```

```
    ll::sensors::init();

    loop {
        // Read sensor data
        let sensor_data = ll::sensors::read();

        // Perform real-time control based on sensor data
        ll::robotic_arm::control(sensor_data);

        // Meet precise timing requirements
        ll::timing::delay_microseconds(1000);
    }
}

// Ouput

// Robotic arm controlled with sensor data: 42
// Robotic arm controlled with sensor data: 42
// Robotic arm controlled with sensor data: 42
.
.
.
```

In this **main.rs** file, we use the functions provided by our fictional **some_low_level_library** to initialize the robotic arm and sensors, read sensor data, control the robotic arm, and implement a delay to meet precise timing requirements.

In the provided example, we've assumed the use of a hypothetical low-level library for real-time control. The code initializes and configures the robotic arm and sensors, reads sensor data, and controls the robotic arm based on the sensor readings, all while meeting strict timing requirements. Notably, the **#![no_std]** attribute is used to indicate that the standard library is not utilized, a common practice in real-time systems with strict resource constraints.

Rust's versatility in the world of real-time systems extends across diverse domains, encompassing industrial automation, robotics, automotive control systems, and embedded devices. Capitalizing on its unique blend of low-level hardware access and robust safety mechanisms, Rust equips us with the tools necessary to engineer real-time systems capable of interacting with devices in a secure, predictable, and dependable manner. These systems play a pivotal role in applications where precision and adherence to strict timing requirements are crucial, ensuring that actions emerge precisely as assigned within predefined timeframes. Rust's rich feature set and advanced capabilities render it a powerful choice for orchestrating real-time device input and output operations.

Conclusion

In this comprehensive chapter, we have explored a wide array of topics, from handling files and filesystem operations to device I/O and network programming. This comprehensive journey through system-level programming in Rust has equipped you with valuable knowledge and practical skills for building robust and efficient software.

We began by delving into advanced file operations, including working with file metadata, symbolic and hard links, file locking, and memory-mapped files. These concepts are fundamental for managing data and resources on various systems.

This chapter then took us into the world of device I/O, where we discussed device drivers and kernel modules in Rust. While challenging, writing device drivers in Rust offers the benefits of memory safety and strong typing, enhancing the security and reliability of system-level code.

Transitioning into the world of network programming, we explored the integration of network communication with device I/O. We saw how Rust's features and libraries can facilitate remote device management, real-time data acquisition, and distributed control over networks.

Security considerations for networked devices were highlighted, emphasizing the importance of input validation, data encryption, access control, and other best practices to protect networked devices and systems.

This chapter also covered the significance of parallelism and concurrency in system programming, especially when dealing with device I/O. Rust's concurrency model and support for parallel execution enable efficient management of concurrent device tasks, enhancing system responsiveness and throughput.

Furthermore, we discussed real-time systems and how Rust's low-level capabilities and safety features make it an ideal choice for developing software that meets strict timing requirements in device control and data acquisition.

As you progress in your journey as a system programmer in Rust, you'll encounter a wide array of scenarios and challenges, from managing files and devices to optimizing network communication and real-time control. Rust equips you with the tools and safety features needed to tackle complex tasks with confidence.

The practical examples and best practices discussed here will serve as valuable assets as you embark on real-world projects in the world of systems and low-level programming.

In the next chapter, we will explore iterators and closures in Rust, essential for efficient data processing. This chapter will provide a comprehensive understanding of these constructs and their practical application, including working with iterators for data processing, writing closures, and applying these concepts to real-world problem-solving.

Resources

To deepen your understanding of working with devices I/O in Rust, you can explore the following resources:

- *Tokio I/O Documentation*: Refer to the official documentation for Tokio's I/O module. Tokio provides a powerful asynchronous runtime for Rust, and its I/O module offers abstractions and utilities for efficient device I/O operations. - *https://docs.rs/tokio/latest/tokio/io/index.html*
- *Async IO Documentation*: Explore the documentation for the Async IO crate, which provides asynchronous I/O primitives for Rust. This crate offers a set of tools for working with devices asynchronously, enabling efficient and non-blocking I/O operations. - *https://docs.rs/async-io*
- *Rust Standard Library - I/O module*: Delve into the I/O module of the Rust Standard Library documentation. Understanding the foundational I/O concepts in Rust's standard library is crucial for working with devices and managing I/O operations efficiently. - *https://doc.rust-lang.org/std/io/index.html*
- *Mio Documentation*: Explore the official documentation for the Mio crate, a lightweight asynchronous I/O library for Rust. Mio provides the building blocks for building scalable and efficient event-driven systems, making it well-suited for device I/O scenarios. - *https://docs.rs/mio*
- *Cortex-M Repository*: Explore the GitHub repository for the Cortex-M project, which provides support for ARM Cortex-M microcontrollers in Rust. This repository includes HAL implementations and examples for working with devices on Cortex-M platforms. - *https://github.com/rust-embedded/cortex-m*
- *Embedded HAL Documentation*: Delve into the documentation for the Embedded HAL crate, a trait-based Hardware Abstraction Layer for embedded systems in Rust. This crate defines a common interface for working with devices across different embedded platforms. - *https://*

docs.rs/embedded-hal

- *Target ATSAMD Microcontrollers using Rust Repository*: Explore the GitHub repository for the Tiny USB project on ATSAMD, which demonstrates USB device support on ATSAMD microcontrollers in Rust. Studying this repository can provide insights into implementing USB device I/O in Rust. - *https://github.com/atsamd-rs/atsamd*
- *Tokio Serial Documentation*: If working with serial communication is part of your device I/O requirements, explore the documentation for the Tokio Serial crate. This crate provides asynchronous serial port support within the Tokio runtime. - *https://docs.rs/tokio-serial*

These resources offer a comprehensive view of working with devices I/O in Rust, providing practical guidance and documentation to help you master the complexities of interacting with devices and managing I/O operations efficiently.

Multiple Choice Questions

Q1: Which Rust module is responsible for file operations like opening, reading, and writing?

a) `std::fs::file`

b) `std::io::file`

c) `std::file::io`

d) `std::fs`

Q2: How does Rust handle errors in file operations, such as file opening?

a) Rust crashes the program if an error occurs

b) Errors are ignored, and the program continues execution

c) Rust uses the Result type to elegantly manage errors

d) Errors trigger an infinite loop in the program

Q3: What does the `BufRead` trait facilitate in Rust file I/O?

a) Reading binary data from a file

b) Reading files line by line efficiently

c) Creating a new file in buffered mode

d) Writing data to a file with buffering

Q4: What is the purpose of the std::fs::rename function in Rust?

a) Creating a new file

b) Renaming and moving files

c) Reading file metadata

d) Checking file permissions

Q5: Which Rust feature plays a pivotal role in reducing security risks when interacting with hardware directly?

a) Cross-compilation

b) Ownership

c) Memory safety and thread safety

d) File locking

Q6 What is the role of device drivers in the interaction between software and hardware layers?

a) Control hardware peripherals

b) Enable cross-compilation

c) Facilitate communication and coordination

d) Create symbolic links

Q7: Which Rust crate is used for controlling GPIO pins in the provided code sample?

a) i2cdev

b) rppal

c) fs2

d) std

Q8: In hardware programming, what is the purpose of creating hard links?

a) Enable communication with sensors

b) Provide shared behaviors for types

c) Share underlying data on the storage device

d) Ensure memory safety

Q9: What advantage do memory-mapped files offer when handling large files or optimizing performance?

a) Sequential I/O operations

b) Random access to file contents

c) Limited data manipulation

d) Linear data storage

Q10: Which Rust crate provides a valuable tool for efficiently harnessing the capability of memory-mapped files?

a) `io`

b) `std`

c) `memmap`

d) `file`

Q11: What is a key benefit of utilizing memory-mapped files for data access in Rust?

a) Sequential data access

b) Linear file processing

c) Elimination of traditional I/O bottlenecks

d) Reduced memory usage

Q12: What does the code snippet using File::create demonstrate in the context of file I/O best practices?

a) Reading from a file

b) Handling errors during file creation

c) Changing file permissions

d) Creating a backup of a file

Q13: In file I/O best practices, what does the term "Cross-Platform Compatibility" refer to?

a) Ensuring files are compatible with different programming languages

b) Avoiding file sharing between platforms

c) Handling differences in file systems between various platforms

d) Ensuring compatibility with different file formats

Q14: What is the purpose of the Arc and Mutex constructs in Rust's concurrency model?

a) Ensuring data safety through ownership

b) Enforcing static typing

c) Facilitating safe data sharing between multiple threads

d) Controlling access to device I/O

Q15: In the context of real-time systems, why is timing crucial in Rust?

a) To introduce unpredictability

b) To achieve low-level control over hardware

c) To enforce strict data ownership

d) To prevent the use of asynchronous operations

Answers

1. d) std::fs
2. c) Rust uses the Result type to elegantly manage errors
3. b) Reading files line by line efficiently
4. b) Renaming and moving files
5. c) Memory safety and thread safety
6. c) Facilitate communication and coordination
7. b) rppal
8. c) Share underlying data on the storage device
9. b) Random access to file contents
10. c) memmap
11. c) Elimination of traditional I/O bottlenecks
12. b) Handling errors during file creation

13. c) Handling differences in file systems between various platforms
14. c) Facilitating safe data sharing between multiple threads
15. b) To achieve low-level control over hardware

Key Terms

- **BufRead:** A trait in Rust that provides buffered reading capabilities, allowing efficient reading of data, especially line by line.
- **Metadata:** Information about a file, including attributes such as size, modification time, and permissions.
- **Automatic File Closing:** A feature in Rust where files are automatically closed when the file handle goes out of scope, enhancing safety and reliability in file operations.
- **std::fs::rename:** A Rust function used for renaming and moving files, ensuring atomic and reliable file system operations.
- **Device Drivers:** Software components that serve as intermediaries between the operating system and hardware devices, facilitating communication and coordination.
- **GPIO (General-Purpose Input/Output) Pins:** Pins on a device that can be configured as either input or output and are commonly used for tasks such as turning LEDs on and off or reading button states.
- **Cross-compilation:** The process of compiling code on one platform and producing executable code that can run on a different platform or architecture.
- **Symbolic Links:** Also known as symlinks, these are references to other files that act as pointers or shortcuts, directing users to the actual file's location.
- **Hard Links:** File references that point to the same underlying data on the storage device as the original file, creating multiple file entries that share the same content.
- **File Locking:** A mechanism to prevent multiple processes or threads from simultaneously accessing and modifying a file, ensuring data consistency and integrity.
- **Memory Safety:** A feature in Rust that prevents common programming errors related to memory access, reducing the risk of security vulnerabilities.
- **Thread Safety:** A feature in Rust that ensures safe concurrent access to data by multiple threads, preventing data races and related issues.

- **I2C (Inter-Integrated Circuit):** A communication protocol used for connecting and communicating with various devices, such as sensors, in hardware programming.
- **Memory-Mapped Files:** Files that provide a mechanism for mapping a file directly into memory, allowing random access to file contents and eliminating traditional I/O bottlenecks.
- **Resource Management:** Leveraging Rust's ownership and scope management to handle resource cleanup, ensuring that file handles are automatically closed when they go out of scope.
- **Permissions and Security:** Being aware of file permissions and security considerations, with Rust providing mechanisms to set and check file permissions, as shown in the code snippet changing file permissions.
- **Backup and Version Control:** Implementing mechanisms for backing up and versioning important files, such as the example of a simple backup function using `std::fs::copy`.
- **Performance Optimization:** Exploring techniques like memory-mapped files or buffered I/O for large files or performance-critical tasks to maximize efficiency, as recommended in file I/O best practices.

CHAPTER 10

Iterators and Closures

Introduction

In Rust, there are two crucial concepts that hold the key to efficient data processing: iterators and closures. These fundamental building blocks are at the core of Rust's design philosophy, which prioritizes safety, performance, and expressive code. As we kick off our enlightening journey through the following sections, we will delve deep into the complex world of iterators and closures, discovering their nuances and uncovering plenty of ways they can be utilized to tackle real-world problems.

Closures, one of Rust's most remarkable features, are a mechanism that allows us to create anonymous functions equipped with the power to access their enclosing scope. These dynamic constructs are at the heart of a wide array of tasks in Rust, ranging from sorting data to handling concurrency. Throughout the course of this chapter, we will explore the universe of closures, gaining an understanding of their different types, mastering their integration with standard library functions, and delving into the art of variable capture. As we explore this domain, we will also uncover the essential traits that define closures in Rust.

What makes this journey truly fascinating is the complex connection between iterators and closures. In Rust, these two concepts are often seen working in coordination, with closures seamlessly integrated into iterators to process data in a manner that's not only highly expressive but also exceptionally efficient. Let us begin this exploration by examining each of these concepts in more detail, starting with the powerful world of iterators.

Structure

In this chapter, we are going to explore the following topics:

- Working with Iterators for Efficient Data Processing in Rust
- Writing Closures and Capturing Variables in Rust
- Applying Iterators and Closures to Practical Examples

Iterators

Iterators play a crucial role in Rust's standard library, serving as a fundamental tool for handling collections in a manner that is both user-friendly and expressive. These constructs empower us to manipulate data in a highly efficient manner while saving us from getting stuck in the nitty-gritty complexities of how collections work beneath the surface. The result? Code that is not only more efficient but also much more readable and comprehensible. To begin our journey into this fascinating world, let's start by taking a closer look at the world of iterators.

Anatomy of an Iterator

At its core, an iterator is a value that generates a sequence of values, which can be conveniently used in loops or other operations. Rust's standard library provides a wide range of iterators tailored for different data types, including vectors, strings, hash tables, and more. Notably, you can create custom iterators to meet your specific requirements, giving you full control over your data.

An iterator comes with a set of methods that allow us to traverse a collection of items one by one. It provides the following fundamental methods:

- **`next()`**: The `next()` method is like turning the pages of a book, one page at a time. It lets you retrieve the next item in a sequence, almost like unwrapping a present. If there's an item waiting for you, it hands it over with a cheerful **"Here's something for you!" in the form of `Some(item)`**. But if you've reached the end of the sequence, it kindly informs you with a polite **"Sorry, nothing more to see here" by returning `None`**.
- **`for_each()`**: Think of **`for_each()`** as a handy tool for your to-do list. This method goes through each item in an iterator, and for every item, it performs a specific action. It's like an orchestra conductor, directing each musician to play their part. You provide a closure or code to execute for each element, and **`for_each()`** takes care of the rest, ensuring that every item gets its moment in the spotlight.

- `map()`: Imagine `map()` as your personal transformation artist for your iterator. It takes each item in the iterator and applies a special transformation, almost like a makeover. The result is a brand-new iterator with all the items modified by the provided closure. It's like taking a dry painting and having a talented artist give it a fresh, vibrant look. `map()` lets you reshape the items in your iterator with ease, allowing you to create a whole new set of values while keeping the essence of the original.
- `filter()`: The `filter()` method is your handy filter for finding specific elements in a collection of items. It creates a new iterator, much like a magnifying glass, and focuses on only the items that meet particular criteria or satisfy a given predicate. It's like sifting through a collection of marbles and picking out only the shiny, colorful ones. `filter()` helps you declutter your iterator, leaving you with only the items that truly matter for your task at hand.
- `collect()`: Think of `collect()` as the method that gathers all your scattered ingredients and organizes them neatly into a well-prepared dish. It accumulates the items in your iterator, much like a chef collecting all the ingredients for a recipe. But instead of making a meal, it puts them together in a collection type, such as a `Vec` or `HashMap`. `collect()` simplifies your iterator into a convenient and structured form, making it ready for further use or analysis.
- `chain()`: The `chain()` method is like linking two different stories into one epic tale. It allows you to concatenate two iterators, effectively chaining them together for sequential processing. It's as if you're combining two threads into a single, complex pattern. `chain()` merges the content of two iterators, allowing you to seamlessly traverse through them one after the other.

These methods serve as the backbone of an iterator's functionality, offering a powerful suite of tools for efficient data manipulation, filtering, and aggregation. They encapsulate the essence of concise and expressive coding, simplifying complex operations into elegant, easily readable solutions.

To delve deeper, consider a scenario where you're tasked with calculating the sum of the first '`n`' prime numbers. A seemingly complex problem becomes remarkably elegant when you leverage Rust's iterators. These methods are like an orchestra conductor, ensuring that every instrument plays its part to perfection. They demonstrate how Rust's iterator system can transform complex challenges into streamlined and graceful solutions, making your code not just powerful but a true joy to work with.

Listing 10.1 A simple program that demonstrates iterators usage.

```
fn is_prime(n: u32) -> bool {
    if n <= 1 {
        return false;
    }
    for i in 2..(n / 2 + 1) {
        if n % i == 0 {
            return false;
        }
    }
    true
}

fn sum_of_primes(n: u32) -> u32 {
    (2..).filter(|&x| is_prime(x)).take(n as usize).sum()
}

fn main() {
    let n = 10;
    let result = sum_of_primes(n);
    println!("The sum of the first {} prime numbers is: {}", n, result);
}
```

Let's dive into the complexities of this code and explore the **`is_prime`** function, which plays a crucial role in our objective to find and add up prime numbers.

Before delving into the nitty-gritty of our prime number-seeking program, we started with a helper function called **`is_prime`**. This function serves as a sort of detective for numbers, specifically tasked with determining whether a given number qualifies as a prime number. Prime numbers, for the uninitiated, are those special numerical entities that possess the unique property of being divisible only by themselves and the number one, like 2, 3, 5, and so on. Think of them as the loners of the number world, standing apart from the crowd of divisible digits.

Now, let's explore the heart of our operation: the **`sum_of_primes`** function. Picture this function as a skilled chef in a kitchen, and the ingredients are numbers. Its magic lies in setting up a conveyor belt of numbers, starting from 2. Each number passes through the **`is_prime`** function, which works like a skilled chef checking if it's a prime number. If it is, it's like a valuable ingredient added to our recipe.

The **`sum_of_primes`** function is clever because it not only spots prime numbers but also keeps the sum of them. Think of this sum as a pot on the stove, and each prime number is a unique spice that enhances our dish. What's brilliant about this code is how it utilizes Rust's iterators, freeing us from the hassle of writing lengthy and complex loops. Instead, we smoothly loop through our numbers, accumulating prime numbers along the way.

This example is like a thrilling journey where Rust's iterators serve as our reliable guides, making complex math tasks feel as effortless as cooking a happy meal. It highlights how Rust's iterators not only promote efficiency but also make coding an enjoyable experience.

Key Traits: `Iterator` and `IntoIterator`

To understand iterators, we must first explore two fundamental traits: **`Iterator`** and **`IntoIterator`**.

The **`Iterator`** trait defines the structure of an iterator in Rust. It specifies an associated type, **`Item`**, which represents the type of values the iterator produces. The most important method in this trait is **`next`**, which retrieves the next value as an **`Option<Self::Item>`**. The **`next`** method returns **`Some(value)`** when there are more values to produce and **`None`** when the sequence ends.

On the other hand, the **`IntoIterator`** trait allows types to be treated as iterable. It's defined by the **`into_iter`** method, which returns an iterator for the type. Implementing **`IntoIterator`** for your custom types enables them to be used in Rust's **`for`** loop, making your code more idiomatic.

Let's consider an example to illustrate these traits. Suppose you have a custom data structure called **`MyCollection`** and you want to make it iterable. Here's how you can implement these traits:

Listing 10.2 A basic program that demonstrates custom iterators in action.

```
struct MyCollection {
    data: Vec<i32>, // ①
}

impl MyCollection { // ②
    fn new() -> Self {
        MyCollection { data: Vec::new() }
    }

    // Add an integer to the collection
    fn add(&mut self, value: i32) {
        self.data.push(value);
```

```
    }
}

impl IntoIterator for MyCollection { // ③
    type Item = i32;
    type IntoIter = std::vec::IntoIter<Self::Item>;

    fn into_iter(self) -> Self::IntoIter {
        self.data.into_iter()
    }
}

fn main() {
    let mut collection = MyCollection::new();

    collection.add(42);
    collection.add(100);
    collection.add(7);

    for item in collection { // ④
        println!("Item: {}", item);
    }
}
```

① Here, we define the **MyCollection** struct, which contains a field **data** of type **Vec<i32>**. This field is like a container that holds a sequence of 32-bit integers (**i32**).

② In this section, we implement methods for the **MyCollection** struct. The **new()** method is responsible for creating a new instance of **MyCollection**, initializing an empty **Vec** to hold our integers. The **add()** method allows us to insert integers into the **Vec**, effectively adding them to our collection.

③ Here, we delve into the implementation of the **IntoIterator** trait for our **MyCollection** struct. We specify the associated types: **Item** represents the type of items in our collection (**i32** in this case), and **IntoIter** indicates how to create an iterator for our collection. The **into_iter()** method defines how our collection can be used as an iterator, enabling us to loop through its contents.

④ In the **main** function, we create an instance of **MyCollection** called **collection**, add some integers to it, and then use a **for** loop to iterate through the collection. With each iteration, we print out the item. It's as if we're opening our collection and revealing its contents one by one, displaying each integer as we encounter it.

This illustrative code example demonstrates how Rust's expressive syntax and powerful iterators simplify the manipulation of custom data structures. The true marvel, however, lies in the application of iterators, which streamline the process of traversing the **`MyCollection`** data structure, rendering the code more elegant and comprehensible. The utilization of Rust's type system and the **`IntoIterator`** trait underscores the language's strength in creating clear and functional solutions, facilitating seamless integration with Rust's versatile iterator ecosystem. In essence, this code showcases Rust's exceptional capacity to deliver efficiency, clarity, and beauty in the world of software development.

Creating Iterators with `from_fn` and `successors`

One fundamental approach in programming is to create sequences of values, and closures offer a versatile way of achieving this. Closures are self-contained blocks of code that can be executed whenever required, encapsulating specific logic to generate values on demand. These closures serve as handy tools for various applications, from data processing and simulations to algorithm design and statistical analysis. They allow us to abstract complex operations into concise and reusable blocks of code, enhancing code clarity and maintainability. In Rust, closures are pivotal for achieving flexibility in value generation.

In addition to closures, Rust's standard library provides the **`std::iter::from_fn`** function, which extends the capabilities of value sequence generation. This function empowers us to create custom iterators by repeatedly invoking a closure to produce items. It's like a dynamic conveyor belt, where the closure operates as a worker consistently contributing new items to the flow. As an illustrative example, consider the task of generating the lengths of 1000 random line segments with endpoints uniformly distributed across the interval [0, 1]. Using **`std::iter::from_fn`**, this can be efficiently accomplished, as the closure acts as a generator, seamlessly creating each segment's length as needed. This approach simplifies the process of generating a significant number of random values while maintaining precise control and optimal resource utilization, making it a valuable technique for a wide array of applications, from scientific simulations to statistical analysis and beyond.

Listing 10.3 A basic program that demonstrates the `from_fn iterator usage.`

```
use rand::random;

use std::iter::from_fn;

let lengths: Vec<f64> =
    from_fn(|| Some((random::<f64>() - random::<f64>()).abs())) // ①
    .take(1000) // ②
    .collect(); // ③
```

① We're also using the standard library's **from_fn** iterator, which allows us to create an iterator that produces values based on a function. In this case, we've provided a closure **|| Some(random::<f64>() - random::<f64>(random::<f64>() - random::<f64>(.abs())** as the function. This closure generates random floating-point numbers, calculates the absolute difference between them, and returns the result as a **Some** option. Because the closure always returns **Some**, the iterator produced by **from_fn** continues indefinitely, creating a potentially infinite sequence of random numbers.

② The **take** method is used to limit the infinite sequence we created with **from_fn**. It ensures that we only take the first 1000 elements from that sequence.

③ Finally, we use the **collect** method to gather the 1,000 random numbers into a vector of type **f64**. This vector, named **lengths**, contains the first 1000 random floating-point numbers from our limited sequence.

The following code snippet demonstrates how to generate a sequence of random floating-point numbers, constrain the sequence to a specific length, and collect the results into a vector for further use. It's like filling a bucket with exactly 1000 randomly chosen values from an endless stream of numbers, and the **collect** method neatly organizes them for easy access and manipulation.

Here's an example of rewriting the **escape_time** function for plotting the Mandelbrot set using **successors**:

Listing 10.4 A basic program that demonstrates the successors iterator usage.

```
use num::Complex;
use std::iter::successors;

fn escape_time(c: Complex<f64>, limit: usize) -> Option<usize> {
    let zero = Complex { re: 0.0, im: 0.0 };

    let result = successors(Some(zero), |&z| Some(z * z + c)) // ①
        .take(limit) // ②
```

```
        .enumerate() // ③
        .find(|(_i, z)| z.norm_sqr() > 4.0); // ④

    match result {
        Some((i, _z)) => Some(i),
        None => None,
    }
}

fn main() { // ⑤
    let c = Complex { re: -0.7, im: 0.27015 };
    let limit = 1000;

    match escape_time(c, limit) {
        Some(steps) => println!("Escaped after {} steps.", steps),
        None => println!("Did not escape within {} steps.", limit),
    }
}

// Output

// Escaped after 96 steps.
```

① In this code, we utilize the **successors** function. It generates a sequence of points on the complex plane by repeatedly applying the provided closure to the previous point (starting from the origin) and adding the parameter **c**. This process continues until the **limit** is reached or until a point escapes from the origin. The closure **|&z| Some(z * z + c)** represents squaring the complex number and adding **c** to it in each iteration.

② The **take(limit)** method limits the sequence to a specified number of iterations, ensuring that we don't continue indefinitely.

③ The **enumerate()** method pairs each point in the sequence with its index.

④ The **find** method looks for the first point in the sequence that escapes from the origin, as indicated by having a squared norm greater than 4.0. If such a point is found, it returns its index and the corresponding complex number. If no escaping point is found within the specified limit, the **find** method returns **None**.

⑤ In the **main** function, we calculate the escape time for a specific complex number **c** and a limit. Depending on whether an escape is detected, we print the number of steps taken to escape or indicate that the escape did not occur within the given limit. In this example, the output states, "Escaped after 96 steps".

Both **from_fn** and **successors** accept **FnMut** closures, allowing your closures to capture and modify variables from the surrounding scopes.

Listing 10.5 A basic Fibonacci implementation using iterators.

```
fn fibonacci() -> impl Iterator<Item = usize> {
    let mut state = (0, 1); // ①
    std::iter::from_fn(move || { // ②
        state = (state.1, state.0 + state.1); // ③
        Some(state.0) // ④
    })
}

fn main() {
    let result: Vec<usize> = fibonacci().take(8).collect(); // ⑤

    let expected = vec![1, 1, 2, 3, 5, 8, 13, 21]; // ⑥

    assert_eq!(result, expected); // ⑦

    println!("Fibonacci sequence (first 8 numbers): {:?}", result); // ⑧
}

// Output

// Fibonacci sequence (first 8 numbers): [1, 1, 2, 3, 5, 8, 13, 21]
```

① We initialize a tuple called **state** to keep track of the current and next Fibonacci numbers.

② We create an iterator using **std::iter::from_fn()** with a closure.

③ Inside the closure, we calculate the next Fibonacci number and update the **state** tuple.

④ We yield the current Fibonacci number.

⑤ In the **main()** function, we generate the first 8 Fibonacci numbers and collect them into a vector.

⑥ We define the expected Fibonacci sequence for comparison.

⑦ We use assert_eq! to check if the generated sequence matches the expected one.

⑧ Finally, we print the generated sequence of the first 8 Fibonacci numbers.

While **from_fn** and **successors** offer flexibility and can replace many other iterator patterns, it is essential to remember the clarity and standard naming conventions provided by other iterator methods. Ensure you're familiar with other iterator methods before heavily relying on **from_fn** and **successors**.

Drain Methods

Numerous collection types, like vectors, provide a valuable method known as the **drain** method. This method, when invoked, requests a mutable reference to the collection and in return offers an iterator. The distinctive feature of this iterator is that it transfers ownership of each element to the recipient. Unlike the **into_iter** method, which entirely consumes the collection itself, **drain** merely borrows a mutable reference to the collection.

The essential distinction here is that the collection doesn't vanish; it remains accessible but temporarily suspended as the **drain** iterator does its work. However, it's essential to note that when this **drain** iterator concludes its operation and is dropped, it carries out one last task before departing, it cleans up after itself. Any remaining elements within the collection that it had initially borrowed are effectively removed. As a result, the collection is left empty, almost as if it's been tidied up, ready for a new set of items or a new purpose. In essence, **drain** not only facilitates element transfer but also takes responsibility for the cleanup, ensuring the collection is left undefiled when it has fulfilled its role.

On collection types that support indexing by range, such as Strings, vectors, and VecDeques, the **drain** method takes a range of elements to remove, rather than draining the entire sequence:

Listing 10.6 A basic program that demonstrates the drain method usage.

```
let mut outer = "Earth".to_string(); // ①

let inner = String::from_iter(outer.drain(1..4)); // ②

assert_eq!(outer, "Eh"); // ③

assert_eq!(inner, "art"); // ④
```

① We start by creating a mutable String called **outer** and initialize it with the value "Earth". This initializes a variable 'outer' with the text "**Earth**."

② The **inner** String is created by extracting characters from the **outer**. The **drain** method is used to remove characters from the **outer** based on the range **1..4,** excluding the character at index 4. The result is stored in the **inner**, effectively taking a portion of the **outer** and placing it in the **inner**.

③ We verify that **outer** now contains "**Eh**" by using the **assert_eq!** macro, which checks whether the value of the **outer** matches the expected value "**Eh**".

④ Similarly, we assert that **inner** contains "**art**" to ensure that the extracted characters are correctly stored in the **inner**.

If you need to drain the entire sequence, you can use the full range, **..**, as the argument.

Other Iterator Sources

In addition to the methods discussed so far, there are many other types in Rust's standard library that support iteration. Here's a summary of some of these types and their iterator sources:

Type or Trait	Iterator Expression	Description	Example
`std::fs::DirEntry`	`std::fs::read_dir(path)`	Produces directory entries from the specified path	`std::fs::read_dir("/path/to/directory")`
`std::path::PathBuf`	`path.iter()`	Iterates over the components of a path as **PathBuf** instances	`"/path/to/file".iter()`
`std::env::VarError`	`env::vars().map(|(key, value)| (key, value))`	Maps environment variables to a tuple of key and value	`std::env::vars().map(|(key, value)| (key, value))`
`Option<T>`	`Some(42).iter()`	Behaves like a vector whose length is either 0 (**None**) or 1 (**Some(v)**)	`Some(42).iter()`
`Result<T, E>`	`Ok("success").iter()`	Similar to **Option**, producing **Ok** values	`Ok("success").iter()`

Vec<T, Slice	**v.windows**	Produces every contiguous slice of the given length, from left to right. The windows overlap	**v.windows(5)**
	v.chunks	Produces non-overlapping, contiguous slices of the given length, from left to right	**v.chunks(10)**
	v.chunks_mut	Like chunks, but slices are mutable	**v.chunks_mut(256)**
	v.split	Produces slices separated by elements that match the given predicate	**v.split(|elem| elem > 5)**
	v.rsplitn	Like **split**, but produces slices from right to left with a maximum of 2 slices	**v.rsplitn(2, …)**
String, &str	**s.bytes**	Produces the bytes of the UTF-8 form	**"sample text". bytes()**
	s.chars	Produces the characters represented in UTF-8	**"sample text". chars()**

	s.split_whitespace	Splits the string by whitespace and produces slices of non-space characters	**“split by spaces”.split_whitespace()**
	s.lines	Produces slices of the lines of the string	**“line 1\nline 2\nline 3”.lines()**
	`s.split	Splits the string on a given pattern, producing the slices between matches. Patterns can be characters, strings, or closures	**“item1,item2,item3”.split(‘,’)**
	s.matches-(char::is_alphabetic)	Produces slices matching the given pattern	**“abc123xyz”.matches-(char::is_alphabetic)**
std::collections::HashMap, std::collections::BTreeMap	**map.keys()**	Produces shared references to keys of the map	**your_map.keys()**
	map.values()	Produces shared references to entries’ values	**your_map.values()**
	map.values_mut()	Produces mutable references to entries’ values	**your_map.values_mut()**
std::collections::HashSet, std::collections::BTreeSet	**set1.union(set2)**	Produces shared references to elements of the union of set1 and set2	**set1.union(set2)**

	set1.intersection(set2)	Produces shared references to elements of the intersection of set1 and set2	**set1.intersection(set2)**
std::sync::mpsc::Receiver	**recv.iter()**	Produces values sent from another thread on the corresponding Sender	**recv.iter()**
std::io::Read	**stream.bytes()**	Produces bytes from an I/O stream	**your_io_stream.bytes()**
	stream.chars()	Parses the stream as UTF-8 and produces characters	**your_io_stream.chars()**
	bufstream.lines()	Parses the stream as UTF-8 and produces lines as Strings	**your_buf_stream.lines()**
	bufstream.split(10)	Splits the stream on a given byte and produces inter-byte Vec<u8> buffers	**your_buf_stream.split(10)**
std::fs::ReadDir	**std::fs::read_dir("/my_directory")**	Produces directory entries	**std::fs::read_dir("/my_directory")**
std::net::TcpListener	**listener.incoming()**	Produces incoming network connections	**listener.incoming()**

your_custom_ type	**your_iter_ method()**	Implement your custom iterator for your specific type	`your_custom_type.iter()`

Table 10.1: *Types in Rust's standard library that support iteration*

Iterator Adapter Methods

Rust's standard library offers a wide array of iterator adapter methods that empower us to transform and manipulate iterators, enhancing their power and expressiveness. These adapter methods are valuable tools in functional programming, enabling elegant and efficient data processing. We'll delve into some of the most commonly used iterator adapter methods to comprehend their functionalities and practical applications.

Starting with the **`map`** method, it is a versatile adapter that applies a provided closure to each item produced by an iterator. It then generates a new iterator with the transformed values. This transformation process is performed lazily, meaning the actual computation occurs only when you access the elements. Let's illustrate the **`map`** method with an example:

Listing 10.7 A basic program that demonstrates the map adapter usage.

```
fn main() {
    let numbers = vec![1, 2, 3, 4, 5]; // ①

    let squared: Vec<i32> = numbers.into_iter().map(|x| x * x).col-
lect(); // ②

    println!("{:?}", squared); // ③
}
```

In this code:

① We start by creating a Rust vector named **`"numbers"` `and populate it with integers`** `1`, `2`, `3`, `4`, and `5`. Vectors, as we learned from *Chapter 4*, *Rust Built-In Data Structures*, are dynamic collections in Rust that can store multiple values of the same data type, and in this case, they hold a sequence of integers.

② Next, we convert the **`"numbers"` `vector into an iterator using into_iter`**. The **`map`** method is then applied to each element in the iterator, squaring the integers using a closure **`|x| x * x`**. The squared values are collected into a new vector called "squared". This demonstrates Rust's power in data transformation using iterators and closures, resulting in concise and expressive code.

③ To conclude the code, we print the "squared" vector to the console using the **println!** macro. This step displays the squared values obtained from the previous transformation. Printing the results with **println!** is a common practice in Rust for visualizing and verifying code execution outcomes, aiding in debugging and understanding the program's behavior.

This code illustrates the creation of a vector, the transformation of its elements using Rust's iterator methods, and the display of the squared values.

Another crucial iterator adapter is **filter**, which enables the selective extraction of items from an iterator based on a provided predicate. It constructs a new iterator containing only the elements that satisfy the given condition. The **filter** operation is also performed lazily, ensuring efficient and on-demand computation. Let's examine how **filter** can be used to select even numbers from a range:

Listing 10.8 A basic program that demonstrates the filter adapter usage.

```
fn main() {
    let numbers = 1..=10; // ①

    let evens: Vec<i32> = numbers.into_iter().filter(|x| x % 2 == 0).col-
lect(); // ②

    println!("{:?}", evens); // ③
}

// Output

// [2, 4, 6, 8, 10]
```

① The code begins by defining a range of numbers using Rust's range notation, specifically from 1 to 10 (inclusive). This range represents a sequence of integers that will be the basis for further operations.

② In the subsequent statement, we introduce the **filter** method. This method is a vital iterator adapter in Rust, enabling selective extraction of items based on a given condition. In this case, we use it to selectively extract even numbers from the defined range. The result is a new vector named "**evens**", which exclusively contains the even values from the original range.

③ To wrap up the code, we utilize the **println!** macro to display the contents of the "**evens**" vector in the terminal. This output represents the successful filtering of even numbers from the initial range, demonstrating the effectiveness of the filtering criteria, which is provided as a closure, `|x| x % 2 == 0`. This closure ensures that only elements meeting the condition of being even are included in the output vector.

These are merely a glimpse of the iterator adapter methods available in Rust's standard library. Each of these methods serves a specific purpose, and by combining them, you can create complex and efficient data processing pipelines. Other noteworthy adapter methods such as **collect**, **fold**, **zip**, and **enumerate** offer various ways of transforming, aggregating, and manipulating data within an iterator, enhancing the expressiveness and flexibility of Rust's iterator ecosystem. The key advantage of these adapter methods is that they promote clean, concise, and declarative code, contributing to the readability and maintainability of your Rust programs.

Building Custom Iterators

While Rust's standard library offers a wide range of iterator methods, there may be cases where you need to create custom iterators tailored to your specific needs. Rust makes it straightforward to implement your own iterators by defining a custom struct and implementing the **Iterator** trait for it.

Here's an example where we create a custom iterator for prime numbers called **PrimeGenerator**. Our custom iterator will effectively identify and deliver prime numbers as we request them. The **PrimeGenerator** iterator prime generates numbers on-the-fly and demonstrates how you can create your iterator logic:

Listing 10.9 A basic program that demonstrates building custom iterators.

```
struct PrimeGenerator { // ①
    current: u32,
}

impl Iterator for PrimeGenerator { // ②
    type Item = u32;

    fn next(&mut self) -> Option<Self::Item> {
        loop {
            self.current += 1;
            if is_prime(self.current) {
                return Some(self.current);
```

```
            }
        }
    }
}

fn is_prime(num: u32) -> bool { // ③
    if num <= 1 {
        return false;
    }

    for i in 2..(num / 2 + 1) {
        if num % i == 0 {
            return false;
        }
    }

    true
}

fn main() { // ④
    let prime_sequence = PrimeGenerator { current: 1 }; // ⑤

    for prime in prime_sequence.take(10) {
        println!("{}", prime);
    }
}

// Ouptut

// 2
// 3
// 5
// 7
// 11
// 13
// 17
// 19
// 23
// 29
```

① First, we begin by creating our specialized iterator. This custom iterator, named **PrimeGenerator**, is designed with a specific objective: to dynamically generate prime numbers. As we saw in previous sections, prime numbers hold a distinct quality – they can only be divided without any remainder by 1 and themselves. Our custom iterator is tailored to effectively recognize and generate these prime numbers precisely when they are required.

② Next, we proceed to implement the **Iterator** trait to our **PrimeGenerator** struct. As we saw earlier, this particular trait equips our struct with the capabilities of an iterator, enabling us to use methods like **next()** to fetch the next item in the sequence. In our example, this **next** item generates the next prime number in line.

③ We also need to include a helper function known as **is_prime**. This function serves the purpose of examining whether a given number qualifies as a prime number. This helper function is implemented separately.

④ With the **PrimeGenerator** iterator now complete, it can generate prime numbers one at a time. To start utilizing it, we establish an instance of our custom iterator within the **main** function.

⑤ Lastly, we're ready to set our custom prime number generator into action. In the "main" function, we create an instance of our **PrimeGenerator** iterator and initialize it with an initial value of 1. Subsequently, we employ a **for** loop to extract the first 10 prime numbers and display each of them on the console.

This example serves as a demonstration of how we can create a custom iterator to efficiently generate prime numbers. Our **PrimeGenerator** iterator has the capability to calculate prime numbers on-the-fly, offering flexibility and resource efficiency for various applications. It highlights the power of creating tailored iterators to suit specific data generation needs.

Lazy Evaluation

One of the key advantages of iterators in Rust is lazy evaluation. This means that an iterator doesn't compute and store all its values in memory upfront. Instead, it generates values on-the-fly as you request them. This lazy evaluation makes iterators highly memory-efficient and allows you to work with potentially infinite sequences.

Consider the following code snippet:

Listing 10.10 A basic program that demonstrates the lazy evaluation concept.

```
fn main() {
    let numbers = vec![1, 2, 3, 4, 5]; // ①

    let doubled: Vec<i32> = numbers.iter().map(|x| x * 2).collect(); // ②

    println!("Doubled: {:?}", doubled); // ③
```

}

In this code snippet:

① We begin by creating a vector named **`numbers`** that contains the values **`1`**, **`2`**, **`3`**, **`4`**, and **`5`**.

② Moving forward, we generate a new vector named **`doubled`** through the application of a technique known as "**mapping**". This method is put into action on the **"`numbers`"** vector, where it takes each element and performs a doubling operation. It's worth highlighting that this doubling process doesn't happen instantly for the entire vector. Instead, it takes place one element at a time, precisely when it's needed.

This concept is known as "*lazy evaluation*". It means that the code doesn't compute all the values in one go. Instead, it waits until you ask for the results. In this case, it's only when we call **`collect()`** that the results are calculated and gathered into a new vector, which we've named **`doubled`**.

③ We display the contents of the **`doubled`** vector by printing it to the terminal. This line, **`println!("Doubled: {:?}", doubled);`**, shows the doubled values in the **`doubled`** vector.

This code demonstrates Rust's clever use of lazy evaluation in iterators. It ensures that calculations are performed only when necessary, leading to efficient and memory-conscious code. The **`map`** method is a powerful tool in transforming data, and it shines when working with large datasets where you want to perform operations on each element without loading everything into memory at once.

Advanced Techniques: `flat_map`, `take`, `skip`, and `peekable`

Once you've grasped the basics of iterator adaptation, it's time to dive into more advanced techniques. Let's explore the **`flat_map`**, **`take`**, **`skip`**, and **`peekable`** adapters.

`flat_map`

The **`flat_map`** adapter is your key to managing nested iterators and dealing with collections of collections. It allows you to transform each item into an iterator and then flatten the results into a single sequence. Here's an example that demonstrates the **`flat_map`** adapter:

Listing 10.11 A basic program that demonstrates the flat_map adapter.

```
fn main() {
    let words = vec!["Rust", "is", "awesome"]; // ①

    let letters: Vec<char> = words.iter() // ②
        .flat_map(|&word| word.chars())
        .collect();

    assert_eq!(letters, vec!['R', 'u', 's', 't', 'i', 's', 'a', 'w',
'e', 's', 'o', 'm', 'e']); // ③
}
```

① The code starts with the creation of a Rust vector called **"words"**. This vector is initialized with a sequence of string literals, specifically `"Rust"`, `"is"`, and `"awesome"`. These strings will be the source of further transformation.

② In the subsequent step, we introduce the `flat_map` method, an indispensable iterator adapter within the Rust programming language. It serves a crucial role in flattening nested iterators, making it particularly valuable for handling complex data transformations. In this specific scenario, we utilize `flat_map` to convert a collection of words into a comprehensive collection of individual letters. This transformation unfolds as follows: we initiate the process by utilizing the `iter()` method on the `words` vector, creating an iterator that allows us to traverse its elements systematically. Subsequently, we apply the `flat_map` method, utilizing a closure denoted as `|&word| word.chars()`. This closure effectively disassembles each word into its corresponding characters. The outcome is a newly created vector named `letters`, which contains all the individual characters extracted from the original words.

③ To conclude the code, an `assert_eq!` macro is used to verify that the `letters` vector indeed contains the expected sequence of characters. This assertion ensures that the transformation, which utilized the `flat_map` method, correctly converted the words into their corresponding letters.

This code exemplifies the transformation of a collection of words into a collection of their individual characters using the `flat_map method.`

take and skip

The `take` and `skip` adapters give you control over the number of elements you want to process from your iterator. `take` allows you to consume a specific number of elements from the start, while `skip` enables you to bypass a set number of elements before processing the rest. Here's an example that showcases the use of **take** and **skip** together:

Listing 10.12 A basic program that demonstrates the take and skip adapters.

```
fn main() {
    let numbers = vec![1, 2, 3, 4, 5, 6, 7, 8, 9, 10];

    let selected_numbers: Vec<i32> = numbers.iter() // ①
        .skip(3) // ②③
        .take(4) // ②③
        .cloned() // ④
        .collect();

    assert_eq!(selected_numbers, vec![4, 5, 6, 7]); // ⑤
}
```

① This code excerpt introduces the **take** and **skip** iterator adapters, offering a way to precisely control the number of elements you wish to process from an iterator. With the **take** adapter, you can selectively consume a specific number of elements from the iterator's outset, while the **skip** adapter allows you to escape a predetermined number of elements before processing the subsequent items.

② We employ both the **take** and **skip** adapters. At the outset, we have a vector named **numbers**, containing a series of integers ranging from 1 to 10. The primary objective here is to demonstrate the effective control and manipulation of the desired range of elements you wish to work with.

③ We utilize the **numbers** vector by creating an iterator with the **iter()** method. We first apply the **skip(3)** method, which means we skip the first three elements in the iterator. Following that, we use the **take(4)** method, which allows us to capture the next four elements in the sequence. This combined action precisely controls the range of elements we want to process.

④ After performing the desired operations, we call **.cloned()** to clone the selected elements, creating a new vector called **selected_numbers**. This vector contains the elements we've precisely controlled through the use of **take** and **skip** adapters.

⑤ Finally, we employ the **assert_eq!** macro to validate that **selected_numbers** aligns with the anticipated outcome. In this context, the anticipated outcome corresponds to a vector that includes the integers 4, 5, 6, and 7. This validation step guarantees the code operates as intended and successfully accomplishes the meticulous selection process.

This code serves as a practical example of how the **take** and **skip** adapters can be used together to precisely manage the range of elements you wish to process from an iterator.

peekable

The **peekable** adapter is like a clever trick for your iterators. It lets you look ahead at the next thing in line without actually using it. This can be super handy when you need to decide what to do based on what's coming up next in the sequence. For example, imagine dealing with a big list of items and you want to process them in a special way, but your decision depends on what's coming next. Without **peekable**, you'd have to move through the list to see what's next, which could be wasteful and slow. But with **peekable**, you can take a sneak peek, make smart choices, and keep your code working efficiently. It's like giving your code a little crystal ball to see into the future!

Listing 10.13 A basic program that demonstrates the peekable adapter usage.

```
fn main() {
    let mut numbers = vec![1, 2, 3, 4, 5].into_iter().peekable(); // ①

    if let Some(&next_number) = numbers.peek() { // ②
        println!("The next number is: {}", next_number);
    } else { // ③
        println!("No more numbers to process.");
    }

    let _ = numbers.next(); // ④

    if let Some(&next_number) = numbers.peek() { // ⑤
        println!("The next number is: {}", next_number);
    } else {
        println!("No more numbers to process.");
    }
}

// Output

// The next number is: 1
// The next number is: 2
```

In this code snippet:

① We begin by creating an iterator called **numbers** using the **vec!** macro, which initializes a vector containing integers 1 to 5. We then call **into_iter()** to obtain an iterator over this vector and wrap it with **peekable()**. This creates a **'peekable'** iterator, which allows us to look ahead at the elements in the sequence without consuming them.

② Next, we use a conditional statement to check if there's a value when we 'peek' at the next element using **numbers.peek()**. If there is a value, we print a message indicating what the next number is.

③ In case there are no more elements to process (that is, the iterator is exhausted), we print a different message.

④ After that, we consume the first number in the iterator using **numbers.next()**. This means we move to the next item in the sequence, effectively progressing our position.

⑤ Following the consumption of the first number, we once again **peek** at the next element using **numbers.peek()**, and if there's a value, we print a message indicating the next number. If there are no more elements, we print the corresponding message.

This code snippet illustrates how **peekable** iterators are utilized to make informed decisions based on upcoming data, all while efficiently managing the iterator's position and ensuring that we process the data in the desired manner. It's a clever way to work with iterators in Rust, offering fine-grained control and enhanced expressiveness in your data processing tasks.

By mastering these advanced techniques and combining them with the foundational **map** and **filter** adapters, you gain fine-grained control over your iterators, making your data processing tasks more efficient and expressive.

filter_map, fuse, and flatten

As we delve deeper into the world of iterator adapters, let's explore **filter_map**, **fuse**, and **flatten**, which take your sequence manipulation skills to the next level.

filter_map

The **filter_map** adapter is a powerful tool that combines the capabilities of filtering and mapping in a single step, allowing us to gain precise control over iterators. This adapter permits the application of a custom function to each item in the sequence, enabling the choice of either transforming it into a new item or discarding it altogether. In practical terms, consider a scenario where you have a collection of strings with a mix of numeric and non-numeric data, and your goal is to extract and parse the numeric values while bypassing the invalid entries. The **filter_map** adapter seamlessly handles this task by filtering out non-numeric data and mapping the valid entries to their numeric equivalents in one efficient operation. It streamlines data extraction, ensuring that you obtain the desired information while maintaining code elegance and performance efficiency, making it an invaluable asset in data processing and programming tasks.

Listing 10.14 A basic program that demonstrates the filter_map adapter usage.

```
use std::str::FromStr;

fn main() {
    let text = "The numbers are: 42, 19, invalid, 27, 33";

    let parsed_numbers: Vec<i32> = text
        .split(',') // ①
        .map(str::trim) // ②
        .filter_map(|s| { // ③
            let s = s
                .chars()
                .skip_while(|&c| !c.is_digit(10))
                .collect::<String>();
            if !s.is_empty() { // ④
                i32::from_str(&s).ok() // ⑤
            } else {
                None
            }
        })
        .collect();

    assert_eq!(parsed_numbers, vec![42, 19, 27, 33]);
}
```

In this Rust code snippet, our goal is to work with a text string that contains a mix of numbers and non-numeric characters and extract and parse the valid numbers while filtering out the invalid ones. To accomplish this, we've implemented a series of string manipulation techniques and made use of the **filter_map** adapter, which proves to be a clever tool for this data processing task.

① We begin by splitting the input text using commas as delimiters with **.split(',')**. This results in a sequence of substrings, each representing a portion of the original text.

② Subsequently, we apply the `.map(str::trim)` operation to each of these substrings. This means we're trimming any leading or trailing whitespace from each substring, ensuring that we're working with clean data.

③ The clever part happens in the `filter_map` operation. We're creating an anonymous function (a closure) that performs the following steps:

- First, we utilize `.chars()` to turn the trimmed substring into an iterator over its individual characters.
- Then, we use `.skip_while(|&c| !c.is_digit(10))` to skip characters until we find the first digit. This helps us locate the start of a potential number.
- We collect the remaining characters into a `String`.

④ We then check if the collected string is not empty. This check ensures that we only proceed with non-empty strings, as empty strings would not represent valid numbers.

⑤ When the string we've collected isn't empty, we attempt to transform it into an `i32` integer using the `i32::from_str(&s).ok()` method. Here's how it works: this method tries to convert the string `s` into an `i32`. If the conversion is successful, it returns `Some(parsed_number)` with the parsed integer; however, if the conversion fails, it gracefully returns `None`.

The result is a `Vec<i32>` called `parsed_numbers` containing the successfully parsed and filtered values. In this specific code, the `assert_eq!` statement confirms that the `parsed_numbers` vector indeed contains the expected numbers, namely `[42, 19, 27, 33]`. The `filter_map` adapter, in combination with the other string manipulation techniques, proves to be a clever and efficient way to extract and process valid numerical data from a text string while ignoring invalid entries.

fuse

The `fuse` adapter serves as a fail-safe mechanism when working with iterators, preventing unexpected behavior that can occur when you continue to use an iterator after it has reached its end. When you apply `fuse` to an iterator, you effectively lock it into a state where it will always return `None` once it has reached the end of its elements, regardless of how you try to use it. This capability proves invaluable in situations where you need to ensure that your code behaves predictably and consistently, preventing any unintended consequences.

Imagine you have an iterator that goes through a sequence of elements, and you're working on a task that relies on knowing when the iterator is exhausted.

Without the **fuse** adapter, the iterator might not always behave as expected, potentially leading to errors or unpredictable outcomes. By applying **fuse**, you ensure that the iterator will reliably signal its end, making your code more robust and easier to reason about. It's like having a fail-safe mechanism that keeps your code on the right track. Here's a simple example:

Listing 10.15 A basic program that demonstrates the fuse adapter usage.

```
struct Unpredictable(bool);

impl Iterator for Unpredictable {
    type Item = &'static str;

    fn next(&mut self) -> Option<Self::Item> {
        if self.0 {
            self.0 = false;
            Some("totally the last item")
        } else {
            self.0 = true;
            None
        }
    }
}

fn main() {
    let mut unpredictable = Unpredictable(true);
    assert_eq!(unpredictable.next(), Some("totally the last item"));
    assert_eq!(unpredictable.next(), None);
    assert_eq!(unpredictable.next(), Some("totally the last item"));

    let mut reliable = Unpredictable(true).fuse();
    assert_eq!(reliable.next(), Some("totally the last item"));
    assert_eq!(reliable.next(), None);
    assert_eq!(reliable.next(), None);
}
```

In this code snippet, we have an iterator, **Unpredictable**, that behaves unpredictably after producing its first item. When we use **fuse**, it ensures that the iterator consistently returns **None** after the first termination.

flatten

The **flatten** adapter is a versatile and invaluable component of Rust's iterator ecosystem, designed to address the challenges associated when working with nested sequences effectively. It comes into its own when dealing with iterators that produce sequences of their own, which often introduce complexity due to the nesting of data structures. The core function of **flatten** is to simplify the process by unwrapping these nested sequences, resulting in a coherent, linear sequence of elements.

To comprehend the significance of the **flatten** adapter, let's consider a scenario where you need to consolidate various sequences of cities, possibly organized by geographical regions or other criteria, into a unified, comprehensive list of all cities. Without the **flatten** adapter, this task might entail complex and error-prone code, involving nested loops and conditional logic. However, **flatten** streamlines this operation significantly, offering a cleaner, more efficient, and concise solution. It gracefully merges the city sequences, resulting in a flat list that is much more manageable, enhances code readability, and simplifies data processing. Here's an example demonstrating how to merge several sequences of cities into a single list:

Listing 10.16 A basic program that demonstrates the flatten adapter usage.

```
use std::collections::HashMap;

fn main() {
    // Create a data structure representing students and their courses
    let mut student_courses = HashMap::new();
    student_courses.insert("Alice", vec!["Math", "Physics"]);
    student_courses.insert("Bob", vec!["Computer Science", "Chemistry"]);
    student_courses.insert("Charlie", vec!["Physics", "Biology"]);

    // Calculate the number of students enrolled in each course
    let course_enrollment: HashMap<&str, usize> = student_courses
        .values() // Extract the course lists
        .flatten() // Flatten the nested lists into a single iterator of
course references
        .fold(HashMap::new(), |mut enrollment, course| {
            *enrollment.entry(course).or_insert(0) += 1;
            enrollment
        });

    // Print the course enrollment
    for (course, count) in &course_enrollment {
        println!("Course: {}, Students Enrolled: {}", course, count);
    }
}
```

```
// Output

// Course: Biology, Students Enrolled: 1
// Course: Physics, Students Enrolled: 2
// Course: Computer Science, Students Enrolled: 1
// Course: Math, Students Enrolled: 1
// Course: Chemistry, Students Enrolled: 1
```

In this code example, think of it as managing a list of students and the courses they are attending, similar to a school schedule. The idea is to figure out the number of students in each course, such as how many students are in math, how many in physics, and so on. We use some special tools to make this task easier, similar to using the right tools for solving a puzzle. These tools help us organize the information and count the students in each course, so we can then show the results neatly, like saying, "*There are 20 students in Math and 15 in Physics*". It's a way to make handling and understanding this data more straightforward.

We start by extracting the course lists using **values()**. Next, we flatten the nested lists into a single iterator of course references with **flatten()**. We use **fold()** to accumulate the enrollment data in a new HashMap. Within the fold closure, we update the count for each course in the **HashMap**.

Finally, we print the course enrollment, displaying the course name along with the number of students enrolled in each course. This example demonstrates the power of Rust's iterator adapters in managing and transforming complex data structures, providing precise control over data processing, and making the code more expressive and efficient.

The initial sections of this chapter have taken us through the world of iterator adapters, from the foundational **map** and **filter** to advanced techniques like **flat_map**, **take**, **skip**, **peekable**, **filter_map**, **fuse**, and **flatten**. These adapters empower us to manipulate our sequences with precision, making Rust's iterators a powerful tool for crafting and transforming data sequences. Now, it is time to explore the world of closures.

The Magic of Closures

In Rust, closures are like special functions that can grab and use variables from their surroundings. They're super useful, especially when working with lists of data. Closures make your code neat and reusable, and they play a big role in how you work with collections of information, letting you do all sorts of custom stuff to your data, which makes your code work better and stay easy to understand.

Closure Syntax

Rust offers us a trio of different syntax options for defining closures, allowing for versatile and efficient code construction. The first syntax, represented as `|| { /\* code here \*/ }`, caters to scenarios where a closure necessitates no input arguments. This minimalistic approach is ideal for crafting concise, argumentless closures, making it a handy tool in situations that call for simple and straightforward implementations.

The second syntax, `|x| { /\* code here \*/ }`, is geared towards closures that take a single argument. This syntax is ideal when you need to pass one specific parameter to your closure. It allows you to specify the input argument clearly and concisely, making your code more expressive and self-documenting.

Lastly, the third syntax, `|x, y| { /\* code here \*/ }`, offers the flexibility of accepting multiple arguments within a closure. This versatility is invaluable for cases where complex interactions between multiple variables or parameters are essential. By allowing closures to take multiple arguments, Rust empowers us to create complex and comprehensive solutions.

The selection of the appropriate closure syntax is based on the specific requirements of the task at hand. Rust's comprehensive range of closure syntaxes grants you the freedom to write code that not only meets your project's demands but also enhances the readability and efficiency of your programs. This adaptability is a testament to Rust's commitment to providing us with the tools we need to create robust, well-structured, and maintainable code.

Variable Capture in Closures

In Rust, closures can capture variables from their surrounding environment, and this capture can be accomplished either by reference (borrowing) or by value (moving), depending on the closure's intended behavior and the usage requirements of the variables involved. Capturing by reference allows for shared access to the variable, making it suitable for read-only operations and facilitating concurrent access, while capturing by value transfers ownership, enabling modifications within the closure but preventing further use in the outer scope. This flexible approach to variable capture is a fundamental aspect of Rust's design, providing us with ways to balance performance and memory safety, and making it a preferred choice for systems programming where both are critical.

Borrowing Variables

When a closure borrows a variable, it keeps a reference to that variable without taking ownership. This allows the closure to read and use the variable without consuming it. Let's explore an example:

Listing 10.17 A basic program that demonstrates borrowing variables within closures.

```
fn main() {
    let multiplier = 5; // ①
    let numbers = vec![1, 2, 3, 4, 5]; // ①

    let multiplied: Vec<i32> = numbers.iter().map(|x| x * multiplier).
collect(); //②

    println!("Multiplied: {:?}", multiplied); // ③
}

// Output

// Multiplied: [5, 10, 15, 20, 25]
```

① The program starts by initializing two variables: **multiplier** and **numbers**. The **multiplier** variable is set to the value **5**, while the **numbers** variable is created as a vector containing the integers **1, 2, 3, 4, 5**.

② Subsequently, the code introduces a new variable called **multiplied**, which is designed to store the outcome of an operation applied to the **numbers** vector. Here's what takes place within this line:

- **numbers.iter()**: This converts the **numbers** vector into an iterator. Iterators facilitate the step-by-step traversal of elements within a collection.
- **.map(|x| x * multiplier)**: The **map** method is invoked on the iterator, accompanied by a closure. For each element **x** within the iterator, the closure performs a multiplication operation by multiplying **x** with the **multiplier** value, which is set at **5**. This operation results in the creation of a new iterator where the elements are the product of this multiplication.
- **.collect()**: Finally, the **collect** method is utilized to gather the elements from the iterator into a new vector. The end result of this entire expression is a vector containing the elements sourced from the **numbers** vector, with each element being the result of multiplication by **5**.

③ The last segment of the code is focused on the display of the **multiplied** vector. To achieve this, the **println!** macro is employed to format and print the contents of the **multiplied** vector.

The program's output showcases the elements contained within the **multiplied** vector. Each of these elements corresponds to the original numbers derived from the **numbers** vector, with each number having been multiplied by the **multiplier** value, which is set to **5**. This code effectively illustrates how Rust can leverage iterators and closures to apply a specific operation to each element within a collection; in this case, the multiplication of elements by a constant value.

Moving Variables

Closures can also take full ownership of variables, effectively moving them into the closure's scope. This is useful when you want to transfer ownership of a variable to the closure. Let's illustrate this with an example:

In Rust, closures provide the flexibility to either borrow variables by reference or take full ownership of them, effectively moving the variables into the closure's scope. This allows you to control how variables are accessed and manipulated within the closure. Let's delve into an example that illustrates the concept:

Listing 10.18 A basic program that demonstrates ownership within closures.

```
fn main() {
    let message = "Hello, Rust!".to_string(); // ①

    let greet = || { // ②
        let message = message;
        println!("{}", message);
    };

    greet(); // ③

    // greet(); // ④
}

// Output

// Hello, Rust!
```

In this code:

① We start by creating a variable called **`message`**, which holds the string "**`Hello, Rust!`**" as a String type.

② We then define a closure named **`greet`** using the **`||`** syntax, capturing the **`message`** variable within the closure's scope. In this case, capturing means taking full ownership of **`message`** and moving it into the closure. This ownership transfer means that **`message`** can no longer be accessed outside of the closure's scope.

③ When we call the **`greet`** closure using **`greet()`**, it successfully prints the message "Hello, Rust!" to the terminal, as it explicitly consumes the variable within its scope.

④ However, if we attempt to call the closure a second time by uncommenting the line **`greet();`**, we encounter a compilation error. This error is due to the fact that **`message`** has already been moved into the closure, and it's no longer accessible in the outer scope. The error message, "Use of moved value: **`message`**", highlights this behavior.

This example demonstrates the difference between borrowing and moving variables within closures. By moving a variable into a closure, you explicitly transfer ownership, which can be useful for scenarios where you want to ensure exclusive access to a variable within the closure, but it also means the variable is no longer accessible outside of the closure's scope.

Closures and `Fn`, `FnMut`, `FnOnce` Traits

In Rust, closures fall into three categories based on how they capture variables: **`Fn`**, **`FnMut`**, and **`FnOnce`**. These traits determine the closure's ability to access and modify captured variables:

- **`Fn`**: Closures that capture variables immutably, allowing read-only access to the captured data.
- **`FnMut`**: Closures that capture variables mutably, enabling both read and write access to the captured data.
- **`FnOnce`**: Closures that consume variables, taking complete ownership of the captured data and preventing any further use of those variables.

To specify the desired trait for a closure, you can use the **`move`** keyword in combination with the **`Fn`**, **`FnMut`**, and **`FnOnce`** traits, as needed.

Let's explore these traits through practical examples.

Fn Closures

In Rust, closures provide flexible ways to capture variables from their surrounding scope. In the following example, we create a closure that captures a variable immutably and increments its value:

Listing 10.19 A basic program that demonstrates Fn closures usage.

```
fn main() {
    let counter = 0; // ①

    let print_counter = || { // ②
        println!("Counter: {}", counter); // ③
    };

    print_counter(); // ④

    // counter += 1; // ⑤
}
// Output

// Counter: 0
```

In this example:

① We declare the **counter** variable as immutable by not using the **mut** keyword. This means that **counter** cannot be modified once it's assigned a value.

② We create a closure named **print_counter** that captures the **counter** variable as an immutable reference. This means the closure can read the value of **counter**, but it cannot modify it.

③ Inside the closure, we use **println!** to print the value of **counter**.

④ When we call the **print_counter** closure, it successfully reads and prints the value of **counter**.

⑤ If we attempt to modify the **counter** variable, as shown in the commented-out line, it will result in a compilation error because the variable is borrowed as immutable, and Rust enforces that immutably borrowed variables cannot be modified while they are borrowed.

The important point to note in this code is that the closure **print_counter** captures the **counter** variable immutably, which means it can read the value of "**counter**", but it cannot modify it directly within the closure. Despite this immutability, the closure can access and print the updated value of "**counter**" after each call.

This example demonstrates how closures can capture variables from their enclosing scope and interact with them, respecting Rust's ownership and borrowing rules. In this case, the variable **counter** is borrowed immutably by the closure, allowing it to read the variable's value.

FnMut Closures

In this example, we define a closure that captures a variable mutably, enabling us to modify the captured data:

Listing 10.20 A basic program that demonstrates FnMut closures usage.

```
fn main() {
    let mut counter = 0; // ①
    let mut increment = || { // ②
        counter += 1; // ③
        println!("Counter: {}", counter); // ④
    };

    increment(); // ⑤
    increment(); // ⑥
}

// Output

// Counter: 1
// Counter: 2
```

In this code:

① We begin by declaring a mutable variable named **counter** and initializing it with the value **0**. The **mut** keyword signifies that this variable can be modified.

② Subsequently, we define a closure called **increment** using the **||** syntax, which represents a closure that takes no arguments. Within this closure:

③ We increment the "**counter**" variable by 1 using **counter += 1**. This operation modifies the value of "**counter**".

④ We then use **println!** to print the updated value of "**counter**", displaying it as **"Counter: {value}"**.

⑤ We call the **increment** closure for the first time using **increment()**. This results in the closure incrementing the "counter" and printing the updated value.

⑥ We call the **increment** closure a second time with **increment()**, which once again increments the "counter" and displays the updated value.

The closure **increment** captures the **counter** variable mutably, granting both read and write access to the captured data. Consequently, we can increment the **counter** variable within the closure, and the changes are reflected outside the closure as well.

FnOnce Closures

FnOnce closures in Rust are a type of closures that have the unique ability to consume variables, taking full ownership of the captured variables. This means that when a FnOnce closure captures a variable, that variable cannot be used anywhere else in the code after the closure has been called. This consumption behavior is demonstrated in the following Rust code snippet:

Listing 10.21 A basic program that demonstrates FnOnce closures usage.

```
fn main() {
    let numbers = vec![1, 2, 3, 4, 5]; // ①
    let consume_numbers = || { // ②
        let numbers = numbers; // ③
        let sum: i32 = numbers.iter().sum(); // ④
        println!("Sum: {}", sum); // ⑤
    };

    consume_numbers(); // ⑥
    // consume_numbers(); // ⑦
}
```

In this code:

①We begin by defining a **numbers** variable and assigning it a **Vec** that contains a list of integers from 1 to 5. This **Vec** is stored in memory and holds ownership of its elements.

② Next, we define a closure named **consume_numbers** using Rust's closure syntax, denoted by **||**. This closure does not take any arguments and does not explicitly return a value.

③ Inside the closure, we encounter a line that appears to create a new variable named **numbers**. However, what's happening here is not the creation of a new variable but the shadowing of the outer **numbers** variable. The closure consumes and takes ownership of the **numbers** variable from the outer scope. This means the original **numbers** variable outside the closure is no longer accessible, and any attempt to use it after this point will result in a compilation error.

④ Continuing inside the closure, the **numbers** variable is used to create an iterator, and the **sum** of the elements in the **Vec** is calculated and stored in a new variable named **sum**. This variable **sum** is a local variable within the closure's scope.

⑤ After calculating the sum, the closure prints the result to the terminal, displaying the total sum of the elements in the captured **Vec**.

⑥ We then call the **consume_numbers** closure, which is a valid operation. The closure has consumed the **numbers** variable and can access it as long as it remains within the closure's scope.

⑦ If we uncomment the second call to **consume_numbers** and attempt to invoke the closure again, a compilation error occurs. This is because the **numbers** variable has been moved into the closure during the first call, and it cannot be used again in the outer scope. This error demonstrates the concept of variable ownership in Rust and the behavior of FnOnce closures, which fully consume the variables they capture.

FnOnce closures in Rust allow for the consumption of variables, taking full ownership of those variables and preventing them from being used elsewhere in the code. This can be a powerful feature for ensuring safe and predictable behavior in Rust programs, as it enforces strict rules on how variables are accessed and modified within closures.

These traits provide a way to specify the behavior of closures, allowing you to control variable access and modification based on your needs.

Iterators for Efficient Data Processing

Iterators in Rust provide a powerful mechanism for efficiently processing data, and in this section, we'll dive deep into their usage to explore how to perform various data operations effectively. We will investigate different iterator methods and techniques for filtering, mapping, and collecting data, along with their applications. Furthermore, we will explore how iterators can be used to work with infinite sequences and perform advanced operations on collections, enhancing the expressiveness and efficiency of Rust code.

Accumulating Data with fold

The **fold** method, often referred to as **reduce** in other programming languages like Python (*https://docs.python.org/3/library/functools.html?highlight=reduce#functools.reduce*), allows you to accumulate values from an iterator into a single result. You provide an initial value and a closure that specifies how to combine the current accumulated value with the next element.

Listing 10.22 A basic program that demonstrates the fold method usage.

```
fn main() {
    let numbers = vec![1, 2, 3, 4, 5]; // ①

    let sum: i32 = numbers.iter().fold(0, |acc, x| acc + x); // ②

    println!("Sum: {}", sum); // ③
}

// Output

// Sum: 15
```

In this code snippet:

① We start by creating a **numbers** variable and assigning it a **Vec** containing a sequence of integers, namely, 1, 2, 3, 4, and 5. This **Vec** is essentially an iterable collection in memory.

② Moving forward, we introduce the **sum** variable of type **i32**. To calculate the sum of all elements within the **numbers** vector efficiently, we make use of the **fold** method. This method requires two primary arguments: the initial value for accumulation (in this case, 0), and a closure that specifies how each element should be combined with the accumulated result. This closure, represented as **|acc, x| acc + x**, instructs the iterator to add each element (**x**) to the current accumulated sum (**acc**). As the iterator iterates through the elements, it applies this closure repeatedly, updating the accumulated sum with each element.

③ Subsequently, we utilize the **println!** macro to display the final result. The sum of all elements in the **numbers** vector, calculated using the **fold** method, is printed to the terminal. This showcases a compact and efficient way to perform aggregation operations on collections in Rust, thanks to the **fold** method.

Accumulation operations are a common necessity in data processing, and the **fold** method offers an elegant and efficient solution for such tasks. It allows for the gradual accumulation of values while providing control and flexibility through the closure, ensuring that you can achieve the desired result with minimal code. This, in turn, promotes readable and expressive Rust code, making data processing tasks more approachable and maintainable.

Chaining Iterators with chain

Chaining iterators with the **chain** method is a versatile approach in Rust, allowing you to seamlessly concatenate two iterators, effectively creating a single, unified sequence for further processing. This is especially useful when you have multiple sources of data that you want to process as a cohesive whole. Let's break down the provided Rust code to understand how this technique works and its significance.

Listing 10.23 A basic program that demonstrates the chain method usage.

```
fn main() {
    let numbers1 = vec![1, 2, 3]; // ①
    let numbers2 = vec![4, 5, 6]; // ①

    let combined: Vec<i32> = numbers1 // ②
        .iter()
        .chain(numbers2.iter())
        .map(|x| x * 2) // ③
        .collect(); // ④

    println!("Combined and doubled: {:?}", combined); // ⑤
}

// Output

// Combined and doubled: [2, 4, 6, 8, 10, 12]
```

① The code begins by defining two **Vec** variables, namely **numbers1** and **numbers2**, each containing sequences of integers. **numbers1** holds the values [1, 2, 3], and **numbers2** contains the values [4, 5, 6]. These vectors represent iterable collections of data in memory.

② We proceed by creating a new variable called **combined**, which is explicitly typed as a **Vec<i32**. This variable will store the results of our combined and processed sequence. To achieve this, we employ the **chain** method, which allows us to concatenate the iterators generated from **numbers1** and **numbers2**. By chaining these iterators together, we create a unified sequence that includes

elements from both `numbers1` and `numbers2`. This is a powerful mechanism for treating data from different sources as if they were part of a single sequence.

③ Continuing with the data processing, we use the `map` method to apply a transformation to each element in the combined sequence. The transformation is specified within the closure, denoted as `|x| x * 2`. This closure instructs the iterator to double each element it encounters, effectively multiplying every value in the combined sequence by 2.

④ Finally, we utilize the `collect` method to gather the processed elements into a new `Vec<i32`, which is then stored in the `combined` variable. This action creates a vector containing the doubled values resulting from the transformation applied through the `map` method.

⑤ To conclude, we use the `println!` macro to display the content of the `combined` vector. The output will show the elements in the sequence after they have been doubled. This demonstrates the efficiency and elegance of chaining iterators in Rust, allowing for the smooth and efficient processing of data from multiple sources as if they were a single stream.

Chaining iterators and employing iterator methods like `map` open up powerful possibilities for combining and processing data from diverse origins. Rust's iterator ecosystem, with its composable and functional nature, offers an elegant way to achieve such operations, promoting code readability, maintainability, and efficiency in data processing tasks.

Applying Iterators and Closures to Practical Examples

In this section, we'll explore the practical utility of iterators and closures in Rust through various real-world use cases. These powerful language features enhance code efficiency, readability, and expressiveness. We will take a deep dive into each example, providing comprehensive explanations and context for how iterators and closures contribute to code improvement.

Use Case 1: Text Analysis

Text analysis plays a pivotal role in fields like natural language processing and data mining, often necessitating the computation of word frequencies within a text document. Rust's iterators and closures offer an elegant solution for this task. The following code snippet dissects the process step-by-step:

Listing 10.24 A basic program that demonstrates closures usage in text analysis.

```
use std::collections::HashMap;

fn main() {
    let text = "Rust is a language that makes it easy to learn Rust and
Rust programming is fun when you learn Rust"; // ①

    let word_freq: HashMap<String, u32> = text // ②
        .split_whitespace() // ③
        .map(|word| word.to_lowercase()) // ④
        .filter(|word| !word.is_empty()) // ⑤
        .fold(HashMap::new(), |mut map, word| { // ⑥
            *map.entry(word.to_string()).or_insert(0) += 1;
            map
        });

    println!("Word Frequencies: {:?}", word_freq); // ⑦
}

// Output

// Word Frequencies: {"language": 1, "when": 1, "that": 1, "you": 1,
"fun": 1, "it": 1, "easy": 1, "makes": 1, "and": 1, "rust": 4, "is": 2,
"a": 1, "to": 1, "learn": 2, "programming": 1}
```

In this Rust code:

① We start by defining a string **text** containing a sentence about Rust programming. This text will be analyzed to calculate word frequencies.

② We create a **word_freq** variable as a **HashMap** that will store the word frequencies. The key will be a string (representing a word), and the value will be a 32-bit unsigned integer (representing the frequency).

③ To break down the text into individual words, we use the **split_whitespace()** method. This method returns an iterator over the words in the text, splitting it by whitespace characters like spaces and tabs.

④ The **map()** method is applied to transform each word to lowercase using a closure. This step ensures that the analysis is case-insensitive and prevents duplicate entries for the same word with different letter cases.

⑤ The **filter()** method is used with a closure to eliminate any empty words. This filtering step improves the quality of the word frequency analysis by excluding non-word characters or extra spaces.

⑥ Finally, we utilize the **`fold()`** method to accumulate the word frequencies within a **`HashMap`**. The closure provided to **`fold()`** takes the current **`HashMap`** (**`map`**) and each word, increments its frequency in the **`HashMap`**, and returns the updated **`HashMap`**. The **`or_insert()`** method is used to insert a new key-value pair if the word is not already present in the **`HashMap`**.

⑦ The code concludes by printing the resulting **`word_freq`** HashMap, displaying the word frequencies for the input text.

This code demonstrates how Rust's iterators and closures can be applied to perform efficient text analysis, making it case-insensitive, removing non-word characters, and accumulating word frequencies using a clear and expressive approach.

Use Case 2: Image Processing

Image processing tasks often involve pixel-level operations, which range from basic transformations to intricate filters. In this particular use case, our objective is to double the RGB (Red, Green, Blue) values of pixels within an image. The following code snippet exemplifies how iterators and closures in Rust can simplify this task efficiently and elegantly:

Listing 10.25 A basic program that demonstrates closures usage in image processing.

```
#[derive(Debug)]
struct Pixel { // ①
    red: u8,
    green: u8,
    blue: u8,
}

fn main() {
    let mut image: Vec<Pixel> = vec![ // ②
        Pixel {
            red: 100,
            green: 50,
            blue: 25,
        },
        Pixel {
            red: 200,
            green: 100,
            blue: 50,
        },
```

```
        // ... more pixels
    ];

    image.iter_mut().for_each(|pixel| { // ③
        pixel.red = pixel.red.wrapping_mul(2); // ④
        pixel.green = pixel.green.wrapping_mul(2); // ④
        pixel.blue = pixel.blue.wrapping_mul(2); // ④
    });

    println!("Image after processing: {:?}", image); // ⑤
}

// Output

// Image after processing: [Pixel { red: 200, green: 100, blue: 50 },
Pixel { red: 144, green: 200, blue: 100 }]
```

In this code:

① We begin by defining a **Pixel** struct that represents individual pixels in the image. Each pixel is characterized by separate red, green, and blue components.

② The image itself is represented as a vector of **Pixel** instances, held within the **image** variable. Each **Pixel** instance specifies the initial RGB values for the respective pixel.

③ To manipulate the pixel data in place, we utilize the **iter_mut()** method, which provides a mutable iterator over the **image** vector. This iterator allows us to modify the pixel values directly.

④ Within the closure provided to the **for_each()** method, we double the values of the red, green, and blue components for each pixel. This is achieved through the **wrapping_mul()** method, which not only multiplies the values but also gracefully handles any potential overflow that might occur due to the doubling operation.

⑤ The code concludes by printing the modified **image** vector, displaying the updated RGB values for each pixel after the processing.

In this use case, the code demonstrates how Rust's iterators and closures can efficiently handle pixel-level transformations in image processing. It's a simplified example, but in practical image processing scenarios, more complex operations and filters would be applied. Rust's iterators and closures enable you to tackle such complexities while maintaining code readability and clarity.

Use Case 3: Data Filtering and Transformation

Working with product datasets is a common task in e-commerce and inventory management applications. This use case explores how iterators and closures in Rust can be effectively employed to handle data filtering and transformation tasks.

Listing 10.26 A basic program that demonstrates closures usage in data manipulation.

```
#[allow(dead_code)]

#[derive(Debug)]
struct Product { // ①
    name: String,
    price: f64,
    in_stock: bool,
}

fn main() {
    let products = vec![
        Product {
            name: String::from("Widget A"),
            price: 10.0,
            in_stock: true,
        },
        Product {
            name: String::from("Widget B"),
            price: 15.0,
            in_stock: false,
        },
        // ... more products
    ];

    let discount = 0.2; // ②

    let discounted_products: Vec<Product> = products // ③
        .into_iter() // ④
        .filter(|product| product.in_stock) // ⑤
        .map(|mut product| { // ⑥
            product.price -= product.price * discount;
            product
        })
        .collect(); // ⑦
```

```
    println!("Discounted Products: {:?}", discounted_products); // ⑧
}

// Output

// Discounted Products: [Product { name: "Widget A", price: 8.0, in_
stock: true }]
```

① The code begins by defining a **Product** struct to represent individual products, each characterized by attributes such as name, price, and in-stock status. The product data is stored in a vector called **products**, which represents the available items for sale.

② To apply a discount to products in stock, a discount percentage is defined.

③ A new vector, **discounted_products**, is created to store the products that will be discounted. This vector will contain the modified products after the transformation.

④ We use the **into_iter()** method to obtain an iterator that takes ownership of the **products** vector. This is done because we want to modify the product prices in place, and using **into_iter()** allows us to move out of the vector.

⑤ The **filter()** method is applied with a closure that checks if a product is in stock. This method filters and retains only the products with **in_stock** set to **true**.

⑥ The **map()** method is used with a closure to adjust the price of each product by applying the discount. The **map()** method transforms each product by calculating the new discounted price.

⑦ The end result is a new vector, **discounted_products**, which contains the modified products. This vector represents the products after applying the discount.

⑧ The code concludes by printing the **discounted_products** vector, displaying the modified products with the applied discounts.

This use case demonstrates how closures within iterators can efficiently handle data filtering and transformation tasks in Rust. While this example is simplified, in real-world applications, data filtering and transformation tasks can involve more complex operations, and Rust's iterators and closures are powerful tools for such scenarios.

Use Case 4: Processing Sensor Data

Processing sensor data is a common requirement in various domains, from the Internet of Things (IoT) to scientific research. It frequently involves analyzing data to identify trends or anomalies. In this use case, we explore how iterators and closures in Rust can be harnessed effectively for processing sensor data.

Listing 10.27 A basic program that demonstrates closures usage in data processing.

```
#[allow(dead_code)]

#[derive(Debug)]
struct SensorReading { // ①
    timestamp: u64,
    value: f64,
}

fn main() {
    let sensor_data = vec![ // ②
        SensorReading {
            timestamp: 1,
            value: 20.0,
        },
        SensorReading {
            timestamp: 2,
            value: 22.0,
        },
        SensorReading {
            timestamp: 3,
            value: 23.0,
        },
        // ... more readings
    ];

    let threshold = 22.0; // ③

    let anomalies: Vec<&SensorReading> = sensor_data
        .iter() // ④
        .filter(|&reading| reading.value > threshold) // ⑤
        .collect(); // ⑥

    println!("Anomalous Readings: {:?}", anomalies); // ⑦
}
```

```
// Output

// Anomalous Readings: [SensorReading { timestamp: 3, value: 23.0 }]
```

① We start by defining a **SensorReading** struct, designed to represent individual sensor readings. Each reading includes a timestamp (as an unsigned 64-bit integer) and a value (as a floating-point number, **f64**). This struct enables us to model and process sensor data effectively.

② The **sensor_data** vector is created to store a collection of **SensorReading** instances, mimicking actual sensor data readings. In this scenario, it's important to note that the readings represent some form of data that the sensor is measuring, such as temperature, pressure, or any other measurable quantity.

③ A threshold value (**threshold**) is established to identify anomalous readings in the sensor data. In this example, any reading with a value greater than this threshold is considered an anomaly.

④ Rust's iterators and closures are employed to filter the sensor data efficiently. The **iter()** method is utilized to obtain an iterator over the **sensor_data** vector. This iterator allows us to traverse the readings while keeping the original data intact.

⑤ Within the **filter()** method, a closure is applied to each reading, checking whether the reading's value exceeds the specified threshold. The **filter()** method retains the readings that meet this condition, effectively filtering out anomalies.

⑥ The outcome of this processing is a new vector called **anomalies**. This vector contains references to the **SensorReading** instances that have values exceeding the threshold.

⑦ The code concludes by printing the **anomalies** vector, providing insight into the readings that are identified as anomalous. While the output in this simplified example includes only one anomalous reading, real-world sensor data analysis often involves more complex algorithms and criteria for detecting anomalies.

This use case serves as an illustration of how Rust's iterators and closures can efficiently process sensor data, facilitating the identification of anomalies or trends. In practical sensor data analysis, these language features can be applied to uncover valuable insights and patterns in a wide range of domains, from environmental monitoring to industrial quality control.

Use Case 5: Financial Calculations

Financial applications often entail complex computations and data transformations, particularly when dealing with tasks like tracking account balances based on a series of financial transactions. In this use case, we delve into how iterators and closures in Rust can be leveraged to perform financial calculations with efficiency and clarity.

Listing 10.28 A basic program that demonstrates closures usage in finance.

```
#[derive(Debug)]
struct Transaction { // ①
    amount: f64,
    transaction_type: String,
}

fn main() {
    let transactions = vec![ // ②
        Transaction {
            amount: 100.0,
            transaction_type: String::from("Deposit"),
        },
        Transaction {
            amount: -50.0,
            transaction_type: String::from("Withdrawal"),
        },
        // ... more transactions
    ];

    let balance = transactions.iter().fold(0.0, |acc, transaction| { //
③⑤
        if transaction.transaction_type == "Deposit" {
            acc + transaction.amount // ④
        } else {
            acc - transaction.amount
        }
    });

    println!("Final Balance: {:?}", balance); // ⑥
}
```

```
// Ouptut

// Final Balance: 150.0
```

① The code starts by defining a **Transaction** struct, which serves to represent individual financial transactions. Each transaction carries an amount, represented as a floating-point number (**f64**), and a transaction type denoted as a string.

② An array, **transactions**, aggregates a collection of financial transactions, which can encompass deposits, withdrawals, or various financial operations.

③ To calculate the final balance based on these financial transactions, the code leverages Rust's iterators and closures. Specifically, it utilizes the **fold()** method, a suitable tool for accumulating values through an iterative process.

④ Within the **fold()** method, an initial accumulator, **acc**, is set to 0.0. This accumulator acts as a running sum of the balance as we iterate through the transactions.

⑤ The closure provided to **fold()** is responsible for inspecting the transaction type for each individual transaction. If the transaction type is "Deposit", the amount is added to the accumulator (**acc**); On the other hand, if the transaction type is "Withdrawal", the amount is subtracted from the accumulator. This conditional logic ensures the determination of the final balance based on the series of transactions.

⑥ The outcome is the final balance, which is subsequently printed to the console. This use case exemplifies how closures integrated within iterators facilitate the effective handling of complex financial operations, including conditional calculations.

In real financial applications, additional complexities such as interest rates, fees, and currency conversions may introduce further intricacies to the calculations. However, Rust's iterators and closures remain versatile and readable tools, well-suited to manage a diverse array of financial scenarios with efficiency and precision.

Use Case 6: Sorting

Closures in Rust offer a powerful tool for sorting data, making it a versatile solution for numerous use cases. In this specific scenario, we assume you possess a collection of custom Product structs and intend to sort them in ascending order based on their prices.

Listing 10.29 A basic program that demonstrates closures usage in sorting.

```
struct Product { // ①
    name: String,
    price: f64,
}

fn main() {
    let mut products = vec![ // ②
        Product {
            name: "Laptop".to_string(),
            price: 799.99,
        },
        Product {
            name: "Headphones".to_string(),
            price: 149.99,
        },
        Product {
            name: "Smartphone".to_string(),
            price: 599.99,
        },
    ];

    products.sort_by(|a, b| a.price.partial_cmp(&b.price).unwrap()); //
③④

    for product in &products { // ⑤
        println!("Product: {} - Price: ${}", product.name, product.
price);
    }
}

// Output

// Product: Headphones - Price: $149.99
// Product: Smartphone - Price: $599.99
// Product: Laptop - Price: $799.99
```

① The code begins by defining a **Product** struct, which characterizes each product with a name (as a string) and a price (as a floating-point number, **f64**).

② A mutable vector, **products**, is established to hold a collection of **Product** instances. Each instance specifies the product's name and price.

③ To sort the products based on their prices in ascending order, the code employs the **sort_by** method. This method allows us to specify a sorting criterion using a closure. The closure captures two product references, denoted as **`a`** and **`b`**, and compares their prices.

④ The comparison within the closure utilizes the **`partial_cmp`** method to perform a partial comparison of the prices. The **`unwrap`** method is then used to safely extract the result of the comparison, which is necessary because **`partial_cmp`** returns an **`Option`**. This comparison ensures that the products are sorted in ascending order based on their prices.

⑤ Subsequently, the code iterates through the sorted products and prints their names and prices to the console, demonstrating the successful sorting of the **`Product`** instances.

This use case illustrates how closures within iterators are instrumental in facilitating data sorting operations. While this example simplifies the scenario of sorting by a single criterion, real-world sorting tasks may involve more complex criteria and multiple fields. Nevertheless, Rust's iterators and closures offer the flexibility and expressiveness needed to tackle various sorting challenges efficiently.

Conclusion

This chapter has provided an extensive exploration of iterators, closures, and their complex role within Rust's programming paradigm. Iterators stand as a foundational concept in Rust, serving as a backbone for efficient and expressive data processing. By creating, adapting, and harnessing iterators from Rust's standard library and in your custom code, you gain access to a powerful toolkit for handling data sequences. Throughout this chapter, you've acquired a robust understanding of iterators, from the utilization of standard iterator adapter methods to the craft of custom iterators tailored to your specific requirements. These skills will prove invaluable as you navigate the multifaceted landscape of Rust, enabling you to craft clean, idiomatic, and efficient code.

Closures, another focal point of our exploration, represent a powerful feature within Rust, allowing for the creation and use of anonymous functions with access to their surrounding context. These dynamic functions play a pivotal role in various programming tasks, encompassing sorting, filtering, and concurrent programming. This chapter has meticulously examined the different ingredients of closures, from their fundamental syntax to their complex relationship with variables in the surrounding scope. Closures prove to be not only a convenient coding tool but also a performance-oriented one, designed to minimize overhead and enable efficient usage, even within performance-critical code segments.

Understanding the nuanced `Fn`, `FnMut`, and `FnOnce` traits has been presented to you with the ability to control the behavior of closures and dictate how they interact with captured variables, amplifying the flexibility of Rust's closure system.

As you advance in your Rust journey, the comprehension and mastery of iterators and closures will continue to be indispensable in your programming toolkit. These constructs enable you to tackle a wide spectrum of data processing tasks with confidence, facilitating the creation of robust, maintainable, and expressive software. Beyond iterators and closures, further chapters will delve into Rust's rich ecosystem, extending your knowledge and skills, and equipping you to navigate the complexities and nuances of this powerful language.

In the next chapter, we'll dive into Unit Testing in Rust. Testing is crucial in software development, and this chapter focuses on unit testing. You'll learn to write test functions and modules, run tests, interpret results, and practice Test-driven development (TDD) in Rust. Topics covered include writing test functions and modules, executing tests, and TDD. This chapter enhances your testing skills and code reliability in Rust.

Resources

To deepen your understanding of iterators and closures in Rust, you can explore the following resources:

- *Rust Book - Chapter 13: Functional Language Features*: Dive into Chapter 13 of the official Rust Book, which focuses on functional language features, including iterators and closures. Gain a solid foundation in using iterators and closures for concise and expressive Rust code. - *https://doc.rust-lang.org/book/ch13-00-functional-features.html*
- *Rust Standard Library - Iterator Trait Documentation*: Delve into the documentation for the Iterator trait in the Rust Standard Library. Understanding the Iterator trait is essential for working with Rust's powerful iterator framework, enabling you to perform operations on sequences of data efficiently. - *https://doc.rust-lang.org/std/iter/index.html*
- *Itertools Crate - Iterator Extension Trait Documentation*: Explore the documentation for the Itertools crate on crates.io. This crate extends the functionality of Rust iterators, providing additional methods and combinators to simplify complex iteration patterns. - *https://docs.rs/itertools*

- *Rust By Example - Closures*: Explore the "Closures" section in Rust By Example for hands-on examples and exercises that reinforce your understanding of closures. This resource provides a practical and interactive approach to learning closures in Rust. - *https://doc.rust-lang.org/rust-by-example/fn/closures.html*
- *RFC 2394 - Closures and Async/Await*: Review RFC 2394, which discusses closures and their interaction with async/await in Rust. This RFC is foundational for understanding how closures play a role in asynchronous programming in Rust. - *https://github.com/rust-lang/rfcs/blob/master/text/2394-async_await.md*

These resources offer a comprehensive view of iterators and closures in Rust, providing practical guidance and documentation to help you master these fundamental concepts for writing expressive and efficient Rust code.

Multiple Choice Questions

Q1: Which of the following best describes closures in Rust?

a) Special iterators

b) Blocks of code that can capture and use variables from their surrounding scope

c) Standard library functions

d) Mutable references to collections

Q2: What role does the `map()` method play in Rust iterators?

a) Filters elements based on a predicate

b) Applies a transformation to each item in the iterator

c) Concatenates two iterators

d) Creates a new iterator with a specific length

Q3: Which trait is responsible for defining the structure of an iterator in Rust?

a) Iterator

b) IntoIterator

c) Option

d) Result

Q4: What is the main purpose of the `drain` method for collection types in Rust?

a) Consumes the entire collection

b) Transfers ownership of each element to the recipient

c) Iterates over the elements in reverse order

d) Filters elements based on a given predicate

Q5: Which method is used to retrieve the next item in an iterator sequence in Rust?

a) `` `collect()` ``

b) `` `for_each()` ``

c) `` `next()` ``

d) `` `map()` ``

Q6: Which iterator adapter method in Rust is used for selective extraction of items based on a provided predicate?

a) `map`

b) `filter`

c) `collect`

d) `zip`

Q7: What does the `peekable` adapter in Rust allow you to do?

a) Modify elements in the iterator

b) Look ahead at the next element without consuming it

c) Skip a specific number of elements

d) Flatten nested iterators

Q8: Which iterator adapter is used for managing nested iterators and dealing with collections of collections in Rust?

a) `take`

b) `skip`

c) `flat_map`

d) `peekable`

Q9: What is lazy evaluation in Rust iterators?

a) Computing and storing all values in memory upfront

b) Generating values on-the-fly as requested

c) Consuming elements without any condition

d) Applying operations eagerly to the entire sequence

Q10: Which iterator adapter serves as a fail-safe mechanism, preventing unexpected behavior when using an iterator after it has reached its end in Rust?

a) `flatten`

b) `filter`

c) `fuse`

d) `map`

Q11: What does the `flatten` adapter do in Rust's iterator ecosystem?

a) Filters elements based on a given condition

b) Unwraps nested sequences, producing a linear sequence of elements

c) Skips a specified number of elements

d) Applies a function to each element

Q12: In Rust closures, what does the `FnMut` trait signify?

a) Immutably captures variables

b) Mutably captures variables

c) Consumes variables, taking ownership

d) Applies only to closures with no arguments

Q13: What is the role of the `fold` method in the context of Rust iterators?*

a) Skips elements in the iterator

b) Collects elements into a new iterator

c) Folds elements into a single value using a closure

d) Unwraps nested sequences

Q14: Which iterator method is used for accumulating values from an iterator into a single result in Rust?

a) `` `map` ``

b) `` `filter` ``

c) `` `fold` ``

d) `` `chain` ``

Q15: What is the purpose of the `chain` method in Rust iterators?

a) To filter elements based on a condition

b) To concatenate two iterators

c) To map elements to a new value

d) To accumulate values into a single result

Q16: In Rust, what does the `partial_cmp` method return?

a) `Boolean value`

b) `Option`

c) `Result`

d) `usize`

Q17: What does the `wrapping_mul` method in Rust handle?*

a) Division by zero

b) Overflow and underflow

c) Floating-point errors

d) String concatenation

Answers

1. b) Blocks of code that can capture and use variables from their surrounding scope
2. b) Applies a transformation to each item in the iterator

3. a) Iterator
4. b) Transfers ownership of each element to the recipient
5. c) `next()`
6. b) filter
7. b) Look ahead at the next element without consuming it
8. c) flat_map
9. b) Generating values on-the-fly as requested
10. c) fuse
11. b) Unwraps nested sequences, producing a linear sequence of elements
12. b) Mutably captures variables
13. c) Folds elements into a single value using a closure
14. c) `fold`
15. b) To concatenate two iterators
16. b) Option
17. b) Overflow and underflow

Key Terms

- **Iterator Trait:** A trait in Rust that defines the structure of an iterator. It specifies methods such as `next()` and an associated type `Item` representing the type of values the iterator produces.
- **IntoIterator Trait:** A trait in Rust that allows types to be treated as iterable. It is defined by the `into_iter` method and enables the use of types in Rust's `for` loop, making code more idiomatic.
- **Drain Method:** A method provided by some collection types in Rust, such as vectors, that offers an iterator, which transfers ownership of each element to the recipient. It leaves the collection empty after the operation.
- **Closures:** Anonymous functions in Rust that can capture and access variables from their enclosing scope. They are a powerful feature, often used for concise and reusable code blocks.

- **Map Method:** An iterator method in Rust that applies a transformation to each item in the iterator, creating a new iterator with the modified values.
- **Iterator Methods (`next`, `for_each`, `collect`, `map`, `filter`):** Methods associated with iterators in Rust, providing a suite of tools for efficient data manipulation, filtering, and aggregation. They contribute to concise and expressive coding.
- **Successors Function:** A function in Rust's standard library (`std::iter::successors`) that extends the capabilities of value sequence generation. It creates custom iterators by repeatedly invoking a closure to produce items.
- **Drain Iterator Cleanup:** The cleanup process performed by the `drain` iterator in Rust after it concludes its operation. It removes any remaining elements within the collection it had initially borrowed, leaving the collection empty.
- **Iterator Adapter Methods:** Methods in Rust's standard library that empower developers to transform and manipulate iterators for efficient data processing.
- **Lazy Evaluation:** A feature in Rust iterators where values are generated on-the-fly as requested, leading to memory-efficient and potentially infinite sequences.
- **`flat_map`:** An iterator adapter in Rust used for managing nested iterators and dealing with collections of collections by flattening the results into a single sequence.
- **`filter_map`:** A powerful iterator adapter in Rust that combines filtering and mapping in a single step, allowing precise control over iterators by transforming or discarding items based on a custom function.
- **`Fn`, `FnMut`, `FnOnce`:** Traits in Rust that categorize closures based on their ability to capture variables immutably, mutably, or by consuming ownership.

Chapter 11

Unit Testing in Rust

Introduction

Software testing plays a pivotal role in the complex landscape of the software development lifecycle, serving as an important component to ensure the integrity and functionality of software. As a complex process, it strives to guarantee that the developed software operates as intended, meets the specified requirements, and puts up with the challenges of evolving technological landscapes. Within the Rust ecosystem, the commitment to quality extends to testing, as evidenced by the provision of a robust testing framework that empowers developers to verify the correctness of their code. This chapter unrolls a comprehensive exploration into the universe of unit testing in Rust, where the spotlight is on inspecting individual components or units of the codebase, thereby strengthening the foundation of reliable and resilient software.

Unit testing in Rust exceeds being a mere best practice; it stands as a foundational cornerstone in the hunt for developing software of the highest quality. The act of crafting tests in Rust is not just a checkbox exercise but an essential investment in the long-term viability and maintainability of software projects. As we embrace the discipline of unit testing, we not only validate the immediate functionality of our code but also establish a safeguard against regressions and unintended consequences as the codebase evolves. This chapter takes an immersive journey into the art and science of unit testing in Rust, starting with foundational principles and progressively navigating through advanced concepts and techniques. Through this exploration, you gain not only proficiency in the Rust testing framework but also a profound understanding of how robust testing practices contribute to the resilience and adaptability of your software creations.

Structure

In this chapter, we are going to explore the following topics:

- Writing Test Functions and Test Modules in Rust
- Executing Tests and Understanding Test Results
- Practicing Test-Driven Development (TDD) in Rust

Unit Testing

Before we immerse ourselves in the specifics of unit testing in Rust, it's essential to understand why testing is crucial in software development. Testing fulfills several pivotal roles, including:

- Verification of the correctness of your code.
- Early detection and resolution of bugs and defects.
- Providing a safety net for refactoring and modifications.
- Documentation of the expected behavior of your code.
- Encouraging robust, maintainable software.

In Rust, where the language's design principles focus on safety, testing takes on even more significant importance. Rust's robust type system and ownership model work diligently to reduce runtime errors, but unit tests serve as a powerful instrument to ensure that your code adheres constantly to its expected behavior.

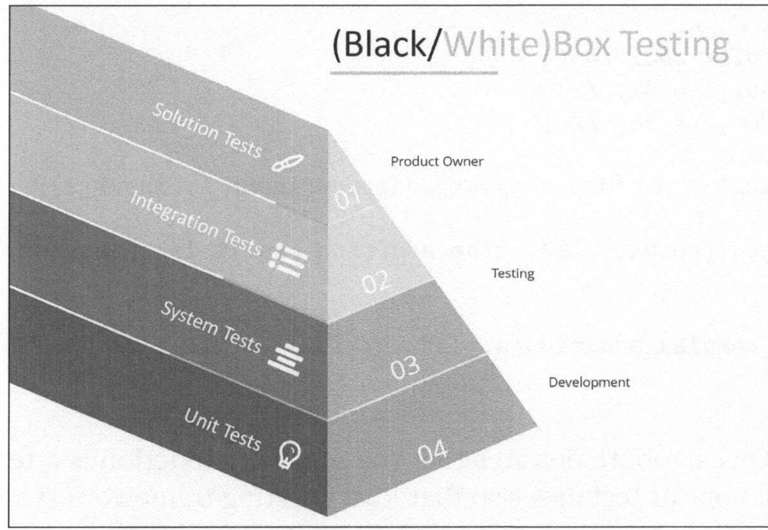

Figure 11.1: Black and white box testing hierarchy

Writing Test Functions and Modules

In Rust, testing your code is like making sure everything works smoothly and fits together well. Imagine you're an artist, and each piece of your code is like a stroke of your paintbrush. Rust lets you create specific tests, like little checks, for each stroke. These checks make sure that each part of your code does what it's supposed to do. But Rust goes further. It lets you organize your tests into groups called modules. Modules are like chapters in a book. They help you organize your tests neatly so you can check different parts of your code separately.

What's really cool is that writing these tests in Rust feels a lot like writing the actual code. It's not a separate, boring task, it's built right into the process of creating your software. This makes it easier to catch mistakes early on and ensures that your code works smoothly, like a well-tuned melody.

Now, let us delve into the complexities of crafting test functions in the Rust programming language.

Writing a Basic Test Function

A test function in Rust is, at its core, a standard Rust function decorated with the **#[test]** attribute. This attribute signifies to the Rust compiler that the function is a test and should be included in test runs. Here's an example of a test function:

Listing 11.1 A basic test function in Rust.

```
#[test] // ①
fn test_complex_addition() { // ②
    let input_1 = 42; // ③
    let input_2 = 58; // ③

    let result = perform_complex_addition(input_1, input_2); // ④

    assert_eq!(result, 100, "The addition result is incorrect."); // ⑤
}

fn perform_complex_addition(a: i32, b: i32) -> i32 { // ⑥
    a + b
}
```

① **[test]**: This attribute denotes that the following function is a test. It's used to mark functions as test cases so that Rust's testing framework recognizes and executes them when you run tests with **cargo test**.

② **`fn test_complex_addition()`** defines the test function named **`test_complex_addition`**, adhering to Rust's naming conventions for test functions. It's responsible for testing the **`perform_complex_addition`** function.

③ The lines that follow, including **`let input_1 = 42;`** and **`let input_2 = 58;`**, are part of the "Arrange" phase in the AAA pattern. During the "**`Arrange`**" phase, you prepare the input data and any necessary conditions for the test. In this specific case, **`input_1`** and **`input_2`** are assigned particular values, which serve as inputs to the **`perform_complex_addition`** function.

④ `let` **`result = perform_complex_addition(input_1, input_2);`**: This line is part of the "`Act`" phase in the AAA pattern. During the "`Act`" phase, you execute the actual operation or function that you want to test. In this case, it calls the **`perform_complex_addition`** function with the input values from the "Arrange" phase and stores the result in the **`result`** variable.

⑤ **`assert_eq!(result, 100, "The addition result is incorrect.");`**: This line is associated with the "`Assert`" phase. In the "`Assert`" phase, you verify the result of the operation against the expected outcome. The **`assert_eq!`** macro is used to check if the **`result`** is equal to **`100`**. If the assertion fails (that is, **`result`** is not equal to **`100`**), the specified error message, "**`The addition result is incorrect`**", will be displayed.

⑥ The **`perform_complex_addition`** function, which performs the addition of two **`i32`** integers, represents the actual logic being tested in the "**`Act`**" phase. The structured AAA pattern provides clarity and ensures that the test functions are organized and easy to understand, making it simpler to identify and address issues in the code under test[1].

The test function **`test_complex_addition`** follows the Arrange, Act, Assert (AAA) pattern. It prepares input data, performs a more complex addition operation using the **`perform_complex_addition`** function, and verifies that the result matches the expected outcome using the **`assert_eq!`** macro. This structured approach to testing helps ensure that the code behaves correctly and helps catch potential issues or regressions.

Test Modules

Organizing your test functions into test modules is a valuable practice for keeping your tests well-structured and manageable, especially as your codebase grows. To create a test module, use the **`mod`** keyword and define your tests within it.

[1]Khorikov, V. (n.d.). Unit testing principles, practices, and patterns. O'Reilly Online Learning. *https://www.oreilly.com/library/view/unit-testing-principles/9781617296277/*

Listing 11.2 A basic test module structure.

```
mod mod_tests {
    #[test]
    fn test_addition() {
        let input_1 = 42;
        let input_2 = 58;

        let result = perform_addition(input_1, input_2);

        assert_eq!(result, 100, "The addition result is incorrect.");
    }

    fn perform_addition(a: i32, b: i32) -> i32 {
        a + b
    }
}
```

The preceding code snippet introduces the concept of test modules in Rust and demonstrates how they can be used to maintain organized and manageable test suites. In this particular example, a test module named **`mod_tests`** is defined to encapsulate the **`test_addition`** test function. This organizational structure aligns with the best practices in Rust unit testing and follows the principle of structuring tests in a modular and maintainable manner.

The purpose of creating a test module like **`mod_tests`** is to group related test functions and organize them according to specific areas or features of the code under test. This modularity is especially valuable as your project grows and the number of tests increases. By separating tests into different modules, you can maintain clarity and ease of navigation within your codebase.

Within the **`mod_tests`** module, you'll find the **`test_addition`** test function, which mirrors the structure of the previous example. This test function follows the Arrange, Act, Assert (AAA) pattern, where the "Arrange" phase involves setting up the necessary input data and conditions, the "Act" phase executes the operation being tested, and the "Assert" phase verifies the result against the expected outcome. This structured approach to testing is vital for comprehensibility and maintainability, as it clearly defines the purpose and components of each test.

The creation of test modules like **`mod_tests`** in Rust is a practice that promotes code organization and ensures that your tests are grouped logically. This not only aids in maintaining the quality of your tests but also simplifies the process of running specific sets of tests when needed. As your project evolves and new features are added, this modular approach will prove indispensable in keeping your testing suite manageable and comprehensible.

Tests and Test Results

Creating tests marks the initial phase of the development process, but it merely serves as the starting point on the path toward ensuring the reliability of your code. Beyond the act of writing tests, a crucial step involves the execution of these tests and the subsequent addition of a profound comprehension of the outcomes. Rust, as a programming language, provides inherent tools that facilitate the seamless execution of tests and the extraction of invaluable feedback. It is through this comprehensive examination of test results that we can identify potential issues, validate the functionality of the code, and enhance the overall reliability of the software.

Running Tests

Rust simplifies the process of running tests. The **`cargo test`** command is your go-to command, executing all the tests within your project. To run your tests, navigate to your project directory and execute the following command:

```
$ cargo test
```

When you execute this command, Cargo, Rust's package manager, identifies your tests and runs them. Cargo collects the results and presents a summary, indicating which tests passed and which ones failed.

When you're coding in Rust and need to run tests, **`cargo test`** provides several options and features for controlling the execution of your tests. One common scenario is running tests by specifying their names. To do this, you can use the following syntax:

```
$ cargo test test_fn_name
```

By providing the name of the test, you instruct **`cargo test`** to filter and execute tests that contain the specified **`test_fn_name`**. This feature is particularly useful when you want to focus on specific tests within your codebase.

In cases where the specified **`test_fn_name`** matches multiple tests, **`cargo test`** would execute all of them. However, there might be situations where you only want to run one specific test, and to achieve this, you can add **`--exact`** as an argument:

```
$ cargo test test_fn_name -- --exact
```

The **`--exact`** flag ensures that **`cargo test`** runs only one test that exactly matches the provided **`test_fn_name`**, helping you avoid unintended multiple executions.

However, if your test functions are within modules, you need to specify the full namespace path to the test you want to run. You can do this with the following command:

```
$ cargo test test_mod_name::test_fn_name -- --exact
```

With this command, `cargo test` ensures that it runs the specified test function within the specified module, providing the necessary granularity when dealing with organized code.

In more complex projects with multiple packages, you might want to target tests in a specific package. You can achieve this by using the `--package` flag in combination with specifying the test name, as follows:

```
$ cargo test --package package_name test_fn_name -- --exact
```

This command will run tests with the name `test-name` in the package specified by `package_name`, ensuring that tests are executed within the desired package.

When dealing with projects containing multiple packages and various modules, you may encounter tests with the same name in different locations. To address this, you can use the `--package` flag and provide the full path to the test, ensuring that you are targeting the correct package and module:

```
$ cargo test --package package_name test_mod_name::test_fn_name -- --ex-
act
```

The capabilities and choices provided through the `cargo test` command empower you to finely adjust the execution parameters of your tests. This functionality proves invaluable by enabling you to concentrate on particular segments of your codebase, ensuring a targeted and efficient testing process. This becomes especially crucial in scenarios where multiple tests share similar names, as it guarantees the precise selection and execution of the intended tests. The ability to customize the testing process with such granularity proves to be particularly advantageous when dealing with larger codebases characterized by complex testing demands. These features not only streamline the testing workflow but also enhance the reliability and accuracy of the testing outcomes in complex software projects.

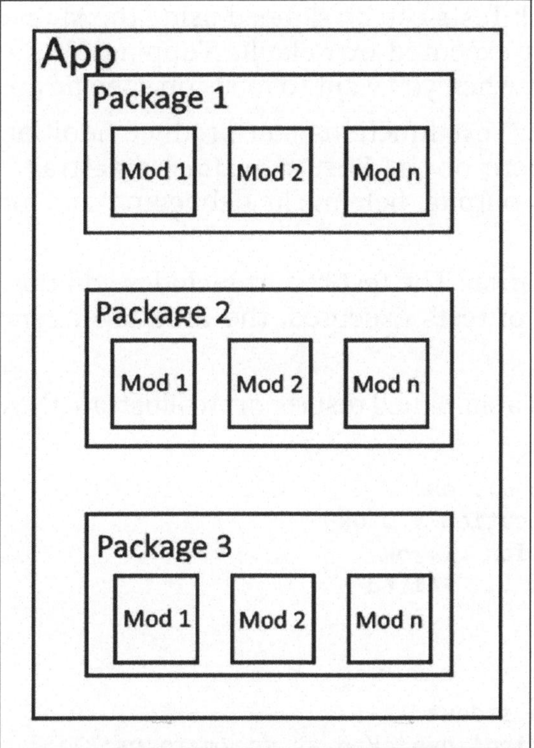

Figure 11.2: *Package, modules, unit tests hierarchy*

Interpreting Test Results

Following the execution of your tests, a detailed report will be generated to provide a comprehensive summary of the results. This report will offer a thorough analysis, identifying the tests that have successfully passed, those that have encountered failures, and any supplementary information essential for a more in-depth examination. This breakdown within the test results aims to equip you with a clear understanding of the overall performance and functionality, allowing you to pinpoint areas of success and those that may require further attention or analysis. Here's a breakdown of what you might encounter in the test results:

- **Test Passed**: When a test successfully satisfies its assertion, it's marked as "`passed`". This indicates that the code under inspection behaves as expected.
- **Test Failed**: A test is marked as "`failed`" when the assertion within the test function doesn't hold true. A failing test implies a potential issue or regression in the code.

- **Test Skipped**: Tests can be skipped using the `#[ignore]` attribute. These tests are not executed by default. Skipping tests can be useful during development when you want to focus on specific areas of your codebase.
- **Test Output**: Test functions can produce additional output using the `println!` macro or the Rust `std::io::Write` trait. The test report will include this output, helping in debugging and providing context for failing tests.
- **Test Information**: The test report includes additional information about the number of tests executed, the time taken, and any other relevant data.

Here's an example of a simplified test report to illustrate these different elements:

```
running 4 tests
test test_addition ... ok
test test_multiplication ... ok
test test_subtraction ... ok
test test_division ... FAILED

failures:

---- test_division stdout ----
thread 'test_division' panicked at src/main.rs:37:5:
assertion `left == right` failed
  left: 4
 right: 3
note: run with `RUST_BACKTRACE=1` environment variable to display a
backtrace


failures:
    test_division

test result: FAILED. 3 passed; 1 failed; 0 ignored; 0 measured; 0 fil-
tered out; finished in 0.00s

error: test failed, to rerun pass `--bin file`
```

In the given code snippet, a total of four tests were executed, with three of them successfully passing, denoted by the "ok" status. However, one specific test, identified as `test_division`, did not meet the criteria for success and consequently failed. The accompanying report offers further insights into the unsuccessful test, providing information such as the precise location of the assertion failure. Additionally, the report extends a recommendation to rerun the particular test, thereby facilitating the identification and rectification of the underlying issue.

This comprehensive test reporting enables you to identify issues quickly, understand their root causes, and work toward resolutions. Regular testing and analysis play a critical role in maintaining code quality.

Assertions

Assertions are the core elements that make unit testing effective. In Rust, the standard library provides a variety of macros for creating assertions, each catering to different scenarios. Here are some commonly used assertion macros:

- **`assert!(condition)`**: This macro verifies that the provided condition is **`true`**. If the condition is **`false`**, the test fails.
- **`assert_eq!(left, right)`**: This macro checks whether the values of **`left`** and **`right`** are equal. If they are not, the test fails.
- **`assert_ne!(left, right)`**: This macro checks whether the values of **`left`** and **`right`** are not equal. If they are equal, the test fails.
- **`assert!(expression, "message")`**: Similar to the **`assert!(condition)`** macro, this variant provides an optional custom error message to clarify the assertion failure.
- **`assert_eq!(left, right, "message")`**: This macro allows you to provide an optional custom error message along with the equality check.
- **`assert_ne!(left, right, "message")`**: Similar to **`assert_eq!`**, this macro adds a custom error message to the inequality check.

Using these assertion macros, you can validate different conditions, such as whether a particular value matches an expected result, whether an error condition is handled correctly, or if a function returns the expected output.

Here's an example of how these assertion macros are applied in test functions:

Listing 11.3 Different test assertions usage.

```
#[test] // ①
fn test_assertions() { // ②
    assert_eq!(add(2, 2), 4); // ③

    assert_ne!(subtract(5, 2), 5); // ④

    assert!(is_even(4)); // ⑤
```

```
    assert!(!is_odd(6)); // ⑥
}

fn add(a: i32, b: i32) -> i32 { // ⑦
    a + b
}

fn subtract(a: i32, b: i32) -> i32 { // ⑧
    a - b
}

fn is_even(n: i32) -> bool { // ⑨
    n % 2 == 0
}

fn is_odd(n: i32) -> bool { // ⑩
    n % 2 != 0
}
```

Let's break down the preceding code snippet that demonstrates the use of assertion macros in test functions:

① **#[test]**: This attribute marks the following function, **test_assertions**, as a test function, indicating that it should be executed as part of the test suite when running tests with **cargo test**.

② **fn test_assertions()**: This line defines the test function named **test_assertions**. Within this function, various assertion macros are used to validate different conditions.

③ **assert_eq!(add(2, 2), 4);**: This line employs the **assert_eq!** macro, which checks if the result of the **add** function, called with arguments **2** and **2**, is equal to **4**. If the equality check fails, it will indicate a test failure.

④ **assert_ne!(subtract(5, 2), 5);**: Here, the **assert_ne!** macro is used to verify that the result of the **subtract** function, called with arguments **5** and **2**, is not equal to **5**. This checks for inequality, and a failure will be reported if the values are equal.

⑤ **assert!(is_even(4));**: The **assert!** macro is used to confirm that the **is_even** function, called with **4**, returns **true**. This macro checks if a given expression is true and reports a test failure if it evaluates to false.

⑥ **assert!(!is_odd(6));**: In this line, the **assert!** macro is used to assert that the **is_odd** function, called with **6**, returns **false**. The **!** operator is used to negate the condition. If the condition is not false, it will result in a test failure.

⑦ **`fn add(a: i32, b: i32) → i32 { a + b }`**: The code defines the **`add`** function, which takes two integer arguments, **`a`** and **`b`**, and returns their sum.

⑧ **`fn subtract(a: i32, b: i32) → i32 { a - b }`**: The **`subtract`** function is defined to take two integer arguments, **`a`** and **`b`**, and return their difference.

⑨ **`fn is_even(n: i32) → bool { n % 2 == 0 }`**: This function, **`is_even`**, takes an integer **`n`** as input and checks whether it's even by evaluating the expression **`n % 2 == 0`**, returning a boolean result.

⑩ **`fn is_odd(n: i32) → bool { n % 2 != 0 }`**: The **`is_odd`** function takes an integer **`n`** and checks if it's odd by using the expression **`n % 2 != 0`**, returning a boolean result.

This example demonstrates a test function, **`test_assertions`**, that uses various assertion macros to verify different conditions. These macros include **`assert_eq!`** for equality checks, **`assert_ne!`** for inequality checks, and **`assert!`** to verify whether conditions are true or false. These assertions are essential for validating the behavior of functions in your code during testing. If any of these assertions fail, the corresponding test will be marked as failed.

Using these assertion macros helps ensure the correctness of your code by comparing actual outcomes to expected results, and it provides clarity about what your test is evaluating.

Custom Error Messages

Utilizing Rust's assertion macros presents a notable advantage in the form of custom error messages, which prove invaluable in comprehending the reasons behind test failures. These tailored error messages contribute essential contextual information, helping us pinpoint the root cause of the failure. An illustrative example can be observed in the following test function where the **`assert_eq!(add(2, 2), 4)`** line is not only asserting the equality of the result but also augmented with a descriptive error message:

Listing 11.4 Assertion with error message.

```
assert_eq!(add(2, 2), 4, "The addition result is incorrect.");
```

When this assertion fails, the error message is included in the test report, helping in debugging and pinpointing the issue. Custom error messages are particularly useful when you have complex or non-obvious assertions that require detailed explanations.

Running Tests with Options

Rust's testing framework provides various options to configure and customize test runs. These options allow you to fine-tune your testing process according to your needs. Here are some essential options for running tests in Rust:

- **`--test-threads`**: You can specify the number of threads used for test execution with the **`--test-threads`** option. This allows you to control the level of parallelism when running tests. For example, if you want to run tests with a single thread, you can use:

  ```
  $ cargo test -- --test-threads=1
  ```

Alternatively, you can set the number of threads in your **`Cargo.toml`** file under the **`[profile.test]`** section:

```
[profile.test]
nthreads = 1
```

This can be useful when running tests on code that might have thread-safety concerns.

- **`--release`**: By default, tests are run in debug mode. To execute tests in release mode, which can help uncover optimization-related issues, you can use the **`--release`** flag:

  ```
  cargo test --release
  ```

- **`-- --ignored`**: Tests marked with the **`#[ignore]`** attribute are not executed by default. If you want to run only the ignored tests, you can use the **`-- --ignored`** flag:

  ```
  cargo test -- --ignored
  ```

- **`--quiet`** and **`--nocapture`**: The **`--quiet`** option suppresses test output, making the test run less verbose. On the other hand, the **`--nocapture`** option allows you to see the output produced by the tests themselves, which can be helpful for debugging and understanding the context of test failures.

  ```
  $ cargo test -- --quiet
  $ cargo test -- --nocapture
  ```

- **`--color`**: The **`--color`** option lets you specify whether to use colored output for test results. You can use **`auto`**, **`always`**, or **`never`** as values. By default, Cargo attempts to detect whether your terminal supports colors.

  ```
  $ cargo test -- --color=always
  ```

These options provide flexibility when running your tests, enabling you to tailor the testing process to your specific requirements and debugging needs.

Fixtures and Setup Code

Executing unit tests frequently demands a meticulously defined and consistent environment. There are instances where it becomes imperative to establish particular conditions or allocate resources prior to initiating a test. Moreover, there may arise a need to utilize the same fixture across numerous tests to ensure uniformity and coherence in testing scenarios. To accomplish this, a fixture function can be created, and designed to produce the required fixture value. Subsequently, this fixture function can be seamlessly referenced and applied across various tests, thereby streamlining the process and promoting consistency in the testing framework. This approach not only enhances the efficiency of unit testing but also facilitates the maintenance of a standardized testing environment.

Here's an example of sharing a fixture across multiple tests:

Listing 11.5 A basic fixtures and setup code.

```
use std::collections::HashMap; // ①

fn create_fixture() -> HashMap<String, i32> {
    let mut fixture = HashMap::new();
    fixture.insert("foo".to_string(), 42);
    fixture.insert("bar".to_string(), 37);
    fixture
} // ②

#[test]
fn test_contains_foo() {
    let fixture = create_fixture();
    assert!(fixture.contains_key("foo")); // ④
} // ③

#[test]
fn test_contains_bar() {
    let fixture = create_fixture();
    assert!(fixture.contains_key("bar")); // ④
} // ③

#[test]
fn test_contains_baz() {
    let fixture = create_fixture();
    assert!(!fixture.contains_key("baz")); // ⑤
} // ③
```

The preceding code snippet exemplifies a common testing pattern inside a fixture, represented by a HashMap containing predefined key-value pairs, which is shared across multiple test functions.

① The code begins with the import statement, bringing the HashMap type from the standard library into scope for usage in the subsequent code.

② The function **`create_fixture`** is defined to construct and return a **`HashMap<String, i32>`**. Within this function, an empty HashMap named **`fixture`** is instantiated, and two key-value pairs, **`("foo", 42)`** and **`("bar", 37)`**, are sequentially inserted into the fixture. The function concludes by returning the populated fixture. This design choice ensures a consistent initial state for the subsequent tests.

③ Subsequently, three test functions, namely **`test_contains_foo`**, **`test_contains_bar`**, and **`test_contains_baz`**, are implemented. Each test creates a fixture using the **`create_fixture`** function, thereby ensuring that the tests share a common initial state. This approach promotes code modularity, reduces redundancy, and facilitates the isolation of specific test cases.

④ The first two tests, **`test_contains_foo`** and **`test_contains_bar`**, assert the presence of the keys "**`foo`**" and "**`bar`**" in the created fixture, respectively. These tests validate that the initial state contains the expected elements, serving as positive test cases for key existence.

⑤ The third test, **`test_contains_baz`**, verifies that the fixture does not contain the key "**`baz`**". This negative test case ensures that the created fixture lacks a specific key, demonstrating the flexibility of the testing approach in handling different scenarios.

The structured approach to testing with a shared fixture enhances code maintainability and coherence, providing a robust foundation for validating different aspects of the program's functionality across multiple test cases. By defining a separate fixture function, you ensure that the fixture setup is consistent across all tests that use it, promoting test isolation and a controlled environment.

While Rust does not natively provide fixtures, you can also achieve this using the **rstest** crate, which allows you to create fixtures and parameterized tests with ease.

To create fixtures and set up parameterized tests, follow these steps:

- Add the **rstest** crate to your project's dependencies in the **Cargo.toml** file:
  ```
  [dependencies]
  rstest = "0.5"
  ```
- Define parameterized test functions using the **#[rstest]** attribute and specify the input parameters.
- Use the **fixture** argument within your test function to access the fixture data.

Here's an example illustrating how to set up fixtures and create parameterized tests using the **rstest** crate:

Listing 11.6 A basic unit test example using rstest fixtures.

```
use rstest::{rstest, fixture}; // ①
use std::fs;
use tempfile::TempDir; // ①

#[fixture]
fn temp_dir() -> TempDir { // ②
    // Code to create and return a TempDir goes here
    TempDir::new().expect("Failed to create temporary directory")
}

#[rstest]
fn test_with_temp_dir(temp_dir: TempDir) { // ③
    // You can use the temp_dir fixture within this test.
    let file_path = temp_dir.path().join("example.txt"); // ④
    fs::write(&file_path, "Test data").expect("Failed to write to the
file"); // ④

    assert!(file_path.exists()); // ⑤
    assert_eq!(fs::read_to_string(&file_path).expect("Failed to read
file"), "Test data"); // ⑤
}
```

① The code begins by importing necessary crates and modules: **rstest** for parameterized testing, **fixture** for declaring fixtures, and **TempDir** from the **tempfile** crate for managing temporary directories.

② The **temp_dir** fixture is declared using the **#[fixture]** attribute. This fixture function creates and returns a **TempDir** instance, representing a temporary directory. The implementation uses **TempDir::new()** to create the directory and panics with an error message if the creation fails.

③ The **test_with_temp_dir** function is decorated with the **#[rstest]** attribute, indicating that it is a parameterized test. The test function takes a parameter **temp_dir** of type **TempDir**, which is automatically provided by the test framework.

④ Inside the test function, a file path is constructed within the temporary directory using **temp_dir.path().join("example.txt")**. Subsequently, the test writes "**Test data**" to the file, handling potential write errors with the **expect** method.

⑤ Two assertions follow: the first checks whether the file path exists (**assert!(file_path.exists())**), ensuring the file was created successfully. The second assertion verifies that the content of the file matches the expected "Test data" (**assert_eq!(fs::read_to_string(&file_path).expect("Failed to read file"), "Test data")**).

This code showcases the usage of the **rstest** crate to create a parameterized test (**test_with_temp_dir**) with the help of a fixture (**temp_dir**). The fixture provides a **TempDir** instance for each test case, allowing consistent handling of temporary directories. This approach enhances code organization and readability, particularly when dealing with complex test environments requiring setup and cleanup.

Unit tests often require a well-defined and consistent environment in which to execute, and sometimes it's necessary to set up specific conditions or resources before running a test. While Rust's standard testing framework does not natively provide built-in attributes or mechanisms for setup and teardown, you can manually structure your tests with setup and teardown functions to achieve the desired functionality. Let's consider an example:

Listing 11.7 A custom test setup and teardown example.

```
fn setup() -> String { // ①
    let resource = "Some resource".to_string(); // ②
    println!("Setting up: {}", resource);
    resource // ③
}

fn teardown(resource: String) { // ④
    println!("Tearing down: {}", resource); // ⑤
}
```

```
#[test]
fn test_with_setup_and_teardown() { // ⑥
    let resource = setup(); // ⑦

    let result = format!("Test using: {}", resource); // ⑧

    assert_eq!(result, "Test using: Some resource"); //⑨

    teardown(resource); // ⑩
}

// $ cargo test -- --show-output

// running 1 test
// test test_with_setup_and_teardown ... ok

// successes:

// ---- test_with_setup_and_teardown stdout ----
// Setting up: Some resource
// Tearing down: Some resource


// successes:
//     test_with_setup_and_teardown

// test result: ok. 1 passed; 0 failed; 0 ignored; 0 measured; 0 filtered
out; finished in 0.00s
```

In this illustrative code, we delve into the process of manually implementing a setup and teardown mechanism within Rust tests. This mechanism is particularly valuable when you need to establish specific preconditions for your tests, manage resources, or conduct cleanup tasks once the tests have concluded.

Within the code, we define a series of functions that collectively enable us to set up a controlled testing environment and conduct necessary cleanup. The procedure for creating such tests encompasses the definition of setup and teardown functions, the creation of test functions, and the strategic invocation of these functions.

Let's break down the various components within the code starting with the **setup** function:

① The first step involves the creation of a function named **setup**. This function serves the pivotal role of initializing a resource, which is integral to the testing scenario.

② Within the **setup** function, we initiate the actual setup process. We instantiate a variable of type **String** named **resource**, populating it with the value "**Some resource**". This resource is fundamental to our test and represents an entity we wish to manipulate.

③ In order to maintain clarity and insight into the setup process, we include a **println!** statement within the **setup** function. This statement outputs a message that effectively indicates the initiation of the setup phase, accompanied by the value of the **resource**. Subsequently, we return the **resource** value, ensuring it is available for the test functions.

As we proceed to the **teardown** function, which plays a pivotal role in the cleanup aspect of our testing mechanism:

④ The **teardown** function is introduced to handle post-test operations, specifically the cleanup of resources. It is defined with a single parameter, a **String** variable named **resource**, which signifies the resource we intend to clean up.

⑤ Within the **teardown** function, we employ a **println!** statement as well. This statement performs an essential role in signaling the beginning of the teardown process. The message it produces conveys the intent to clean up, and it includes the **resource** value.

Subsequently, the **test_with_setup_and_teardown** test function is presented, revealing how these setup and teardown functions are integrated and operational:

⑥ The **test_with_setup_and_teardown** test function is meticulously defined to showcase the practical application of our setup and teardown mechanisms.

⑦ Within the test function, we initiate the setup process by invoking the **setup** function. This action is vital for creating the necessary testing conditions and acquiring the **resource** value, which will be central to the test.

⑧ Subsequently, we proceed with the test logic, generating a **result** variable that encapsulates the **resource**. This step is crucial to validate the interactions and manipulations of the resource during the test.

⑨ To assert the test's validity, we employ the **assert_eq!** macro, comparing the **result** with the expected value, "**Test using: Some resource**". This comparison forms the core of our test, affirming that the test logic successfully operates on the resource as anticipated.

⑩ Finally, after the test function's logic has been executed, we initiate the teardown phase by invoking the **teardown** function. By passing the **resource** as a parameter, we ensure the cleanup operation is consistently carried out. This is essential for maintaining a controlled and predictable testing environment, where resources are initialized and cleaned up in a structured manner.

This code exemplifies how to manually establish a setup and teardown mechanism within Rust tests. Through the creation of setup and teardown functions, paired with the strategic invocation of these functions within a test function, we can systematically set up a controlled testing environment, conduct test-specific operations, and ensure that cleanup is consistently performed. This approach provides a level of predictability and structure in testing that is especially valuable when dealing with complex testing scenarios involving resources and specific setup conditions.

Test fixtures are a powerful tool for sharing common setup code across multiple tests, ensuring that tests can be isolated and predictable. By defining fixture functions and marking them with the appropriate attributes, you can create clean and well-organized test suites.

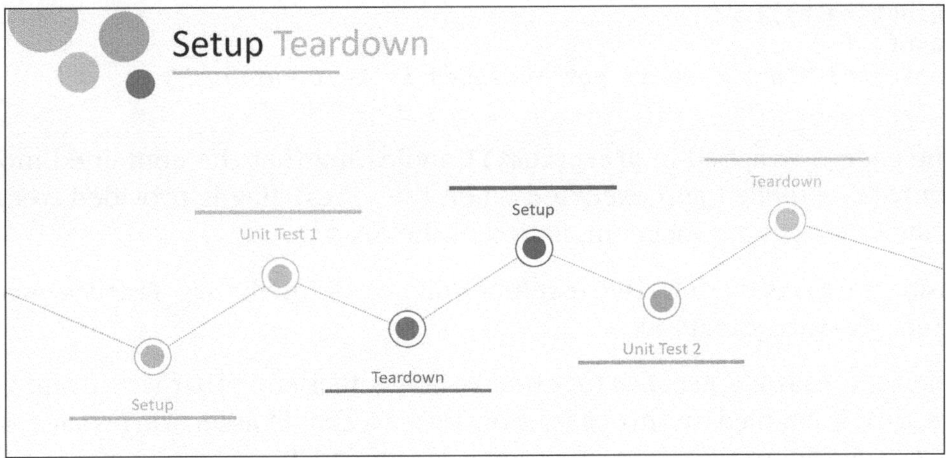

Figure 11.3: *Setup and teardown tests illustration (from left to right)*

Conditional Tests

Sometimes you may want to run tests conditionally based on specific criteria. Rust's testing framework allows you to do this with the `#[cfg(test)]` attribute and conditional compilation.

Here's an example of conditional testing in Rust:

Listing 11.8 An example of conditional testing in Rust.

```
#[cfg(test)] // ①
mod tests { // ②
    #[test]
    fn test_feature_enabled() { // ③
        // Test code for the feature when it's enabled.
        assert_eq!(1 + 1, 2);
    }

    #[test]
    fn test_feature_disabled() { // ④
        // Test code for the feature when it's disabled.
        assert_eq!(2 * 3, 6);
    }
}

#[cfg(not(test))] // ⑤
fn main() {
    println!("This code is not included in test builds.");
}
```

① The code is wrapped in **#[cfg(test)]**, indicating that the contained module will only be compiled and executed when the **--test** flag is provided to **cargo**. This allows for conditional compilation of the tests.

② Inside the **tests** module, two test functions are defined: **test_feature_enabled** and **test_feature_disabled**.

③ The **test_feature_enabled** function contains test code that is relevant when the feature is enabled. In this case, it performs a simple assertion (**assert_eq!(1 + 1, 2)**) to validate that the sum of 1 and 1 is indeed 2.

④ Contrarily, the **test_feature_disabled** function contains test code for the scenario when the feature is disabled. It includes an assertion (**assert_eq!(2 * 3, 6)**) that checks if the product of 2 and 3 is equal to 6.

⑤ The **main** function is wrapped in **#[cfg(not(test))]**, so it won't be included in the test build.

This code demonstrates the use of conditional compilation in tests. The tests inside the **tests** module will only be compiled and run when the **--test** flag is provided to **cargo**, allowing for the testing of different scenarios based on the presence or absence of specific features. This approach is useful for writing tests that are selectively executed based on the configuration or feature flags, providing flexibility in testing various code paths.

If you have a feature flag, `my_feature`, that determines whether the tests should be run or not, you can use conditional compilation as follows:

Listing 11.9 An example of conditional testing with features in Rust.

```
#[cfg(all(test, feature = "my_feature"))]
mod tests {
    #[test]
    fn test_feature_enabled() {
        // Test code for the feature when it's enabled.
        assert_eq!(1 + 1, 2);
    }

    #[test]
    fn test_feature_disabled() {
        // Test code for the feature when it's disabled.
        assert_eq!(2 * 3, 6);
    }
}
```

To test the functions, `test_feature_enabled` and `test_feature_disabled`, under the condition `feature = "my_feature"`, you need to enable the feature during the test build. Here are the steps to achieve this:

- Make sure your `Cargo.toml` file includes the necessary configuration for the feature:

  ```
  [features]
  my_feature = []
  ```

This indicates that a feature named "`my_feature`" is defined. To run the tests with the feature enabled, use the following command:

```
$ cargo test --features my_feature
```

This command tells Cargo to include the "`my_feature`" feature during the test build. If you want to run a specific test, you can use the test function name:

```
$ cargo test --features my_feature test_feature_enabled
```

Replace `test_feature_enabled` with the name of the specific test you want to run.

By adopting this method, you can verify that the tests located within the `tests` module go through compilation and execution only when the "`my_feature`" feature is activated. This strategy offers the flexibility to selectively initiate tests dependent on the existence or non-existence of particular features within your codebase. By incorporating this conditional testing framework, you gain a valuable mechanism to control the execution of tests in alignment with the specific features you choose to enable, contributing to a more targeted and efficient testing process. This selective approach ensures that the testing suite is closely aligned with the configuration and feature set of your codebase, thereby enhancing the overall precision and relevance of your testing procedures.

Asynchronous Testing

Rust additionally facilitates asynchronous testing to accommodate code that incorporates asynchronous operations. When writing asynchronous tests in Rust, we have the option to leverage the **tokio** or **async-std** crates, both of which provide dedicated asynchronous runtime environments. These crates serve as valuable tools in ensuring the effective testing of code that relies on asynchronous functionalities. By utilizing these asynchronous testing frameworks, we can comprehensively assess the performance and reliability of our asynchronous code, enhancing the overall robustness of our applications. This capability underscores Rust's commitment to providing a versatile and robust ecosystem that supports different programming paradigms, including the increasingly powerful asynchronous programming model.

Here's an example of writing an asynchronous test using **tokio**:

```
[dev-dependencies]
tokio = { version = "1.34.0", features = ["full"] }
```

Listing 11.10 An example of asynchronous testing using tokio.

```
#[tokio::test]
async fn test_async_function() {
    // Perform asynchronous operations here.
    let result = async_function().await;
    assert_eq!(result, 42);
}

async fn async_function() -> i32 {
    // Simulate an asynchronous operation.
    tokio::time::sleep(tokio::time::Duration::from_secs(1)).await;
    42
}
```

In this example, the **tokio** crate is employed to create an asynchronous test marked by the **#[tokio::test]** attribute, designating the test function as asynchronous. The test involves the execution of the asynchronous function **async_function** and subsequent assertion of the expected result. Utilizing the **tokio** crate streamlines the asynchronous task execution, providing a robust foundation for efficient and concurrent Rust applications. This example showcases the practical application of asynchronous testing with **tokio** and highlights the significance of specialized tools in addressing the challenges of asynchronous programming.

Likewise, you can use the **async-std** crate if you prefer that runtime environment:

```
[dev-dependencies]
async-std = { version = "1.12.0", features = ["attributes"] }
```

Listing 11.11 An example of asynchronous testing using async_std.

```
#[async_std::test]
async fn test_async_function() {
    // Perform asynchronous operations here.
    let result = async_function().await;
    assert_eq!(result, 42);
}

// An example asynchronous function to test.
async fn async_function() -> i32 {
    // Simulate an asynchronous operation.
    async_std::task::sleep(std::time::Duration::from_secs(1)).await;
    42
}
```

These code snippets illustrate the implementation of asynchronous tests using the **tokio** and **async-std** runtimes. Asynchronous testing is essential for scenarios involving non-blocking I/O, concurrent code, and the integration of async/await constructs. Leveraging the versatility of these runtimes, we can efficiently handle different asynchronous functionalities within Rust applications. The code highlights the significance of asynchronous testing in capturing the nuances of asynchronous workflows and assessing the behavior of code under parallel execution, particularly crucial for high-performance applications. Additionally, it showcases the seamless integration of **async/await** constructs, emphasizing their synergy in creating robust and scalable Rust applications.

Mocking Dependencies

In Rust testing, isolating code for accurate evaluation often involves mocking external dependencies. The **mockall** crate is a widely used tool for creating mock implementations of these dependencies, enabling precise control over their behavior during testing. This ensures that the focus remains on evaluating the logic of the code being tested. For example, when a Rust module interacts with an external service, using **mockall** allows us to seamlessly integrate mock implementations, simulating various scenarios and responses without invoking the actual external service functionalities. Here's an example of how to use **mockall** for mocking dependencies in tests:

```
[dev-dependencies]
mockall = "0.8"
```

Listing 11.12 An example of mocking dependencies using mockall.

```
use mockall::automock;

#[automock]
pub trait ExternalDependency {
    fn do_something(&self) -> i32;
}

#[cfg(test)]
mod tests {
    use super::*;

    #[test]
    fn test_with_mocked_dependency() {
        // Create a mock instance of the dependency.
        let mut dependency = MockExternalDependency::default();

        // Set expectation for the method
        dependency.expect_do_something().returning(|| 42);

        // Use the mock dependency in the code you're testing.
        let result = code_under_test(&dependency);

        // Verify that the code under test behaves as expected.
        assert_eq!(result, 42);
    }

    fn code_under_test(external_dep: &dyn ExternalDependency) -> i32 {
        // Call the dependency's method.
        external_dep.do_something()
    }
}
```

In this example, the **ExternalDependency** trait serves as a crucial abstraction for representing external dependencies in a software system. The introduction of the **automock** attribute streamlines the testing process by automatically generating mock implementations for the specified trait. The **test_with_mocked_dependency** function exemplifies this approach, creating a mock instance, setting expectations on its behavior, and integrating it into the code under test. This automated mocking process enables us to isolate our code from external dependencies effectively, allowing tests to focus exclusively on the specific behavior of the code and ensuring a more efficient and targeted testing strategy.

The use of **automock** enhances the precision of testing by isolating the code under test from the complexities of external dependencies. This isolation promotes a streamlined testing approach, enabling us to concentrate on verifying the internal logic and functionality of our code without being overwhelmed by the complexities of external systems. By creating a controlled environment through mock implementations, **automock** facilitates a more systematic and reliable testing process, contributing to the development of robust and maintainable code.

Testing Private Functions

In Rust, it's generally a good practice to test the public API of your modules and structures. However, there may be cases where you want to test private functions for better code coverage or to verify the correctness of implementation details. While you can't directly test private functions, you can use the **cfg(test)** attribute and the **[allow(dead_code)]** attribute to make them testable. Here's an example of testing a private function in Rust:

Listing 11.13 An example of testing private functions.

```
#[cfg(test)]
mod tests {
    // Import the private function from the main module for testing.
    use super::private_function;

    #[test]
    fn test_private_function() {
        // Call the private function for testing.
        let result = private_function(3);
        assert_eq!(result, 6);
    }
}
```

```
// The private function that you want to test.
#[allow(dead_code)]
fn private_function(x: i32) -> i32 {
    x * 2
}
```

In the given example, the utilization of the private function `private_function` underscores a deliberate design choice within the given function that is intentionally excluded from the module's public API. To facilitate the testing of this private function, a test module is instantiated within the same module scope. The `use super::private_function` statement is employed to import the targeted private function into the test module, providing the necessary access for testing purposes. Significantly, the inclusion of the `#[allow(dead_code)]` attribute serves as a strategic directive to the compiler, instructing it to stop issuing warnings related to unused code. This approach not only permits the seamless execution of tests for private functions but also safeguards against the unintentional exposure of these internal components within the library's public interface. The utilization of testing modules, coupled with attribute annotations, thus exemplifies a sophisticated strategy for maintaining a clear distinction between a module's internal implementation details and its externally visible API.

However, keep in mind that testing private functions is generally discouraged. It's better to test the public interface of your code as this provides a clear contract for users of your library or module. Testing private functions can lead to fragile tests that break when you refactor your code. If you find that you need to test a private function extensively, consider whether it should be part of the public API or refactor your code to make it more testable at the public level.

Effective test writing in Rust involves a comprehensive approach encompassing various key aspects. Leveraging fixtures provides predefined data sets to systematically evaluate different scenarios, while conditional tests enable the validation of code behavior under diverse conditions and edge cases. Rust's support for asynchronous testing is crucial in assessing code involving asynchronous operations, reflecting the demands of modern concurrent programming. Mocking dependencies allow the isolation of code for focused testing by substituting external components with controlled, simulated versions. Additionally, the ability to test private functions ensures a thorough evaluation of internal logic within modules. Overall, comprehensive testing in Rust is crucial for ensuring code correctness and reliability, and the Rust testing ecosystem provides a range of tools to facilitate these efforts, empowering us to create robust and maintainable software.

Benchmarking

Rust features an integrated benchmarking framework that simplifies the evaluation of code performance. This is made possible by the `[bench]` attribute, a tool allowing us to construct benchmark tests, helping in pinpointing performance bottlenecks and monitoring improvements over time. Typically, we integrate benchmark tests into the same module as our regular tests. The following example illustrates the process of writing benchmarks.

Listing 11.14 An example of benchmark test.

```
#![feature(test)] // Enable the test feature to use the test crate

extern crate test; // Import the test crate

use test::Bencher; // Import the Bencher trait

#[bench]
fn bench_example(b: &mut Bencher) {
    // The code you want to benchmark
    b.iter(|| {
        // Code to be benchmarked
        let result = expensive_computation();
        assert!(result > 0);
    });
}

fn expensive_computation() -> i32 {
    // Simulate an expensive computation.
    (1..1_000).sum()
}
```

In this code snippet, the `test` feature is activated, and the `test` crate is imported to leverage the `Bencher` trait for benchmarking. A benchmark function, marked with `[bench]`, is defined to encapsulate the code under testing. Inside this function, `b.iter()` is employed to specify the code snippet to be benchmarked and encapsulated within a closure. This systematic setup enables efficient testing and optimization of code performance in your applications.

When running your tests with `cargo test`, you can also run benchmarks using `cargo bench`. This will execute your benchmark functions and provide you with performance measurements and statistics.

Code Coverage

Code coverage tools are essential for assessing test effectiveness in software development, providing insights into code coverage by tests. In Rust, a popular choice is **tarpaulin**. To integrate it, install it as a global CLI. This enables seamless code coverage analysis, helping identify untested or inefficiently tested code sections. **Tarpaulin** plays a key role in ensuring robust and reliable Rust applications by enhancing test coverage and identifying potential vulnerabilities.

```
$ cargo install cargo-tarpaulin
```

You can then generate code coverage reports using **tarpaulin**:

```
$ cargo tarpaulin --out Xml
```

This command will generate an XML code coverage report that you can use in CI/CD pipelines or view in code coverage visualization tools.

Continuous Integration

Continuous Integration (CI) plays a pivotal role in automating testing processes and maintaining code quality. For Rust projects, leveraging various CI platforms such as Travis CI, GitHub Actions, GitLab CI/CD, and others is essential. The setup process involves crafting configuration files that define the steps for building, testing, and potentially deploying the project.

Let's delve into an example configuration file, **.travis.yml**, tailored for Travis CI:

Listing 11.15 Basic Travis CI Rust setup.

```
language: rust
rust:
  - stable
  - beta
  - nightly
cache: cargo
script:
  - cargo test
```

In this configuration:

- **language: rust** specifies the programming language being used.
- **rust** lists the Rust versions against which the project should be tested, stable, beta, and nightly, covering a range of compiler versions.

- **`cache: cargo`** optimizes the CI process by caching Cargo dependencies, speeding up subsequent builds.
- **`script: - cargo test`** defines the command to run, in this case, executing **`cargo test`** to ensure all tests pass.

Similar configuration files can be created for other CI platforms, like circleci, tailoring them to the specific requirements of your Rust project. Each CI system will have its syntax and conventions, but the core concepts remain consistent.

By seamlessly integrating CI into your development workflow, you establish a process where your code undergoes automated building and testing with every commit. This proactive approach ensures the reliability and bug-free nature of your codebase, fostering a robust and efficient development pipeline.

Writing tests in Rust is essential for ensuring the correctness and reliability of your code. Rust's testing ecosystem provides a range of tools and best practices to help you write comprehensive unit tests and benchmarks, including:

- **Fixtures:** Share common setup code across tests.
- **Conditional Tests:** Run tests conditionally based on criteria.
- **Asynchronous Testing:** Write tests for asynchronous code.
- **Mocking Dependencies:** Isolate your code by mocking external dependencies.
- **Testing Private Functions:** Test private functions using attributes.
- **Benchmarking:** Measure code performance with benchmarks.
- **Code Coverage:** Analyze code coverage with tools like **`tarpaulin`**.
- **Continuous Integration:** Automate testing with CI platforms.

By following these practices and integrating them into your development workflow, you can create robust and reliable applications. Remember that thorough testing helps prevent bugs and unexpected behavior, making it a vital part of software development in Rust or any other programming language.

Conclusion

In this chapter, we've taken a comprehensive journey into the world of unit testing in Rust. We started by emphasizing the significance of unit testing in Rust, aligning with its commitment to safety and reliability. We explored the basics, from writing test functions and modules using the **`[test]`** attribute to organizing tests effectively.

Our exploration extended to executing tests with `cargo test` and interpreting results, crucial for identifying and resolving issues in your code. Beyond the fundamentals, we delved into advanced techniques, including Test-driven Development (TDD), asynchronous testing, mocking, property-based testing, and optimal test organization.

Unit testing, as demonstrated, is a critical practice ensuring the reliability and correctness of your codebase. Whether you're developing a small project or a large-scale system, a solid testing strategy is your key to catching bugs early, documenting code, and maintaining robustness.

As you progress in your Rust development journey, remember that testing is an ongoing process. Continuously refine your testing skills and adopt best practices, leveraging the rich set of tools and libraries within the Rust ecosystem. .

Now armed with the knowledge of unit testing in Rust, you are well-prepared to create robust and reliable applications that adhere to the high standards set by the Rust programming language. Whether you're building systems software, web applications, or any other Rust-based project, unit testing is by your side in delivering quality and reliability.

In the next chapter, we'll dive into network programming in Rust. You'll learn to build networked applications, working with TCP and UDP protocols, managing Asynchronous Network Operations with async/await, among many others.

Resources

To enhance your expertise in unit testing within the Rust ecosystem and elevate your testing proficiency, you can explore the following resources:

- *Rust Testing Book*: Explore the official Rust documentation providing a comprehensive guide to testing in Rust, covering both fundamentals and advanced topics. - *https://doc.rust-lang.org/book/ch11-00-testing.html*
- *Proptest Documentation*: Delve into property-based testing using **proptest** with insights and guidance from the official documentation. - *https://docs.rs/proptest/*
- *Mockito Documentation*: Learn how to mock HTTP services in Rust with the guidance provided in the **mockito** documentation. - *https://docs.rs/mockito/*

- *Async Programming in Rust*: Take a deeper dive into asynchronous programming in Rust with the async book, exploring advanced techniques. - *https://rust-lang.github.io/async-book/*
- *nextest*: A testing library for Rust, designed to be concise and expressive, allowing for efficient unit testing. - *https://github.com/nextest-rs/nextest*
- **mockall:** Widely-used for creating mock implementations of dependencies, the **mockall** crate is a valuable tool in the Rust testing ecosystem. - *https://docs.rs/mockall*
- *criterion*: Utilize the **criterion** crate for benchmarking your Rust code, ensuring performance optimization. - *https://crates.io/crates/criterion*
- *Criterion Documentation*: Delve into the detailed documentation of criterion to master the art of writing effective benchmarks in Rust. - *https://bheisler.github.io/criterion.rs/book/*
- *assert-approx-eq*: Ensure precision in your numeric tests using the **assert-approx-eq** crate. - *https://docs.rs/assert-approx-eq*

Multiple Choice Questions

Q1: Why is unit testing important in software development?

a) To increase code complexity

b) To slow down the development process

c) To verify the correctness of code

d) To avoid documentation efforts

Q2: What does the `#[test]` attribute signify in Rust?

a) It denotes a data structure definition

b) It marks a function as a test case

c) It provides default implementations for functions

d) It restricts access to data

Q3: What is the purpose of the AAA pattern in unit testing?

a) To organize test functions alphabetically

b) To structure tests into Arrange, Act, and Assert phases

c) To enforce strict coding standards

d) To prevent code duplication in tests

Q4: How can you run a specific test function named `test_function` using `cargo test`?

a) `cargo test --function test_function`

b) `cargo test --name test_function`

c) `cargo test --test-function test_function`

d) `cargo test test_function`

Q5: What is the purpose of test modules in Rust?

a) To define new programming constructs

b) To organize test functions into groups

c) To provide default implementations for tests

d) To restrict access to test data

Q6: What does the `--exact` flag do when running tests with cargo test?

a) It runs all tests

b) It runs tests with exact matches only

c) It skips running tests

d) It sets the number of threads for test execution

Q7: Why would you use custom error messages in Rust assertions?

a) To confuse developers

b) To make the code longer

c) To provide additional context for test failures

d) To speed up test execution

Q8: What does the `--release` flag do when running tests with cargo test?

a) It runs tests in debug mode

b) It skips running tests

c) It sets the number of threads for test execution

d) It runs tests in release mode

Q9: What is a fixture in the context of unit testing?

a) A bug in the code

b) A piece of code that performs arithmetic operations

c) A consistent environment or set of initial conditions for tests

d) A tool for code profiling

Q10: What does the `--ignored` flag do in cargo test?

a) Skips all tests

b) Runs only ignored tests

c) Ignores test output

d) Enforces strict naming conventions

Q11: What is the purpose of the setup function in the setup and teardown example?

a) To define a test case

b) To clean up resources

c) To initialize a resource for testing

d) To disable a feature

Q12: Which command is used to enable a specific feature during the test build?

a) `cargo run`

b) `cargo build`

c) `cargo test`

d) `cargo test --features`

Q13: What is the role of the teardown function in the setup and teardown example?

a) Initializes resources

b) Performs post-test cleanup

c) Defines test logic

d) Checks for feature flags

Q14: How can conditional testing be achieved in Rust?

a) Using the #[`test`] attribute

b) Wrapping tests in #[`conditional`] blocks

c) By defining conditional functions

d) Using #[`cfg(test)`] and conditional compilation

Q15: Which attribute is used to mark a function as an asynchronous test in Rust using the tokio crate?

a) `#[async]`

b) `#[tokio::test]`

c) `#[async_test]`

d) `#[tokio]`

Q16: What does the automock attribute do in Rust when using the mockall crate?

a) Generates documentation for mocks

b) Automatically generates mock implementations for specified traits

c) Marks a trait as a mockable trait

d) Enables automatic mocking of dependencies

Q17: Which tool is commonly used for code coverage analysis in Rust?

a) `tarpit`

b) `tarpaulin`

c) `coveralls`

d) `codecov`

Q18: What is the purpose of the [bench] attribute in Rust?

a) Marks a function as a benchmark test

b) Generates benchmark documentation

c) Specifies test dependencies

d) Enables conditional testing

Q19: What is the role of the Bencher trait in Rust benchmarking?

a) Defines asynchronous benchmarks

b) Represents a benchmarked function

c) Provides methods for benchmarking

d) Enables conditional benchmarking

Q20: Which command is used to generate an XML code coverage report with tarpaulin?

a) `cargo coverage`

b) `cargo report`

c) `cargo tarpaulin --out Xml`

d) `tarpaulin --report xml`

Answers

1. c) To verify the correctness of code
2. b) It marks a function as a test case
3. b) To structure tests into Arrange, Act, and Assert phases
4. b) `cargo test --name test_function`
5. b) To organize test functions into groups
6. b) It runs tests with exact matches only
7. c) To provide additional context for test failures
8. d) It runs tests in release mode
9. c) A consistent environment or set of initial conditions for tests

10. b) Runs only ignored tests
11. c) To initialize a resource for testing
12. d) `cargo test -features`
13. b) Performs post-test cleanup
14. d) Using `#[cfg(test)]` and conditional compilation
15. b) `#[tokio::test]`
16. b) Automatically generates mock implementations for specified traits
17. b) tarpaulin
18. a) Marks a function as a benchmark test
19. c) Provides methods for benchmarking
20. c) `cargo tarpaulin --out Xml`

Key Terms

- **Unit Testing:** The practice of testing individual components or units of code to ensure they function correctly. In Rust, unit testing is facilitated by the built-in testing framework and the use of test attributes.
- **AAA Pattern:** An abbreviation for Arrange, Act, and Assert, a structured approach to writing unit tests. It helps organize test functions into phases where input is prepared (Arrange), the actual operation is performed (Act), and the result is verified (Assert).
- **Test Module:** A grouping mechanism in Rust for organizing test functions. Modules help maintain a structured and manageable organization of tests, especially as the codebase grows.
- **Assertion Macros:** Macros in Rust's testing framework used for making assertions about the expected behavior of code. Common assertion macros include **`assert!`**, **`assert_eq!`**, and **`assert_ne!`**.
- **Fixture:** A predefined and consistent set of data used in unit testing to ensure a controlled and reproducible testing environment. Fixtures are commonly shared across multiple tests.
- **Test Execution Options:** Configuration settings and flags used with **`cargo test`** to customize the testing process. Examples include **`--test-threads`**, **`--release`**, **`--ignored`**, and **`--quiet`**.

- **Test Report:** A detailed summary generated after running tests, providing information on tests passed, failed, and skipped. It includes output, errors, and additional information for debugging.
- **Custom Error Messages:** Messages associated with assertions in Rust tests that provide additional context when a test fails. Custom error messages aid in understanding the reason behind test failures and assist in debugging.
- **Conditional Compilation:** A Rust feature that allows code to be conditionally included or excluded during compilation based on specific attributes, such as feature flags or test configurations.
- **Setup Function:** A function in testing responsible for preparing the necessary environment or resources required for the execution of a test.
- **Teardown Function:** A function in testing responsible for performing cleanup operations after the execution of a test, ensuring that resources are properly released.
- **Parameterized Test:** A type of test in which the test function is executed multiple times with different sets of parameters, allowing for efficient testing of various input scenarios.
- **Automock:** An attribute used in Rust with the `mockall` crate to automatically generate mock implementations for specified traits.
- **Benchmarking:** The process of measuring the performance of code using benchmarks to identify bottlenecks and monitor improvements over time.
- **Code Coverage:** A measure of how much of your code is covered by tests, analyzed using tools like `tarpaulin` in Rust.
- **`#[feature(test)]`:** A Rust feature that enables the test crate for benchmarking, allowing the use of the `test` feature in benchmarks.
- **`#[bench]`:** An attribute in Rust used to mark a function as a benchmark test, facilitating the evaluation of code performance.

CHAPTER 12

Network Programming

Introduction

Delving into the world of constructing networked applications proves to be a pivotal and, at times, demanding aspect within the modern landscape of software development. This complex process revolves around the meticulous creation of systems capable of effortlessly exchanging information across networks, thereby facilitating distributed and collaborative functionalities. Our journey through this chapter is marked by an extensive investigation into the complexities of network programming, with a particular focus on leveraging Rust - a programming language that is celebrated for its commitment to performance, safety, and concurrency.

As we uncover the layers of network programming, it becomes evident that the landscape is universal with challenges and complexities that demand a complex approach. The ingenuity of network programming lies in the ability to orchestrate seamless communication between diverse systems, promoting a harmonious exchange of data that supports collaborative functionalities. Rust, with its unique set of features, emerges as an integral choice for navigating this complex landscape. Its emphasis on performance ensures that networked applications can operate with optimal efficiency, while its commitment to safety safeguards against potential vulnerabilities that may arise in the complex web of interconnected systems. Moreover, Rust's concurrency model becomes a clever tool for handling the dynamic nature of networked environments, enabling us to create applications that seamlessly juggle multiple tasks concurrently.

As we get deeper into this topic, you'll see that making programs talk to each other over networks isn't always straightforward. It's a bit like orchestrating a conversation between different friends who speak different languages. Rust becomes our helpful friend here, bringing its own set of skills to the table. It's like having a friend who not only helps the conversation flow smoothly but also makes sure everything happens efficiently and without any hiccups. So, in this chapter, we're not just learning about how to make systems talk; we're discovering the smart ways Rust makes this happen, making our journey into network programming both fun and fascinating.

Structure

In this chapter, we are going to explore the following topics:

- Building Networked Applications with Rust
- Working with TCP and UDP Communication
- Managing Asynchronous Network Operations with async/await

Network Programming

Rust's robust features make it an excellent choice for developing networked applications. As we learned from previous chapters, the ownership system and borrow checker play a pivotal role in ensuring memory safety, which is crucial for preventing common issues like null pointer dereferencing and data races. When building networked applications with Rust, we have the flexibility to leverage the standard library or choose from a variety of third-party libraries tailored to specific networking requirements.

Building Networked Applications

Choosing between *the standard library* and third-party crates depends on the complexity of the networking tasks at hand. The standard library provides a solid foundation for basic networking operations, making it suitable for simpler applications. Third-party crates, such as **tokio**, **async-std**, **socket2**, **rocket**, or **hyper**, offer more advanced features like asynchronous I/O and convenient abstractions for handling complex networking scenarios.

In the world of fundamental networking operations, we can harness the capabilities of modules like **std::net** and **std::io** within the standard library. These modules provide indispensable tools for managing sockets, addresses, and input/output operations. To illustrate the practical application of these modules, let's delve into an example featuring a straightforward TCP server implemented using the standard library.

Consider the following use case where we showcase a basic TCP server, operational on **`127.0.0.1:8080`**, and engineered to deliver a simplistic HTTP response. The focal point of this illustration is the **handle_client** function, designed to efficiently process incoming data from the client and generate a straightforward HTTP reply.

Listing 12.1 A basic TCP server using the standard library.

```
use std::net::{TcpListener, TcpStream};
use std::io::{Read, Write};

fn handle_client(mut stream: TcpStream) {
    println!("Handling client connection...");

    let mut buffer = [0; 512];
    stream.read(&mut buffer).unwrap();

    // Convert the received bytes to a string for better readability
    let request = String::from_utf8_lossy(&buffer[..]);
    println!("Received request:\n{}", request);

    let response = b"HTTP/1.1 200 OK\r\n\r\nHello, Rust!";
    stream.write(response).unwrap();

    println!("Response sent.");
}

fn main() {
    let listener = TcpListener::bind("127.0.0.1:8080").unwrap();
    println!("Server listening on 127.0.0.1:8080...");

    for stream in listener.incoming() {
        match stream {
            Ok(stream) => {
                println!("Accepted a new connection");
                std::thread::spawn(|| handle_client(stream));
            }
            Err(e) => {
                eprintln!("Error: {}", e);
            }
        }
    }
}
```

```
// Output

// Server
// $ cargo run
// Server listening on 127.0.0.1:8080...
// Accepted a new connection
// Handling client connection...
// Received request:
// GET / HTTP/1.1

// Response sent.
```

This practical example encapsulates the essence of leveraging Rust's standard library for networking tasks. The modules, **std::net** and **std::io**, seamlessly integrate into the development process, offering a foundation for addressing low-level networking concerns. This not only simplifies the implementation of common networking functionalities but also promotes a robust and standardized approach to network programming.

The heart of the example lies in the simplicity of the TCP server's design. By binding to the address **127.0.0.1:8080**, the server actively awaits incoming connections. Once a connection is established, the **handle_client** function takes charge, efficiently reading data from the client and responding on time with a basic HTTP message. This encapsulates the core workflow of a minimalistic server-client interaction, highlighting the seamless integration of Rust's standard library into the development of networked applications.

Netcat (**nc**) is a handy command-line tool for interacting with network services. It can be a valuable asset during the development and testing phases of a networking application. In the case of our Rust TCP server, you can use **netcat** to simulate a client connecting to the server and sending HTTP requests.

Assuming your Rust TCP server is running and listening on **127.0.0.1:8080**, open a new terminal window and use **netcat** to connect to the server:

```
$ nc 127.0.0.1 8080
```

This command establishes a connection to the server at **127.0.0.1** on port **8080**. You can then interact with the server by typing an HTTP request and pressing Enter. For example:

```
GET / HTTP/1.1
```

Press Enter again to send the request. You should receive the HTTP response from your Rust server, which, in this example, is a simple message:

```
HTTP/1.1 200 OK

Hello, Rust!
```

Using **netcat** in this way allows you to manually test your Rust TCP server and observe its behavior in response to different client requests. This kind of testing is particularly useful during development to ensure that your server correctly handles incoming connections and produces the expected responses.

By integrating **netcat** into your testing workflow, you can simulate various scenarios and assess how your Rust server performs under different conditions, contributing to the overall reliability and robustness of your networked application.

Third-party crates like **tokio** and **async-std** cater to more advanced networking scenarios, particularly those involving asynchronous I/O. These crates provide abstractions for asynchronous programming, making it easier for developers to write non-blocking, concurrent code. Let's explore a simplified example using **tokio** to create an asynchronous TCP server:

Listing 12.2 A basic TCP server using the tokio crate.

```
use tokio::net::TcpListener;
use tokio::io::{AsyncReadExt, AsyncWriteExt};

#[tokio::main]
async fn main() {
    let listener = TcpListener::bind("127.0.0.1:8080").await.unwrap();
    println!("Server listening on 127.0.0.1:8080...");

    while let Ok((mut socket, _)) = listener.accept().await {
        println!("Accepted a new connection");

        tokio::spawn(async move {
            let mut buffer = [0; 512];
            socket.read(&mut buffer).await.unwrap();

            // Convert the received bytes to a string for better read-
ability
            let request = String::from_utf8_lossy(&buffer[..]);
            println!("Received request:\n{}", request);

            let response = b"HTTP/1.1 200 OK\r\n\r\nHello, Rust!";
            socket.write_all(response).await.unwrap();
            println!("Response sent.");
        });
```

```
    }
}

// Output

// Server
// $ cargo run
// Server listening on 127.0.0.1:8080...
// Accepted a new connection
// Received request:
// GET / HTTP/1.1

// Response sent.

// Client
// $ nc 127.0.0.1 8080
// GET / HTTP/1.1
// HTTP/1.1 200 OK

// Hello, Rust!
```

In this illustration, the utilization of **tokio** is showcased to construct an asynchronous TCP server in Rust. The presence of the **tokio::main** attribute signifies the asynchronous nature of the application's entry point. This distinctive attribute designates the initiation of an asynchronous runtime environment using Tokio, a widely used asynchronous runtime for Rust. Within this asynchronous context, the server handles incoming connections in an asynchronous manner, employing specialized asynchronous I/O operations for reading and writing data.

To encapsulate, Rust's robust ownership system and borrow checker play pivotal roles in the development of memory-safe and concurrent networked systems. The ownership system, where each value has a unique owner responsible for its lifecycle, prevents issues like dangling pointers and data races, as we saw in *Chapter 1, Systems Programming with Rust*. The borrow checker, operating at compile time, enforces strict rules on references and lifetimes, thus preventing potential runtime errors.

Looking ahead, the exploration continues into communication protocols such as *Transmission Control Protocol* (TCP) and *User Datagram Protocol* (UDP). These protocols constitute the backbone of networked communication, and understanding their complexities is vital for proficient network programming in Rust. Furthermore, the narrative extends to the world of managing asynchronous network operations using *the async/await syntax*, a powerful paradigm that enhances the readability and maintainability of asynchronous code in Rust. Throughout the upcoming sections, a comprehensive understanding of network programming in Rust will be well-informed, enlightening you to craft efficient and reliable networked applications.

Communication Protocols: TCP and UDP

At the core of networked applications lie communication protocols, essential frameworks that lay down the rules and conventions governing how different pieces of technology share information. These protocols act as the backbone, ensuring a structured and orderly exchange of data between various entities within a networked environment. Among the multitude of protocols, two stand out prominently, each serving unique purposes in the complex world of network communication.

First in the spotlight is the Transmission Control Protocol (TCP), a heavyweight contender known for its reliability and precision. TCP operates on the principle of establishing a connection before data exchange, creating a virtual link between the sender and the receiver. It meticulously manages the flow of information, confirming the delivery of data packets and retransmitting any lost or corrupted bits. This level of assurance makes TCP the go-to choice for applications where data accuracy and completeness are non-negotiable, such as file transfers, email communication, and web browsing.

On the flip side, we encounter the User Datagram Protocol (UDP), a lightweight and speed-oriented player in the network protocol domain. Unlike TCP, UDP does not require establishing a connection before transmitting data. It opts for a faster, more direct approach, sending data packets without any confirmation of receipt. This speed advantage makes UDP an ideal candidate for applications where real-time communication and quick data transfer take precedence over guaranteed delivery, as seen in online gaming, video streaming, and voice-over-IP (VoIP) services.

The duality of TCP and UDP encapsulates the diverse needs of networked applications. TCP's meticulous and reliable nature suits scenarios where accuracy is crucial, while UDP's quick and straightforward approach caters to situations where speed and real-time responsiveness are the name of the game. Together, these protocols form the dynamic framework that promotes the vast array of interactions within the ever-expanding world of network communication.

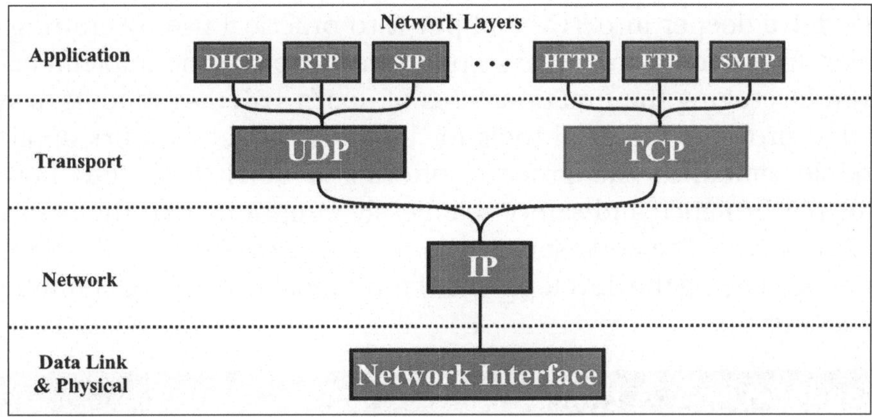

Figure 12.1: *TCP/IP Conceptual Model*

Transmission Control Protocol (TCP)

TCP, short for Transmission Control Protocol, operates as a connection-oriented communication method, meaning it takes a careful and thorough approach to ensure the reliable and properly sequenced transfer of data between devices. Unlike some other protocols, TCP goes the extra mile by first establishing a solid and reliable connection before even thinking about sending data. This upfront commitment is what sets TCP apart in the world of network communication. It guarantees that the packets of information being sent not only reach their destination but also arrive in the right order, ensuring the integrity and coherence of the transmitted data. While this commitment to reliability is commendable, it does come at a cost, TCP introduces additional overhead due to its meticulous approach, making it especially well-suited for applications where the accuracy and completeness of data are non-negotiable.

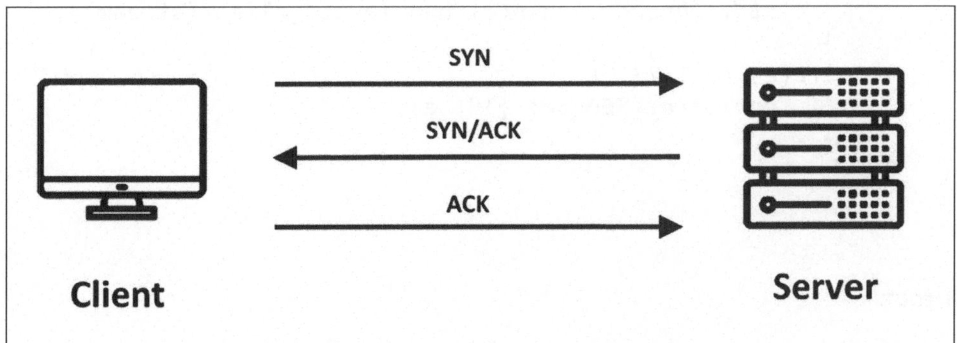

Figure 12.2: *Three-way handshake (TCP)*

Now, let's delve deeper into TCP and put it to practical use by crafting a basic TCP server. In the following code snippet, we'll explore the implementation of this server, leveraging the functionalities of Rust's **std::net** module, a versatile toolbox that provides essential tools for building robust network applications. This module simplifies the process, offering a quick look into how Rust's design for performance and safety seamlessly integrates into the creation of a reliable TCP server. The code serves as a testament to Rust's ability in network programming, making the development of functional and secure communication systems accessible.

Listing 12.3 A basic TCP server using the standard library.

```
use std::net::{TcpListener, TcpStream};
use std::io::{Read, Write};

fn handle_tcp_client(mut stream: TcpStream) { // ①
    let mut buffer = [0; 512]; // ②
    stream.read(&mut buffer).unwrap();

    let request = String::from_utf8_lossy(&buffer); // ③
    println!("Received TCP request: {}", request);

    let response = b"HTTP/1.1 200 OK\r\n\r\nHello, TCP!"; // ④
    stream.write(response).unwrap();
}

fn main() { // ⑤
    let listener = TcpListener::bind("127.0.0.1:8080").unwrap(); // ⑥
    for stream in listener.incoming() { // ⑦
        match stream {
            Ok(stream) => { // ⑧
                std::thread::spawn(|| handle_tcp_client(stream));
            }
            Err(e) => { // ⑨
                eprintln!("Error: {}", e);
            }
        }
    }
}

// Output

// Server
// $ cargo run
// Received TCP request: GET / HTTP/1.1
```

```
// Client
// $ nc 127.0.0.1 8080
// GET / HTTP/1.1
// HTTP/1.1 200 OK

// Hello, TCP!
```

In this illustrative code snippet, the complexities of server-client communication are elegantly emerged:

① At the heart of the code, the **handle_tcp_client** function takes center stage, encapsulating the core functionality responsible for orchestrating the communication with a TCP client. It encompasses reading incoming data, processing it, and returning a suitable HTTP response to be sent back to the client.

② Within the scope of the **handle_tcp_client** function, a pivotal step involves reading data from the TCP client and capturing it within a designated buffer. This process lays the groundwork for subsequent data manipulation and response crafting.

③ The received data, now residing in the buffer, goes through a casting process as it is converted into a String. This step not only highlights Rust's adaptability in handling diverse data types but also highlights the language's commitment to providing us with flexible and expressive tools for data manipulation.

④ As a testament to the basics of server-client interaction, a straightforward yet illustrative HTTP response is methodically constructed within the **handle_tcp_client** function. This practical demonstration serves as a foundation for understanding the fundamental principles of communicating between server and client entities.

⑤ The entry point of the program, the **main** function, orchestrates the initial setup and execution of the server. It serves as a centralized hub from which various functionalities are initiated, directing the flow of the program's execution.

⑥ A pivotal component in the networking infrastructure is revealed as a TCP listener is instantiated, binding to the specific address "`127.0.0.1:8080`". This marks the inception of the server's ability to listen for incoming connections on the designated port.

⑦ The program seamlessly transitions into a loop, awaiting incoming TCP connections. This iterative process ensures that the server remains observant and responsive to potential clients, initiating a thread for each successful connection to manage concurrent communication channels.

⑧ With each successfully accepted connection, a new thread is spawned, introducing a parallel execution paradigm. This new thread, in turn, invokes the **`handle_tcp_client`** function, signifying a dynamic approach to handling multiple client interactions concurrently.

⑨ A layer of robustness is presented in the code through the incorporation of error-handling mechanisms. This ensures that any potential issues arising during the connection acceptance process are methodically addressed, with relevant error messages being carefully printed. This commitment to error management amplifies the server's resilience, enhancing its ability to gracefully handle unexpected scenarios.

This code snippet exemplifies not only the fundamental principles of network programming but also showcases Rust's ability in providing a robust and expressive framework for building efficient and reliable server-client applications. The careful orchestration of functions, the emphasis on concurrency, and the meticulous incorporation of error-handling mechanisms collectively contribute to a codebase that not only functions effectively but also incorporates best practices in software development.

TCP's reliability and ordering guarantees make it suitable for applications such as file transfers, web browsing, and email communication. However, the connection-oriented nature introduces latency, making it less ideal for real-time applications where low latency is crucial.

User Datagram Protocol (UDP)

Unlike TCP, User Datagram Protocol (UDP) is a connectionless protocol that focuses on simplicity and reduced overhead. It operates on a "*fire-and-forget*" principle, where data packets are sent without establishing a connection, and there is no guarantee of delivery or order. This makes UDP suitable for scenarios where low latency and minimal overhead are priorities.

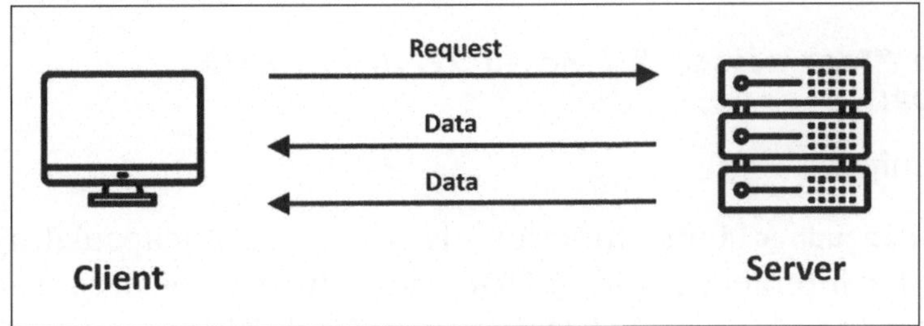

Figure 12.3: *A conceptual UDP workflow*

Let's explore a detailed explanation of UDP and implement a basic UDP server in Rust. The following code snippet demonstrates a simple UDP server using the **std::net** module:

Listing 12.4 A basic UDP server using the standard library.

```
use std::net::UdpSocket;

fn handle_udp_client(socket: UdpSocket) { // ①
    let mut buffer = [0; 512]; // ②

    let (_, client_address) = socket.recv_from(&mut buffer).unwrap(); // ③

    let request = String::from_utf8_lossy(&buffer); // ④
    println!("Received UDP request from {}: {}", client_address, request);

    let response = b"Hello, UDP!"; // ⑤
    socket.send_to(response, client_address).unwrap();
}

fn main() { // ⑥
    let socket = UdpSocket::bind("127.0.0.1:8080").unwrap(); // ⑦

    loop { // ⑧
        handle_udp_client(socket.try_clone().unwrap()); // ⑨
    }
}

// Output

// Server
// $ cargo run
// Received UDP request from 127.0.0.1:35213: Test message
```

```
// Client
// $ echo -n "Test message" | nc -u 127.0.0.1 8080
// Hello, UDP!
```

In this code snippet:

① The **`handle_udp_client`** function is defined, encapsulating the core functionality for interacting with a UDP client. It receives data from the client, processes it, and sends a simple UDP response back. This function plays a pivotal role in managing the communication protocol.

② Within the **`handle_udp_client`** function, a buffer is initialized to store the data received from the UDP client. This buffer acts as a temporary storage space for efficiently handling incoming data.

③ The function proceeds to receive data from the UDP client using the **`recv_from`** method, simultaneously extracting the client's address during the process. This step establishes the groundwork for understanding the source of the incoming data.

④ The received data, residing in the buffer, goes through processing as it is converted into a String. This conversion, facilitated by Rust's flexible handling of data types, prepares the data for further analysis or response construction.

⑤ Subsequently, a simple UDP response, denoted by the byte string "Hello, UDP!", is formulated and sent back to the UDP client using the **`send_to`** method. This marks the completion of the server's communication cycle with the UDP client.

⑥ The entry point of the program is marked by the **`main`** function, serving as the central hub orchestrating the server's execution.

⑦ A UDP socket is created, binding to the specified address "`127.0.0.1:8080`". This initialization step establishes the server's readiness to listen for incoming UDP messages on the designated port.

⑧ The program seamlessly transitions into a loop, indicating its perpetual readiness to handle incoming UDP messages continuously.

⑨ Within this loop, a new thread is spawned for each incoming UDP message, invoking the **`handle_udp_client`** function to manage the communication. This approach ensures a concurrent and responsive handling of multiple UDP clients.

This code snippet exemplifies the fundamental processes involved in server-client communication using the UDP protocol. The careful orchestration of functions, the utilization of buffers for data storage, and the continuous handling of incoming messages within a loop collectively contribute to a robust and responsive UDP server implementation. The code exemplifies Rust's capability to handle low-level networking complexities while providing us with expressive tools for building efficient and reliable networked applications.

TCP and UDP are foundational protocols for network communication, each serving specific use cases based on reliability and latency requirements. You must choose the appropriate protocol for your application's needs.

Asynchronous Network Operations

Asynchronous programming, which we are going to explore in more detail in *Chapter* 14, is essential in network programming to efficiently handle concurrent operations without blocking the execution of other tasks. Rust provides native support for asynchronous programming through the **`async/await`** syntax, enabling us to write non-blocking code with ease.

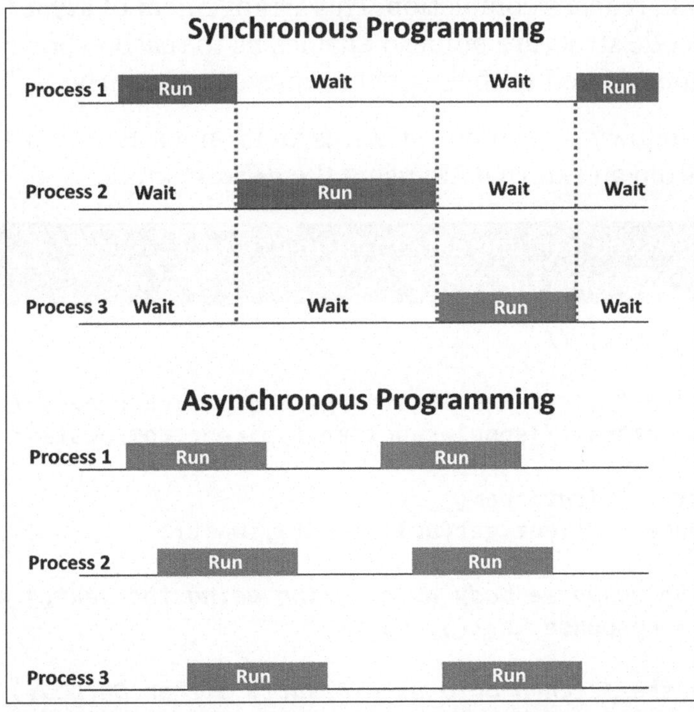

***Figure* 12.4:** *Synchronous versus Asynchronous programming*

Asynchronous Programming

Delving into the world of asynchronous programming opens the door to a paradigm where multiple tasks can operate concurrently, without the necessity to wait for each other's completion. This approach proves especially advantageous in the context of network programming, where scenarios such as managing numerous client connections or concurrently dispatching requests to external services are commonplace. The essence of asynchronous programming lies in the ability to efficiently juggle these tasks, enhancing the overall responsiveness and throughput of applications dealing with concurrent operations.

In Rust, the introduction of the **async/await** syntax revolutionizes the way we approach asynchronous coding. This syntax offers a more intuitive and synchronous-style representation, making the development of asynchronous applications more accessible and comprehensible. The pivotal tool in this syntactical evolution is the **async** keyword, which signifies the initiation of an asynchronous function. Complcmenting this, the **await** keyword emerges as a powerful control mechanism, strategically halting the execution of an asynchronous function until a specific operation, such as an I/O operation or a network request, reaches completion. This arrangement of **async/await** not only simplifies the code structure but also enables us to reason about asynchronous tasks in a manner related to their synchronous counterparts.

Consider the following example of an asynchronous function that simulates fetching data from an external API using the **reqwest** crate:

Listing 12.5 Async fetching data from an external API using the reqwest crate.

```
use reqwest::Client; // ①

async fn fetch_data() -> Result<String, reqwest::Error> { // ②
    let url = "https://jsonplaceholder.typicode.com/posts";

    let client = Client::new(); // ③
    let response = client.get(url).send().await?;

    // Read the response body as a string using the text() method.
    let body = response.text().await?;

    // Return the fetched data as a Result, either Ok(body) or Err
(reqwest::Error).
    Ok(body)
}
```

```
#[tokio::main]
async fn main() { // ④
    match fetch_data().await {
        Ok(data) => println!("Fetched data: {}", data), // ⑤
        Err(e) => eprintln!("Error fetching data: {}", e), // ⑥
    }
}

// Output

// Fetched data: [
//   {
//      "userId": 1,
//      "id": 1,
//      "title": "sunt aut facere repellat provident occaecati excepturi optio reprehenderit",
//      "body": "quia et suscipit\nsuscipit recusandae consequuntur expedita et cum\nreprehenderit molestiae ut ut quas totam\nnostrum rerum est autem sunt rem eveniet architecto"
//   },
//   {
//      "userId": 1,
//      "id": 2,
//      "title": "qui est esse",
//      "body": "est rerum tempore vitae\nsequi sint nihil reprehenderit dolor beatae ea dolores neque\nfugiat blanditiis voluptate porro vel nihil molestiae ut reiciendis\nqui aperiam non debitis possimus qui neque nisi nulla"
//   },
// ...
```

① The code begins with an import statement, bringing the **reqwest** crate into our program's scope. This crate is assumed to be used for handling HTTP requests in the code.

② The asynchronous function **fetch_data** is defined, encapsulating the process of simulating data fetching from an external API. It returns a **Result<String, reqwest::Error>** where the **`String`** represents the fetched data, and **reqwest::Error** represents any potential errors that may occur during the HTTP request.

③ The **tokio::main** attribute marks the entry point of the asynchronous application. This attribute indicates to the Tokio runtime that this is the main function for an asynchronous program.

④ Within the asynchronous context, the **fetch_data** function is called using the **await** keyword. This keyword pauses the execution of the function until the asynchronous HTTP request initiated by **client.get(url).send().await?** completes.

⑤ If the data fetching is successful (resulting in an **Ok** variant), the fetched data is printed to the console.

⑥ If an error occurs during data fetching (resulting in an **Err** variant), the error message is printed to the console using **eprintln!**. This demonstrates a robust error-handling approach, providing insights into any issues that may arise during the asynchronous data fetching process.

The previous code exemplifies the implementation of an asynchronous function designed to simulate the process of fetching data from an external API. The **fetch_data** function showcases the power of Rust's asynchronous programming capabilities, employing the **reqwest** crate to handle HTTP requests in a non-blocking fashion. The use of the **await** keyword strategically pauses the function's execution until the asynchronous HTTP request is complete, ensuring efficient and responsive handling of asynchronous tasks.

Asynchronous TCP Server

Now, let's explore how to implement an asynchronous TCP server using Rust's **async/await** syntax and the **tokio** runtime. The following code snippet demonstrates a simple asynchronous TCP server:

Listing 12.6 Async TCP server using tokio.

```
use tokio::net::TcpListener; // ①
use tokio::io::{AsyncReadExt, AsyncWriteExt};

async fn handle_async_tcp_client(mut socket: tokio::net::TcpStream) { // ②
    let mut buffer = [0; 512]; // ③
    let bytes_read = socket.read(&mut buffer).await.unwrap();

    let request = String::from_utf8_lossy(&buffer[..bytes_read]); // ④
    println!("Received asynchronous TCP request: {}", request);

    let response = b"HTTP/1.1 200 OK\r\n\r\nHello, Asynchronous TCP!"; // ⑤
    socket.write_all(response).await.unwrap();
}
```

```
#[tokio::main] // ⑥
async fn main() {
    let listener = TcpListener::bind("127.0.0.1:8080").await.unwrap(); // ⑦

    while let Ok((stream, _)) = listener.accept().await { // ⑧
        tokio::spawn(handle_async_tcp_client(stream)); // ⑨
    }
}

// Output

// Server
// $ cargo run
// Received asynchronous TCP request: GET / HTTP/1.1


// Client
// $ nc 127.0.0.1 8080
// GET / HTTP/1.1
// HTTP/1.1 200 OK

// Hello, Asynchronous TCP!
```

① The code begins by importing the necessary modules from the Tokio asynchronous runtime, enabling the use of asynchronous I/O operations for networking.

② We then define an asynchronous function, **handle_async_tcp_client**, responsible for managing communication with TCP clients using the async/await syntax.

③ Within the **handle_async_tcp_client** function, we asynchronously read data from the TCP client into a buffer, showcasing the asynchronous nature of the operation.

④ We then process the received data asynchronously, converting it into a String, emphasizing the flexibility of Rust's asynchronous capabilities.

⑤ The code asynchronously sends a response back to the client, demonstrating the seamless integration of asynchronous write operations.

⑥ The code defines the main asynchronous function using the **[tokio::main]** attribute, marking it as the entry point for the asynchronous runtime.

⑦ The program creates an asynchronous TCP listener bound to a specific address, utilizing the async/await syntax for asynchronous setup.

⑧ The program asynchronously accepts incoming TCP connections, entering into a loop to handle each connection asynchronously.

⑨ For each successfully accepted connection, the program spawns a new asynchronous task, invoking the `handle_async_tcp_client` function to handle communication asynchronously. This dynamic approach ensures the concurrent handling of multiple client connections, aligning with the principles of asynchronous programming.

Asynchronous programming in Rust, combined with the `async/await` syntax and asynchronous runtimes like `tokio`, enables us to write scalable and efficient networked applications. This is particularly beneficial when dealing with a large number of concurrent connections or when performing I/O-bound operations.

Real-World Use Cases: Handling HTTP Requests

In real-world scenarios, Rust's application in network programming spans a multitude of contexts, with a notable use case being the development of web servers tailored to handle HTTP requests and serve web applications. Rust's distinctive attributes, including high performance and rigorous memory safety, position it as an exceptional choice for constructing robust web servers. Its performance benefits, derived from low-level control over system resources, make it proficient at meeting the demands of modern, data-intensive applications. Simultaneously, Rust's emphasis on memory safety through strict ownership and borrowing rules enhances its suitability for building secure systems, guarding against common pitfalls like null pointer dereferences and buffer overflows, as we saw in *Chapter 1, Systems Programming with Rust.*

Consider a scenario where a web server is designed to serve a simple static website. The server can utilize the `hyper` crate, a popular asynchronous HTTP library for Rust. The following is an illustrative example:

Listing 12.7 HTTP server using Hyper.

```
use hyper::service::{make_service_fn, service_fn}; // ①
use hyper::{Body, Request, Response, Server};
// ②
async fn handle_request(_: Request<Body>) -> Result<Response<Body>, hy-
per::Error> {
    // Process the request and generate a response
    let response = Response::new(Body::from("Hello, Rust Web Server!"));
```

```
    Ok(response)
}

#[tokio::main]
async fn main() { // ③
    let addr = ([127, 0, 0, 1], 8080).into(); // ④

    let make_service = make_service_fn(|_conn| { // ⑤
        async { Ok::<_, hyper::Error>(service_fn(handle_request)) }
    });

    let server = Server::bind(&addr).serve(make_service); // ⑥

    println!("Rust Web Server running on http://{}", addr); // ⑦

    if let Err(e) = server.await { // ⑧
        eprintln!("server error: {}", e);
    }
}
```

In this code example:

① The **hyper** crate is employed to facilitate the creation of an asynchronous HTTP server. Modules like **make_service_fn**, **service_fn**, **Body**, **Request**, **Response**, and **Server** are imported to enable the construction of the server and handle HTTP requests.

② The **handle_request** function is defined as an asynchronous function. It processes incoming HTTP requests, and for simplicity, it generates a response that includes the message "**Hello, Rust Web Server**!".

③ The **main** function, marked with **[tokio::main]**, serves as the primary entry point for the program. This annotation signals the use of the Tokio runtime for handling asynchronous tasks.

④ The server address to bind to is defined as **([127, 0, 0, 1], 8080).into()**, representing the IP address 127.0.0.1 and port 8080.

⑤ A **make_service** closure is created to build a service for each connection. It utilizes the **service_fn** function to employ the **handle_request** function for processing incoming requests.

⑥ The hyper server is instantiated using **Server::bind(&addr).serve(make_service)**, combining the specified server address and the **make_service** closure.

⑦ The server address is printed to the console, providing a convenient reference for accessing the Rust Web Server.

⑧ The server is started with **server.await**, and any potential errors during its execution are captured and printed to the console. The server runs indefinitely, continuously handling incoming HTTP requests and generating responses. This example demonstrates Rust's capability in managing networked applications, showcasing its versatility in the context of serving web content.

This simple web server showcases the versatility of Rust in handling networked applications, even in the context of serving web content.

Networked Chat Application

Another real-world scenario involves implementing a networked chat application. In the domain of a networked chat application, where the simultaneous exchange of messages among multiple users is crucial, Rust's ability to handle concurrency becomes crucial for creating a responsive and efficient system. By employing the **tokio** library, we can effortlessly orchestrate asynchronous tasks, ensuring that the chat server remains responsive even under the load of numerous concurrent connections. Additionally, the **serde** library proves invaluable in serializing and deserializing data, streamlining the communication process between clients and the server. The following is a high-level example that encapsulates the essence of how Rust, with its concurrency and asynchronous capabilities, can serve as an ideal language for building robust and performant networked chat applications:

Listing 12.8 Async chat app using tokio and serde.

```
use tokio::net::{TcpListener, TcpStream};
use tokio::io::{AsyncReadExt, AsyncWriteExt};
use tokio::sync::broadcast;
use serde::{Deserialize, Serialize};
use std::net::SocketAddr;

#[derive(Debug, Serialize, Deserialize, Clone)] // ①
struct ChatMessage {
    username: String,
    content: String,
}

async fn handle_chat_client( // ②
    stream: TcpStream,
    username: String,
    sender: broadcast::Sender<ChatMessage>,
) {
    println!("New client connected: {}", username);
```

```
    // Clone the sender to send messages to all clients
    let mut receiver = sender.subscribe();

    let (mut reader, mut writer) = tokio::io::split(stream);

    tokio::spawn(async move { // ③
        loop {
            let mut buffer = [0; 512];
            if let Ok(bytes_read) = reader.read(&mut buffer).await {
                if bytes_read == 0 {
                    break;
                }

                // Deserialize the received message
                if let Ok(message) = serde_json::from_slice::<ChatMes-
sage>(&buffer[..bytes_read]) {
                    // Broadcast the message to all clients
                    sender.send(message.clone()).unwrap();
                }
            }
        }
    });

    while let Ok(message) = receiver.recv().await { // ④
        // Exclude the current client from receiving its own messages
        if message.username != username {
            let response = serde_json::to_string(&message).unwrap();
            writer.write_all(response.as_bytes()).await.unwrap();
            println!("Sent message to {}: {}", username, message.con-
tent);
        }
    }

    println!("Client disconnected: {}", username);
}

#[tokio::main] // ⑤
async fn main() {
    let (sender, _) = broadcast::channel::<ChatMessage>(100); // ⑥

    let addr: SocketAddr = "127.0.0.1:8080".parse().unwrap(); // ⑦
    let listener = TcpListener::bind(&addr).await.unwrap();

    println!("Chat Server running on {}", addr);
```

```
    loop { // ⑧
        let (stream, _) = listener.accept().await.unwrap();

        let mut buffer = [0; 512]; // ⑨
        let bytes_read = stream.peek(&mut buffer).await.unwrap();
        let username = String::from_utf8_lossy(&buffer[..bytes_read]).
trim().to_owned();
        println!("Received connection request from: {}", username);

        tokio::spawn(handle_chat_client(stream, username.to_string(),
sender.clone())); // ⑩
    }
}


// $ telnet 127.0.0.1 8080
// {"username": "Alice", "content": "Hello, server!"}
```

① The code snippet begins by defining a struct named **ChatMessage** marked with the **Debug**, **Serialize**, **Deserialize**, and **Clone** traits. This struct encapsulates the structure of messages used for chat communication. The **Debug** trait allows for debugging printouts, while the **Serialize** and **Deserialize** traits enable the conversion of the struct to and from JSON. Lastly, the **Clone** trait allows for creating independent copies of instances of **ChatMessage**.

② The asynchronous function **handle_chat_client** is a cornerstone of the server, responsible for managing each connected chat client. It takes parameters including the client's **TcpStream**, their **username**, and a **broadcast::Sender<ChatMessage>**. As a new client connects, the server prints a welcoming message indicating the successful connection. A clone of the broadcast sender is created, enabling the sending of messages to all connected clients.

③ Inside this function, the client's stream is split into a reader and a writer, facilitating the handling of incoming and outgoing messages separately. Concurrently, a new asynchronous task is spawned to continuously read incoming messages from the client in a loop. These messages are deserialized using the **serde_json** crate and subsequently broadcasted to all clients, ensuring a seamless exchange of information within the chat server.

④ Simultaneously, the function receives messages from other clients via the broadcast channel. To prevent the client from receiving its own messages, the sender's username is compared with the current client's username, and if they differ, the message is sent back to the client. The outgoing messages are serialized into JSON format before being written to the client's stream. The server logs each successfully sent message along with its content. As the client disconnects, a message is printed, indicating the departure of the client associated with the given username. This function encapsulates the dynamic and concurrent nature of managing multiple chat clients in an asynchronous environment.

⑤ ⑥ The **`main`** function serves as the entry point for the chat server. It begins by creating a broadcast channel using the **`broadcast::channel`** function from the **`tokio::sync`** module. This channel is tailored for transmitting instances of the **`ChatMessage`** struct, with a capacity set at 100, ensuring efficient communication among connected clients.

⑦ The server's address, defined as **`127.0.0.1:8080`**, is parsed into a **`SocketAddr`** and subsequently used to bind the TCP listener using **`TcpListener::bind`**. A welcoming message is printed, announcing the successful launch of the chat server at the specified address.

⑧ ⑨ The server then enters into an infinite loop, continuously accepting incoming connections. For each new connection, a new **`TcpStream`** is obtained, and the username of the connecting client is extracted by peeking into the stream. This username extraction process helps in uniquely identifying and addressing each client within the chat system.

⑩ A new asynchronous task is spawned for each connected client using **`tokio::spawn`**. This task invokes the **`handle_chat_client`** function, passing the client's stream, extracted username, and a cloned broadcast sender. This mechanism ensures that each client is handled concurrently, fostering a responsive and scalable chat server.

This code snippet demonstrates a robust and scalable chat server utilizing asynchronous programming principles and the Tokio runtime. The handling of chat clients is orchestrated with finesse, leveraging broadcast channels for efficient message distribution. The modular design and integration with external crates, such as **`serde`** for serialization, showcase Rust's versatility in building high-performance and concurrent network applications.

File Transfer Server

Building a file transfer server is a practical application of network programming, enabling clients to seamlessly upload and download files across a network. In this section, we demonstrate the creation of a straightforward yet robust file transfer server using Rust's standard library. Rust's emphasis on performance, safety, and concurrency proves instrumental in crafting a server that efficiently handles file exchanges. This example underscores the versatility of Rust in simplifying network programming tasks, showcasing its capacity to provide a secure and streamlined solution for facilitating file transfers in various scenarios, from local networks to broader internet environments.

Listing 12.9 FTP server using the standard library.

```
use std::net::{TcpListener, TcpStream};
use std::io::{Read, Write};
use std::fs::File;

fn handle_file_transfer_client(mut stream: TcpStream) {
    let mut filename_buffer = [0; 128]; // ①
    stream.read(&mut filename_buffer).unwrap();
    let filename = String::from_utf8_lossy(&filename_buffer)
        .split_terminator('\0') // ②
        .next() // ③
        .unwrap_or_default() // ④
        .trim() // ⑤
        .to_string();

    let mut file = File::create(&filename).unwrap(); // ⑥

    let mut buffer = [0; 1024]; // ⑦
    loop {
        let bytes_read = stream.read(&mut buffer).unwrap();
        if bytes_read == 0 { // ⑧
            break;
        }
        file.write_all(&buffer[..bytes_read]).unwrap();
    }

    println!("File '{}' received successfully.", filename);
}

fn main() {
    let listener = TcpListener::bind("127.0.0.1:8080").unwrap(); // ⑨
    println!("File Transfer Server listening on 127.0.0.1:8080...");

    for stream in listener.incoming() { // ⑩
        match stream {
            Ok(stream) => {
                println!("Accepted a new connection for file transfer");
                std::thread::spawn(|| handle_file_transfer_client(stream));
            }
```

```
                Err(e) => {
                    eprintln!("Error: {}", e);
                }
            }
        }
}
```

Breaking down the complexities of this code snippet, the **`handle_file_transfer_client`** function forms the core of the file transfer server's functionality.

① Within this function, the process begins by reading the filename from the client and managing the reception of both the filename and the file content. The subsequent step involves storing the received file on the server side, thereby establishing a basic foundation for file transfer.

② The filename is initially read into a buffer, and this line of code strategically splits the filename at null bytes, assuming null termination – a common practice in network communication.

③ The **`next`** method plays a pivotal role in retrieving the first part before the null byte, effectively extracting the filename from the received data.

④ An error prevention plan is in place if no valid characters are present. In such cases, an empty string is utilized as a default, ensuring that the process can adapt to varying input scenarios.

⑤ Further refinements involve trimming leading and trailing whitespaces from the filename, enhancing the robustness and cleanliness of the extracted information.

⑥ Following the extraction of the filename, the server proceeds to create the file on the server-side for writing. This step is crucial in preparing the destination for storing the incoming file content.

⑦ To optimize the transfer process, data is read and written in chunks. This chunked approach enhances efficiency, especially when dealing with potentially large files.

⑧ The looping structure incorporates a break condition triggered by the encounter of a null byte. This signifies the conclusion of the file transfer process, ensuring that the server can efficiently handle files of varying lengths.

⑨ Shifting the focus to the main function, it initiates the creation of a TCP listener on the address "`127.0.0.1:8080`". This serves as the entry point for incoming connections.

⑩ The main function excels in handling the dynamic nature of network communication by accepting incoming connections and allocating a new thread for each. The use of **std::thread::spawn** ensures concurrent handling of multiple clients, adding a layer of scalability to the file transfer server.

This well-structured file transfer server not only allows clients to transmit filenames and corresponding file content but also ensures the secure storage of files on the server side. Its design showcases Rust's capabilities in managing network communication intricacies and handling concurrency. By offering a solid foundation for file transfer systems, this implementation highlights Rust's versatility in crafting robust and efficient network applications.

Remote Command Execution Server

Another compelling use case for Rust lies in constructing servers that facilitate remote command execution by clients. This situation frequently arises in distributed computing environments or when dealing with remote system administration, where the need for seamless interaction with remote systems is crucial. In Rust, a simple yet powerful example of such a server can be crafted to handle the execution of commands issued by clients from afar. By leveraging Rust's capabilities in network programming, concurrency, and system-level interactions, this server becomes a robust tool for orchestrating remote command execution. This functionality proves invaluable for scenarios where the efficient management and control of systems across networks are essential, showcasing Rust's versatility in addressing real-world challenges in distributed computing and remote administration.

Listing 12.10 RCE server using the standard library.

```
use std::net::{TcpListener, TcpStream};
use std::io::{Read, Write};
use std::process::{Command, Stdio};

fn handle_remote_command_client(mut stream: TcpStream) {
    let mut command_buffer = [0; 512]; // ①
    stream.read(&mut command_buffer).unwrap();
    let command_str = String::from_utf8_lossy(&command_buffer)
        .split_terminator('\0') // ②
        .next() // ③
        .unwrap_or_default() // ④
        .trim() // ⑤
        .to_string();
```

```
    let output = Command::new("sh") // ⑥
        .arg("-c")
        .arg(&command_str)
        .stdout(Stdio::piped())
        .output()
        .unwrap();

    stream.write_all(&output.stdout).unwrap(); // ⑦
}

fn main() {
    let listener = TcpListener::bind("127.0.0.1:8080").unwrap(); // ⑧
    println!("Remote Command Execution Server listening on 
127.0.0.1:8080...");

    for stream in listener.incoming() { // ⑨
        match stream {
            Ok(stream) => {
                println!("Accepted a new connection for remote command 
execution");
                std::thread::spawn(|| handle_remote_command_cli-
ent(stream)); // ⑩
            }
            Err(e) => {
                eprintln!("Error: {}", e);
            }
        }
    }
}

// Output

// Server
// $ cargo run
// Remote Command Execution Server listening on 127.0.0.1:8080...
// Accepted a new connection for remote command execution

// Client
// $ nc 127.0.0.1 8080
// ls src
// main.rs
```

Let's delve into the complexities of this code snippet, which exemplifies the creation of a basic remote command execution server:

① The **handle_remote_command_client** function is responsible for processing client commands. It reads a command from the client, trims, and processes it, executes the command using the system shell, captures the output, and sends it back to the client.

② The received command is split at null bytes, allowing for multiple commands to be sent in a single transmission.

③ The **next** method retrieves the first part of the split command, ensuring that the server works with the provided command.

④ If there are no valid characters, the **unwrap_or_default** method ensures that an empty string is used to avoid issues.

⑤ The **trim** method removes any leading or trailing whitespaces from the command.

⑥ The command is executed using the system shell (**sh -c**), and its output is captured.

⑦ The server then sends the output of the executed command back to the client.

⑧ In the **main** function, a TCP listener is created and bound to the address "**127.0.0.1:8080**".

⑨ The server listens for incoming connections in a loop, accepting each connection and spawning a new thread to handle the client.

⑩ A new thread is spawned for each accepted connection, invoking the **handle_remote_command_client** function to process client commands concurrently.

Illustrated here is a straightforward yet robust instantiation of a remote command execution server in Rust, underscoring the language's adeptness in managing both network communication and concurrent execution seamlessly. The incorporation of threads serves as a pivotal element, providing the server with the ability to efficiently manage numerous clients concurrently. This not only enhances the server's efficiency but also positions it as a versatile and pragmatic solution for diverse remote command execution scenarios. Rust's unique features shine through, providing a solid foundation for the development of such networked applications, where the need for both responsiveness and scalability is crucial. This example stands as a testament to Rust's capabilities in crafting solutions that balance simplicity and power, particularly in the world of network programming and command execution.

Peer-to-Peer File Sharing

Facilitating the direct exchange of files between users without reliance on a central server, *peer-to-peer (P2P) file sharing* systems represent a decentralized approach to file distribution. Rust, with its robust concurrency features and adept low-level networking capabilities, emerges as a fitting choice for the development of P2P applications. The language's concurrency support allows for efficient handling of multiple tasks simultaneously, a crucial aspect in the dynamic environment of P2P file sharing. In the absence of a central intermediary, Rust's capabilities empower us to create resilient and responsive P2P file-sharing servers. The following example provides a simplified glimpse into the construction of such a server, showcasing how Rust's strengths align seamlessly with the demands of decentralized file-sharing systems:

Listing 12.11 P2P file sharing using the standard library.

```
use std::net::{TcpListener, TcpStream};
use std::io::{Read, Write};
use std::fs::File;
use std::thread;
use std::env;

fn handle_p2p_client(mut stream: TcpStream) {
    let mut filename_buffer = [0; 128]; // ①
    stream.read(&mut filename_buffer).unwrap();

    let filename = String::from_utf8_lossy(&filename_buffer) // ②
        .split_terminator('\0') // ③
        .next() // ④
        .unwrap_or_default() // ⑤
        .trim() // ⑥
        .to_string();

    println!("Server working directory: {:?}", env::current_dir());

    println!("Received request for file: {}", filename);

    let file = File::open(&filename); // ⑦
    let response: Vec<u8> = match file {
        Ok(mut file) => {
            let mut buffer = Vec::new();
            file.read_to_end(&mut buffer).unwrap();
            buffer
```

```
        }
        Err(_) => {
            println!("File not found: {}", filename);
            Vec::new() // ⑧
        }
    };

    stream.write_all(&response).unwrap(); // ⑨

    println!("Sent response to the client for file: {}", filename);
}

fn main() {
    let listener = TcpListener::bind("127.0.0.1:8080").unwrap(); // ⑩
    println!("P2P File Sharing Server listening on 127.0.0.1:8080...");

    for stream in listener.incoming() { // ⑪
        match stream {
            Ok(stream) => {
                println!("Accepted a new connection for P2P file shar-
ing");
                thread::spawn(|| handle_p2p_client(stream)); // ⑫
            }
            Err(e) => {
                eprintln!("Error: {}", e);
            }
        }
    }
}

// Output

// Server
// $ cargo run
// P2P File Sharing Server listening on 127.0.0.1:8080...
// Accepted a new connection for P2P file sharing
// Server working directory: Ok("/home/mahmoud/chapter-12/p2p")
// Received request for file: file.txt
// Sent response to the client for file: file.txt

// Client
// $ nc 127.0.0.1 8080
// file.txt
// line 1
// line 2
// line 3
//
```

Let's delve into each part of this code snippet for the P2P file-sharing server:

① The **`handle_p2p_client`** function is the core of the server's file-sharing functionality. It reads the filename from the client over a TCP connection.

② The obtained filename may contain null bytes. To ensure a clean filename, null bytes are removed from the buffer.

③ The **`split_terminator`** method is used to split the filename at null bytes, creating an iterator.

④ The **`next`** method retrieves the first part of the split, representing the filename before the null byte.

⑤ The **`unwrap_or_default`** method ensures that an empty string is used if there are no valid characters in the filename.

⑥ The **`trim`** method removes leading and trailing whitespaces from the filename, providing a clean and formatted result.

⑦ The server's working directory and the received filename are printed to the console for informative purposes.

⑧ The server attempts to open the file specified by the client for reading. If successful, the file's content is read into a buffer.

⑨ The file content is then sent back to the client over the TCP connection, completing the file-sharing process.

⑩ In the **`main`** function, a TCP listener is created and bound to the address "**`127.0.0.1:8080`**."

⑪ The server enters a loop to accept incoming connections. For each connection, a new thread is spawned to handle the client concurrently.

⑫ Each accepted connection triggers the spawning of a new thread using **`thread::spawn`**, where the **`handle_p2p_client`** function is executed to manage the client's file-sharing request. This threading approach enhances the server's ability to handle multiple client connections simultaneously.

In this P2P file-sharing server, clients can request a file by sending its filename, and the server responds by sending the file content. This simple example lays the foundation for more advanced P2P systems.

Real-Time Collaborative Editing

Network programming in Rust can be applied to build real-time collaborative editing systems, where multiple users can edit a shared document simultaneously. This example uses the **WebSocket** protocol through the **tungstenite** crate for communication:

Listing 12.12 Real-time collaborative editing using tokio and tungstenite.

```
use futures_util::StreamExt; // ①
use futures_util::stream::TryStreamExt;
use tokio::net::TcpListener;
use tokio_tungstenite::accept_async;
use futures_util::SinkExt;

#[tokio::main]
async fn main() {
    let addr: std::net::SocketAddr = "127.0.0.1:8080".parse().expect
("Invalid address"); // ②

    let listener = TcpListener::bind(&addr).await.expect("Failed to bind
to address");
    println!("Real-Time Collaborative Editing Server listening on {}",
addr); // ③

    handle_editor_connection(listener).await; // ④
}

async fn handle_editor_connection(stream: TcpListener) { // ⑤
    while let Ok((socket, addr)) = stream.accept().await {
        println!("Accepted a new connection from: {}", addr);
        tokio::spawn(handle_editor_client(socket, addr)); // ⑥
    }
}

async fn handle_editor_client(socket: tokio::net::TcpStream, addr: st-
d::net::SocketAddr) { // ⑦
    let ws_stream = match accept_async(socket).await { // ⑧
        Ok(ws_stream) => {
            println!("WebSocket connection established with: {}", addr);
            ws_stream
        }
        Err(e) => { // ⑨
            eprintln!("Error during WebSocket handshake with {}: {}",
```

```
addr, e);
                return;
            }
        };

    let (mut write, mut read) = ws_stream.split(); // ⑩

    tokio::spawn(async move { // ⑪
        while let Ok(Some(message)) = read.try_next().await {
            println!("Received message from {}: {}", addr, message.to_
text().unwrap_or_default()); // ⑫


            if let Err(e) = write.send(message).await { // ⑬
                eprintln!("Error sending WebSocket message to {}: {}",
addr, e);
                break;
            }
        }

        if let Err(e) = write.close().await { // ⑭
            eprintln!("Error closing WebSocket connection with {}: {}",
addr, e);
        }

        println!("WebSocket connection with {} closed", addr);
    });
}

// Output

// Server
// $ cargo run
// Real-Time Collaborative Editing Server listening on 127.0.0.1:8080
// Accepted a new connection from: 127.0.0.1:38154
// WebSocket connection established with: 127.0.0.1:38154
// Received message from 127.0.0.1:38154: Hello, WebSocket server!

// WebSocket connection with 127.0.0.1:38154 closed

// Client
// $ websocat ws://127.0.0.1:8080
// Hello, WebSocket server!
// Hello, WebSocket server!
// ^C
```

Let's explore the complexities of the preceding code snippet that sets up a server to handle WebSocket connections for real-time collaborative editing. The code utilizes several libraries, including **futures_util, tokio**, and **tokio_tungstenite**, to streamline asynchronous operations and WebSocket handling. The main function, marked with `[tokio::main]`, serves as the entry point, defining the server's address, binding it, and initiating the handling of editor connections.

① The code begins by importing the necessary libraries, including those for handling futures, asynchronous streams, TCP connections, and WebSocket operations.

② The server's address is defined as "`127.0.0.1:8080`".

③ The TCP listener is bound to the specified address, and the server's readiness is printed to the console.

④ The `handle_editor_connection` function is called to initiate the handling of incoming editor connections.

⑤ The `handle_editor_connection` function is defined to loop over incoming connections, accepting them and spawning a new task for each.

⑥ Each new connection triggers the spawning of a new task to handle the WebSocket connection using the `handle_editor_client` function.

⑦ The `handle_editor_client` function is defined to handle individual editor clients, attempting to establish a WebSocket connection.

⑧ The WebSocket stream is split into read and write parts, allowing separate handling of incoming and outgoing messages.

⑨ Errors during the WebSocket handshake are handled, with appropriate messages printed to the console.

⑩ A new task is spawned to process incoming WebSocket messages asynchronously.

⑪ Within this asynchronous task, incoming messages are processed, and a placeholder logic (commented as ⑫) is provided for handling collaborative editing, such as document updates.

⑬ The received message is broadcasted to all connected clients, and potential errors in sending are handled.

⑭ The WebSocket connection is closed gracefully, and any errors during the closing process are reported.

This code snippet serves as a comprehensive foundation for building a real-time collaborative editing server, with a focus on handling WebSocket connections and processing messages between clients. We can customize the collaboration logic according to specific project requirements. The code showcases the power of asynchronous programming in Rust, leveraging libraries like **tokio** and **tokio_tungstenite** to streamline network operations effectively.

To interact with this real-time collaborative editing server, we can use **websocat** from the command line interface (CLI).

First, ensure that you have **websocat** installed on your system. You can install it using a package manager like **cargo**, which is Rust's package manager:

```
$ cargo install websocat
```

Assuming you have saved the Rust code in a file named **main.rs**, you can use **cargo** to build and run the code. Navigate to the directory containing your Rust code in the terminal and run:

```
$ cargo run
```

This will compile and execute your Rust program, starting the WebSocket server on **127.0.0.1:8080**.

Now, open another terminal window and use **websocat** to connect to the WebSocket server. Run the following command:

```
$ websocat ws://127.0.0.1:8080
```

This command tells **websocat** to establish a WebSocket connection to the server running at **127.0.0.1:8080**. You should see a message indicating a successful connection in the terminal where **websocat** is running.

With the WebSocket connection established, you can now send and receive messages. Anything you type in the **websocat** terminal will be sent to the server, and any messages received from the server will be displayed in the terminal.

For example, type a message and press Enter. You should see the message being processed by the server, and if the collaborative editing logic (as a placeholder in the code) involves broadcasting, you might see the message echoed back to you:

```
Hello, WebSocket server!
```

The server's terminal where you ran **cargo run** will also display messages about received and broadcasted messages.

To close the connection, you can simply close the **`websocat`** terminal. This will trigger the WebSocket server to handle the closure gracefully, as per the logic in the code.

These real-world use cases demonstrate the versatility of Rust in network programming, showcasing its capabilities in building diverse and sophisticated applications.

Conclusion

Throughout this comprehensive exploration of network programming with Rust, we've traversed the vast landscape of real-world use cases, demonstrating the remarkable versatility of Rust in tackling diverse networking scenarios. From the construction of web servers and chat applications to the nuanced utilization of the **`tokio`** crate for different networking tasks, Rust has proven itself as a robust foundation for the development of efficient and reliable networked applications.

As you navigate the dynamic field of network programming, Rust offers a spectrum of choices. The high-level abstractions provided by Rust's standard library, complemented by third-party crates like **`tokio`** and **`hyper`** for asynchronous and HTTP-based applications, present flexible options. Simultaneously, the **`socket2`** crate empowers us with fine-grained control over socket configurations, enabling tailored solutions for specific networking requirements.

Armed with the insights gained from this chapter, you are well-prepared to tackle the complexities of network programming in Rust. The knowledge gathered here serves as a robust toolkit, equipping you to construct networked applications that are not only performant and scalable but also adept at navigating the complex challenges posed by modern networking environments. Whether opting for high-level abstractions or delving into low-level socket interactions, Rust emerges as a crucial tool in the pursuit of building resilient and efficient networked systems.

As we conclude our exploration of networking in Rust, the upcoming chapter will delve into the world of unsafe coding. This chapter will take us to the riskier aspects of Rust, where greater control is possible, but caution is essential. We'll investigate the reasons behind the existence of unsafe code and when it's appropriate to employ it. Whether it's dealing with unique data types or performing advanced operations, we'll uncover how Rust empowers us to accomplish potent tasks while maintaining a commitment to safety.

Resources

To deepen your understanding of Network Programming with Rust, you can explore the following resources:

- *Rust Book - Building a Multithreaded Web Server*: Follow the official Rust documentation to build a multithreaded web server, gaining insights into practical applications of network programming. - *https://doc.rust-lang.org/book/ch20-00-final-project-a-web-server.html*
- *Tokio Tutorial*: Learn asynchronous programming in Rust with Tokio, a popular runtime for building scalable and efficient network applications. - *https://tokio.rs/tokio/tutorial*
- *Async-std Documentation*: Explore the documentation for the **`async-std`** crate, which provides asynchronous versions of standard Rust library types, essential for async network programming. - *https://docs.rs/async-std/*
- *Hyper Documentation*: Delve into the documentation of the **`hyper`** crate, a widely-used HTTP library in Rust, to understand building robust and performant HTTP servers. - *https://docs.rs/hyper/*
- *Tungstenite Documentation*: Learn about WebSocket programming in Rust by exploring the documentation for the **`tungstenite`** crate, a key tool for real-time communication. - *https://docs.rs/tungstenite/*[
- *Serde Documentation*: Understand how to serialize and deserialize data for network communication using the **`serde`** crate with insights from the official documentation. - *https://docs.rs/serde/*
- *Warp Documentation*: Delve into the documentation of the **`warp`** crate, a powerful web framework for Rust that simplifies building RESTful APIs and web applications. - *https://docs.rs/warp/*
- *Reqwest Documentation*: Learn how to make HTTP requests from Rust applications with the **`reqwest`** crate, exploring the documentation for insights into client-side networking. - *https://docs.rs/reqwest/*
- *async-raft*: Dive into the **`async-raft`** crate for building distributed systems with Raft consensus, expanding your knowledge of networked applications in Rust. - *https://github.com/async-raft/async-raft*
- *Network Programming in Rust Book*: Explore this book for a comprehensive guide to network programming in Rust, covering a wide range of topics and practical examples.

- *Are We Game Yet? - Networking*: Stay updated on the networking ecosystem in Rust with the "Are We Game Yet?" website, providing a curated list of networking-related crates and tools. - *https://arewegameyet.rs/ecosystem/networking/*

These resources cover various aspects of network programming in Rust, from building web servers to handling asynchronous communication and exploring popular crates for networking tasks.

Multiple Choice Questions

Q1: Which Rust feature plays a pivotal role in ensuring memory safety in networked applications?

a) `Async/await` syntax

b) Ownership system and borrow checker

c) Tokio runtime

d) Third-party crates

Q2: When building networked applications with Rust, the choice between the standard library and third-party crates depends on:

a) The popularity of the crate

b) Personal preference of the developer

c) The complexity of the networking tasks

d) The size of the development team

Q3: What is the purpose of the `handle_client` function in the TCP server example?

a) Initiating a new TCP connection

b) Reading data from the client and generating an HTTP response

c) Closing the TCP connection

d) Handling errors during the connection

Q4: Which protocol is known for its reliability and precision, confirming the delivery of data packets and retransmitting any lost or corrupted bits?

a) Transmission Control Protocol (TCP)

b) User Datagram Protocol (UDP)

c) Hypertext Transfer Protocol (HTTP)

d) File Transfer Protocol (FTP)

Q5: Which crate is commonly used for asynchronous programming in Rust?

a) `serde`

b) `tokio`

c) `hyper`

d) `rustc`

Q6: In the networked chat application example, what is the role of the `broadcast::channel` function?

a) It defines the structure of chat messages.

b) It handles communication with TCP clients.

c) It creates a channel for transmitting chat messages among clients.

d) It restricts access to the server address.

Q7: What does the `tokio::main` attribute signify in the chat server example?

a) It defines the structure of the main function.

b) It provides default implementations for asynchronous tasks.

c) It marks the main function as the entry point, signaling the use of the Tokio runtime.

d) It restricts access to the server address.

Q8: What does the `serde` library facilitate in the chat application example?

a) It defines the structure of chat messages.

b) It handles communication with TCP clients.

c) It serializes and deserializes data for communication.

d) It restricts access to the server address.

Q9: In the chat server example, what does the `tokio::spawn` function do?

a) It defines the structure of the main function.

b) It provides default implementations for asynchronous tasks.

c) It spawns a new asynchronous task for each connected client.

d) It restricts access to the server address.

Q10: What is the role of the `handle_file_transfer_client` function in the file transfer server example?

a) Initiating the TCP listener

b) Handling incoming connections and managing file transfers

c) Creating a file on the client side

d) Writing data to the file on the server side

Q11: What does the `split_terminator` method do in the file transfer server code?

a) Splits the file content into chunks

b) Splits the filename at null bytes

c) Terminates the server's execution

d) Terminates the client's connection

Q12: How does the file transfer server handle the termination of file transfer?

a) Using a specific termination character in the file content

b) Closing the connection abruptly

c) Encountering a null byte in the filename

d) Detecting zero bytes read during file content transfer

Q13: Why is the `stdout(Stdio::piped())` method used in the remote command execution server?

a) To redirect standard output to a pipe

b) To close the standard output

c) To print output to the console

d) To capture standard error output

Q14: How does the P2P file-sharing server handle a request for a non-existent file?

a) Terminates the server's execution

b) Sends an error message to the client

c) Prints an error message to the console

d) Sends an empty response to the client

Q15: What is the purpose of the `accept_async` function in the real-time collaborative editing server?

a) Accepts incoming TCP connections

b) Accepts incoming WebSocket connections

c) Accepts incoming file transfers

d) Accepts incoming command executions

Q16: How does the real-time collaborative editing server handle WebSocket message transmission errors?

a) Terminates the server's execution

b) Prints an error message to the console

c) Sends an error message to the client

d) Closes the WebSocket connection

Answers

1. b) Ownership system and borrow checker
2. c) The complexity of the networking tasks

3. b) Reading data from the client and generating an HTTP response
4. a) Transmission Control Protocol (TCP)
5. b) `tokio`
6. c) It creates a channel for transmitting chat messages among clients
7. c) It marks the main function as the entry point, signaling the use of the Tokio runtime.
8. c) It serializes and deserializes data for communication.
9. c) It spawns a new asynchronous task for each connected client.
10. b) Handling incoming connections and managing file transfers
11. b) Splits the filename at null bytes
12. d) Detecting zero bytes read during file content transfer
13. a) To redirect standard output to a pipe
14. d) Sends an empty response to the client
15. b) Accepts incoming WebSocket connections
16. d) Closes the WebSocket connection

Key Terms

- **Tokio:** A widely used asynchronous runtime for Rust, facilitating the development of non-blocking, concurrent code.
- **Standard Library:** The set of modules and functionalities that come bundled with the Rust programming language, providing essential tools for common programming tasks.
- **Third-party Crates:** External libraries in Rust that can be added to a project to extend its functionality, often created and maintained by the Rust community.
- **Transmission Control Protocol (TCP):** A reliable and connection-oriented communication protocol that ensures the accurate and ordered transfer of data between devices.

- **User Datagram Protocol (UDP):** A connectionless and lightweight communication protocol that prioritizes speed and minimal overhead, suitable for real-time applications.
- **Asynchronous Programming:** A programming paradigm in Rust that allows multiple tasks to operate concurrently without waiting for each other's completion, enhancing responsiveness and throughput.
- **Hyper:** A popular asynchronous HTTP library for Rust, used for building web servers and handling HTTP requests.
- **Serde:** A Rust library for serializing and deserializing data, commonly used in networked applications for efficient communication.
- **Broadcast Channel:** A communication channel in Rust that allows sending messages to multiple receivers, commonly used for broadcasting messages in concurrent systems.
- **P2P (Peer-to-Peer) File Sharing:** Decentralized file-sharing systems that allow direct exchange of files between users without reliance on a central server.
- **`accept_async`:** A function in the real-time collaborative editing server that accepts incoming WebSocket connections asynchronously.
- **WebSocket:** A communication protocol that provides full-duplex communication channels over a single, long-lived connection, used for real-time collaborative editing in the server example.

CHAPTER 13

Unsafe Coding in Rust

Introduction

In Rust, knowing how to handle unsafe code is super important. Rust really cares about keeping things safe with memory and making programs efficient. But sometimes, to do special things, we have to use unsafe code. This chapter is like a guide to help you understand what unsafe code is all about, and when and why you might need to use it.

Rust is known for being super careful about keeping your computer's memory safe. It has rules in place to prevent common mistakes that can make programs crash or cause other problems. This helps make Rust programs reliable and fast. However, in certain situations, especially when dealing with low-level tasks or connecting with other languages, following these super strict rules can get in the way. That's where unsafe code comes in handy, but it's like handling a powerful tool that needs careful attention to make sure everything stays in good shape.

Knowing why and when to use unsafe code is like having a superpower for us. This chapter not only talks about the ideas behind unsafe code but also gives real examples to show when and why you might need it. Understanding the situations that make unsafe code necessary helps us make smart choices, using its power when needed while still sticking to the main rules of Rust. As we go through the world of unsafe code in Rust, the goal is to help you have the knowledge and good judgment to handle it safely and effectively.

Structure

In this chapter, we are going to explore the following topics:

- Introduction to unsafe code
- Exploring some of the unsafe block scenarios
- Performance and safety considerations of an unsafe code
- Real world examples of unsafe code
- Memory safety violations
- Case studies

Unsafe Code

Unsafe code in Rust allows us to bypass the safety guarantees normally enforced by the compiler. It provides a way to perform operations that would be considered risky within the limits of safe Rust. To comprehend when it's necessary, it's essential to appreciate Rust's commitment to safety and the situations where circumventing those safeguards becomes imperative.

Unsafe blocks are a powerful feature, but they should not be approached casually. They are reserved for scenarios where the benefits of bypassing Rust's safety checks outweigh the risks. This includes situations where interfacing with external languages or performing low-level system operations necessitates a departure from the safety net provided by the language. Let's consider the following example:

Listing 13.1 Unsafe code block example.

```
fn main() {
    let safe_variable = 42; // ①

    println!("This is safe code: {}", safe_variable); // ②

    unsafe {
        let raw_pointer: *const i32 = &safe_variable; // ③
        println!("Unsafe raw pointer value: {}", *raw_pointer); // ④
    }
}

// Output

// This is safe code: 42
// Unsafe raw pointer value: 42
```

① In this line, a new variable named **`safe_variable`** is declared and assigned the value **`42`**. The **`let`** keyword is used for variable declaration, and in this case, the variable is immutable, indicated by the absence of the **`mut`** keyword. The value **`42`** is a placeholder, and the variable is of type **`i32`**, a 32-bit signed integer. This line represents a standard and safe initialization of a variable in Rust.

② The following line utilizes the **`println!`** macro to print a message along with the value of **`safe_variable`**. This line exemplifies safe Rust code, adhering to the language's memory safety guarantees. The macro takes a format string with a placeholder **`{}`**, which is replaced by the actual value of **`safe_variable`** during execution.

③ Inside the unsafe block, a raw pointer is introduced with the declaration **`let raw_pointer: *const i32 = &safe_variable;`**. The **`*const i32`** type signifies a raw pointer to an immutable integer of type **`i32`**. The **`&safe_variable`** syntax retrieves the memory address of **`safe_variable`**, and the raw pointer is initialized with this address. It's important to note that the creation of raw pointers is inherently unsafe in Rust, as it sidesteps the language's usual safety checks.

④ The unsafe block proceeds to dereference the raw pointer using **`*raw_pointer`** to access the value it points to. This value is then printed using the **`println!`** macro. Dereferencing raw pointers is marked as unsafe because it involves interacting with raw memory addresses without the safety guarantees provided by Rust's ownership system and borrowing rules. It's a powerful feature but requires careful consideration and should only be employed in scenarios where the benefits outweigh the risks.

This code snippet introduces a scenario where the use of unsafe code, specifically raw pointers, becomes necessary for low-level operations. The safe code preceding the unsafe block demonstrates adherence to Rust's safety principles, while the subsequent unsafe block showcases a deliberate departure from these safety guarantees to achieve a specific goal, illustrating the controlled and purposeful nature of unsafe code in Rust.

We must have a deep understanding of the potential risks involved in using unsafe code. This includes the possibility of causing undefined behavior, memory safety violations, or data races. Before diving into unsafe blocks, one should thoroughly evaluate whether the specific scenario genuinely validates their use and if there are alternative, safer approaches.

Unsafe Blocks Scenarios

One of the primary scenarios that might result in the use of unsafe code is when interfacing with external languages. Rust's safety guarantees are built around its own abstractions, and interacting with foreign languages, especially those without Rust's safety features, may necessitate the use of unsafe code.

Low-level system operations, such as direct memory manipulation or interactions with hardware, also often demand the use of unsafe code. Rust's ownership system and borrowing rules, while powerful for ensuring memory safety, can be too restrictive for certain system-level tasks.

Listing 13.2 Safe Rust code calling an unsafe external function.

```
extern "C" {
    fn external_function(); // ①
}

fn main() {
    unsafe {
        external_function(); // ②
    }
}
```

① In this code snippet, an external function is declared using the **`extern "C"`** block. This signals the usage of the C calling convention, a crucial aspect of Rust's Foreign Function Interface (FFI). The **`extern "C"`** block defines the interface for interacting with functions from external languages, particularly those using the C ABI (*Application Binary Interface*). This inclusion allows Rust to seamlessly integrate with and call functions written in languages like C. The function **`external_function`** is a placeholder, representing an external function written in the C language.

② The **`main`** function demonstrates the invocation of the external function within an **`unsafe`** block. The use of **`unsafe`** here is indicative of the potential risks associated with FFI. When Rust calls functions from external languages, especially those lacking Rust's safety features, it introduces uncertainties and risks that cannot be comprehensively verified by the Rust compiler. The **`unsafe`** block serves as a marker, signaling that the interaction involves operations beyond Rust's usual safety guarantees.

In the broader context of interfacing with external languages, this code snippet highlights Rust's FFI capabilities and the need for the **`unsafe`** block when engaging in such interactions. FFI is a powerful tool that enables Rust to communicate with codebases written in other languages seamlessly. However, the use of FFI introduces potential risks, and we must exercise caution and careful consideration when incorporating external functions, as indicated by the `unsafe` block. This underlines the controlled and deliberate nature of unsafe code in Rust, especially when exploring the world of foreign function interfaces.

Continuing with this theme, it's essential to delve into the specifics of the scenarios where Rust's safety mechanisms might become too restrictive. This could include cases where a developer needs direct access to hardware or when dealing with complex data structures that the borrow checker struggles to navigate.

Performance and Safety Considerations

The decision to use unsafe code is often a delicate balancing act between performance and safety considerations. In scenarios where the performance is critical and the overhead of safe abstractions becomes prohibitive, we may opt for unsafe code to squeeze out every bit of efficiency.

While the temptation to prioritize performance is strong, it's essential to approach this decision with caution. The potential risks and consequences of unsafe code must be thoroughly evaluated, and the trade-offs carefully considered.

Listing 13.3 Unsafe but performant for loop.

```
fn main() {
    let data = vec![1, 2, 3, 4, 5]; // ①

    for &value in &data { // ②
        println!("Value: {}", value);
    }

    unsafe {
        let raw_pointer = data.as_ptr(); // ③
        for i in 0..data.len() {
            println!("Value at index {}: {}", i, *raw_pointer.add(i)); // ④
        }
    }
}
```

```
// Output

// Value: 1
// Value: 2
// Value: 3
// Value: 4
// Value: 5
// Value at index 0: 1
// Value at index 1: 2
// Value at index 2: 3
// Value at index 3: 4
// Value at index 4: 5
```

① The code begins by creating a vector named **data** containing five integers. As we learned from *Chapter 4, Rust Built-In Data Structures*, Vectors are a dynamic array-like data structure in Rust. The elements of the vector are initialized with the values **1**, **2**, **3**, **4**, and **5**.

② A safe code block follows, employing a **for** loop to iterate over the vector **data**. The loop variable **value** is assigned the reference to each element of the vector in turn, and the values are printed using the **println!** macro. This demonstrates the typical and safe method of iterating over a collection in Rust.

③ Transitioning into an unsafe code block, a raw pointer **raw_pointer** is created using the **as_ptr()** method on the vector **data**. This method returns a raw pointer to the first element of the vector. It's important to note that using raw pointers introduces the potential for unsafe behavior since it circumvents Rust's usual safety checks.

④ Within the unsafe block, another **for** loop is utilized to iterate over the elements of the vector using pointer arithmetic. The expression ***raw_pointer.add(i)** dereferences the raw pointer and adds the index **i** to it, effectively accessing the value at that index in the vector. This method of direct memory access can offer performance benefits but is marked as unsafe due to the lack of Rust's usual safety guarantees.

In the broader discussion of balancing performance and safety considerations, this code snippet serves as an illustrative example. The safe code demonstrates the standard, secure approach to iterating over a vector. However, the subsequent unsafe code block showcases an alternative, more performance-oriented approach using raw pointers. It emphasizes that the decision to use unsafe code should be approached with caution, and the potential risks and consequences must be thoroughly evaluated. The benefits of performance optimization through unsafe code should be well-understood and justified against the safety mechanisms provided by Rust's abstractions.

Real-World Examples

To solidify our understanding, let's delve into real-world examples that highlight the necessity of unsafe code in certain scenarios. Consider a situation where a Rust project needs to interact with a legacy C library that lacks the safety features inherent in Rust.

In such cases, employing unsafe code becomes a pragmatic choice. It allows us as Rust developers to integrate with existing codebases without compromising the safety of the entire project. These examples will underscore the practical implications and utility of unsafe code in overcoming challenges presented by external dependencies.

Example 1: Database Interaction using FFI

Rust's versatility extends beyond its core language features, making it expert at seamlessly interacting with external libraries and languages through the Foreign Function Interface (FFI). In scenarios where Rust applications need to interface with established databases or leverage legacy codebases, FFI serves as a crucial bridge, allowing the integration of Rust's modern syntax with the often lower-level and memory-unsafe APIs of external libraries. The following example demonstrates database interaction using FFI, focusing on a practical illustration involving the integration of Rust with the SQLite database, a widely used embedded relational database management system.

Listing 13.4 sqlite3 interaction using FFI.

```
unsafe extern "C" fn select_data_callback(
    data: *mut std::ffi::c_void,
    columns: i32,
    values: *mut *mut i8,
    _names: *mut *mut i8,
) -> i32 {
    let data = data as *mut Vec<Vec<String>>; // ①

    let mut row_data = Vec::new(); // ②
    for i in 0..columns {
        let value = std::ffi::CStr::from_ptr(*values.offset(i as isize)).
to_string_lossy();
        row_data.push(value.into_owned());
    }

    println!("Row Data in Callback: {:?}", row_data); // ③
```

```
    let data = &mut *data; // ④
    data.push(row_data);

    0 // Continue processing rows
}

fn advanced_database_interaction() {
    unsafe {
        let mut db: *mut rusqlite::ffi::sqlite3 = std::ptr::null_mut(); // ⑤
        let result = rusqlite::ffi::sqlite3_open(":memory:\0".as_ptr() as
*const i8, &mut db); // ⑥
        println!("SQLite database connection result: {}", result);
        println!("SQLite database pointer: {:p}", db);

        if result != rusqlite::ffi::SQLITE_OK { // ⑦
            println!("Error opening SQLite database");
            return;
        }

        let create_table_query =
            "CREATE TABLE IF NOT EXISTS users (id INTEGER PRIMARY KEY,
name TEXT);\0"; // ⑧
        let create_table_query_ptr = create_table_query.as_ptr() as
*const i8;
        let mut create_table_err_msg: *mut i8 = std::ptr::null_mut();
        let create_table_result = rusqlite::ffi::sqlite3_exec(
            db,
            create_table_query_ptr,
            None,
            std::ptr::null_mut(),
            &mut create_table_err_msg,
        );

        println!("Create table result: {}", create_table_result);
        println!(
            "Create table error message pointer: {:p}",
            create_table_err_msg
        );

        if create_table_result != rusqlite::ffi::SQLITE_OK { // ⑨
            println!("Error creating table: {:?}", create_table_err_
msg);
            rusqlite::ffi::sqlite3_free(create_table_err_msg as *mut st-
d::ffi::c_void);
            return;
        }
```

```
        let insert_data_query = "INSERT INTO users (name) VALUES ('Mah-
moud Harmouch');\0"; // ⑩
        let insert_data_query_ptr = insert_data_query.as_ptr() as *const
i8;
        let mut insert_data_err_msg: *mut i8 = std::ptr::null_mut();
        let insert_data_result = rusqlite::ffi::sqlite3_exec(
            db,
            insert_data_query_ptr,
            None,
            std::ptr::null_mut(),
            &mut insert_data_err_msg,
        );

        println!("Insert data result: {}", insert_data_result);
        println!(
            "Insert data error message pointer: {:p}",
            insert_data_err_msg
        );

        if insert_data_result != rusqlite::ffi::SQLITE_OK { // ⑪
            println!("Error inserting data: {:?}", insert_data_err_msg);
            rusqlite::ffi::sqlite3_free(insert_data_err_msg as *mut st-
d::ffi::c_void);
            return;
        }

        let select_data_query = "SELECT * FROM users;\0"; // ⑫
        let select_data_query_ptr = select_data_query.as_ptr() as *const
i8;
        let mut select_data_err_msg: *mut i8 = std::ptr::null_mut();
        let mut select_data_result: Vec<Vec<String>> = Vec::new();
        let select_data_callback = Some(
            select_data_callback
                as unsafe extern "C" fn(
                    *mut std::ffi::c_void,
                    i32,
                    *mut *mut i8,
                    *mut *mut i8,
                ) -> i32,
        );
        let data_ptr = &mut select_data_result as *mut Vec<Vec<String>>
as *mut std::ffi::c_void; // ⑬
        let select_data_result = rusqlite::ffi::sqlite3_exec(
            db,
            select_data_query_ptr,
            select_data_callback,
```

```
            data_ptr,
            &mut select_data_err_msg,
        );

        println!("Select data result: {}", select_data_result);
        println!(
            "Select data error message pointer: {:p}",
            select_data_err_msg
        );

        if select_data_result != rusqlite::ffi::SQLITE_OK { // ⑭
            println!("Error selecting data: {:?}", select_data_err_msg);
            rusqlite::ffi::sqlite3_free(select_data_err_msg as *mut
std::ffi::c_void);
            return;
        }

        rusqlite::ffi::sqlite3_close(db); // ⑮
        println!("SQLite database connection closed");
    }
}

fn main() {
    advanced_database_interaction(); // ⑯
}

// Output

// SQLite database connection result: 0
// SQLite database pointer: 0x5629b9ed5c08
// Create table result: 0
// Create table error message pointer: 0x0
// Insert data result: 0
// Insert data error message pointer: 0x0
// Row Data in Callback: ["1", "Mahmoud Harmouch"]
// Select data result: 0
// Select data error message pointer: 0x0
// SQLite database connection closed
```

Now, let's explore each step of this code snippet:

① The **data** pointer, initially of type **`*mut std::ffi::c_void`**, is cast to a mutable reference of **`Vec<Vec<String>>`**, providing a safe Rust representation. This is a crucial step in bridging the gap between the unsafe world of raw pointers and Rust's ownership system. By casting the raw pointer to a typed reference, we gain the ability to interact with it using idiomatic Rust, ensuring type safety and memory safety.

② A loop iterates through the raw values, converts them to **String** using **CStr::from_ptr**, and adds them to the **row_data** vector. Here, the raw values, representing individual columns in a database row, are transformed into Rust's String type. This conversion is essential to bring the data into a format that Rust can manage safely. The loop ensures that each column's value is correctly converted and added to the **row_data** vector.

③ The **row_data** vector, containing the values of a row, is printed to the terminal for debugging purposes. Printing the row data allows us to inspect and verify that the data retrieved from the SQLite database is correctly captured in the Rust environment. This step helps in identifying potential issues with the data transformation process or the SQLite interaction.

④ The **data** pointer is recast to its original type, and the row data is pushed to the vector of results. After processing a row, the **data** pointer is transformed back to its original type (**Vec<Vec<String>>**). This step is necessary as the callback function's signature requires the original type, and pushing the row data to the vector of results ensures that the processed data is retained for further analysis or use.

⑤ A raw pointer to the SQLite database, **db**, is declared and initialized to **std::ptr::null_mut()**. This initializes a raw pointer that initially points to null, indicating that it doesn't currently point to a valid memory location. This pointer will be later used to manage the SQLite database connection.

⑥ The **sqlite3_open** function is called to open an SQLite in-memory database, and the result is printed to the terminal. Opening the database is a critical step, and the result of this operation is checked to ensure the database connection is successfully established. If successful, the SQLite database pointer, **db**, will point to a valid SQLite database instance.

⑦ If an error occurs in opening the database, an error message is printed, and the function returns. Handling errors during database connection is vital for robustness. If the database cannot be opened, printing an error message provides insight into the issue, and returning from the function prevents further execution, avoiding potential issues with an invalid database connection.

⑧ A query to create a table for storing user data is defined, and the **sqlite3_exec** function is used to execute it. This step involves executing a SQL query to create a table within the SQLite database. The **sqlite3_exec** function is a versatile SQLite function that can be used to execute various SQL commands. Here, it is employed to execute the query for creating a user table.

⑨ If an error occurs in creating the table, an error message is printed, and the function returns. Similar to the error handling during the database opening phase, if creating the table fails, it is essential to print an error message for diagnosis and return from the function to prevent further operations on an incomplete or corrupted database state.

⑩ A query to insert sample data into the table is defined, and the **`sqlite3_exec`** function is used to execute it. This step involves populating the previously created table with sample data. The SQL query for data insertion is executed using the **`sqlite3_exec`** function.

⑪ If an error occurs in inserting data, an error message is printed, and the function returns. Ensuring that data insertion is successful is crucial for maintaining the integrity of the database. If the insertion operation fails, an error message is printed, and the function returns to prevent subsequent operations on potentially corrupted data.

⑫ A query to select all data from the users table is defined. This step involves preparing a query to retrieve all rows and columns from the users table.

⑬ The **`sqlite3_exec`** function is used to execute the select query, with the **`select_data_callback`** function serving as the callback for processing selected rows. Executing a select query involves retrieving data from the database, and the specified callback function (**`select_data_callback`**) is invoked for each row of the result set. This callback function processes the raw data and transforms it into a Rust-friendly format.

⑭ If an error occurs in selecting data, an error message is printed, and the function returns. Similar to the error handling during database creation and data insertion, if selecting data fails, an error message is printed for diagnosis, and the function returns to prevent further operations on potentially incomplete or corrupted data.

⑮ The **`sqlite3_close`** function is used to close the SQLite database connection. Properly closing the database connection is essential for resource management. This step releases any resources associated with the SQLite database, preventing memory leaks and ensuring a clean shutdown of the database connection.

⑯ The **`advanced_database_interaction`** function is invoked as the main entry point for testing the advanced database interaction functionality. This function encapsulates the entire process of interacting with an SQLite database, from opening a connection to querying and manipulating data. Invoking this function in the **`main`** function serves as a practical way to test and demonstrate the advanced database interaction capabilities in a Rust program.

This code snippet exemplifies a comprehensive and controlled interaction with an SQLite database, showcasing the need for unsafe code in certain scenarios. The **advanced_database_interaction** function orchestrates various steps, from opening an SQLite database to performing operations such as table creation, data insertion, and data selection.

The usage of unsafe code becomes apparent in the callback function, **select_data_callback**, which interfaces with the raw pointers received from SQLite's C API. Through careful casting and manipulation, the raw pointers are converted into a Rust-friendly representation (**Vec<Vec<String>>**), emphasizing the controlled and deliberate nature of unsafe code in bridging the gap between Rust's safety guarantees and the low-level operations required for interacting with external C libraries.

The example further highlights error handling practices, ensuring that potential issues during database connection, table creation, data insertion, and data selection are appropriately reported. This meticulous error management contributes to the overall robustness of the database interaction, preventing undefined behavior and maintaining the integrity of the Rust program.

While the use of unsafe code is justified in this scenario for interfacing with the SQLite C API, it's essential for us to approach such usage with caution. A thorough understanding of the external library's API, careful casting, and adherence to best practices are crucial aspects of leveraging unsafe code in a controlled manner. Overall, this example serves as a practical illustration of Rust's ability to seamlessly integrate with existing C libraries while maintaining a balance between performance and safety.

Example 2: Advanced Image Processing

In this example, we will delve into the details of interfacing with OpenCV's C API, emphasizing the need for unsafe code when dealing with external libraries. The step-by-step breakdown of image processing operations provides insights into the application of OpenCV's functionality within a Rust context. Let's explore how Rust's safety features are balanced with the need for efficient and low-level manipulation required for advanced image processing.

Listing 13.5 Advanced image processing using OpenCV.

```
extern crate opencv;

use opencv::prelude::MatTraitConst;
use opencv::core::{BORDER_DEFAULT, CV_8UC3};
```

```
use std::ffi::c_void;

fn image_processing() {
    unsafe {
        // Create sample data
        let sample_data: Vec<u8> = vec![0; 480 * 640 * 3]; // Assuming 3 
channels

        let mut image: opencv::core::Mat = opencv::core::Mat::new_rows_
cols_with_data(
            480, 640, CV_8UC3, sample_data.as_ptr() as *mut c_void, 0,
        ).unwrap(); // ①

        println!(
            "Original Image: Rows={}, Cols={}, Channels={}",
            image.rows(),
            image.cols(),
            image.channels()
        );

        let mut blurred_image = opencv::core::Mat::default();
        opencv::imgproc::blur(
            &image,
            &mut blurred_image,
            opencv::core::Size::new(5, 5),
            opencv::core::Point::new(2, 2),
            BORDER_DEFAULT,
        )
        .unwrap(); // ②

        // Move the temporary variable back to the original variable
        std::mem::swap(&mut image, &mut blurred_image);

        println!(
            "Image after Gaussian Blur: Rows={}, Cols={}, Channels={}",
            image.rows(),
            image.cols(),
            image.channels()
        );

        let mut gray_image = opencv::core::Mat::default();
        opencv::imgproc::cvt_color(
            &image,
            &mut gray_image,
            opencv::imgproc::COLOR_BGR2GRAY,
            0,
        )
```

```
        .unwrap(); // ③

        // Move the temporary variable back to the original variable
        std::mem::swap(&mut image, &mut gray_image);

        println!(
            "Image after Grayscale Conversion: Rows={}, Cols={}, Chan-
nels={}",
            image.rows(),
            image.cols(),
            image.channels()
        );

        // Canny edge detection with a temporary variable
        let mut canny_image = opencv::core::Mat::default();
        opencv::imgproc::canny(
            &image,
            &mut canny_image,
            50.0,
            150.0,
            3,
            false,
        )
        .unwrap(); // ④

        // Move the temporary variable back to the original variable
        std::mem::swap(&mut image, &mut canny_image);

        println!(
            "Image after Canny Edge Detection: Rows={}, Cols={}, Chan-
nels={}",
            image.rows(),
            image.cols(),
            image.channels()
        );
    }
}

fn main() {
    image_processing(); // ⑤
}
```

```
// Output

// Original Image: Rows=480, Cols=640, Channels=3
// Image after Gaussian Blur: Rows=480, Cols=640, Channels=3
// Image after Grayscale Conversion: Rows=480, Cols=640, Channels=1
// Image after Canny Edge Detection: Rows=480, Cols=640, Channels=1
```

① In this line, an OpenCV `Mat` object named `image` is created within an unsafe block. The `opencv::core::Mat::new_rows_cols_with_data` method is called to initialize the `Mat` object with a size of 480x640 and pixel type `CV_8UC3`, representing an 8-bit unsigned integer image with three channels (color).

② Subsequently, a Gaussian blur is applied to the image using the `opencv::imgproc::blur` function. This introduces a more advanced image processing step, showcasing the ability to manipulate pixel data with unsafe code.

③ The image is then converted to grayscale using the `opencv::imgproc::cvt_color` function, expanding the complexity of the image processing pipeline. The conversion involves a color transformation, emphasizing the flexibility of Rust's unsafe code in handling complex operations.

④ Further enhancing the image processing, Canny edge detection is applied to the grayscale image. The `opencv::imgproc::canny` function introduces edge detection algorithms, showcasing the integration of more sophisticated OpenCV functionality within the Rust codebase.

⑤ The `main` function is invoked to test the advanced image processing functionality with OpenCV. This function serves as the entry point for executing and observing the behavior of the code responsible for interfacing with the OpenCV library. It encapsulates the advanced image processing functionality for focused testing and validation.

Example 3: Custom Memory Management

Let us explore a Rust project dealing with a custom data processing pipeline that requires efficient memory management. In certain cases, using unsafe code for custom memory allocation and deallocation might be necessary. This example demonstrates a simplified scenario where a custom memory manager is used to handle data buffers efficiently.

Listing 13.6 Custom memory management processing pipeline example.

```
struct CustomMemoryManager { // ①
    allocate: unsafe extern "C" fn(size: usize) -> *mut u8,
    deallocate: unsafe extern "C" fn(ptr: *mut u8, size: usize),
}

fn process_data_with_custom_memory_manager(data: &[u8], memory_manager:
&CustomMemoryManager) { // ②
    unsafe {
        let buffer_size = data.len() * 2;
        let custom_buffer = (memory_manager.allocate)(buffer_size);

        println!("Allocated {} bytes at {:p}", buffer_size, custom_buffer);

        std::ptr::copy_nonoverlapping(data.as_ptr(), custom_buffer, data.
len());

        // Additional data processing using the custom buffer would hap-
pen here

        (memory_manager.deallocate)(custom_buffer, buffer_size);

        println!("Deallocated {} bytes at {:p}", buffer_size, custom_buffer);
    }
}

fn main() { // ③
    let custom_memory_manager = CustomMemoryManager {
        allocate: custom_allocate,
        deallocate: custom_deallocate,
    };
    let input_data = vec![1, 2, 3, 4, 5];
    process_data_with_custom_memory_manager(&input_data, &custom_memory
_manager);
}

unsafe extern "C" fn custom_allocate(size: usize) -> *mut u8 { // ④
    let ptr = std::alloc::alloc(std::alloc::Layout::from_size_align
(size, 1).unwrap());
    println!("Allocated {} bytes at {:p}", size, ptr);
    ptr
}

unsafe extern "C" fn custom_deallocate(ptr: *mut u8, size: usize) { // ⑤
```

```
    println!("Deallocating {} bytes at {:p}", size, ptr);
    std::alloc::dealloc(ptr, std::alloc::Layout::from_size_align(size,
1).unwrap());
}

// Output

// Allocated 10 bytes at 0x559447656bc0
// Allocated 10 bytes at 0x559447656bc0
// Deallocating 10 bytes at 0x559447656bc0
// Deallocated 10 bytes at 0x559447656bc0
```

① At the core of this Rust code lies the definition of a struct named **CustomMemoryManager**. This struct serves as a container, encapsulating two function pointers essential for the orchestration of memory within the program. These function pointers, namely **allocate** and **deallocate**, are designated as unsafe external functions, emphasizing their involvement in low-level memory management operations. The struct's purpose is to act as a cohesive unit, providing a modular and organized approach to handling memory-related tasks within the broader context of the Rust program.

② The focal point of this Rust script revolves around the **process_data_with_custom_memory_manager** function. This function contains the utilization of the custom memory manager defined earlier. In essence, it serves as the orchestrator for a sequence of operations involving memory: allocation, data processing, and deallocation. The use of the **unsafe** keyword outlines the potential hazards associated with these low-level memory operations, underlining the gravity of the code's interaction with memory management complexities. The function represents the controlled and deliberate use of unsafe code to achieve specific goals related to memory within the Rust programming paradigm.

③ Moving on, the **main** function takes center stage. Within this entry point of the program, an instance of the custom memory manager is instantiated. This instantiation marks the integration of the struct into the program's runtime, where its designated functions will control memory-related operations. The main function proceeds to execute a sample data processing scenario, showcasing the practical application of the custom memory manager in a real-world context. This entire approach to memory management underscores Rust's commitment to not only safety but also flexibility in handling low-level operations.

④ The **custom_allocate** function emerges as a critical component in the orchestration of memory allocation within this program. This function encapsulates a hypothetical implementation of the memory allocation logic, adhering to the unsafe and external nature of memory-related operations.

Within its code block, the function employs the standard Rust allocator to allocate a block of memory, showcasing a practical example of how memory can be allocated in a controlled and monitored manner. The function's role is not merely useful but also helpful, providing insights into the complexities of memory allocation within the Rust language.

⑤ In parallel with its counterpart, the **`custom_deallocate`** function plays a symmetrical role in the memory management symphony. This function represents a hypothetical implementation of the memory deallocation logic, including the counterpart to the allocation process. The use of the standard Rust deallocator within the function underscores the language's commitment to structured and safe memory management practices. As the function executes, it prints information about the deallocation, promoting a transparent and informative approach to memory handling. This hypothetical implementation not only demonstrates the mechanics of deallocation but also serves as a tool, highlighting the combination between allocation and deallocation within the Rust programming paradigm.

These examples emphasize the diverse scenarios where unsafe code can be employed, ranging from database interaction using FFI to custom memory management for specialized data processing pipelines. We should exercise caution, thoroughly document unsafe code usage, and adhere to best practices to ensure the safety and robustness of Rust applications.

Continuing the discussion, it's important to address the importance of thoroughly understanding the external code being interfaced with. We must not only consider the technical aspects of the integration but also the potential implications of using unsafe code in the broader context of their project's goals and safety requirements.

Best Practices for using Unsafe Code

Given the inherent risks associated with unsafe code, it is imperative to establish best practices for its careful use. As we explore this domain, we must follow guidelines that mitigate potential pitfalls and ensure a level of safety that aligns with Rust's overarching principles.

One key best practice is to encapsulate unsafe code within safe abstractions, minimizing its surface area and potential impact. This categorization helps binding the risks to specific modules or functions, allowing the rest of the codebase to remain safely within the limits of Rust's guarantees.

Listing 13.7 Encapsulating unsafe code within safe abstractions.

```
mod unsafe_module {
    // Safe Rust function
    pub fn safe_function(data: &mut Vec<i32>) {
        // Safe Rust code
        data.push(42);
        println!("Safe function: {:?}", data);
    }

    // Unsafe Rust function
    pub unsafe fn unsafe_function(data: &mut Vec<i32>) {
        // Unsafe code encapsulated within a safe abstraction
        let reference = data.as_mut_ptr();
        *reference.offset(0) = 10;
        println!("Unsafe function: {:?}", data);
    }
}

fn main() {
    let mut data = vec![1, 2, 3, 4, 5];

    unsafe_module::safe_function(&mut data); // ①

    unsafe {
        unsafe_module::unsafe_function(&mut data); // ②
    }

    println!("Main function: {:?}", data); // ③
}

// Output

// Safe function: [1, 2, 3, 4, 5, 42]
// Unsafe function: [10, 2, 3, 4, 5, 42]
// Main function: [10, 2, 3, 4, 5, 42]
```

① In this line, the safe function **safe_function** from the **unsafe_module** module is called. This function manipulates the vector **data** in a safe manner, pushing the value **42** onto it and printing the modified vector. Importantly, this function does not require an **unsafe** block when called.

② The unsafe function **unsafe_function** is called within an **unsafe** block. This function encapsulates unsafe code by obtaining a mutable raw pointer to the vector's first element and modifying the data using pointer arithmetic. The use of an `unsafe` block signals that the code within may violate Rust's safety guarantees, and it should be used with caution.

③ After calling the unsafe function, the modified data is accessed and printed in the `main` function. This line demonstrates that changes made by the unsafe function are observable in the main context. It's crucial to understand that using unsafe code can have an impact beyond the immediate unsafe block.

This code exemplifies best practices for using unsafe code carefully. By encapsulating unsafe functionality within a module and providing a safe interface (such as `safe_function`), we can isolate and control the usage of unsafe code, limiting potential risks to well-defined boundaries. The modular approach aligns with Rust's emphasis on safety and facilitates collaborative development practices, including code reviews and knowledge sharing. We should exercise caution when using unsafe code, follow best practices, and leverage safe abstractions whenever possible to maintain the integrity and safety of Rust codebases.

In the broader context of best practices, the modular approach demonstrated in this code snippet aligns with the Rust community's recommendation to isolate and control the usage of unsafe code. By encapsulating unsafe functionality within modules or functions, we can constrain the potential risks, limiting their impact to well-defined boundaries. Furthermore, the code underscores the importance of code reviews and collaborative practices when dealing with unsafe code. Multiple sets of eyes can inspect such code, identifying issues, ensuring adherence to best practices, and promoting knowledge sharing within the development team. This collaborative approach is crucial in maintaining the integrity and safety of Rust codebases, especially when exploring the world of unsafe code.

Memory Safety Violations

One of the most critical concerns when dealing with unsafe code is the potential for memory safety violations. Rust's ownership system and borrow checker play a pivotal role in preventing such issues, but when operating in the world of unsafe code, we must take extra precautions.

Memory safety violations can lead to a wide range of problems, from subtle bugs to severe security vulnerabilities. Understanding the complexities of memory management within the context of unsafe code is crucial to avoiding these pitfalls.

Listing 13.8 Modification of data through direct raw pointer.

```
fn main() { // ①
    let mut data = vec![1, 2, 3, 4, 5]; // ②

    let reference = data.as_mut_ptr(); // ③

    unsafe {
        *reference.offset(0) = 10; // ④
    }

    println!("Modified data: {:?}", data); // ⑤
}

// Output

// Modified data: [10, 2, 3, 4, 5]
```

① The **main** function is the entry point of the Rust program.

② A mutable vector **data** is created with elements **[1, 2, 3, 4, 5]**.

③ In this line, we safely obtain a mutable raw pointer (***mut i32**) to the data vector's first element.

④ Within the **unsafe** block, the code attempts to modify the data through the mutable reference using pointer arithmetic. ***reference.offset(0) = 10;** assigns the value **10** to the first element of the vector. This operation is considered unsafe due to the direct manipulation of memory without adhering to Rust's ownership principles.

⑤ The modified data is printed. This line serves to demonstrate that modifications made through the raw pointer affect the original vector, potentially leading to unexpected behavior.

In this example, the unsafe code poses a risk of violating Rust's ownership principles, potentially resulting in undefined behavior and memory safety issues. It's important to use unsafe code carefully and with a thorough understanding of the potential risks involved.

Expanding on the example, it's important to discuss alternative approaches that maintain memory safety. This might involve using safe abstractions, such as the **iter_mut** method provided by the standard library, which allows safe iteration over mutable references without resorting to unsafe code. Here's an example that demonstrates this approach:

Listing 13.9 Safe iteration over mutable references without using unsafe code.

```
fn main() {
    let mut data = vec![1, 2, 3, 4, 5]; // ①

    for element in data.iter_mut() { // ②
        *element = *element + 10; // ③
    }

    println!("Modified data: {:?}", data); // ④
}

// Output

// Modified data: [11, 12, 13, 14, 15]
```

① A mutable vector **data** is created with elements **[1, 2, 3, 4, 5]**.

② The **iter_mut** method is used to obtain a mutable iterator over the elements of the vector. This allows safe iteration over mutable references without resorting to unsafe code.

③ Within the loop, each element is modified through the mutable iterator. In this example, we add **10** to each element.

④ The modified data is printed, demonstrating that modifications made through the safe iterator affect the original vector.

Using safe abstractions like **iter_mut** helps ensure memory safety by adhering to Rust's ownership and borrowing rules. It allows you to perform operations on mutable references in a controlled and safe manner, eliminating the need for unsafe code in many cases.

Case Studies

In order to enhance our comprehension of the potential consequences of unsafe coding practices, let us delve into case studies that illuminate real-world scenarios. These illustrative cases will offer concrete examples that vividly demonstrate the impact of employing unsafe code within software systems. By analyzing these instances, we aim to underscore the critical importance of exercising caution, thoughtful consideration, and thorough testing when dealing with unsafe code. Through these practical examples, we seek to emphasize the imperative for developers to grasp the gravity of their coding decisions and the far-reaching effects they may have on the reliability and security of software systems.

Case Study 1: Heartbleed Vulnerability

The Heartbleed vulnerability within the OpenSSL library serves as an illustration of the real-world consequences associated with unsafe code practices. This notorious security flaw enabled malicious actors to exploit a critical weakness, permitting unauthorized access to sensitive data residing in the memory of affected systems. The fundamental issue at the heart of this vulnerability lay in the absence of a robust bounds check within the implementation of the OpenSSL Heartbeat extension. This oversight facilitated the unauthorized extraction of highly confidential information, including private keys and passwords, posing a severe threat to the security and integrity of systems relying on the compromised OpenSSL versions [1].

The Heartbleed incident underscores the importance of rigorous code audits, thorough testing, and the critical role that the correct and safe use of memory plays in the security of software systems. It serves as a reminder that vulnerabilities introduced through unsafe code can have severe and far-reaching consequences.

Listing 13.10 Simulating the Heartbleed vulnerability in Rust.

```
use std::collections::HashMap;

struct Server {
    user_data: HashMap<String, String>, // ①
}

impl Server {
    fn get_user_data(&self, username: &str) -> Option<&String> { // ②
        self.user_data.get(username)
    }

    unsafe fn unsafe_heartbleed(&self) { // ③
        let buffer: Vec<u8> = self
            .user_data
            .values()
            .flat_map(|s| s.as_bytes().to_vec())
            .collect(); // ④

        let mut response = Vec::new(); // ⑤
        response.resize(buffer.len(), 0); // ⑥
        response.copy_from_slice(&buffer); // ⑦
```

[1]Synopsys, Inc. *http://www.synopsys.com/*. (2020, June 3). Heartbleed bug. *https://heartbleed.com/*

```
        send_response(response); // ⑧
    }
}

fn send_response(response: Vec<u8>) { // ⑨

    let response_str = String::from_utf8_lossy(&response); // ⑩

    println!("Sending response: {}", response_str); // ⑪
}

fn main() {
    let server = Server {
        user_data: [
            ("Mahmoud".to_string(), "password123".to_string()),
            ("Prime".to_string(), "secret456".to_string()),
        ]
        .iter()
        .cloned()
        .collect(), // ⑫
    };

    unsafe {
        server.unsafe_heartbleed(); // ⑬
    }
}

// Output

// Sending response: password123secret456
```

① The **Server** struct serves as a representation of a server within the program, designed specifically to manage sensitive user data. The user data is stored in a **HashMap**, a collection type in Rust that allows efficient key-value pair associations.

② The **get_user_data** method is a safe function associated with the **Server** struct. It is designed to provide a secure means of retrieving user data based on a given username. By leveraging the safety guarantees of Rust's ownership system, this method ensures that the user data is accessed in a controlled and secure manner, adhering to Rust's borrowing rules.

③ The **unsafe_heartbleed** method is marked as unsafe, signaling that it involves operations that deviate from Rust's usual safety guarantees. This method simulates the infamous Heartbleed vulnerability, a critical security flaw that occurred in the OpenSSL library. The purpose of this simulation is to illustrate the potential risks associated with unsafe code when handling sensitive data.

④ In this line, a buffer is created from the user data. The buffer is constructed by flattening the byte representations of each string in the user data. This step is crucial for simulating the Heartbleed vulnerability, as it mimics the scenario where sensitive information is exposed through a memory buffer.

⑤ The **`response`** variable is a mutable vector specifically crafted to store the simulated response. In the context of the Heartbleed simulation, this vector represents the data that might be leaked due to the vulnerability.

⑥ The **`resize`** method is employed to ensure that the **`response`** vector has the same length as the buffer. This operation initializes the vector with zeros, creating a space for the simulated response data. Proper bounds checking is omitted, reflecting the unsafe nature of the Heartbleed simulation.

⑦ The **`copy_from_slice`** method is utilized to copy data from the buffer to the **`response`** vector. This operation is performed without proper bounds checking, emulating the behavior that led to the Heartbleed vulnerability, where an attacker could potentially retrieve sensitive information beyond the intended bounds of the buffer.

⑧ The **`send_response`** function is called, representing the point at which the simulated response is sent. In the context of the Heartbleed simulation, this action symbolizes the potential leakage of sensitive user data to an external entity.

⑨ The **`send_response`** function is defined to simulate the actual process of sending a response. While the implementation is simplified for the purpose of this simulation, it highlights the point at which sensitive data could be exposed in a real-world scenario, such as the Heartbleed incident.

⑩ The **`response`** vector, now containing the simulated data, is converted to a readable string format using the **`String::from_utf8_lossy`** method. This step is essential for presenting the leaked data in a human-readable form, emphasizing the severity of the potential consequences.

⑪ The readable response is printed to the terminal. This step is a symbolic representation of the sensitive data being leaked or exposed, illustrating the impact of the Heartbleed vulnerability and emphasizing the importance of secure coding practices.

⑫ In the **`main`** function, an instance of the **`Server`** struct is created to simulate a server with sensitive user data. The user data is initialized with fictional information, including usernames and corresponding passwords.

⑬ The unsafe method **`unsafe_heartbleed`** is called within an **`unsafe`** block in the **`main`** function, representing the intentional invocation of the simulated Heartbleed vulnerability. This action emphasizes the critical need for caution and adherence to safety guidelines when dealing with unsafe code, especially in scenarios involving sensitive data.

This simulation exposes the pitfalls of unsafe code by representing a **`Server`** struct designed to protect sensitive user data, yielding a simulated Heartbleed vulnerability. While the **`get_user_data`** method showcases secure data access, the **`unsafe_heartbleed`** method becomes a focal point of risk, replicating Heartbleed's conditions without Rust's usual safeguards. Buffer creation, vector manipulation, and response generation lacking proper bounds checking symbolize potential data leakage. The intentional invocation of **`unsafe_heartbleed`** underscores the inherent risks of unsafe code, emphasizing the need for rigorous code audits, thorough testing, and secure memory management to strengthen software security. This simulation serves as a stark reminder that unsafe code vulnerabilities can have severe consequences, urging us to prioritize safety guidelines and secure coding practices for resilient software systems.

Case Study 2: Ariane 5 Flight 501 Failure

The failure of the Ariane 5 Flight 501 in 1996 is another case study highlighting the consequences of unsafe code in a safety-critical system. The incident occurred just 39 seconds after liftoff when the rocket's guidance system failed due to an integer overflow in the software. The software used in the Ariane 5 was inherited from the previous Ariane 4 model, and its lack of proper error handling and safeguards led to the catastrophic failure [2].

This case study underscores the importance of careful code reviews, testing methodologies, and the need for safety-critical systems to adhere to strict coding standards. In the context of Rust, it reinforces the significance of avoiding undefined behavior, especially in systems where human lives or substantial financial investments are at stake.

Continuing with case studies, it's valuable to explore examples that highlight not only the consequences of unsafe code in security-critical or safety-critical systems but also instances where performance-critical systems faced challenges due to unsafe coding practices. This might include scenarios where premature

---

[2] Systmes, R. E., Lann, G. J. L., Systmes, T. R. E., & Reflecs, P. (1997). The Ariane 5 Flight 501 Failure - A Case Study in System Engineering for Computing Systems. ResearchGate. *https://www.researchgate.net/publication/2637332_The_Ariane_5_Flight_501_Failure_-_A_Case_Study_in_System_Engineering_for_Computing_Systems*

optimizations in unsafe code led to maintenance nightmares, and introduced subtle bugs that were challenging to diagnose.

Listing 13.11 Simulating the Ariane 5 Flight 501 failure in Rust.

```
use std::sync::atomic::{AtomicBool, AtomicUsize, Ordering};
use std::sync::Arc;
use std::thread;

struct GuidanceSystem {
    safe_mode: AtomicBool, // ①
    unsafe_counter: AtomicUsize, // ②
}

impl GuidanceSystem {
    fn safe_critical_calculation(&self, payload_mass: f64) -> i32 {
        if self.safe_mode.load(Ordering::SeqCst) {
            let result = (32767.0 * 9.81 / payload_mass).round(); // ③

            if result >= i32::MIN as f64 && result <= i32::MAX as f64 {
                result as i32 // ④
            } else {
                if result > 0.0 {
                    i32::MAX
                } else {
                    i32::MIN
                }
            }
        } else {
            (32767.0 * 9.81 / payload_mass) as i32 // ⑤
        }
    }

    unsafe fn unsafe_use_result(&self, result: i32) {
        self.unsafe_counter
            .fetch_add(result as usize, Ordering::Relaxed); // ⑥

        println!("Using result in guidance system: {}", result); // ⑦
    }
}

fn main() {
    let guidance_system = Arc::new(GuidanceSystem {
        safe_mode: AtomicBool::new(false), // ⑧
        unsafe_counter: AtomicUsize::new(0), // ⑨
    });
```

```
    let guidance_system_thread = Arc::clone(&guidance_system); // ⑩

    let handle = thread::spawn(move || {
        let payload_mass = 0.0000000001; // ⑪
        let result = guidance_system_thread.safe_critical_calcula-
tion(payload_mass); // ⑫
        println!("Result of safe critical calculation: {}", result); // ⑬

        unsafe {
            guidance_system_thread.unsafe_use_result(result); // ⑭
        }
    });

    let handles: Vec<_> = (0..4)
        .map(|_| {
            let guidance_system_thread = Arc::clone(&guidance_system);
// ⑮
            thread::spawn(move || {
                let payload_mass = 0.1; // ⑯
                let result = guidance_system_thread.safe_critical_calcu-
lation(payload_mass); // ⑰
                unsafe {
                    guidance_system_thread.unsafe_use_result(result); // ⑱
                }
            })
        })
        .collect();

    handle.join().unwrap(); // ⑲

    for handle in handles {
        handle.join().unwrap(); // ⑳
    }

    println!(
        "Unsafe Counter Value: {}",
        guidance_system.unsafe_counter.load(Ordering::SeqCst)
    );
}

// Output

// Result of safe critical calculation: 2147483647
// Using result in guidance system: 2147483647
```

```
// Using result in guidance system: 3214442
// Using result in guidance system: 3214442
// Using result in guidance system: 3214442
// Using result in guidance system: 3214442
// Unsafe Counter Value: 2160341415
```

① This line of code declares the **safe_mode** field within the **GuidanceSystem** struct. It is of type **AtomicBool**, which means it is an atomic boolean variable. An atomic boolean ensures that operations on this variable are atomic, providing thread safety. This specific boolean is crucial for representing the current operational mode of the guidance system, signaling whether it is in a state considered safe.

② Here, the **unsafe_counter** field is declared within the **GuidanceSystem** struct. This field is of type **AtomicUsize**, indicating an atomic unsigned size variable. The purpose of this counter is to keep track of the number of operations that are potentially unsafe. Being atomic ensures that multiple threads can increment this counter concurrently without causing data races or inconsistencies.

③ Within the **safe_critical_calculation** method, this line performs a mathematical calculation for a critical operation. The result is determined based on the payload mass, gravity, and a constant value. This calculation is designed with safety in mind to prevent integer overflow and guarantee that the result fits within the representable range of a 32-bit integer.

④ In this line, the calculated result is returned as a 32-bit integer if it falls within the valid range of **i32::MIN** to **i32::MAX**. It includes a check to ensure that if the result exceeds the maximum representable value, it returns **i32::MAX**; if it goes below the minimum representable value, it returns **i32::MIN**. This ensures that the returned result remains within the bounds of a 32-bit integer.

⑤ If the guidance system is not in safe mode, this line performs the critical calculation without the safety checks applied. It directly converts the result to a 32-bit integer, potentially risking integer overflow or other unsafe behavior. This represents a scenario where safety measures are bypassed, and the calculation is performed without constraints.

⑥ Within the **unsafe_use_result** method, this line increments the **unsafe_counter** by the value of the result. The **fetch_add** operation is atomic, ensuring that multiple threads can safely increment the counter without causing data races. This counter serves as a tally for potentially risky operations performed by the guidance system.

⑦ This line prints a message indicating the usage of the result within the guidance system. While in this simulation, it merely prints a message, in a real-world scenario, this section of the code would contain the actual implementation for utilizing the calculated result within the guidance system.

⑧ Here, the **safe_mode** field of the **guidance_system** instance is initialized. The atomic boolean is set to **false**, signifying that at the beginning of the simulation, the guidance system is not in a safe operational mode.

⑨ The **unsafe_counter** field of the **guidance_system** instance is initialized with an atomic unsigned size set to **0**. The counter starts at zero, reflecting the absence of any unsafe operations initially.

⑩ This line creates a cloned reference to the guidance system using **Arc::clone(&guidance_system)**. The **Arc** (atomic reference count) ensures shared ownership across multiple threads. Each thread can now safely access and modify the guidance system without causing data races or synchronization issues.

⑪ A small payload mass is simulated for the critical calculation in the main thread. This parameter is crucial for the calculation of critical operations in the guidance system.

⑫ The **safe_critical_calculation** method is invoked on the guidance system thread, passing the simulated payload mass. This method calculates the result of the critical operation in a safe manner, considering the current status of the safe mode.

⑬ The result of the safe critical calculation is printed in the main thread. This step allows observation and analysis of the calculated result during the simulation.

⑭ The **unsafe_use_result** method is invoked within an **unsafe** block, simulating the usage of the calculated result in an unsafe manner. This step illustrates the potential consequences of unsafe operations within the guidance system.

⑮ For each thread spawned in the loop, a cloned reference to the guidance system is created. This ensures that each thread has its own reference to the shared guidance system, preventing potential conflicts between threads.

⑯ A larger payload mass is simulated for the critical calculation in the spawned threads. Each thread uses a different payload mass, introducing diversity in the scenarios being simulated.

⑰ The **safe_critical_calculation** method is invoked on each spawned thread, passing the simulated payload mass. Each thread independently calculates the result of the critical operation in a safe manner.

⑱ The `unsafe_use_result` method is invoked within an `unsafe` block for each spawned thread. This simulates the usage of the calculated result in an unsafe manner, emphasizing the potential risks associated with unsafe operations.

⑲ The `join` method is used to wait for the guidance system thread (the first spawned thread) to finish its execution before proceeding with the rest of the main thread. This ensures proper synchronization and observation of the simulation.

⑳ The `join` method is used in a loop to wait for each of the spawned threads to finish their execution before proceeding with the rest of the main thread. This step ensures that all threads complete their tasks before finalizing the simulation.

The final value of the `unsafe_counter` is printed to observe the cumulative count of potentially unsafe operations performed by the guidance system. This provides insights into the impact of unsafe operations during the simulation.

These simulations are designed to capture the complex aspects of vulnerabilities like Heartbleed and the unfortunate incident with Ariane 5 Flight 501. They underscore the critical need for meticulous consideration and thorough testing when handling unsafe code in real-world situations. The goal is to emphasize the potential consequences of overlooking safety measures, encouraging us to approach unsafe code with caution and thoroughness to avoid similar issues in practical applications.

Risks Associated with Unsafe Coding

In order to traverse the landscape of unsafe code in a careful manner, it is imperative to familiarize ourselves with the common pitfalls and risks inherent in unsafe coding practices. Navigating this domain demands a comprehensive awareness of potential challenges that may arise, and a clear understanding of the risks involved is crucial. By delving into the complexities of these risks, we empower ourselves to make informed decisions when opting for the use of unsafe code in our projects. Recognizing these hazards serves as a foundation for developing strategies to proactively mitigate potential issues, ensuring that the advantages of utilizing unsafe code can be harnessed while concurrently safeguarding against undesirable consequences.

Risk 1: Null Pointer Dereferencing

Null pointer dereferencing, as we saw in *Chapter 1: Systems Programming with Rust*, is a common source of bugs in many programming languages, leading to crashes or undefined behavior. While Rust's ownership system largely eliminates the risk of null pointers, unsafe code can reintroduce this danger. We must exercise caution when working with raw pointers and ensure they are not mistakenly dereferencing null or dangling pointers.

Listing 13.12 Null pointer dereferencing.

```
fn main() {
    let null_pointer: *const i32 = std::ptr::null();

    unsafe {
        let value = *null_pointer; // ①
        println!("Dereferenced value: {}", value); // ②
    }
}

// Output

// Dereferenced value: 0
```

① Within an unsafe block, the code attempts to dereference a null pointer (`null_pointer`). Dereferencing a null pointer is a precarious operation that can lead to undefined behavior, as it points to an invalid or nonexistent memory location.

② The dereferenced value is then printed. However, since the pointer was null, trying to use the dereferenced value may result in crashes or unpredictable behavior. This example serves as a cautionary illustration of the risks associated with null pointer dereferencing in unsafe Rust code.

Handling null pointers in Rust requires utmost care, especially within unsafe blocks. Dereferencing a null pointer can lead to undefined behavior, putting at risk the stability and predictability of the program. It is essential for us to exercise caution, thoroughly validate pointers, and employ safe alternatives to avoid potential crashes and security vulnerabilities. Rust's emphasis on safety is a crucial aspect, and the use of unsafe blocks should be approached with a deep understanding of the associated risks and responsibilities.

Risk 2: Buffer Overflows

Buffer overflows are a classic security vulnerability that can result in data corruption, crashes, or even remote code execution. Rust's safe abstractions protect against buffer overflows, but in unsafe code, we must be meticulous in managing memory bounds to avoid overstepping the allocated space. Failure to do so can lead to unpredictable behavior and security vulnerabilities.

Listing 13.13 Buffer overflows.

```
fn main() {
    let data: [u8; 5] = [1, 2, 3, 4, 5];

    unsafe {
        let value = *data.get_unchecked(10); // ①
        println!("Value obtained from buffer overflow: {}", value); // ②
    }
}

// Output

// Value obtained from buffer overflow: 0
```

① Attempting to access an element outside the bounds of the array, causing a buffer overflow.

② Trying to use the value obtained from the out-of-bounds access, which can lead to data corruption or crashes.

This example highlights the dangers of buffer overflows in Rust, especially within unsafe code. Accessing elements outside the bounds of an array can result in unpredictable behavior, data corruption, and even security vulnerabilities. We should exercise extreme caution, ensure proper bounds checking, and consider alternative strategies to prevent buffer overflows and maintain the integrity of our programs. Rust's emphasis on memory safety remains crucial, and understanding the risks associated with unsafe practices is essential for responsible programming in this language.

Risk 3: Use-After-Free Errors

Use-after-free errors occur when a program continues to use a pointer after the memory it points to has been freed. Rust's ownership model eliminates many instances of use-after-free errors, but in the realm of unsafe code, we must carefully manage the lifetimes of objects to prevent inadvertent use after they are deallocated.

Listing 13.14 Dangling reference example.

```
fn main() { // ①
    let data = Box::new(42); // ②

    let raw_pointer = Box::into_raw(data); // ③

    unsafe {
        drop(Box::from_raw(raw_pointer)); // ④
        println!("Value at raw pointer: {}", *raw_pointer); // ⑤
    }
}

// Output

// Value at raw pointer: 1492189596
```

① The **main** function is the starting point of the Rust program.

② A box (**Box**) is used to allocate memory on the heap and store the value **42**.

③ The **into_raw** method is employed to convert the box into a raw pointer (***mut i32**).

④ The **drop** function is called, which deallocates the memory associated with the box. This step simulates the scenario where the memory is freed.

⑤ Within the **unsafe** block, an attempt is made to access the value at the raw pointer after the associated memory has been deallocated. This situation can lead to undefined behavior.

In this example, the unsafe code attempts to use a raw pointer after the associated memory has been deallocated, resulting in a potential use-after-free error. This underscores the importance of careful management of object lifetimes when working with unsafe code. Mitigating such risks involves understanding the consequences of unsafe operations and employing strategies to prevent memory safety violations.

Continuing the discussion on common unsafe coding practices, it's essential to explore strategies for mitigating these risks. This might involve leveraging safe abstractions wherever possible, conducting thorough code reviews with a focus on unsafe code, and utilizing tools like the Rust compiler's **unsafe** linting features to catch potential issues early in the development process.

Conclusion

The landscape of working with unsafe code in Rust represents a powerful yet complex domain that demands deep comprehension and wise application. Navigating this space requires us to find a fine line, striking a delicate balance between optimizing performance and upholding safety. This delicate equilibrium becomes particularly critical as we make decisions tailored to the specific requirements of our projects, where the trade-offs between efficiency and security become apparent.

This chapter has undertaken an exploration of the foundational aspects of unsafe code, unraveling its necessity in diverse scenarios such as interfacing with other languages, undertaking low-level system operations, and addressing performance-critical situations. Real-world examples and case studies have been employed to underscore the pragmatic utility of unsafe code and illuminate the potential consequences stemming from its misuse. By delving into practical applications, developers gain insights into when and how to employ unsafe code effectively, while remaining attuned to the pitfalls that may arise if it is not wielded with care.

Furthermore, the chapter has proactively engaged with best practices that govern the wise use of unsafe code, addressing the associated risks universal to common coding practices that might compromise safety. Strategies for identifying and mitigating potential issues have been explained, emphasizing the importance of comprehensive code reviews, rigorous testing, and the adoption of static analysis tools. Through these measures, we are equipped to harness the power of unsafe code carefully, effectively balancing its advantages with the imperative to minimize risks.

As Rust continues its evolutionary journey, we are encouraged to stay alongside emerging best practices, leverage the wealth of resources available within the Rust community, and actively contribute to the ongoing discourse surrounding safe and efficient systems programming. Approaching unsafe code with a mindset grounded in respect, caution, and a commitment to excellence allows us to unlock the inherent potential while being determined to uphold Rust's fundamental principles of safety and performance. This relationship between leveraging the power of unsafe code and maintaining the core tenets of Rust's design philosophy positions us to navigate the complexities of modern systems programming with both efficacy and responsibility.

In the next chapter, we will delve into the complexities of Asynchronous Programming in Rust, a crucial paradigm for developing responsive and efficient applications. The exploration centers around Rust's async/await syntax, exploring its nuances and providing you with a comprehensive understanding of its application. Additionally, we will navigate the landscape of the Tokio library, a prominent asynchronous runtime in Rust, exploring its features and capabilities. Whether a seasoned developer or a newcomer to Rust, the insights gained here will empower you to create performant applications very good at handling concurrent and parallel tasks with finesse.

Resources

To deepen your understanding of Unsafe Code in Rust, you can explore the following resources:

- *Rust Book - Unsafe Rust*: Refer to the official Rust documentation on unsafe Rust, exploring the intricacies of using unsafe code and understanding the scenarios where it is necessary. - *https://doc.rust-lang.org/book/ch19-01-unsafe-rust.html*
- *The Rustonomicon*: Dive into "The Rustonomicon," a resource that delves into the dark arts of unsafe Rust, providing in-depth insights into advanced programming techniques and considerations. - *https://doc.rust-lang.org/nomicon/*
- *Rust Reference - Undefined Behavior*: Explore the Rust reference on undefined behavior, gaining a deeper understanding of the consequences of unsafe code and how to avoid common pitfalls. - *https://doc.rust-lang.org/reference/behavior-considered-undefined.html*
- *Unsafe Rust and Miri by Ralf Jung - Rust Zürisee June* 2023: Watch the RustConf 2023 talk on "Unsafe Rust and Miri" by Ralf Jung, providing practical insights and examples of using unsafe code in Rust. - *https://www.youtube.com/watch?v=svR0p6fSUYY*
- *Too Many Lists*: Explore the "Too Many Lists" guide, which provides a practical approach to learning Rust and includes sections on unsafe Rust, ownership, and borrowing. - *https://rust-unofficial.github.io/too-many-lists/index.html*
- RFC 2585 - *Allow unsafe blocks in unsafe functions*: An RFC which proposes allowing the use of unsafe block in an unsafe function. - *https://github.com/rust-lang/rfcs/blob/master/text/2585-unsafe-block-in-unsafe-fn.md*

These resources cover various aspects of unsafe code in Rust, providing both theoretical knowledge and practical insights into using unsafe code responsibly and effectively.

Multiple Choice Questions

Q1: When might developers choose to use unsafe code in Rust?

a) For all programming tasks to maximize performance

b) Only when dealing with high-level abstractions

c) When interfacing with external languages or performing low-level operations

d) To enforce strict memory safety

Q2: What does the unsafe keyword indicate in Rust?

a) That the code is error-prone

b) That the code violates Rust syntax rules

c) That the code requires special attention and may bypass safety checks

d) That the code is inefficient

Q3: In the context of Rust, when might the use of FFI (Foreign Function Interface) with unsafe code be necessary?

a) To enhance code readability

b) When developing purely in Rust without external dependencies

c) When interfacing with external languages lacking Rust's safety features

d) To enforce strict adherence to Rust's borrowing rules

Q4: What is a potential risk of using unsafe code in Rust?

a) Improved code performance

b) Undefined behavior, memory safety violations, or data races

c) Enhanced code readability

d) Compatibility with all Rust versions

Q5: In the context of Rust, what does a raw pointer represent?

a) A high-level reference to data

b) A type-safe pointer

c) A pointer with strict lifetime rules

d) A direct memory address without safety guarantees

Q6: How does Rust's ownership system contribute to memory safety?

a) By allowing unrestricted access to memory

b) By enforcing strict borrowing rules

c) By automatically managing memory allocation and deallocation

d) By permitting multiple parts of code to modify data simultaneously

Q7: What is the purpose of the as_ptr() method in Rust?

a) To convert a pointer to a reference

b) To perform arithmetic operations on a pointer

c) To obtain a raw pointer to the first element of a collection

d) To cast a pointer to a different type

Q8: When might a developer choose to use unsafe blocks in Rust?

a) Always, for all programming tasks

b) Only for tasks involving high-level abstractions

c) When the benefits of bypassing safety checks outweigh the risks

d) When following strict safety rules is not important

Q9: What is the primary consideration when balancing performance and safety in Rust?

a) Prioritizing performance without any safety considerations

b) Ignoring potential risks and consequences of unsafe code

c) Evaluating whether the benefits of performance outweigh the risks of unsafe code

d) Ensuring maximum safety without any regard for performance

Q10: In the given example of advanced image processing with OpenCV, what is the purpose of the opencv::imgproc::blur function?

a) Grayscale conversion

b) Gaussian blur

c) Canny edge detection

d) Image resizing

Q11: In the custom memory management example, what is the role of the CustomMemoryManager struct?

a) It defines image processing operations.

b) It encapsulates two function pointers for custom memory allocation and deallocation.

c) It represents a data structure for storing pixel values.

d) It is responsible for handling database interactions.

Q12: What is the purpose of the custom_allocate function in the custom memory management example?

a) It performs image resizing.

b) It handles database queries.

c) It allocates custom memory using the standard Rust allocator.

d) It defines traits for data structures.

Q13: What is the purpose of the iter_mut method in the alternative approach example?

a) To define shared behaviors

b) To allocate custom memory

c) To obtain a mutable iterator over elements without using unsafe code

d) To restrict access to data

Answers

1. c) When interfacing with external languages or performing low-level operations
2. c) That the code requires special attention and may bypass safety checks
3. c) When interfacing with external languages lacking Rust's safety features
4. b) Undefined behavior, memory safety violations, or data races
5. d) A direct memory address without safety guarantees
6. b) By enforcing strict borrowing rules
7. c) To obtain a raw pointer to the first element of a collection
8. c) When the benefits of bypassing safety checks outweigh the risks
9. c) Evaluating whether the benefits of performance outweigh the risks of unsafe code
10. b) Gaussian blur
11. b) It encapsulates two function pointers for custom memory allocation and deallocation.
12. c) It allocates custom memory using the standard Rust allocator
13. c) To obtain a mutable iterator over elements without using unsafe code

Key Terms

- **Unsafe Code:** Code in Rust that bypasses the usual safety guarantees provided by the compiler, allowing for operations that would be considered risky within the limits of safe Rust.
- **Raw Pointer:** A direct memory address without safety guarantees, often used in unsafe code for low-level operations where fine-grained control over memory is necessary.
- **Foreign Function Interface (FFI):** A mechanism in Rust that enables interaction with code written in other languages, allowing seamless integration with external libraries and languages, often requiring the use of unsafe code.
- **Memory Safety:** A key characteristic of Rust that prevents common programming errors such as null pointer dereferences, buffer overflows, and data races by enforcing strict ownership and borrowing rules.

- **Undefined Behavior:** Undesirable and unpredictable outcomes resulting from the execution of code that violates the language's rules, often associated with the misuse of unsafe code.
- **Borrow Checker:** A component of the Rust compiler that enforces ownership and borrowing rules, ensuring that references to data are valid and preventing data races.
- **Performance Optimization:** The process of enhancing the efficiency of a Rust program, often involving trade-offs between performance and safety, with careful consideration of the benefits and risks associated with unsafe code.
- **Gaussian Blur:** An image processing technique used to reduce noise and detail in images, as demonstrated in the OpenCV example, by applying a convolution operation with a Gaussian filter.
- **Custom Memory Manager:** A struct, as demonstrated in the custom memory management example, responsible for orchestrating custom memory allocation and deallocation operations in a data processing pipeline.
- **Canny Edge Detection:** An advanced image processing technique demonstrated in the OpenCV example, used to detect edges in an image by identifying areas of rapid intensity changes.
- **Modular Approach:** A best practice in Rust programming that involves encapsulating unsafe code within safe abstractions, minimizing its surface area and potential impact on the codebase.
- **Memory Safety Violations:** Risks associated with unsafe code that can lead to undefined behavior and security vulnerabilities by violating Rust's ownership and borrowing rules.
- **`iter_mut` Method:** A safe abstraction in Rust's standard library used to obtain a mutable iterator over elements, providing a controlled and safe way to perform operations on mutable references.

CHAPTER 14
Asynchronous Programming

Introduction

In the ever-evolving landscape of application development, the importance of asynchronous programming cannot be overstated. As our digital world demands applications to be both responsive and efficient, understanding and mastering asynchronous programming becomes a cornerstone for developers. This chapter unfolds as a comprehensive guide, navigating through the complexities of asynchronous programming in Rust, with a specialized focus on leveraging Rust's async/await syntax and the powerful `tokio` library.

Kicking off this exploration of asynchronous programming in Rust is like setting off on a thrilling journey of discovery. It all begins with exploring the unique characteristics of Rust's `async/await` methodology, a dynamic combo that enables programs to carry on with tasks without waiting for each one to finish. Imagine it as a cool technique where your program effortlessly juggles multiple tasks, keeping things moving quickly. This chapter highlights Rust's async/await style, guiding you through the process of crafting programs that are not only fast and responsive but also handle a multitude of tasks concurrently with ease. In essence, it's about making your program a multitasking expert, ensuring it operates with efficiency.

By the end of this chapter, you will not only have a comprehensive understanding of the fundamental principles and techniques underpinning asynchronous programming but will also be equipped with the skills needed to construct robust applications that leverage the power of concurrency. As we delve into the complexities of asynchronous programming in Rust, we aim to demystify the complexities, providing practical insights and examples that empower you to create applications that excel in both responsiveness and efficiency.

Structure

In this chapter, we are going to explore the following topics:

- Learning asynchronous programming with async/await in Rust
- Utilizing the Tokio library for building asynchronous applications

Fundamentals of Rust's `async/await` Syntax

Rust's **`async/await`** syntax introduces a fundamental shift in the way we structure and execute code. The **`async`** keyword serves as the gateway to creating asynchronous functions, transforming them into entities capable of running concurrently with other tasks. Asynchronous functions enable the interleaved execution of code, allowing the program to progress while awaiting the resolution of asynchronous operations. This marks a departure from traditional synchronous programming, where operations typically block the execution flow until completion.

Let's explore the following example illustrating the basic structure of an asynchronous function using Rust's **`async/await`** syntax:

Listing 14.1 A basic structure of an asynchronous function

```
async fn example_async_function() { // ①
    // Asynchronous code goes here
    let result = async_operation().await; // ②
    // ③
}
```

① The function **`example_async_function`** is declared with the **`async`** keyword, signaling its asynchronous nature. This declaration enables non-blocking execution, allowing the function to perform asynchronous operations without halting the program's progress.

② Within the function body, the variable **`result`** is assigned the value returned by the asynchronous operation **`async_operation`**. The **`await`** keyword is a crucial element here, as it gracefully pauses the function's execution, enabling the runtime to switch to other tasks while awaiting the completion of **`async_operation`**.

③ After the asynchronous operation is completed, the function resumes execution at this point. Here, we can seamlessly continue with the result obtained from the asynchronous operation. This elegant syntax enhances code expressiveness, allowing us to integrate asynchronous logic seamlessly into our applications, a mark of Rust's elegant **async/await** syntax.

To delve deeper into the complexities of Rust's **async/await** syntax, let's examine a more elaborate example that showcases the versatility of this paradigm. The following code snippet illustrates an asynchronous function with nuanced complexity:

Listing 14.2 A slightly complex structure of an asynchronous function

```
async fn complex_async_function() { // ①
    let result_1 = async_operation_1().await; // ②

    if result_1 { // ③
        let result_2 = async_operation_2().await; // ④

        match result_2 { // ⑤
            Ok(value) => { // ⑥
                println!("Result: {}", value); // ⑦
            }
            Err(error) => { // ⑧
                eprintln!("Error: {}", error); // ⑨
            }
        }
    } else { // ⑩
        println!("Operation 1 failed"); // ⑪
    }
}
```

① The function **complex_async_function** is declared as asynchronous, indicating that it can execute asynchronously. This designation allows for the incorporation of asynchronous operations without blocking the program's flow.

② The variable **result_1** is assigned the value returned by the asynchronous operation **async_operation_1()**. The **await** keyword pauses the function until the completion of this operation, ensuring non-blocking execution.

③ Conditional branching occurs based on the value of **result_1**. If it evaluates to true, indicating success, the block inside the if statement is executed; otherwise, the else block is executed.

④ Within the if block, **`result_2`** is assigned the value of another asynchronous operation, **`async_operation_2()`**. Again, the **`await`** keyword is instrumental in managing the asynchronous nature of this operation.

⑤ The **`match`** statement is employed to handle the potential outcomes of **`result_2`**. This construct allows for exhaustive pattern matching, covering both successful and error scenarios.

⑥ In the case of a successful result, the code within this arm of the match statement is executed, processing and printing the result.

⑦ The successful result is processed here, demonstrating the seamless integration of asynchronous logic into the application. The elegance of Rust's async/await syntax becomes apparent.

⑧ In the event of an error, the code within this arm of the match statement is executed. Error handling is an integral part of robust asynchronous programming.

⑨ The error case is handled here, with an appropriate error message printed to the standard error stream. This exemplifies Rust's commitment to safe and expressive error handling.

⑩ If **`result_1`** evaluates to false, indicating a failure in the first asynchronous operation, the code within the else block is executed.

⑪ In the else block, the program handles the case where the first operation failed, printing a corresponding message. This comprehensive example showcases not only the elegance of Rust's **`async/await`** syntax but also its capability to handle complex asynchronous workflows, including conditional branching and error handling.

Furthermore, it's crucial to recognize that the **`await`** keyword serves as a key element in this asynchronous task. It gracefully pauses the execution of the current function, allowing the runtime to switch to other tasks until the awaited operation completes. This non-blocking nature is pivotal in achieving efficient concurrency, ensuring that the program progresses unrestrained even while certain operations are awaiting resolution.

Asynchronous programming in Rust is not merely about syntax; it's a mindset shift that opens doors to efficient, parallel execution. Embracing this paradigm empowers us to create responsive and scalable applications, where the interleaved execution of tasks blend seamlessly, resulting in enhanced performance and responsiveness.

Exploring the Dynamics of `async/await`

To gain a profound understanding of **`async/await`** mechanics in Rust, let's explore it through the complex process that governs the execution of asynchronous functions. Imagine you're orchestrating a distributed system, and certain operations, such as fetching data from multiple remote servers simultaneously, would greatly benefit from asynchronous execution.

When an asynchronous function, let's call it **`fetchDataFromServers`**, encounters an **`await`** expression, it gracefully steps aside in its execution journey. This temporal pause is like a conductor temporarily halting the performance, allowing other musicians (asynchronous tasks) to take center stage. In the context of Rust's async/await, this suspension is intentional and strategic, promoting a cooperative multitasking job.

`fetchDataFromServers() Execution`

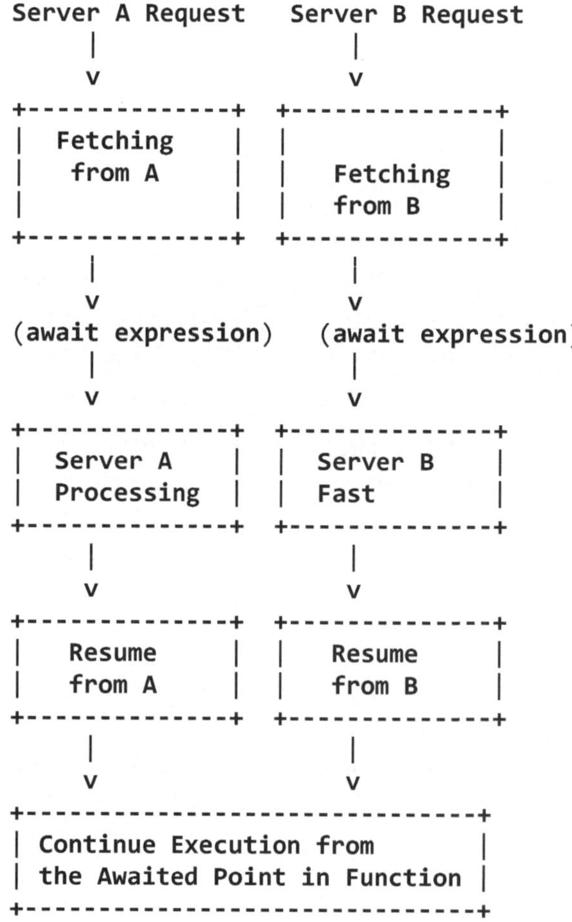

Consider this scenario: **`fetchDataFromServers`** initiates a request to Server A, hits the **`await`** expression, and gracefully pauses. Meanwhile, the Rust runtime, like a seasoned conductor, directs the spotlight to other ongoing tasks, ensuring a harmonious symphony of concurrent operations.

Now, let's say Server B has a speedy response time. While Server A is still processing, Server B's data retrieval quickly finishes. Rust's runtime, leveraging the power of the **`await`** expression, seamlessly resumes the execution of **`fetchDataFromServers`** precisely from where it left off. The function regains control, processing Server B's data without missing a beat.

Crucially, Rust's ownership system acts as a conductor in this performance, ensuring memory safety and preventing data races. Each asynchronous task holds ownership of its data, eliminating the risk of conflicts and harmonizing the orchestration of tasks. This meticulous choreography, orchestrated by **`async/await`** and guided by Rust's ownership principles, grants the program responsiveness and efficiency without resorting to traditional blocking calls.

Async/await in Rust is not just a syntactic feature; it's a symphony of cooperative multitasking, where the conductor (Rust's runtime) orchestrates a seamless performance, allowing asynchronous functions to harmoniously yield and resume, creating a melody of efficient, concurrent execution.

Utilizing the tokio Library

Within the Rust ecosystem, the **`tokio`** library distinguishes itself as a robust and widely embraced asynchronous runtime. Offering essential tools and abstractions, tokio proves to be an outstanding selection for the effective orchestration of asynchronous tasks, thereby becoming a preferred solution for crafting high-performance applications. At the core of tokio's capabilities is its comprehensive runtime, encompassing features like a scheduler, an event loop, and other integral components.

To use tokio in a Rust project, you need to add the following dependencies to your **`Cargo.toml`** file:

```
[dependencies]
tokio = { version = "1.34.0", features = ["full"] }
```

With tokio integrated, we can leverage its runtime to spawn asynchronous tasks, manage concurrency, and handle I/O operations efficiently.

Using Async for Responsiveness

As you kick off the journey of learning asynchronous programming, the primary motivation often revolves around enhancing the responsiveness of applications. Rust's async/await syntax acts as a powerful tool in achieving this goal, allowing you to design systems that efficiently handle I/O-bound operations without sacrificing performance.

Let's explore an example where multiple asynchronous functions collaborate to download and process data concurrently:

Listing 14.3 An example of multiple asynchronous functions workflow.

```
use tokio::time::Duration;


async fn fetch_data() -> Result<String, reqwest::Error> { // ①
    tokio::time::sleep(Duration::from_secs(2)).await; // ②
    Ok::<String, _>("Data fetched successfully".to_owned()) // ③
}

async fn process_data(data: String) { // ④
    println!("Processing: {}", data); // ⑤
}

async fn main_async_workflow() { // ⑥
    let fetch_task = tokio::spawn(fetch_data()); // ⑦
    let process_task = tokio::spawn(process_data("Sample Data".to_
owned())); // ⑧

    let fetch_result = fetch_task.await.expect("Failed to fetch data");
// ⑨
    let _ = process_task.await; // ⑩

    println!("Fetch Result: {:?}", fetch_result); // ⑪
}

#[tokio::main] // ⑫
async fn main() {
    main_async_workflow().await; // ⑬
}
```

```
// Output

// Processing: Sample Data
// Fetch Result: Ok("Data fetched successfully")
```

① The **fetch_data** function is defined to simulate an asynchronous HTTP request. It returns a **Result** with the fetched data or an error of type **reqwest::Error**.

② Within **fetch_data**, an asynchronous delay of 2 seconds is introduced using **tokio::time::sleep**. This emulates the asynchronous nature of an HTTP request that takes time to complete.

③ The function concludes by returning the fetched data as a successful result using **Ok("Data fetched successfully".to_owned())**.

④ The **process_data** function is declared to asynchronously handle the processing of fetched data.

⑤ Within **process_data**, a simple operation is performed, printing the processed data to the console.

⑥ The **main_async_workflow** function orchestrates the overall workflow, demonstrating how to coordinate multiple asynchronous tasks.

⑦ The **tokio::spawn** function is used to spawn an asynchronous task for the **fetch_data** function, enabling concurrent execution.

⑧ Similarly, another task is spawned for the **process_data** function, showcasing the ability to perform multiple asynchronous operations concurrently.

⑨ The completion of the fetch task is awaited, extracting the result or panicking with an error message if fetching fails.

⑩ The processing task is awaited as well. The underscore (_) indicates that we are not interested in the result, as it happens concurrently.

⑪ The function concludes by printing the result of the fetch operation, showcasing the asynchronous coordination and execution of tasks. This example underscores how Rust's `async/await` syntax, combined with an asynchronous runtime like tokio, can significantly enhance the responsiveness of applications.

Rust's `async/await` syntax, when coupled with asynchronous runtimes like tokio, provides a powerful paradigm for building concurrent and responsive applications. In this extended example, the orchestration of asynchronous tasks to fetch and process data showcases the elegance and expressiveness of Rust's asynchronous programming model. The ability to seamlessly integrate asynchronous operations into the workflow enhances code readability and facilitates the creation of efficient, non-blocking applications. As we embrace this paradigm, we unlock the potential for building scalable and performant systems that harness the benefits of parallelism.

Error Handling in Asynchronous Code

While Rust's `async/await` syntax simplifies the expression of asynchronous logic, navigating the complexities of async programming requires a profound understanding of potential challenges and their solutions. Asynchronous code introduces complexities such as handling errors, managing task lifetimes, and orchestrating concurrent operations effectively.

Error handling in asynchronous code involves considerations beyond traditional synchronous error handling. Rust provides mechanisms, such as the **`Result`** type and the **`?`** operator, to propagate errors through the asynchronous call stack. Additionally, the **`tokio::task::spawn`** function returns a **`tokio::task::JoinHandle`** that can be used to await task completion and handle potential errors.

Listing 14.4 Error handling in an asynchronous program.

```
use std::error::Error; // ①

async fn async_with_error_handling() -> Result<(), Box<dyn Error +
Send>> { // ②
    let handle = tokio::task::spawn(async { // ③
        Ok::<(), Box<dyn Error + Send>>(()) // ④
    });

    let _ = handle.await.map_err(|error| { // ⑤
        Box::new(error) as Box<dyn Error + Send> // ⑥
    })?;
    Ok(()) // ⑦
}

#[tokio::main]
async fn main() { // ⑧
    match async_with_error_handling().await { // ⑨
        Ok(_) => println!("Async operation completed successfully"), // ⑩
        Err(error) => eprintln!("Error during async operation: {}", er-
ror), // ⑪
    }
}
```

```
// Output

// Async operation completed successfully
```

① The code begins with importing the necessary module **std::error::Error**, providing functionalities related to error handling in Rust.

② The function **async_with_error_handling** is declared as an asynchronous function, returning a **Result** with an empty tuple **()** and a boxed trait object representing any type that implements **Error** and is **Send**.

③ Inside the asynchronous function, a new asynchronous task is spawned using **tokio::task::spawn**. This task encapsulates the asynchronous logic and is set up to return an **Ok** result of type **()**.

④ The asynchronous logic within the spawned task is a placeholder, and you should replace it with actual asynchronous operations that may yield errors. The result type is explicitly specified as **Ok<(), Box<dyn Error + Send>>**.

⑤ After spawning the task, the code awaits its completion using the **await** keyword. The **map_err** method is employed to handle any potential errors that might occur during the execution of the asynchronous task.

⑥ In case of an error, the error is wrapped in a **Box<dyn Error + Send>** to meet the return type requirement, allowing different types of errors to be captured uniformly.

⑦ The overall function returns an **Ok** result with an empty tuple **()** if the asynchronous task completes successfully, effectively signaling the absence of errors.

⑧ The **main** function is annotated with **tokio::main**, indicating that it will serve as the entry point for the tokio runtime, a popular asynchronous runtime for Rust.

⑨ Within the **main** function, the **async_with_error_handling** function is invoked using the **await** keyword, initiating the asynchronous operation.

⑩ If the asynchronous operation completes without errors, a success message is printed to the console.

⑪ In the event of an error during the asynchronous operation, an error message is printed to the console using **eprintln**.

This example demonstrates the utilization of Rust's async/await syntax in conjunction with the tokio runtime to handle asynchronous tasks with built-in error propagation. The concise yet powerful combination of **`tokio::task::spawn`**, **`await`**, and the **`?`** operator facilitates efficient and clean asynchronous programming, offering us a robust foundation for building responsive and error-aware applications.

Concurrent Task Lifetimes

Concurrent programming introduces the challenge of managing the lifetimes of asynchronous tasks and ensuring efficient resource utilization. Rust's ownership system, coupled with tokio's runtime, offers a robust solution to these challenges. The ownership system ensures that references to data are valid for the duration of the asynchronous task, preventing data races and memory safety issues.

We should be mindful of the ownership rules when sharing data between asynchronous tasks. Utilizing tools like **`Arc`** (*Atomic Reference Counting*) to create a thread-safe reference-counted pointer becomes essential when multiple tasks need to access shared data concurrently.

Listing 14.5 Asynchronous program with shared data.

```
use tokio::sync::Mutex;
use std::sync::Arc;

async fn async_with_shared_data() { // ①
    let shared_data = Arc::new(Mutex::new(0)); // ②

    let task1 = tokio::spawn(async_with_shared_data_task
(Arc::clone(&shared_data))); // ③
    let task2 = tokio::spawn(async_with_shared_data_task
(Arc::clone(&shared_data)));
// ④
    println!("Task 1 and Task 2 spawned.");

    task1.await.expect("Task 1 failed"); // ⑤

    println!("Task 1 completed successfully.");

    task2.await.expect("Task 2 failed"); // ⑥

    println!("Task 2 completed successfully.");

    println!("Continuing with the results.");
    // ⑦
}
```

```
async fn async_with_shared_data_task(shared_data: Arc<Mutex<i32>>) { //
⑧
    let mut data = shared_data.lock().await; // ⑨

    println!("Task acquiring lock on shared data.");

    *data += 1; // ⑩
    println!("Task modifying shared data: {}", data);
}

#[tokio::main]
async fn main() { // ⑪
    async_with_shared_data().await; // ⑫
    println!("Main function completed.");
}

// Output

// Task 1 and Task 2 spawned.
// Task acquiring lock on shared data.
// Task modifying shared data: 1
// Task acquiring lock on shared data.
// Task modifying shared data: 2
// Task 1 completed successfully.
// Task 2 completed successfully.
// Continuing with the results.
// Main function completed.
```

① The asynchronous function **async_with_shared_data** orchestrates the sharing of data among multiple tasks.

② An Arc-wrapped Mutex, **shared_data**, is created to safely share an integer (initialized to 0) among the asynchronous tasks.

③, ④ Two asynchronous tasks are spawned, each invoking the **async_with_shared_data_task** function with a cloned reference to the shared data.

⑤, ⑥ The **await** keyword is used to wait for the completion of both tasks, and any potential errors are handled using the **expect** method.

⑦ After the tasks are completed, the function continues with the results.

⑧ The **async_with_shared_data_task** function takes an Arc-wrapped Mutex as a parameter to operate on the shared data.

⑨ Within this function, a lock is acquired on the shared data using the **lock** method, ensuring exclusive access.

⑩ The shared data is modified in a synchronized manner, incrementing its value by 1.

⑪ The **main** function, annotated with **[tokio::main]**, serves as the entry point for the tokio runtime.

⑫ The **async_with_shared_data** function is executed within the tokio runtime using the **await** keyword within the **main** function.

To enhance clarity, let's illustrate this example using a simple diagram:

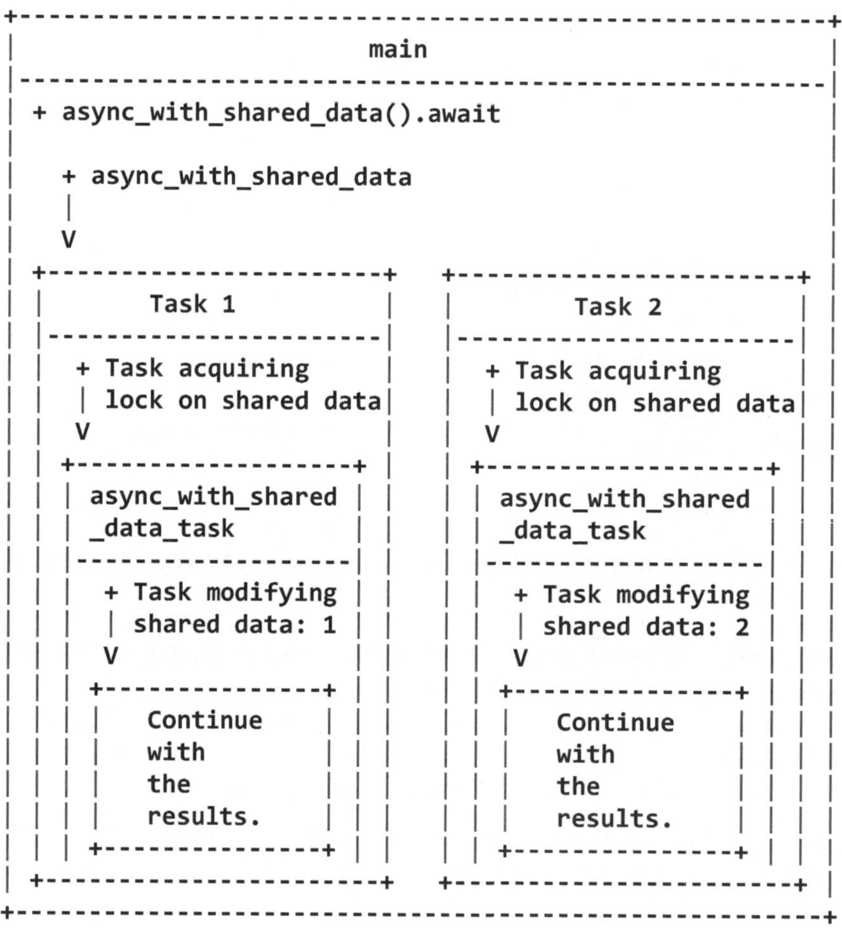

The + symbol is used to denote the presence of a component, like methods.

This code snippet exemplifies the power of asynchronous programming with shared data using the `async/await` syntax. The use of Arc-wrapped Mutex ensures safe concurrent access to shared resources, and tokio's async runtime facilitates the coordination of asynchronous tasks. This paradigm allows for efficient and synchronized manipulation of data across concurrent operations, showcasing Rust's capability to build robust and concurrent applications.

Advanced Patterns in Async Programming

Asynchronous programming in Rust transcends the foundational `async/await` syntax, delving into advanced patterns that augment both expressiveness and efficiency. These sophisticated patterns are crucial for addressing complex scenarios and optimizing the performance of asynchronous applications. In this domain, one notable and crucial abstraction is the use of asynchronous streams, a mechanism that represents a sequence of values produced over time. As we explore these advanced patterns, we unlock new possibilities for managing concurrency, handling asynchronous events, and designing more intricate and responsive systems.

Asynchronous Streams

One of the key advanced patterns in Rust's asynchronous programming landscape is the concept of *asynchronous streams*. Unlike synchronous iterators that produce a finite sequence of values in a blocking fashion, asynchronous streams enable the asynchronous generation of values over time. This is particularly advantageous in scenarios where data is continuously produced, such as event streams, sensor data, or real-time updates.

To facilitate working with asynchronous streams, the **`tokio_stream`** crate comes into play, offering a range of modules and utilities. These tools empower us to seamlessly manipulate, transform, and consume asynchronous streams, unlocking a rich set of possibilities for building responsive and scalable applications.

To illustrate the power of asynchronous streams, let's delve into a practical example. Consider a scenario where we want to generate an asynchronous stream of random numbers at regular intervals. This use case highlights the flexibility and expressiveness that asynchronous streams bring to the table, allowing us to model dynamic and continuous data sources efficiently.

The following code snippet showcases the creation of a custom asynchronous stream named **`MyInterval`**, leveraging the tokio runtime and the **tokio_stream** crate. This stream emits instances of **tokio::time::Instant** at specified intervals, creating a dynamic sequence of time-related values. Additionally, a **`map`** operation is applied to transform each emitted item into a random **u32**, showcasing the composability and versatility of asynchronous stream operations.

Listing 14.6 Asynchronous streams using the `tokio_stream` crate.

```
use std::pin::Pin; // ①
use std::task::{Context, Poll}; // ②
use tokio::time::Duration; // ③
use tokio_stream::{Stream, StreamExt}; // ④


struct MyInterval { // ⑤
    interval: tokio::time::Interval,
}

impl MyInterval { // ⑥

    fn new(duration: Duration) -> Self {
        Self {
            interval: tokio::time::interval(duration),
        }
    }
}

impl Stream for MyInterval {
    type Item = tokio::time::Instant; // ⑦


    fn poll_next(mut self: Pin<&mut Self>, cx: &mut Context<'_>) ->
Poll<Option<Self::Item>> { // ⑧

        match Pin::new(&mut self.interval).poll_tick(cx) { // ⑨
            Poll::Ready(instant) => Poll::Ready(Some(instant)),
            Poll::Pending => Poll::Pending,
        }
    }
}

#[tokio::main] // ⑩
async fn main() {

    let mut random_number_stream =
        MyInterval::new(Duration::from_secs(1)).map(|_| rand::random::
<u32>()); // ⑪
```

```
    for _ in 0..5 { // ⑫
        if let Some(random_number) = random_number_stream.next().await
{ // ⑬
            println!("Random Number: {}", random_number);
        }
    }
}

// Output

// Random Number: 2968165177
// Random Number: 3728492754
// Random Number: 3705231156
// Random Number: 2459930473
// Random Number: 3383401261
```

① The code begins by importing the **Pin** type from the standard library, which is a fundamental element utilized for handling self-referential structs. This becomes crucial when dealing with structures that contain references to their own fields, a common scenario in asynchronous programming.

② Following that, the code imports the **Context** and **Poll** types from the standard library's **task** module. These types play a pivotal role in asynchronous task execution, providing the necessary tools for managing the execution context and polling tasks for completion.

③ The **Duration** type is imported from the tokio runtime. This type is utilized for specifying time intervals, a fundamental aspect when dealing with asynchronous programming and tasks that are scheduled to occur at regular time intervals.

④ The code imports essential components from both the tokio runtime and the **tokio_stream** crate. This step ensures access to the asynchronous runtime environment and stream-related functionalities required for building asynchronous streams.

⑤ The **MyInterval** struct is introduced, serving as a custom representation of an interval-based stream. This struct encapsulates the functionality required for emitting items at specified intervals.

⑥ The **new** method is implemented for the **MyInterval** struct. This method facilitates the creation of a new instance of **MyInterval** with a user-defined duration, enabling flexibility in configuring the time intervals between emitted items.

⑦ The associated type **Item** for the stream is specified as **tokio::time::Instant**. This indicates that the stream emits instances of **Instant**, representing points in time, adding a temporal dimension to the stream's output.

⑧ The **Stream** trait is implemented for the **MyInterval** struct. This implementation includes the definition of the **poll_next** method, responsible for handling the emission of items in the stream.

⑨ Within the **poll_next** method, the code utilizes the **poll_tick** function on the underlying **tokio::time::Interval**. This function checks for the availability of the next instant in time and signals whether it is ready or still pending.

⑩ The main asynchronous function is introduced, marked with the tokio runtime attribute. This function serves as the entry point for asynchronous execution and orchestrates the usage of the custom interval-based stream.

⑪ An instance of **MyInterval** is created within the main function, configured with a one-second interval. Additionally, a **map** operation is applied to the stream, transforming each emitted item to a random **u32**, showcasing the versatility of asynchronous stream operations.

⑫ The code enters a loop, iterating over the stream for a fixed number of times. This loop represents the consumption of asynchronous stream items in a controlled manner.

⑬ Within the loop, the code awaits the arrival of the next random number from the stream using the **next** method and prints the received random number. This demonstrates the asynchronous nature of the stream, where items are produced and consumed asynchronously.

To enhance clarity, let's illustrate this example using a simple diagram:

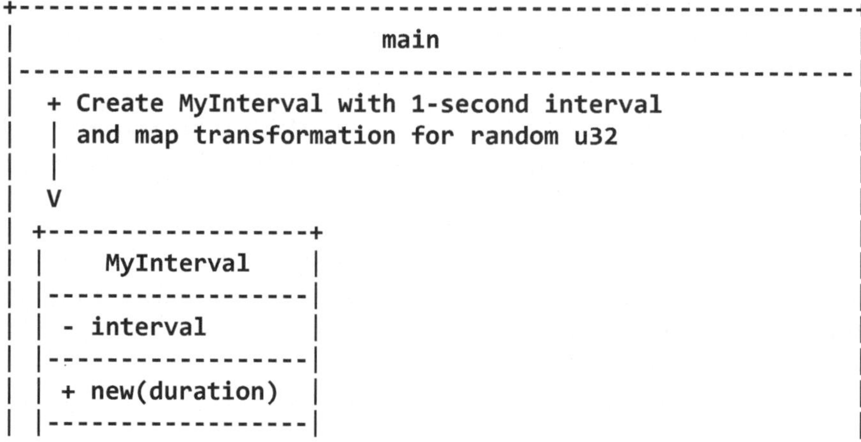

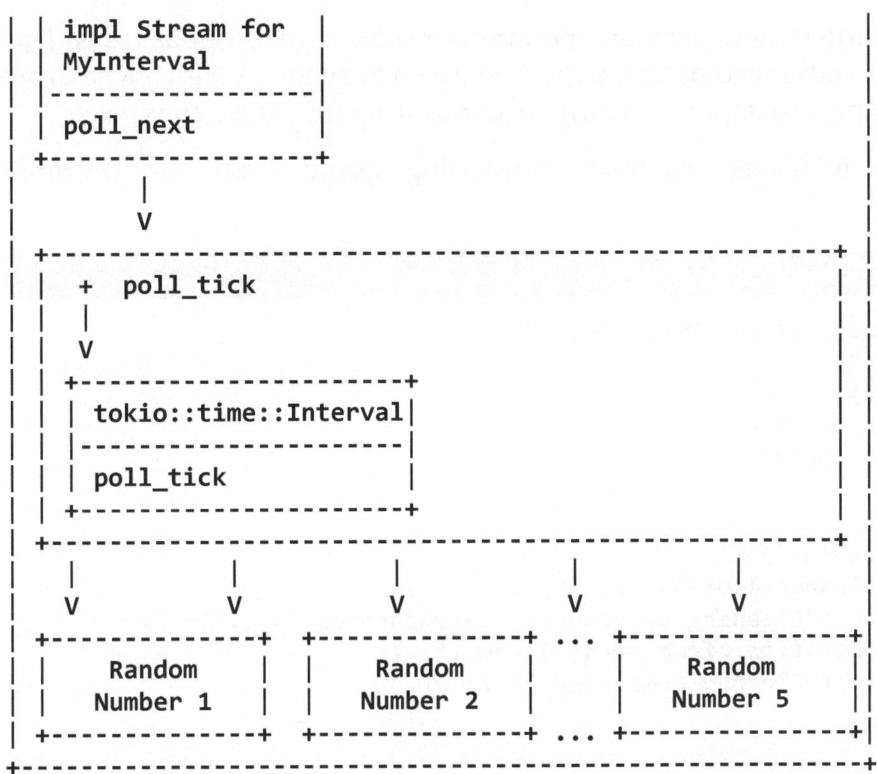

The + symbol is used to denote the presence of a component, like methods.
The - symbol indicates a relationship or association between components, like structs fields, and so on.

This code snippet exemplifies the construction and utilization of an asynchronous stream, showcasing the power of the tokio runtime and stream processing. The `MyInterval` struct encapsulates an interval-based stream, emitting instances of `tokio::time::Instant` at specified time intervals. Through the main function, an instance of this stream is created, and its items are consumed in a controlled loop, each transformed into a random `u32`. This code illustrates the seamless integration of asynchronous patterns, time handling, and stream operations in Rust, contributing to the development of efficient and expressive asynchronous applications.

Resource Management with Async Drop

Async Rust introduces the concept of asynchronous dropping, allowing you to manage resources asynchronously during the drop lifecycle. This is particularly useful for scenarios where cleanup operations involve asynchronous tasks. This section explores advanced patterns for resource management with async drop, demonstrating how to implement asynchronous drop for a custom type.

Consider the following example showcasing async drop for resource management:

Listing 14.7 Resource management with async drop.

```
use tokio::time::{sleep, Duration}; // ①

#[derive(Clone)] // ②
struct AsyncResource {
    // Resource fields
}

impl AsyncResource {
    async fn cleanup(&self) { // ③
        println!("Cleaning up resources asynchronously..."); // ④
        sleep(Duration::from_secs(1)).await; // ⑤
        println!("Cleanup completed"); // ⑥
    }
}

#[tokio::main] // ⑦
async fn main() {
    let resource = AsyncResource { /* Initialize resource */ }; // ⑧

    let task_handle = tokio::spawn({
        let _resource = resource.clone(); // ⑨
        async move {
            println!("Asynchronous task started"); // ⑩

            sleep(Duration::from_secs(2)).await; // ⑪
            // Actual asynchronous work would go here...

            println!("Asynchronous task completed"); // ⑫
        }
    });

    task_handle.await.expect("Task failed"); // ⑬

    // At this point, async drop has completed cleanup for the resource
    resource.cleanup().await; // ⑭
    println!("Main function completed"); // ⑮
}
```

```
// Output

// Asynchronous task started
// Asynchronous task completed
// Cleaning up resources asynchronously...
// Cleanup completed
// Main function completed
```

① The initial action involves the importation of imperative components from the tokio runtime, specifically those related to the management and handling of time.

② Following this, the code proceeds to define the **AsyncResource** struct, which serves as a blueprint for a resource equipped with asynchronous cleanup logic, underlining the significance of structured resource management.

③ Within the defined struct, a pivotal asynchronous cleanup method is implemented, representing the orchestrated process of resource cleanup through asynchronous execution.

④ Subsequently, a log message is generated to signify the start of the asynchronous cleanup logic, offering insight into the code's progression and execution flow.

⑤ The asynchronous cleanup logic is then emulated through the introduction of a sleep function, deliberately configured to simulate cleanup work lasting for a duration of 1 second.

⑥ Upon the completion of the asynchronous cleanup, a corresponding log message is dispatched, marking the conclusion of the resource cleanup process and contributing to the overall code transparency.

⑦ The primary asynchronous function, crucial to orchestrating the resource management scenario, is introduced, distinctly marked by the utilization of the tokio runtime.

⑧ Within this asynchronous function, an instance of the previously defined **AsyncResource** is created and initialized, establishing the foundational state of the resource.

⑨ To facilitate the subsequent asynchronous task, a cloned reference to the initialized resource is crafted, ensuring the preservation of the original state for effective resource management.

⑩ A log message is strategically positioned to signal the initiation of the asynchronous task, providing valuable contextual information for understanding the code's runtime behavior.

⑪ The asynchronous task starts in simulated work, emulating a time-consuming process with a sleep duration set to 2 seconds, mimicking real-world asynchronous operations.

⑫ As the asynchronous task finishes its execution, a log message is dispatched, underscoring the completion of the task and contributing to the comprehensibility of the code.

⑬ The main function diligently awaits the completion of the asynchronous task, incorporating error handling measures to address any potential issues that might arise during execution.

⑭ Post-task completion, the asynchronous cleanup method of the resource is invoked, leveraging the async drop mechanism to ensure thorough cleanup actions are undertaken.

⑮ Finally, a conclusive log message is emitted, signaling the overall completion of the main function and encapsulating the entire asynchronous resource management scenario within the tokio runtime.

This code snippet exemplifies a meticulous approach to asynchronous resource management within the tokio runtime, marked by a sequence of clearly annotated steps. From importing essential components and defining the asynchronous resource struct to orchestrating tasks, simulating operations, and ensuring proper cleanup, each phase is thoughtfully documented. The code not only showcases the efficient utilization of asynchronous Rust features but also underscores the significance of structured resource management in building robust and maintainable asynchronous applications. Through detailed logging and methodical execution, this example provides a valuable template for you if you want to implement effective asynchronous resource handling in your Rust projects within the tokio runtime.

Fan-Out and Fan-In with Async Streams

Async streams facilitate *fan-out* and *fan-in* patterns, enabling us to efficiently distribute work across multiple asynchronous tasks and aggregate results. This section explores advanced patterns for **`fan-out`** (parallelizing tasks) and **`fan-in`** (collecting results) using async streams through the **`tokio_stream`** crate.

Let's explore the following example illustrating fan-out and fan-in with async streams:

Listing 14.8 Fan-Out and Fan-In using Async Streams.

```
use tokio_stream::{self as stream, Stream, StreamExt}; // ①
use tokio::time::{sleep, Duration}; // ②

async fn async_task(id: usize) -> usize { // ③
    sleep(Duration::from_secs(id as u64)).await; // ④
    id * 2 // ⑤
}

fn fan_out_tasks() -> impl Stream<Item = usize> { // ⑥
    stream::iter(0..5).then(async_task) // ⑦
}

#[tokio::main]
async fn main() { // ⑧
    fan_in_results().await; // ⑨
}

async fn fan_in_results() { // ⑩
    let result_stream = fan_out_tasks(); // ⑪

    tokio::pin!(result_stream); // ⑫

    while let Some(result) = result_stream.next().await { // ⑬
        println!("Received result: {:?}", result); // ⑭
    }
}

// Output

// Received result: 0
// Received result: 2
// Received result: 4
// Received result: 6
// Received result: 8
```

① Import necessary libraries, including **tokio_stream** and **tokio::time**, to facilitate asynchronous stream operations.

② Import the **sleep** function and **Duration** struct from the **tokio::time** module, crucial for introducing delays in asynchronous tasks.

③ Define an asynchronous task named **async_task** that simulates work by sleeping for a duration based on the task's ID and then returning a result.

④ Use the **sleep** function to pause the asynchronous task for a duration specified by the task's ID, introducing an artificial delay.

⑤ Multiply the task's ID by 2, representing a simple computation, and return the result.

⑥ Declare a function **fan_out_tasks** that returns a stream of asynchronous tasks, generated using **stream::iter(0..5).then(async_task)**.

⑦ Utilize **stream::iter** to create a stream of values ranging from 0 to 4, and then apply the **then** combinator to transform each value into the result of the **async_task** function.

⑧ In the **main** function, the coordination of fan-out and fan-in is initiated.

⑨ Invoke the **fan_in_results** asynchronous function, which handles the fan-in aspect of collecting and processing results concurrently.

⑩ Define the asynchronous function **fan_in_results** responsible for the fan-in operation.

⑪ Obtain a stream of asynchronous task results by calling the **fan_out_tasks** function.

⑫ Pin the result stream into a **Box** using **tokio::pin!** to enable efficient asynchronous handling.

⑬ Use a **while let** loop to iterate over the asynchronous results using **result_stream.next().await**.

⑭ Print each received result, showcasing the concurrent processing of asynchronous tasks and the **fan-in** operation.

This example illustrates the power of asynchronous programming, offering a glimpse into the seamless orchestration of concurrent tasks for enhanced performance in modern software development.

To enhance clarity, let's illustrate this example using a simple diagram:

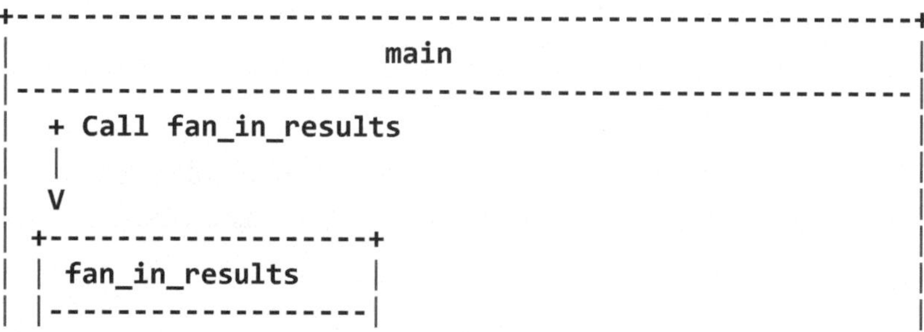

```
| | + fan_out_tasks   |                                  |
| |-------------------|                                  |
| |  + result_stream  |                                  |
| |  |                |                                  |
| |  V                |                                  |
| | +-----------------------+                            |
| | |     tokio::pin!       |                            |
| | |-----------------------|                            |
| | | result_stream.next()  |                            |
| | +-----------------------+                            |
| |  |                      |                            |
| |  V                      |                            |
| | +--------------------+--|                            |
| | | Received result:   |  |                            |
| | |       ...          |  |                            |
| | +--------------------+  |                            |
| +-------------------+-----+                            |
| | fan_out_tasks     |                                  |
| |-------------------|                                  |
| |  + stream::iter   |                                  |
| |  |                |                                  |
| |  V                |                                  |
| | +---------------+ |                                  |
| | |   async_task  | |                                  |
| | +---------------+ |                                  |
| +-------------------+                                  |
+--------------------------------------------------------+
```

Cancelation and Timeout Handling

Async Rust provides robust mechanisms for canceling asynchronous tasks and handling timeouts effectively. This section explores advanced patterns for canceling tasks and implementing timeouts, crucial for building responsive and fault-tolerant applications.

Consider the following example demonstrating cancelation and timeout handling:

Listing 14.9 Cancelation and timeout handling in an async program.

```
use tokio::time::{sleep, timeout, Duration};

async fn async_task() { // ①
    sleep(Duration::from_secs(5)).await; // ②
    println!("Task completed"); // ③
}
```

```
async fn cancelable_task() { // ④
    timeout(Duration::from_secs(2), async_task()) // ⑤
        .await // ⑥
        .unwrap_or_else(|err| { // ⑦
            eprintln!("Error: {}", err); // ⑧
        });
}

#[tokio::main]
async fn main() { // ⑨
    cancelable_task().await; // ⑩
}

// Output

// Error: deadline has elapsed
```

① The **async_task** function is declared as an asynchronous function, and it simulates a time-consuming asynchronous operation. Here, the **sleep** function is employed with a duration of 5 seconds, representing the duration of the simulated task.

② Within **async_task**, the **sleep** function is used to introduce a delay of 5 seconds, effectively simulating the asynchronous nature of the task.

③ After the asynchronous delay, a simple message, "**Task completed**," is printed, indicating the completion of the simulated task.

④ The **cancelable_task** function is declared, which leverages the **timeout** function to set a timeout of 2 seconds for the execution of the **async_task**.

⑤ The **timeout** function is invoked, wrapping the **async_task()** function call. This function returns a **Result** that either contains the result of the task if it completes within the specified timeout or an error if the timeout is exceeded.

⑥ The **await** keyword is used to await the completion of the **timeout** operation, and the program continues based on the result.

⑦ The **unwrap_or_else** method is employed to handle potential errors. If an error occurs, the provided closure is executed, printing an error message to the standard error stream.

⑧ Inside the error-handling closure, the program prints an error message to the standard error stream, providing visibility into any issues that may arise during the execution of the cancelable task.

⑨ The **main** function is declared as an asynchronous function using the **[tokio::main]** attribute. This attribute sets up the tokio runtime, allowing asynchronous code to run within the **main** function.

⑩ The **cancelable_task** is invoked within the **main** function using the **await** keyword. This demonstrates the execution of a cancelable asynchronous task, showcasing how to gracefully handle cancelation and timeouts in the context of asynchronous Rust programming.

This example showcases how Rust's **async/await** syntax, combined with tokio's asynchronous runtime, enables the development of cancelable asynchronous tasks with built-in timeout handling. This capability enhances the resilience and responsiveness of asynchronous Rust applications, allowing you to manage and control the execution of time-sensitive operations in a structured and efficient manner.

Dynamic Task Management

Managing a dynamic set of asynchronous tasks with varying lifetimes requires advanced patterns. The **FuturesUnordered** type from the **futures** crate provides a powerful solution. This section explores dynamic task management using **FuturesUnordered** for scenarios where tasks are added and removed dynamically.

Consider the following example showcasing dynamic task management:

Listing 14.10 Dynamic task management.

```
use futures::stream::FuturesUnordered; // ①
use futures::StreamExt; // ②
use tokio::task::spawn; // ③
use tokio::time::{sleep, Duration}; // ④

async fn dynamic_task_manager() { // ⑤
    let task_manager = FuturesUnordered::new(); // ⑥

    for id in 0..5 {
        let task = spawn(async move { // ⑦
            sleep(Duration::from_secs(id as u64)).await; // ⑧
            id * 3
        });

        task_manager.push(task); // ⑨
    }

    tokio::pin!(task_manager); // ⑩
```

```
    while let Some(result) = task_manager.next().await { // ⑪
        println!("Task result: {:?}", result.unwrap()); // ⑫
    }
}

#[tokio::main]
async fn main() { // ⑬
    dynamic_task_manager().await; // ⑭
}

// Output

// Task result: 0
// Task result: 3
// Task result: 6
// Task result: 9
// Task result: 12
```

① The code begins by importing the necessary dependencies, including the **FuturesUnordered** stream, which is integral for managing dynamic asynchronous tasks efficiently.

② Similarly, the **StreamExt** trait is imported, providing additional functionality for working with asynchronous streams.

③ The **spawn** function from the **tokio::task** module is imported, allowing the creation of asynchronous tasks that can run concurrently.

④ Importing **sleep** and **Duration** from **tokio::time** sets the stage for simulating asynchronous work by introducing delays.

⑤ The **dynamic_task_manager** function is declared, serving as the epicenter of dynamic task management.

⑥ Within this function, a **FuturesUnordered** instance, named **task_manager**, is created to efficiently manage dynamically added asynchronous tasks.

⑦ A loop iterates over a range of task identifiers, spawning asynchronous tasks using the **spawn** function. Each task simulates dynamic asynchronous work by introducing a sleep duration based on the task identifier.

⑧ The **sleep** function introduces delays, creating a staggered execution pattern, crucial for simulating dynamic asynchronous workloads.

⑨ The spawned tasks are then added to the **FuturesUnordered** stream using the **push** method, dynamically populating the task manager.

⑩ The `tokio::pin!` macro is employed to pin the `task_manager` stream, ensuring stable memory locations for efficient polling.

⑪ The `while let` loop continuously polls the task manager for completed tasks using the `next` method, reflecting the non-blocking nature of asynchronous operations.

⑫ As completed tasks are encountered, their results are unwrapped and printed, showcasing the order in which they finish execution.

⑬ The `main` function, annotated with `` `tokio::main` ``, sets the stage for the asynchronous runtime to execute the dynamic task manager.

⑭ Finally, the dynamic task manager is executed within the `main` function, bringing the entire orchestration of dynamic asynchronous tasks to life.

This code snippet exemplifies an elegant and efficient approach to managing dynamic asynchronous workloads in Rust. Leveraging the `FuturesUnordered` stream and the `spawn` function from the tokio runtime, it showcases a flexible and scalable pattern for handling asynchronous tasks with varying execution times. This dynamic task management paradigm proves valuable in scenarios where the set of tasks is not known in advance, providing us with a powerful tool for building responsive and efficient asynchronous systems.

Integrating Async Code with Sync Code

In real-world applications, it's common to have both asynchronous and synchronous code coexisting. **tokio** provides mechanisms to seamlessly integrate asynchronous and synchronous code, allowing us to leverage existing synchronous libraries and components.

The function **tokio::task::block_in_place** stands as a crucial asset when it comes to executing synchronous code within an asynchronous environment. Its primary purpose lies in safeguarding against potential blocking of the asynchronous runtime, thus ensuring the continued responsiveness of the application. By employing this function, we can strategically integrate synchronous operations without disrupting the efficiency of the asynchronous execution model. This approach becomes particularly significant in scenarios where certain portions of code require synchronous handling but need to seamlessly coexist within an overall asynchronous framework. The utilization of **tokio::task::block_in_place** contributes to the overall responsiveness and smooth functioning of the application, striking a balance between the worlds of synchronous and asynchronous programming paradigms.

Listing 14.11 Integrating async code with sync code.

```
use tokio::task; // ①
use tokio::time::{sleep, Duration}; // ②

#[derive(Clone)] // ③
struct AsyncResource {
    // Resource fields
}

impl AsyncResource {
    async fn cleanup(&self) { // ④
        // Asynchronous cleanup logic
        println!("Cleaning up resources asynchronously...");
        // Simulate cleanup work
        sleep(Duration::from_secs(1)).await;
        println!("Cleanup completed");
    }
}

async fn async_and_sync_integration() {
    let handle = task::spawn(async {

        println!("Asynchronous code: Start");

        sleep(Duration::from_secs(2)).await;

        println!("Asynchronous code: End");

        tokio::task::block_in_place(|| { // ⑤

            println!("Synchronous code: Start");

            for i in 1..=3 {
                println!("Synchronous iteration: {}", i);
            }

            println!("Synchronous code: End");
        });

        println!("Continuing with asynchronous logic");
    });

    handle.await.expect("Task failed");
}
```

```
#[tokio::main] // ⑥
async fn main() {
    async_and_sync_integration().await;

    println!("Main function completed");
}

// Output

// Asynchronous code: Start
// Asynchronous code: End
// Synchronous code: Start
// Synchronous iteration: 1
// Synchronous iteration: 2
// Synchronous iteration: 3
// Synchronous code: End
// Continuing with asynchronous logic
// Main function completed
```

① In this line, we are including essential components from the tokio runtime library that are specifically related to task handling. As we saw previously, by importing these components, we gain access to functionalities that facilitate the management and execution of asynchronous tasks.

② Similarly, in this line, we are importing components from the tokio runtime that are focused on time handling. The **time** module from tokio provides utilities for dealing with time-related operations in asynchronous code, such as introducing delays or scheduling tasks to run after a certain duration.

③ Here, we define a struct named **AsyncResource**. This struct is designed to represent a resource that includes asynchronous cleanup logic. **AsyncResource** is intended to model an entity with asynchronous cleanup capabilities, which can be crucial in asynchronous programming to efficiently manage resources.

④ Within the implementation of the **AsyncResource** struct, we find an asynchronous method named **cleanup**. This method defines the logic for asynchronously cleaning up resources.

⑤ In this line, we utilize the **tokio::task::block_in_place** function to execute synchronous code within an asynchronous context. **block_in_place** ensures that the synchronous code runs without disrupting the responsiveness of the asynchronous runtime, maintaining the overall efficiency of the application.

⑥ Finally, we define the main asynchronous function named **async_and_sync_integration**. This function showcases the integration of asynchronous and synchronous code within a tokio runtime. It spawns a new asynchronous task, executes asynchronous code, introduces a synchronous block using **`block_in_place`** for specific operations, and then continues with asynchronous logic. This illustrates how we can leverage both asynchronous and synchronous paradigms in a cohesive manner using tokio.

Mastering the integration of asynchronous and synchronous code, as demonstrated in this Rust code snippet using tokio, is essential for building efficient and responsive applications. By combining the strengths of asynchronous and synchronous programming, you can achieve a balance that optimizes resource utilization and responsiveness, leading to more robust and scalable software solutions.

Conclusion

In this chapter, we explored the world of asynchronous programming with Rust, focusing on the foundational concepts encapsulated within the async/await syntax. By delving into the complexities of async/await, you gained a solid grasp of the syntax's fundamentals and mechanics. We explored the tools at our disposal for effective error handling, proficient resource management, and the implementation of advanced patterns such as async streams.

This introductory section served as a compass, guiding you through the landscape of Rust's asynchronous capabilities, with a particular emphasis on the tokio library. Understanding tokio's role as an asynchronous runtime became crucial, laying the foundation for the exploration of its powerful features in this book and beyond.

Looking forward, the journey continues into deeper layers of Rust and tokio. Reading the official documentation will unfold more advanced concepts, presenting in-depth insights and practical examples. By expanding your knowledge on this topic, you will not only have consolidated your understanding of asynchronous programming but will also possess the tools and knowledge necessary to build responsive and high-performance applications. As we move forward, the goal is to empower you to leverage Rust and Tokio effectively, bringing the benefits of asynchronous programming to success in your projects.

Resources

To enhance your understanding of asynchronous programming in Rust, consider exploring the following resources:

- *Tokio Documentation*: Refer to the official documentation for the Tokio runtime, a powerful asynchronous runtime for Rust. Explore the features, modules, and guides provided to master the art of asynchronous programming with Tokio. - *https://docs.rs/tokio*
- *The Async Book*: Dive into "The Async Book," an official resource that comprehensively covers asynchronous programming in Rust. Gain insights into async/await syntax, futures, and the broader ecosystem supporting asynchronous development. - *https://rust-lang.github.io/async-book/01_getting_started/01_chapter.html*
- *Tokio Blog*: Read the Tokio blog, introducing the Tokio Preview release. Stay updated on the latest features, improvements, and advancements in the Tokio asynchronous runtime. - *https://tokio.rs/blog*
- *Tokio Stream Crate*: Explore the official Tokio Stream crate on crates.io. This crate provides essential utilities for working with asynchronous streams in Rust, offering a range of functions and modules to streamline stream processing. - *https://crates.io/crates/tokio-stream*
- *Futures - Stream Trait Documentation*: Delve into the documentation for the Stream trait in the Futures crate. Understanding the Stream trait is fundamental to working with asynchronous streams in Rust. - *https://docs.rs/futures/latest/futures/stream/trait.Stream.html*
- *Rust Book - Reference Cycles and Memory Leaks*: Refer to the official Rust documentation on reference cycles and memory leaks. Understanding these concepts is crucial for effective resource management in Rust. - *https://doc.rust-lang.org/book/ch15-06-reference-cycles.html*
- *The Async Book - Workarounds to Know and Love*: Explore "Workarounds to Know and Love", a chapter in The Async Book that provides insights into dealing with errors in asynchronous programming and managing resources effectively. - *https://rust-lang.github.io/async-book/07_workarounds/01_chapter.html*
- *Async Std GitHub Repository*: Explore the GitHub repository for the Async Std project, an asynchronous runtime for Rust. Async Std provides essential tools and utilities for asynchronous programming, contributing to resource management practices. - *https://github.com/async-rs/async-std*
- RFC 2394 - *Async Await*: Review RFC 2394, which proposes the introduction of async await in Rust. This RFC is foundational to understanding the concept of asynchronous programming and its impact on resource management. - *https://github.com/rust-lang/rfcs/blob/master/text/2394-async_await.md*

These resources offer a comprehensive view of advanced patterns in asynchronous programming, providing practical guidance and documentation to help you master the complexities of working with asynchronous streams and designing responsive systems in Rust.

Multiple Choice Questions

Q1: Which keyword is used to declare an asynchronous function in Rust?

a) `sync`

b) `async`

c) `await`

d) `async/await`

Q2: In Rust's `async/await` syntax, what does the await keyword do?

a) Pauses the program's execution indefinitely

b) Blocks the execution flow until completion of the asynchronous operation

c) Terminates the asynchronous function

d) Allows the program to skip the asynchronous operation

Q3: What does the tokio library provide in the context of asynchronous programming in Rust?

a) A programming language

b) A web framework

c) An asynchronous runtime

d) A database management system

Q4: How is concurrent execution achieved in Rust's `async/await` syntax?

a) By using parallel threads

b) By using synchronous functions

c) By leveraging the `` `await` `` keyword

d) By avoiding asynchronous operations

Q5: What is the purpose of the Result type in asynchronous error handling in Rust?

a) To indicate success without any value

b) To indicate failure with an error message

c) To propagate errors through the asynchronous call stack

d) To handle errors only in synchronous code

Q6: What does the Arc (Atomic Reference Counting) do in Rust's asynchronous programming?

a) Ensures atomic operations on data

b) Enables asynchronous execution

c) Manages lifetimes of asynchronous tasks

d) Provides a thread-safe reference-counted pointer for shared data

Q7: What does Rust's ownership system ensure in the context of asynchronous programming?

a) Memory leaks

b) Data races

c) Non-blocking execution

d) Thread safety

Q8: What is the primary benefit of using asynchronous programming in Rust?

a) Improved data structures

b) Synchronous execution

c) Efficient concurrency and responsiveness

d) Reduced code expressiveness

Q9: Which crate is mentioned as a tool for working with asynchronous streams in Rust?

a) `tokio::sync`

b) `async-streams`

c) `tokio-stream`

d) `async-util`

Q10: What is the purpose of the async drop feature introduced in Async Rust?

a) To define asynchronous functions

b) To manage resources asynchronously during the drop lifecycle

c) To handle errors in asynchronous code

d) To create asynchronous streams

Q11: What is the primary advantage of using asynchronous streams over synchronous iterators in Rust

a) Asynchronous streams can produce an infinite sequence of values

b) Asynchronous streams enable the asynchronous generation of values over time

c) Synchronous iterators have better performance

d) Synchronous iterators are more versatile

Answers

1. b) async
2. b) Blocks the execution flow until completion of the asynchronous operation
3. c) An asynchronous runtime
4. c) By leveraging the await keyword
5. c) To propagate errors through the asynchronous call stack
6. d) Provides a thread-safe reference-counted pointer for shared data
7. d) Thread safety
8. c) Efficient concurrency and responsiveness
9. c) tokio-stream
10. b) To manage resources asynchronously during the drop lifecycle

11. b) Asynchronous streams enable the asynchronous generation of values over time

Key Terms

- **Async/Await Syntax:** Rust's syntax for asynchronous programming, introducing the **async** and **await** keywords to create non-blocking functions and pause execution until asynchronous operations are complete.
- **Result Type:** A Rust type used in asynchronous error handling to represent the result of an operation, either indicating success with a value or failure with an error message, allowing error propagation through the asynchronous call stack.
- **Arc (Atomic Reference Counting):** A Rust type providing a thread-safe reference-counted pointer, essential for sharing data among multiple asynchronous tasks, ensuring efficient resource utilization and preventing data races.
- **Concurrency:** The execution of multiple tasks or operations in overlapping time intervals, a key aspect of asynchronous programming in Rust that enables efficient parallel execution.
- **Task Lifetimes:** In the context of asynchronous programming, the duration during which asynchronous tasks execute and the challenge of managing their lifetimes efficiently to prevent issues like data races.
- **Responsive Applications:** The primary goal of asynchronous programming in Rust, aiming to design systems that efficiently handle I/O-bound operations without sacrificing performance, resulting in applications that respond promptly to user interactions.
- **Futures:** In the context of asynchronous programming, a fundamental building block representing a value or an error that may be available in the future, allowing for efficient composition of asynchronous operations.
- **Poll:** A method used in Rust's asynchronous programming model to check the status of a **Future** or **Stream**, indicating whether the value is ready, pending, or an error has occurred.
- **Executor:** An abstraction in asynchronous programming responsible for scheduling and executing tasks, ensuring that asynchronous operations are executed efficiently and in a non-blocking fashion.
- **Async Mutex:** A synchronization primitive in Rust that provides exclusive access to data across asynchronous tasks, preventing data races and ensuring safe concurrent access.

- **Pin:** A type in Rust used to indicate that a value should not move in memory, particularly relevant in asynchronous programming when dealing with self-referential structures.
- **Tokio Runtime:** The runtime environment provided by the Tokio library in Rust, encompassing an event loop, task scheduler, and other components for managing asynchronous tasks.
- **Async/Await Desugaring:** The process in Rust's compiler where async/await syntax is transformed into lower-level Future and Stream combinators, allowing for seamless integration with the asynchronous runtime.
- **Backpressure:** A mechanism in asynchronous programming that regulates the flow of data between producers and consumers, preventing overwhelming the system with too much data.

Chapter 15
Web Assembly with Rust

Introduction

WebAssembly (Wasm) stands as a groundbreaking technology in the web development domain, fundamentally altering the landscape of code execution within web browsers [1]. Unlike the conventional approach of interpreting JavaScript, WebAssembly offers the capability to execute low-level code at speeds approaching native machine code. This chapter provides a comprehensive exploration of the core principles of WebAssembly, shedding light on the benefits it introduces to web applications.

WebAssembly is rapidly transforming how web applications deliver high-performance computing capabilities. Its binary instruction format enables the execution of code from high-level programming languages, including C, C++, C#, and Rust, directly within web browsers [2]. This marks a departure from traditional JavaScript execution, opening doors to extraordinary performance gains and a broader range of language choices for developers.

The WebAssembly format is designed to be efficient for both downloading and execution, making it a powerful tool for improving web application performance [3]. Its compact representation ensures faster loading times compared to traditional JavaScript files, optimizing the initial user experience. This efficiency extends to execution, enabling near-native speeds for computationally intensive tasks.

---

[1]WebAssembly. (n.d.). *https://webassembly.org/*

[2]WebAssembly | MDN. (2023, December 6). MDN Web Docs. *https://developer.mozilla.org/en-US/docs/WebAssembly*

[3]WebAssembly High-Level Goals - WebAssembly. (n.d.). *https://webassembly.org/docs/high-level-goals/*

Structure

In this chapter, we will cover the following topics:

- Introduction to WebAssembly and its benefits
- Configuring Rust for WebAssembly development
- Integrating Rust code with JavaScript using WebAssembly

Advantages of WebAssembly

The advantages of WebAssembly are numerous, with one of the pivotal benefits being its high performance. Through the provision of a low-level binary format, WebAssembly minimizes the need for extensive parsing and interpretation by browsers, resulting in accelerated execution speeds. This performance boost proves particularly advantageous for tasks demanding substantial computational power, such as graphics rendering, data processing, and scientific simulations.

Moreover, WebAssembly offers language independence, allowing you to compose code in your preferred high-level languages [4]. As long as a WebAssembly compiler for a specific language is available, the code seamlessly integrates into web applications. This flexibility promotes the utilization of existing codebases and facilitates the incorporation of diverse programming languages into web applications.

WebAssembly's performance advantages are emphasized by its efficient use of system resources, making it an ideal choice for resource-intensive applications. We can refer to the WebAssembly System Interface (WASI), a standard interface designed to run WebAssembly applications on any platform, for further insights into resource management and system interactions.

Security constitutes another critical aspect enhanced by WebAssembly. The technology executes code within a sandboxed environment, ensuring that even if a WebAssembly module contains vulnerabilities, it cannot compromise the overall security of the browser or the user's system. This robust isolation of WebAssembly code adds an additional layer of protection to web applications, contributing to a more secure web ecosystem.

---

[4]WebAssembly | MDN. (2023, December 6). MDN Web Docs. *https://developer.mozilla.org/en-US/docs/WebAssembly*

WebAssembly Limitations

While *WebAssembly* has undoubtedly revolutionized web application performance, it isn't immune to a set of challenges. Ongoing development aims to tackle these challenges, shaping a more robust platform for developers. Grasping these current limitations becomes crucial for informed decision-making in the development journey.

Limited Browser Support

WebAssembly's journey encounters challenges concerning browser support, particularly in older browsers lacking the global WebAssembly object crucial for module instantiation and loading. This limitation raises compatibility concerns, as older browsers may not fully support WebAssembly modules.

To address this, experimental polyfills utilizing asm.js serve as a fallback mechanism, utilizing asm.js if the WebAssembly object is absent. However, the WebAssembly Working Group currently lacks plans for an official polyfill. Developers relying on WebAssembly in projects with a broad user base must weigh the implications of limited support in older browsers.

The connection between asm.js and WebAssembly is noteworthy, as asm.js, a subset of JavaScript designed for performance, can serve as an alternative in the absence of WebAssembly support. While providing performance gains, it's crucial to weigh trade-offs, considering asm.js does not offer the same level of optimization and efficiency as native WebAssembly modules.

Checking current browser support for WebAssembly becomes a pivotal step in project planning. The *Can I Use* website provides an up-to-date overview of browser compatibility with WebAssembly features. This resource empowers developers to make informed decisions based on the target audience, ensuring a seamless user experience across diverse browser environments.

Indirect DOM Manipulation

Another notable limitation in WebAssembly lies in its inability to directly access the Document Object Model (DOM). Unlike the seamless and direct DOM manipulation in JavaScript, WebAssembly requires an indirect approach through JavaScript or tools like Emscripten for DOM manipulation.

This limitation comes from design choices prioritizing performance and security over direct DOM access. The aim is to prevent potential security vulnerabilities arising from unregulated access to the DOM. While ensuring a secure execution environment, this approach adds complexity for developers bridging the gap between WebAssembly and the DOM through intermediary languages.

Plans are underway to introduce direct referencing of DOM and other Web API objects in WebAssembly, currently in the proposal phase. This enhancement seeks to simplify the interaction between WebAssembly and the DOM, potentially streamlining web development processes and broadening accessibility to a diverse range of developers.

Developers leveraging WebAssembly for web applications reliant on dynamic DOM manipulation may encounter challenges due to the current limitations. The need for intermediary steps introduces potential points of failure and complexity, underscoring the importance of evaluating project requirements before choosing WebAssembly for DOM-intensive tasks.

Memory Management Challenges

WebAssembly's adoption of a linear memory introduces a unique memory management challenge. This approach demands explicit memory allocation for code execution, setting it apart from languages like C and C++, favored for the MVP due to their inherent memory management capabilities. The exclusion of high-level languages like Java initially comes from their reliance on garbage collection (GC).

Garbage collection, like an automated memory collector, reclaims memory occupied by objects no longer in use. In contrast, manual memory allocation, resembles to driving a car with a manual transmission, offers more control but demands meticulous handling. WebAssembly's active work on supporting GC languages hints at a future where automated memory management coexists with its performance ability, yet the timeline remains uncertain.

The absence of garbage collection in WebAssembly means you must exercise precision in managing memory to prevent potential issues. While manual memory allocation can optimize performance, it demands a deeper understanding and careful handling, lacking the forgiving nature of languages with built-in garbage collection.

Moreover, the ease of programming in garbage-collected languages, exemplified by JavaScript, allows us to focus on logic without the constant worry of memory complexities. Integrating garbage collection support in WebAssembly aims to unite performance with the convenience of automated memory management, promoting a more accessible and developer-friendly environment.

Rust for WebAssembly Development

Rust, with its emphasis on performance, memory safety, and concurrency, stands out as an ideal language for WebAssembly development. The following sections take us on an in-depth exploration of the complex process of configuring Rust for seamless integration with WebAssembly. From the installation of essential tools to the creation of a new project and the meticulous building and testing of WebAssembly modules, every step is meticulously covered to empower you in unlocking the full potential of these technologies.

Installing Rust and WebAssembly Toolchain

Kicking off the journey into Rust for WebAssembly development involves the installation of both the Rust programming language and the WebAssembly toolchain. The Rustup installer appears as a pillar in this process, streamlining the installation of Rust and managing associated tools. It is a versatile tool that facilitates the effortless management of Rust versions and allows us to switch between them effortlessly. Having Rust installed, the integration of the WebAssembly target into the Rust toolchain becomes important. A pivotal Rustup command achieves this seamlessly:

```
$ rustup target add wasm32-unknown-unknown
```

This command expands the capabilities of the Rust toolchain, incorporating the WebAssembly target, a prerequisite for compiling Rust code into efficient and optimized WebAssembly modules.

Delving deeper into the installation process, Rustup ensures a straightforward setup experience. You can download and execute the Rustup installer, gaining access to the Rust compiler (`rustc`) and package manager (`cargo`). The flexibility provided by Rustup extends to version management, enabling us to effortlessly switch between different Rust versions, making it an indispensable tool in the Rust ecosystem.

Following the successful installation of Rust and the WebAssembly toolchain, you are equipped with a robust foundation, ready to kick off an exciting journey of WebAssembly development.

Setting Up a New Rust Wasm Project

With the Rust and WebAssembly toolchain in place, the next logical step involves creating a new Rust project tailored specifically for WebAssembly development.

This process entails a command designed to initialize a new Rust project and configure it appropriately:

```
$ cargo generate --git https://github.com/rustwasm/wasm-pack-template

// Output

// ·   Project Name: wasm-rust
// ·   Destination: /home/mahmoud/my_wasm_project/wasm-rust ...
// ·   project-name: wasm-rust ...
// ·   Generating template ...
// ·   Moving generated files into: `/home/mahmoud/my_wasm_project/wasm-rust`...
// ·   Initializing a fresh Git repository
// ✨   Done! New project created /home/mahmoud/my_wasm_project/wasm-rust
```

This cargo command collectively laid the foundation for a new Rust project named **`wasm-rust`**. The **`cargo generate`** command initializes the project from a template, and generates the essential files. These files, which include configuration files and scripts, are instrumental in streamlining various aspects of WebAssembly module development, such as building, testing, and packaging.

A deeper understanding of this setup process is crucial for us, as it establishes the initial structure and configuration of the Rust project. The **`cargo generate`** command is not only responsible for creating the project but also for setting up the necessary files and directories that form the basis for subsequent development tasks. Navigating into the project directory (**`cd wasm-rust`**) positions us for further customization and exploration of WebAssembly capabilities.

The generated project structure provides a starting point for us to build upon, featuring essential components such as the **`src`** directory for Rust source code, a **`Cargo.toml`** file for project configuration, and a **`tests`** directory for writing test files. Familiarity with these elements is crucial for effective project management and development.

Building and Testing WebAssembly Modules

Having laid the groundwork for a Rust project tailored for WebAssembly, the subsequent stage involves the compilation of the WebAssembly module. This critical step is facilitated through the utilization of the **`wasm-pack`** tool:

```
$ wasm-pack build --target web

// Output

// [INFO]: · Checking for the Wasm target...
// [INFO]: · Compiling to Wasm...
// [INFO]: · Installing wasm-bindgen...
// [INFO]: Optimizing wasm binaries with `wasm-opt`...
// [INFO]: Optional fields missing from Cargo.toml: 'description', 're-
pository', and 'license'. These are not necessary, but recommended
// [INFO]: ✨   Done in 13.01s
// [INFO]: ·   Your wasm pkg is ready to publish at /home/mahmoud/my_
wasm_project/pkg.
```

Executing this command triggers the WebAssembly packager, a powerful tool that orchestrates the compilation of Rust code into a WebAssembly module. The resulting module is then deposited within the **pkg** directory of the project, representing a tangible output ready for further testing and integration.

The testing phase is equally important, ensuring the reliability and functionality of the WebAssembly module. We can make use of the provided test suite through the following command:

```
$ wasm-pack test --headless --firefox

// Output

// [INFO]: · Installing wasm-bindgen...
// no tests to run!
//       Running tests/web.rs (target/wasm32-unknown-unknown/debug/deps/
web-f725b10a03a23af1.wasm)
// Set timeout to 20 seconds...
// Running headless tests in Firefox on `http://127.0.0.1:45011/`
// Try find `webdriver.json` for configure browser's capabilities:
// Not found
// running 1 test

// test web::pass ... ok

// test result: ok. 1 passed; 0 failed; 0 ignored
```

This command not only initiates the execution of tests but does so in a headless Firefox browser, simulating real-world conditions to validate the WebAssembly module's adherence to expected behavior. Testing serves as a crucial quality assurance step, instilling confidence in the module's performance and functionality.

Now that the development environment is configured, let's explore writing Rust code for Web Assembly. Rust's syntax is expressive, and leveraging its features ensures efficient and safe code execution within the Web Assembly runtime.

Writing Wasm Rust Functions

With the WASM development environment configured, the subsequent step involves crafting Rust functions and binding them to Web Assembly (Wasm). This process establishes a robust connection between the strength of Rust and the adaptability of the web. Let's delve into a straightforward yet illustrative Rust code snippet dedicated to computing the Fibonacci sequence. The code snippets starts with the **fibonacci** function, a recursive method designed for computing Fibonacci numbers. In Rust's expressive syntax, we utilize pattern matching through the **match** keyword, managing both base cases and recursive calls.

Listing 15.1 A simple Rust Wasm fibonacci function.

```
fn fibonacci(n: u32) -> u32 {
    match n {
        0 => 0,
        1 => 1,
        _ => fibonacci(n - 1) + fibonacci(n - 2),
    }
}

#[wasm_bindgen]
pub extern "C" fn calculate_fibonacci(n: u32) -> u32 {
    fibonacci(n)
}
```

This snippet isn't merely Rust; it serves as a gateway to the Wasm world. The **calculate_fibonacci** function is decorated with **\#[wasm_bindgen]**, indicating its readiness for invocation from Web Assembly. This straightforward yet powerful integration illustrates how Rust functions effortlessly transform into fundamental building blocks within the dynamic landscape of web development.

Testing the Web Assembly Module

Now, as the Rust functions ready, it's time to put them to the test within the Web Assembly module. An important step in this exploration is creating an HTML file to act as a playground for your newly created Wasm capabilities. Create an **index.html** file in your project's root directory for web experimentation.

Listing 15.2 Index.html entry point file for the rust Wasm app.

```
<!DOCTYPE html>
<html lang="en">
<head>
    <meta charset="UTF-8">
    <meta http-equiv="X-UA-Compatible" content="IE=edge">
    <meta name="viewport" content="width=device-width, initial-scale=1.0">
    <title>Web Assembly with Rust</title>
</head>
<body>
    <script type="module">
        import init, { calculate_fibonacci } from './pkg/wasm_rust.js';

        async function loadWasm() {
            try {
                await init('/pkg/wasm_rust_bg.wasm');
                const result = calculate_fibonacci(12);
                console.log('Result from Web Assembly:', result);
            } catch (error) {
               console.error('Failed to load WebAssembly module:', error);
            }
        }
        loadWasm();
    </script>
</body>
</html>
```

This HTML snippet orchestrates the interaction between your Rust functions and the web environment. The asynchronous **loadWasm** function ensures a smooth initiation, handling potential errors with grace. The script imports the Wasm module and calls the **calculate_fibonacci** function, with the result echoing in the console.

To serve this HTML file using a server of your choice, let's opt for the **http.server** pythonic module to make our app accessible to the browser:

```
python3 -m http.server 8080
```

Figure 15.1: *The Result of the wasm fibonacci sequence of 12*

Next, inspect the browser console to explore the result, revealing the calculated Fibonacci sequence. This testing phase not only solidifies your understanding but also sets the stage for broader exploration.

Congratulations! You've successfully orchestrated a combination of Rust functions, Web Assembly, and HTML, laying the foundation for an exciting journey into the intersection of systems-level programming and web development.

In the next section, we are going to explore some real-world applications of Rust and WebAssembly.

Real-world Applications of WebAssembly

WebAssembly's potential extends beyond theoretical exploration, finding practical application in various real-world scenarios. This section delves into concrete use cases where Rust and WebAssembly shine, from enhancing browser-based applications to enabling high-performance computational tasks in the browser. You will gain valuable insights into the domains where the combination of Rust and WebAssembly offers significant advantages, inspiring creative solutions for diverse application domains.

Use Case 1: Image Processing

In this example, we will delve into a practical use case that showcases the efficiency of Rust and WebAssembly in handling complex computational workloads. Our focus will be on image processing, a domain where the performance advantages of Rust and the portability of WebAssembly can be particularly pronounced.

The heart of this example lies in a Rust file named **lib.rs**. This file contains Rust code that utilizes the **image** crate to apply grayscale conversion to an RGBA image. The

apply_grayscale function, exposed to WebAssembly using **wasm-bindgen**, takes an input RGBA image represented as a **Vec<u8>**, performs the grayscale transformation, and returns the processed image as another **Vec<u8>**. The code showcases Rust's strong typing and safety features, ensuring a robust image processing pipeline.

Listing 15.3 A simple rust wasm image processing logic.

```
use image::RgbaImage;
use wasm_bindgen::prelude::*;

#[wasm_bindgen]
pub fn apply_grayscale(input: Vec<u8>, width: u32, height: u32) ->
Vec<u8> {
    let mut img = RgbaImage::from_vec(width, height, input).expect
("Invalid image dimensions");

    for pixel in img.pixels_mut() {
        let gray_value =
            pixel.0[0] as f32 * 0.299 + pixel.0[1] as f32 * 0.587 + pixel.
0[2] as f32 * 0.114;
        pixel.0 = [
            gray_value as u8,
            gray_value as u8,
            gray_value as u8,
            pixel.0[3],
        ];
    }

    let output = img.into_raw();
    output
}
```

After crafting the Rust code, the next step involves compiling it to WebAssembly. This can be achieved by running the following **wasm-pack** in the terminal:

```
$ wasm-pack build --target web --release

// Output

// [INFO]: · Checking for the Wasm target...
// [INFO]: · Compiling to Wasm...
//    Compiling image-processing v0.1.0 (/home/mahmoud/image-processing)
```

```
//     Finished release [optimized] target(s) in 0.15s
// [INFO]: ·  Installing wasm-bindgen...
// [INFO]: Optimizing wasm binaries with `wasm-opt`...
// [INFO]: Optional fields missing from Cargo.toml: 'description', 're-
pository', and 'license'. These are not necessary, but recommended
// [INFO]: ✨   Done in 0.54s
// [INFO]: ·   Your wasm pkg is ready to publish at /home/mahmoud/im-
age-processing/pkg.
```

This process ensures that our Rust image processing logic is encapsulated into a WebAssembly module, ready to be seamlessly integrated into web applications.

To test our WebAssembly module, we create an HTML file named **index.html**. This file includes an input for selecting an image file, two canvases for displaying the original and processed images, and JavaScript code that orchestrates the interaction between the HTML file, the WebAssembly module, and the user.

Listing 15.4 Index.html entry point file for the rust wasm app.

```
<!DOCTYPE html>
<html lang="en">
  <head>
    <meta charset="UTF-8" />
    <meta http-equiv="X-UA-Compatible" content="IE=edge" />
    <meta name="viewport" content="width=device-width, initial-scale=1.0" />
    <title>Image Processing with Rust and WebAssembly</title>
  </head>
  <body>
    <h1>Image Processing with Rust and WebAssembly</h1>
    <input
      type="file"
      accept="image/*"
      id="imageInput"
      onchange="processImage()"
    />
    <canvas
      id="originalCanvas"
      width="300"
      height="300"
      style="border: 1px solid #000"
    ></canvas>
    <canvas
```

```
    id="processedCanvas"
    width="300"
    height="300"
    style="border: 1px solid #000"
  ></canvas>

  <script type="module" defer>
    import init, { apply_grayscale } from "./pkg/image_processing.js";

    async function loadWasm() {
      try {
        await init();
        window.processImage = processImage;
      } catch (error) {
        console.error("Failed to load WebAssembly module:", error);
      }
    }

    function processImage() {
      const imageInput = document.getElementById("imageInput");
      const originalCanvas = document.getElementById("originalCanvas");
      const processedCanvas = document.getElementById("processedCanvas");

      const ctxOriginal = originalCanvas.getContext("2d");
      const ctxProcessed = processedCanvas.getContext("2d");

      const reader = new FileReader();

      reader.onload = function (event) {
        const img = new Image();
        img.src = event.target.result;

        img.onload = function () {
          // Display the original image
          ctxOriginal.clearRect(
            0,
            0,
            originalCanvas.width,
            originalCanvas.height
          );
```

```
    ctxOriginal.drawImage(
      img,
      0,
      0,
      originalCanvas.width,
      originalCanvas.height
    );

    // Get image data from the original canvas
    const imageData = ctxOriginal.getImageData(
      0,
      0,
      originalCanvas.width,
      originalCanvas.height
    );

    // Convert image data to grayscale using Rust WebAssembly
    const inputArray = new Uint8Array(imageData.data);
    const outputArray = apply_grayscale(
      inputArray,
      originalCanvas.width,
      originalCanvas.height
    );

    // Create a new ImageData object with the processed data
    const processedImageData = new ImageData(
      new Uint8ClampedArray(outputArray),
      originalCanvas.width,
      originalCanvas.height
    );

    // Display the processed image
    ctxProcessed.clearRect(
      0,
      0,
      processedCanvas.width,
      processedCanvas.height
    );
    ctxProcessed.putImageData(processedImageData, 0, 0);
  };
```

```
        };

        // Read the selected image file
        const file = imageInput.files[0];
        reader.readAsDataURL(file);
      }

      loadWasm();
    </script>
  </body>
</html>
```

The JavaScript code within **index.html** establishes the necessary connections. It initializes the WebAssembly module, defines a **processImage** function to handle user interactions, and dynamically updates the canvases to display the original and processed images.

To serve our files and test the image processing functionality, a Python HTTP server is employed. Running the following command in the terminal launches a server, making our application accessible at **http://localhost:8080**.

```
python3 -m http.server 8080
```

Upon navigating to the specified URL, you can choose an image using the file input. The web page will display both the original and processed grayscale versions of the selected image. This example illustrates a sophisticated application of Rust and WebAssembly in real-time image processing directly within the browser.

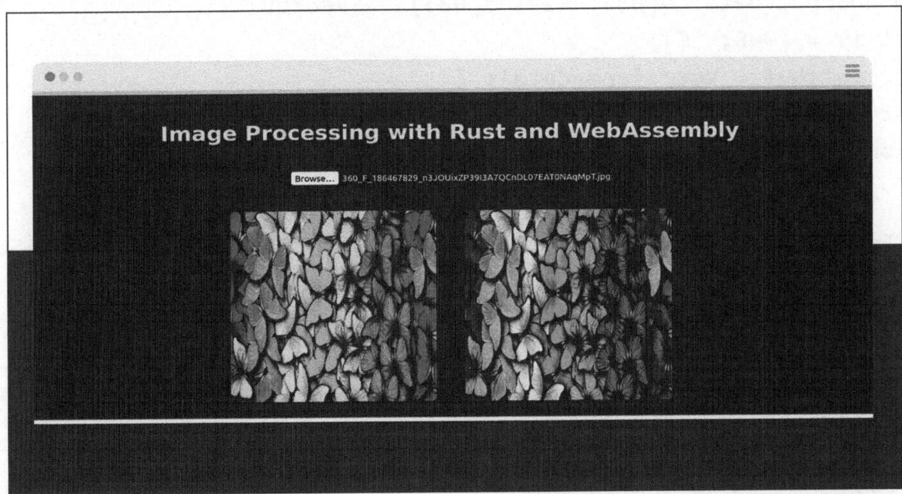

Figure 15.2: *A simple image processing application with Rust and WASM*

By delving into this example, you've gained valuable insights into the coordination of Rust's efficiency and safety features with WebAssembly's portability. This example establishes a robust foundation, empowering the creation of sophisticated image-processing applications. It highlights the substantial potential inherent in the combination of Rust and WebAssembly for handling computationally intensive tasks, thereby unlocking new possibilities for web-based applications that require cutting-edge, high-performance image processing capabilities.

Use Case 2: Cryptographic Operations

In this use case, we will explore advanced cryptographic operations using Rust and WebAssembly. The implementation involves encrypting data using the Advanced Encryption Standard (AES) algorithm in Electronic Codebook (ECB) mode. Rust is well-suited for handling cryptographic tasks.

Listing 15.5 A simple cryptographic rust wasm function.

```
use aes::cipher::{block_padding::Pkcs7, BlockEncryptMut, KeyIvInit};
use cbc::Encryptor;
use wasm_bindgen::prelude::*;

type Aes128CbcEnc = Encryptor<aes::Aes128>;

#[wasm_bindgen]
pub fn encrypt(data: &[u8], key: &[u8]) -> Vec<u8> {
    let iv = [0u8; 16];
    let mut buf = Vec::from(data);
    let cipher = Aes128CbcEnc::new(key.into(), (&iv).into());
    cipher.encrypt_padded_vec_mut::<Pkcs7>(&mut buf)
}
```

After crafting the Rust code, the next step involves compiling it to WebAssembly. This can be achieved by running the following `wasm-pack` in the terminal:

```
$ wasm-pack build --target web --release

// Output
// [INFO]: · Checking for the Wasm target...
// [INFO]: · Compiling to Wasm...
//    Compiling crypto v0.1.0 (/home/mahmoud/crypto)
//     Finished release [optimized] target(s) in 0.20s
```

```
// [INFO]: ·  Installing wasm-bindgen...
// [INFO]: Optimizing wasm binaries with `wasm-opt`...
// [INFO]: Optional fields missing from Cargo.toml: 'description', 're-
pository', and 'license'. These are not necessary, but recommended
// [INFO]: ✨   Done in 0.67s
// [INFO]: ·   Your wasm pkg is ready to publish at /home/mahmoud/cryp-
to/pkg.
```

This process ensures that the Rust cryptographic operations logic is encapsulated into a WebAssembly module, ready to be seamlessly integrated into web applications.

Listing 15.6 Index.html entry point file for the rust wasm app.

```
<!DOCTYPE html>
<html lang="en">
  <head>
    <meta charset="UTF-8" />
    <meta http-equiv="X-UA-Compatible" content="IE=edge" />
    <meta name="viewport" content="width=device-width, initial-scale=1.0" />
    <title>Cryptography with Rust and WebAssembly</title>
  </head>
  <body>
    <h1>Cryptography with Rust and WebAssembly</h1>
    <textarea id="inputText" placeholder="Enter text to encrypt..."></
textarea>
    <textarea
      id="outputText"
      placeholder="Encrypted result will appear here..."
      readonly
    ></textarea>
    <button onclick="encryptData()">Encrypt</button>

    <script type="module" defer>
      import init, { encrypt } from "./pkg/crypto.js";

      async function loadWasm() {
        try {
          await init();
          window.encryptData = encryptData;
        } catch (error) {
```

```
        console.error("Failed to load WebAssembly module:", error);
      }
    }

    function encryptData() {
      const inputText = document.getElementById("inputText").value;
      const key = "abcdefghijklmnop"; // Must be of length 16 chars

      const inputArray = new TextEncoder().encode(inputText);
      const keyArray = new TextEncoder().encode(key);
      const outputArray = encrypt(inputArray, keyArray);

      const outputText = new TextDecoder().decode(outputArray);
      document.getElementById("outputText").value = outputText;
    }

    loadWasm();
  </script>
 </body>
</html>
```

The HTML file includes input and output text areas along with a button to trigger the encryption process. The JavaScript code establishes the necessary connections, initializes the WebAssembly module, and defines the **encryptData** function to handle user interactions.

To test our WebAssembly module, we serve the files using a Python HTTP server. Running the following command in the terminal launches a server, making the application accessible at **http://localhost:8080**.

```
python3 -m http.server 8080
```

Upon navigating to the specified URL, you can enter text in the input area, click the "Encrypt" button, and observe the encrypted result in the output area. This example illustrates the application of Rust and WebAssembly in advanced cryptographic operations within a web environment.

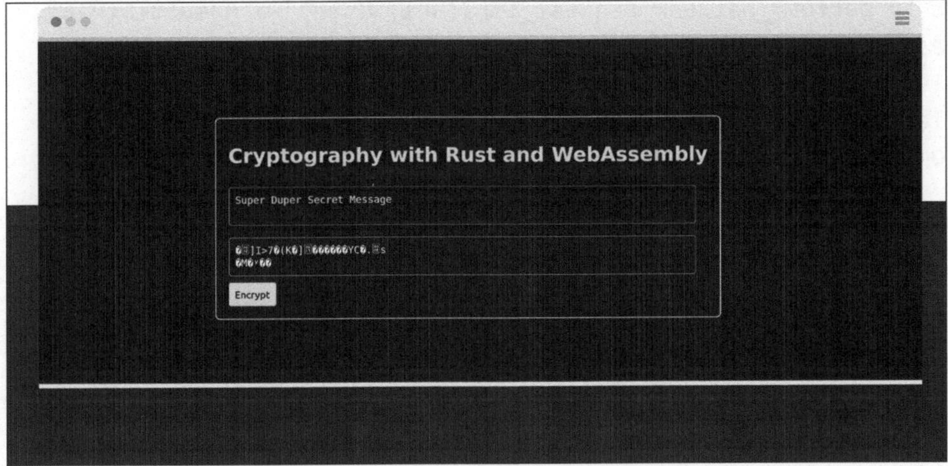

Figure 15.3: *A simple cryptographic application with Rust and WASM*

By delving into this illustrative example, you've acquired a deeper understanding of how Rust seamlessly merges its performance and safety features with WebAssembly's portability. This coordination creates a powerful framework, laying the groundwork for constructing cryptographic applications that are both secure and highly efficient. This demonstration underscores the immense potential of combining Rust and WebAssembly to tackle complex cryptographic tasks, thereby serving as a solid foundation for the development of secure and resilient web-based applications.

Use Case 3: Network Request Handling

In this use case, we'll explore how Rust and WebAssembly can be employed for efficient network request handling within a web application. The scenario involves making asynchronous HTTP requests to a remote server, processing the responses in Rust, and updating the web page dynamically. Rust's safety and performance features are harnessed to create a robust networking component, showcasing the seamless integration with WebAssembly for web applications.

Listing 15.7 A simple request handling rust wasm logic.

```
// network_handler.rs

extern crate wasm_bindgen;
use wasm_bindgen::prelude::*;
use reqwest;
```

```
async fn perform_network_request_impl(url: &str) -> Result<String,
reqwest::Error> {
    let response = reqwest::get(url).await?;
    let body = response.text().await?;
    Ok(body)
}

#[wasm_bindgen]
pub async fn perform_network_request(url: &str) -> JsValue {
    match perform_network_request_impl(url).await {
        Ok(response_body) => JsValue::from_str(&response_body),
        Err(error) => JsValue::from_str(&format!("Error: {:?}", error)),
    }
}
```

After crafting the Rust code, the next step involves compiling it to WebAssembly. This can be achieved by running the following **wasm-pack** in the terminal:

```
$ wasm-pack build --target web --release

// Output
// [INFO]: · Checking for the Wasm target...
// [INFO]: · Compiling to Wasm...
//     Finished release [optimized] target(s) in 0.06s
// [INFO]: · Installing wasm-bindgen...
// [INFO]: Optimizing wasm binaries with `wasm-opt`...
// [INFO]: Optional fields missing from Cargo.toml: 'description', 're-
pository', and 'license'. These are not necessary, but recommended
// [INFO]: ✨   Done in 3.47s
// [INFO]: ·   Your wasm pkg is ready to publish at /home/mahmoud/net-
working/pkg.
```

This process ensures that the Rust network request handling logic is encapsulated into a WebAssembly module, ready to be seamlessly integrated into web applications.

Listing 15.8 Index.html entry point file for the rust wasm app.

```
<!DOCTYPE html>
<html lang="en">
  <head>
    <meta charset="UTF-8" />
```

```
    <meta http-equiv="X-UA-Compatible" content="IE=edge" />
    <meta name="viewport" content="width=device-width, initial-scale=1.0" />
    <title>Request Handling with Rust and WebAssembly</title>
  </head>
  <body>
    <h1>Request Handling with Rust and WebAssembly</h1>
    <button onclick="handleNetworkRequest()">Fetch</button>
    <div id="result"></div>

    <script type="module" defer>
      import init, { get_request } from "./pkg/networking.js";

      async function loadWasm() {
        try {
          await init();
          window.handleNetworkRequest = handleNetworkRequest;
        } catch (error) {
          console.error("Failed to load WebAssembly module:", error);
        }
      }

      async function handleNetworkRequest() {
        const resultDiv = document.getElementById("result");

        // Call the Rust WebAssembly function for network request handling
        const url = "https://jsonplaceholder.typicode.com/posts/1";
        const response = await get_request(url);

        // Display the network request result
        resultDiv.innerText = `Response: ${response}`;
      }

      loadWasm();
    </script>
  </body>
</html>
```

The HTML file includes a button for triggering the network request and a result div to display the response. The JavaScript code establishes the necessary connections, initializes the WebAssembly module, and defines the **handleNetworkRequest** function to handle user interactions.

To test our WebAssembly module, we serve the files using a Python HTTP server. Running the following command in the terminal launches a server, making the application accessible at **`http://localhost:8080`**.

```
python3 -m http.server 8080
```

Upon navigating to the specified URL, you can click the "**`Fetch`**" button, and the web page will display the response from the asynchronous HTTP GET request. This example illustrates the application of Rust and WebAssembly in handling network requests within a web application, showcasing the efficiency and safety features provided by Rust in a web context.

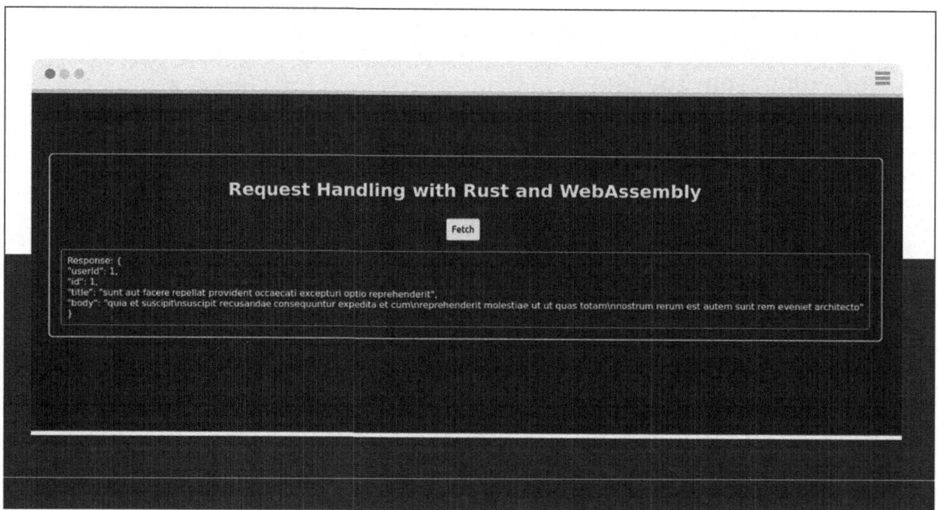

Figure 15.4: *A simple request handling application with Rust and WASM*

Exploring these real-world applications of Rust and WebAssembly offers a profound comprehension of the versatile solutions they bring to specific challenges and the augmentation they provide to user experiences across various domains. Rust, combined with WebAssembly's ability to execute code at near-native speed in web browsers, unlocks a lot of possibilities. From empowering web applications with high-performance functionalities to enabling the development of computationally intensive tasks in a browser environment, the interaction of Rust and WebAssembly has proven invaluable. As these technologies advance, the landscape of potential applications will continue to expand, promising new opportunities that leverage their combined strengths to redefine and optimize digital experiences.

Conclusion

In this chapter, we understood that while WebAssembly unfolds significant benefits in performance and portability, we must navigate its limitations with ingenuity. Memory management complexities, indirect DOM manipulation, and limited browser support demand thoughtful consideration in the decision-making process. Staying alongside ongoing developments in the WebAssembly ecosystem is key to unlocking its full potential while effectively managing potential challenges.

As a developer, you have to explore what's beyond syntax and libraries; it's a journey into the heart of systems-level programming and web interactivity. The integration of Rust with Web Assembly becomes a powerful toolset, equipping you to build applications that push the boundaries of what's possible on the web.

From the inception of Rust functions to the integration with JavaScript, each step has unfolded new dimensions of understanding. The testing phase served as a practical demonstration of the seamless coordination between Rust and the web environment. The exploration of advanced features elevated your proficiency, unlocking the true potential of Rust in a web context.

Building real-world applications marked the peak of your journey, where theory transformed into practice. The canvas of real-world development allowed you to apply your knowledge, navigate challenges, and create applications that stand as a testament to the capabilities of Rust and Web Assembly.

As you conclude this chapter, reflect on the skills acquired, the challenges overcame, and the exciting path ahead. The intersection of Rust and the web is a landscape of continuous learning and innovation. Embrace the possibilities, push the boundaries, and let the journey into Rust with Web Assembly be a perpetual source of inspiration in your web development projects.

Additional Resources

To deepen your understanding of WebAssembly and Rust and harness their potential in various applications, consider exploring the following resources:

- *The Rust and WebAssembly Book*: The official guide that provides a comprehensive overview of integrating Rust with WebAssembly, offering insights into building efficient and high-performance web applications. - *https://rustwasm.github.io/docs/book*

- *Rust and WebAssembly Runtimes*: Explore the **`wasmer`** project, a versatile and extensible runtime for WebAssembly that supports Rust, enabling seamless integration and execution. - *https://github.com/wasmerio/wasmer*
- *Wasmer*: Visit the official website of Wasmer, a universal WebAssembly runtime, to explore its features, use cases, and community resources. - *https://wasmer.io/*
- *wasm-bindgen*: Learn about **`wasm-bindgen`**, a tool that facilitates seamless communication between Rust and JavaScript in WebAssembly projects, enhancing interoperability. - *https://rustwasm.github.io/wasm-bindgen/*
- *WebAssembly Official Documentation*: Dive into the official WebAssembly documentation to gain in-depth knowledge about the specifications, tools, and resources for leveraging WebAssembly in various development scenarios. - *https://webassembly.org/*
- *wasmtime Documentation*: Explore the documentation for **`wasmtime`**, a standalone WebAssembly runtime, providing details on its features and capabilities. - *https://docs.rs/wasmtime/*
- *Yew Framework*: Discover the Yew framework, a Rust framework for building modern web applications with WebAssembly, offering a reactive and component-based approach. - *https://github.com/yewstack/yew*

Multiple Choice Questions

Q1: What is the key advantage of WebAssembly over traditional JavaScript execution in web browsers?

a) Faster loading times

b) Improved security

c) Direct DOM manipulation

d) Compatibility with older browsers

Q2: In WebAssembly, what role does the WebAssembly System Interface (WASI) play?

a) It defines the binary instruction format.

b) It facilitates direct DOM manipulation.

c) It provides a standard interface for resource management and system interactions.

d) It focuses on high-level programming languages.

Q3: What is a significant benefit of WebAssembly's language independence?

a) It restricts developers to using a specific programming language.

b) It limits the range of tasks that can be performed in web applications.

c) It allows the integration of code written in different high-level languages.

d) It enforces the use of JavaScript for all web applications.

Q4: How does WebAssembly enhance security in web applications?

a) By executing code in a sandboxed environment

b) By restricting access to the Document Object Model (DOM)

c) By enforcing the use of garbage collection

d) By providing a global WebAssembly object

Q5: What is a limitation of WebAssembly concerning browser support?

a) Limited memory management

b) Inability to execute computationally intensive tasks

c) Compatibility issues with newer browsers

d) Challenges in older browsers lacking the global WebAssembly object

Q6: How does asm.js relate to WebAssembly?

a) It is a replacement for WebAssembly.

b) It serves as a competing technology.

c) It is a subset of JavaScript designed for performance.

d) It provides better memory management than WebAssembly.

Q7: What is a current limitation of WebAssembly concerning DOM manipulation?

a) Direct and seamless access to the DOM

b) Indirect access through JavaScript or Emscripten

c) Automatic memory allocation for DOM operations

d) Inclusion of DOM objects in the binary instruction format

Q8: What is the purpose of the WebAssembly System Interface (WASI)?

a) To optimize code execution

b) To enhance browser security

c) To provide a standard interface for running WebAssembly applications on any platform

d) To directly access the Document Object Model (DOM)

Q9: What is a unique memory management challenge in WebAssembly?

a) Automatic garbage collection

b) Linear memory allocation

c) Reliance on languages with garbage collection

d) Exclusion of high-level languages like C and C++

Q10: Why is the absence of garbage collection in `WebAssembly` significant?

a) It simplifies memory management.

b) It improves performance without trade-offs.

c) It allows for automatic memory reclamation.

d) It requires meticulous manual memory allocation.

Q11: What is the benefit of integrating garbage collection support in `WebAssembly`?

a) Improved security

b) Simplified memory management

c) Enhanced compatibility with older browsers

d) Faster loading times

Q12: Which Rust tool is crucial for incorporating the WebAssembly target into the Rust toolchain?

a) `Cargo`

b) `rustc`

c) `wasm-pack`

d) `rustup`

Answers

1. a) Faster loading times.
2. c) It provides a standard interface for resource management and system interactions.
3. c) It allows the integration of code written in different high-level languages.
4. a) By executing code in a sandboxed environment.
5. d) Challenges in older browsers lacking the global WebAssembly object.
6. c) It is a subset of JavaScript designed for performance.
7. b) Indirect access through JavaScript or Emscripten.
8. c) To provide a standard interface for running WebAssembly applications on any platform.
9. b) Linear memory allocation.
10. d) It requires meticulous manual memory allocation
11. b) Simplified memory management
12. d) `rustup`

Index

A

B

C

D

E

H

I

L

M

N

P

R

U

V

W